CHILD STAR

CHILD STAR

AN AUTOBIOGRAPHY

Shirley Temple Black

McGRAW-HILL PUBLISHING COMPANY
New York   St. Louis   San Francisco   Auckland   Bogotá   Hamburg
London   Madrid   Mexico   Milan   Montreal   New Delhi   Panama
Paris   São Paulo   Singapore   Sydney   Tokyo   Toronto

4 5 6 7 8 9 DOC DOC 8 9 2 1 0 9 8

ISBN 0-07-005532-7

LIBRARY OF CONGRESS CATALOGING-IN-PUBLICATION DATA

Temple, Shirley, 1928–
    Child star / by Shirley Temple Black.
        p.   cm.
    Includes index.
    ISBN 0-07-005532-7
    1. Temple, Shirley, 1928–   2. Motion picture actors and
actresses—United States—Biography.   I. Title.
PN2287.T33A3   1988
791.43'028'0924—dc19
[B]   88-23286
                                                CIP

Book design by Eve L. Kirch

Acknowledgments

I would like to acknowledge the existence of several dozen books, past and current, purporting to describe my life as a child star and in some cases recording as fact gross inaccuracies first composed well over fifty years ago. Now I am happy to share my true experiences and emotions as a child star.

Exceptional thanks are due to Mary and Wallace Stegner, whose appraisal, admonitions and advice guided the book from its onset; to Elizabeth Denys, Graham Greene, and Christopher Hawtree for their consent to quote materials relating to the *Night and Day* controversy; to Lester and Irene David for permitting me to use published excerpts not otherwise available; to Harold Ober Associates and Random House, Inc. for permission to quote correspondence of F. Scott Fitzgerald; to Dick Moore for sharing his recollections; to my good friend Herb Caen, columnist for the *San Francisco Chronicle*, for permitting me to repeat his humor; to Daniel Mayer Selznick for arranging permission to quote from his father's personal papers; to Warner Bros. Music Corp. for permission to repeat lyrics from songs in my early movies; and to Anita Colby for her consent to use material from her book. Quoted conversations are either taken from reliable documentary origins or reconstructed from recollections of what actually transpired.

Gratitude for photographs used in this book is due to, among others: Acme News Pictures (New York), Jack Albin, The American Academy of Motion Picture Arts and Sciences, Max Munn Autrey, Ernest A. Bachrach, Wendell Bishop, Columbia Pictures, Culver Pictures, Curtis Camera Press (London), Edward S. Curtis Studios (Los Angeles), John Engstead, The Ettinger Company (Hollywood), Hyman Fink, Bert Fix, Gene Kornman, *Life* magazine, *Look* magazine, McFadden Publications, John Miehle, *The News* (New York), Paramount Productions, Inc., Penguin Photo (Penguin), Robert Perkins, Press Association, RKO Radio Pictures, "Morgan" and Eugene Robert Richee, Phil Roettinger, *San Francisco Examiner*, Selznick International Films, Earl Theisen, Twentieth Century-Fox Film Corp., Anthony Ugrin, United Press International, Warner Bros. (Hollywood), and Wide World.

Had I not enjoyed the confidence of my agents Robert Lantz and Joy Harris, my task would surely have been more difficult. It would have been impossible without the assistance from Virginia L. Jenny and Joyce Adams to assemble my longhand manuscript, and without the skilled support from the McGraw-Hill Publishing Company. Above all, I thank my husband and children for their understanding and patience.

Dedication

Human memory comes in many varieties. Some are disorderly or fuzzy, some selective or short. Mine is long.

Sixty years ago the California coastal town of Santa Monica was remindful of the picture-book Mediterranean seashore, a panorama of sun-drenched stucco bungalows crowned with red tile roofs, its streets lined with sentinel palms whose fronds rustled pleasantly in the constant onshore breeze. Hollywood lay a distant twelve miles eastward through scattered buildings and orange groves.

My earliest recollection is of a pioneer ride in a wicker baby carriage. Although old enough to sit, I could not stand, and true to Mother's ritual for infant health, I was naked in the kindly sunshine.

I knew my mother was there because I heard her, humming softly. Secure in the knowledge of her love and guiding grip on the buggy handles, I was totally free.

To one side tidy lawn patches gave up a cool, damp scent of freshly cut grass. On the other marched an army of palm trunks casting a ladder of thin shadows across my path. Down the gentle slope ahead stretched a receding chain of squared cement patches of gray, and as I clung to the siderail my fingers sensed the repeated, soft pulse as my buggy tires passed creases in the sidewalk.

Indelibly fixed in my mind's eye today is a vision of beauty, motion, and excitement, a profound, tingling joy in my newfound world dappled with sunlight and shade. Stretched ahead lay my pathway, taut as a string into an unclear distance.

My buggy, me in charge, but not alone.

Lovingly, I dedicate *Child Star* to my mother.

☆ ☆ ☆ ☆ ☆ ☆ ☆ ☆

CHILD STAR

☆ ☆ ☆ ☆ ☆ ☆ ☆ ☆

1

"If you cannot get rid of the family skeleton, make it dance!"

—George Bernard Shaw

In 1931, when I was barely three years old, Mother led me up the path from a quiet street in Santa Monica, California, to the doorway of Mrs. Meglin's Dance Studio. It was a first small step to several disparate careers: movies, television, twice a housewife, thrice a mother, politician, and diplomat. Mrs. Meglin greeted me with that unctuous behavior reserved by teachers for the presence of parents, and ushered me into a classroom. I could learn dancing or how to bang a big bass drum. Either would cost the Temple parents 50 cents a week, a fee not wholly without self-interest.

First, it provided mutual back scratching between the small branch bank where Father was manager and Mrs. Meglin a valued customer. Second, it served as an organized outlet for my brimming energy. Underlying the whole idea, however, was a calculated decision by Mother: I should be trained as a professional dancer, something to capitalize on my overflowing enthusiasm, natural sense of physical coordination, and rudimentary sense of rhythm. Her motivation was benevolent, to encourage tender shoots of talent. Of less importance, the vision of me as prima ballerina was an undisguised gratification of her own reverence for the dance, lifelong and continuously thwarted.

Sometimes one scores a bull's-eye purely by chance. Dancing happened to be symbolic in my parents' life. During 1910 they had met in Los Angeles surroundings much like Meglin's, at Henry K. Kramer's

1

dancing cotillion for adults. In a large, well-lit public ballroom staffed with solicitous instructors, music poured from scratchy gramophone records, but the aura of dance professionalism belied Kramer's multiple purpose. Some surely came solely for the exhilaration of social dancing. Others may have used the ballroom as a rendezvous with friends. Some surely came to seek youthful companionship, without appearing to stalk or play the coquette. Mother went, I'm confident, only to dance. Father, I am equally sure, was looking for a girl.

As a young man of twenty-three, George Francis Temple wore pearl-gray spats, a detachable collar, and a three-piece suit. Short, muscular, and compact, he danced with a self-conscious disdain for such an unmanly activity. Having abandoned school at fourteen, he was employed by Southern California Edison electric utility company and lived quietly with his widowed mother, a maiden sister, and two brothers.

Shy and wily as most high school juniors, Gertrude Amelia Krieger arrived holding hands with a girl classmate, both recently from Chicago. Seventeen and willowy, she towered over George. Appraising her jet-black hair piled on top of her head, eyes atwinkle, and a carefully cultivated half-smile, George may have misread her interest as extending beyond dancing.

As an earlier Indianapolis grammar school student in 1907, she had despaired of her singing voice but fancied herself a ballerina. Behind cautiously bolted doors, she strained up on tiptoe and swirled in sweeping pirouettes, her long hair flying. She found little encouragement at home. Mingled in her bloodline were the stern inclinations of German and the frugality of Irish parents, neither of whom regarded her fascination with sympathy. Instruction was too expensive, and dancing was frivolous. Self-discipline and hard work were virtues, not the emotional and physical gratification they equated with dancing. Go find yourself a nice young man, they urged, preferably someone German.

Time can obscure cords which bind generation to generation. Behind her stern, Lutheran facade, Gertrude's mother, Maude, nurtured her own secret talents by painting still lifes and floral bouquets, pleasing examples of delicacy and precision, and by embroidering petit-point portraits—often featuring femme fatales, with lips parted and colorful flower garlands wreathed in their hair. Her taste for languid hairstyles accentuated by an occasional tight pin curl may well have been Mother's subconscious model for the spit curls she later designed for me.

Intentions often melt in the face of unexpected opportunity. Before many Kramer sessions had passed, Gertrude, who came to dance, began to pay attention to George. To better qualify himself in her favor, he was forced to learn dancing. Circling the dance floor with his free arm a pump handle of activity, and she smiling with her head tilted back, they soon replaced their box step with cow eyes. It seemed a good match, and so it proved over the next sixty years.

During their early married years they struggled and coped like any other couple of modest means and narrow interests. However, by 1927, George could point to a short list of personal satisfactions. Standing in the driveway was an auto, something reserved for weekend drives up the coast and useful as a parked refuge in which to contentedly smoke his cigar, blow rings, and think.

Their stucco bungalow at 948-24th Street in Santa Monica was small, but boasted a radio, elevating the Temples among the one-third of Americans so blessed. Babe Ruth was going to hit sixty home runs. Amelia Earhart, a slip of a girl with the same middle name as his wife's, had flown solo from Newfoundland to Wales. Americans were on the move. Everywhere there was a sense of vitality, a heady, reckless spirit along what seemed an endless road of good times. That a third of American income funneled into pockets of only 5 percent of our population did not trouble George, any more than the national avalanche of goods and services which increasingly neither he nor anyone could long afford to buy. The rich had cash. The poor had credit. He had a good job as manager of a California Bank branch. Financial credit was a benign convenience, not an ugly monster poised to pounce.

Their best friends were the Isleibs and the Fergusons. Harry Isleib addressed all life as he did banking, with studied respect for detail, punctuality, and cautious conduct. His curvaceous blond wife, Aileen, was imaginative, emotional, and energetic, particularly effective at buying and selling residential real estate, not excepting her own. On several occasions Harry returned home to learn she had just sold their house. Close friends joked that her current house was never listed with brokers but always for sale. Impermanence was her way of life but always at a profit.

Jack Ferguson was as industrious as Harry but more outgoing, and his words tumbled amid little expectant giggles, as if even mundane topics were humorous. Fay, his wife, was a golden-plated madcap, frisky and chatty, an old-fashioned woman in every sense. Although she was born mimic, no trace of off-color innuendo crept into her impromptu performances. Mother and these two women regarded loyalty to each other as the highest virtue.

In 1915, Gertrude had borne the first of two sons closely spaced, both now beyond childhood. George, Jr., was muscular and athletic; Jack, lean and sensitive like his mother. Both boys were growing by leaps and bounds when, in 1926, Gertrude's world was upended. What rattled her satisfied concept of family resulted from actions of those two close friends, almost to the day. First, Fay bore Catherine, a beautiful baby girl with naturally curly blond hair. Next, Aileen bore Mary Lou, an infant of exactly the same description. Gertrude's pride had been tweaked, twice. Alone of their triumvirate she had produced no comparable baby girl, with or without naturally curly blond hair.

One summer day in 1927, in her thirty-fourth year, she announced her intention to produce a baby girl. To ensure against possible failure to father a child of that sex, George sought counsel from his good friend Dr. Leo J. Madsen.

Stay in top physical shape, the doctor advised, and let's get those tonsils out right now. George went home with a sore throat. Nothing happened about a baby, but his tonsils grew back. The doctor cursed and took George off to a proper hospital. Again George opened wide and returned home. This time Gertrude got pregnant, the initial milestone in my long journey.

Pregnancy was only a starter for Gertrude, who believed devoutly in self-determination. The female sex and artistic interests of her own child must be established long before birth. Her scheme involved preempting the name Shirley, for no particular reason, with Jane added to honor her paternal grandmother. To endow her unborn child with a sense of self-discipline, she switched from beloved chocolates to raw carrots. Marshaling her array of feminine instincts, although unable to carry a tune herself, she kept the radio blaring out classical orchestral programs, read good literature aloud, toured local museums, purposely pausing to admire architectural beauty along the way, bathing herself in color, form, and aesthetics. Occasionally she attended a local movie, exposing her unborn child to sounds and sensations of romantic films such as Janet Gaynor's *Seventh Heaven* and *Street Angel* as she dabbed away her sympathetic tears. She walked down to the ocean, remarking on the natural beauty in flowers, and listened to the rhythmic thump of sea surf, the rustle of palm fronds in the Pacific wind, and the happy babble as she passed public playgrounds. It was her mystical, Teutonic conviction that noble thoughts, beautiful sights, and pleasant sounds could somehow imprint themselves directly on her child, a prenatal blitzkreig.

On the twenty-third of April 1928 her basic plan reached a major milepost. I was indeed a baby girl. I arrived at nine in the evening, too late for dinner, so I started out one meal behind. (Ever since I've tried to make up for that loss.)

Like many newborn infants, my head was shiny and bald, my face broad but short, and the tips of my ears inclined outward like a flying mouse. My only unique trait was one deep dimple in the right cheek. Three days later a second dimple appeared on the left side. At last I seemed balanced, and ready.

Soon I had become a roly-poly child with barely a wisp of curly blond hair. When I cried my face was wrinkled and unattractively florid, but at least my bottom was always carefully clothed in ruffled lace. Long before I learned to stand, Mother instituted a sequel to her prenatal campaign of artistic endowment. More than once I crawled across the playpen on hands and knees and peered through the wooden bars in astonishment. The radio was turned up to music, and around the living room she swooped, rattling a tambourine and silently mouthing accompaniment to her own private dancing demonstration. It looked like something fun to do, if only I could walk.

Professionalism requires training, and Meglin's was one of many such schools sprouting in Los Angeles and offering instruction in dramatic and musical arts. Anyone could enroll in the band or learn to sing or dance. Whatever the selection, each child automatically became a Famous Meglin Kiddie, the polyglot group led with martial authority by the headmistress herself.

A compact woman with glistening eyes, Mrs. Meglin was her own best saleslady. Every healthy child loves to dance, she enthused. The finest exercise to build up health and bodily vigor.

To the beauties of artistry and health she added the tantalizing comment that "dancing also provides an exceptional entree into the entertainment field, with all its rich financial rewards." Mrs. Meglin and I were a perfect match. I wanted to learn, and she wanted to teach.

Before dancing I was briefly introduced to music. Mother had developed my knack for hitting notes in a baby key, so I joined the unharmonious chorus with more than a little volume and energy. However, dancing does not demand voice training, which required an extra fee my parents could ill afford, so our attention was soon directed to our feet. Sternly admonished to silence and obedience, we lined up before a mirrored wall and practiced balancing books on top of our heads. Next we tried fast turns, swiveling around with eyes fixed on a single point, theoretically not falling down but in fact producing a hilarious gaggle of small, blue-clad bodies twirling off and heaping up in piles. Undismayed, Mrs. Meglin seized the opportunity to demonstrate how to fall gracefully. Arms should be canted just so, and each hand confidently relaxed, no matter our personal consternation.

As an initial dance routine came simple tap, the time-step, and some soft-shoe fundamentals. On sand scattered over the floor we slipped and scuffled around, later on learning the strut, a hornpipe, and how to make an exit doing a shuffle-off-to-Buffalo.

Mastery of a particular step seemed less important than variety when it came to periodic reassurance to our mothers that the time was well spent. Flubs or mixing up steps were acceptable sins so long as new ground was being broken. Piling in on top of each other came waltz, clog, buck-and-wing, the Charleston, tango, and rhumba, none mastered completely. Even ballet basic positions were tried—with the masse grand plié providing another pileup—our ankles aching but spirits high.

Along with sand on the floor, the long mirror-wall was critically important. Lined up by Ben Bard, Mrs. Meglin's agile, unsmiling assistant, and ordered to move right, half our mirror images moved left. For some the dilemma of reverse images really never wore off. The moment of supreme truth came when he gave the order to dance without looking down at our feet. Some children dissolved in tears of frustration. A few sneaked peeks downward. Others tried doggedly, as I did while sucking away on my lower lip.

As an early thumb sucker, I found sucking away at something comforting. A sloppy habit which deforms your teeth, Mother had warned, and ingeniously fashioned a metallic contraption from a champagne cork as a restrainer to fit over my thumb. Who wants to suck a grid of wire? So I quit. Too bad thumb-sucking is noted only for its drawbacks.

Chaotic though Meglin's may have occasionally appeared, an underlying message echoed. Our job was to master a craft, in my case, dancing. Lesson after lesson, the dance routines were drilled and repeated. There were no shortcuts. It was just repeated practice until every motion of each dance became as reflexive and natural as walking or standing. It could have been one big bore, had I not really enjoyed myself.

I was destined to remain at Meglin's for two and a half years. It took me that long to learn how to dance naturally.

Learning about activity and its requisite self-discipline was not something first taught at dancing school, but a result of what Mother had already done. She was no namby-pamby. In fact, my first spoken phrase—"Don't do 'at!" was probably in mimicry of what she said to me. Always inside that velvet glove was a hard hand, a symbol of linkage between command and obedience. Initially my response was not just contented gurgles. I was quick to protest, and knew how to project a good yell, buffeting my family with aimless yowls. Unable to afford the luxury of a baby-sitter, once Mother left older brother Jack in charge. When bedtime stories failed to stanch my sobbing, he disguised himself in Mother's bathrobe and cradled me in his arms as he had seen her do. The ruse failed. Instead of the cushiony comfort of a breast, I detected only a bony chest, well worth screaming about.

Despite my initial resistance, Mother's knack for making a joy of obligatory behavior was a blessing. To teach the alphabet and numbers, she keyed her lesson to spoonsful of my morning cereal, never my favorite food. Locked in my high chair, I would recite an appropriate sequence and be rewarded with a mouthful. There was one hazard. Time and again we both got lost in our game, until finally I would just overflow. It was a messy business, but in the process, I began to draw some conclusions about life. First, it was better if I set my own speed, and stopped when full. Next, a product of the strange alchemy of childhood, I believed that the first bowl represented a necessary duty to achieve the reward of my second. Trouble, therefore, became a prerequisite to reward. On one other point I had little doubt: everyone always had two bowls of cereal.

Shocking experiences likewise taught useful lessons. Two years before Meglin's, at my parents' New Year's Day wedding anniversary party,
everything began and ended early in our kitchen. Maternal grandmother
Maude perched me on a stool to witness how she prepared country
gravy from lamb drippings. Unlike Mother, she was sharply opinionated
and took charge at each slight opportunity, edging herself into the fabric
of our household.

Although intrusive and usually stubborn, Maude also had a streak
of pragmatic flexibility. Seeking a bonanza, she and her husband, Otto,
had left Chicago with their young daughter and son for golden California. Instead of riches, he soon suffered severe financial reverses as
a jewelry salesman. His sudden final demise surprised everyone, but
not Otto. Philosophically, Maude interred him in a cemetery located
next door to their bungalow and for $12 purchased an adjoining plot
for herself.

When anti-German public opinion ran high during World War I, she
had simply altered the spelling of her name from the unmistakably
German *Krieger* to the French-sounding *Cregier*, and told strangers she
was from Toronto. When son Ralph was packed off to the San Quentin
State Penitentiary for secretly borrowing money from his employer, she
once again balanced grief with prudence by gulping enough iodine to
arouse sympathy but not enough to kill herself.

Edged in beside Maude at the stove, Mother was leaning over a
double boiler cooking lemon filling for chiffon pie. With a sudden,
metallic pop, the pot exploded, sending a cascade of boiling sauce up
across Mother's shirtfront. Gasping with pain, she fell to the floor, clawing
the blouse material away and exposing both her naked breasts, where
the scalded skin was already brilliant pink.

Clutching firmly onto the sides of my stool, I stared in dismay. I had
always regarded her as invincible, an assumption now ripped asunder
as surely as the bodice. This was not my only surprise. I never recalled
seeing my mother's bare breasts. Like any new sight, their shape and
coloration fascinated me, all too briefly, for Father quickly wrapped her
in a shawl and sped her to the hospital. Bandaged and gray-faced, she
finally returned, never glanced in my direction, climbed stiffly upstairs,
and crawled into bed. Don't bother her, Maude instructed. Where before
I had fancied myself at the center of things, suddenly I was pushed
aside, irrelevant.

Too late for notification, anniversary guests arrived, each bearing some gaily wrapped gift, brimful of cheer. Instantly, everything was reduced to a somber tableau. The women filed singly on tiptoe up to Mother's bedside, speaking in hushed voices. Left outside the door, I could only stare jealously as each person passed in solemn procession. Why couldn't I visit my own mother, I asked Maude, who had obviously taken charge. Because I say so, she said. Isolation from my wounded mother had two predictable effects on me: first, it sharpened my love by denying me access, and second, it helped me realize that only I could make things be the way I wanted. Certainly Maude was little help. There was no joy in our house that night, no gravy, and no dessert.

As a distraction for me later that evening, Maude demonstrated how to do a jigsaw puzzle, while Father sat behind his newspaper and my brothers lolled on the rug listening to the radio turned low.

"Grandma, when you have no clothes on, do you look like me?" I asked.

She peered at me from under thick, arched eyebrows. "Why do you ask?"

"Because I don't know." I had never seen anyone naked, except me.

"Ask him," she said, gesturing toward Father.

"Does he look the same as me?" I persisted. Both brothers had begun to snicker.

"Pay attention to the puzzle," she ordered.

That's just what I was doing, I thought. What people looked like naked was not the point. Solving puzzles was. But once again I recognized I would have to find answers by myself.

Balanced against such experiences emphasizing independent action, one physically painful experience showed that exuberant behavior can have disastrous implications. On my third birthday, once again it was a festive family dinner table. Before my cake was brought in, dirty dishes had to be removed. So far I had been assigned few family chores, but I wanted to help. Fearing a condescending turndown from Mother, I whispered to Grandmother for permission. A chain-smoker, Maude was puffing on a cigarette, holding it between thumb and index finger with palm opened outward. Quietly nodding approval, she exhaled a long smoke plume from the side of her mouth in Mother's direction. It's a wonder all of us could eat together at all without smashing up the crockery.

Delighted to be acting independently, like a grown-up, I slipped from my chair, took a few joyous skips, tripped, and smashed my mouth against the table edge. Blood gushed from my lower lip, smeared the white tablecloth, and dribbled over my chin onto my party dress.

At the Santa Monica emergency room, the doctor had a face like a mouse, with prominent upper teeth, a sleek receding chin, and a balding forehead.

"Have to sew this one up," he muttered. Father carried me into an adjoining operating room. Why carry me? I wondered. Nothing wrong with my legs.

Clicking on his operating light, the doctor fitted a long strand of thread into a curved needle and began to suture, while Father reassuringly clutched my hand.

"Does it hurt?" the doctor asked in a bored tone. Of course it did, but I wasn't going to let on.

Suddenly Father's hand had released its grip. I glanced sideways and saw him slump to his knees on the green tile floor, then slowly tip over in a dead faint.

"Damn," cursed the doctor, putting down his needle. "Don't move, kid."

Getting down on the floor, he waved a jar of smelling salts back and forth under Father's nose, and finally pulled him into a sitting position. My lip hurt and my tongue still tasted of blood, fresh and bitter. The unfinished suture hung out of my mouth. There was nothing I could do about myself or Father. How could I blow out the candles on my birthday cake? I wished I hadn't tried to clear the dishes, at least not that night.

While I was mastering dance basics at Meglin's with no future sought or in sight, 3,000 miles away, at New York's Paramount Theatre, a veteran black performer was tap-dancing back and forth across the stage with no clear vision of what lay ahead. For twenty years he had performed in vaudeville acts, but since 1929 and the advent of Warner cinema sound, a coup de grace had been dealt his medium of entertainment. Those who could fled vaudeville for Broadway, and he was one. *Blackbirds,* his first stab at legitimate theatre, was a year-long success. In 1930 he scored again in *Brown Buddies.* But an even more lucrative and attractive refuge was motion pictures. Unfortunately, opportunity for any black man in movies was limited, but the odds did not dismay him. A sporting type who loved a wager, he didn't drink or chase women, was happily married, and trusted Lady Luck implicitly. He just kept on dancing, one eye cocked westward for the big chance. Nobody, least of all Bill "Bojangles" Robinson, would have detected that his professional salvation lay in the babble and confusion created by a bunch of babies at Mrs. Meglin's Dance Studio.

2

Through summer and fall of 1931, Mother faithfully escorted me to Meglin's. Seated with other mothers on folding chairs against the wall, she waited, knitted, and gossiped, perhaps occasionally speculating about her child and motion pictures. The proximity of Santa Monica to Hollywood provided an advantage for aspiring child dancers, but the notion of movie stardom would have seemed bizarre to Mother. A different version of Mother's attitude appeared many years later, offered by Hal Roach, producer of the most durable and appealing current child-actor series, the *Our Gang* comedies.

"About Shirley Temple," Roach later recalled, "her mother brought her in five or six times, I understand. Nobody'd let her get beyond the outer office.... The casting director apparently didn't think Shirley Temple had anything to offer the gang...."

I recall nothing of what Roach describes, and to her dying day forty-six years later, Mother scoffed at his claim. In fact, nothing relating to movies happened to me until one day at Meglin's late in 1931, when I was three and a half years old. Among my possessions I have a letter Mother wrote to Maude.

. . . The Wednesday morning before Thanksgiving, Shirley had to go to her dancing lesson at nine o'clock instead of ten. I didn't take the usual amount of time to curl her hair, and she just wore her little blue rehearsal costume and her play shoes.

After her lesson, I put on her little pink coat and cap and started out of the studio when I was called back by the music teacher. There were some directors coming from one of the studios looking for two little girls and ten little boys for a series of pictures. She thought I should let them see Shirley. There must have been about two hundred children there from two years to six or seven years old. Some little girls all dressed up to beat the band, in chiffon, etc. Hair all curled and everything. All the mothers had to leave the room.

Little old Shirley walks in through the crowd holding onto another little girl's hand with her little cap over one ear and her elkskin play shoes on, and evidently knocked them for a loop.

When the children came out, Shirley said they had talked to her, asked her her name and how old she was.

The man with slicked black hair seemed to pay me scant attention, but the other kept coming back to stare at me. I didn't like his face at all, moon-shaped, jowly, and moist-looking, so I crawled under the piano, the only hiding spot in the room. "We want that one," the man said to his partner, so I had cringed back against a piano leg and held on.

Mother's letter continued:

Six days later I got a telephone call to take her to Hollywood for a screen test. She was crazy about the whole performance, not a bit frightened, did everything they told her to. A few days later the Universal Studio called George and me in and told us they wanted Shirley under a two-year contract for a series of twenty-six pictures. She is to be the pretty little leading lady, all the rest being funny-looking little boys, and one other very plain, homely little girl.

She will have a very good dramatic teacher train her, a little kitchen and nursery for her to sleep in, so her daily routine will not be upset very much.

The pictures are to be "take-offs" on big pictures, the first to be *The Front Page*, only called *The Runt Page*. The second will be *What Price Gloria*, a take-off on *What Price Glory*, etc.

In fact, no drama coach, kitchen, or nursery materialized, nor seem to have been intended. Although generally a heavy-handed spoof, the films were a cynical exploitation of our childish innocence, and occasionally were racist or sexist. Mother had no cause to disbelieve the promises nor presume a mean-spirited character in the films themselves. Her suspicions related to money.

> Of course every good thing has to have a joker ... there won't be a great deal of money at first. I think they said at the rate of $50 a week, but only paid for the days she works. George has been inquiring around; that is the way all the moving-picture contracts are worded. The salaries always sound a great deal higher than they really are.
>
> If Shirley makes good and other studios want her, then Universal will loan her out at a much higher salary and we will receive a certain percentage of that. But she could not go to another studio no matter how much they offered her until her two years were up. Maybe by that time she will be worth a lot of money. Who can tell?
>
> Of course, this all sounds like a fairy story to me. I haven't been able to sleep nights and I look like the "dickens."
>
> Every six months the contract is to be renewed and I am going to see that after the first six months, if she makes good, she has an increase in salary, and so on every six months until the two years are up.
>
> I will always have to be on call whenever they want me. ...

The men Mother characterized as directors associated with Universal Studios were far lesser lights. Jack Hays and Charles Lamont were from Educational Films Corporation, a minor organization making two-reel comedies and program fillers and located on "Poverty Row," a hodgepodge of production facilities scattered along outer Santa Monica Boulevard west of Hollywood.

If my selection surprised Mother, she never blinked. The one-reel shorts were titled *Baby Burlesks*. Educational underwrote 75 percent of the cost and Hays dug up the remaining 25 percent from advertising tie-ins and peddling us as models for promotional gimmicks and publicity photographs. In due course, and without credit, my photo touted corn flakes for health, Baby Ruth candy bars for pleasure, and was emblazoned on five million gum wrappers for kids and on cigar rings for grown-ups.

Rehearsals took a week or two, with no pay. Each film was then shot at lightning speed in two days. As a star, I got $10 a day. For her maternal services, Mother collected $5.00 per week, a real bargain for the studio. Not only was she business agent and chauffeur, she was hairdresser and seamstress. Each evening she put up my hair in an imaginative collection of ringlets. Always clever at the current fad of home dress-making, she would run up each of my *Baby Burlesk* costumes. Only half was needed. From the waist up, we were costumed as adults. From the waist down, we wore only bulky flannel diapers secured by a safety pin large enough to have come off a horse blanket.

Oftentimes she would measure me up for her own design, then settle under a bright lamp with needle and thread, patiently attaching each spangle, tying every ostrich feather at an aesthetically pleasing angle. Her creativity in sewing was no surprise. Artistic to her fingertips, still she could tackle any household chore, always wearing a clean apron and with never a strand of hair out of place.

Shortly after New Year's, 1932, Mother again wrote Maude:

Shirley started rehearsing for the first picture a week before Christmas . . . finished last Saturday night. Poor little Shirley was all in . . . had a raging cold for the last ten days. Last Thursday night she awakened with an earache . . . the hospital had to pierce her ear drum . . . a game little soul. I stayed with her all night.

The worst part . . . they *had* to have her at the studio the next day. Mr. Hays, the producer, was almost crazy and so was I.

To think that after all our trips to town for rehearsals, which we were not paid for, Shirley would not be able to be in the picture. They wanted her especially for the first picture, because if this picture is a success, they are going on with the rest of the series and star her through the whole thing.

I begged them to wait until today (Monday) to finish the picture, but it absolutely had to be finished Saturday. We didn't leave the studio until that night. She went through her lines as if nothing had happened.

In the studio eleven hours and a half. She had two naps there, which helped. This business of being mother to a budding star is no joke. I think I look ten years older and have lost quite a little weight.

But we all think the picture is going to be a big success.

However, employment conditions here seem very bad. The stores seem almost empty, and have just a few clerks on each floor. George is also very worried, as our financial condition is pretty bad. . . .

The Runt Page, contrary to Mother's high hopes, added another sour note. A dismal failure in the marketplace, its sale was abandoned, but not before the producers sensed my potential.

On January 23, 1932, my parents signed a contract without benefit of an attorney. On its surface it merited their hope. For two years Hays would have unrestricted right to use or loan me out as he might choose for screen, stage, and radio performances, with an option to extend for another two. Half my earnings in excess of $50 per week were his. In return for his exclusive control, Hays was obligated to provide training, advertising, and publicity, but only five weeks of annual employment. My earning potential therefore was $250 per year. A four-year lock upon these terms seems harsh, but perhaps I really was no bargain. As an actress, I had little experience. As a child, I was afflicted with a boil, a sty, and the flu. However, it was progress. Although still only three years old, I at least had a job.

As Mother had implied to Maude, down at his branch bank Father became increasingly aware of hard times. As investment capital dried up, customers offered increasingly chancy propositions, asking for loans. Mining projects and real estate speculations seemed to excite him most, and were received with optimism more characteristic of a grubstake prospector than a cautious banker. With the Depression surging in full tide, almost everyone was ferreting out ways to beat the pinch of shrinking financial credit.

Not far away from Santa Monica, the agony of William Fox's film company was no exception. In 1930 he had defaulted on repayment of $55 million worth of short-term borrowings, while cheerily reporting annual net earnings of $10,200,000, an increase from the previous year. One skeptical San Francisco brokerage firm recomposed the numbers on the Fox statement, using generally accepted accounting principles, then declared that the reported earnings were only a smoke screen for awful news. Not only was Fox delinquent in its debt repayment, read the report, it posted an actual operation *loss* of $1 million.

Fox share prices had plummeted. Creditors yelped. In a desperate grab at financial salvation, Fox paired its two highest money-makers, Janet Gaynor and Will Rogers, in *Cavalcade*, a monster spectacle with 15,000 extras, three directors, and 140 speaking parts. Critics acclaimed it a triumph, and it was a giant at the box office. When profits were computed, however, it proved a pigmy.

Among those alarmed by the course of events was Chase National Bank of New York, to whom the company owed a reported $150 million. In a drastic shakeup, Chase placed its nominees on the Fox board of directors and demanded all existing contracts be repudiated and no new ones valid unless countersigned by the full board. This was a direct slap at vice president-general manager Winfield Sheehan, whose sole authority had previously reigned unquestioned. Amid yowls of executive resentment, the Chase nominees reluctantly retreated, but not before imposing a $350,000 ceiling on all new features and paring annual operating budgets by $8 million.

Despite such draconian measures, Fox sales plummeted 30 percent to $24 million, while operating deficits soared to a net annual loss of $15 million. The company was a waterlogged ship in mountainous seas. Who could have suspected salvation in the guise of a baby girl skipping across the stormy waves with a corporate lifeline?

3

The Great Depression continued to strike America with a series of thunderbolts. The stock market crash on Black Thursday, October 23, 1929, had wiped out $30 billion of investment on the New York Stock Exchange, an augury of the disaster that had overtaken America by 1932. The whole economy was in an appalling collapse. Optimism and vigor so typical of the twenties were supplanted by a creeping sense of national despair, misfortune, and human adversity. It was an era of bread lines, soup kitchens, and Apple Annies.

From outside, the Fox Criterion Theater in Santa Monica loomed as a typical marble and gilt palace of dreams. Inside on that cold, rainy evening of December 9, 1932, was packed an audience come to help Hollywood stars raise money for the Unemployed Citizens' League. Midway in the program, Will Rogers sauntered onstage in relief duty as master of ceremonies. He wore leather cowboy chaps, chewed gum, and twirled two ropes at the same time. At the end of his intricate spinning-rope trick he wisecracked, the audience laughed appreciatively, and he then waved me onstage and stood aside. When my dance routine was finished, he grabbed my hand, and we joined in an impromptu encore, his chaps flapping and boots clumping beside my bare legs and white pumps. The audience thundered approval as I ran offstage, but he called me back for an encore. I didn't know any.

18

Backstage, he wiped his forehead with the back of his hand and peered down. "What's your name again?"

Tipping my head back, I looked up. "Shirley Jane Temple," I answered, "and this is my mommy. What's yours?"

Winter melted away into spring, and we Meglin Kiddies trouped with our mothers where we were told. A spring fashion show at the Los Angeles Athletic Club featured a mock wedding procession. In advance, Mother explained weddings, with bride and groom always kissing after the ceremony and living happily ever afterwards. I believed this was the real thing. Five bridesmaids were identically dressed in ruffles and lace skirts, and five ushers appeared in black tailcoats with white vests. Showing the only bare leg in the house, I led the procession, smiling my best and tossing rose petals left and right. Nobody had kissed anyone else yet. Backstage, the bride shrugged out of her veil and the groom removed his tailcoat and threw it on a chair. Still there was no kiss. In fact, not one word of conversation passed before each departed separately out the door. With a shock I realized it was all an act, like my one movie.

Following five months silence, in June 1932, Hays summoned me back for my second film, retitled *War Babies* from *What Price Gloria*, but it was director Charles Lamont who herded us together for his welcoming speech.

"Kids, this is business." His face was a full moon and his nose knobbed up at the end. "Time is important. Don't waste it."

With his lower lip protruding beneath the upper and chin sloping sharply away into his collar, his appearance was sharklike and ominous. He swept us with one accusatory stare and said, "This isn't playtime, kids. It's work."

Anyone four years old absorbs experience like a blotter. Our minds are still a blank map. We can draw our own lines. Stage jargon hit me first: apprehension at the cry "Put the baby in the fireplace," which only meant a small spotlight with narrow focus, or guarded delight to hear "Bring the dolly," which, instead of playtime, really referred to tracks for portable cameras.

Arranging us on the set required we learn about chalk marks on the floor to indicate where we should be sequentially. For someone only thirty-six inches tall, peripheral vision and peeking proved helpful in hitting one of those marks, but I soon found stage lighting an even more reliable friend.

Lighting technicians, I learned, employ an arsenal of different lights, ranging from the ponderous arc lights called "ash cans," down through a family of lights, lenses, and shutters, to provide different intensities and focus. Any film stage properly lit becomes a veritable crisscross of unseen light beams. These soon became my secret tools for correct positioning. Realizing that my facial skin was sensitive to subtle differences in emission of heat from various combinations of light beams, I came to correlate and memorize the patterns of heat and action established during rehearsal and used this knowledge to maintain correct changes of position during filming. What I recalled was a rehearsed pattern of heat. My knack involved sensing the difference between a patch of skin on my forehead and a cooler area on my cheek. Combining this fact with my memory of where I had been in rehearsals, I could even sense if my head was held in the right position. Occasionally light intensity was dimmed or raised between rehearsal and actual filming, but even this rarely threw me off. In later years I grew to know lights and marks as well as I recognized my paycheck. Without the former ability, there would have been no latter pleasure.

During those early times dramatic instruction was minimal. What there was came doled out by Lamont, or more often by producer Jack Hays. A stringy man with a long nose, dark, round eyes, and protruding ears, Hays brushed his black hair, glistening with pomade, straight back. Sensing his impatience and distaste with erratic behavior, I instinctively was wary.

Both men would drill us, one script line at a time, demonstrating how to move around, loosen up our arms, and use facial contortions for emphasis. Our task was basically mimicry. We were expected to be a collection of mannequins with good memories.

My real acting direction came at home. Again and again Mother's instructions included the word "sparkle." Arching eyebrows and rounding the mouth in an expression of surprise was "sparkling," by her definition. So was frowning with an outthrust lower lip, or a knowing half-smile with head cocked to the side. Her verbal definition connoted more than posing. It was a word covering a total attitude, an emotional stance. When she said "sparkle" it meant energy, an intellectual intensity which would naturally translate itself into vivid and convincing gesture and expression.

Before long, acting in *Baby Burlesks* demonstrated some fundamental lessons of movie life. It is not easy to be a Hollywood starlet. Starlets have to kiss a lot of people, including some unattractive ones. Often, starlets are knocked down to the floor or pricked by their diaper pins. The hours are long. Some of the positions that must be assumed are downright uncomfortable. Your hair and teeth must always be clean, and the same goes for your white socks.

Often starlets are required to wear scanty costumes and suffer sexist schemes, such as walking around with a silver arrow stuck through your head.

Like a Girl Scout, starlets must be cheerful and obliging, particularly to directors, producers, and cameramen. Like a Boy Scout, starlets must always be prepared, whether to recite lines, give a benefit performance, or become the butt of a joke.

Starlets must be constantly alert. Weak theatrical talent must be compensated by strong instincts for survival. Above all, starlets must cultivate the talent of tenacity.

Lesson One: Being a starlet is a complicated life, especially when you are four years old.

Lesson Two: Disobedience carries its price. The price was penalty time in a large, black box. Lamont was keeper of the key. Two dozen children under six years old can become a rabble more easily than two dozen adults. However menacing, Lamont's visage and manner were insufficient alone to establish his authority. He had a clincher to ensure our good behavior.

The 1927 advent of talking motion pictures had created the first such box, a portable work station for sound technicians, six feet to a side, mounted on rubber-tired wheels and with sole access through a narrow, soundproofed door. Inside there was a thick glass viewing port screened by a heavy curtain. There appeared to be no way to construct it so that it would be both soundproof and ventilated, so the air inside remained humid, hot, and heavy.

Two boxes were available for us, only one to be used for sound mixing. The other was empty, save for a large block of ice, its diabolic, dark interior waiting expectantly for some troublesome child to be thrust inside for punishment not always befitting the crime. The ice chilled the stale air and steadily melted. No child wants to lie down in a cold puddle, yet standing grows tiresome. As a final satanic option, the ice block provided the only place to sit.

Before utilizing this black box, however, our production staff had to temporarily separate mothers and offspring. That problem was easily solved. Mothers were officially excluded from the set at all times, on the pretext that their exclusion would avoid tumult, noise, and divided authority. Under this policy of exclusion, mothers were no longer chaperones but simply chauffeurs, hairdressers, and seamstresses. At the stage door mothers were redirected to an adjacent waiting room, where they sewed, chatted, or otherwise frittered away the waiting hours. As mothers patted us good-bye a child welfare supervisor theoretically took charge, smiling benignly. Across the threshold we would all troop, and the big, airtight doors of the soundstage would close behind us with a soft whoosh!

The presence of the child welfare supervisor represented another problem and a different tack was employed to neutralize her. Once our gaggle of children was without mothers present and in custody of the supervisor, she, too, disappeared. Adjourned to a nearby dressing room tastefully outfitted with radio, magazines, refreshments, and a soft couch, seldom would she reappear until end of work and time to reopen the soundstage door. Rested and refreshed, she would dutifully release us back into the custody of our waiting mothers.

Several times I wound up banished inside Lamont's black box. It was really a devilish punishment. Take one small, obstreperous child. Heat it under bright Kleig lights until perspiration starts. Remove child directly to the chill of the black box. Close access door tightly and leave child in box until sufficiently cooled and chastened. Remove child, reheat under the glare of Kleig lights, and carry on with work. The box proved the ultimate enforcer. Increased obedience followed as night follows day.

The process also proved a slick way to induce ear infections, a sty, some boils, or intestinal flu, items of only slight concern to our film mentors, save where production was thereby delayed. Child health was for mothers to cope with.

One obvious loose end in the scheme remained. What if some child complained to Mother? Hays and Lamont covered that open base by warning us that anyone who tattled would be recommitted to the box for disobedience. Despite Lamont's order of silence, I confided in Mother. Although intensely disliking my punishment status, I had come to uneasy terms with the total darkness, the ice block and the sense of locked confinement. The reason I turned to Mother was that I always had, but what I related was so alien to her patient, loving style, she brushed off my weird tale as if make-believe all day had overstimulated my imagination. I resolved the dilemma the only way left. The game was clear. Pay attention. Be alert. Do as I was told, when, and how. Get it right the first time. No mistakes, and no wasted time.

So far as I can tell, the black box did no lasting damage to my psyche. Its lesson of life, however, was profound and unforgettable. Time is money. Wasted time means wasted money means trouble. Time spent working is more fun than standing in any icy black box and getting an earache.

Although bits of stagecraft came pelting down at me during those early days, the experiences also began to teach me about myself. As a hard-boiled French bar girl in *War Babies*, I dressed in an off-the-shoulder blouse and trademark diaper, a giant rose perched over one ear. Entertaining Yanks en route to the Western front, I toasted them with buttermilk and postured nondescript kootchy dances. Where France was, I had no idea, let alone anything about the world war.

"Me, monsieur?" I said coyly, as one diaper-clad doughboy yanked me to his side. A jealous Frenchman dropped a scoop of ice cream down my shirt back making my dance solo a heartfelt cross between a shimmy and a samba. I rather enjoyed all the international flirtation, but my foot hurt to dance, right under the instep strap of my Mary Jane shoe.

Three days earlier I had been playing barefooted on our back porch and watched Father's ritual replacement of our jug of bottled spring water. Proud of his strength and coordination, he hoisted up a fresh, ten-gallon bottle stenciled with the supplier's logotype, a small red arrowhead. He misjudged. Slowly the dispenser tipped, dumping the bottle in a watery smash of glass fragments. Blood oozed up on top of my foot and dribbled onto the porch floor. With the crash Mother had burst through the kitchen screen door. Seeing a jagged shard of glass still lodged on my instep, she kneeled, eased it out, and mopped at the blood with her dishrag. The outline of the puncture was the same as the red arrowhead emblem on the bottle.

"She has to dance on that foot Saturday." The words had been thrown impatiently over her shoulder as she carried me inside.

During rehearsal and filming of the barroom dance I winced, causing Hays to rebuke me before the other children.

"Never mind if it hurts," he ordered. "Around here, the show must go on." More concerned about criticism before my peers than the pain, I ignored my problem and kept on dancing.

Dual stardom is unnatural, certainly in Hollywood, and there always lurks an urge to diminish a rival. Saying what one felt could also run one into trouble. I was no exception on either count. During rehearsals for *The Pie-Covered Wagon*, mine was the first sally.

"His shirt is dirty," I accused, pointing a stubby finger at co-star Georgie Smith. "I won't rehearse unless he gets a clean one." Everyone ignored me.

Later in our film parody I was captured by Indians, bound to a stake, and pelted with dirt clods. As rehearsed, Georgie was supposed to rush in, scatter the Indians, and rescue his loved one. On cue, through a shower of debris, I yelled for help, but Georgie stood unmoving on the sidelines, a grin on his face. I shut my eyes tight against the barrage. Two could obviously play at the game I started. It turned out a grubby lesson.

FDR's political New Deal was announced simultaneously with another of my films, *Polly Tix in Washington*. I was a strumpet on the payroll of the Nipple Trust and the Anti-Castor Oil Lobby. Mine was the task of seducing a newly arrived bumpkin senator. Nipples and castor oil I understood, but seduction I took on faith. Decked out in a black satin and lace gown created by Mother, I swayed stiff-legged up to the senator and cooed, "Aw, c'mon, Senator, you can be had."

Flashing what I presumed was a seductive smile, I roughly drew the senator into my embrace. With a deep breath and my mouth tightly pursed, I squashed my lips hard against his. There we froze, the senator and the vixen, nobody moving or breathing. Despite my aggressive charms, the senator's incorruptibility asserted itself. Thrusting me away, he grabbed one arm and swung me in a broad arc across the room.

Like snap-the-whip, my feet went out and I hit the floor and slid. Scrambling back up, I faced him with my arms akimbo and lower lip outthrust. This was not in the rehearsal. Hereafter I would have to hold back something of myself until camera time. Actors were not necessarily friendly, and sometimes competitive.

Actually it was the second time I had wound up knocked down by a little boy. Earlier it was on the Santa Monica beach, a place offering free and healthy recreation for the Temple family. As usual, my preferred playmates were boys. I was attracted by both their outgoing, boisterous behavior and my unique feminine status in their midst. John was a little older than I, square-shouldered and built like a rock, a snarling beach bully quick to flex his knobby little muscles. Challenged too directly by something I said one sunny day, he threw me facedown and straddled my back. Grabbing a fistful of hair, he began pounding my head into the sand. Unable to wiggle free, I yelled bloody murder for Father, who came loping across the beach as my tormentor fled into a nearby swirl of youngsters. Getting knocked down was uncomfortable and humiliating. Unless your father is around, it's hard to get up. Far better to stay alert and avoid the problem. I wiped the sand out of my mouth, but as for John, I resolved to get even someday. It took thirty-eight years. By then I was serving on the United States delegation to the first World Environmental Conference in Stockholm, Sweden. John Ehrlichman was visiting us from Washington, where he was an assistant to President Richard M. Nixon. My chance with him came in a group including several particularly gossipy, feminist types. When I recalled our bout on the beach, he took it in ill grace. Sensing blood, the women taunted that such a highly placed White House official could not appreciate my colorful recollection, while he sat square-jawed and defiant, the beach-bully scowl still in place.

Taken together, the *Baby Burlesks* could have been arduous for a child unable or unwilling to rapidly adjust to the realities of movie-making. Being locked in a black box, pelted while tied to a stake, or knocked flat were but a prelude to *Kid in Africa*, my last in the series of eight.

Rehearsal for a jungle skirmish between two groups of barefoot black children painted with white stripes like a mob of tiny zebras called for the bad guys, fleeing down a twisting jungle path, to be suddenly felled by a barrage of arrows from pursuing good guys. The action during rehearsal must not have been convincing enough. Before the live camera was used a thin piano wire was secretly rigged shin-high across the trail. Down the path bolted the bad guys. Racing into the disguised trip wire, the whole bunch cartwheeled heads over heels into one squirming heap, with yowls rising from the pileup of small bodies. Some shins were bleeding. Out of pure sympathy I burst into tears, my first cry on a movie set. Lamont was laughing above the wailed chorus of pain. By then I had begun to suspect how powerful and purposeful the people were who ran things on the set. Self-interest dominated; compassion was secondary. Those coming from home environments like mine, where kindness is cultivated side by side with ambition, could find themselves ill-prepared to accept this reality, as was I when my time came with the ostrich.

A long, black sleeve of canvas covered its head as it stood patiently while a trainer eased up the traces of our spindly little surrey and strapped the harness securely. Everything about the bird's appearance seemed out of harmony. The feathers sheathing its snakelike neck were a tight, woolly-white covering, while those on its body fluffed loose, dark and long, like a broad canopy. Beneath protruded its bare, leathery legs, with knobbed knees and evil, two-toed talons. From where I sat in the surrey the ostrich appeared to crouch rather than stand. Upon signal the cameras whirred and the bird's hood was snatched free. Around swiveled its head, an eye the size of a glass baseball coldly inspecting Georgie, who held the reins, and me who held the cart seat with one hand and Georgie with the other. Suddenly we bolted forward at top speed. Straight toward the camera we plunged, the bird's long neck extended and our cart careening among chairs, scattering the crew, and jouncing over lighting cables. Circling toward the back set, we swerved into the shadows behind some scenery, the bird looping with great strides that left its feathery body almost motionless. Leaned back and sawing away at the reins, Georgie failed to slow us down, only provoking the ostrich to turn its bald, leathery face to the side, beak slightly parted. Bursting from behind the scenery, we raced back across the set, the bird's long legs reaching out, neck thrust forward. The trainer was frantically waving his arms and shouting unintelligible orders at the bird. The director yelled at Georgie to haul in on the reins. Others either dodged away or shouted their own advice. As excited and confused as everyone else, the ostrich zigzagged back through the toppled light standards and overturned chairs and smashed headlong into a wall, collapsing in a stunned heap of feathers, while our cart overturned and pitched us skidding across the floor. The trainer raced up and pulled the black sack over the bird's head and unstrapped the harness. Someone picked Georgie and me up, could find no blood or broken bones, and left us. The director bellowed that both bird and trainer were fired and ordered them off the set. Despite our collision with the wall, I was far more excited than fearful. However harrowing the experience, not everyone is paired with a runaway ostrich. Before I could reconcile my bruises with my joy, the director had posed a new experience by jubilantly calling for someone to "bring on the elephant!" Sure enough, in stalked a real circus elephant, and before I knew it, I was hoisted aboard and sent plodding around the set for our next scene.

Beyond the soundproof stage door our mothers knitted and chatted. Whatever happened was something apparently only between us and the animals.

Anyone consulting entrails in the roster of *Baby Burlesks* could have foreseen the future.

Kid in Hollywood cast me as a lowly, ambitious scrubwoman, rocketed in one blinding instant from anonymity to movie stardom. Within one year this preposterous theme would be fact.

Kid in Africa foretold events forty years later when, in what I still regard as one of the best jobs of my life, I served in Africa as U.S. Ambassador to the Republic of Ghana.

Even the spangles of *War Babies* and *Polly Tix in Washington* could be read as omens of international striped-pants diplomacy and my roles as U.S. Representative to the United Nations, the first woman Ambassador and U.S. Chief of Protocol, and appointment as an Honorary Foreign Service Officer.

Midway in the whole series, producer Hays had recognized that the risk of box-office flops had passed, all underscored in my parents' ignorance that California contracts with minors are invalid until confirmed by the State Superior Court. Time had come to officially lock up Georgie and me with court approval. We and our families trooped together into the paneled courtroom of Superior Court Judge Parker Wood.

Queried what his business was, Georgie answered, "I make love."

"And I act," I added.

Writing the date, October 7, 1932, he showed us where to sign. Not knowing how to write words, I scratched in an "X." Hays and I shared the same objective, that I act. Capitalizing on the tiny commodity he now controlled, he farmed me sideways to Educational Pictures, Inc., for roles in short comedy series with titles like *Frolics of Youth* and *Dora's Dunking Doughnuts*. Employing as it did the same sets and crews as did *Baby Burlesks*, the loan-out seemed just another day of predictable work and fun with now well-recognized friends.

Getting shunted around town was a different story. To quicken his return, Hays also offered me to commission agents Gene Mann and Jimmy Valentine, the latter moonlighting from his local trade magazine, *Hollywood Low-Down*.

My first audition came at Columbia Studios in a tiny part for a potboiler film, *Red Haired Alibi*. Mann was busy, so my parents waited in the car while one of his associates led me onto a stage being set up for an afternoon shooting. Sitting me down on a rolled-up rug, he explained I wasn't yet hired. That's the director's job, he said. Go out and tell him you want a job.

Used to doing as I was told, I walked out, carefully stepping over electrical cables as I had been taught. The director was reading and didn't look up, even though I was squarely before him.

"I'm Shirley Temple," I started. "I take good direction. If you want me, please tell me what time, and what to wear."

Looking bored, he gestured for someone else and returned to his reading. Repeating myself to several more people, I finally was told yes. For my two days work Hays received $50, deducted a commission of $15, and gave Mother the rest.

Never high on peddling me, agent Mann's enthusiasm soon waned, so Mother started reading trade magazines, watching for casting calls, and zigzagging our car about Hollywood for bit-part tryouts. Habitually late, we hurtled around at forty miles per hour in a perpetual state of expectation, collecting a tapestry of speeding citations as we went. The rules were simple. Hang on, keep tap shoes at the ready, and don't spill milk in the car.

Nothing I did took much time.

Mandalay, at Warner Brothers, was a steamy, sensual tropical yarn, but my fleeting part was as a homey prop, held for an instant in someone's arms. Tested as a child version of Joan Crawford for her MGM *Dancing Lady* with newcomers Fred Astaire and Nelson Eddy, I flunked. Back at Warner's, I cavorted briefly with nine other children in *As the Earth Turns*. Agent Valentine got me a preliminary audition for the role of Marky in *Little Miss Marker*, then being cast. They took one look, watched me dance, and rejected me without a smile.

Universal Studios gave me two and a half days work in a comedy titled *Out All Night* (later titled *Niagara Falls*) replacing Cora Sue Collins, who was judged too big to be carried around like a baby, so I got to hear ZaSu Pitts recite the big bad wolf eating up Red Riding Hood. It was a sad story, so I cried on cue, then went home.

The good part of this frenetic rushing around was its sense of being busy, being needed. If my filmed expression occasionally was vague, perhaps I was unsure where I was, who I was supposed to be, and who all those strange people were. Having been hoisted, held, and passed from hand to hand like a basketball, at day's end I might have tried to wriggle free if Father had taken me up in his arms.

Passage of President Roosevelt's National Recovery Act in 1933 provided Paramount a title for its two-reel featurette *New Deal Rhythm*, another bit part. Being called someone else's name usually left me looking so blank, the director switched the character's name in the script to Shirley. With hindsight, Paramount later claimed this was my screen test for *Little Miss Marker*, a contention difficult to accept. I had already tried out for that film directly and been told to go away.

My first and only bit part, minuscule at that, was in *To the Last Man*, on location in a rustic setting at Big Bear Lake, complete with pine trees, cowboys, box lunches, and a gaggle of geese. Dashing Randolph Scott was leading man but my eye fastened on a lesser light, a cowpuncher older than my father, but with a wide smile, flashing white teeth, and bandy legs. Trailing him around across the fallen pine needles, I possessively clung to his giant-sized hand at every chance, and several times got hoisted up onto his saddle, where he strummed his guitar and crooned, "I'm heading for the last roundup." His song was prophetic. Soon afterward my hero was surprised in a love tryst and stopped a slug from his irate wife's revolver, smack between his eyes.

Wedged into this erratic schedule, I had a tiny cameo as a sharecropper's daughter in Janet Gaynor's film *Carolina*, as my first-time-ever on the Fox lot. It was not even a walk-on, but another lift-up in someone's arms. No costume, no makeup, a minute of stage direction, and a moment on camera. Our soundstage insulated us from the figurative explosions erupting in nearby Fox executive offices.

The company now owed a staggering $42 million. Box-office receipts were flat, and it faced bankruptcy, the recent fate of both RKO Radio and Universal Studios. Drastic action was needed.

Chase National Bank agreed to write off $55 million of its original investment in a losing Fox affiliate, General Theatres Equipment, and operating chief Sheehan came under tremendous pressure to find new stars to fuel a financial turnaround. In an ironic coincidence, Will Hays, former U.S. Postmaster General, had just arrived in Hollywood to "restore the days of decency to the screen, to make movies a clean and virginal thing, the mind of a child." They could have found me at their feet. Nearby on their own soundstage confusion for *Carolina*, somebody cuddled me, I looked loving, and the scene ended. Collecting her check, Mother took my hand and we went out through the studio gate and away into street traffic, unnoticed.

On September 28, 1933, Jack Hays filed personal bankruptcy. In an instant, my world changed. No more studios, loan-outs, lift-ups, nothing. Although vaguely aware that everything was changed, and with the resilience common to children, I resumed all my routines with the neighborhood gang.

By this time my parents more clearly understood the implications of the contract so enthusiastically signed earlier. Bankruptcy had rearranged the hazards. Ownership of my contract, along with its leverage over my professional and private life, could be passed to Hays's unknown creditors. It was a chilling prospect. Through banking contacts Father discreetly negotiated with the court-appointed trustee in bankruptcy, who agreed to sell my contract for $25. The trustee knew nothing of the contract, as Hays had failed to declare it among his assets, so he had nothing to deliver to Father. However, he accepted cash and noted the sale for his records.

Later, Hays trumpeted that this was all illegal, but at the time he said nothing. For insurance, Father wrote Hays on October 25, 1933, confirming his ownership of the contract, which was still in Hays's physical

possession, and in Father's mind effectively abrogated the tenuous relationship with agent Mann. It was a strange transaction, but again Hays
said nothing. Perhaps I wasn't worth the bother.

From the day I learned to walk, almost half my life had been working
in movies. Almost all I knew came from Meglin's Dancing School, eight
Baby Burlesks, five comedy shorts, six walk-ons, and one bit part. My
earnings were $702.50, but unfortunately my employer was now bank-
rupt. I was out of a job with no future in sight, and still too young to
get into kindergarten. All in all, it was a tough spot for any five-year-
old.

4

Good luck needs no explanation. Fox and I came shambling backwards into each other one Thanksgiving evening.

The preview of my final *Frolics of Youth* was sandwiched between the newsreel and main feature. As the departing audience streamed past, I waited under the theatre marquee, doing a little impromptu jig and staring at a movie poster while Mother chatted with someone nearby. Jay Gorney, a New York songwriter recently hired by Fox, chanced by in the crowd. Recognizing me from the film, he asked where my mother was. Pointing, I returned to examine the poster and kept dancing.

Several days later, on December 7, 1933, we left home together. Mother's shoes had pointy, shiny toes and her broad-brimmed hat was cocked at a stylish angle. As usual, I didn't know where we were going, but we were late. Pulled to a stop at the Fox gate, we were refused entry by the guard. Mother protested that Mr. Gorney had requested we come to the studio for a tryout. With a wan smile, the guard sent off a messenger, who soon returned and escorted us to a nearby cream-colored bungalow with a tar-paper roof.

"You wait over here, Mrs. Temple," Gorney directed, and led me into an adjoining small rehearsal room. Behind a battered old piano lounged a man with slick black hair, bushy eyebrows, his shirt sleeves rolled to the elbow, and a stubby, unlit cigar stuck between his teeth. Gorney casually mentioned the other man as Mr. Brown, actually associate producer on the new film *Stand Up and Cheer*, a Depression-era fantasy, inspired by Will Rogers, in which a federal Department of Amusement instills public self-confidence through vaudeville on the theory that compulsive cheerfulness is better than facing life's dreary realities. Gorney, composer of "Brother, Can You Spare a Dime," had already written the music.

Brown yawned and stared at his piano keys. "What do you know, kid?" he asked.

"Lazy Bones," I answered. Gorney lifted me on top of the piano. I smoothed my skirt and began before the first chord. We finished together, so I rolled over on one hip and slid off to the floor. My panties had showed, but it was too late to worry.

Nobody said anything, both men staring at me silently. Finally Brown shook his head and turned to Gorney.

"Too late," he said, referring to his studio chief, "Sheehan's high on the other kid."

Gorney started to pace back and forth. "Unnatural, precocious," he said, "a revolting little monster."

Brown nodded agreement. They talked while I stood and waited, totally ignored. Finally Brown sighed and called for Mother and told her I could have the bit part. Surprised to learn I had no agent, he wearily observed that studios preferred not to do business with mothers, but he produced a minimum contract. It called for $150 a week, a two-week work guarantee, and I must provide my own shoes and socks. Show up for work tomorrow, he said.

The film was already well into production so I had lots to do, but first I did it in bed. There Mother read me the whole script, pausing occasionally to explain why people were doing what they did and what some new words meant. My job was to come tap-dancing across stage wearing a starched polka-dot dress, thread through a rank of sequin-clad chorus girls, and crawl between actor Jimmy Dunn's legs for a song-and-dance duet. It all looked like another, slightly different bit part, but ahead lay two tumultuous days in my life.

Rehearsals were conducted by the dance director, Sammy Lee, an intense, wiry man wearing a large silk bow tie and sleeveless sweater. Bursting onto the set in a run, he instantly was issuing orders in a loud voice and with broad gestures.

"Simon Legree," muttered one dancer.

"Who?" I asked.

The dancer stared down at me. "A mean guy who whips niggers," he hissed. "Shut up, kid."

When he got around to me, Lee announced there was no time to teach me the routines already mastered by Dunn, so he would use what I already knew from my Meglin routines. Although I had on my own black shoes, he loaned me a more suitable pair, white Mary Janes with shiny brass buckles and metal taps fitted into the soles.

Dunn would have been a standout Meglin pupil, except for perspiring so much. He wrapped a white towel around his neck to keep things dry.

Buoyed by my apparent success with Dunn and basking in the pleasure of my new tap shoes, I returned to the set and noticed another dancer rehearsing a little jig. His moves seemed pretty tentative, so I challenged him to a contest. Arching his eyebrows at my insolence, he agreed but told me to go first.

Weaving together all my most intricate Meglin routines, I ended with a cascade of rifle-shot taps with my new shoes and stood confidently aside. Starting with a clumsy routine, he suddenly stopped, turned his head slowly toward me, then executed a back flip, landing gracefully on both feet. I disliked the feeling of having lost, and decided to be more cautious in the future.

Called "Baby Take a Bow," the number was performed in two pieces. First came the recording of the song, then the dance filming. Although I had learned the tune, nobody had given us the lyrics. At the last moment director Hamilton McFadden hastily scribbled them on a piece of paper, and Mother taught me the words during breaks in my final dance rehearsal with Dunn. The hectic nature of it all may have worried Mother, but I found the pressure exhilarating.

Just before noontime of my first day, we entered the cavernous sound studio, where a large orchestra was tuning up with little squibs of music. Technicians were bustling around, and a few people lounged around with nothing better to do, including one Mother recognized as actor Harold Lloyd.

Dunn went to the microphone first, sang a chorus, stumbled on some phrasing and was asked to start over. Failure breeds failure. After a dozen tries he finally made it all the way through without error, again sweating and mopping away at his face. Tenor voices had never been my favorites, too nasal and unmasculine, but his troubles left me saddened and somewhat apprehensive about myself.

With one reassuring kiss from Mother, I climbed up on the stool and stared down at the microphone. Following the introductory musical vamps, I started off with as clear and unfaltering a tone as I could muster. All went according to plan until my last word, a "bow." The voice broke up into an unexpected falsetto note. My spirits sagged. While I was left standing on the stool, a hurried consultation was taking place between the director and his sound technicians. Finally, someone told me to get down. My only thought was, I've ruined it.

Mother ignored my final flub. Taking my hand, she steered me off to the Café de Paris studio commissary for something to eat before actual filming began. This was getting to be more complicated than previous jobs. I think both of us realized over our hot soup that my first chance to act and sing together might be my last.

Leaving, I waved good-bye to our waiter, who replied with "Break a leg, kid," theatre argot for "good luck." As I skipped down the steps I slipped on the metal clogs of my borrowed shoes and plunged headfirst onto the red-brick paving. A small cut on my forehead began oozing blood. The waiter wrapped some ice cubes in a napkin and pressed them on my face, repeating he had only said "break a leg." The lump grew larger as the ice cubes melted. Filming was due to start, so in desperation Mother pulled one of my loose curls across the bump and plastered it down as a spit curl. It would have to do. Dressed in my costume of white organdy, a frilly, starched thing appliquéd with giant red polka dots, I realized I didn't look my best, but Mother kissed my cheek and whispered "Sparkle!" just as the number began.

I came on dancing, my borrowed shoes feeling like part of my bare feet. What nobody but Mother and I knew was how much I really *loved* to sing and dance.

There was one tricky part. During this filming I was required to synchronize my lips and facial expressions with the lyrics and music recorded earlier and now flooding the set. I am sure I tried very hard, but somehow it was not difficult. Mimicry is not an unusual talent in a child, and I had no appreciation for what a nasty problem such synchronization presents for many actors. Lloyd was standing near Mother. "Good Lord!" she heard him exclaim. "A feminine Jackie Coogan!"

As we finished Lew Brown came over to Mother. "Stick around, Mrs. Temple," he said, "the boss may want to see you," and he trotted off toward the Administration Building.

Later Mother confessed she had entered Sheehan's office with her knees knocking. It was a large room dominated by a long desk and tables piled with papers. Stepping carefully across the polished floor to disguise my taps, I climbed into an armchair and let my legs dangle. Sheehan's eyes glistened bright blue. With his rosy cheeks and square chin, a white beard would have made him look like Santa Claus. The comparison was more apt than I realized. Mother sat motionless, her feet tucked together and handbag clutched in her lap.

"My people say Shirley has potential," he began in grandfatherly tones. A faint little smile began at Mother's lips. "Unfortunately, she needs lots more training."

Swinging my legs a little, I kept staring down at the shoes, wiggling them sideways. In color, weight, and style they were very pleasing.

"It will cost us a lot to train her," Sheehan was saying, "but we can risk it. The same $150 per week for a year, then an option for seven years. . . ."

Looking up from my shoes, I could see Mother looked pleased.

"And for you, Mrs. Temple," he said, smiling benevolently, "we make a supplementary contract for taking care of her. Another $25 a week." His manner was cautious and comforting.

"Then it's settled," he declared. "We destroy yesterday's contract and make two new ones."

It was only three days ago the gate guard wanted to turn us away, and now obviously something important had happened. Mother's mouth was held in a tight little smile, pleased, yet alert.

"Thank you," she replied in the same cordial tone I had heard her use with salesmen at our door.

Inside the tap shoes I wriggled my toes. Would I get to keep the shoes?

5

Sheehan moved swiftly to tighten his hold. If things worked out, I was both a potential financial gold mine for Fox and insurance for his own job. On December 21, 1933, my parents and I were ceremoniously ushered into an office in the Fox legal department. Father signed the contracts with a banker's flourish, followed by Mother's ratification executed in a precise, flowing script.

"Where do I write?" I asked. Everyone turned toward me in astonishment. Giggling uneasily, Father said he had signed my name for me.

"Can't I write somewhere too?" I repeated, creating a moment of confusion in the scene of otherwise mutual felicity. Although Mother had now taught me to write my name, along with how to read *Dick and Jane*, and *See Spot Run*, to see me anxious to sign my own contract must have startled her. Shaped in her own parents' Victorian attitudes, she viewed haggling after money and the scrabble of commerce as unladylike. Business was man's domain.

Riffling through the document, the lawyer found an unused line. There I printed my name, starting with a backward "S," veering away from my parents' signatures, and barely missing superimposition on the Fox treasurer's name.

Two weeks later we were hustled down to the Los Angeles Superior Court for Judge Marshall F. McComb's official approval of the contract. As we entered his courtroom I spotted uniformed bailiff Pat Soren, a full-bellied figure with holstered pistol, glinting badge, and handcuffs dangling at his belt. Everyone else seemed to want to lift me up, and this one looked better than most. I ran down the aisle, holding out my arms, and leaped into his startled embrace, calling out that I liked policemen.

With the judge, I was more wary. When he picked me up to inspect me at close range, I just smiled.

Going to court cost my family only gasoline. They had no professional counsel and no lawyer. Since Father's reacquisition of my contract, they also had no theatrical agent. Both went to Fox's bosom like hungry, trusting children. With official court approval, the studio could be excused for rubbing its corporate hands with glee. Based on what they already knew about my singing, dancing, and acting from *Stand Up and Cheer*, they sensed they had a winner, and at their price. It had been a surgically quick procedure, a coup. For my family it was the first in a series of clouds to hover darkly over the next seven years.

Sniffing the sweet aroma of opportunity, agent Gene Mann reappeared suddenly to remind my parents that his prior assignment from Hays entitled him to a slice of my earnings. Father was offended. Regarding Mann simply as an inconvenience who resurfaced after a consummated deal in which he had had no role, Father decided to ignore him.

When it comes to rumors, Hollywood is a seine. By January 6, 1934, Educational Productions head E. H. Allen knew of my initial success and announced plans for me to rejoin his own *Frolics of Youth* series, as if the Hays contract were still in force. On January 19, Mother was advised by the Fox casting director that I was being loaned back to director Charles Lamont for another film starting the next week. Although seemingly going in all directions at once, to step backwards from a major film to shorts on Poverty Row was quite acceptable to my parents if Fox so directed. Nor did it seem to trouble them when Fox attorneys abruptly reversed course, declaring that Father's repurchase of the Hays contract eliminated further obligation to both Hays and Educational. It was comfortable for him to shrink behind the Fox coattails, now amply spread in protection. Our family good fortune obscured the import of such festering wrangles, but Fox seemed omniscient.

Certainly no clue of disharmony between my family and Mann and

Fox was evident in Mann's public advertisement of December 23, 1933, sending "Happy New Year" to everybody. "Little Shirley Temple," it proclaimed, "five years old, wishes to thank Fox and O'Reilly-Mann."

Two weeks later, I became a year younger. Always a competitor, Sheehan manipulated the numbers, announcing on January 13, 1934: "*Four*-year-old Shirley Temple has been given a long-term contract."

Actually, I was almost six. Faking youth is practiced in more places than Hollywood, but Sheehan had me on dangerous turf. At my age, I had no years to spare.

A minor forgery completed Sheehan's age-reduction plot. My official birth certificate was cleverly altered, advancing my legal birth year by one, thereby authenticating my precocity. Enthused with the prospect of fashioning me to their specification, the studio set about to rewrite my whole history, brief though it was.

Some Hollywood publicists cherish a poetic vision of childhood, a place where talent gushes like a pure spring, awaiting only discovery by some canny producer. No matter that I really was a child who had already suffered dronelike tedium while mastering the basic crafts of dance and acting. Ignore all the scrounging for the shorts and fillers. Far better for eventual box office that I be suddenly "discovered" than seen trudging slowly along the dusty path of self-development. Shirley must be recreated as a natural phenomenon, someone without formal training. That required that my entire Meglin history be expunged, a process in which Mother was enlisted. Asked how her daughter could have developed such appealing competence, she dutifully replied, "She comes by it naturally. She has a natural flair."

The concept was lyric. A tiny flower found under a protective Hollywood leaf, amid dew drops. My abilities sprang naturally, like each blond curl. All untrue, except for the hair color.

Hollywood may produce such mythology, but its creators are seldom believers. It takes a miraculous mix of innocence and self-deception to believe that dancing and acting skills derive solely from genetics or maternal wishful thinking. Skeptics quickly pecked away at the studio scenario. How does anyone learn stylized buck-and-wing dancing routines without some training? To help explain away this precocity, the studio enrolled me in the Elisa Ryan School of Dancing, a Meglin competitor with more chic credentials. Ryan served two purposes: first to explain my ability while cutting out Meglin's, and second, to scatter a little high-class stardust over my plebeian origins.

Obviously, I learned swiftly. Two weeks after entering, I had acquired for a second time the dancing tricks already mastered from the previous two years at Meglin's. Upon leaving Ryan's, unwitting and uncaring of the purpose behind my enrollment, I was suffering from another problem, unrequited love. A lanky and agile Gower Champion was due for his own dancing debut at the Cocoanut Grove theatre-restaurant in Los Angeles. Happy and handsome, he had instantly become my idol, then disappeared.

Shifting my age and provenance was the studio's business. Learning what to say to reporters was mine. At first I tried to scatter dust in their eyes. One early visitor was George Lewis of the *New York Post*.

"You have it all over your more statuesque colleagues," he began. "Those great round eyes, curly blond hair, and pink, chubby cheeks. And your voice, a mixture of bells and baby whispers. Miss Temple, what is your opinion of the motion picture industry?"

Rolling my eyes up at him, I thrust my hands deep in my overcoat pockets. Peeking toward Mother for surreptitious guidance, I found none. "Like to," I replied.

He looked startled. "Like to what?" he asked.

"Yes," I replied, thinking hard.

"Yes, what?"

"Yes, sir," I said. Polite but safe.

Lewis could see he was on the wrong track, so he began all over again. "Do you believe there is any future for a girl in *Stand Up and Cheer*?"

My attention had conveniently wandered to the tip of my shoe. I knelt down for a more critical inspection. "My shoe," I explained.

"May I have your shoe?" he asked.

"No," I said, adding scornfully, "you got shoes."

"So I have," he admitted. He could see I was disgusted about something and considered our interview closed.

"Well," he explained, "I must go."

"Yes," I replied.

"Good-bye, Miss Temple" he said. "I hope your picture is a big success."

"Like to," I said, and went back to my shoe.

If there were any clouds, they drifted far too high to obscure the brilliance of that January day in 1934 when I marched onto Fox studio property as a regular employee. Everywhere were bustle, glitter, excitement, and a cavalcade of strangers. Grips and gaffers, costume and makeup people, and executives in matching coats and pants hustled purposefully by. Despite all the waved hands, smiles, and apparent camaraderie, I sensed the studio lot was strange territory, filled with potholes for the unwary. It was a time for deep caution.

6

Riding the tide of public acclamation, Fox writers plunged into a film story capitalizing on the "Baby Take a Bow" tune and my fortuitously cracking voice. To keep the telltale song fresh in the public ear, crooner Rudy Vallee was delegated to sing it on a national radio hookup, an unlikely surrogate were we not both employees of the same company. To create some semblance of activity I was assigned a bit part in *Now I'll Tell*, as daughter of Spencer Tracy playing New York City gangster Arnold Rothstein.

While the new Fox script was in preparation, Mother benignly overlooked the exclusivity provision of my contract. Having heard Paramount was ready to start Damon Runyon's *Little Miss Marker*, and ignoring my earlier turndown for the lead role, she read the story and was impressed. Touts and dolls on the racetrack fringe, a canny little girl deposited with gamblers as a $20 IOU, a little missionary who converts hard-boiled crooks and cynical molls into a chorus of saints, it seemed made in heaven for me.

Somehow she wrangled a meeting with Alexander Hall, director-designate for the film. Pledging me to her game of secrecy, one noon-time she drove me over to the tall, filigree iron gates at Paramount. I enjoyed the conspiratorial mood, even if I knew little of her scheme.

As I was always told to do when meeting adults, I extended my right hand for a ritual handshake with Hall, a man I had not met during my

42

previous aborted audition for the same role. Giving Mother a copy of his script, he requested she return the next morning.

The next day Hall auditioned me, first requesting that Mother wait in an anteroom. Unseen by him, she edged her chair close to the half-opened door, the brim of her hat just visible to me.

Seated facing one another, Hall said, "Say, 'Aw, nuts.' "

"Aw, nuts!" I repeated.

"Scram!" he said.

"Scram!" I echoed.

"Okay," he said, rising.

"Okay," I continued with undiminished enthusiasm.

"No, kid! Stop!" he said. "We're finished. Let's go see Mother." It was as quick as that.

In its official request for my loan-out, Paramount offered Fox $1,000 a week for my services. Representing a neat 600 percent markup on what Fox paid me, it was agreed, on one condition: I must fulfill a trivial walk-on part in *Change of Heart*, a Janet Gaynor film then in production. What promised to be only a brief delay dragged on. The catch was, my scene occurred indoors, but because California sunshine continued to beam, the studio elected to shoot outdoor scenes first. We needed divine assistance. As I always did in both gratitude and entreaty, I pinched my eyes shut, kneeled, and clasped my hands. Dear God, I prayed, send us rain next Monday.

Providence listened, and a storm came slashing in. Shooting moved indoors. I walked through my film segment, and on March the first found myself at Paramount being fitted with Dr. Denton pajamas, a tiny shroud of soft flannel with built-in feet, a comforting prospect. Jamming a leg inside, I yelped in surprise, and backed out. Two straight pins were stuck into my tender sole like porcupine quills. It was a good lesson in caution.

In 1934, Edith Head was in charge of Paramount's costume design. An exceptionally talented artist, she was trained originally in art and languages. Fresh from *She Done Him Wrong*, the filmed version of Mae West's stage hit *Diamond Lil*, Head had decided to make my costumes from scratch instead of drawn off the studio rack. This would require many try-ons while she created exactly the desired impression. With a toe and one eye still peeled for pins, I reinserted my foot with newfound caution and in absolute silence, a practice I followed faithfully thereafter. Head obviously was pleased. Fortunately, she later observed, I was too young to talk much; nobody realized how much that helped.

Damon Runyon's classic lines for *Little Miss Marker* were riddled with insolence, as captivating to adult audiences in a theatre as they would have been infuriating in real life. Smart-aleck behavior was not my normal style, but I plunged into my task with something more than professional verve. One of my early rehearsals was with Dorothy Dell, the warm-hearted blond gun moll called Bangles. Stuck as my foster mother on behalf of her mob, Dell was attempting to get me to eat breakfast and behave like her version of a lady.

"Don't you like mush, Marky?" she asked.

"Naw," I drawled, slumped back in my chair.

"No, thank you, Bangles," she corrected. "Say it like that. No—thank you—Bangles."

"What for?" I asked sharply.

"You used to say 'thank you,'" Bangles observed.

"Aw, I used to be a sissy," I replied in disgust.

The slang bothered Bangles. "Where did you get that?" she asked.

"Ain't telling," I retorted. "Don't want no mush! Take it away! Scram!"

Such insolence was a delight. Duty obliged me to speak in an otherwise prohibited way, and still kept me blameless.

Dell burst into unrehearsed giggles, stopping the scene. We held hands, enjoying the sense of impromptu gaiety. I felt treated as an equal, the same as with the Big Bear Lake cowhand, and with Jimmy Dunn. Time and again during the film she turned out to be a splendid foil for my energy and exuberance. My special affection for her was based on this positive attitude, one which made me feel inches taller than I was.

Adolphe Menjou's film character was a hard-bitten, lovable gambler who liked Marky, but off-camera he treated me with the reticence adults commonly reserve for children, sometimes staring at me fixedly without comment. In one rare exception he offered to show me how to play hide-and-seek, something I already knew well and which I regarded as an outgrown infant pastime, not nearly so adult as cops-and-robbers. His gesture was so obviously kind, I feigned enthusiasm while he hid behind pieces of scenery and I sought him with only half a heart. Beyond that one instance, he spent little time directly with me, always preferring to watch me from a distance.

He realized we were on to something good with the film. Reportedly he offered to forgo all of his $40,000 salary in exchange for a percentage of the film's profits, a proposition the studio declined. It, too, knew a good thing. Turning about-face, Paramount offered Fox $50,000 to buy my contract outright. Sheehan was another canny character, and declined.

"This child frightens me," Menjou openly confessed. "She knows all the tricks. She backs me out of the camera, blankets me, grabs my laughs. She's making a stooge out of me. She's an Ethel Barrymore at six! If she were forty years old, she wouldn't have had time to learn all she knows about acting."

I wouldn't have recognized all those tricks by his definition. Perhaps he underestimated the capability of a child to learn a trade. Starting with only empty, unbounded curiosity, I had been in training for three years, half my life. Generally a child of six is long on curiosity and naturally clever but too restless to sustain prolonged concentration. Luckily for me I could maintain a high level of attention over a considerable period of time, something vitally important in every aspect of acting. Part of my incentive for concentrating was to assure myself that I wouldn't blow my lines. Learning everything cold was the best protection for my professional pride.

Well aware of my ability for absorption, Mother had gradually evolved an effective system to teach me not only my lines but my role. At bedtime I lay with eyes closed while she read the entire story aloud, her voice acting out all the parts. Then she retraced and read all my individual cue lines, and I would respond. When she came to scenes scheduled for shooting the next day, I would recite my own lines, and she again played all the other parts. By this time my rapport with the whole story was so intense that I had learned not only my lines but most of everyone else's too. We routinely repeated our run-through three times, followed by a good-night kiss and lights-out while all those fresh visions of the story still danced in the darkness. In one variation or another, this bedtime system served me well always.

Refinements of expression and gesture were left to me. Mother never coached me at home, and seldom did a director offer specific instruction. Because of my early training in the basic craft, I was free to make up my own interpretations of character. My versions were naturally and invariably how I felt as a child, not how I suspected it would be as an adult. If ever there were instances where I tried to superimpose unwarranted maturity of inflection or expression, Mother was sure to raise a skeptical eyebrow. Although she seldom tried to dominate, neither did I balk. We each knew who we were, with or without each other.

Largely as a result of my complete grasp of the entire script, each day was no problem for me, even when the director might skip around for shooting convenience. I knew it all, backwards, forwards, and in pieces. The one drawback to my mastery of the script came if someone rewrote dialogue in midstream. Minor changes gave me little trouble, but anything major destroyed my sense of coherence and sent my memory into a heap. Little could be salvaged, and Mother and I would simply have to go off to memorize privately and anew.

"How do you learn your lines?" a reporter asked. Nodding toward Mother, I answered with a grin, "She reads and reads and reads, and I talk and talk and talk."

Of course there were some things that study in bed did little to prepare me for, such as getting bucked off a rearing horse or undergoing a blood transfusion. One scene in *Little Miss Marker* called for me to be thrown from Dream Prince, a Thoroughbred of uncertain age but of so sedate a disposition he never even turned his head as I was lifted into the saddle. Special effects had fashioned an almost invisible harness attached through two holes cut through the back of my long, red masquerade gown and trailing headdress. Ignoring my initial protests to such wanton destruction of so beautiful an outfit, they explained how I was to be lifted rather than tossed from the horse as it bucked, immediately convincing me that the costume sacrifice was justified.

Hall started the rehearsals. Dream Prince reared on cue and upward the wires jerked me, out of the lights and into the shadowy upper stage. There I hung suspended in midair like a puppet while the scene continued below. Looking around, I could see on every side a fascinating new world of scaffolding, catwalks, and anchored equipment. Among the shadows I could spot figures, rumpled men in work shirts and crushed fedoras. One grinned at me across the space. His front teeth were missing. It was almost anticlimactic to be lowered when the scene ended.

"You're supposed to be scared," said Hall. "Next time, don't grin."

Submerging my delight was asking a lot. I would gladly have rehearsed all day.

If the director had difficulty wiping off my grin in the bucking scene, he had no such problem when I was critically wounded and needed a blood transfusion. The donation was to be reluctantly offered by Charles Bickford, an otherwise nasty hood nudged on at gunpoint by more humanitarian crooks.

Stretched out on a hospital gurney, shrouded in a white sheet up to my neck, and my head swaddled in white bandage, I looked like some accident victim in a coma.

"Now, shut your eyes. Lie absolutely still," ordered Hall. "Not an eyelash moves. In a minute we're going to fix a needle to your left arm. That's so blood can flow from Big Steve's arm into yours."

The line between reality and make-believe blurred. My heart raced. A needle with me immobilized summoned painful recollections. When I was barely one year old, Mother became fearful of polio, for which no vaccine then existed, and agreed to one of those pointy-head clinical trials for immunity using an inoculation made from Father's whole blood. The prospect of the needle was enough to make me bolt for the door, but fourteen-year-old brother Jack blocked my way. Helping strip me naked, he held me facedown on a pillow while my bared buttock received the plunge of the doctor's needle. Maybe the serum helped, but the event had an impact transcending any medical benefit.

The point of my objections was not the humiliation of my position. Baby girls are not so vain. My concern was not where the needle went, but how and when. What distressed me acutely was being held down in a frightening, painful experience without any control whatsoever of my own fate. I detested the moment.

Since then, however, with Mother's help I had devised a plan to minimize the sting of inoculations. Each first sniffle was sure to produce family pediatrician Dr. Russell Sands, a humorless, balding, moon-faced man with a hawk nose and a bulging black medicine bag. Peering at my upper arm through gold-rimmed glasses, he would wait patiently, his filled syringe pointed toward the ceiling.

"Remember," I would always remind, "you don't do it until *I say* I'm ready!"

My plan blunted the worst of the pricking. I was in charge. I said when. No surprise thrust by an impatient doctor. No arm grasped in a powerful pinch. No euphemisms about this not hurting a bit. It was my arm, my sensation, and my decision.

At Paramount all these criteria were missing. Once again I was immobilized, ordered to remain mute and motionless. I was angry, then surprised when the needle was being attached. Why did I feel no pain? Was blood really pumping into me? When the scene ended I turned and watched as they untaped my arm. The needle was not even stuck in. My annoyance vanished, replaced by an even more keen sense of chagrin. Once again someone was treating me like a child to be tricked because of lack of understanding and self-control. I felt even younger than I was, and unhappier than I should have. My eagerness to stand on my own feet must have stemmed from learning so early to dance on them.

Not all responsibility was greeted with joy, although I seldom dodged it. It was Mother's style not to permit love to stifle my growth as an individual. Her touch on this was so gentle that at times I felt responsible for her, not vice versa. I well recall the large local department store where we had gone so I could purchase candy for her birthday surprise. After winding through a labyrinth of showcases and aisles clogged with shoppers, we arrived at the candy counter, where I selected chocolates wrapped in a pink bow and handed up a fistful of coins to the saleslady. Receiving my wrapped package, I turned to grasp Mother's hand. She was gone. To perpetuate the fiction of the purchase, she had moved away in a jumble of feet, legs, handbags, and belt buckles.

"Nowhere, and she won't get to eat her candy," I recall mumbling. "She's got lost." It never occurred to me that I was the one lost.

Director Hall was calling for resumption of work, and again resorted to deception. First dispatching Mother on some errand, he took me aside. "Your mother is gone," he whined sadly.

Behind my back he signaled to cameramen already poised to shoot. "Kidnapped by an ugly man! All green, with blood-red eyes!"

I glanced around. Sure enough, she was gone. Hall's scary vision was more than enough. Testing my independence while within her loving shadow was one thing. If she was actually borne away by an evil monster, that was another. My face crinkled up and genuine tears poured down over my cheeks. The camera whirred, and I kept crying.

"Good, good," Hall murmured.

However excellent his scene, I could not stop. "Where's my mommy?" I continued to wail until she came bustling back onto the stage. Gasping and blubbering, between sobs I repeated the kidnap tale.

Mother was furious. Turning to Hall, she gave him the sharp edge of her tongue. I stopped crying and watched, amazed. Part of Mother's usual charm was always an underlying streak of naiveté. She believed making movies should be a pleasant experience. In my case, it should also be a training ground for later life, a school where common virtues could be instilled and emphasized. Untruth, whatever its technical justification, always shocked her.

"Besides, Shirley can cry on cue," she insisted. "She could have done even better if you had done it our way."

Crying on cue had to be an acquired skill. Jackie Coogan's father reportedly took him aside and told him his dog had died. Mother had tried all sorts of tricks, even conjuring up sad thoughts until, theoretically, my eyes should have brimmed over. Perhaps I had nothing really to be sad about. Instead of being in anguish, we usually wound up in frustrated hilarity, mirth often so intense, it produced the tears that were proving so elusive.

Eventually we devised a more reliable technique. The night before a crying scene we did the usual reading, but without the real cry. While still fresh in the image of my role, I clicked off the lights for our "good night." That bedtime script imprint remained unaltered as I slept. At morning I rose and dressed quietly. There was no frivolity at breakfast, and minimum talk in the car. Every effort was made to avoid diluting my subdued mood. On mornings like that the stage crew soon learned to accommodate my problem, ignoring me or speaking in modulated tones and reducing stage clatter to a minimum until the crying scene had passed.

One such morning Buster Crabbe, whom I had first met on *To the*

Last Man, breezed noisily onto the set. Unaware of his intrusion, he challenged me to a game of pretend.

"I can't play now," I gravely informed him, and turned away. "I'm going to be sad."

As the moment approached, my trick was to concentrate, but on absolutely nothing. I let my mind go blank. A few seconds before the cue for crying, I switched my concentration to the physical process of generating tears. It sounds harder than it is. There was no necessity for the usual application of glycerine on the cheek or irritant puffed into the eye. Unfailingly, the system produced instant grief.

One aspect of this technique did present a problem which was to prove insoluble. My nose wouldn't run, as any blubbering child's should, an inadequacy which offended me. However, it pleased the camera, which prefers eyes that run but noses that remain dry. Visible tears and a dry upper lip allow for a stoic smile with the mouth held in an attractive shape, not contorted in a glistening caricature of grief. I recognized it was a good technique, yet that telltale dry nose always reminded me that my performance was imperfect.

As further support to my crying requirements, the studio gradually scheduled all such scenes for mornings. This arbitrary priority continued to annoy some directors, whose scheduling prerogatives were being compromised. "Why?" one complained.

"Because," I replied, "crying is too hard after lunch." The truth.

☆

In three weeks at only one theatre, the Paramount in New York City, *Little Miss Marker* grossed $100,000, thus returning half its original cost. During the next two weeks at the nearby Roxy, it piled up another $60,000, and went on to become a smash hit, packing theatres all over America. We had all latched onto a skyrocket.

While speaking well of the script, *Washington Post* film critic Nelson Bell hedged his enthusiasm about my acting:

"... poised and completely captivating ... remarkable brightness of feature ... vivacity of spirit ... qualities which may disappear at any time."

In a way his skepticism was warranted. During the evening of our film preview I was seated in the dark between my parents, watching everything carefully and occasionally joining in the audience laughter. Toward the end of the film Mother spoke to me but received no response. At bedtime it takes a very good picture to keep anyone awake. I had fallen sound asleep.

When a child abruptly quadruples her family's income, some changes may be expected. First, we moved several blocks away into a bungalow roofed in red tile in the style of a Mexican farmhouse. A slightly larger home, it folded itself around an open courtyard with a water fountain lipped by glazed tiles. Inside and out, it was festooned with a jungle of hanging plants in wrought-iron pots. A small shed was installed as my backyard playhouse. The interior decorator commissioned a dominating mural across my bedroom wall of Bo-Peep and her flock of lambs, irrelevant companions I promptly learned to ignore.

My favorite aspect of the new house was a canary named Twink, a full-throated little thing whose cage hung by the sunny French doors in our dinette. Each day I changed the floor paper and replenished the seed and water dishes, each task and every peep and trill reminding me of the bird's dependence. One morning Mother put Twink's cage outside to give the bird some fresh air and sunshine. A passing blue jay stuck his beak between the cage bars and pecked Twink stone dead. For someone just discovering the joy of controlling things to be suddenly confronted with a grotesquely mangled corpse was a severe jolt.

To free Mother from mundane household chores, a hired housekeeper appeared. Tall, slim, and wearing oversized eyeglasses, she ordered me around with a long, bony index finger and a nasal twang.

When the mailman began to deliver fan letters, Mother and my two older brothers would slit envelopes as well as paste clippings in scrapbooks, but when the mail began to arrive by the sackful, the task was shunted off for Fox to answer. As the weekly deluge approached 4,000 letters everyone gave up, so a full-time secretary was hired.

Steady income and increased space in the new house combined to allow Mother to indulge her taste for the delicacy and beauty of decorative miniatures. Our living-room shelves were soon studded with runty little glass animals, colorful but fragile porcelain birds, dozens of Lilliputian people posed alongside ceramic palm trees, and rows of tiny teacups balanced on small saucers.

Matching my size with her figurines, Mother assigned me the job of dusting, posing a twin dilemma. The miniatures subtly accentuated my size. Second, dusting was tedious, something to get done when there was nothing better to do. The work was hazardous, a perpetual challenge to avoid breakage. A coating of dust was proof that more useful things were being accomplished. My time at those shelves ruined me forever for both miniatures and dusting.

As sudden reflected limelight caught Father in its glow, he found it a mixed blessing. Certainly it endowed him with notoriety uncommon for a branch bank manager, particularly one whose formal education had ended at age fourteen. A life-sized photograph of me handing him my first paycheck stood at the bank door. Savings deposits leaped upward 20 percent. Anxious mothers got in line to meet the father of the child, and dozens of other children were sent dancing across his marble foyer to demonstrate their skill. At home one evening he recounted how a lady had offered him a stud fee to produce another Shirley, an anecdote predictably met with icy silence around the table.

As his unquenchable good cheer flowed on, so did his sense of fatherly affection. We had long been "secret best friends," and we visited the local jail, toured fire houses, and sneaked thick, chocolate milk shakes. In private moments he would hold me astraddle his lap and croon his only song: "... you are the ideal of my dreams... I've known you forever it seems... I love you, love you, love you..." Although his voice was thin, tight, and flat, it is recalled now as music from an angel.

Surging bank deposits and personal fame were not Father's only windfall from my popularity. Salesmen, cranks, and theatrical agents began to sidle up, attracted by the scent of earnings. Legitimate risk opportunities were mingled with wildly speculative temptations and several outright bribes for Father to do this or that. Probably unable to digest the volume and complexity of all these propositions, he fortunately was stunned into inaction.

By late spring I had again returned to Fox, where *Baby Take a Bow* was being readied, and Sheehan had developed some ideas as to how I should change. Summoning us to view rushes from actress Simone

Simon's film *Girls' Dormitory*, he used her as an example of what I should be.

In 1934 foreign female faces had become fashionable in the movies. Simone was the Fox entry in the femme-fatale movie sweepstakes, a rebuttal to stars from other studios like Dietrich, Garbo, and Danielle Darrieux. From the neck down, Simone looked unexceptional and compact, but in her face she had exquisite balance, a visage aglow with feminine promise.

"See how she pouts. She makes magic with that face. Misty eyes. Shirley, you do it too," Sheehan enthused.

His instruction was the first of several attempts studio executives would make to reshape me. At first Mother argued strenuously against what she regarded as mimicry. Trying to alter what I was by nature risked confusing my personality, but she finally agreed that I should try. The mouth was no problem. Mine had a perpetual pout, tight at the corners, lower lip outthrust when required. If anything, mine needed modulation, not stimulation.

Misty eyes were another matter. No matter how I tried to copy Simone's expressions, the result only made me giggle. I gave up, and Mother fell back on her earlier nonspecific advice to "sparkle," leaving me to supply the rest, whatever came naturally.

By this time I regularly knew everyone's lines, including my own, and was busy as an ant. My cosmos was the studio and my universe the soundstage. Merriment, particularly with the working crew, with whom I felt widespread compatibility, was the keystone of my behavior. Coming to work in the morning I rejoiced, and sorrowed when day ended. Viewed from the director's chair and from Sheehan's front office, however, my animated behavior and frolicsome attitude had a troubling edge.

Exploring and mingling, I was developing a habit of wandering away from the set between takes and slowing things down until somebody came to get me for a scene. Director Harry Lachman started using a duck call to decoy me back within range when I was needed. Initially it brought me at full speed, but soon I turned it into a game, delaying, hiding, or sneaking up beside him unnoticed. There were lots of things to do besides being prompt.

One day Will Rogers had wandered over to watch us during a break from *David Harum*, which was being made on an adjoining soundstage. His black felt hat was crumpled and tipped back, allowing a shock of hair to spill over his forehead. Hooking both thumbs in his suspenders and rocking back and forth on his heels, he was a picture of cheerfulness and vitality.

"They tell me we're going to make a movie together about rail-roading when I get back from Alaska."

"Where's Alaska?" I asked. He gestured for me to sit down with him on a pile of boards. Taking up some little chips of wood, he arranged them on the cement floor to show where Alaska was. Apart from his revelations, I liked him. He wasn't good-looking like some other actors, but his speech had an appealing cadence, and he laughed a lot. I didn't hear Lachman's duck call.

Rogers was my sort of favorite. As I had been born into a middle-class family without pretense, my natural preference went toward out-going, accessible people like Rogers and the workingmen around the soundstage. There may have been an administrative caste system divid-ing such specialties as actors, stage crew, technicians, and executives, but to me everyone was equal and subject to my own criteria of worth. Withdrawn, vain people left me totally cold. Grouches were ignored. Contemplative types bored me. Humor was sure to get attention. Anyone interested in games was a sure winner with me.

The duck call was sounding insistently, so I got up and ran.

This time Lachman's patience had boiled over. The following Sat-urday, Lachman's wife, Chai, invited us to a luncheon celebrating Chinese Day. A stylish woman with jet-black hair and square-cut bangs touching her eyebrows, she had been commissioned to reinforce Lachman's insistence that I be more attentive.

"Oh, lovely face," she cooed, her hands reaching down, long fin-gernails dipping and curving toward me, gleaming blood-red. "You must listen more to the director."

I cringed away, out of range.

Later, Mother scolded me, saying I shouldn't shrink back.

"Well, if I didn't," I said, "she'd put out my eye."

Lachman's frustration may have been shared with Sheehan, for he summoned Mother for a conference. From their first meeting he must have sensed Mother's ingrained awe of authority, for he consistently employed this advantage to superimpose his opinion on hers. What transpired I learned from her immediately after she returned, agitated and talkative.

Sheehan had begun by noting favorable press reviews of my films, but quickly noted that some experts were already warning of pitfalls ahead. Reading from one report, he said that although I knew how to steal a picture and how to be beloved by adult members of cast and crew, my cuteness would not last much longer. Striking where he knew Mother was most vulnerable, he asked if my ego were inflated by this adulation, how would I ever be able to take my place with children my own age. My career might well be brief, and at its conclusion, my personality a shambles.

To further underscore his point, he had given her a commentary written by a veteran child welfare supervisor, a document Mother still held in her hand.

"During my nine years," she read to me aloud, "I've had every juvenile star in pictures at one time or another. There is no antidote to the corroding effect of Hollywood hubbub. It is impossible for children to remain impervious or unchanged."

The problem, Sheehan had gone on, was the degree of liberty I was enjoying on the set. Too many compliments from fellow workers, too much conviviality. All corroding.

"She can't get spoiled, Mrs. Temple," he had warned. "She gets spoiled, it shows in the eyes."

When Mother suggested that I was only showing self-confidence, not inflated ego, Sheehan rolled over her comment, sharpening his criticism of me and insisting that she exert greater control over me, an attack which eventually reduced her almost to tears. Now dry-eyed but still angry, she began rummaging in her oversized handbag.

"Sparks flew out of his eyes." Her voice quavered. "Where's my essence of peppermint?"

All fairly abstract, Sheehan's comments were quickly followed by instructions intended to save me as a person, and of course as a corporate asset. As a start, no longer could I eat my meals in the studio commissary with everyone else.

The Café de Paris enjoyed an almost exclusively grown-up clientele, with mature banter, drinks, and ribald humor. Any child was a toy, something to be fawned over, manipulated into carrying adult jokes between tables, or to be lifted onto a lap and kissed. Banning me was probably a good idea.

To simulate a child's normal home environment, Sheehan also ordered that henceforth I would not be free to spend spare time on the set but would occupy a private cottage. It had been used the previous year by Lillian Harvey, a capricious personality who decorated everything in ermine and gilt and rhapsodized that the cottage was "La Maison des Rêves." Both her dreams and tenancy had ended when her career faltered.

Next had come Gloria Swanson, completing *Music in the Air* and conducting a torrid romance with actor Herbert Marshall, so the record now suggests. I had seen Swanson only once. An aloof woman clothed in satin, with eyes that darted like a cat, and her body jiggling beneath her long, satiny skirt, she had hurried past me without a word.

Swanson and sophistication departed the cottage together, her past layered over with fresh paint. In came Humpty Dumpty and Mother Goose murals, dolls, and wheeled toys. Down came the musty velvet drapes and up went pleated chintz. A sandbox appeared in the tiny backyard, a place where I was content to dig away with a trowel, but not deep enough. An oil deposit lay directly underneath, and today a cantilevered pump handle rocks away on the site of my sandbox.

Like a movie set, the whole thing was instant cottage. Nothing was an old friend to me except my toothbrush. In marched an army of undersized furniture, a Freudian slip, as no provision was made for the time when I would outgrow my chairs and table. Nobody expected me to grow up.

Now all our lunches would be carried over from the Café de Paris on a busboy's aluminum tray and left on the crossed-leg tray rack in our tiny kitchenette. Although Mother could order from the menu, my diet seemed ordained: every day, roast chicken, baked potato, and peas and carrots. For a change there was chicken potpie, but as in roulette, I never knew which day it would come.

Sheehan's final arrangement was schooling. State law required school attendance, an impossibility off the lot if I were to keep working on it. Although the studio conducted what amounted to a one-room schoolhouse for all the other children, he elected to keep me isolated and created a schoolroom nook in a corner of the cottage. To approximate the real thing, an ornate cast-iron desk with a drop seat and inkwell was obtained from the school system, with texts and study materials identical to those provided Los Angeles public schools. My mandatory three hours of supervised daily lessons were strung together in an irregular succession of time segments fitted to the erratic priorities of rehearsal and shooting film.

As my teacher I got a Phi Beta Kappa honor student and linguist, Miss Lillian Barkley, who was preceded by a reputation for proficiency rather than playfulness. Her exceptional credentials were matched by a steely intention to drum into me the fundamentals of reading and writing. A wiry woman, with her hair brushed close to her head like a cap of feathers, and dressed in silk print dresses and sensible low heels, she always regarded me with her head tilted quizzically to one side. The instant she arrived I liked her eyes and her calm, patient gaze, like a bird sizing up a worm.

My preschool preparation had been spotty. I knew about alphabets, autographs, and something about signing a contract. I could count well beyond 100, if it was coins. As for geography, mine was primitive. Hollywood, of course, was the center of the universe. California and Alaska were wood chips arranged between Will Rogers's feet. There were more important things in life than the world. Like making a movie.

Despite my repeated efforts to superimpose hilarity on her school lessons, Miss Barkley never met me more than halfway. With the fine little wrinkles across her brow deepening but never a strand in her wavy hair ruffled, she would redirect me back to basics, using only her facial expressions to command.

After preschool, kindergarten was a snap. I graduated within days. A couple of months in first grade were sufficient to pass the mandatory final exam. Mother and she agreed that the pace should be set by me, not some statutory norm, so Miss Barkley announced I would really start school in second grade. That sounded fine to me. The higher the grade, the older I felt.

Despite studio arrangements to isolate me from contaminating contacts and reduce headstrong behavior, I still had a mind of my own at home, once disastrously triggered by a doorbell. Any prospect of fans as visitors was mildly annoying. If I failed to flee quickly enough to some refuge like the bathroom, or circle the house and ignore the summons, I would usually be trapped into an impromptu performance for strangers standing on the front steps. This attitude had deeper roots than just childish intransigence. I enjoyed singing and dancing in privacy, and of course any performance before a camera was gratifying. Although unsure of how much, I knew there was some sort of recompense. However, singing and dancing for just anyone was unrewarding. Work belonged in the workplace. Work deserved appropriate professional recognition and tangible reward, at least something beyond gaping mouths and adoring smiles from strangers who chanced to ring our front doorbell. Being a windup toy was distasteful.

That afternoon Mother had summoned me into the front hall, where I was confronted by a clot of self-conscious strangers. When she asked me to give them a little song-and-dance routine, I stuck out both my chin and lower lip and shook my head.

Apologizing profusely, Mother bid them good-bye and steered me into another room, one stiff finger between my shoulder blades.

"Take down your pants," she commanded, and produced a wooden yardstick from her cupboard of sewing materials. "Bend over!" She was not fooling.

So far as I knew, few people had inspected my bottom bare. It was not my most impressive feature, and my instinct always was to hide it. I was mortified to be hunched over, staring at a wooden floor with my nude bottom upended.

Her yardstick fell with a sharp thwack. It really didn't sting, but I didn't laugh and didn't straighten up. It was ineffective punishment; my bottom, then and now, made me the original dead-end kid. The second time her stick cracked in two, sending the broken end clattering across the floor. I turned and peered up. Mother was staring at the shattered stub still clutched in her hand, her eyes glistening.

Slowly I eased off her lap and pulled up my panties. She had started crying silently, so I put my arms around her and nestled one cheek close against her chin. In a moment she dropped the broken stub to the floor and put her arms around me, tears dampening both her face and mine. The moment was a watershed, in more ways than one. We remained in our embrace a long time, silent symbolism of the love and sense of partnership which would characterize our lifelong relationship. It was my first spanking from her, but not the last.

Brother Jack had the misfortune a few weeks later to take a swipe at my passing bottom over some petty frustration. Summoned by one indignant yowl, Mother boxed his ears and forbade him ever to strike at me again under threat of a worse thrashing for him. From that instant on Jack recognized a new social order in our household. His sister was his mother's pet project. When it came to an argument with me, he was bound to lose.

My film personality continued to convey what the public wanted. *Baby Take a Bow* premiered in New York on Adolf Hitler's birthday in 1934. Like his, my career was attracting considerable attention. Even President Roosevelt took favorable note of mine, saying "When the spirit of the people is lower than at any other time during this Depression, it is a splendid thing that for just 15 cents, an American can go to a movie and look at the smiling face of a baby and forget his troubles."

Laudatory comments from the White House may have delighted Fox, but hardly more than the cheering company financial results. Profits from my second film were doubly heartening in the face of plunging theatre attendance nationwide. Among the fondest in Hollywood's galaxy of myths was the thesis advanced by the President that Americans would still flock to movies in bad times. A comforting thought, but perhaps not true. For the three years since the start of the Depression in 1930, both overall numerical American movie attendance and dollar box-office receipts had plunged by a third. Twenty-four thousand jobs had disappeared in the industry, swelling the tide of national unemployment and deprivation. Against this dismal backdrop each studio fought to capture a bigger slice of a shrinking box-office total. This was the real significance of the success of my film. Suddenly I was catapulted up beside the two Fox leading stars, Janet Gaynor and Will Rogers, in our corporate swim upstream against rising currents of adversity.

In addition to using the symbolism of childhood and reborn hope as antidotes to the personal despair and disillusion of the Depression, Hollywood had also been looking to its morals. Here, too, an innocent child proved immensely useful. Our film was cited fondly by those yearning for indications of new trends toward higher levels of movie morality, although not everyone regarded *Baby Take a Bow* sufficiently pristine.

"... Too much about paroled prisoners," said some, "too many detectives trying to link them up with crimes, too many escaped prisoners. What a pity," went one wail, "to associate this child with so many racketeers."

The German government went even one step further. "Berlin Bans Temple Film," proclaimed *Reichsanzeiger*, the official legal gazette, citing that gangsterism and gunplay were excessively portrayed. Germany was then awash in pride over the epic *Triumph of the Will*, a documentary film depicting the 1934 Nazi Nuremberg party rally. Directed and produced by Leni Reifenstahl, a prodigiously talented woman and one of the dozen most creative geniuses ever to work in the film medium, the film employs aesthetically stunning shots of roaring crowds and speakers in an oratorical frenzy. To deplore with one tongue my depraved associations and with another to exult in the pageantry and icons of Naziism remains a chilling commentary on the times.

For weeks both *Little Miss Marker* and my two Fox films continued to rack up stunning attendance everywhere, tempting Paramount once again to pyramid on my popularity. As my next Fox film was still rattling its way uncertainly between typewriters, Sheehan transmuted his creative lag into cash, sending me again underneath the Romanesque archway at Paramount to be teamed with Carole Lombard and Gary Cooper in *Now and Forever*, directed by Henry Hathaway, coincidentally, director of my earlier *To the Last Man*.

Undismayed by the German disapproval, this new film concerned international swindlers, plus a seductive traveling companion. All this interstudio incest earned Sheehan $3,500 per week, twenty-three times what he paid me.

I had never met Cooper before the first day of rehearsal. We were standing side by side when someone asked what I thought of him.

"How do I know what I think," I answered, peering up. Anyone three feet tall has a problem with people six feet tall. In a group of standing adults, my vision necessarily centered on belt buckles, tie clasps, and handbags. Of course a lot can be learned from this level. Hands and wrists sticking out of sleeves, for example. Thin wrists on a man were not good. Thick fingers and fleshy palms meant strength and authority. Footwear helped describe the owner. Work boots laced to the calf indicated reliability; thin-soled shiny shoes meant someone crafty.

Seeing the problem, Cooper squatted down to my eye level, smiled, and drawled, "Hi, Wiggle-Britches!" I liked him from then on, particularly because his jaw was square and he had laugh wrinkles at his eyes. Later producing his autograph book, he asked me to sign, which turned out a scrawl across the page from top to bottom. "Looks like an inscription copied from the pyramids," he chuckled. Collecting autographs had always seemed silly to me, but in this case the principle of fair exchange controlled. I demanded his in return.

Several days later he brought in some beautiful toys, which he arranged in the center of our set before my arrival. A pure white, mechanical cat walked and meowed, curling its tail realistically, and a jack-in-the-box popped up and down. While I exclaimed over each one, Cooper sat nearby in a canvas chair, an unfolded newspaper partially hiding his face while he sneaked peeks around the edge to see my reaction. He really knew how to ensure my undying devotion.

On another day he produced some drawing paper and colored pencils and sketched a house with smoke coming out of its chimney. An art student at Grinnell College, he had originally come to Hollywood to draw caricatures. With a fistful of pencils stuck out between his fingers like multicolored porcupine quills, he demonstrated how to blend colors and stay inside the lines. Somebody interested in showing me new things to do, who also had a deep voice and a manly face, could almost obliterate my affectionate memory of Jimmy Dunn. Standing or sitting, Cooper had become his romantic replacement.

Like Dorothy Dell during my earlier Paramount film, Carole Lombard was a prankster, a lovely, funny, generous lady. Easily dropping down to her knees, she echoed my jubilant yelps about all sorts of nonsense, her great expressive eyes crinkling at the corners and her high forehead glistening where it reached the blond hairline. Others have since suggested she had a rough tongue. If she really employed bawdy humor or truck-driver expletives, it was never within my hearing. Wherever she went she seemed to wear a halo of crystalline happiness.

Of course all was not personal felicity at Paramount. Menjou's earlier allegation concerning my competitive attitude obviously was well remembered. Before many days passed other actors on the film were fiercely crowding me at every turn with confounding new tricks. However, I was not without a strong ally. Perched quietly on her stool apart from the main activity, knitting unobtrusively but keeping track, Mother was a superlative auditor of events. Privately we tried to devise ways to obstruct each theft. Perhaps simply moving right or left at the last moment did the trick, or a sudden slight head movement to gain camera attention, although rarely did she suggest exactly a specific gesture or precise facial expression. Each time we plotted my defense she would remind me of the verity that movie success gets built only on professional achievement, not a bag full of fancy tricks. But at the same time we must watch out for me.

While resisting the urge to depend on artifice, sometimes it proved impossible to cope with competition. In one beach scene complete with sand and a big, standing umbrella, I was posed beside Cooper, who was dressed in a snap-brim Panama, garishly checked jacket, and double-pleated billowing trousers. Clustered in the background, around a large beach ball were several children. During my spoken lines one girl suddenly moved, straddled the beach ball and began to bounce gently up and down, a sure-fire attention-getter.

Director Hathaway saw it, and immediately stopped the scene. The kid on the beach ball had to quit it, he said. From her chair by the wall a black-haired woman moved quickly to the girl's side, whispered in her ear, and scurried back out of camera range. Before the scene started the girl climbed carefully on top of the ball, where she sat motionless.

Following a repeat of my lines, I sneaked a backward glance as the camera continued to roll. The girl was bouncing again. Against the wall, the black-haired woman was smiling and nodding her head in approval.

"Woman's intuition is what contributes to Shirley's success," Hathaway observed. "Surprising mentality, inexhaustible energy. Fine memory, but the key is her adult understanding."

He may have missed the boat. My intuition was like any kid's, as was my energy level. In truth, he had someone trained in the fundamentals and ready to work hard. Most important of all, I was at peace with myself. At home and on the set, I was bathed in a nourishing glow of affection. Father was unfailingly jolly and deferential to Mother, and both brothers were protective and reconciled to the attention I was receiving. Above all, Mother was a constant resource of love, ladled out in equal measures of encouragement and restraint. Beneath what Hathaway regarded as a naturally joyous and curious personality was someone with growing self-confidence. I seldom struggled to remember lines, nor blew them. There were no emotional hang-ups. I just stood there in my socks, paid attention, and worked with an uncluttered sense of purpose. Whatever role feminine intuition played in my success, it was minor. Love was the thing that freed me from nagging uncertainty, allowing me to do my job better than the next kid. Love was my philosopher's stone, a constant companion of good cheer.

One morning a studio official introduced a girl with dark brown bangs and some front teeth missing, someone I vaguely recalled from our ranks at Meglin's. She was to be my stand-in. Nobody had done that for me before, and I truly had no idea what to expect nor why a stand-in was needed. Rumors instantly blamed Mother for seeking my professional parity with other stars who had stand-ins. Others whispered that the request was mine, really nonsense. Kids are not like that. Every instant on the set was a delectable experience. Limitation of my working time was something I would have avoided, not sought.

In truth, a stand-in simply made good business sense for Paramount. State law limited me to four hours work each day, plus the three hours of school. Setting up a scene might take forty-five minutes; actual camera shooting would consume only five minutes. Using my time for setup simply squandered my legal availability before the camera. When asked, however, I explained the whole deal in terms removed from economics.

"Marilyn is my stand-out-in," I said. "She works while I rest, I work while she rests. We don't get very tired, either of us, do we, Marilyn?"

"No," she answered. "My sister has a dog. He found a mouse in the kitchen and killed it."

"Our cat had kittens," I countered. "We're going to the dressing room now. Not that I'm going to take a nap, though. Marilyn and I can play house."

"I'm going to be the mother of twins," she said.

"No," I retorted, "I'm going to have the twins. You are going to have two babies, one white and one black."

Although the stand-in program suggested that Mother might now encourage my contact with other children on the set, such was not so. As a general rule, circumstances involving me professionally with other children were something she scrupulously avoided. Whether actually her idea or the studio's, the logic was that any other child appearing in my photographs, for example, would dilute my aura of uniqueness and thereby diminish my professional potential.

Some encounters were inescapable, however. Once, in the Paramount commissary, actress Marlene Dietrich came threading her way through the tables, propelling a small girl ahead of her.

"This is my daughter, Maria," she announced, speaking with low-pitched inflections and a mysterious accent. "Imagine, only eight years old, and playing me as a child in *The Scarlet Empress*." I tried to look impressed.

Mother was obviously uneasy, confronted by the very luminous star I had so spoofed two years earlier as "Morelegs Sweettrick" in a *Baby Burlesk*. Fortunately the subject was avoided by all, Mother effusively directing all conversation toward Maria, reducing Dietrich and me to bystanders. We glanced at each other a lot. Her eyelashes were so long and stiff, they should have locked together as she batted them, but her mouth formed tight, pleasing little half-smiles. Not until the encounter was almost ending did Maria start talking to me.

"You know, I can't have still photos taken of me," she said. I looked puzzled. "One side of me is no good."

"Let me see why?" I asked. She cocked her face one way, then the other.

"They look the same to me," I said, mystified.

Looking slightly annoyed, Dietrich reached down for Maria's hand, said a cool, quick good-bye, and melted back among the tables.

Although I sidestepped other children on the lot, by no means was I short of playmates at home. There we had a gang of regulars on our block, kids who had shared my rough-and-tumble long before the hours of my work began to make me less accessible after their weekday school. Limited contact with studio children may have helped focus my affection solidly on special adult friends, as in the case of Dorothy Dell, my frolicsome cohort from *Little Miss Marker*. She was working on the stage next to mine during the filming of *Now and Forever*, and on several occasions she visited our set, rekindling my personal affection for her as well as reinforcing my sense of belonging to a broad studio family beyond my immediate set. Midway in our film Dell was killed in a gruesome nighttime automobile accident. Although explicit reports leaked around the whole lot, everyone was aware of my affection for her, and for a time the crew kept me unaware of the tragedy.

We were doing a dramatic bedtime scene where my father is discovered to have lied to me about being a jewel thief. Grief-stricken by this breach of faith, I was required to fling myself on the pillows, crying. We were set to film when someone, perhaps advertently, spilled the sad news about Dell. I burst into tears. Mother was momentarily off the set, so everyone milled around helplessly. Everyone but the director, who quickly called for a camera to focus on me where I lay slumped, sobbing away. First a close-up, then a medium shot. Mother returned, observed the splendid performance, and remained watching while the camera continued to roll. Only I knew it was more fun to shed fake tears than real ones.

7

On the good ship Lollipop
It's a sweet trip to a candy shop,
Where bon-bons play,
On the sunny beach of Peppermint Bay...
—Richard Whiting, *Bright Eyes*, 1934

Those lyrics were an instant hit when I sang them as the lead song from *Bright Eyes*. Four hundred thousand copies of the sheet music were sold, topping the previous all-time records of crooner Bing Crosby and soprano Jeanette MacDonald. That lollipop trademark was due to stick like lifelong glue although this was actually my second encounter with one. The first was in the *Baby Burlesk* movie *War Babies* at the Lolli-Pop Inn, featuring me as a French bar girl thieving from diaper-clad Yanks en route to the Western front.

For most people the song conjures up an image of a benevolent seagoing vessel. Actually it was a plane. To hasten my education carpenter friends knocked together a toy plane from a hogshead with two stubby wings, a fake propeller, and perilous balance. I was supposed to just rock, but I immediately rolled the whole contraption over, pinning myself in the cockpit. For my own protection, the toy was disassembled.

At Grand Central Air Terminal in nearby Glendale, it was a real plane. Hoisted into the open front cockpit for photographs, I could wiggle the joystick while posing in a red leather flying jacket and airman's cap with dangling earflaps and a propeller insignia with each vane curved like a pinwheel. Joy was complete when a pilot climbed into the rear cockpit, a mechanic spun our propeller to life, and away we clattered and jounced to the far end of the runway and back. With my unbuttoned earflaps flying in our own wind, it was the closest I could get to the real thing. Mother wanted no part of flying, and the fine print in my Lloyds accident insurance policy voided claims resulting from "any kind of aeronautics and/or aviation of any description, or resulting from being in an aircraft. . . ."

Our aircraft scenes were cooperative ventures with two private companies. American Airlines and Douglas Aircraft Company provided a DC-2 passenger airplane to taxi us back and forth on the tarmac while cameras ground away. Later American flew distribution film copies to New York with pomp and publicity, proclaiming the potential of air freight, still in its infancy.

Will Rogers had taken a special interest in what we were doing and often hung around our stage. An unofficial cheerleader for aviation, Rogers had written, "There were eight people killed [in planes] all over America on Sunday, and it's headlined in every paper today. When will newspapers give aviation an even break? If there's a safer mode of transportation, I have never found it." One year later he was dead in an air crash.

My first onstage flying experience was in a sliced-open interior mock-up of a DC-2 aircraft. Passengers on our plane were all volunteers from the football team from nearby University of Southern California. As stagehands slowly pulled a painted panorama of clouds past the windows and others heaved and rocked our mock-up in simulated, bouncy travel, I wandered along the aisle singing cheerfully.

My second trip was more hazardous, a stowaway on Dunn's plane delivering documents through a violent storm when the mechanical controls failed. Before the plane was to crash I appeared from hiding to hitch a ride on Dunn's parachute as we bailed out. Harnessed together, we were hoisted up among the catwalks and soundstage rafters. Bolts of fake lightning flashed, wind machines howled a gale, sending us swinging like a pendulum while overhead sprinklers swirled a deluge. Camera! Our billowing chute was released and downward we drifted toward the ring of upturned faces. Just as we hit the floor someone entered the soundstage through the securely air-locked door. Our synthetic gale immediately exhausted toward the opening, sucking up our parachute and its tangled web of cords. With Dunn and me still strapped in our embrace, it dragged us across the floor through collapsed chairs and overturned light standards; he gallantly on his back while I kept riding on top. Every actor for himself.

Despite his reedy tenor voice, Dunn was again my current favorite. A Hollywood maxim is that you always fall in love with the person playing opposite you; in my case again with Dunn. He liked games, was cheerful, and never used baby talk. At the outset my affection had hardly been reciprocated.

"All actors dislike working with children," Dunn had wailed when we were first matched up several months earlier. "My worst fears were justified the minute I set foot in front of the camera with her." Later he mellowed.

"It's ridiculous," he mused. "A child can't understand dramatic import in film lines and grasp what the business of the studio is all about. Yet, she behaves exactly as though she did."

Occasionally someone else tried to butt into what I considered my romantic monopoly. One day actress Alice Faye swooped past me without a nod, her blond hair blindingly pale in the glare of Kleig lights. An eye-catching woman in an elegant velvet costume, she dropped herself into Dunn's lap, where she remained, giggling, fluffing at his hair, and playfully chucking his chin. I was annoyed, considering Dunn to be my special property, at least for a while.

When Faye finished and departed I had no time to lose. Into Dunn's vacant lap I climbed, and slipped both arms around his neck. Time for my trump card.

"I'll marry you, Jimmy," I said, moving my head so as to shake its curls, the only feminine thing I had to shake.

When he told me it was a deal, I knew those curls were an asset. Something progressively devised by Mother, my curls were originally to thwart a tendency to frizziness induced by seashore humidity. Later they evolved into a collection of loosely rolled sausage curls for the *Baby Burlesks*, augmented by one flat spit curl Mother created to hide the forehead bruise just prior to filming my *Baby Take a Bow* theme song, and finally settling down to fifty-six unvarying pin curls. Occasionally bystanders reached out to tug at my hair to test its authenticity. The family of one famed makeup expert claimed he attached human hair ringlets to what was a sparsely endowed scalp, just as he had provided fake ringlets for Mary Pickford. That expert would have had to rise from his grave for the job. He had died in 1931, even before I entered Meglin's.

Fake hair might have been less of a chore. Every weekday night my hair had to be pinned up, and on Sunday, Mother washed it in my bathroom basin. Not a simple procedure. The soap was carved off a corner of a white bar of laundry Castile, melted in a pan on the stove, and applied warm and mushy. The scrubbing ended with an odorous vinegar rinse, which stung my eyes and diminished my later appreciation for tart salad dressings.

While Mother dipped her fingers in water and rolled up curls, Father perched on my closed toilet seat and read aloud from one of the *Oz* books by L. Frank Baum. Wicked witches and Munchkin people became familiar friends.

"I'd like to go to Kansas and see Dorothy," I said one evening. "The one blown away in the cyclone."

Mother was preoccupied, applying a cotton swab of peroxide to restore original blond to a curl threatening to grow up darker.

"Someday," she mused, "I want you to play Dorothy."

I thought about her comment for a moment. "How could I *play* Dorothy," I replied. "She's real. What I'd like to do is *visit* her."

Particularly with children, a powerful empathy and vivid imagination easily create reality where none exists. Yet drawing a line without disillusion is not easy. Commencing with chitchat during hair washing, Mother began the delicate process of defining make-believe without destroying its charm, eventually helping me construct a mental fence, something low enough to hop yet high enough to establish a separation between fact and fantasy.

☆

Before having approved *Bright Eyes*, Sheehan must have become leery of continuing me in roles of unadulterated goodness, for he concocted a challenge, a girl slightly older than I and several times more assertive. To pull it off Sheehan combined the assets of Fox from its two shooting locations, the feature-film home lot and a second lot for lower-budget productions on Western Avenue, referred to as Fox Hills. For our producer Sheehan mustered Sol M. Wurtzel, chief of the Fox Hills operation, a man who reminded me of Reynard the Fox, with his arrowhead face, broad across the top, narrow at the bottom, with big, expressionless eyes, and a long sharp nose. For someone detestable to enhance my innocence by comparison, Wurtzel brought along Jane Withers. We were on location in a Pasadena mansion, and she was combative in the film from the outset.

"There really isn't any Santa Claus," she sneered. When I insisted there was she screwed her face in disgust and flounced away. I really still wanted to believe the Christmas myth, and the certainty with which she delivered the line was saddening. A clever little girl, Withers then started mimicking me to whoever would listen offstage. Put on the defensive by all this self-confident, noisy humiliation, both Mother and I tried politely to sidestep Withers's mother and, whenever possible, Withers herself by always having something else to do.

As a timely foil to this tactic, Mary Lou Isleib had arrived as my stand-in, replacing Marilyn Granas, whose mother had refused to bleach her dark hair to match mine. Daughter of Mother's old and dear friend, Aileen, Mary Lou was one of the preceding babies with "naturally curly blond hair" that had inspired Mother to have me. A look-alike in hair color, height, and weight, she was docile and patient, well suited to her task, one which would last throughout my movie career. As a dividend for Mother, Aileen was often on the lot, anchoring two old friends in a shifting sea of new acquaintances.

As cast, Withers was noisy, arrogant, and rich, constantly humiliating me as the shy, stubborn poor girl. For props we were each issued a doll, mine modest and frumpy, befitting my role, and hers a giant glorious Lenci from Italy with dangling blond curls and exquisitely costumed in ruffles and a velvet bonnet garlanded with lifelike flowers. Offstage I admired the clothing, and following her stage role, Withers became possessive, denying me even a peek, clutching it and turning away. Ultimately it developed into a quiet offstage competition for something she really did want, but I did not.

Growing impatient with what seemed a petty competition, Mother quietly explained the unworthiness of my unqualified envy. When someone wanted something she should be prepared to give something, a precept I immediately tested in another context.

Madame Ernestine Schumann-Heink, seventy-four-year-old grand lady of the opera in Hollywood for her film debut in *Here's to Romance*, had come gliding onto the set as though on wheels.

"I'm just a beginner," the body thundered but only the lips moved. "You are so experienced. How do you remember your lines?"

"Oh, that's easy," I replied, and recounted our bedtime system, reserving enough detail to preserve our secrets.

"Will you help me with my lines, and coach my acting?" she asked.

That wasn't yet the fair exchange Mother had mentioned.

"Well, yes," I replied, "but then you will have to teach me how to sing like you do."

With one big rolling laugh, she hurried off somewhere else. Obviously I would never make it as a diva, but then she might never become an actress. As she disappeared Mother squeezed my hand in approval.

Toward the end of *Bright Eyes*, Sheehan caught wind of the doll competition and offered Mother the Lenci doll in order to gain her cooperation on some other minor matter. Believing I really coveted it, Mother accepted his bribe, thinking perhaps to employ the doll in some secondary inducement with me. Her hope vanished when Sheehan publicly announced that I was starting a doll collection with the Lenci as my first. This action was tantamount to removing a finger from the dike. From all over the box-office world a thousand dolls of every type and nationality flooded in. In fact, the concept of a collection of anything beyond slingshots had no appeal whatsoever. It was a Pyrrhic victory; winning the Withers war imposed the unwelcome burden of becoming curator for an unwanted collection.

Aided by the earnings from my films, Fox seemed to be struggling free from the grip of financial quicksand but could hardly ignore an enormous exposure. Its basket of champions still held only two stars and a half: Janet Gaynor, Will Rogers, and me. To memorialize its principal current assets, the studio commissioned Peruvian painter Alberto Vargas to do a mural for the Café de Paris executive dining room depicting its lead stars. An immaculately groomed dandy in the Rudolf Valentino mold, with pomaded hair and mustache pencil-thin, Vargas was widely known for seminude, sensuous ethereal creatures, sometimes prone. It took several sketches of me to get Mother's penciled okay. It also took personal redirection for this sophisticated voluptuary to paint the virginal innocence which to this day still smiles down from that wall.

Chosen as master of ceremonies, Will Rogers pulled the string, and down fluttered the veil, disclosing me as the central figure in the group.

"The greatest squawkie entertainer in the world today," he quipped, chewing his gum, "but still pint-sized." I grinned, but close-mouthed.

Noticing my strained expression, he asked: if I liked the painting, why wasn't I smiling?

"My tooth fell out yesterday," I answered, covering my mouth, "right in front."

It had happened at the worst time. For rising movie stars it was noblesse oblige to register hand and footprints in wet cement in the forecourt plaza of Grauman's Chinese, an ornate movie theatre fronting on Hollywood Boulevard. A wall of gaping people pressed in to gawk at my investiture. At this moment of maximum exposure, out fell my first baby tooth, an incisor, right in the middle of my smile. Furtively, I spit it into my hand.

"Smile for the photographers," Mother whispered, unaware. With lips pursed, I grinned. The cameras were all on my face.

Jean W. Klossner, ex-mason inspiration for the whole showy ritual, was beside me in his flowing robe and medieval beret and pointed to a square of glistening wet cement where I should place my foot.

A-ha, the foot! Get all those cameras and eyes off my face and onto something else.

"These shoes make my feet too big," I mumbled behind my palm. "Can I do it barefoot?"

Slowly removing one shoe and sock, I wiggled the bare toes to catch camera attention, holding my face pointed down at all times.

My story finished, Rogers shifted his gum and bent down. "You're lucky," he said, and opened his mouth. "See, one of mine fell out yesterday! At least yours grow right back!"

"Not very quickly," I said, and told him about my dentist. Presiding over an unusual practice, he did dental plates and caps. No appointments required. Everything done quickly. Assume the chair, open wide for an impression. Within several hours a matchbox-size package would arrive at the studio with a new tooth and a can of adhesive powder for Mother to glue in the fake. He needed me, and I needed him. For years my teeth continued to fall out, one by one, and for years I was sneaked in and out of that office, like an incognito criminal.

So far as the audience could tell, my baby teeth never did fall out. Like me, they were timeless.

Bright Eyes was an instant hit, returning its $190,000 cost three weeks after release. Besides a financial bonanza, the film worked a medical miracle. A young girl from Romford, England, named Kathleen Robinson, congenitally mute for twelve years, became so excited watching the film that her ability to speak was suddenly restored.

Fox net profits now crept toward $1,270,000. By year's end the company had $4 million cash on hand. The turnaround looked dramatic, and its shares moved sharply upward on Wall Street. Not least among major Fox creditors, Chase National Bank breathed relief, and a delegation from the board of directors arrived in California to confirm the reported progress. Included were heavy-hitters Winthrop W. Aldrich and Nelson A. Rockefeller.

To honor the visitors a welcoming dinner was scheduled, with required attendance by key Fox stars. Janet Gaynor came over when I was getting dressed in the wardrobe department.

"You're a real trouper," she enthused. "Eight films in one year! Will you sign this picture for me?"

Six movies, not eight, I thought, counting them up. I took her pen and began to scratch out the letters of my name. Two nearby wardrobe mistresses chimed in, requesting autographs for themselves.

"You can all have them," I agreed, "but somebody has to wait. I can only sign two a day. My printing is too slow."

With white tablecloths and candlelight, everything at dinner moved like a well-rehearsed movie, although black actor Stepin Fetchit caused one small ripple, loudly drawling that it looked like a "swell spot for a crap game."

After dessert Will Rogers rose and ribbed the honored guests with an anecdote comparing bankers to scarecrows, saying both wore sincere suits and waved sleeves in the wind, but only the banker failed to scare anyone. Everyone laughed and clapped at the jest except Aldrich.

Rogers's lariat had been thrown high and wide. Rising and leaning forward on his chair back, Aldrich launched into an ill-disguised, sobering rebuttal. While humor had its place, he said, Chase directors had not spent five days by train to California from New York to be ridiculed.

Hardly the useless evil portrayed by Rogers, banks were indispensable partners in any real-life financial success.

I was getting sleepy. Not so one Fox official, who had slunk over and now crouched down between Mother and me.

"Get Shirley to do something," he whispered to her. "Kiss him."

When Mother told me what to do, I was bug-eyed. My kissing any adult offstage was anathema to her, the epitome of all the pushy, obnoxious qualities common in movie children. But kissing was permitted before the cameras, so I rationalized that this situation must be another aspect of work.

Going around behind Aldrich, I waited for him to finish and sit down, then tapped his shoulder.

"Mr. Aldrich, may I sit in your lap?"

Turning toward me, he flashed a wan smile, adequate invitation for me to climb up. As laps go, his was not comfy. The legs felt hard and thin, and he couldn't decide whether to keep them tight together or slightly spread. Twisting around, I reached up and kissed his cheek. Letting out a little "whoof" of surprise, he put both hands securely at my waist as if to anchor me on his lap a safe distance from his face.

The deed had been done, but without the desired result.

"Can I sing you something?" I asked. He raised his eyebrows in surprise and arched his head back, staring out from the bottoms of his eyes. He hadn't said no, so I started.

My song finished to an outburst of applause from the partisan and obviously relieved table. Taking that cue, I launched off into an encore, followed by more loud cheers and handclaps. So I tried a third time.

By then the appreciative contagion of the moment had apparently softened Aldrich's annoyance. We chatted animatedly about nothing until Rockefeller, who was sitting a few seats away, leaned over and complained that I had not tried his lap.

It turned out to be fatter, and I remained there until no longer able to stifle my yawns. For anyone seven years old it was the end of a long day, way past regular bedtime. Besides, the job was done, and frankly I had been on more comfortable laps.

☆

Although Fox seemed to be working its way out of the financial woods, a thicket of trouble awaited within the movie industry. In early 1934 from Poverty Row rose the voice of Educational Studio again, clamoring for me to fulfill the Hays commitment to them for more comedies in the *Frolics of Youth* series. Answering the veiled threat of court action, Fox lawyers dangled a lump-sum settlement offer, noisily declined by Educational. Fox strategy appears to have been to keep me fully assigned or loaned out. It was simply a matter of possession. Physically, Fox had me. However, as reasonable antagonists often do, both organizations recognized that impasse is not a solution. Once the two studios decided not to bite each other, it would have been folly to keep barking. Educational agreed to combine all my *Baby Burlesks* and *Frolics of Youth* in one film package to be called the "Shirley Temple Special," set a price far in excess of what each film could command separately, and appointed Fox as exclusive distribution agent for a fee. I was the same wine in a new bottle at a higher price, with profits for all except me.

Monogram Studios then prepared *Million Dollar Baby*, a spoof riddled with specific references to my name. Again, Fox lawyers poured out to battle like a swarm of hornets, successfully thwarting the idea by brandishing threats of legal injunction and monetary damages.

Forthright solutions proved more elusive for Father, however. First, it was outright commercial piracy of my name and image. A fan magazine affiliate released a line of dresses bearing my name. A fashion book contained my endorsement without my having been asked. The studio was either tolerating or encouraging other commercial endorsements as adjuncts to its publicity programs. In a General Electric model kitchen I reached on tiptoe for the handle of a "double-door GE Monitor refrigerator." Beside a model Packard Motors six-cylinder car I smiled my confident endorsement, surely the least likely driver of the year. When Father purchased a $5,000 policy on me from Lincoln National Life Insurance Company, national publicity appeared implying my personal endorsement for the company as a whole.

Between newspaper ads offering cures for arthritis, varicose veins, and hernias, I appeared holding a giant placard proclaiming a weight-reduction program for $1.00.

Adult bars selling alcoholic beverages began devising variations of a Shirley Temple cocktail, sugary concoctions of grenadine syrup, fruit juices, and soda water, something theoretically to occupy children while accompanying adults imbibed more powerful drinks. Mother objected strongly to the practice. It gave my name currency in the same locale as manhattans and martinis, and could cause cavities as well. The drink looked like diluted blood and tasted worse.

In a rare instance of reciprocity a new four-door maroon sedan appeared from Dodge Motor Car Company in return for Mother's saying she "demanded a safe car for Shirley Temple and admired its 18–24 miles per gallon, its rugged welded-steel body, its amazing brake-action, and its list price of $640."

My name and likeness in testimonials and personal endorsements were being sown like seeds on the wind. Nobody was in charge.

Not really a bone of contention between Father and the studio, the tie-ins might not have provoked him were it not for money matters arising at the same time. Paramount Theatre in New York offered $5,000 for my one-week personal appearance. Fox declined, with Mother's support.

"We intend to keep her natural and unspoiled," she insisted, "even if it costs us $10,000 per week."

Next to be rejected was a food company proposal for $3,500 on a single radio broadcast. Unacceptable, said Fox; radio drains away popularity and diminishes a future in films.

Father was becoming rankled by the glaring disparity between my value as measured in the marketplace and my $150 weekly salary from Fox. After brooding about this privately, he gingerly raised his concern with studio officials. Never mind the offers, he was brusquely told. My salary was fixed by contract, iron-clad.

Our studio relationship came under further tension when Mother innocently took me to join fellow actors in a public appearance on behalf of the Screen Actors Guild (SAG). Still a nascent labor union, the SAG was viewed by some management as a flaming hotbed of Communists. Mother was taken sorely to task for permitting such an appearance.

Our kettle was due to boil over, and in a backhand way the fire was stoked by agent Gene Mann, whose claims to commission had been blithely ignored by Father. In June 1934, Mann served notice he was suing me for breach of contract. All at once Father had his hands full with commercial piracy, thwarted income, and now a legal suit from an ex-agent.

As he would do several times in the future, Father coped with one agent by hiring another. In return for promises from my family of exclusive representation, agent Bern Bernard, a gaunt man with frog eyes, pledged to indemnify them against the claim from Mann. Away we all went the following week for customary court approval of the Bernard contract.

"Will you fix this contract for me?" I appealed, right on cue.

Leaning forward in his chair and scowling over the top of his papers, the judge declined. Excessive and retroactive commissions; total control of my bank accounts; absence of a contract termination date: he shook his head and looked straight at me. That contract simply could not be fixed, he said.

Bernard went home to release an irate statement that Judge Marshall F. McComb was ignorant of the entertainment business, and gratuitously ended his negotiations with my family. Once again we were adrift in unchanged turbulent seas. Too many disconnected levers were being pulled.

Into this confusion then stalked actor Jackie Coogan's mother and his stepfather, Arthur Bernstein, still another theatrical agent.

"They came over to the house," reported Mother, "and he walked up and down our living room waving a check for half a million dollars in my face, saying he had just gotten the check for Jackie. We didn't know anything about the picture business, he shouted, and we needed him to handle all our affairs."

Quoting J. C. Furnas, film critic of the *New York Herald Tribune*, Bernstein argued that I was like Mae West, primarily a stunt. Just something out of the normal run, like roller skating and contract bridge. I was just another pint-sized, short-lived phenomenon. Odds were against either my or Mae West's showing much staying power. Unless we hired him, Bernstein added.

"He talked and talked until we were dizzy," Mother said, "claiming we would certainly be cheated if we didn't let him take care of us. We didn't know where to turn."

Instead of moving along a tranquil causeway of progress and prosperity, my parents were now being harried by voluble strangers and rained on by career complexities beyond their knowledge and control. Both parents agreed that the logical thing to do was to call in the only professional man they knew, our family doctor.

Why they thought a physician could help was an attitude rooted in

Father's family history. At his birth in 1890 in tiny Fairview, Pennsylvania, his father was a family physician and county coroner, and occupied a house between Church and Cemetery streets, thus cornering the local medical market, cradle to grave.

One winter day the doctor, an impulsive man, was outside chopping kindling. Jokingly his wife placed her finger on the block and dared him to chop it off. He did, retrieved the severed finger from the snow, and sewed it back on at the kitchen table. Many times thereafter Father's mother admonished her four children against tempting fate, brandishing her slightly crooked, scarred finger, a lesson which deeply impressed Father with the power of doctors to both damage and repair.

No miracle had seemed beyond the ken of physicians. At four, Father had contracted a digestive disorder which his father judged to be terminal. A man with an eye for recorded history, the doctor bundled his ill child into a horse-drawn carriage and set off for the nearby town of Girard to have a final photo taken. En route they reined up at a roadside store, where the child was curiously attracted to some bananas. In the spirit of the Last Supper, Dr. Temple bought one for his patient, who immediately lost all his morbid digestive symptoms. A frugal man, the doctor turned his horse homeward, saved the cost of a photo, and took to prescribing bananas when all else seemed to fail.

Blessed with such an inheritance, it is not surprising that in Father's household a mystique existed around physicians, a certainty of sagacity, insight, and innovative thought. Medicine was arcane and powerful, and physicians were its apostles. Trapped in their labyrinth of problems, where better for them to seek guidance?

When asked, the doctor was more realistic than Father, and prescribed a lawyer. Through bank connections Father enlisted downtown attorney Loyd Wright, an articulate and ambitious man remembered for his oversized bow ties.

"Now we have a lawyer to help us," explained Mother, "but weren't we lucky to have such a sensible doctor!" It was hardly too soon, and almost too late.

8

Within the first six months of 1934 I had completed four feature films at two major studios, plus minor roles in several other features. Suddenly this frenetic pace came to a halt. Our new lawyer, Loyd Wright, served notice to the studio that the status quo in my employment had become unacceptable.

Fox lobbed their initial firecracker on a hot July 4th Independence Day. In a spirit of generosity and equity my pay was being boosted from $150 per week to $1,000. However, there were preliminary conditions. My parents must free themselves of any theatrical agency contracts which might exist. They must also reject all pending offers for my services, such as a recent one offering $4,000 for a single Chicago personal appearance.

Our return volley ignored the Fox offer. Wright demanded $2,500 per week, a limitation of two films per year, and Mother on the payroll at $100 per week.

Fox adopted a stony silence. With the rope pulled taut and heels dug in on both sides, something had to happen beyond verbal sparring. Father jumped into the action, declaring I would not work until his demands were met. It was not an early summer; it was an early frost. I was put on strike in my backyard, with slingshots, handcuffs, water pistols, and rubber daggers.

Attorney Wright was the bad guy, as far as Fox was concerned. My parents had been well contained before he showed up. That was the message carried by an employee of the Motion Picture Academy of Arts and Sciences. Not directly involved in his visit, I sat and listened. When the man spoke he gesticulated widely with both hands to emphasize his points. Seated perched on the edge of his chair, feet spread wide, he looked as if ready to spring up.

Attorney Wright was a misleading, uninformed influence, the man proclaimed. Allowing him to lead us down the current pathway was suicidal. Father nodded his head, more in courtesy than conviction as it turned out, for nothing was agreed.

The next day a letter arrived from the man restating that multiple opinions were proving to be "terribly disconcerting . . . a bad situation for Shirley." Wright should be dismissed. Advice should come only from a good theatrical agent, preferably himself, counsel which flew in the face of the Fox precondition regarding agents.

My parents continued immobilized, but Wright's hand steadied at the helm as these smallish clouds of confusion passed over. Two weeks after the first salvos were exchanged on Independence Day, everything fizzled out. Unlikely as it was that one small girl could turn Fox studio upside down, there was even less chance I would be long left to sling-shots in my backyard.

On July 18, 1934, Fox and my parents executed two new contracts, one for my services and a second for Mother's. Taken together, this was the legal backdrop against which my next six years would be played. With little fanfare but great alacrity, both contracts were officially endorsed by the State Superior Court and, as petitioned by Fox, promptly withdrawn from court records available to the public. Only three days had elapsed from agreement before both documents were launched into a black hole of privacy, far from prying public eyes.

Obscurity suited both parties. It insulated Fox from both agents and performers culling through records to unearth precedents favorable to themselves. For my parents it answered their concern for my physical security. Deeply impressed by the Lindbergh kidnapping example, they held that silence theoretically reduced criminal incentive to capitalize on my financial bonanza.

Joint formal announcement of the deal oozed platitudes and generalities, but some factual terms leaked from the bottom of Fox files.

Mother would receive $250 weekly, ten times her current salary and more than twice Wright's original request. Her job was to continue as my mother, and specifically to be in charge of my hair. My salary would be increased to $1,000 weekly. Less than half Father's prior adamant proposal, it was still more than six times bigger than before. The contract term would run for seven years, subject to Fox's exercising its annual renewal options.

As part of our deal Fox agreed to provide certain perquisites, such as one rubber-tired scooter, a doll carriage, picture books, assorted blocks, a skipping rope, and a game of jacks. Confirming what Sheehan and Mother had already arranged, I would be barred from the Café de Paris commissary except for special occasions. It was an odd negotiation. Typically performers concentrate on cash and let perquisites take second place. My parents' concern was the reverse, concentrating instead on well-being, privacy, and personal protection.

Three profoundly important areas of the contract remained undisclosed publicly. One related to agents, another to artistic and professional control, and a third involved detailed financial arrangements.

First, Father agreed to forgo any and all theatrical representation for me. Ironically, this flew directly in the face of relevant industry rules in the *Code of Fair Competition in the Motion Picture Industry*, formally adopted by Fox the previous November. Prior to this time studios had been using questionable tactics to restrict star salaries and constrain negotiating rights of talent agents. Studio prohibition against agents was a subtle coup. In any subsequent conflict Fox could watch the chicken, as it were, by representing both sides.

Secondly, the studio retained full and sole authority in all matters relating to artistic control, including scripts, casting, costuming, and exploitation. Always distasteful to performers, such exclusions are not unusual. In addition, however, the studio also obtained total and sole authority over any and all of my appearances, performances in public, including the theatre, and on radio and recordings. To cap off this control, each commercial license negotiated by my parents was subject to written studio consent, but without studio liability. It was a professional lock-up.

The third provision, buried in fine print, was both sweet and sour. For each film completed there would be a $15,000 confidential bonus initially, later more than doubling to $35,000, a stunning windfall. However, the accumulated bonus would be held back from my recorded paychecks until contract termination seven years later. Meanwhile, such sums would be placed in two revocable trusts, with California Trust Company and the Bank of America as trustees. The owner was to remain Fox, with my parents as residual beneficiaries.

Most likely, Father regarded the trusts as hidden assets. It would have been out of character for Mother to ponder their significance, and Father never discussed such matters with her.

For the studio, however, revocable trusts served as a type of compensating balance for extra bank credit, supremely useful in those hard times. Most important, it was also a subtle financial truncheon suspended over my curly head. Tax rates were rising sharply to help finance FDR's New Deal. Each year my reported earnings were reduced by the amount held back. Thus, each year my eventual tax liability increased. In effect, the longer I worked, the more severe my tax penalty would be if I decided to quit. My tiny feet were placed in quicksand.

Two minor disadvantages to Fox still existed but were completely cured in a supplemental contract executed April 10, 1935. In return for a minor salary adjustment for Mother, both parents agreed never again to ask Fox for any salary increases for either Mother or me, nor to seek any further modification of the original contract. To reinforce restrictions on my exposure beyond movies, I was prohibited from "any public appearance of any kind or character whatsoever, either to be introduced or to perform before any audience."

This latter edict was challenged only once, and then by mistake. During our subsequent 1937 Hawaii visit, lyric tenor Tito Schipa had invited us to his evening concert, arranged by a prophetically named promoter, Mr. Clutterbuck. Delaying his start until we arrived, Schipa apparently irritated his large audience, and after we came called me to the stage to be introduced. Mindful of the contract prohibition, Father rose to his feet and refused. The audience booed. Ringed by animosity, he then marched us all up the aisle and out of the hall. It was not one of my better nights.

With the Fox contract at last put to bed, Father confided he would probably have to leave his job at the bank in order to take proper care of my financial affairs.

"Even if I took only an agent's fee of ten percent, it would be more than I am earning," he remarked candidly. "As Shirley's natural guardian I suppose I could charge more, if I so desired." Somehow he had forgotten the specific ruling laid down by the State Superior Court when approving the Fox contracts which prohibited what he was suggesting.

Asked what he planned to do with all the money, Father puffed away at his cigar. "Invest it. So when she gets older and falls in love, some punk can't marry her and go south with the cash."

Asked how he felt as the father of a six-year-old earning over $1,000 per week, he fingered the gold watch chain he wore draped at a rakish angle between upper and lower vest pockets. "Very foolish," he replied.

No useful purpose is served in overlooking Father's flaws nor in making a virtue of them, as he often did. He believed everyone else to be as openhearted as he regarded himself. Each turn of the Fox negotiation had been assessed in the context terms of his own expectations. Disturbing nuances failed to dampen his hopes. Snuggled in a comforting corporate embrace, he anticipated both relief from stinging problems and a guarantee of endless amity. He was hopelessly out of touch with reality.

Dressed in a dark suit and wearing his glowing smile, he signed with a flourish. The partnership was perfect. Actually it was a cruel false dawn of unity. It was far too late for Father to rub his eyes free of the blear which obscured how others had played their hand. What he was executing was a strange sort of due bill. It was his to enjoy, but I would have to pay.

Nobody should sneer at Fox for pursuing their legitimate self-interest in a skillful, relentless fashion. Yet in abandoning rights to representation, accepting exclusion from all professional and artistic control, and overlooking the quirky financial aspects of the deal, my parents were terribly ill-advised. Above the obvious blessings of the agreement these three errors in judgment would continue to loom like a trio of ghosts at the feast.

9

Jubilant with resolution of the Fox wrangle, Father unloaded on Loyd Wright's shoulders the plaguing and disorderly jumble of my financial, legal, and business affairs. Some pattern of family cash operations had already been established. Basic family expenses were being met by my earnings, including salaries for housekeeper and fan-mail secretary. Allowances and educational tuition for my older brothers were included, Jack at Santa Monica Junior College and George at New Mexico Military Institute. A monthly allowance went to Grandmother Maude Cregier, living nearby. On top of her contractual earnings from Fox, Father paid Mother an additional $25 a month for petty cash. My monthly allowance was $13, half dutifully deposited in a piggy bank for my future.

Although money was already sloshing in and out, it was over a jumbled rockpile of financial records. Wright helped sort all this out, establishing a system of accounting to keep accurate track of family cash flow for tax purposes. Next he engineered an out-of-court settlement of $1,000 with Gene Mann on his breach-of-contract suit over unpaid commissions. Father's delaying tactic had proved costly. The settlement was roughly double Mann's claimed commission had he been paid in the first place.

Finally Wright addressed the chaos of my public endorsements, sent off a flurry of threatening letters to flagrant commercial pirates, and began to establish an orderly system so that with his help my parents could execute licenses of major potential.

The American toy business was becalmed. Seeing me as a life preserver, Ideal Toy and Novelty Company in New York negotiated a license for dolls, the first model to be patterned on the red polka-dot dress from *Stand Up and Cheer*. Soon Ideal had contracted for the entire output of the nation's largest wigmaker. Two large dress-goods firms were consolidated to stitch up costumes. Company employment bounded upward 50 percent, yet production continued to lag three weeks behind the flood of orders. Within a year Ideal would be selling me in six baby sizes, and seven sizes as a little girl. Before 1941 the public would have invested $45 million in Shirley Temple dolls.

Apart from product sales, my face was useful as a merchandising tool. General Mills Corporation obtained a license to use my image stenciled on sturdy cobalt-blue mugs, plates, and pitchers given away as a box-top premium with Wheaties breakfast food. "A sure-fire way to get children to drink more milk," read the promotion. Forty years later this apparently indestructible blue glassware would be a collector's item.

"My favorite souvenir is a quite rare Shirley Temple blue pitcher," wrote Herb Caen, *San Francisco Chronicle* columnist. "It has her picture on the side in white and is perfect for martinis, with the following foolproof formula: gin to the chin, vermouth to the tooth."

Clutching holiday bouquets from billboards, I urged passing motorists to send flowers by Postal Telegraph. From life-sized supermarket displays I offered recipes for my six favorite desserts, "All made with Sperry Drifted Snow Flour." The Grunow Teledial radio was so easy to operate, I proclaimed, even I could tune it. Radiating enthusiasm, I pushed the healthful attributes of Quaker Puffed Wheat cereal. Privately I ate it solely because its advertising said it was "shot out of guns."

Licenses were awarded for dresses, hair ribbons, and headbands, all to help transform other girls into my curly-haired likeness. Along came hats and berets to cover up those same heads. To cloak the small bodies, overcoats were available with my face on the label. Soap novelties ensured clean hands and faces on those little bodies newly dressed, beribboned, hatted, and cloaked. A torrent of hodgepodge items flooded the marketplace. Cutout books, dishware, sheet music, sewing sets, pocket mirrors, paper tablets, playing cards, anklets, barrettes, candy molds, and all sorts of novelties swirled across sales counters.

Before 1935 ended my license royalty income would reach $100,000, doubling my earnings from movies. During the next year licensing income would crest in a floodtide of over $200,000.

Finally, corralling my commercial opportunities with doll, dress, and paperbook companies had one ironic twist. Rather than tidying up the marketplace, it spawned a new tier of violators. An army of unlicensed dolls, clothing, and oddities came marching onstage, a mechanical doll from Maine playing a pipe organ and another doing a jig. Spanish cigar bands featured my face. Bracelets came spiraling in from Denmark, floppy cloth dolls from England, books and assorted figurines from Germany and France. Tiaras, charms, and rings rained down. Costs to pursue this band of elusive commercial scoundrels made no economic sense. A swarm of small-time thieves, they peddled where they could, pocketed the cash, and melted into the murk of their origins.

The volume of things being sold suggested an exploding demand, but not everyone held a sanguine view of products endorsed by me. In Washington, Paraguayan Minister Enrique Bordenave cited the deluge as the one thing he didn't like about our country.

"I have become a victim of Shirley Temple," he wailed. "I have to take my children to see all her pictures. I must buy dresses, pajamas, and hats, all modeled after her. I am glad we have no Shirley Temple in Paraguay!"

In the world of movie personalities the distance between popularity and politics is short. California voters were seething in a race for the statehouse, pitting seventy-year-old acting governor Frank S. Merriam against flamboyant but appealing challenger Upton Sinclair, author of a socialist utopian scheme entitled "End Poverty in California" (EPIC). Under EPIC a footage tax would be assessed on all motion pictures and the proceeds diverted into unspecified projects for the common good. Led by Joseph M. Schenck of Twentieth Century Pictures, Inc., the owners of movie companies recognized a dangerous new cost in their future. Mandatory levies on paychecks of studio workers helped management raise a political kitty for Merriam, and I was among stars dispatched to attract him favorable publicity.

In the state capitol at Sacramento, the governor presented me with some papers and a welcoming proclamation festooned with golden seals and multicolored ribbons. Cameras flashed but nobody offered to read the documents to me.

"Funny papers," I muttered.

Merriam ignored my comment. "Are you Republican or Democrat?"

"What are they?"

"Well, are you going to vote for me or Upton Sinclair?"

"I'm going to vote for the boss," I answered.

Hoisting me onto his lap, surprisingly bony considering his jowls and rounded stomach, he said complimentary things such as that I was the only performer who could get him to steal away and attend what he called a "picture show." He seemed uninformed, so I kept quiet.

"What do you think of yourself?" he suddenly asked.

"I don't like me much," I answered, shifting around on his legs.

"I've noticed you seem impervious to flattery."

Mother interjected, saying I was suspicious of praise and promises, and preferred to wait and see. She explained that the trait had appeared about two years before. Perhaps someone had promised something, a doll or a dog, failed to deliver, and stimulated me to be wary next time. In the alchemy of childhood perhaps this experience had converted disappointment into a shield against subsequent expectation.

"Let's hope her future disappointments have as good an influence," was the way the governor put it, and switched subjects to say 10,000 people were expected at that evening's rally, mostly because of me. Mother reacted politely but firmly, saying I could not attend because my contract prohibited such events.

"Besides, I don't want her to get into politics," she added, "at least until she can spell the word."

Held securely on his uncomfortable lap, slightly bored listening to why I was the way I was, and why I could not do something, I might have misled Merriam with my silence. Actually I was tongue-tied with respect. Nobody could have existed in our disciplined soundstage environment without acknowledging both the nature and necessity of authority. Alongside grew an appreciation for the hierarchical nature of things. All bosses were unequal. At home Mother was my boss. Zanuck bossed us both at the studio. Now that I knew who he was, Merriam was a superboss for all California.

My understanding of such relationships proved unequivocal a few days later. The man's name had meant nothing to me, just another visitor. Heavy-jowled and wearing a buttoned black overcoat, he sat slumped and silent until the scene ended. Introducing him, Mother explained he was a writer who believed science-fiction wars were coming. He continued to stare, eyes expressionless as a bird's. And a world-famous historian, too, she added. Waiting for him to say something, I noticed his necktie knot had loosened, revealing the collar button. Something intervened before he spoke to me, if that was his intent, and he went away.

"That was H. G. Wells," Mother intoned, looking after him. "One of the world's greatest living men."

"Oh, no, he isn't," I answered, my Sacramento trip still fresh in mind. "God is the greatest man. After him comes the Governor."

My respect for institutions extended to the insurance business as well, although this time slightly diluted by my frolicsome nature. Under a $25,000 face-value accident insurance policy underwritten by Lloyds of London, exclusions on my behavior were rigorous, voiding coverage if I were dismembered or disabled while dueling, or during insanity, drunkenness, or military service. Printed on oversized paper, the document was emblazoned with wax seals and appended by several long sheets bearing impressive inked signatures.

Weekly submission of my urine sample was also a condition of coverage. In consequence each Friday a drab little man would bustle into the cottage, usually mopping his head with a handkerchief, and wait for me to accommodate. One day he arrived unexpectedly. As usual I took his bottle into the bathroom, but I remained dry as a bone. Idly canvassing the cabinet where Mother kept her things, my eye fixed on a tall urn-shaped bottle of Shalimar toilet water, light yellow-colored. Obviously the expedient answer was substitution. Soon the messenger was gone on his perspiring way.

Several days later he returned, more moist than usual and deeply annoyed. Requesting I leave the room, he spoke cryptically with both Mother and Miss Barkley, and all three then joined to present a fresh glass bottle for my immediate attention. Wrapping the eventual submission in a brown paper bag, he departed, face glistening and rock-hard.

"Don't ever do that again," Mother scolded. "Those samples are needed by the 488 prominent people who signed your insurance policy," adding in a tone of reverence, "including seventeen lords and earls!"

Her argument was awesome. With such an international obligation to nobility and distinguished commoners in faraway London, could I do less than endow their process with authenticity? Toying with the insurance business, I had gone as far as I could go.

With the Shirley Temple police force, however, I had no limits. After contemplating the linkage between duty and obligation as applied to urine samples, I hit upon the idea of creating my own force, with me as chief, making the rules. It was really not designed to police anything, but rather was an organized system of obligations from whomever I was able to shanghai into membership. Fines were arbitrarily collected for infraction of rules, such as flubbing a line or delaying a scene. Insignia of membership were paper clips, until director David Butler later re-supplied us with gilded Junior G-man badges from a toy store. I was chief. I was judge. There was no appeal. At last I had designed an ideal balance between authority and obligation. As an autocracy, it was perfect.

10

The preeminent legendary giant of motion picture history is D. W. Griffith. By 1935, with his important career waning, he had written Winfield Sheehan at Fox proposing a controversial idea.

"There is nothing, absolutely nothing, calculated to raise the gooseflesh on the back of an audience more than that of a white girl in relation to Negroes," he said.

That such a proposal would emanate from Griffith should surprise no one. In his films, spanning thirty-eight years of filmmaking, bigotry and inhumanity are enduring themes of conflict. *Birth of a Nation*, in 1915, created a rage of controversy over its alleged Ku Klux Klan and anti-black bias. The following year *Intolerance* dwelled on man's inhumanity to man. In 1918 his *Greatest Thing in Life* aroused bitter dissension, showing an intolerant white snob overcome by battlefield passion and kissing a dying black soldier.

What weight Sheehan accorded the Griffith suggestion is unclear, but not what he did. Traveling to New York, he scouted black tap dancer Bill "Bojangles" Robinson, then on the Paramount Theatre stage. Sheehan haggled with agent Marty Forkins over whether Robinson could act as well as dance. Although a vaudeville performer, Robinson had appeared twice before movie cameras, in a 1930 cameo appearance in RKO's *Dixiana* and in a role in an all-black experiment called *Harlem Is Heaven*. Eventually they settled for a deal that was void if Robinson failed his Fox dramatic test. Sheehan was willing to give Griffith's "gooseflesh" theory a try.

The Little Colonel was to be produced by Buddy G. de Sylva. A mysterious scar ran from de Sylva's right nostril down over his upper lip. Sadly for me, any sinister connotation of the scar vanished with his explanation that he cut his face falling off a play cart when he was eight years old. Probably aware that this was a letdown, he observed that the scar had saved him from lots of brawls because others figured he'd gotten it in a knife fight.

It was de Sylva who introduced Bill Robinson, waiting outside our cottage with his wife, Fannie. The first thing I noted was the way his arms and legs moved with a silky, muscular grace. He was square-jawed and shiny-cheeked, his great round eyes showing whites all around. I was instantly attracted. Mr. Robinson will show you how to do the dances, was the way de Sylva put it.

Following introductory chitchat, we all started across the lot. Robinson walked a step ahead of us, but when he noticed me hurrying to catch up, he shortened his stride to accommodate mine. I kept reaching up for his hand, but he hadn't looked down and seemed unaware. Fannie called his attention to what I was doing, so he stopped short, bent low over me, his eyes wide and rows of brilliant teeth showing in a wide smile. When he took my hand in his, it felt large and cool.

For a few moments we continued walking in silence. "Can I call you Uncle Billy?" I asked

"Why, sure you can," he replied. After a few steps he again stopped.

"Mr. Robinson doesn't fit anyway." He grinned broadly. "But then I get to call you darlin'."

It was a deal.

From then on whenever we walked together it was hand in hand, and I was always his "darlin'."

☆

At first we practiced in the regular mirrored rehearsal hall. Then we found it more convenient to use a contraption that when folded looked like a wooden box, but when unfolded, became three steps, up one side and down the other. At any spare moment, anywhere, we could practice.

"We'll have a hand-squeeze system," he proposed. "When I give you three quick squeezes, means we're coming to a hard part. One long squeeze, really good, darlin'! No squeeze at all? Well, let's do it again."

Before long his system of signals became superfluous. "Now we just let those hands hang loose," he instructed. "Limp wrists, loose in the shoulders. There, that's it! Copacetic! Now let's get your feet attached to your ears."

It was the same message as from Mrs. Meglin, but with a superlative teacher, imperturbable and kind, but demanding. Although bubbling with energy, his physical motions were so controlled and fluid, they came out looking relaxed. He made it look easy, but was not one to pick his way gingerly. I must be guided solely by muscular memory. I must visualize my own sounds, not think about them. It must all be reflexive and unthinking, the sound of my taps telling me how I am doing, setting the pace and controlling the sequence. Every one of my taps had to ring crisp and clear in the best cadence. Otherwise I had to do it over.

That sort of repetitive rehearsal lay behind our familiar staircase dance in the southern plantation mansion in *The Little Colonel*. We made an unusual couple. A raggedy urchin with tousled curls paired with a regal black man in striped vest and brass buttons and patent-leather shoes. Every sound matched, every gesture, the scuffle, the staccato tap, a sharp-toed kick to the stile, a triple-time race up and down the staircase, tapping as we went. The smile on my face was not acting; I was ecstatic.

Fondest memories of dancing with Uncle Billy come not only from our camera takes but from rehearsals, up and down that portable stile, or in any convenient corner. Practicing until each move became unthinking was a joy. Learning, an exhilaration. In devising some nuance of movement or sound to make the dance only ours lay the ultimate satisfaction. Once we had reached the point of "roll 'em," each of our routines had been perfected, ready for only a final moment of elation in a long sequence totally devoid of drudgery.

But making movies is not all rehearse-and-perform. We sat around a lot, talking about boxing, for instance, and diamonds. Uncle Billy enthused about Joe Louis, then only a promising fighter from Detroit, and demonstrated uppercuts and vicious hooks while I watched transfixed.

"A dancer just like us," he said, bouncing around on tiptoe and jabbing out at an unseen opponent. "One day he'll beat Max Baer. He's world champion. But then, so am I," and he went on to describe how in Olympic Games tryouts he had won a 100-yard sprint in fourteen seconds, but running backwards.

Directors always reminded Uncle Billy to remove his ring before shooting. It was a brilliant diamond, and time and again we crouched like two mystics over his hand while he flicked his finger to catch the light and spun tales of African mines and bejeweled crowns. To him, diamonds were endowed with powers unrelated to monetary value. Perhaps that is why he gave me a gold-plated chief's badge for my police force. In the center was mounted his talisman, a small diamond.

The Little Colonel is an amalgam of southern plantations, pinafores, Spanish moss, and banjos plinking away with Civil War songs. At the outset director David Butler took me over to meet our southern colonel, Lionel Barrymore. It wasn't really a meeting. Barrymore didn't take my extended hand, and with one brief downward glance, he turned to speak with someone else. There is a big difference between being seen and being acknowledged.

During our first rehearsals a large blackboard was wheeled onstage and all Barrymore's cues and lines chalked up. I asked Mother why he couldn't learn his lines at home like everyone else, but she hushed me, explaining that he was a famous stage actor and would be hurt if he heard such comments.

Our first scene together went well enough, but I noticed his breath had a rich, fruity aroma vaguely remindful of the alcohol rub Mother gave me when I had a fever.

"It's because he's in pain," she explained later. "You must learn to be more sympathetic."

From the start Barrymore seemed weak on his lines, stumbling a lot over phrasing, and arguing with Butler over small points of emphasis. I mistakenly considered us both confederates acting in concert, not boiling up to our own civil war. One time, having as usual learned everyone's lines, I prompted him.

"Dammit!" he exploded. "I'm thirty years in this business!"

Watching from the sidelines, Miss Barkley filled the momentary silence with a shrill professorial warning: "Don't swear in front of the child or I'll order her off."

Barrymore glowered briefly in her direction and started to walk toward the door.

"Quiet!" exclaimed Butler, his arms extended like wings.

"No swearing," called Miss Barkley after Barrymore's retreating figure.

"Everyone take a break," said Butler, shaking his head, "This sort of deal just shouldn't happen."

For a few minutes everyone milled around waiting, then Butler left. Returning shortly, he took both Mother and me aside.

"Bad news," he said. "He's complaining she made him look ridiculous. He told me to get somebody else to do the picture."

In the pit of every true crisis there exists a moment of utter loneliness. Although acutely aware of being the cause of the dilemma, I could only stand aside, forlorn and silent. Finally Butler and Mother gave me their opinion. I must go alone and make up with him. I had no option.

When I rapped on Barrymore's dressing-room door, he let me in without a word and closed the door behind us. The place was cluttered. A half-completed landscape painting sat on an easel with paint tubes and brushes nearby. Some bottles stood on a worktable beside a copper etching plate. I asked him what was in the bottles and he replied, "Chemicals," watching me with his hands on his hips. Going from paints to etching plate and back to bottles, I asked questions of myself, and now and then he commented, curtly.

"Uncle Lionel," I said, addressing him that way for the first time. "I know you're the best actor in the world." He shot me an incredulous glance, but I kept on. "May I have your autograph?"

He shrugged his shoulders, sighed once, then sat down at his table. "To my favorite little niece," he wrote. "Your Uncle Lionel."

Examining motivations is a murky business, not the least through a prism of fifty intervening years. However, in the Barrymore incident two forces were at work. Having caused a problem, I had to work out of it. But in addition there was an underlying reason for my backhanded apology, a powerful sense of community purpose. Stuck together we would succeed; pried apart, we failed. Even my new police force had symbolized this belief in unity of effort.

Commitment to a common objective did not, however, mean total self-effacement. Our bunch of children were in a southern baptism scene. The bank of our man-made stream was muddy, lined with potted trees and shrubs disguised with collars of mossy turf. Everything smelled swampy. Draped in white sheets, another girl and I were knee deep in water, washing sins away. We were supposed to dunk Nyanza, a small black boy with his hair braided pickaninny style. During rehearsals I had realized he kept watching me, eyes rounded in a fixed gaze. In the spluttering and commotion of filming he missed his cues and was speechless. The more the director cajoled and the more we dunked him, the more flustered he became, a pitiful figure, dripping and bedraggled.

Making little progress, the director called a break and scolded Nyanza sharply. Mother, however, sensed the problem. Someone had gotten him tongue-tied at the prospect of acting with a name star, so she suggested I help him.

Taking his small hand in mine, I led him into a corner to rehearse. He really knew his lines, and the more we talked as two children do, the more self-assured he became. Convinced he finally had it, we dressed in dry sheets and waded back down into the stream. Nyanza said his lines without a falter. We dunked him. Surfacing, he said some more. Again he got dunked. The director seemed happy.

"Was I perfect?" Nyanza asked as we splashed up out of the stream.

"Sure," I answered, glad to have helped but unwilling to give him all the credit. "We all were! We did it together!"

The flare-up with Barrymore and tiny snags like Nyanza may have been structural reasons for delay in filming, but so was plain fun. In a play-within-a-play based on *Uncle Tom's Cabin*, I was cast as Little Eva, suffering a terminal fever contracted by fleeing across an ice-clogged river. Placed in bed to die, I was attended only by my father, John D. Lodge, a patrician by birth. Lodge's grandfather and brother were both U.S. senators. Admirals, generals, and Secretaries of State and Navy dangle from his family tree, but the sole suggestion of any artistic heritage was his poet father. Following Harvard and an unsatisfactory fling at practicing law, Lodge had bolted to become a movie actor. Success came rapidly, with *Women Accused, Little Women*, and the male lead opposite Dietrich in *The Scarlet Empress*. After all those sophisticates, playing father to Little Eva must have been a big switch.

Kneeling by my bedside, Lodge sobbed convincingly and pounded his fists into the bedding. Raising my head torturously one last time, I let it fall back, my face impassive, while Lodge wailed and pounded anew as life ebbed away. Unfortunately, I could not suppress a grin. On the retake I again smiled through my death mask. Lodge's passionate thumping on the bed was bouncing my head on the pillow, and the vision of my head pulsing off to death in synchrony with his flailing fists was too weird not to seem hilarious.

Joking around on a movie set is an insider's prerogative, a subtlety overlooked by Father until too late. Occasionally he visited the studio, mingling and joshing in his own way. An unrelenting punster, he may have inherited this streak. Among my possessions are an 1894 letter from his father, a doctor, and a home concoction called Elixir of Youth, a restorative derived from extracts of lamb testicles.

"I used it on three patients today," he wrote. "Confidentially, they will all be running around town tomorrow bleating and butting every-thing.... Now I must go to Blake's slaughterhouse and superintend killing a lamb for material to make more elixir with.... Today I took injections myself, but don't feel any more sheepish than usual."

Everyone else on the set had a job to do, so frequently Father's stream of colorful and cheerful interjections fell on ears not ready for his humor. This was the case the day word came from the Ambassador Hotel that Prince Purachatra, brother of the King of Siam, wished to visit. A studio car was requested to pick him up, but when the guest arrived it was by his own taxi, and he was in a state of princely annoyance. Misunderstanding instructions, the dispatcher had sent not a sedan for the Siam prince but a pickup truck for film *prints*. Father made much of the pun involved, until it was really stale.

At the end of his visit the Prince had a request.

"Miss Temple, may I take a home movie?"

I offered a deal. "Okay, if you tell me about Siamese temples."

The opportunity was too much for Father, who commented, "The Siamese wants to know about Temple, and Temple wants to know about Siamese temples."

For director Butler, Father was one Temple too much. Within a few minutes a small black boy, one of our extras, ran up and suddenly wiggled onto Father's lap. Clutching him around the neck, the child began shouting "Daddy, Daddy!"

A picture of genuine discomfort, Father struggled to release the entwined little fingers while Butler pointed and hooted his derision.

Like many pranksters, Father took a joke poorly, and on this occasion he was offended by its context.

"Daddy, Daddy," continued the little boy, dogging Father's footsteps all the way to the door, then returning holding aloft the quarter Butler had given him for the extra job.

Two things about the incident left me puzzled. Having no concept of racial prejudice, I saw no joke worth a laugh in a black son perched on a white father's lap. The other thing I did not understand was the coin. People always got something for doing something. That was simply fair exchange. But it looked as if the boy had gotten something extra for doing as directed. Confused, I let the matter trail away, forgotten for the time being.

Audiences cheered *The Little Colonel*, described by Andre Sennwald in the *New York Film Review* as "all adrip with magnolia, whimsy, and vast unashamed portions of synthetic Dixie atmosphere ... a nostalgic flight in times of stern realities." During its long, lucrative smash run at New York's Fifth Avenue Theatre, the film was sandwiched between a *March of Time* commentary on Adolf Hitler's edicts to scrap the hated Treaty of Versailles ending World War I and form a new Nazi army of a half million men and a feature covering the trial of Bruno Hauptmann, alleged kidnapper of the Lindbergh baby.

The film produced two innovations, only one of which seemed important to me at the time. Our fleeting use of experimental Technicolor required me to wear makeup. Measured against today's rainbow spectrum, our film color was heavy on red hues, conveniently well matched for the pink party scene where it was employed, but leaving us with highly flushed faces on film. To correct this imbalance we all received bold applications of rouge, mascara, and lipstick, producing a comic gang of clown faces. Enjoying the experience so vividly was lucky; it was my first and last makeup at Fox.

The more significant innovation concerned Uncle Billy Robinson and me. As Griffith had earlier surmised, gooseflesh did rise among some preview audiences, notably in southern states. In our staircase dance we had touched fingers. To avoid social offense and assure wide distribution, the studio cut scenes showing physical contact between us. But for the rest of the world we provided a watershed. We were the first interracial dancing couple in movie history.

11

The ant is knowing and wise,
But doesn't know enough to take a vacation.
—*This Simian World*, Clarence Day, 1960

A ccolades for *The Little Colonel* came from an unexpected quarter. On a cool February evening in 1935 the Academy of Motion Picture Arts and Sciences convened its seventh Annual Awards banquet at the Los Angeles Biltmore Hotel. Under the great, curved porte cochere arrived a procession of limousines discharging wave after wave of sleek, glittering cargo. Searchlights sent thin, long, probing fingers of celebration into the clear evening sky.

Scattered among gawkers lining the nearby sidewalks could be seen several hand-held placards protesting the ceremony.

"Harebrains," scoffed our accompanying studio executive. "Writers Guild nuts. A witless mob, dupes of the Commies."

Despite the hoopla, the Academy was tottering, a pawn in a festering war between studio management and nascent labor guilds. Labor strategy was to deny producing companies the worldwide publicity potential of the Academy, particularly its award ceremony. The ranks of gilded Oscar statuettes faced five long years of being straddled by a withering crossfire.

But inside all was cheerful, dinner tables sparkling with crystalware and silver. Elegantly clad guests swirled in a babble of animated conversation. Actors William Powell, Ronald Colman, and Clark Gable were pointed out to me. Each one, I noted, sported an identical thin mustache. Everyone eyed everyone else. My dress was pink batiste trimmed in white, showing lots of leg. Following current styles, all the other skirts seemed to drag on the floor. Seated nearby was Jean Harlow, wearing a long, white crepe evening dress. Her white ermine wrap seemed alive, first draped over one shoulder, then the other. Whatever her technique, it was proving effective, and certainly better than mine in France, had I known.

". . . Shirley Temple is amusing," critic Maurice Debache had written in *L'Echo de Paris*, "but her precocity leaves me sad. By contrast, Harlow sets the Frenchman palpitating. . . . With sex appeal, there are no national boundaries."

As the formal recitation of nominees and awards dragged on, I collected crumbs from nearby partially eaten hard rolls and made symmetrical little piles on the tablecloth. Honoring his thirty-eight-year history of profoundly important contribution to character and growth of the international motion picture art form, D. W. Griffith was presented an honorary Oscar.

The drone from the podium was suddenly interrupted by a commotion near the ballroom entrance. Actress Claudette Colbert was just being announced as winner in the best actress category for her role in *It Happened One Night*. Right on cue, she entered carrying a mink coat and dressed in a tailored suit and hat better suited to a departure on a railroad train, which happened to be exactly the case.

Acknowledging her award with dramatic hesitation, she said, "I'm afraid I'm going to be foolish and cry!" That sounded exciting, but unfortunately she remained quite dry-eyed. Following this flurry of excitement I again slumped in my chair, heavy-lidded and bored.

". . . One great towering figure in the cinema game," humorist Irvin S. Cobb read, "one giant among the troupers . . . for monumental, stupendous, elephantine achievements in 1934 . . . a special award for . . . Shirley Temple!"

I recognized my name but with total surprise. Nobody had even hinted I might win anything. Having watched the earlier succession of winners, I knew what to do. Leaping to my feet, I ran up the ramp to the stage. Right behind me in ladylike haste came Mother, with Father hard on her heels. I reached out for the small Oscar statuette, but Cobb withdrew it from my outstretched hand. He had a white, goatish face.

"I'll give you this if you'll give me a kiss," he said. The audience howled in appreciation.

As he spoke I could see little showers of moisture fly out in my direction, each droplet reflecting as a speck in the spotlight before disappearing somewhere on me or my hair. Damp, casual kisses are one of my intense dislikes, but with an eye on the Oscar I turned my cheek upward. Cobb leaned down while the audience cheered. Just as he kissed me I got a firm handhold on the statuette.

"Thank you all very much," I called upwards toward the microphone, not letting go. "Mommy, can we go home now?"

Circling just beyond Cobb's outstretched reach, I ran back down the ramp ahead of my parents.

"You-all ain't old enough to know what this is all about!" he called after me.

He was right. With the applause still in my ears, I stood the statuette beside my pile of bread crumbs. It was less than half the size of the other Oscars being handed out.

"What did I get this for, good acting?" I asked Mother.

"For making the most pictures of anyone last year. For quantity, not quality."

There was more to her explanation. During the 1934 nominations for best actress, a vicious cat fight had erupted. My name was on the nomination list and odds-makers had me an almost certainty to win. Myrna Loy (*The Thin Man*) and Bette Davis (*Of Human Bondage*) had both been ignored in the nominations and write-in campaigns had been threatened. This quarrelsome affair had forced Academy officials to rescind both my nomination and the Academy rules against write-ins and devise a compromise. I would be excluded from the best actress category altogether. A diminutive Oscar would be awarded me in a special-award category, one whose only previous recipients had been Charlie Chaplin in 1927 for *The Circus*, Warner Brothers for revolutionizing movies with sound in *The Jazz Singer*, and Walt Disney for Mickey Mouse.

Someone's cute idea to match my height with a shrunken Oscar badly misfired. If mine was really a commendable job done, why not a big Oscar like everyone else's? I immediately concluded that the award was somehow not genuine. Not being particularly prideful, however, I was not offended. The miniature statuette and adjacent pile of bread crumbs were regarded with almost equal indifference. Symbolic of where things stood, as we departed the hall I held Mother's hand, she carried the Oscar, and Father bore the coats.

☆

My sixth birthday found me deluged with gifts from well-meaning fans, almost entirely passed on to local charities. Occasionally special problems arose, as with Tillie the calf from Tillamook, Oregon, who stood around dropping manure clods on our driveway until Mother persuaded our milkman to remove it to his employer's farm.

From Australia a film distributor's organization released headline news that my 1935 birthday gift from down under would be a live kangaroo. Learning of this, Mother visibly paled. Having just taken care of the Oregon calf, she sent word. Thanks, but no thanks.

"If not the kangaroo," came the Australian rejoinder, "how about a wallaby?" The question was moot. Before she could reply word came that two wallabies were en route from Sydney aboard the SS *Mariposa*, with caretaker S. S. Crick.

All three from Australia appeared outside my studio bungalow. Upon their release from the shipping crate, both wallabies eluded the custodial clutch of Mr. Crick and went bounding out my garden gate. Selecting the studio main street, they went leaping off like the diminutive kangaroos they were, followed in hot pursuit by Crick, me, and a crowd who had joined the chase. Darting in tandem around building corners and doubling back, they easily eluded their pursuers. Still searching for some refuge, they came leaping zigzag toward the studio restaurant, before which stood a decorative fountain and pool drained for repairs. Over the edge both wallabies sailed, landing with a thud on the bare cement, where they both lay stunned in a trap of their own choosing.

"Wouldn't they be happier in the California Zoological Gardens?" Mother asked, a question with but one answer.

Going on seven years old, I was less interested in calves and wallabies than in love, the kind that exists between people. Kissing, marriage, breakup, and reconciliation had been fundamental plot elements in almost all my films. Tender dialogue and hugs were only flesh on the important romantic skeleton I was constructing. Selectivity did not seem important. My general approach was to fall in love whenever possible, preferably with someone nearby. Affection should be something transferable. Love seemed central to what adults did, and I resolved to give it a try.

Opportunity came with Joel McCrea, my lanky, deep-throated co-star in *Heaven's Gate*, itself a soap-opera tale of unrequited affection. McCrea measured up to my usual criteria, abundant masculinity and effervescent humor, but from its outset this romance had problems.

First, my only purely personal opportunities with McCrea came when I was squeezed between him and a driver in a limousine front seat. Riding in front always afforded a sense of control impossible when dragged along in a distant back seat.

"Morning," he said, and immediately started rereading his script.

"What does 'morn' mean?" I asked.

"Where did you hear that, Butch?" Like Gary Cooper before him, he used a nickname.

"A word from a song in *The Little Colonel*."

He pursed his lips. "It probably means morning."

"If they mean morning, why don't they call it morning?"

He nodded unthinkingly and returned to his reading.

"Mr. McCrea," I again interrupted, "where do faces come from?"

"From the stork, I suppose."

"That's not what I mean," I persisted. "Why don't all faces look alike?"

From the back seat Mother had been eavesdropping. "Don't bother him," she called.

"It's okay." He smiled over his shoulder and closed his script. "She doesn't seem to care for baby talk. Some of these questions would keep H. G. Wells guessing."

"What I mean is," I whispered, "are people with one kind of face happier than people with different ones?"

"Now, Shirley," Mother again admonished. Like mine, her ears were sharp.

Our outdoor location was a springtime glade appropriately named Hidden Valley, a grassy field studded with gnarled oak trees and creased by a meandering brook. My puppy, Sniff, and I were examining a grasshopper at close range. Suddenly I sneezed. Two front porcelain dental caps fluttered off into space and disappeared among the dry grass blades.

Without them filming could not proceed, so everyone crawled around gently fingering through the stubble to recover my caps, a search in vain.

Rather than being charmed, McCrea was annoyed at the delay, particularly when director John Robertson was forced to cancel all filming and sent us home again for my "instant" dentist to practice his magic. En route, I was seated beside McCrea; a loose tooth dislodged itself into my hand. It is hard to carry on a romantic reconciliation with one's teeth falling out.

The next morning at Hidden Valley, the air was so frosty chill, even our breath came out foggy. McCrea and I were waiting for light reflectors to be adjusted. Our mark was standing near a rustic bridge, which arched over the brook babbling along underneath.

"Is it really true you're married to someone else?" I asked.

"Yes," he answered. My eyes must have clouded, for he added, "But you're still my special friend." Under the circumstances it was the best arrangement.

Our delay was long. The men kept fussing with their light levels, our conversation petered out, and the only noise was the cheery, cold gurgling from the brook. Suddenly I became aware of lukewarm moisture in my socks. Peeking down, I saw both legs lined with wet, shiny streaks. Overflow from my shoes was creating a dark stain on the dry dirt where I stood. The realization was sudden and terrifying. I stood rooted, too mortified to move. Somebody noticed, and pointed.

"Never mind, Mugwump," said Robertson, urgently gesturing for Mother to come take over. McCrea stared ahead. I burst into tears. High and low, I was one wet kid.

Led despairingly to the refuge of my portable dressing trailer, I undressed. A wardrobe mistress found me fresh underpants and socks. Propping both my shoes before a heater, she also used a hair blower to accelerate drying. Outside the crew and cast stood around in little knots, drinking coffee and waiting.

Inside the trailer I suffered a thousand agonies. Not to reappear was impossible. There was no back door to slink out. Mother gave a little speech about accidents and courage. Finally I mustered enough confidence to open the door, but only by convincing myself the whole thing had never happened. Someone had mercifully scuffed dry dirt over the two damp spots. The accident was no Oscar performance. My reappearance was.

That everything had occurred while standing beside McCrea erected a tombstone over further flirtation. First, the falling teeth, now another problem of older performers, incontinence. Oh well, I reasoned, my love was due to end with the picture anyway.

In final editing Fox feared public revulsion with the title *Heaven's Gate*, suggestive of a cemetery, and switched the title to *Our Little Girl*. By either name I forgot it as soon as possible.

Elsewhere, events were no less turbulent. Toyland was going to war. Small-time commercial pirates could be tolerated, but when major companies began to infringe, tin soldiers and log forts went to red alert and my licensees mounted the battlements.

In the first barrage my doll licensee, Ideal Novelty and Toy Company, filed a $100,000 infringement suit against Lenora Doll Company for making and selling Shirley Temple dolls without authorization, citing me as co-plaintiff. Complicating matters, the New York courts rejected my parents as guardians because they were not New Yorkers. Fortunately, Sidney R. Rosenau, a native of the city, was available. A pleasant man with leonine features, he evidenced keen interest in the doll suit. Small wonder. He was my exclusive licensee for dresses.

"There's nothing new under the sun," said the *Boston Post*. "Seeing the success of 'Little Colonel' dolls licensed to Ideal, pirates of the industry put imitations on the market immediately. The most successful manufacturer is the one who can steal the most . . . the greatest bunch of thieves outside prison. . . . The industry hopes Shirley will assist in providing a code of ethics to bring order out of chaos."

The industry also enlisted reinforcements. In the tiny town of Callander, Ontario, the previous year a startled farmer had stood beside his wife's delivery bed viewing the first surviving quintuplets in history.

"I already have five children," he had wailed. "I'm broke. The farm is mortgaged. A man like me should be in jail."

Instead of a jailer he met promoters. The Chicago Exposition offered the farmer's parish priest 7 percent of the gate receipts to help sign up the girls.

"It's a miracle!" the priest reportedly urged. "The parish needs a new roof. Take it!"

Manufacturers of cribs, high chairs, and dolls had bloomed like weeds, all without license. The Quints and I were joined as plaintiffs in the suit against Lenora Doll.

Peace was without victory. After extended argument, we six girls settled for an amount unknown to me but pocketed by Ideal and its corporate co-plaintiffs. The industry made no further attempt to use our example to establish a code of ethics, leaving another generation of pirates free to roam and pillage.

Lawyers were also busy in the California state legislature, where theatre owners had embarked on a campaign to amend existing child-labor laws prohibiting children under eight, like me, from appearing in concerts and performances onstage. Clouds of political rhetoric and public debate preceded the final vote, but at day's end the law was amended to legitimize appearances of children, with particular reference to me. Some attorney had not done his homework. Never mind what law permitted. My contract already prohibited theatre appearances.

For a couple of years writers and critics had enjoyed wrestling with one slippery question about my films: Why were they so enormously popular? Technical answers did not wholly satisfy. Screenplays like *Little Miss Marker* were delectable, but *Curly Top*, my latest in production, was uncomfortably banal. Both were hits. The values in direction, production, and supporting cast were often remarkable but variable. I could sing, dance, act, and dimple, but probably there were others around who could do equally well and far better in some categories.

Certainly of help was a pleasing personality, which after all most children have anyway. Having a knack for projecting myself into make-believe situations without abandoning the reality of my true self was a strength, sparing me that disastrous corkscrewing which occurs when a child tries to adapt to unnatural reactions in fictional circumstances. Then and now, however, this answer seems too abstract.

Another opinion blamed the audience for my success. Contrasting life inside and outside a theatre, people preferred to wallow comfortably before the untrue happiness on the screen, rather than confront reality in the street outside where the Depression continued to grind life down.

Nobody seemed able to grasp the touchstone of "Why?" And of

course I was no more help then than now. While *Curly Top* was filming in 1935, one writer's opinions demonstrated the difficulty when contrasted with the sort of thing actually going on.

"It is as an actress that Shirley Temple is primarily interesting," Gilbert Seldes wrote in *Esquire* magazine.

In fact, I had faltered. The monologue in *Curly Top* was particularly long, and midway I had suddenly looked cross-eyed and stopped speaking. Irving Cummings, the director, was listening rather than watching.

"I thought you were One-Take-Temple," he said.

"I am," I insisted, standing stock-still. "But there is a fly sitting on my nose."

"As a close second," Seldes had continued, "she is interesting because of something rude and rowdy. . . ."

There he was getting closer to the mark. Our *Curly Top* scene was in an orphanage. I had borrowed the black bowler and oversized overcoat of a crotchety trustee and was mimicking his gravel voice and pompous behavior. For a finale I tripped over the coattails in an acrobatic pratfall. Quite apart from acting, the slapstick fitted my personality like a glove.

". . . Instead of apologetic giggles or an ingratiating ripple, her laughter is positively boisterous, a sort of hoot at pomposity. . . ."

One of the film's songs is "When I Grow Up," performed in a succession of roles depicting different stages of life, first as my sweet-sixteen period and then as a bride. I entered carrying an orange-blossom bouquet with trailing satin ribbons and sending coquettish glances through a lace veil. Inside my bodice, falsies rounded up like two small kumquats.

". . .The door opened," the Seldes article continued, "and she came through with precisely an air of command, the certainty that you will never again look at another woman. . . ."

What appeared as composure and control was in fact a secret sense of pleasure, plowing a furrow through virginal ground. For the first time I was playing someone older than I was.

". . . The roar of male approval is not for what is sweet. It is for what is mocking, hearty and contemptuous. . . ."

It was an old woman in a rocking chair, white wig peeping out from under a lace cap, with embroidery needles and yarn in her lap. Peering over the top of rimless eyeglasses, she sang in a croaky rasp. Nobody was more relieved than I when the decrepit old lady finally raised her skirt, exposing white bobby socks, and tap-danced offstage.

"...At her good moments, something like a growl of satisfaction rises from the men in the audience...."

In actor John Boles's dream I am a naked cupid, smeared hairline to feet in gilt paint. Like the male audience, I, too, experienced supreme excitement. The makeup people had described how the paint sealed my skin pores and would suffocate me unless the scene was completed rapidly. Racing against time, I plunged a mythical dart into Boles's heart as he sang sleepily, "It's All So New to Me." Me, too.

Trying to come to grips with the daunting question of why my films packed them in was obviously disheartening, so with a rumble of distant thunder the writer took refuge in a prediction and a recommendation:

"... I feel moderately certain she is good for two more pictures. What she needs most of all is a firing squad at daybreak with her directors against the stone wall."

East was not West where movies were concerned. Although banned from theatres in Denmark for unspecified "corruption," in China *Curly Top* pleased Madame Chiang Kai-shek, who requested repeat private screenings. Everywhere the film racked up big earnings, pacing the buoyant 1935 Fox financial recovery, which almost tripled the previous year's profits. Thus window-dressed, the company was merged into the hitherto rival movie studio of Twentieth Century Pictures. Although current Fox president Sidney Kent would retain his position in the new company, it was curtains for Winfield Sheehan.

Widely regarded as a keystone in Fox revitalization, Sheehan got some mud kicked on his reputation and a reported settlement of a half million dollars for hurt feelings. Exalted and inaccessible, he had been my Zeus. When he spoke my world trembled. His abrupt disappearance, however, seemed unremarkable, like a good-bye to a stage crew at a film's completion. There was little finality in farewell.

Into vacant executive chairs swept the dynamic duo from Twentieth Century, Joseph M. Schenck as chairman of the board and Darryl R. Zanuck as vice-president and head of production. Both would be new key players in my life.

Earlier, Zanuck had authored movie scripts for the dog Rin Tin Tin and had also fathered the Warner Bros. era of gangster films. On both counts his taste was for raw drama, straight from the headlines. By reputation he was blessed with a huge vitality and the ability to spin off ideas like a pinwheel. On self-command he could be either a sledge-hammer or a man of the world. Concentrating his charm on Mother, he immediately jumped her salary to $1,000 per week, providing verbal assurances that he would continue her on the payroll even if I were, God forbid, ever put on suspension. In another note to her, handwritten by Schenck, the same sanguine theme rang:

"Please don't permit anything to worry you. We will cooperate with you, one hundred percent."

Zanuck raced to announce his overall program. In 1936 sixty pictures would be in production, representing an investment of $15 million. In addition to the fifteen existing soundstages, five more would be con-structed, permitting simultaneous production on ten feature pictures. For a company snatched from the brink of ruin it was a thundering proclamation of sharply increased production budgets, huge capital facilities expansion, and, of course, high hopes. But the next thing that happened was that the studio shut down for summer vacation.

The concept of vacation was almost meaningless for me. Routines of work and pleasures of leisure had always been commingled. In fact, this was what the studio had in mind—piggyback a maximum publicity program on our private plans for a Hawaiian vacation. Photographic opportunities and official contacts were carefully interwoven with press and radio interviews. Intense public exposure was the objective, at minimum cost. It would be our vacation, and so were all the expenses.

For our ship's arrival in Honolulu, 20,000 people clogged Aloha pier and spilled onto city streets. I debarked astride the shoulders of Duke Kahanamoku, famed Olympic Games swimming and surfing champion.

"Watch out," someone cried. "Duke is our sheriff."

"That's all right," I called down. "I'm a police chief."

"Everything seemed under control," wrote Mother. "... then the crowds broke ... we were mobbed. The police finally cleared a way for the car. Shirley was the only calm one in the bunch." Ecstatic, Mother, not calm, as I sailed high above the tumult.

Both parents detested mobs of people, for different reasons. I was always picked up by someone and got carried a lot. But like any man, Father was constantly annoyed by being crowded aside by someone intent on getting close to me, and he usually got left behind in the process. Like any woman wearing high heels, Mother seldom could keep pace and always got a lot of pushing, shoving, and stray elbows.

Outside the arrival building the crowd was even thicker. Police had already contained them behind wooden barricades, rank upon rank of cheering, waving people. Perched on the back seat in an open sedan, chin high in fragrant flower leis, I was slowly driven up Fort Street. Absent was the helter-skelter confusion outside a theatre premiere. This was a happy crowd, as well organized as a scene for some movie.

Told by the acting territorial governor that we had rushed away from the ship so rapidly that many were deprived of any adequate glimpse, we accepted his idea of an appearance at Iolani Royal Palace. Another throng of 10,000 was already waiting. It was my first physical contact with so large an audience. Obviously everyone had overlooked the prohibition against such appearances in the supplemental contract signed only months earlier. Circling the upstairs verandah, I sang the lollipop song four times while the packed crowd below listened and cheered, calling my name. Surely just that song didn't warrant so enthusiastic a reaction, so I asked Mother what made them applaud and shout approval. Her reply was simple. Because I made them happy.

With Fox Movietone News cameramen never far behind, I inspected military parades, posed astraddle field guns wearing billed officers' caps, then switched to a sailor's hat at Pearl Harbor while inspecting the destroyer USS *Gamble* and a submarine.

Blaring military bands, guns and warships, the order and discipline, the stamping of shiny black boots and the sparkle of brass buttons and braid, for me it all amounted to heaven. Perhaps my enthusiasm traced back to earlier visits with firemen and jailers in Santa Monica, symbols of protection from evil and catastrophe. At that time there had been practical reasons for my jubilation: the trucks and cars had sirens, there were handcuffs, handguns, and billy clubs. To cap things off, the police had uniforms with colorful swatches, shiny badges, and for the firemen, coal-scuttle hats.

Father himself might have provided some impetus to my affection for uniforms. Volunteering late in World War I, he had drilled in a drafty post office but got no farther than maneuvers on nearby Catalina Island before the armistice ruined his hopes of becoming a hero. Uniforms always commanded his respect, regardless of who wore them. Some of this may have rubbed off on me, for later I would marry uniforms twice, first an army sergeant, then a naval commander.

My zest for uniforms in 1935 extended even to swimming outfits. Posed on our palm-fringed hotel verandah with an honor guard of ten tanned beachboys with surfboards held at attention, I was solemnly recruited into the Waikiki Beach Patrol and presented with a T-shirt embroidered with a gigantic patrol insignia and a small surfboard inscribed with each beachboy's signature.

Those tangible mementos were important, far more than the event. Things to heft, feel, and take away gave an air of permanence to what happened. If they were martial, so much the better.

Only one other time in Hawaii did another organization provide trappings. On a later trip in 1939, during a military review at Scofield Barracks, I was outfitted by the 27th "Wolfhound" Infantry Regiment in a symbolic uniform: corduroy cartridge bandoliers crossed over my chest and a gaudy ceremonial sash striped in black and orange wrapped around my waist. Tipped over my eye at a jaunty angle, my cossack felt hat was emblazoned with their regimental emblem, a snarling wolf with bared teeth. Standing rigidly at attention, I let my mind reel with heroic visions. Waiting to parade, horses hitched to caissons pawed and shifted nervously, as a breeze sent regimental pennants snapping at their flag-staffs, bugles called, and gruff marching orders were passed down the line. Rank after rank passed in review, a mixed noise of jangling harness, heavy breathing of horses and men, laced boots thumping in unison across the grassy turf. They made me an honorary colonel, but had anyone asked, I would have enlisted on the spot as a private.

And then in Hawaii in 1935 there was the swimming.

". . . So many people on the sands waiting for Shirley," Mother complained. "I haven't found courage to go out on the beach. Maybe they will get tired of waiting and we can take a dip in the ocean without half the population of Honolulu watching us. . . ."

At crowded Waikiki Beach someone inevitably suggested a swim. Every child knows about the bogeyman who gets you if you don't watch out. Open the closet door and out he steps, all teeth and eyes. My personal bogeyman was a swim cap designed and installed by Mother.

Scrapbook snapshots show her as a younger woman with tousled and windblown long black hair. Then came diphtheria, and it all fell out, a crushing blow to any young woman's vanity. When it grew back, thick and curly, Mother must have regarded her blessing in a newly protective light. Since then wind and water had become vandals, destroyers of the flowerlike harmony of her hair, and now, by heredity, mine. Against these natural enemies she had devised a defense. First, pin curls in a routine set; bind a gasket seal of soft kid leather tightly around the head at hairline; flatten curls carefully with a tight silk-stocking hat; encase everything under two separate rubber swim caps, one placed on top of the other, both securely buttoned under the chin. Everyone else on Waikiki Beach went bareheaded. I wore a rigid helmet.

Barefooted, with his trousers rolled up, Father stood knee deep. Holding his hand, I edged into the water sideways, like a crab. I knew how to swim but was no fish. On the beach a swimsuited crowd had quickly collected and stood watching, snapping pictures, and pointing. Bending over, eyes closed, I dove, surfacing immediately, spluttering and regaining a foothold.

"How's the surfing, Shirley?" someone shouted.

"Fine!" I called back, rubbing my eyes. "It's the headaches I get tired of."

"Can you really swim?" yelled another.

"Sure!" I said. "If somebody holds my chin!"

The crowd grew thicker, gaping and discussing me among themselves, so we called off the swim. Judged by the mixture of smiles and derisive laughter, there were two bodies of beach opinion. Those who hoped I'd swim and those who hoped I'd drown. Each had some reason to be satisfied. And the hair got wet anyway.

Swimming publicly was for me no casual activity. It was a performance, no less than before studio cameras. On the beach I simply had insufficient skill to perform. The gawking crowd was no less an audience than in some movie theatre. Mine was a matter of professional pride, not self-consciousness. Until I was competent to perform before an audience, I would avoid it.

Dawning of boat day, when guests both arrived and departed, found the hotel lobby clogged. The air was heavy with a fragrance from the tropical flower leis piled around the necks of both guests and well-wishers.

I was standing near the elevator when the door slid back, revealing a portly, balding man draped chin-high in leis, who turned out to be Postmaster General James A. Farley, political confidant of FDR. I had never noticed him before.

"Hello, darling," he said, "how are you?" Photographers' bulbs were flashing, so I struck a friendly smile and held it.

Circling me with one protective arm, Farley posed until the photographers were gone. "Gee, Shirley," he said, "you're a wonder!" Leaning down, he kissed my cheek.

"Why?" I asked.

"Anyone who can smile so much this early in the morning is a *world* wonder!" I thought it was a dumb reason. Raising his finger like a teacher, he said, "Mark my words, I've been watching you. You talk like a Democrat. You act like one. For sure, you'll be a Democrat."

Except for its certainty of expression, the statement was not worth remembering. Already I had been several dozen people. Being a Democrat would be another role I could play.

Hawaii was rustling cocoanut palms, languid music, and the tantalizing thump of surf. But vacation it was not, merely work in balmy surroundings. Under no illusion about the purpose of the trip, I was spared disappointment. As our ship steamed offshore I observed the Hawaiian tradition to guarantee a return by dropping each of my goodbye flower leis overboard and letting them swirl away in our wake. Honolulu might be a nice place to just visit someday, I mused. Fifteen years later it was.

12

Every child should have mudpies ... Any child who has been deprived of these has been deprived of the best part of education.

—Luther Burbank, as quoted in
A Garden Touched With Genius,
Peter Dreyer, 1985

Near Point Barrow, Alaska, at 8:15 p.m. on August 15, 1935, a low-winged red monoplane crashed in the slush ice. Dead in the wreckage was Wiley Post, who the previous year had circumnavigated the earth in the record time of seven days and eighteen hours. Accompanying him on this last, fatal flight was Will Rogers. Ripples from this arctic accident reached Hollywood with telling impact.

For newly born Twentieth Century-Fox, Rogers's death was a catastrophe. Lead horse in the studio stable of stars, he had been cited in the authoritative *Motion Picture Herald* poll as the biggest money-making star of 1934, although not among the most popular ten. Only lukewarm reception had attended Janet Gaynor's recent films, slipping her completely out of top-ten ratings.

In all this darkness flickered one pinprick of hope. Although only number eight, I suddenly was the only studio performer among the top ten. A 1935 national juvenile survey of boys reported that the leading "I-want-to-be" male figure was Charles Lindbergh. For the girls, however, I rated first, followed by aviatrix Amelia Earhart and Mrs. Eleanor Roosevelt. Another national survey to give the studio hope was among aspiring young journalists, this one concerned with name recognition. In only two cases were names recognized by everyone polled, Richard Hauptmann as kidnapper of the Lindbergh baby and me as an actress.

As companion to such surveys, the studio could take heart from a marketplace indication of my current professional value. A "reputable source" guaranteed Father $416,000 for two years of my radio broadcasts and personal appearances. When told of my exclusive studio contract, the source airily replied, "Never mind that. It will be handled."

As further benchmarks of value, the Texas Centennial Exhibition commissioned me, *in absentia*, an officer of the Texas Rangers, dangling at the same time $10,000 for a week-long personal tour in Dallas. Promoters from the New Jersey State Fair topped that, offering $12,500 for a single day.

All this unsolicited bidding was not lost on Zanuck, who decided to physically protect his potential asset by detailing burly John Griffith as my combination chauffeur-bodyguard.

"Watch the kid like a hawk," Zanuck instructed him. "If anything happens to her, this studio might as well close up."

An ex-carnival roustabout, Griff had saved Zanuck's life in a Nebraska boyhood swimming accident, and ever since had basked in Zanuck's gratitude. He squinted a lot, sending darting glances around as if searching for danger beyond our normal ken, and made no effort to disguise the hard bulge of a holstered .38-caliber pistol near his armpit, nor the flat leather belt case that held folded handcuffs. Griff seldom smiled, but then protecting me was no laughing responsibility.

My perspective was quite different. I regarded him as a playmate. His primary task was to keep me in sight. Naturally, mine was to escape. His feet were flat, his wind short, and he huffed like an elephant. In any game of pursuit, I was the easy winner.

In the process, however, we gradually became friends. Feigning reluctance, he showed me how his pistol worked, unloaded of course, then snapped me in and out of his handcuffs. But his playfulness had limits. When I locked him in his own cuffs and then hid the key, his patience ran out with a rush.

Thereafter we concentrated on more subtle aspects of illegality and law enforcement. Squatting in the garage corner, hidden from Mother, he taught me card playing. Rounding off my education, he showed how to cheat. With eyes narrowed and voice lowered to a conspiratorial whisper, he demonstrated how to double deal, palm cards, and reverse the deck. When one's hands are small such legerdermain is not easy, but I soon mastered the fundamentals. Cheating was never presented as immoral, simply a tactic for winning. From then on I rarely lost to him in cards.

Before releasing children on an Easter-egg hunt, Griff secretly reconnoitered hiding places and devised a set of silent signals between us. Head gestured right or left steered me, eyes heavenward meant an egg nearby. Other boys and girls got suddenly bowled aside as I beelined to an indicated bush and beat them to the egg. I always won, and never felt remorse. Any contest called for using resources and skills at hand. I was too young for ethics.

Relief from her daily driving chores by Griff's presence was only one dividend for Mother. When later we moved into a larger house, he occupied an attached apartment with his wife, Mabel, whom Mother promptly hired as a personal maid.

Griff the bodyguard and Mabel the maid as members of our household had implications for Zanuck beyond my security and Mother's comfort. Good business calls for keeping close track of your assets. Their intimate employment ideally positioned Zanuck to know details of what we did as a family, when, and with whom. No specific instance points a finger at Griff as a tattletale, nor diminishes the competence of his service. Yet, to ignore his long personal allegiance to Zanuck as employer and benefactor would be naive. If occasionally they found themselves trapped between the tug of two competing loyalties, Griff and Mabel can be forgiven.

A personal bodyguard was only one aspect of the studio's coherent plan to preserve my value. In case of my demise, they would be well paid. Life insurance in the amount of $795,000 was placed through a syndicate headed by Federal Life Insurance Company of Chicago, with the studio named as sole beneficiary.

"We welcome this risk," said vice president L. D. Cavanaugh. "She is . . . sheltered, supervised, lives in a fine home . . . addicted to neither alcohol nor tobacco . . . and has gained twenty pounds in two years. . . ."

With me physically monitored, personally protected, my value insured, Zanuck passed instructions to maintain my upward artistic momentum. Keep her skirts high. Have co-stars lift her up whenever possible to create the illusion now selling so well. Preserve babyhood.

Although gratified by my popularity as measured by box office, polls, and cash offers, Mother clung to her general apprehension born of the horrifying Lindbergh baby kidnapping in 1932. Presumed wealth and international prominence might attract kidnappers. Her general concern was fueled by several events, perhaps mild in themselves but viewed by her as harbingers of evil.

During the time of the heavily publicized kidnapping of an heir to the wealthy Weyerhaeuser family in Washington State a boy appeared at our home. Scruffily dressed and ill at ease, he told Mrs. Brackett, our housekeeper, he had an urgent message. The same gang that had kidnapped Weyerhaeuser intended to make me its next victim. Turning, he fled.

In a hopeful euphemism, the studio announced that some delinquent had created a "disturbance" while counseling me on my career, small solace to Mother in her frame of mind.

In Texas, a youthful prisoner was cut down by the jailer while attempting to hang himself with a light cord. Nearby lay a despairing note of love for me, touching enough to get him bundled off to a mental institution. Again, Mother's apprehension deepened. As a fan of horrifying stories the incident caused me no particular alarm.

The middle 1930s were seeing an upsurge in social brutality. Radio mirrored the times, with drama regularly veering to the side of violence. There were 30 million radios in America broadcasting over 600 stations, easily the most powerful communication medium in history. Thugs, cops, and weirdos speckled my radio dial. I was a voracious, indefatigable listener, and radio was my most important porthole on the world. This devotion had two principal origins. First, living as I did in crowded family circumstances, almost everything I did was done with something else going on. Perhaps it was conversation, or general bustle, kitchen clamor or living-room hum typical of any small home. Doing something with background activity was normal. Movie studios, with all the complexity of overlapping activity, merely intensified my ability to work in a busy environment. At home and at work I concentrated best in the presence of background noise. I decried utter silence. Feeling this way, it was natural, if not necessary, to click on the radio whenever I could.

Once the radio was on, invariably it was tuned to drama. Mother had been a fan of *Little Orphan Annie*, and my playpen was exposed to the booming voice of Daddy Warbucks, the guttural tones of Punjab as he wielded a gigantic scimitar and the spine-tingling sign-off, "Leapin' lizards! Orphan Annie may die! Now for tomorrow's clue!" With the possible exception of arithmetic instructions, absolutely everything at the studio was susceptible to some dramatic interpretation, so tuning in to evening and weekend radio programs was simply an extension of weekday daytime life.

Can a simple girl from a small mining town in the West find happiness as the wife of a British lord? Incidentally, we never did find out. Jack Armstrong, the all-American boy, rattled a boxful of Wheaties breakfast food. Captain Midnight piloted his plane in daring deeds to save souls. In *Gangbusters* the FBI solved murder most foul in the convent, and to the haunting melody of "Some Day I'll Find You," Mr. Keen traced lost persons.

Wanting to listen to two programs at once on one radio, I started flicking the dial, and soon could follow both. Mad scientists with disintegration-ray guns ran parallel to the lonely *Whistler*, who set spines a-tingling. What better way to spend an evening than to flip the dial between the squeaking hinges of *Inner Sanctum* and the demented laugh of *The Shadow* confirming that evil lurks in the hearts of men. Kidnap, even mine, seemed pale by comparison.

The Lone Ranger offered a three-speed bike in a slogan contest on bicycle safety. I signed my entry S. J. Temple and won. When the sponsor asked if I was any relation to myself, the studio told them any publicity about the award would infringe on their exclusivity to the use of my name. With that, the sponsor reversed its decision and gave the bicycle to somebody else. Undaunted I sent in Puffed Wheat Cereal box tops plus a dime for a Dick Tracy eighteen-piece detecto kit for fingerprints and invisible writing, and another box top for a sunburst-shaped decoder pin that glowed in the dark and unraveled secret messages sent over the radio.

Although I was comfortably spellbound by bizarre possibilities, my parents continued to fret about kidnapping. As their concern for increased security and privacy coincided with increased finances, our modest, curbside bungalow was put up for sale and a more isolated four-acre piece of wooded property in nearby Brentwood was acquired. By coincidence the plot was located adjacent to the home of actress ZaSu Pitts, in whose 1933 film I had cried for the predicament of Red Riding Hood in the forest.

At eighteen months,
me and ball
*(Twentieth Century-
Fox)*

Cheesecake, posed by me for Father, Santa Monica, California, 1930
(Author's private collection)

My second film, *War Babies*, Educational Films, costume by Mother, 1932 *(Culver Pictures)*

My fifth birthday, with Mother, 1933 *(Author's private collection)*

Morelegs Sweettrick, *Kid in Hollywood*, costume by Mother, 1933 *(Culver Pictures/Curtis Camera Press)*

With Georgie and ostrich, *Kid in Africa*, 1933   *(Author's private collection)*

With producer Jack Hays
and my first leading man
Georgie Smith, 1932
*(Culver Studios/Curtis
Camera Press)*

Femme fatale, 1933 vintage   *(Culver Service)*

"Lazy Bones" audition with Lew Brown, Fox studio, 1933 *(Twentieth Century-Fox)*

My first dance routine in a major film. With Jimmy Dunn, *Stand Up and Cheer*, 1934 *(Culver Pictures/Curtis Camera Press)*

Will Rogers visiting from *David Harum*, Fox studio, 1934 *(Twentieth Century-Fox)*

Contract signed. Father and I at Fox studio, summer 1934 *(Twentieth Century-Fox)*

My all-time favorite photo: waif in *Little Miss Marker*, 1934   *(Paramount Productions, Inc.)*

Conciliatory pony
ride after being
spanked by brother
Jack   *(Author's
private collection)*

Encounter with Marlene Dietrich, Paramount studio
commissary, 1934   *(Paramount Productions, Inc.)*

The 24th Street neighborhood gang: Bernard Arnold, Dorothy Arnold, Richard Allen, John Matzinger, Mark Allen, Jean Arnold, myself, 1934 *(Twentieth Century-Fox)*

Carole Lombard and Gary Cooper at Paramount, *Now and Forever*, 1934 *(Hyman Fink, McFadden Publications)*

Mary Lou Isleib,
my friend and
stand-in
*(Twentieth
Century-Fox)*

Ceremonial bare
footprint, forecourt
of Grauman's
Chinese Theatre,
1934 *(Twentieth
Century-Fox)*

Initial dolls in an unexpected collection, 1934 *(Twentieth Century-Fox)*

Promotional
breakthrough, New
Year's, 1935   *(Twentieth
Century-Fox)*

Hand in hand with Uncle Billy "Bojangles" Robinson, 1935   *(Twentieth
Century-Fox)*

A rumble: prompting
Lionel Barrymore in
The Little Colonel,
1934 *(Twentieth
Century-Fox)*

Staircase dance from
The Little Colonel,
with Uncle Billy
Robinson *(Twentieth
Century-Fox)*

Big crush on
Joel McCrea,
Our Little Girl,
1934
*(Twentieth
Century-Fox)*

Diminutive Oscar award, with
Irvin S. Cobb, 1935   *(Twentieth
Century-Fox)*

The most comfortable
shoulders in history: those of
Duke P. Kahanamoku,
Hawaii, 1935 *(Author's private
collection)*

Piping aboard the
USS *Gamble*, Pearl
Harbor, 1935
*(Twentieth
Century-Fox)*

Two early Shirley Temples in costume from *The Little Colonel*, 1934
(Twentieth Century-Fox)

Spotted among native California live oaks and looming eucalyptus, long ago introduced from Australia, stood pepper trees, branches heavy with gaudy clusters of red berries, silvery green cedars, conical evergreens, and exotic pines with giant cones. The ground was stubbled with thickets of rust-colored manzanita, madrone, and fallen limbs, providing a vision of my own forest primeval. While the architect and my parents were occupied discussing the eventual house orientation, I wandered off behind some scrubby bushes, snapping twigs underfoot, and immediately flushed a covey of quail. Running with heads unswerving, chests puffed, and curlicue topknots lending a regal character to their haste, they paused, then rocketed upward, legs tucked tight beneath them, and vanished among the trees ahead.

Looking down, I had almost bumped into a rose bush shaped like a short-stemmed wineglass and sheeted with tiny pink blooms. Carefully I detached one blossom and took it back, and Mother exclaimed that it was her favorite Cecil Breuner rose.

It was a good augury. And indeed the bush became a secret resource of happiness for me too. Later an interior decorator did my bedroom in multiple hues of blue: ice-blue tiles in the bath, deep French blue carpeting, woodwork trim and moldings sky-blue, the two-inch border on my chintz curtains gray-blue, and even my bedspread quilts, hand-embroidered by a ninety-two-year-old fan, depicted little girls in blue poke bonnets. Beautiful but cool, all this blue cried out for warmth, and soft pink roses from my wild bush had a habit of appearing in a water glass on a table, by my chaise longue, or floating in saucers.

Well before this time I had been taken to the local Frank's Flower Nursery, a family enterprise. Regarding it as safe territory, Griff would let me wander along the narrow earthen aisles separating swatches of brilliant color and powerful fragrance to each side, and let me explore in the steamy greenhouse dense with tropical orchids, broad-leafed banana plants, exotic creepers, and dangling trumpet flowers.

Frank was a lean, wiry little Japanese with muscular forearms and trousers always bagged at the knees. An open-air philosopher, he fussed around, rearranging pots and snipping flower stems. Asked if pruning did not kill things, he crinkled up his eyes and grinned through gapped front teeth. "No cut, no new bloom. Cut flowers mean happiness, not sadness."

From him I learned his cosmic theory of cut-flower arrangement, creating tiers by stem length, shape, and color to signify earth, moon, sun, and stars. In later years I adapted another level for Frank's floral constellation. Rather than discard flowers with stems cut short, I fashioned a lowest level of downward-looking blooms, preferably flame-colored.

"You've created the level of hell," Mother laughed, "with all those primary flowers."

Subtle I was not. The sight of a weird lily with tangled yellow petals and yawning ruby throat made me feel exhilarated. Having flowers around was a true stimulant. Each was a vibrant and beautiful being, counterpoint to an otherwise lifeless room environment of metal, wood, paint and cotton.

In good time a shingle-roofed English country house arose on the wooded lot, with a view from its windows of the distant Pacific Ocean. On clear days, thirty miles beyond, Catalina Island barely smudged the horizon. Flagstone terraces and pathways linked the main house with a swimming pool, a poolside guest cottage, and beyond a rustic stable and riding ring sheltered among towering eucalyptus and dense pines.

By the day we moved in an eight-foot-high chain-link fence had been installed, snaking its way through brush and trees on the three wooded sides of the property. Along the street frontage, however, stonemasons were still laying up an imposing fieldstone-and-mortar wall. In Hollywood tradition, our house was promptly included on itineraries for the familiar sight-seeing buses. All day on the hour another fresh busload of tourists were disgorged outside along our wall with cameras clicking. Speaking through a megaphone, the tour driver recited everything he knew about us and the house, while his customers snatched leaves and small branches from the shrubbery as souvenirs, sometimes even scooping up pebbles and fistfuls of dirt for a remembrance. Whenever the buses arrived I would crouch out of sight, peek, and listen, but before long I realized that the coincidence of a steady supply of mortar from the masons' work and the repeated presence of souvenir-conscious sightseers presented an irresistible business opportunity.

With Griff watching protectively, arms akimbo, I struck a deal with the stonemasons to share their wet mortar, which I formed into small pies, using tins borrowed from our kitchen. When the first bus arrived

I had a supply of damp pies ready at curbside, priced from a nickel to 25 cents, depending on size. I sold out instantly. One tourist wanted my handprint, so I made a special pie on the spot, imprinted my hand, and charged 50 cents, plus another 50 cents for the pie tin carried away. I was in business. The driver was enthusiastic, but the demand was only partially met, so I set about making fresh pies for the next bus.

Griff, sensing risk in every stranger, told Mother, who came bustling to the gate and shut me down.

"No more mud pies."

"They aren't," I replied. "They're cement."

Mud, cement, no matter. She ushered me back inside the unfinished wall, issuing stern reprimands about dangers in fraternizing with strangers. My objection that strangers were customers willing to pay me money made scant impression.

Later Griff tried to excuse his tattling. "After all, you get a weekly allowance. Everybody knows all your money goes into a trust fund. You don't need any more, ever."

His explanation was slight consolation. "Maybe she's fixed up everything so I'll never be poor, but I only get four dollars a week. I'd rather be rich now."

In addition to Griff's presence, a photoelectric eye guarded my bedroom door, and every window was fitted with electric circuit sensors leading to local police headquarters. An elaborate outdoor security system was installed, automatically linking our nocturnal patrol guards, keyed time clocks located around the property, and the local police station. Any aberration from check-in schedule and the police would arrive, sirens blazing.

During his rounds one night our guard was twirling his key on a thong when off it flew, splashing into a fishpond thick with water lilies. Groping unsuccessfully in the tangle of watery roots and soft slime, he missed checking in at the next time clock. Police squad cars roared away from the local station and officers came storming in the driveway, guns drawn to apprehend some villain. Instead they confronted only a watchman, bare-legged, stooped and elbow deep in a fishpond protesting he was only searching for a lost key. Wedged safely between my pajama-clad parents at an upstairs bathroom window, I enjoyed the excitement far more than the participants did.

False alarms and cement pies could hardly sustain my interest for long. I genuinely missed studio work during our customary summer shutdown and in another example of restlessness, I played apprentice carpenter for guests.

A small playhouse was being erected near our pool as an Owens-Illinois Glass Company demonstration on how glass brick could be used for Art Deco accent in construction. Watching how the masons laid up a level course of brick using a taut string as a guide, and how the carpenters planed door and window frames to fit, I decided to help.

Picking up a wood plane and selecting a board, I mimicked the carpenters. It was hard pushing, so I switched to a sharp-edged wood chisel and hammer and began hacking away noisily at the wood. The noise bothered Mother. "Don't play with that," she called.

"I'm not playing," I answered. "I'm working!" A wishful truth.

Perhaps best of all, the new home provided ideal country for target practice. By now my trunkful of juvenile armaments had few items more prized than my slingshot collection. A weapon tolerated by Mother, the original slingshot had been augmented by an understanding studio propman. Targets were usually tin cans, tree trunks, and fence posts. Birds were always off limits, but I could hit a Coke bottle at twenty feet. Someone told Edwin Burke, who did the screenplay of *The Littlest Rebel*, so he wrote in a special sequence featuring my slingshot.

Selecting a favorite medium-range weapon, I had it tucked under the belt of my dress as detestable Union soldier Jack Holt and his squad of soldiers galloped onto our southern plantation, intent on capturing my Confederate Army father, John Boles. My job was to pepper Holt with volleys of round pebbles, all on target the first time with no rehearsals and no double needed. In an offhand remark an assistant director observed that pebbles didn't hurt Holt and that slingshots were good only for birds. I objected strongly. There was a big difference between bad guys and birds, and the man's attitude lay heavily on my mind as the next scenes came around.

In the film we had a war going, replete with cavalry charges, thundering cannon fire, and infantry locked in hand-to-hand combat. An acrid pall of black gunpowder fogged across the set and death and destruction were everywhere, at least until quitting time. The action then dissolved to a military prison, where the only sounds were heavy footfalls and clanking keys as a Union jailer moved along the tier, stopping at last before my father's cell.

"I'm afraid I've got bad news, Captain," he said softly.

Suddenly from offstage rose a mournful cooing noise from some caged doves already used in a happy plantation scene.

"Cut," muttered director David Butler. "Somebody get those birds out of here!"

While a grip went to move the cage, I walked up to Butler.

"Why can't they stay?" I asked. "They make a pretty sound!"

"Not in a military prison," he replied impatiently. "Doves go with peace, not war, like..." He seemed distracted. "Well, like down in Africa."

Noting my puzzled expression, he stopped what he was doing and explained how the radio was just reporting Mussolini's invasion of Ethiopia.

"Why doesn't someone make Mussolini stop?"

"Take your places," Butler called, then turned to me. "We can talk later."

We didn't, but someone overheard our exchange, and national wire services carried my forthright solution, a news item predestined to sit poorly with the local Italian consul general. When Mother wrote asking him to obtain Il Duce's autograph, she was haughtily informed he could not be bothered accommodating people critical of Italian foreign affairs.

Months before I had been troubled by the little black boy who got an extra quarter for calling my Father "Daddy," and the same sort of event arose to plague me on *The Littlest Rebel*.

In one children's war game I appeared wearing a Confederate cap and posing as drill sergeant. As I marched at the head of a gaggle of black children, we were supposed to straggle and appear inept, but one soldier overdid it. Finally I saw the director offer the child a 50-cent coin if he would only concentrate, and the next take was perfect.

Afterward I raised the subject with Uncle Billy Robinson, again teamed with me. "Why don't I get some extra money for doing a good job?" I asked.

"Good job is what we all get a salary for," he said.

"Doesn't he get a salary too?" I asked. Uncle Billy nodded. "Then why doesn't he give the extra money back?"

"Because the boy was playing fair and square."

He was obviously finished with the subject, but it kept spinning in my brain, along with visions of the little boy who called Father "Daddy" and Mother's earlier advice about even trades when I coveted Jane Withers's film doll. Was it wrong not to do a good job until paid extra? How could things be right and wrong at the same time? And if you played fair and square, was that all that mattered? Uncle Billy's advice certainly didn't work for me the next week.

Mother had donated a Shirley Temple doll and matching trunk outfitted with special clothes to be raffled off at an Assistance League benefit. As an added attraction, she donated me to draw the winning number. Reaching deep into the boxful of ticket stubs, I pulled my own number. Delighted to have won, I jumped up and down, but out in the audience someone murmured "Hoax," followed by a gabble of protest and polite boos.

"Take another number," whispered Mother.

"I won't," I said. I had helped beat the drums for that auction. The prize itself was of little interest, although the clothes were beautifully made. It was the principle. To win was exciting. I had played fair and square. Why must I surrender what was fairly won?

"You've got to!" Mother insisted, shoving the box toward me. "Take another number!"

"I will not." I remained at the podium, holding my ticket stub tightly. "I won it."

It was an example I would have liked to raise with Uncle Billy, but back on the set I found the timing all wrong. He had suddenly checked into the Hollywood Presbyterian Hospital. Taken there to visit him, I found his ailment difficult to identify. It wasn't contagious or I couldn't have come. No plaster casts, hence no broken bones.

"Are you really sick?" I asked.

He replied no, but that someone just hadn't played fair and square with him.

I had brought a miniature framed picture of myself with an inscription saying, "I'll bet I can beat you tap-dancing now!" He smiled and nodded thoughtfully, climbed carefully out of bed and into a wheelchair, and let me push it up and down the hospital corridor.

After Uncle Billy's return to work, the mystery of his ailment deepened. Within my earshot someone commented that he had been "under the knife" twice in twenty-four hours. First, downtown in Hollywood, then on the operating table.

A portrait photographer later wrote:

As all male dancers do before going onstage, he emptied his pockets. Glancing over to the couch where he'd thrown his coins and keys, I was confounded to see a small .38-caliber revolver! He saw my shocked expression, and told me he had a license. He'd been involved in an altercation on Hollywood Boulevard . . . accosted by hoodlums . . . felt he had to have some basic protection.

When I tried to restart our earlier conversation about winning fair and square, he came up with a new idea about how to win. How would I like to help black boxer Joe Louis whip Max Baer for the boxing championship? Whoever was Uncle Billy's candidate was mine, too, so I said sure. The way we start, he said, was to rub some salt in my hand.

With those sensitive palms inherited from Mother, I hesitated.

"An old trick among us southern folks," he explained. "We can make some things *happen*."

"By just rubbing salt?"

"Betcha, but not just any old salt." He lowered his voice and rounded his eyes until the whites showed all around. "Plain salt has no *magic*."

"Magic?" Now I was whispering as well.

"Yessirree! First you've got to cook some regular salt. Fry it, or just brown it in a pan, or boil it." I was straining to listen.

"Then you got to get a bone from the left rear ankle of a black lady cat." He relaxed one clenched fist so I could peer inside. "Like this one. Take it in your hand."

I was agog. Untying the drawstring of a tiny brown sack, he poured a palmful of what looked like brown salt in my other hand.

"Now close your eyes and squeeze it around real good." I squeezed.

"Keep rubbing around, and think hard. Joe Louis will win!"

With eyes shut, I squeezed, mashed, and rubbed, trying to envision what Louis looked like.

"Is this fair and square?" I asked.

"Sure," he whispered, "but don't tell anyone." He flashed that broad, toothy smile.

Louis probably never realized why he flattened Baer for the championship.

No magic salt was needed to provide *The Littlest Rebel* with a special punch. Within its premiere week at Radio City Music Hall, in New York, the film grossed one half its total original cost of $190,000. In Paris it played with smashing success in twenty-one theatres at the same time. In Germany the government reversed its prohibition on my previous films, allowing it to play simultaneously to overflow audiences in forty-five Berlin theatres. Critics and public agreed it was my finest film to date, and far the best for Uncle Billy. Perhaps our genuine happiness with each other shone through. Certainly whatever we won we had done it fair and square.

Following his death, Will Rogers's estate had given the family home in West Los Angeles to the state as a public museum and park and set about to raise an endowment. The studio helped, cobbling together its stars in public appearances to help raise funds. At a Shrine Auditorium benefit Uncle Billy and I tap-danced up and down the aisles passing the hat, followed by cowboy movie star Leo Carillo twirling his lariat as Rogers used to, and Bing Crosby crooning a sentimental version of "Home on the Range."

At the studio a new soundstage was being dedicated to Rogers's memory on November 15, 1935. Newly elected California Governor Frank Merriam was there. Nevada Senator Pat McCarran came wearing high-heeled cowboy boots and a ten-gallon white hat, and many close friends delivered long eulogies. Joseph Schenck called me from the audience to pull the curtain aside and unveil the memorial plaque.

"Now you say something," he instructed and backed away a pace, his mouth gaping open like a gargoyle's. The others before me had said everything.

"I loved him too," was all I could add.

As our group disbanded, around the corner came a vanguard of carpenters for *Captain January*. Within days the new soundstage would be transformed from an echoing, vacant hall into a fog-shrouded Maine coast, complete with a lighthouse.

Learning my solo tap dance descending a forty-five-foot-high spiral staircase in a lonely lighthouse taught me not only the routine, but also how to multiply. It was all tight steps, like a ballet, a devilishly complicated task. There were three things to do at once: the taps, move down the spiral staircase a step at a time, and synchronize multiplication tables with both taps and movements. Then came an athletic dancing experience with lithe, long-legged Buddy Ebsen over a fifty-yard obstacle course. Somehow in our long, complex sequence he shortened his stride and I learned to fly. Up and down stairs we went, threading our way among bushel baskets of lobsters, leaping up and down off an old rain barrel, all the while wearing unstressed expressions and singing lyrics to "At the Codfish Ball."

That barrel was a problem. I couldn't jump that high. Ebsen solved it by holding me cheek to cheek with my feet dangling, and then vaulting up himself. As he later jokingly told me about those times, he had fallen arches and was wearing steel supports in his shoes. My weight fastened at his neck must have been all he could handle.

The lobsters also concerned me. To prevent them from squirming out of their baskets, the props people had cooked them, turning their color from natural blackish-green to a bright red. To restore their natural hue for the camera, each one had been painted back to its original color. It seemed a ghoulish process, particularly when shooting finished. The crew promptly divided the lobsters, cracked them open with hammers, and consumed them on the spot.

As I sang "Asleep in the Deep," few could realize it was a melancholy requiem for those grotesque, repainted, and helpless creatures. From Hawaii one critic totally misunderstood.

"When you puff out your chest, suck in your chin and sing," he wrote, "I realize you had better take good care of your double chin! It's your greatest asset!"

Lobsters were not the last of it. As a companion to lonely lighthouse inspector Slim Summerville, there appeared a spindle-legged crane standing four feet tall. Costumed with a huge bow ribbon tied around the top of its towering neck, it was standing quietly when I came up from behind, reached to feel its tail feathers, and asked aloud, "Do you remember me?"

Swiveling its neck, the crane stretched its long sliver of bill toward my face, tumbling me backwards in surprise.

"Why *should* the crane remember you?" asked Summerville, helping me up.

"A crane?" I asked. "I thought it was a *stork*."

The bird did not seem to share my humor. Turning in a dainty circle, it took a long step toward me, and naturally I dodged backwards out of range.

"They always go for the eyes," muttered Jonesy the propman. "Keep your distance."

To resolve my problem—or was it the bird's?—a propman tried stretching himself prone out of camera view, holding the bird's feet stationary. He got pecked at for his ingenuity, and wound up hammering flathead nails through the webbing of the crane's feet, anchoring it to a floorboard.

Emphasizing that it was actually painless for the bird, the director pledged everyone to silence about the solution. It worked. We finished the shot, and someone wrenched out the nails with a claw hammer. The crane must have felt fine because in the next scene it danced an unconcerned jig to Summerville's harmonica.

But somebody had snitched. Late that afternoon onto the set bustled an official from the local humane society. I heard no one admit what had happened, and certainly the crane made no complaint. The perforations in his feet were invisible from a distance, and each time the woman tried for a closer inspection, the crane pecked at her too. All the time I averted eye contact with the woman. She never asked me anything, and therefore I was not obliged to lie. Respect for truth was, I believed, inviolate, one of Mother's cardinal rules I shared. Yet team loyalty required we all pull together in whatever direction our leader led. It would have been a tough call.

Where everything really exploded was with my hula. As a nubile island maiden, I wore a hula skirt and brassiere of slippery seaweed fronds, and swayed and swished until my costume seemed alive. Whatever my sin of suggestiveness, reviewers from the Mothers Clubs of America gasped in horror. The hula was immoral.

No studio wants to fly in the face of that sort of charge. The scene was rewritten, the hula deleted, and I was refilmed, dressed this time in tight-fitting trousers with flared bottoms, doing a sailor's hornpipe.

You can't please everyone. Writing for the *The London Spectator*, in his August 7, 1936, review, film critic Graham Greene characterized *Captain January* as "... a little depraved, with an appeal interestingly decadent.... Shirley Temple acts and dances with immense vigor and assurance, but some of her popularity seems to rest on a coquetry quite as mature as Miss Colbert's, and on an oddly precocious body, as voluptuous in grey flannel trousers as Miss Dietrich's."

That dancing could turn out a contentious profession I learned in *Poor Little Rich Girl*, my next film, which came headlong when *Captain January* was completed. In the musical number "I Love a Military Man," I danced in unison between two accomplished pros, Alice Faye and Jack Haley. We were working on a semidarkened recording stage. Our job as a trio was to match our tap noises in synchrony with a long and athletic filmed segment being projected against a screen. Dancing together, it took only one false tap from any of us to ruin the take. Dance director Jack Haskell was a taskmaster for flawless movement and precise timing. Synchronization is not easy, and ours went progressively more poorly.

As we paused to pinpoint some little problem, I stared away, meditatively working my tongue against a precariously loose tooth. Noticing my averted gaze, Haskell brusquely ordered I look at him when he was speaking. Doing two things at once was easy, particularly if one was listening, but his tone of voice introduced a harsh note in trying circumstances.

Haley, in particular, had trouble getting synchrony with his filmed image, and seemed annoyed at me because my taps kept matching perfectly. He obviously knew the mechanics cold, but without music and only a projected image to guide him, his timing remained way off. Even Faye grimaced occasionally, while frustration and fatigue gradually began to erode our basic sense of camaraderie.

At the time, director Irving Cummings had been observing how each of us was reacting under stress. Drawing Mother aside, he told her the studio would have to find better stories for me; I had lost that baby quality and was getting an emotional understanding, "like Helen Hayes when she started." Mother was complimented enough to repeat the remark to me, but it certainly didn't fit my mood at the time.

The recording session dragged on, and by late afternoon my legally permitted workday was soon ending with the dance still not in order. Frustrated herself, Mother made a cutting observation comparing Haley's precision and endurance to mine. It was tinder to a powder keg. Instantly he shot back that I was the problem, not him.

Jumping into the breach, Haskell ordered another break. "We're not going to finish," he proclaimed the obvious. "The law says Shirley can't work at night, so let's get her taps recorded alone now."

Nodding toward Haley and Faye, he suggested they return after dinner and record their own synchrony separately. Sound technicians would then have to match our taps together on one master record.

Like anyone else, I eventually get tired, but seldom in the legs. Haley and Faye stood aside. I wiggled at my tooth and smiled to set my mood. Tap dancers are a prideful lot. Comparatively, singing and acting are natural skills. Tap dancing, however, is an utterly unnatural skill, acquired only with time and great effort. Drawing a deep breath, I began. Once again the projector rolled. Each nerve tap came across crisp and sharp and synchronized on the first try, but I couldn't smile during the last few stanzas. The loose tooth had finally detached, arriving on my tongue like a coughdrop.

"Time to go," said Mother, grabbing my hand and marching past Haley with a long stride I recognized as triumphant.

At Christmastime 1935 Twentieth Century-Fox received a good present. The *Motion Picture Herald* reported I was the biggest money-maker of the year. Not for myself, of course, but for the studio. In the spirit of Santa Claus, however, the studio announced my weekly salary was being doubled from $1,250 to $2,500, and that during 1936 I would be paid $64,000 apiece for four motion pictures, for a total of $256,000. To dramatize the comparative magnitude of my raise, the studio cited $55,000 as my earnings the previous year.

Studios must have arcane reasons for what they say, even when they warp the truth, both ahead and behind. In 1936 I would actually receive $120,499, less than half the amount publicly announced. During the previous year I had actually been paid $71,923, a third *more* than claimed.

If eyebrows rise on a point of accuracy, they should stay elevated on the point of generosity. The average cost for each of my recent films had been $300,000. Because each required about six weeks to make, my cost to the studio at my weekly salary would have been about $7,500. Upon release, each film earned about $1.6 million, leaving studio and exhibitors an even split of about $800,000 apiece. Thus, my $7,500 earnings represented a thin 1 percent slice from the studio's earnings pie. Doubling my salary to 2 percent was gratefully noted by my parents, but it was hardly a sacrifice to the giver.

I had a more important problem with Santa Claus that year. "Please send me a BB gun and a bicycle," I wrote, adding as a cautionary note, "I have too many dolls already."

I got dolls, all sorts. As for the BB gun and bicycle, I concluded Santa Claus simply failed to read his mail.

My two most recent films, *Captain January* and *Poor Little Rich Girl*, racked up booming box office and also a swarm of lawsuits.

L. C. Page & Co., a Boston firm, filed suit against the studio claiming proprietary rights to *Captain January* and asked $250,000 damages, saying it had acquired its rights from Laura E. Richards of Portland, Maine, author of the story forty-six years previous. Although in 1923 movie rights had been sold to Sol Lesser's Principal Pictures Corporation, it was only for a silent film starring child actress Baby Peggy. Even though Lesser had then sold his rights to Twentieth Century-Fox for $50,000, Page claimed its original sale to Lesser was only for silents, not the dialogue in talkies.

Poor Little Rich Girl, too, wound up in its own legal bramble patch. Writers Izola Forrester Page and Mann Page filed suit in New York Superior Court charging the studio had stolen their story outright and demanding an injunction against further showing, plus an accounting of profits and damages. It was their story "Joyous," they claimed, written and submitted to Fox in 1934 specifically for me. Studio writers Gladys Lehman, Sam Hellman and Harry Tugend had stolen the script, they alleged, and rechristened it with a title borrowed from another story, the "Poor Little Rich Girl" of Eleanor Gates, first filmed in 1916 with Mary Pickford.

As if this squabble was not already sufficiently convoluted, Gates herself jumped into the middle. The Pages were partially correct. The borrowed title was indeed hers, but the story was definitely not "Joyous." Rather it was "Betsy Takes the Air" by Ralph Spence.

Obviously my success was getting to be worth a wrangle.

13

The woman standing at our cottage door was reedlike. Glimpsing me, she smiled, disclosing big, even teeth. She wore slacks and a pullover sweater, no makeup, and carried two blue suitcases.

"I'm Amelia Earhart," she said. She put down the bags and gestured like a boy. "These are for you."

Life was developing into a sort of ham sandwich. One piece of bread was work, the other, school. In the middle was the ham, me, and unexpected visitors, the spice.

Earhart's hair was steeply shingled up the back and tousled, an informality which instantly pleased me. The top edge of each ear poked in sight as she stooped, rapped the suitcases with her knuckles, and said they were made of a special light material suitable for air travel. Mother commented she would worry every minute if I were ever airborne, a remark upon which Earhart seized.

"The time to worry is *before* a flight," she said, eyes rounded and sincere. "Worry is a hazard to action. That's why Hamlet would have been a bad aviator."

"Hamlet who?" I interjected.

"Someone who worried too much," she answered.

Continuing to talk about flying, she told how during long, lonely overwater flights she had nothing but soup and hot chocolate. I began swinging my legs back and forth with pleasure.

Earhart's identity as a flying heroine was familiar in our family, and

132

Father had long ago noted that her first name was the same as Mother's middle name.

"Do you like chewing gum?" she suddenly asked, offering me a stick of Beechnut. Stripping off its wrapper, I popped it into my mouth, avoiding eye contact with Mother, who always voiced strong disapproval of gum because it tended to remove my caps and got stuck in my false plate.

With both hands calmly folded together in her lap, Earhart again inclined toward Mother, saying her husband believed in wives doing what they did best, despite the risks. Almost in an offhand manner she mentioned her intention to circumnavigate the Earth. At this Mother inquired why. Because such a flight would both demonstrate aircraft safety and dramatize that women deserved parity with men in aviation.

From Mother's smile, I knew she appreciated the reference to feminine independence, but she reiterated her ambivalent feelings about air travel.

"But women must try to do things," Earhart replied, "just as men do. Even if we fail, our failure still serves by challenging other women to try."

Attempting to derail this topic of conversation, Mother only provoked Earhart to emphasize that exclusion from opportunity in flying was denying women a chance to share in the total human experience. Utterly unaware how women related to aviation, I listened unbelievingly. So far as I knew, everyone could work happily at what he or she did best. Having been emancipated to the workplace at age three, I just listened while much of the rush of feminist chatter sailed comfortably over my head. What captured my attention was Earhart's casual attitude toward mortal risk, her tousled, unaffected appearance, and the chewing gum. She was a notable exception, someone quick to speak about concerns totally alien to my life and therefore provocative.

Success is like currency—it attracts. Visitors had begun to windmill past, for the most part joined in a blurred memory of curious, kindly smiles. Neither surprised nor bothered, I realized I was on exhibit, with a duty to respond not unlike a call for costuming, makeup or camera. I was seldom provided a meaningful advance introduction. What I did was usually extemporaneous, actions modulated by secret instructions from Mother.

Categorizing visitors among those who came to ogle, to bring something, or to get something, Mother had devised a set of private signals to guide what I said, and whether a visit should be stretched or cut short. Her interjection while I was mid-sentence signaled a need to change the subject and to retreat to neutral ground. A squint alerted me to some controversial trap ahead. Eyebrows arched indicated keep going. An averted gaze alerted me that I was already in deep trouble and should get out. Occasionally she interrupted, closing the visit on some pretext and afterwards explaining where I'd gone wrong. Her system struck a nice balance between my independence and her restraint, and was enormously helpful as an international rainbow of strangers continued to appear.

A British vice admiral with a starched line of side boys presented me a commemorative silver spoon from HMS *Norfolk*, described as the same as that used by the royal princess in England. Governor Ben Ross of Idaho commissioned me a lieutenant colonel on his staff. The vision of an army and maybe a uniform delighted me; I was unaware that I was entering politics and that my photo would appear on a poster endorsing Ross as Democratic candidate for reelection.

A delegation of Chilean naval officers, resplendent in golden epaulets and peaked hats with shiny patent-leather bills, christened me their navy mascot and provided a uniform to match my title. Many passed by whom I learned much later to be world-renowned. Conductor Leopold Stokowski held my face between his outstretched fingers and called me "a divine instrument," a description evoking my laughter, to Mother's dismay.

Albert Einstein observed that he, too, was poor at arithmetic, which convinced me he was not very remarkable. U.S. Treasury Secretary Henry M. Morgenthau, Jr., returned three times, and a Missouri politician stole two pencils from my school desk as a souvenir.

Following her visit, the daughter of the Cuban President invited me to come to Havana, her letter buried in a sea of fan mail from overseas. Mistakenly associating her country of origin with poverty, someone declined on my behalf and enclosed two sample Shirley Temple dresses as a charitable gift. The palace never said thank-you.

Only on rare occasions did Mother and I turn out to be at odds over a visitor. In one of those exceptions I had looked forward to meeting General John J. Pershing, leader of American Expeditionary Forces in the world war, but my heart sank a little when he arrived dressed in mufti. Chin high, back ramrod straight, his posture left no way for our eyes to meet until he bent stiffly to kiss Mother's hand in the continental fashion and shot me a sideways glance. His tongue turned out to be almost as inflexible as his spine, as he now and then grunted at me through clenched teeth.

As a diversion I produced the autograph book being maintained by Mother and flipped the pages. Pershing showed little recognition of the names. When he said nothing at Uncle Billy's inscription, I was aghast. Now there was a general who didn't know *anybody*.

My observation was lost on Mother. "When he kissed my hand," she said, "I got gooseflesh!" It was her unfailing barometer of true quality from stage performance to personality.

Wedged into this international montage appeared photographers, reporters, and even a painter, Sir John Lavery, chairman of the English Royal Society of Portrait Painters. Before posing me, he laid down the rules of how I should address him. When he spoke, he commanded, and I obeyed.

Completing rough sketches in California, he executed his final portrait in London and placed it on exhibition at the Royal Institute Galleries. The painting was really a self-portrait: with the artist dressed in high-wing collar, chin elevated, one foot extended to emphasize a two-toned shoe, and his lips parted in a noble overbite. As I linger before him with a croquet mallet held at ease, my face is raised adoringly toward the regal painter.

"Shirley is desperately quick and bright," he told London gallery guests. "Not in the least cheeky, like so many Americans. Most of them addressed me, I deeply regret to say, as Sir Lavery. She, at least, was sufficiently educated to call me Sir *John*." It wasn't education. He told me what to say.

Sometimes a visit called for spontaneous ingenuity, and occasionally one collapsed in failure. Both happened during the appearance of Japanese Ambassador S. Saburo Kurusu. An elegantly dressed man with icy eyes, pomaded hair, and a frozen, toothy smile, he came accompanied by two women, Sachito Chiga, the "Janet Gaynor of Japan," and his ten-year-old daughter, Teru, both rouged and powdered and laden with a bewildering assortment of dolls, fans and shiny lacquer boxes. Believing in the virtue of reciprocal generosity, I was at a loss as to what to give in return, until I remembered my rabbits and presented each of them with one white bunny. By now what had been only a hutch filled with cuddlesome pets with wiggly noses was regarded as a valuable resource, somehow almost inexhaustible.

Two accompanying Japanese photographers then began what seemed to be an extensive photo layout and afterwards posed me with my guests for a memento picture. Look up at us, they said.

"Please tell me who is most important," I replied. "I can't be looking at both of you." We settled on two shots.

As a finale we put in a telephone call for my interview with the editor of *Nitchi-Nitchi*, a Tokyo newspaper. The hookup was not clear, and between his strange accent and the static, the editor's questions were unintelligible.

"I beg your pardon?" I repeated, shouting into the phone.

Mother became fidgety. "Quick, say something else."

"I like Japan," I yelled, just as the telephone line went dead.

Miss Barkley always said she considered me a model student, an inevitable classification, given that my one-pupil school made truancy or classroom mischief quite impossible. When the mandatory national Pitner-Cunningham Intelligence Test rated me in the "genius" category, she told me how exceptional this was, a remark which made little impression. Except in acting, I had limited exposure to other children, and therefore no easy sense of comparison. My yardstick could only be applied against myself. The test reported I "solved mathematics problems up to 1,000." Doubtful; my addition was fair, my subtraction poor. The idea of subtracting anything had always been repugnant, a process of diminishment, of losing something.

My reading, writing and vocabulary were judged equal to those of a child of ten. I should have scored higher than my age. Actually I was a year older than reported, anyway.

One of those momentarily intrigued was Dr. Lewis M. Terman, chairman of the Psychology Department at Stanford. In 1920 he had begun a continuing study to determine the relationship between genetics and genius based on 1,500 of the brightest students in the California school system. Apparently my genius quotient was too little, my genetics unworthy, or I was born too late. Terman came, looked, and left.

On a more personal and pedantic level, Miss Barkley asserted I could disappear from pictures anytime and still grow up successfully as a great dancer, a splendid musician, a successful painter . . . or even a capable farmer. The first three professions were familiar, but in clarifying why farming had come to mind she referred to my recent enthusiastic report about a saleslady of fresh produce in a nearby family market. Always smiling and wearing a spotless apron, the woman had moved up and down in front of her stalls sprinkling the vegetable display from a bright green watering can with a long spout. Everything was left dewy and sparkling. Lettuce looked crinkly fresh, beets glistened, radishes, eggplant, tomatoes, and bunches of green onions all blended in a vivid and mystical composition of beauty. To me, this meant farming.

Patient and invariably kind, Miss Barkley not only coped with scheduling where my studio work took precedence over school, but taught classes at the main studio school. Fluent in several languages, she was constantly drafted as translator for overseas studio communications or interpreter for foreign visitors. Eventually she elected to dump teaching altogether in favor of writing fiction. We were barely getting to be good friends when she kissed me good-bye and waved farewell.

Sudden vacation from schoolwork was brief. Songwriter Harry Revel was visiting with Mother the morning my new schoolteacher, Frances Klampt, appeared. A slight woman who stood with both feet together, she wore a small felt pancake hat tipped at a barely perceptible angle and clutched her handbag directly in front of her. Assigned by the City Board of Education, she had degrees from both UCLA and USC in education, history, and geography. In a calm little voice she inquired what I had been studying. Suddenly Revel, a relaxed, forthright man, interjected, "Miss Klampt . . . that sounds too formal. Let's call you Klammy." And so she remained.

"And for God's sake, take off that hat," he chuckled, "then you'll look like you're *working*!"

With Klammy came an innovation: another pupil, a fictional classmate dubbed Mergotroid. It was Klammy's idea. Someone to provide contrast and competition, if only imaginary.

To teach me French another instructor soon appeared. Gallic from beret to high-heeled pumps, Paula Walling was moonlighting from her job as California correspondent for the Paris newspaper *Ce Soir*.

"To develop zee true French accent," she began, "we shall first put a small piece of chocolate on zee back of your tongue." With that technique she should have been able to teach me anything. But she obviously didn't.

Emboldened by presumed progress, one day I accosted French actress Simone Simon in her native tongue. Bending over courteously, she listened but kept requesting me to repeat. At last she asked me to speak English. I threw up my hands in disgust.

"We just don't speak the same *kind* of French!" I huffed.

On June 5, 1936, Zanuck announced the Dionne Quintuplets and I were being cast together in a blockbuster film to be produced immediately, noting he had signed the Quints under a three-year exclusive contract at $10,000 each child per year. The resulting spray of his publicity emphasized my unquenchable desire to appear with the Quints, hardly the case for me and certainly not for Mother.

What had at first been a glorious human-interest story was deteriorating into a tragedy of greed, exploitation, and insensitivity. A viewing compound had been opened, where the Quints crawled about in a zoo-like environment of asepsis and isolation. Psychologists by the trainload peeked into the compound through one-way windows, as did 12,000 daily visitors.

Perhaps Zanuck was hedging his bet against possible future decline of my popularity, playing to timely news headlines, or hyping his earlier film about the Quints. David Kroll, Canadian government minister and nominal guardian of the Quints, asked would I like to play in a movie with them? I shrugged and replied, "Okay, but too bad they're girls, not boys."

The objective of stardom is broad public response, but on your seventh birthday such affection can turn into a pounding headache. Mine came in the form of 135,000 gifts and greetings. To physically open that many parcels and letters was daunting, so the task devolved on the studio. From Switzerland had come a trained St. Bernard puppy, complete with an empty brandy cask. From Antwerp, Belgium, a hare.

From Ireland, lace enough to trim ten trousseaux. From everywhere an unstanched stream of dolls. Little could be done with such an avalanche beyond sending our thanks and redirecting everything to worthy local children's charities.

Two of these presents, however, warranted my exceptional attention. Both were vehicles.

First, there was a two-wheeled bicycle. Where the Lone Ranger had rejected my winning slogan and Santa Claus turned a deaf ear, my family finally listened. Dancers balance easily, on two wheels or two feet. Griff started to shuffle alongside to steady me but I took off immediately at a strong, wobbly pace, made shortcuts across the lawn and careened along the garden paths, damaging little but occasional flowers.

The second vehicle was even more memorable, a model racing car from Uncle Billy Robinson. Painted pure white with a red leather seat and chrome hood ornament of a leaping antelope, it was powered by a one-cylinder unmuffled lawn-mower motor. There were only two engine controls: a jam clutch to start and a hand brake to stop. On my first solo run on studio grounds, he crouched on the back, showed me how to start, and we leaped forward. Veering into a nearby Fox publicist, I snagged a long tear in his trousers. My first traffic accident.

Once getting the knack of turning corners, pumping the clutch, and ignoring the brake, we raced around the studio grounds with Uncle Billy shouting to clear the track ahead. Belatedly realizing the casualty insurance risks of my driving, the studio insisted the car be licensed to be on the lot, like any other auto.

Eventually the unmuffled, ear-splitting engine noise bothered productions in progress, and no matter how charmed by the sight, few pedestrians relished my charging past. One morning the engine was fitted with a governor to limit my speed and the next day the car was transferred to our home, where the driver was restricted to racing in a circle around her own driveway and soon lost interest.

☆

New York bankers and Wall Street brokers were among those who could take secondary delight in my popularity. Back on June 26, 1936, directors of Chase National Bank in New York had announced they would buy back $50 million of preferred stock issued earlier in the

Depression years. Because the Chase 1935 earnings were only $15,340,000, almost all of it paid out in dividends, it was obvious that the accumulation of $50 million cash for the preferred stock retirement must have stemmed from some other source. Where? Behind the perfunctory announcement lay an improbable tale.

In November 1933, Chase had found itself in such dire financial straits it had defaulted on interest due to shareholders of its preferred stock and deposited the shares with the government-owned Reconstruction Finance Corporation in a form of technical receivership.

Among its moribund assets, Chase held 775,000 shares of Fox preferred stock, 388,000 of its common stock, and additional major holdings in a Fox subsidiary, General Theatre Equipment, Inc. During U.S. Senate testimony, a spokesman for Chase disclosed a proposal to write off as lost $70 million of the value of this $90 million original investment. Its nose gasping for air barely above the surface of bankruptcy, Fox shares were obviously good candidates for such a write-down. National banking authorities endorsed the Chase proposal. Chase shareholdings in Fox and friends were suddenly valued at only $20 million.

Folowing the 1935 merger, Twentieth Century-Fox profits began to accumulate, buoyed principally by my films. This in turn stimulated an upward price movement in Fox shares, which regained much of their previously lost value.

By 1936 the current true market value of Chase's investments in the Fox theatre family was estimated:

775,000 shares of Fox preferred stock @ $35	$27,125,000
388,000 shares of Fox common stock @ $25	9,700,000
General Theatre Equipment, Inc. holdings	15,000,000
	$51,825,000

Sensing its own recovery, Fox had tendered Chase an offer to buy back the General Theatre Equipment stock at a price based on the carrying value on Chase's books. Equally well aware of the favorable outlook for its asset currently in deep sleep, Chase of course declined.

The numbers disclose a roller-coaster recovery. The $90 million original investment, written down to $20 million, had suddenly zoomed back to be worth about $52 million, resulting in a $32 million Chase bonanza, simply because of Fox health. My films were the principal doctor.

Commenting on Chase good fortune and restored healthy financial position, the *Illustrated Daily News* observed:

> It will be taken as an indication of the management shrewdness, which in only a few years has been able to work out of a serious financial predicament. Yet back of it all . . . were bad mistakes, poor judgment and entry into a business of which they knew nothing. To recover from their errors without severe loss is due almost entirely to the nimble feet of a cute little girl with a winning smile. Shirley Temple was the one who poured the profits into coffers of the nation's largest bank.

Knowing it had a good thing going, the studio rushed to keep me working. Abandoning the Quints joint venture, they picked *The Bowery Princess*, a title later judged too coarse for my image, and switched to *Dimples*, something far more symbolic.

The crew kidded me. Anyone could get dimples by sleeping on buttons or twisting a finger in your cheek long enough. But even when at rest my dimples were visible, a slight interruption on otherwise smooth cheeks. More than one makeup man disapprovingly tried to powder them over. One grip lyrically said I was kissed by an angel. He should have said two. Mother insisted they resulted from baby fat. Whatever the reason, they were part of my original equipment, and still are.

Beneath the canopy of shared interest in making each film the best one, all performers know that to focus audience attention on themselves provides the best opportunity to demonstrate professional ability. Conversely, any competent actor is wary of gesture or movement by others which deflects the eye or creates a shadow. It is all curiously impersonal. Actors and actresses are instinctively alert for advantage, combative in defense, and unrelenting. To the degree a child can develop such instincts, I had them. In *Dimples* they were severely tested.

A boisterous tale about gaslit New York with Frank Morgan as a top-hatted swindler, *Dimples* pitted me against an accomplished veteran of the legitimate stage who was not about to let any little curly-headed kid steal his scenes. Competition for camera attention had always been a fact of life for me. The kid and the expert could not help but collide.

Scene stealing is as endemic to movie sets as cameras and lights, but theft requires two people: one to steal, one to give it away. Actors and actresses who without a struggle permit another to unfairly diminish a performance deserve what usually happens—professional oblivion. Performers in a cast are not friendly souls adrift in a comfortable cockleshell. Even when benign winds and following wavelets propel their craft to mutual success, they remain individual competitors in a common cause.

With Morgan even childhood was no refuge. In my close-ups he proved skillful at monopolizing the camera eye. His hands were always at my eye level. When not shooting his cuffs or wiggling a top hat to deflect attention from my face, he could be counted on to toy with white gloves, wring his hands, or flick a handkerchief in some broad gesture. Both of us knew perfectly well what he was doing. There was no way I could cope, short of biting at his fingers.

There I was moving along behind a tabletop with only my face visible. As I entered into camera range Morgan doffed his stovepipe hat and placed it on the table directly between my face and the camera. No way could I see around that hat without moving off my marks, yet if I did nothing, the hat would upstage my face. At such moments the only recourse is to move completely out of the lights. Naturally that spoiled the take and caused us all to start afresh. A few more times and Morgan stopped using that hat to blank me, perhaps electing to let my face appear rather than suffer a dressing-down from the director. Baffled and frustrated, once I tried getting my stage directions changed at the last moment, hoping to thwart Morgan's preplanning.

New York's Central Park, a verdant midsummer scene with a lake bordered by grassy banks and trees, was actually located on our studio back lot. Seated in the foreground by the water's edge under a "No Fishing" sign, I fished. In the background Morgan was being fleeced by confidence men for an antique watch.

Realizing that an unexpected movement from me could steal some attention from Morgan's primary action, I whispered to nearby assistant director "Boots" McCracken to ask if jiggling my pole wouldn't be more lifelike.

"Just fish," he replied, well aware of my motivation.

Morgan overheard. "Just fish!" he echoed and turned to the con men. "Only way to keep her from stealing our scenes."

Only one of my habits—yawning—seemed to baffle Morgan to the end. It was a trick all right, but never premeditated and never precursor to stealing a scene. Yawning was my natural way to relax. Between the call for "roll 'em" and "speed action," that was the moment. Shutting my eyes, I let the yawn build and run its wide-mouthed course. Right afterward my nose usually itched, down at the end. A quick rub with an index finger fixed that little problem, and I was ready to go.

My mannerisms alerted Morgan, probably because few actors can indulge in them. Pancake can show creases after a yawn, and rouge smears, so wide yawns and rubbing the nose are luxuries denied those wearing makeup. My bare face provided latitude to yawn or rub to heart's content. Every time I went through this habitual but involuntary sequence, he would glance down, always with unsatisfied interest and invariably with a sigh in disgust.

Everyone on the set seemed to be following our jousts with silent fascination. One was Helen Westley, a gifted Theatre Guild actress. In a scene together, I stumbled badly. Normally my little mousetrap mind snapped shut on lines and never let go. In this case everything came out as memorized, but it no longer made sense. The lines were gibberish, utterly out of context. Twice I faltered, each time wrecking the scene. Nobody seemed to know what was wrong. Suddenly Westley covered her face with both hands and moaned.

"God forgive me," she said, "I left out a whole speech." Concentrating on my moves, she had skipped a section of script and provided me a cue completely out of phase, but one obviously calling for a response. Her preoccupation with my technique had done us both in. Attempting to put a light touch on the whole matter, she raised the ruffled hem of her skirt, exposing her calf, where a large lump of bills was stuffed into the top of her stocking. "This is one thing nobody around here can steal!" she declared, patting her money.

Streaming onstage during the final moments of *Dimples* came the full two dozen members of the Los Angles County Grand Jury to investigate my working conditions. Their visit reflected a national groundswell of support behind a proposed child-labor amendment to the U.S.

Constitution. Proponents of this measure claimed little people my age were being abused and exploited. Their visit was too late.

Having already survived Morgan's repertoire of abuse, at last I had him in a corner where he had no escape—dancing. When a kid is dancing up a storm, even a pro has enormous difficulty robbing the scene. At the time my Uncle Billy was making a film on an adjacent stage and helped coach me. Aware of my continuing tussle, he added a succession of gestures and rhythmic pauses designed to defeat any attempt by Morgan to deflect attention to himself while I danced.

"You sure do like to dance," Uncle Billy said, wiping his forehead. "You'll never peter out. Guess you'll just grow up."

"I'd much rather dance than act," I replied feelingly.

At noontime following one of the rehearsals, Uncle Billy and I left the set walking hand in hand. A few paces behind came Mother and Klammy. Two little black children, bit-part actors I think, caught his eye. We dropped back a little and he asked them if they had money for lunch. They both shook their heads.

"See you later, darlin'," he said, releasing my hand and gathering up the two boys. "We're going to the snack shop. They aren't allowed in the commissary."

"Neither am I!" I called after him, but he didn't hear.

In our final scene for *Dimples*, William Seiter posed me to sing over Morgan's shoulder. Anchoring Morgan in a chair with the back of his head to the camera was the only way to thwart that wizard. He couldn't wiggle his ears.

Producer Nunnally Johnson witnessed much of Morgan's finesse at scene theft and my stubborn attempts to cope. "When this picture is over," he quipped, "either Shirley will have acquired a taste for Scotch whiskey or Frank will come out with curls."

Big at the box office, *Dimples* still left some critics frustrated by American public taste.

"The Shirley Temple for President Club reconvened yesterday," wrote eminent *New York Times* drama critic Frank Nugent. "It displayed flattering attention to their candidate's latest assault upon the nation's maternal instinct. *Dimples* is an apt title . . . just another word for Little Miss Precocity . . . why they bother with titles, or with plots either, is beyond us." Nugent's sardonic drumfire was perhaps targeted less toward *Dimples* than toward the latest Zanuck film. After three years of monotonous barrage, Zanuck throttled this adversary by hiring him. Lured into the studio stable of screenwriters at three times his *New York Times* salary, Nugent still cannily hedged the Hollywood bet by requesting only one year's leave of absence from the newspaper.

☆

By traditional 1936 definition summertime living was supposed to be easy, a respite from concern, a time of calming restoration of the spirit. For my parents it turned out the reverse. Father had traded in his old LaSalle for a Cadillac, the first of six cars acquired during the next three years, and proposed an auto trip through coastal redwood forests to Vancouver Island, Canada.

Near Willits, then a small rural lumbering town north of San Francisco, we stopped for lunch at a roadhouse. Sobriety is not necessarily a qualification to be a movie fan. From her adjoining booth a woman seemed to be watching, midway between adoration and inebriation. Suddenly she rose on her knees on the seat and, bending over, loudly kissed the top of my head. Surprised, I turned my face, which she then seized in both hands and kissed again, hard and on the mouth. Nobody had ever kissed me there, and I instantly disliked the moist, squishy sensation.

I had been chewing a sandwich and could do little more than hold my breath, squirm, wrench my face from side to side to escape, and claw with my hands. Her embrace was vise-like. Several seconds can seem a lifetime. Freed, I ran to the rest room, got rid of the sandwich, and scrubbed at my mouth.

By nightfall we reached Eureka, a lumber and fishing town, and driving cautiously in the dense coastal fog, we found our small hotel, facing the railroad station. There an urgent message from the studio awaited. I was the subject of a $25,000 extortion threat, it read. Consider returning immediately; exercise extreme caution.

The threat was contained in an anonymous letter posted ten weeks earlier to the studio, where it had become commingled with several thousand fan letters and only recently read. Unless the blackmail money was dropped from an airplane on May 15, 1936, near Grant, Nebraska, my life was in danger. That the deadline had already expired lent urgency to the warning from home. The FBI had assumed jurisdiction since interstate blackmail is a federal crime.

My parents debated what to do. We were already halfway to Canada and moving. Travel itself was a form of security. Yet I was now under a death threat. Mother looked despairing. Father sucked at his teeth. With nothing for me to do, I went down into the tiny lobby with Griff where some fans were waiting, having heard of my presence via the local gossip grapevine. Finding a boy my own age, I challenged him to checkers. Each of us had won a game when Mayor Frank Sweasey, also having been told of our presence, arrived to present a memento of our visit. Reluctant to leave my spot at the checkers table, I gave him my most grateful smile, briefly admired his redwood-burl carving of a teddy bear, and shook his hand.

"You have a very nice city here. It's my move," I said, and returned to checkers. The death threat really was no problem. I knew from *Gangbusters* on radio that the FBI always got their man.

By dawn the sun was shining and my parents had decided to press on. Passing through Grants Pass, Oregon, we were startled to suddenly be surrounded by several dozen men dressed in pelts of deer and bear skin. Prehistoric figures, they leaped up and down around our auto brandishing gnarled wooded clubs, grimacing, and grunting. My parents quickly rolled up the windows and locked the doors. Nobody had forewarned us about the traditional local society of Oregon Cavemen, who only wished to present a scroll of welcome. Already sunk in foreboding, my parents saw ominous portents in everything, as a distant creak on the staircase stimulates frightful imaginings. Father drove on, his glance constantly flickering up in the rearview mirror.

My confidence in the FBI was not ill-placed. On July 31, 1936, a sixteen-year-old Nebraska farmhand was arrested and charged with attempted extortion. Agents sent to stake out the field designated for the earlier air drop of money had encountered him, hoe in hand.

"I didn't mean to go through with it, honest," he pled. "I just did it on impulse after seeing this here picture show about a ransom plot."

Ironically, the sort of film which inspired him had recently received the personal endorsement of FBI Director Hoover. Appearing before a congressional subcommittee, Hoover had expressed support for gangster movies, saying they educated the public that crime is an organized business and that gangsters are "rodents that must be exterminated."

In his one-room farmhouse, the young man's father only shook his head. "Almost as soon as he mailed the letter, he realized it was a crazy thing to do. Now he's arrested. I don't know what to make of it, hardly."

Neither did my parents.

En route by auto ferry between Seattle and Vancouver Island, we encountered another cotton-dense fog. By then we were joined by Wendell B. "Doc" Bishop, Fox publicist, ex-forest ranger, veterinarian, and city editor of the *Los Angeles Herald Express*, a man who knew about wolves and grizzly bears and could spin a tale. Leaning on the ship's railing, he told how the good wolf White Fang sprang to save his human friend while a gale howled and unfriendly wolves snarled defiance. The ship's foghorn sounded a repeated mournful dirge for all malamutes and snowbound prospectors. All seemed in far more desperate straits than I, even when we were greeted upon arrival by another extortion attempt

"Get $25,000," began this letter from Atlanta on August 17. The denominations were specific: $10,000 in $5.00 bills; $10,000 in $20 bills; $5,000 in $1.00 bills.

"The boys are plenty sore, and you'd better get those G-men off my trail. Remember, send money if you want to keep Shirley!"

Events again moved quickly. Father purchased a Colt Special six-shooter and a box of shells. The trip ended abruptly. Southward we sped, toward the presumed sanctuary of home. A wretched mood of anxiety shrouded the front seat, but in the back, where I rode in queenly solitude surrounded by books, there was only a sense of excitement, as if the drama were on radio rather than in my life.

Neither bravado nor escape from reality were involved in my attitude. Risks had always been weighed carefully, and danger sidestepped where possible. And obviously I acknowledged the perils inherent in threats from extortionists.

What was calming, however, was my attitude toward bodily harm. No stoic about little things, by some quirk of thought I had developed a detached philosophical view toward major injury. With the exception of beheading, other catastrophes like dismemberment, broken bones, and having eyes poked out should be taken seriously but were not worth a really major fuss. In this respect, perhaps I saw things through a prism upside down. My "parts" could suffer abuse without hurting the real "me," the inner self inaccessible to injury. This perspective helped convert otherwise terrifying notions into a pleasant form of excitement.

Others resorted to prayer and fairies on my behalf. In distant Java one enterprising film distributor utilized my predicament to build his local box office. Glibly confusing the nature of the threat, he enlisted a prominent local priest to conduct a public prayer to save me from kidnappers. Skeptical of my identity and worthiness, the priest declined until shown *Bright Eyes*. Aware at last, he widely proclaimed his outrage that gangsters were really threatening me, collected 20,000 sympathetic Javanese in a grassy field, and led prayers for my safe deliverance.

From her Hollywood Hotel suite, Carrie Jacobs Bond, optimistic composer of "When you come to the end of a perfect day...," sent me a handwritten note:

"If it should ever get dark and still, light the candle and ring the bell. If the fairies are at home, they will help. I know, because I lighted the candle and rang the bell. The fairies *were* at home!"

Forget the fairies, I reasoned. A better bet, ring for the FBI.

At home each thump in the night sent Father stalking through the house with his gun and Mother tiptoeing to my doorway to verify that I was alive. Griff drove with his unholstered revolver on the seat beside him while I hid in the back seat under a lap robe, my purse nearby stuffed with pebbles and a favorite slingshot.

Just as on *Gangbusters*, on September 15, 1936, the FBI seized its latest public enemy, another sixteen-year-old.

The return address in Atlanta had turned out to be that of a grocery store. Nobody recalled the name at the bottom of the extortion letter. However, the owner did vaguely recall a former part-time clerk inquiring about the expected arrival of a package from Hollywood. The rest was a breeze for the FBI.

Dressed in high-waisted gaucho slacks held up by suspenders, his hair oil-slicked and sporting a gaudy necktie, the boy quickly confessed. The whole idea, he explained, was inspired by a character from a gangster film.

He had thought we would pay right off, he explained, adding that the money was to entertain his sweetheart, whose name he gallantly refused to reveal.

This latest extortionist went free on $500 bail, but before trial date he foolishly jumped bail. Promptly rearrested on a new charge of robbery, he was locked up tight in the city jail.

"We've got enough evidence to send him to the chain gang," declared a city detective.

Like me, this boy had started his career early. At age nine he was packed off to the Alabama Industrial Boys School for Truants. Upon graduation, six years later, he had bungled his first burglary and was remanded to custody of Juvenile Court. Then came his run at me.

On October 6, 1936, a federal judge committed him to further education at the National Training School near Washington, D.C., there to remain until age twenty-one.

"This Atlanta environment," said the judge, "is more to blame than you are."

Life often flows in repeated rhythms, and following our flurry of extortion attempts it was little surprise that my next film, *Stowaway*, was a racing tale of Chinese banditry and smuggling.

For the ring of authenticity, I was required to learn several hundred Chinese phrases. Bessie Nyi was recruited from UCLA to teach me. A beaming, moon-faced student from Shanghai, she taught me by rote, repeating singsong words until my ears knew them by heart. The film required a mob of ethnic extras, largely recruited from local communities near Los Angeles. I welcomed them in my Chinese, but they seemed not to understand. Seeing my desire to learn, however, they soon were providing new words which I took back to try on Bessie. In return she couldn't understand. My problem as translator was that Bessie instructed me in the classic Mandarin dialect of North China and our extras spoke only the dialect of South China. Each of us was spouting a language as mutually unintelligible as if between an Australian aborigine and a reindeer herdsman from Lapland.

Apart from my speaking some Chinese, *Stowaway* was remarkable for providing me for the first time some correlation with a recent experience of my own. The orchestra at our children's school used the same authentic two-stringed cello, Chinese flute, clashing cymbals, and suspended gongs I had recently seen at a Chinese carnival during our brief visit to Vancouver. Our costumes of high-collared silk jackets and coolie straw hats were remindful of Hawaii, as were the pole baskets of woven bamboo and the haunting scent of camphorwood chests and burning punk. Even props like dried ducks hung upside down and unfamiliar oriental vegetables recalled a fleeting memory of passing along Grant Avenue in San Francisco's Chinatown while en route to the Northwest.

Stowaway also called for me to dance with a dummy, something that happens to many people but not with a dummy whose feet are linked to a partner by elastic cord, as mine was.

He was a boy, just my height but pasty-faced, impeccably outfitted in white tie and tailcoat. Pridefully introduced by Tommy Wonder, his creator, the dummy fixed me with a stare, had his arm arranged around my waist in a classic ballroom grip, and away we swooped. As a dancer he was superlative. Leading with uncanny skill, he matched his steps with mine the very first time, every nuance of movement and cadence blended to perfection. He made only one misstep. During one fast whirl the elastic strap binding his foot to mine slipped off my toe, freeing his pants leg to fly around like a weird black pennant, an eye-catching way to steal a scene, even if you are a dummy.

If dawn on *Stowaway* appeared rosy, dusk was not long in coming.

Bandits had killed my missionary parents. Befriended by Robert Young, a rich, wandering playboy, I returned his kindness by arranging for some chop suey of affection between him and luscious Alice Faye. My task as matchmaker complete, I retired to bed singing "Good Night My Love," a delectable ballad by Mack Gordon with Harry Revel with lyrics about Dutch dolls, teddy bears, and my dead daddy.

Faye then reprised my song outside, under a romantic full moon, using mature lyrics sung in her own silky style. Instantly I knew her rendition had finessed mine. Hers was deeper-throated, more resonant, and her facial expressions insinuated much that I sensed was important without knowing why. Yet my proprietary feeling could not so easily be quenched. It was my song. I had sung it first. Why did I lose when she won? Was it due to the back tooth I had just dropped? Even to my own ear the gap back there imparted a peanut vendor's whistle, and plugging the hole with the side of my tongue only deformed the quality of my tones. Perhaps the problem was not my deficiency but her skill. She was older, I brooded, and had beautiful cow eyes to boot.

Thwarted, annoyed, and bothered by my harmonic whistle, I approached my next song in a cloudy mood. "Mammy" had to be sung on bended knee, an imitation of Al Jolson. Watching and listening to him made me wince. As we rehearsed to a scratchy old phonograph disk, I found scant joy in being required to mimic his voice, to say nothing of his gestures. Sandwiched between sultry Faye and nasal Jolson was no place for me to seek satisfaction.

Faye fell ill with influenza, halting *Stowaway* production for two weeks. I seethed in secret; it was the first medical delay in any of my films. Vindictive attitudes have a way of flaring back. The very day she returned I developed a high fever and was sent home. Again film production shut down. For the next two weeks I lay in sickbed with plenty of time to reflect on the possibility of divine retribution for my initial uncompassionate attitude.

At the time of *Stowaway* the studio prayer may well have been to keep me short, unchanging, and static, but not so Mother's. She was concerned about my slow growth, slopey shoulders, stocky legs, and rounded middle, all characteristics remindful of Father. Her willowy grace had left little trace on my looks. In league with Dr. Sands and his innovative pediatrician brother, a program was devised to inject pituitary extract into my knee joints to stimulate leg growth. Hopefully, in place of my compact self would emerge someone tall and leggy. While they were plotting how to make me tall, all over Hollywood mothers were doing everything this side of strapping bricks on the heads of their prodigies to keep them short in my image. I need not have worried. In the end my knees strangled the medical scheme in its crib. X rays proved conclusively that my joints were already fully formed. Despite Mother's impatience and the studio's desire, I was growing up.

14

Of all the forms of genius, goodness has the longest awkward age.

— Thornton Wilder

"Sex can't be important in films," observed savvy columnist Walter Winchell in the fall of 1936. "Remember, the world's leading film attractions remain Charlie Chan, Boris Karloff, and Shirley Temple."

Maintenance of my footing at the pinnacle of popularity was by no means certain. To be sure, optimistic estimates of audience appeal abounded. My motion pictures were estimated to have been seen by 240 million people, double the cumulative audience of venerable Greta Garbo and twice the United States population. For the first time my name was listed in *Who's Who* with a biographical sketch one line longer than that of Governor Alf Landon of Kansas, 1936 Republican candidate for President. Overseas in the United Kingdom, I was the only American film personality to have ever outdrawn then-beloved English star Gracie Fields. The Italian film market for me was strong. In Europe my popularity was still running a dead heat with the ubiquitous Mickey Mouse, born the same year I was.

However, deep and undetected beneath this unruffled surface of success flowed profound freshets of change. One of these was my sense of self-importance. Only an idiot could have lived in the glare of such a central spotlight and been unaware of her prominence. This led to impatience with others, often simply because their work habits did not coincide agreeably with mine. Although digging a tiger trap for others, I was the first to plunge in. Observation had long before taught that the soundstage was no place for outbursts of temperament. At home or in the privacy of my dressing room was another matter. In both places I led myself into trouble.

In my mind, tardiness was tantamount to lack of interest. Punctuality also paid subtle dividends. Arriving early left time to josh informally with the crew and to lean on things. Personal contact with the crew paved the roadway for special little assistances, competitive considerations withheld from other actors more aloof. Standing with one foot raised on an electrical connection box, I could also regard the entry of others with the relaxed confidence of one who had won, even if only the race to work.

In contrast, Mother was habitually late, always running to catch up. The more prominent I became, the longer she required to get dressed and groomed. Each bedtime she carefully put up her hair and sheathed it in netting. Then a succession of facial potions were smoothed on and wiped off. Each fingernail was fastidiously manicured and painted ruby-red, the color of her birthstone.

Each dawn called for base creams, disguise of temporary blemishes, and a meticulous touch of rouge, mascara, powder, and lipstick. Combing out her hair to capture every stray strand, she arranged it in varied but always symmetrical style. Like me, she was cursed with thickening of the skin on her palms. Burnishing with pumice stone and kneading in any new lotion of promise, she never solved the problem, but always lost track of time trying.

Selecting her outfit was another tedious process. First came the girdle. Jiggling flesh annoyed her, and she was confident that without a girdle, skin would sag, stomach distend, bottom droop, and breasts flop. Inheriting her opinion, for years I assumed girdles were necessary for appearance and health. Next came a meticulous matching of hats to dresses, scarves, shoes, brooches, and bracelets. The greater her capacity to purchase, the more varied her closet. The more numerous her available daily options, the later we departed for work.

Usually ready to leave on time and leaning against her doorway, I would ask sardonically, "Why not pick the pin and hat the night before?"

"Go wait in the car," was her standard answer as she fussed with tiny adjustments before her mirror.

Looks nice enough, I often thought, somewhat insolently. After all, I'm the one that's supposed to be working. I was really feeling my oats.

Although Mother's regular delay remained virtually incurable, I stubbornly persisted with snide comments. One morning in a sour mood, watching her scrub her teeth, I accused her of having all false teeth. She knew how to respond, striking hard at my weak spot. Adopting a deeply offended expression, she burst into tears. We had to make up with lots of reassuring hugs, her makeup got ruined, and we set a record for being late.

En route, I would usually urge Griff to drive faster. Just as regularly he would answer he was going as fast as he could. Long before arrival at the studio gate my impatience had devolved into plain ill humor.

If Mother and Griff were the send-off of my irritable attitude, the wardrobe mistress was my lightning rod. Ande was shapeless, sturdy, and devoid of makeup, in an unvarying uniform of dark gabardine skirt with white silk blouse.

"And how are you this morning, darling?" She spoke with a faint Scandinavian accent, inflection falling at the end of each phrase.

"Come on, none of that stuff," I would retort, dodging past her hands outstretched in greeting. "Let's get going."

Until then most of my film clothes were easy to enter or leave, with simply a row of snaps or a zipper down the back. With the Old South, however, came pantalets and hoopskirts, intricate layers of clothing bound together with authentic buttons, clasps, elastic, snaps, and hooks. I reveled in the fabrics: the soft mink collar with matching muff, a vest embroidered in seed pearls, delicate French taffetas, organdies, and exotic lace, materials vibrant with primary colors but soft under the fingertip, silk satins and iridescent velvet, each a joy to the eye and touch. But it all added up to slow dressing, and the high-button shoes were no help.

Ande would kneel at my feet doing up rows of buttons. "You're too slow," I would fret.

"Sorry, darling," she would say, glancing up pathetically. "I'm hurrying." Her eyes were kindly enough but set deep and small, like those of an elephant.

"Not so hard with the buttonhook," I might snap. Mumbling apology, she would crouch still lower.

Even when I was finally dressed, Ande trailed me around carrying a hot iron in case of wrinkles. In period costumes there is no sitting down. To rest I leaned back against a slanted wooden plank, hoopskirts arching into the air with pantalets fully exposed. If schoolwork came between scenes, I would lean on the slant plank, straight and stiff, and recite for Klammy like a small talking corpse not yet fully laid out. Nearby Ande always waited patiently for a wrinkle to appear, her heated iron at the ready.

Ande's problem with me was unrelated to inept fingers or her servile attitude. She never fought back. Occasionally she would wipe away a small tear of frustration or dig her buttonhook a little deeper, but she remained docile. When I sensed weakness, my instinct at the time was to bore in, grind down.

Ande missed teaching me a lesson by failing to retaliate. In fact, she slavishly pursued the opposite course. Collecting remnants of material from each of my film costumes, she dressed model dolls in exact replicas, every detail faithfully duplicated. Each doll was destined to be ignored.

Sensing what was going on and eager to make amends, Mother capitalized on Ande's marriage plans. First she sent her off at our expense to a professional hairdresser for something more feminine than her customary tight bun. Then she organized a bridal shower and embellished her trousseau with hand-sewn lingerie from top designer Jewel Park. As if to expiate my past behavior, I fussed around the fringe of all this activity, a reversal of attitude which surprised everyone, including me.

Ande's role as an instrument of delay was unavoidable, but instead of sparking back, she surrendered without crossing swords. Servility under my fire probably fueled my petulance, and genuine affection got trampled underfoot. That Ande deserved better from me remains one of my prolonged regrets.

Even after the souring morning experiences at home and in wardrobe, one final obstacle to punctuality remained. Outside the air-lock entry door to our shooting stage lay a small lobby with adjoining rest rooms. Afflicted with a chronic bladder weakness and afraid of missing something by leaving the set, Mother always made one final routine stop. There I waited, rehearsed, fully costumed, eager to get started. On the other side of that closed stage door bustled my friends, the crew, among sets newly erected, lights almost rigged and ready. Yet there I stood, stalled two steps from the door handle, forbidden to enter alone. In this instance, Mother's foresight was my extra burden.

If gaining entrance to the soundstage was often grueling, even more so was being pulled away, particularly for still photography sessions. Generally I tolerated the whole process, but sometimes after hours of being dressed, redressed, and posed, photography grew awfully wearisome. Others decided what I would wear, how to stand or sit. I was never consulted as to what might be a good pose. I was an adjustable doll. Fix the eyes on something. Don't dart around. Pay attention to camera angles. Cock the head, face this way, avert your eyes. Now just another one, Shirley.

"You've got enough already," I blurted after one particularly onerous session.

The photographer was offended. It was his job to shoot, mine to comply. Folding both arms across my chest and thrusting out my lower lip, I struck a belligerent pose.

Still photographers are used to bad subjects, but he pleaded for compassion and cooperation for the sake of his livelihood, his wife and his children at home. We struck a bargain. I would stop my bellyaching, but he would take only one shot for each pose. This seemed a good compromise. I did my best to strike the required poses, but raised one finger each time to remind him of the single-shot promise.

Everything happening in my professional life had also rearranged the hitherto parochial borders of Father's existence. As the initial surge of fresh bank deposits stimulated by my success began to taper off, his supervising vice president insinuated that Father might be getting complacent. Sensitive to the core, Father replied sarcastically, saying little new business could be expected from the newest nearby subdivision. Its name was Rosedale Cemetery. Assigned shortly thereafter to a Hollywood branch office of the bank, a transfer not considered a promotion, Father had decided to resign.

It was not the first time he had uprooted himself on a point of pride. Years before, while working as a shipping clerk for a company manufacturing steel storage tanks for the oil industry, he had received a bitter complaint about a slow delivery. The boss decided to pretend the order had been sent and to shift blame to the railroad. Father refused and was hauled before his boss. A cockroach chose that moment to steal out from behind the wainscoting and started across the wall. Ordered to kill it, Father paused, looking for a magazine to use as a weapon. The boss leaped up and with one quick sweep caught the roach in his bare hand. Holding it between his first finger and thumb he crushed it, sending brown droplets against the wallpaper. Dropping the squashed carcass to the floor, he wiped his fingers across his trouser leg and sneered that Father would never be an oilman. Father agreed and quit.

Pride was his downfall on another occasion as well. As a bank clerk working a double shift, his final task each night was to sort, count, and package wads of currency for transfer by bonded messenger to the local Federal Reserve Bank. On a routine check, auditors detected that for some time each stack Father had certified as correct was one $20 bill short. His supervisor ordered Father to restore the money, as if his guilt was assumed. It was a lacerating blow, and again he quit on the spot. When further investigation lodged blame on a delivery boy, he still refused to return to the bank. He was a man readily offended and relentlessly unforgiving.

Thus, pride and pique both played a role in Father's decision to quit the bank and with Ira L. Thomason, a gregarious colleague from the downtown loan department, to set up a partnership to manage business affairs for film personalities. A doughy man with rimless eyeglasses, thinnish red-blond hair, and an affable manner, Thomason easily could be considered a likable bumpkin. When not forcing his smile, however, his mouth turned down at the corners, and for Mother and me it meant gloom and dismal, wearisome talk, even about the weather.

To Father, however, Ira was brainy and reliable. Thomason's Stanford diploma, like a military uniform, automatically connoted qualification, and in fact he did contribute expertise in the arcane skills of taxes and accounting. Above all, Father's self-employment costumed him with an appearance of stability, fiscal wisdom, and managerial competence. On December 9, 1936, they set up Temple-Thomason, Inc., with offices in Hollywood. I was their first client.

Initial ventures were launched through a subsidiary company formed for the purpose, Temple Investments, Inc., with a total of $91,000 capitalization siphoned from my earnings. In association with movie director King Vidor and others, they purchased sixty undeveloped acres in the southwest corner of the city of Beverly Hills, the last undeveloped parcel of the original 3,200-acre Spanish land grant which forms that city. Standing with Mayor Edward Spence, Father smiled confidently as he cut the ribbon christening his project.

Managers of the development were local realtors Read and Wright, a firm that obviously knew how to add and subtract. What happened to his investment is not entirely clear from Father's records, whether cooking the financial books, sour sales, inattentive partners, or simply the burden of his own business innocence. The name of the development was Beverly Green, but for Father it turned out deep red. For the $91,000 originally invested, he recovered $29,000, a 60 percent negative return, tribute to his imperturbable, cheerful naiveté.

In a smaller and less damaging way, both Mother and I were traders and entrepreneurs. Her deal involved a miniature Chinese Pekinese which had first caught my fancy as a prop on *Stowaway*. It was owned by the wife of Landsdowne, a photographer of distinguished men and women. Mother struck an arrangement. I got the dog, promptly rechristened Ching-Ching after my name in the film, and in return Landsdowne not only photographed me but also Father in a Churchillian portrait, provided in thirty elegant, pricey copies.

My own deal was with Jonesy the propman and involved rabbits and cherry tarts. *Ladies in Love*, a film about four women and Don Ameche, required eighteen bunnies as props. Jonesy said he knew I had that many in the runway behind my cottage and asked to borrow them. But how much will you pay to rent them, I asked. He offered a dollar for the lot, but we finally settled on a dollar apiece.

Realizing that even at my age I thought deals were fun, Jonesy put me in business with a garishly painted handcart. Under an overhead billboard proclaiming "Shirley Temple's Pie Factory" he stocked it with several dozen small fruit tarts obtained free from the commissary bakery. A more perfect venture is hard to imagine. No start-up cost. No cost for inventory. My customers all were captive. I went into operation near the soundstage door. Nobody entered or left without buying and paying. Cash only, no credit. Mother collected the coins and made change. My interest was in moving the product.

Among those trapped was Sam Engle, nominal author of my previous film, *Stowaway*. Bending over, he listened to my sales pitch, slack-jawed and breathing through his mouth, head bobbing. His purchase, one cherry tart.

I had almost sold out when a reporter wandered up.

"How do you feel about getting sued?" he asked.

I stared vacantly. "You'll have to talk to my mommy. She takes care of those things." I held up my last pie. "Do you want to buy it? It's a rhubarb!" The flavor was timely. Trouble was indeed brewing for my family.

Sweet circumstance attracts flies to the honey pot. With an unwelcome blast of cold air, Jack Hays, former producer of the *Baby Burlesks*, had filed suit for breach of my January 23, 1932, contract. Asking $1 million as his fair share of my earnings, past and potential, he charged Father with conspiracy in his $25 reacquisition of my contract, for which he now demanded $500,000 damages.

The broadside allegation claimed my parents had "solicited" Hays to train me for motion pictures; that tutors and directors had been engaged to coach me in drama, voice, and cinema technique; that on October 1, 1933, he had placed me at Fox Films through his own efforts, but strictly on a loan. He had also taught me English, Spanish, and French.

Told of this last revelation, my French teacher, Miss Walling, uttered noises of derision, appropriate perhaps but unflattering.

Adding to this pile of moldering bones, Hays also charged that in several particulars the court-appointed backruptcy trustee had unlawfully connived with Father to defraud him in the contract repurchase. There had been no ten-day legal notice of intended sale; no advice to Hays or the bankruptcy referee on the pending sale; no offer to place my contract up for bid; and no transaction conducted in open court.

Hard on the heels of Hays' pursuit of my family came the heavy footfall of other lawyers challenging studio ownership of *Stowaway*'s story and music. The screenplay was stolen from her, charged Joan Storm Dezendorf, saying the tale was her own *Dancing Destiny*, twice submitted to the studio and twice rejected, but allegedly then plagiarized by screenwriter Sam Engle.

All wrong, claimed Stephen Tamas from distant Budapest. It was *his* yarn, copyrighted in Yugoslavia, already published in book form, and serialized in Hungary; the Twentieth Century-Fox representative in London had ordered it from Tamas, then conveniently forgotten the source.

Another suit was filed in New York Federal Court by Charles McCord against songwriters Mack Gordon and Harry Revel charging them with plagiarism of the hit song "Goodnight My Love." Not true, cried Argentine composer Juan Calaby. The song was his, copyrighted. To reinforce his claim, he convened a jury of 700 theatregoers in Buenos Aires who overwhelmingly judged the *Stowaway* song to be a duplicate of Calaby's original rumba "Señorita."

When one is very young, life seems uncomplicated. Home for me was one place, the studio another. Seldom was there interaction. At work every activity was subdivided into compartments. Wardrobe fittings were separate from filming, and both from school lessons. All was tidy, sharp-edged. Gradually I became aware that total separation between studio and home was a fantasy, and commingling the only truth. The sudden appearance of a pony and two horses underscored the point.

Empty stalls in our new stable had stimulated studio boss Joseph M. Schenck to action. Conniving with the Marquis of Donegal, publisher of the *London Sunday Dispatch*, he acquired a Shetland Island pony as a surprise gift. Placed in the care of a retired British Army major, it embarked in the animal hold of the SS *Queen Mary* on her maiden westward transatlantic crossing.

"I'm naming it Samuel of Speen," announced Schenck, and in a rare attempt at humor added, "a biblical character devoted to services for the temple!"

Burdened with a specially made Western saddle with my face tooled into the leather skirts, and attended by a phalanx of publicity staff, Sir Samuel was introduced to me in the railroad freight yards in downtown Los Angeles.

A welcoming flower garland, which it promptly tried to eat, was draped around the pony's neck. Getting saddled, Samuel bucked, then kicked as I was hoisted up.

"Giddap!" I cried.

The pony moved ahead, but the girth was improperly cinched and the saddle started to slip sideways, me with it.

"Whoa!" I ordered, grabbing for a hank of mane and hauling on the reins.

A switch engine tooted just as a line of freight cars came screeching along an adjacent track. The pony whinnied, kicked and reared up, while I held on.

"I'm going to call him Spunky," I shouted above the freight-yard din, patting his neck. "He's not afraid of anything."

Reaching around, he bared his teeth and tried to bite my hand.

A disconsolate Scotsman 8,000 miles from his windswept heather and bracken, Spunky was less a pet than a boarder, one best kept at a distance. Later, the titled English gentlewoman Lady Thelma Furness came visiting. As usual we toured past the stables, where dwelled not only Spunky but Red the Macaw, a boisterous bird with language as gaudy as his plumage. "Bitch!" he called as Lady Furness looked in the tack room. Ignoring the squawked greeting she leaned back against the corral railing. Sir Samuel, titled Scot to his hooves, stretched forward and bit at the bottom of the titled English lady.

When the world learned inaccurately how much I adored Spunky, more gift horses came galloping. Circus rider Betsy King Ross delivered me Roan King II, her trick horse and blue-ribbon winner at the 1934 American Royal Horse Show in Kansas City.

Our stable now had only one unoccupied stall. E. A. Stuart, founder of the Carnation Milk Company, filled it with a five-gaited cow pony trained in Mexico, Missouri, for both riding and hackney and equipped with a cart clearly stenciled "Little Carnation."

One thing leads to another, so to care for our new boarders we hired a young cowboy named Horace. Scrawny and slumped, with thin wrists and unruly straw-blond hair, he let me drive the cart while he perched up behind, his booted feet spread apart on the axle. Around the small dirt track Little Carnation galloped, dark mane flying and tail held at a saucy angle. Skidding at one corner, the cart tipped up, balancing on its outside wheels. With a frantic one-hand grab, Horace got me instead of a handhold on the cart, knocking me headlong over the wheel and into the dirt. With Horace still riding the axle, the cart righted itself and Little Carnation raced on. Landing like a rag doll knocked out my wind, scuffed up my face, and filled my pockets with dirt. Griff had been watching and immediately tattled to Mother.

Explosions followed. Horace was scolded to shreds and placed on probation. The cart was retired. Little Carnation got locked into a stall, and I was grounded, forbidden to use the cart or to ride at all.

Another to capitalize on the overlap between studio life and the outside world was Klammy, in a highly constructive teaching scheme. Mergotroid, my fictional seatmate, had lost her charm, so seizing on both our ceaseless stream of visitors and the topical content of my films, Klammy began to orient much of my optional schoolwork toward people I met and the roles I played. Her first subject was Amelia Earhart. On the first leg of an intended circumnavigation of the earth, Earhart had just flown from Oakland, California, to Hawaii in fifteen hours and fifty-seven minutes. Knowing how impressed I had been by Earhart's earlier exploits, Klammy used her trip as my springboard to world geography, and a fleeting glimpse of other nations as Earhart flew by.

"She's going to delay her trip in Hawaii, then fly westward to a little island called Howland and drop off her navigator," Klammy said, reading from the news. We paused to search our map for Howland Island, a dot in the blue Pacific expanse.

Continuing her reading, she started to laugh. "We hope to heaven when you are packing your grip you put in a pocket comb. Now is the time to get the tangles out and give it a good straightening. In the long, lone watches over the gray and melancholy ocean, comb your hair, kid. Comb your hair!"

Our project tracking Earhart jarred to a temporary stop on May 20, 1937. Her Lockheed Electra plane had collapsed onto the concrete runway during a dawn takeoff from Luke Field in Hawaii. Nobody was injured, but the plane's undercarriage was destroyed. Earhart and navigator Fred Noonan, along with the battered plane, were sailing ignominiously back to California aboard a Matson luxury liner. Earhart's determination to start again fitted neatly into Klammy's parallelism in my studies, so I started learning about Pacific Islands and Southeast Asia, planning to stay one lap ahead of Earhart all the way.

Twentieth Century-Fox corporate profits had reached nearly $8 million during 1936, more than double those of 1935. A $500,000 year-end bonus was distributed to employees. *Dimples* and *Stowaway* had each already grossed over $1 million from American audiences and were assured of more than double that sum from overseas release. Each of my other films was expected to return five times its cost in profits. During 1936, therefore, almost 90 percent of reported corporate net profits were attributable to earnings of my four most recent films.

A heady rejuvenation for an ailing corporation, the turnaround was not without peril. Major corporate eggs were crammed into one small basket. Lacking diversified sources of income, the studio was under an uncomfortable imperative: preserve my earning potential. But that led to one pounding headache of a problem. Exactly what to do with me now?

The answer was also vital to the professional reputation of Zanuck, the man in charge.

"The time has come," wrote one critic, "for Darryl Zanuck to realize that Shirley Temple cannot be expected to carry a poor story all by herself . . . just as bewitching a personality, a better dancer and more skillful actress today than when she first created a sensation . . . yet for two years she has been doing the same thing. Even fanatics are indignant over the implausible stories used to present her as a showoff. . . . Give her more intelligent stories, Mr. Zanuck, and better actors in supporting casts."

Said another analyst, "Zanuck inherited Shirley as a ready-made star. It's up to him to retain her value. If she does not remain a top star, the blame falls directly in Zanuck's lap."

Zanuck hit back, saying, "If we pay attention to Beverly Hills critics, we will be making a grave mistake which may influence Shirley's entire career. If I personally would listen to all the well-meant advice given me, I would be in an asylum."

"In Shirley," he reassured Mother, "you have the greatest star in our business. She will go on forever, in my opinion."

By reputation, Zanuck may have been poorly positioned to understand the problem. Women to him were mostly tramps, a sexy, bitchy, unscrupulous lot who got what they deserved. Of children, his record was blank.

"A clever producer within narrow limits," cautioned one respected critic. "His specialty is rugged, heroic stories built around male stars. Never has he demonstrated any liking for women stars. I have a hunch that deep down inside he feels helpless when confronted with a child star."

Zanuck operated from an exotic cockpit, a narrow, high-ceilinged room painted gold and green, its walls decorated with African hunting trophies. A rhinoceros foot stood by his desk.

"He strode up and down that office nearly as long as an aircraft hangar," wrote one colleague, "swinging a truncated polo mallet at invisible balls on the carpet, full of the euphoria of creation. . . ."

While at Twentieth Century-Fox, Zanuck estimated he alone had "read, revised, cast, filmed, cut, assembled and released one picture every twelve days."

Critics often assess him to have been an arrogant despot, intolerant of criticism, surrounded by stooges and sycophants. Others saw a manipulative genius who used or abused the levers of power. But Zanuck was supreme.

Stardom, at best, is a tricky status. Motion picture stars fall into two broad categories. First, those the public discovered, like Marilyn Monroe. Without studio effort this type ignites its own public reaction, a powerful surge of support which springs naturally and lasts a long time.

In the other category are manufactured stars, such as Jean Harlow. Her portrayal of a sultry sex symbol is believed to have been profoundly different from her true personality. The movie public is fickle, goes one theory. Actors such as Harlow are churned in and out of favor by adroit studio manipulation. With dual personalities cohabiting the same body, such stars depend heavily for success on how skillfully the studio handles the puppet strings.

In this context and in order to intelligently maximize its economic return from me, the studio found it critical to clarify the answers to two questions: first, was my public film image an extension of myself or one created by the industry; and second, did my popularity stem from acting, dancing, or singing, and in what combination?

The answers involved not only artistic judgment but finance. Given its tumultuous corporate past, the studio measured good and bad less by artist achievement than by bottom-line financial results. To accede to recommendations for better casts and stories meant increased costs and reduced profits. It was just that simple. Art had little to do with it.

One way to handle me was to resist change and stay put, a strong argument. My formula was working—perpetual childhood and cheerful resolution to any problem, whether divorce, deceit, mayhem, loneliness, or war. The temptation was awesome. Simply repeat me, again and again. As long as I was a winner, it was relatively effortless and profitable. Afterwards? Forget me.

To remain in a comfortable inertia, however, is seldom a viable option. The process of natural equilibrium would someday see my star decline, not keep rising or hang there. The end was certain. Only in timing and conformation was the future unclear.

How Zanuck resolved such questions can perhaps best be measured by his subsequent actions. First, he must have concluded I was discovered by the public, not manufactured by Hollywood, and therefore relatively immune to constant studio manipulation. Nothing like that seems to have been tried.

Next, in clarifying my talents, everyone seemed to agree I could sing and dance. Zanuck, however, must have wanted a sterner test of my dramatic skills. Were the public to accept me also as a dramatic star, so much the better for the studio in terms of current value and longevity.

Only this sort of analysis could have led Zanuck to call in ace director John Ford, 1935 Academy Award winner for *The Informer*, the thrilling tale of Victor McLaglen as a drunken, boastful Irishman who betrayed his friend for a £20 banknote. A blood-and-thunder mentor of hairy-chested males, Ford was renowned for his shouts, tears, and oaths. By reputation he loathed child actors.

"Now I'm really going to give you something to scream about," Zanuck announced. "I'm going to put you together with Shirley Temple!" Ford later confessed his "face fell to the floor."

"And a million-dollar budget," Zanuck went on. "You can also have McLaglen again." The bait was out.

What Zanuck had in mind was Rudyard Kipling's classic *Wee Willie Winkie*, a racing tale of military heroics on the Afghan border of British colonial India. Had author Kipling not chosen to die one dark London day the previous year, he would have witnessed his little hill-station boy transmuted into a sturdy-legged girl with curls.

15

The elephant did not seem personable. Anna May, a veteran performer for thirty-seven years, stood swaying slightly or tossed clumps of hay around with her trunk. Despite waving my arms in front of her ponderous head, I failed to establish any useful eye contact. I had exchanged more fraternal stares with my canary. Miscellaneous scenes for *Wee Willie Winkie* were being shot out of sequence, using the "Algerian street" back-lot set, a semipermanent jumble of minarets and casbah alleys, sun-drenched, dusty, and mysterious. The elephant had been added for atmosphere, together with a camel.

In contrast to Anna May, the camel had large iridescent eyes, rubbery lips, and a regal bearing.

"Not too close," warned the trainer. "It kicks front, side, and back!"

Carefully measuring the distance, I edged closer to inspect this remarkable beast just as it slowly swiveled its head, curled open its lips, and sent a dollop of brown spittle arching past me onto the packed earth.

"Let's go," called director John Ford.

The actors in the scene took their places. Crouched down against an ancient stone wall was a menacing crowd of turbaned extras. Suddenly the camel gave a loud sigh. Slumping gently to its knees, it slowly rolled over on its side. Its trainer jerked at the halter, to no avail. I had just concluded the beast must be ill when Mother suddenly took my hand and hurried me off the set. Over my shoulder I saw everyone gathered around the fallen camel, which I presumed was dying.

The camel had other ideas, and chose the middle of our Algerian street to deliver her baby. By next day's rehearsal the event had become celebrated around the lot. I didn't miss the birth process nearly as much as glimpsing the finished baby. Mother and child had disappeared.

The camel birth was only one item of unexpected delay to catch front-office attention. There was union trouble. Tensions between management and labor had steadily increased since passage of Roosevelt's National Industrial Recovery Act, guaranteeing the right of employees to organize and bargain collectively, legislation FDR characterized as "the most significant and far-reaching ever enacted." In 1935 the U.S. Supreme Court disagreed, declaring the whole thing unconstitutional, once again plunging the nation into frenzied efforts to resolve its labor-management problems.

By the start of *Wee Willie Winkie*, national unemployment hovered at a bone-chilling ten million people. In one of a number of stunning confrontations, General Motors employees had staged a sit-down strike in Detroit protesting irregular employment, low wages, and speed-up on the automobile assembly line. Under existing law the strike was technically illegal, so police intervened with tear gas and buckshot. This move proved counterproductive, helping spread the strike to sixty other factories in fourteen states. Forty-two days later the employees had returned to work with partial recognition of the United Auto Workers as their bargaining agent. Thereafter union membership rocketed upward tenfold in the space of a year.

Against this backdrop of legal and social conflict, the contagion of unionism had flowered in Hollywood. At the time of the baby camel birth the Screen Actors Guild was becoming certified by the National Labor Relations Board as a sole bargaining agent. The Screen Writers Guild was likewise up for certification, locked in a deathgrip battle with a competing organization claimed by some to be a company union.

At my studio labor-management relations had swerved into this muddy water. The International Alliance of Theatrical Stage Employees and Moving Picture Operators (IATSE), an organization allegedly subverted by infamous labor gangsters such as Willie Bioff, had offered Joseph Schenck at Twentieth Century-Fox a "sweetheart" labor contract in return for a shakedown of cash. Soon Schenck was hip deep in trouble with the Internal Revenue Service, which slapped tax-evasion charges against him for $100,000 of unreported income. Allegedly he had been suckered into personalizing a payoff to IATSE, cashing a personal rather than corporate check with the union and then allowing the cash proceeds to be turned over to Bioff in return for labor peace at Twentieth Century-Fox.

Some days before this peculiar arrangement on our indoor set we had a visit from someone usually unwelcome, a front-office messenger. This one had a repelling personality and seemed impervious to our scorn. Adjusting his fedora squarely, as if to cope with a windstorm, he marched center stage and imperiously raised both hands for quiet.

"At this rate, the picture is never going to come in on time," he thundered, jowls quivering, and stared first right, then left, to let the words sink in. "Each of you had better work harder, and faster."

From high overhead among the shadowy maze of catwalks where lighting equipment was anchored came a disembodied voice:

"We need better conditions. Get some ventilation up here. Shorter hours, that's what we need."

The messenger tipped his head back and squinted upward. "Who said that?" he roared. Up on the catwalks there was neither sound nor movement.

"I'll attend to him later," he snarled, fixing those of us closer at hand with a menacing gaze. "Slovenly and slothful," he shouted. "Are you all here to do a job or just fritter away someone else's money?"

Our attention was diverted from his tirade as the heavy arc light plunged downward. In one ear-splitting crash of metal and splintered glass, it shattered on the cement floor, narrowly missing the messenger. Those of us nearby retreated toward the walls, leaving him standing alone, an unintimidated figure beside the crushed rubble of glass and metal.

"Red bastard," he hissed, staring upward, and with a glum tug at his hat brim and one last scornful glance, he stalked silently from the soundstage.

Intimidation was not unique to our lot. During filming of *Each Dawn I Die* at neighboring Warner Bros., Bioff had reportedly threatened to "drop a light" on Jimmy Cagney if that studio failed to accede to payoff demands. Falling lights appear to have been one of the chosen weapons employed by labor in confrontations with management. *Wee Willie Winkie* was getting off to a shaky start.

Several mornings after the near-miss on the messenger, Mother was telephoned just as we were leaving home for work. Stay away from the studio. Pickets were at the gate. Shrewdly, management elected to avoid confrontation, and instead was rescheduling our next twenty-five days of work on *Wee Willie Winkie* on location at Chatsworth, forty miles distant from Hollywood in open country nestled at the foot of the Santa Susannah Mountains. Although hating to miss the next installment of studio conflict, I was ecstatic. Twenty-five days on location meant twenty-five picnic box lunches.

Location also meant the beginning of intensive direction by John Ford, who made no bones about his indifference toward me, saying, "Working with a child star is a most horrible thing." Mutual cooperation between us was paramount if I were to do a good job, but I also simply wanted Ford to respect me as a professional and like me as a person.

For Klammy, location meant removing our schoolroom into a tent. The film provided her a rich vein of historical and geographic material to mine for her new and unique study program of parallels without neglecting the original spine of her system, Amelia Earhart's circumnavigation of the earth by air.

On our first day at Chatsworth, Earhart had announced completion of repairs on her damaged plane and a reversal of her original routing so as to avoid the onset of seasonally unfavorable weather over sub-Saharan Africa. Her course was now west to east, which called for an early June takeoff in Brazil, thence crossing the south Atlantic to an African landfall. Spreading a world map on our portable school desk, Klammy traced Earhart's intended track in thick blue pencil. By coincidence the track bisected India, site of *Wee Willie Winkie* action, thus enabling Klammy to combine Earhart's travels with the story of my film in her classroom curriculum.

What Earhart's blue line got started, two British actors helped amplify. Heading our colonial army was Sir C. Aubrey Smith, craggy-visaged model for all flame-eating colonels of anybody's regiment. In real life knighted by the King, he was a dignified, energetic ambassador for the empire. As his stand-in the studio hired a retired British general, R. D.

Napier-Raikes, formerly U.K. high commissioner to Nigeria and son of a commander in the Bengal Lancers. If Klammy needed authenticity, she had it in these two, both eager to provide vivid flavor to my history lessons.

The effusive and cordial attitude of my two British generals stood in stark contrast to the reserve of film director Ford. Previous directors had lifted me onto their laps and peppered me with conversation, as friendly as Ford was distant. When not issuing me explicit instructions, Ford usually passed me by, sucking and chewing on his handkerchief, his eyes invisible behind deeply tinted glasses and a Donegal tweed cap with down-turned brim pulled low over his forehead. With everyone else his instructions were sweeping and general, leaving it to the actors to work out the details. With me he was deliberate, as if he knew not what to expect and dared not leave me alone to interpret my role.

Confronted with Ford's elusive personality, I seized every chance to involve him in casual conversation. Borrowing an extra stopwatch from the continuity girl, I went around timing everything I could and eventually interrupted Ford.

"Ford V-8," I said, "did you know you took two minutes and thirty-five seconds to light your pipe that time? The last time you took two minutes and twelve seconds."

Shooting me an annoyed glance, he turned away with grumpy noises and sucked noisily on his pipe.

Later I tried inserting myself into his group discussions. On one occasion he was instructing Victor McLaglen to "bellow like a water buffalo."

"How does a water buffalo bellow?" I interjected.

As usual, Ford answered me with a peevish smile and hollow, un-confident laugh, but nearby someone made a guttural snort. Another person corrected that version with a cross between a lion's roar and a cow's moo. All at once everyone around was in a bellowing contest, not excepting me.

Cheery though the diversion seemed to me, Ford was not overcome with its charm. Despite the warm weather, he was wearing a rumpled tweed coat with collar upturned. Shoving both hands into its already misshapen pockets, he raised his voice to remind everyone within earshot that excessive hilarity had no place in getting the picture in on time and within budget, as the front-office messenger had earlier urged.

If Ford was itched by my provocations, California law must have caused him a rash. Public school regulations still protected me and Douglas Scott, the other cast juvenile, from being exposed to adult swearing. Any oath was technically cause enough to remove me from the set, and repeated offense reason to file an official complaint with child welfare authorities. Of virile habits and intemperate speech, Ford must have swallowed this restriction like unpalatable medicine, but having no recourse, he issued a verbal edict against swearing on the set.

The least likely person to forget Ford's order was Mother. Seated in a shady spot, and rummaging in her purse, she apparently muttered something off-color to herself. Ford overheard. In a public demonstration of evenhandedness, he insisted she stand in mock penance before the full cast and crew. Although this was intended in good humor, I rallied to Mother's defense and determined to catch him in a similar transgression.

Whenever possible I lingered within earshot until finally Francis O'Fearna, his Irish nephew and assistant, inadvertently helped me. Preoccupied in some spirited discussion, they were lacing their exchange with expletives when suddenly I appeared between them. Reminding Ford of his regulation, I called for his public confession and repentance, just as he had ruled for Mother. Doffing his hat and tipping down his dark glasses to better reveal his guileless expression, he pled for another chance.

Unforgiving because of Mother's punishment, I shook my head, led him into a circle of bystanders, and raised my finger in admonition. Taking out my stopwatch, I condemned him to stand in silence for one minute.

Ford's acquiescent attitude was short-lived. Usually he seemed to regard me as someone to be endured, not embraced as a colleague. Not until I began to march around like a soldier did I sense a first small chink in his armor.

"Post *arms!*" barked drillmaster Jack Pennick, former U.S. Marine, soldier of fortune, and now technical adviser on the film. "Atten-*shun!*" he snarled.

Our Black Watch squad was rehearsing the British manual of arms while Ford watched, arms akimbo. My new uniform felt delightfully tight and starchy, and my polished boots winked in the sunlight.

Pennick pointed at me. "Wipe that smile off your face!"

I froze in a scowl, glancing sideways for Ford's approval.

"Eyes front," ordered Pennick. I stared up at him. His face was long and narrow with a smashed, off-center nose and hair shaved high above both ears, one of which showed a deep nick where something had whizzed by. I liked his rugged, mysterious looks and authoritative manner.

Bending low, he bellowed, "Dress down that right hand."

I pressed it tightly against my side, deep into the pleated kilt of my uniform. If not the drilling and marching, that uniform was recompense enough. When I first heard about kilts it had all sounded far too childish and feminine. The costume designer took pains to explain my whole uniform was authentic, only shrunk to my size. At least they couldn't shrink the big brass buttons, I thought. Embellished with a sporran and white puttees, crowned with a Kilkenny hat emblazoned with a green tassel, I was determined to act as martial as I felt.

"Forward . . . march!" shouted Pennick.

Away we went, stiff-backed and stamping in the dust.

"Watch those feet!" Pennick barked. Already ordered to look dead ahead, I laughed out loud at the command.

"Come on, Temple," snapped Ford from the sidelines, "wipe that smile off!"

"Stomachs in," Pennick shouted, "chins out!"

Taking a deep breath, I sucked in my stomach, which automatically caused my chin to duck.

"Chins *out*!" he roared. "Halt!"

Pennick moved directly in front of me, staring down with an unflinching gaze. "Wipe that smile off your face!"

Looking up, I caught his eye and burst into laughter.

"I can't!" I replied, voice slightly strangled by trying to hold my stomach-in, chin-out posture. Pennick was a joy to march for.

Discipline dissolved. The squad broke ranks in laughter. Ford turned away, both arms extended upward as if in supplication.

Marching was something I hated to stop. One afternoon Father arrived on the set at quitting time. Our thoroughly drilled and exhausted squad was disbanding. Like a sheepdog pursuing its flock, I rounded up my fellow soldiers and prevailed upon them to drill one more time for

Father. Pennick stood aside and told me to conduct the squad. Stepping out of ranks, I faced the men as drill sergeant. As Pennick had done, I shouted, "Dress right!"

Ford had joined Pennick and Father to watch.

"Forward march!"

"Halt!"

"To the right oblique, march!" Away we stamped, in top form.

Later Mother told me Ford had muttered, "Nice kid, that."

Trying to earn Ford's respect by physical action had its practical limits. Cast as an imperious Afghan chief, Cesar Romero had captured me. Finding him intransigent to peace, I jabbed him in his ribs with a disgusted backhanded blow from my elbow. Brother George's counsel had always been that for maximum impact, aim the punch for a point deeper than the surface target. Aiming my pointy elbow at a spot on his silk tunic just beneath his rib cage, the first time I struck so hard, he doubled over with a grunt of pain, ruining the take. Winkie was not expected to immobilize the enemy chieftain. Forget the punch to the ribs, Ford said, I was too rough. He directed that next take I only push Romero with both hands.

However modest my progress in mellowing Ford it was arrested by Klammy's announcement that I must be excused from filming to take third-grade school examinations. It took me two hours to pass with high grades, but meanwhile the entire shooting operation was suspended at an idle-time cost of about $5,000. Although I was expecting cheers of congratulations for graduating to fourth grade, only an impatient wave from Ford greeted me. At last we could get to work again.

In fairness, Ford had lots to do besides pal around with me. His directing job was a web of intricate decisions, each with volcanic potential. Back and forth across his stage raced frothing horses and rippling regimental pennants in a tableau of sand, rock, and blood. Woven into the story line were swashbuckling soldiers, a ubiquitous kid, and, back at the barracks, a starched, perfumed lady-love. Ford had much more on his mind than getting to know the kid personally.

Little details of moviemaking had always fascinated me. When not in school, rehearsal, or performance, I usually squirmed into the front rank of onlookers. The mechanics of movies are always a critical ingredient in make-believe. In many ways participation in the process was better than enjoying the eventual product. Well done, mechanics transmute the dross of reality into the gold of imagination. Children like me could clearly see the difference. What a theatre audience eventually sees on the screen is not what we saw at work. From beginning to end how a movie was made captivated me. Day-to-day direction was the crucible in which everything occurred.

Ford could hardly have failed to notice my genuine interest, yet neither by eye contact nor word did he acknowledge my presence, except when routinely calling me up for my scenes and providing me the detailed direction I found so unnecessary.

Halfway through the film several things happened which did seem to catch Ford's attention. Our location site was parched and rocky, dominated by a steep, stony cleft. It was our version of the Khyber Pass, which snakes through the mountains separating India and Afghanistan. A hill-country British garrison had been created, replete with parade ground and barracks crammed with Black Watch soldiers bedeviled by raiding bands of fierce Afghans.

During one bit of rehearsal a stuntman rider came galloping full tilt toward the camera near where I stood watching. Struck by a mythical bullet, the horse reared upright, hooves flailing, as the rider leaped sideways from the saddle. It was pounding, snorting, dusty action. I was so absorbed in how the rider reined his horse backward, and his timing to kick free of the stirrups and leap aside, that I failed to notice Klammy's approach.

"Too dangerous," she said, pulling my hand. "Let's get away from here." I didn't budge.

Ford was standing nearby. He must have heard and seen, but said nothing.

A little later the same sort of thing happened in a rehearsal in which I peered from a window just as a lantern over my head was shot out by a hidden Afghan sniper. Confident in the sharpshooter out of camera range, I resolved not to wince. The shot rang out; a bullet whizzed and smashed the lantern glass into a shower of tiny fragments. I had not moved.

"You're supposed to duck," yelled Ford.

Next time I did, taking pains that it did not appear as a cringe. I hoped he noticed that I was not afraid.

Several days later he asked me directly if I was ready to do a particularly hazardous scene myself or if I preferred a double. The action called for me to flee across a dirt trail and climb quickly to safety on a rocky island directly in the path of a herd of several dozen stampeding horses erupting from the Khyber Pass. Doubles always were an unwelcome thought, their presence connoting professional inadequacy. But additionally, danger was appealing. Imminence of peril does wonders to concentrate the senses. Without split-second timing and sure feet, I knew I could easily be a victim. There lay the attraction. Courage was not a factor in my desire to take the chance. Actors who face a camera lens totally confident are already maimed, if not doomed. Some degree of apprehension is necessary for a convincing performance. Trembling fingers and visibly splotched cheeks are not helpful, but professionals often use insecurity to pump themselves to an acceptable level of intensity before cameras roll. Otherwise the result can be cold mush.

Mother was not keen on the idea, but with my enthusiasm on his side, Ford persuaded her it was photographically vital to the action. Running to the rocks would be no problem if I did not stumble. Once climbing, however, there could be no mistake. Every handhold, every cleft and irregularity had to be perfectly memorized, as well as every physical movement required to reach safety in those rocks.

On Ford's signal I bolted across the path and leaped up among the boulders just as the stampede of wild horses split and thundered by me on both sides in a swirl of snorting and pounding hooves. From my rocky perch I looked through the dust and across at Ford. I could see he was smiling, finger and thumb circled in the traditional gesture of approval.

One day word arrived at our Chatsworth outpost that Zanuck was dissatisfied. Although physically excluding himself from the *Wee Willie Winkie* location, he remained a shrewd spider, poised in the middle of his movie web. Screening each day's film production, he released a flood of written comments which were regarded as tablets from the mountain. Referring to a scene where my stage mother, June Lang, verbally threatens to box my ears for trampling her petunias and falling into a mud puddle, Zanuck sent cryptic word that the action was "not strong enough." A response to this dictum was being debated between

Ford and associate producer Gene Markey as Mother knitted nearby. Her needles suddenly stopped clicking.

"Why don't you get her spanked?" she asked.

"Spanked!" blurted Markey, examining Mother as if she wore horns. "The screen's greatest box-office magnet? The public wouldn't stand for it!"

Markey's credentials on feminine discipline should have been impeccable, based on successive marriages to three highly spirited actresses, Joan Bennett, Hedy Lamarr, and Myrna Loy.

"Nonsense," Mother answered. "Every child gets spanked." She resumed her knitting. "Even *I've* spanked Shirley."

To spank me loomed as so important a decision, it was bucked back for Zanuck's confirmation, thereby spreading the blame for any negative result. "Spank her," Zanuck responded.

Sweet and winsome in her ruffled lace collar and black string tie, Lang surely realized some jeopardy to her career, as well as to my bottom.

"I won't," she said firmly.

From behind his dark glasses Ford fixed her with a long baleful stare, pipe clenched motionless at the down-turned corner of his mouth. Now he had another problem. Only I knew the impasse was unnecessary, well aware where my insensitivity was located.

"Sure, spank me," I said brightly. "Please, Miss Lang. It'll be fun!"

Lang was stuck, pressured from all sides, so up I crawled over her knees and clung white-knuckled to the chair arm. In slow motion she raised her hand and landed a soft slap just where my nightdress began to flare. I puckered up sorrowfully, but Ford had stopped the cameras.

"June, dear," his tone was sarcastic. "Are you dusting her off? Your wrist was as limp as if you were waving good-bye. Let's try it again!"

This time Lang came slapping down with authority, twelve times in a row. I counted aloud, "...six... seven, ouch!... ten, eleven, twelve, ouch!" The camera stopped, so I turned and looked up. She was staring dejectedly at her open palm.

"Don't feel bad," I said reassuringly. "I feel fine."

Looking toward Ford, I whispered, "Bet her hand stings."

Grinning, he tipped up his tinted glasses. His eyes looked watery and sentimental, a hopeful sign of progress.

☆

Labor picketing at the studio having ceased, our company returned for soundstage work. Although growth was taking place all around me, another sort of major change was occurring. Its first indication surfaced during a still photography session at the studio of George Hurrell.

"Shirley carried on professionally," he later observed, "although she must have been tired because of her hectic schedule. She fell asleep while I was changing a background."

Actually what fell asleep was my foot. Rather than disturb it, I joined it.

He raised his voice to waken me. "Do you like still photos, Shirley?" He must have been kidding.

I sighed. "Well, in group pictures it pays to be short. I always get up front."

"That's not what I mean," he replied absently, arranging a new backdrop.

It was Mother who suddenly interrupted. "You attend to your photography, Mr. Hurrell. I'll attend to my daughter."

Both Hurrell and I turned toward her in surprise. Testiness was never her style.

Yet lately her eyes had developed an opaque quality, and often she sat with her shoulders slumped forward, something she had never done before. It was she who really looked bone-tired, although never the type given to self-pity and quick to deplore people who uttered long sighs of ennui or despair. Her typical optimism had been thoroughly shaken by whatever her medical prognosis was. Either swept up in the drama of illness, or worse, death, she laid careful plans for transfer of her maternal responsibilities.

As for my professional career, the studio would have to look after that phase, she wrote.

"It's Shirley as a human entity that worries me . . . how extraordinarily patient she is . . . her well-developed sense of justice . . . a joyous spirit, full of pranks and teasing. Tenderness, warmth, and sensitivity, these are the qualities I want to see guarded and developed."

Dwelling at length on the probability that I would continue to be making films, she expressed grave concern. "Unless surrounded by love and loyalty, any career child is at a tremendous disadvantage. She has to develop extraordinary resources within herself against greed, selfishness, and flattery. I've done my best to lay a foundation but the process must go on."

Candidates as proxy mother included grandmother Maude, but this Mother rejected on two counts: first, Maude was already growing too introspective and morose, vivid contrasts to my outgoing personality. Secondly, she was entitled to the serenity of old age, unlikely with me in her custody.

The final choice was an old and intimate friend, Fay Ferguson, wife of Father's colleague years before at the bank. Unfailingly feisty and ebullient, Fay shared with mother a catlike wisdom about life. Both were self-contained, watchful, and patient.

The evening before Mother was to be admitted to Santa Monica Hospital, I stole beside her as she stood staring up at some books on our library shelf. Slipping my small hand into hers, I asked what was wrong. Nothing, she replied, tightening her lips in a thin smile, but pointing at her stomach, a gesture both nonspecific and ominous.

"Don't be afraid, Mummy," I told her. "God will take care of you."

For the next two weeks gloom settled on my shoulders. Shooting went on as usual, with Fay doing her best to fill in for Mother, but around home everyone spoke in subdued voices. The only cheerful sound to break the unhappy mood came from my canary, who sang on in ignorant good cheer. Each day Fay accompanied me to the studio or location, where everyone adopted a somber air in my presence, one characterized by consideration, quiet talk, and averted glances.

Long before such compassionate conduct had riveted my attention on the severity of Mother's condition, I had tried to cope with the gaping hole caused by her absence. Each bedtime without her usual kiss caused tears to dampen my pillow, leaving me to wallow in a swampland of confusion and helplessness. What bothered me was not that grotesque ogre of despair which sometimes rises at the side of death. That Mother would return I had absolutely no doubt. God would see to that.

What provoked my tears was an ache of regret. How often had I simply accepted her devotion in all its dimension and durability, as if receiving no more than another set of clean bedsheets. Consumed as I was with a succession of daily events in work, school, and growth, I had too often taken her love for granted, too seldom expressed mine.

After two weeks in the hospital she returned, wan and weak, but apparently repaired from something found to be benign. Once again we exchanged our good-night kiss, this time at her bedside instead of mine. I cried harder and longer than on the night she left. In every way the dominant pillar of my young life, she merits and receives my lifelong adoration, deep and indestructible.

Toward the end of studio production, happenstance gave my campaign of credibility with Ford an enormous boost. Victor McLaglen, hard-bitten colossus of a British soldier, was reduced in the course of frontier events to a deep devotion for Winkie, sentiments wholly returned. Mortally wounded in battle, he asked for her. Beside his hospital bed I clutched a small bouquet and sang the Scottish ballad "Auld Lang Syne," a touching farewell to my dying friend.

Death scenes in movies are notorious booby traps. One plucked heartstring too many and everything turns into discord and audience indifference. In this case Ford's direction was unfaltering and supremely sensitive, memorable for both critics and audiences. McLaglen's last gasp did not drag on, and my song was phrased and paced to support the action, not dominate it. With his brawny hero counterposed with an innocent child under the encompassing shadow of death, every nuance of movement and sound coalesced in a scene of power and purity. In a typical Ford touch, the flower bouquet I had brought to the bedside was stolen.

Small bits of timing produce success in such a scene, and one was the afternoon hour selected for filming. Just before the death scene I had eaten a lunch of fried chicken, tomato juice, and an apple. Ford didn't realize it, but crying on a full stomach automatically produced the restraint he required of me.

When the cameras had stopped McLaglen raised on his elbow and placed one massive hand over mine. "If I wasn't already dead," he said, "I'd be crying too."

Ford came over and put his arm around my shoulder, as he would have a boy. My grief had come across with perfect restraint, he said, holding me firmly and punctuating his compliments with gentle hand pressures.

That we could be friends I had never doubted. But now we were colleagues. What had won him over was hard work, sentiment, and a late lunch. In the upshot we remained staunch personal friends, and later he became godfather to my firstborn daughter, Linda Susan.

Although my rendition of the song won the day with Ford, actually it was not authentic, as I learned several days later.

Genuine from tam-o'-shanter to kilt, bared knees and heavy woolen stockings, Scottish Sir Harry Lauder dropped in as one stop on a world singing tour. In his honor I donned my full military costume from the film, complete with pith helmet, demonstrated the manual of arms, told him the story of the Afghan wars, and challenged him to checkers.

"Mon, what a braw bonnie kiltie," he exclaimed. "A wee darlin'! Never did I meet such a nimble child in mind as well as body."

Spotting the tiny pump organ which had come with the cottage, he lowered his ample frame onto the stool and launched into a wailing Highland ballad. Grateful for his final tenor note, I told him about McLaglen's deathbed scene and sang him my "Auld Lang Syne."

"Aye, y'er a lassie with nor cheek nor forwardness," he said politely when I had concluded, "but you dinna know our tongue."

I had expected congratulations, not criticism.

"Now 'syne' means since, and auld lang syne means 'since the days of long ago.' When people of the United States sing our song, they always mistakenly say 'auld lang zine' with a 'zee' sound. You must pronounce it syne, which is correct. Zine, that's wrong.

"Was your friend Victor McLaglen a real true Highlander he would have known that," he concluded dourly.

On completion of the final shooting day of *Wee Willie Winkie*, several people returned with Mother and me to our Brentwood home and tarried outside the front door saying good-bye. Suddenly there was a low whine as some small projectile flew past our group, ricocheted off the stone wall behind us, and landed among nearby rose bushes. Recovering it, Griff announced it was a rifle bullet.

Everyone bolted indoors, as if Afghans were again about to attack. The origin of the shot remains a mystery, but a narrow miss by even a spent bullet was a fitting epitaph on the exploits of Winkie.

☆

The evening of the film's flashy premiere found Mother late for our departure from home, and so I wandered quietly into the downstairs library to kill time. To our mutual dismay, I came face-to-face with brother Jack holding to his lips a glassful of what I knew was whiskey. Not one word to Mother or Dad, he cautioned, knowing well their fury if he was caught drinking.

"I will so," I retorted, feeling as righteous as Winkie.

"Listen," he remonstrated. "George and I aren't even invited to the premiere. Why can't we have some fun too?"

"Drinking is wrong," I repeated, tilting my chin toward him as high as it would go. "I'm going to tell!"

He smacked me hard on the bottom. "Tell, and you get another," he said, then slapped me again for good measure.

Nobody had ever struck me in anger. The situation had potential for a real shambles at the wrong time. I wanted to kick his shin, all because I was right and he was wrong. But why be a tattletale, I rationalized, when I would probably collect another slap, my parents would get upset, and the premiere would be ruined for us. I could get even later, so I strode away.

Over 100,000 gawkers jammed Hollywood streets as we approached the theatre. When actor Tyrone Power introduced me over the national radio hookup, Father muttered that "Fox was a chicken." Recently studio lawyers had rejected a proposition for $7,000 for one radio appearance by me, he groused, and now they were letting me talk for nothing.

Of all my films I rate *Wee Willie Winkie* the best, but for all the wrong reasons. It was best because of its manual of arms, the noisy marching around in military garb with brass buttons, my kilts bouncing. It was best because of daredevil stunts with snipers and stampeding horses. It was also best because I finally seemed to earn the professional respect of someone so blood-and-thunder macho as Ford. Best of all, the watery-blue color of my portable dressing room had been repainted in regimental red.

Although accepted as a film of reeling and ecstatic grandeur, *Wee Willie Winkie* stirred conflicting opinion. Some used it to disinter British arrogance during colonialism. Among those whose pro-England sentiments were barely concealed, Eleanor Roosevelt commented in her "My Day" newspaper column:

I wonder how many people seeing *Wee Willie Winkie* will get the main lesson from it. It took a little child's faith and logic to bring a dangerous tribal chief in India to an understanding with his ancient enemy, the Soldier of the Queen.

No such understanding was evident in Norway, where antipathy to British imperialism went hand in hand with support for tribal resistance. There the government banned our film entirely.

At home the *Literary Digest* reported the film's effect on me. "She was beginning to teeter up there at the top because of a succession of sap pictures. The strength of this film is as much in the yarn as in the girl. Now her drooling is less evident."

In a radio broadcast Victor McLaglen was even more topical when crooner Bing Crosby commented, "Seems odd that you, an Academy Award winner, should be in a supporting role to Shirley."

"Why not?" answered McLaglen. "I've only been in pictures sixteen years. She's been in them all her life!"

Not precisely true, but it had taken me five years to move beyond the talents first developed at Meglin's. In this latest film nobody asked me to dance, and I had sung only one song. At last my role was acting, with winsomeness subordinated to plot. Even I was aware that this was progress.

Wee Willie Winkie was a watershed. Until 1937 my film image had been someone cuddlesome and cute, a matchmaker and problem-solver, a child unsinkable and indestructible, always a paragon of purity. For years I had been almost immune to exacting criticism, except that at moments there seemed too much of me.

Now I had begun to turn one shoulder on childhood, although some people continued to cling tenaciously to their own perception of what I should be. In their own time warp they were not changing much; therefore, neither should I. Not everyone, however, was content to hold me static, particularly the Catholic Church.

Since 1933, when the Catholic League of Decency was created, the Holy See had evidenced increasing concern for the uneasy balance in movies between entertainment and morality. At a recent New York State Convention of the Federated Catholic Charities, Monsignor Amleto Cigognani had delivered a ringing proclamation. A massacre of innocent youth is taking place, he had claimed, hour by hour. How shall crimes attributable to immoral motion pictures be measured? Catholics are called by God, the Pope, bishops and priests to a united and vigorous campaign for the purification of the cinema, he challenged. "Movies have become a deadly menace to morals."

Joining as a powerful ally of the industry-sponsored Hays Office, the League had rapidly become one of the most effective pressure groups in Hollywood history. Its technique was formidable. Films were officially rated according to moral content. All Catholics were urged to sign so-called pledges of decency. To outraged charges of unconstitutional censorship, the League replied it was only "guiding public opinion." The threat of its official boycott continued to hang like a scimitar over actors and studio heads alike.

Curious about the divided public opinion occasioned by my professional growth, the august official Vatican newspaper, *Osservatore Romano*, dispatched church prelate Father Silvio Massante, OSJ, to pay me a visit.

"I have brought you something," Father Massante told us. Opening a coffee-table album of colored lithographic reproductions of paintings by old masters, he slowly turned the pages.

"Do you know any Italian words?" he asked.

"No," I replied, "but I know some Chinese," and recited some lines from *Stowaway*. "Don't worry," I reassured him. "It means 'Are we mice, or are we men?'"

His eyes were fixed on mine, small and unwavering, like a bird staring for a worm, but he made no comment and returned to the book. "These paintings are just as beautiful as when Botticelli painted them hundreds of years ago." The book was long, but he turned every page slowly and waited for my reaction before going on.

At last involving Mother in his attention, he asked what church we attended. Presbyterian, she replied cautiously, although in Santa Monica it was easier to go to a nearby Episcopal church. And sometimes we went to another small village church, she added, unconvincingly forgetting its denomination.

"And her religious instruction?" Father Massante asked.

"I teach her about the Bible and God," Mother answered. Probing personal questions like his always put her on the defensive, so he returned to me with a new topic, asking if I wished to visit Italy. Answering that it would be fun, I observed that we hadn't come to Italy in geography yet.

For about an hour this muddy exchange ran its course, until Mother looked at her wristwatch and finally he rose to leave, remarking he was very happy he had come. The way he stretched out his words suggested he had more to say. Walking toward the door, he stopped for a moment, staring down at his shoes, then deliberately cleared his throat.

"In Italy, as in some other countries of Europe," he said, "there is a persistent rumor that Shirley Temple is no child at all." Mother's eyes widened in astonishment. "The rumor is, Shirley is a midget."

In slow motion both turned to look at me where I stood stock-still in this silent tableau.

"Obviously, she is not," said Father Massante.

When the door had clicked behind our visitor, Mother's irritation bubbled over. "Why don't they *stop* it! All those letters calling you a thirty-year-old midget with a seven-year-old child, and now a priest!"

She stood looking out the window at Father Massante's retreating figure and continued talking as if to herself. "Why do people make out she's not normal! And I *do* wish people would stop saying she has *all* her adult teeth! She only has *eight*!"

Teeth proved the least of it on October 28, 1937, when London's *Night and Day* magazine kicked over a hornet's nest with its film review of *Wee Willie Winkie,* bylined by Graham Greene.

> ... Infancy with her is a disguise, her appeal is more secret and more adult. Already two years ago she was a fancy little piece. (Real childhood, I think, went out after the *Littlest Rebel*.) In *Captain January* she wore trousers with the mature suggestiveness of a Dietrich: her neat and well-developed rump twisted in the tap dance: her eyes had a sidelong, searching coquetry. Now in *Wee Willie Winkie,* wearing short kilts, she is a complete totsy. Watch her swaggering stride across the Indian barrack-square: hear the gasp of excited expectation from her antique audience when the sergeant's palm is raised: watch the way she measures a man with agile studio eyes, with dimpled depravity. Adult emotions of love and grief glissade across the mask of childhood, a childhood skin deep. It is clever, but it cannot last. Her admirers, middle-aged men and clergy-

men, respond to her dubious coquetry, to the sight of her well-shaped and desirable little body, packed with enormous vitality, only because the safety curtain of story and dialogue drops between their intelligence and their desire.

When a major London news distributor refused to handle the magazine issue, the publisher adroitly advertised its ban with posters proclaiming, "Sex and Shirley Temple." In November 1937 local Fox officials, citing the review's "salacious, disgusting character," urged legal action "to give an international aspect to the case and to establish a worldwide precedent to stop similar articles being published." Good reviews are preferable to bad ones, but rather than the statesmanlike motivation expressed, Fox must have seen present danger at the box office.

Characterizing the review as a dangerous concoction of coquetry, immorality, and abnormality handily enlisted my parents as co-plaintiffs in the Complaint, that said Greene had in effect accused the company of "procuring" me "for immoral purposes."

Three months before the suit came to trial during late March of 1938, *Night and Day* had ceased publication, victim more from undercapitalization in competition with venerable *Punch* than from libel actions, of which mine was but one. Acting for the plaintiffs, Sir Patrick Hastings, K.C., declined to read our Complaint aloud to Lord Chief Justice Hewart, rather describing the film review as "one of the most horrible libels one could imagine," and the magazine as "a beastly publication."

Blundering, perhaps, but hardly beastly. Patterned after the erudite *New Yorker*, it was a fleeting jewel of literary intellect and critical humor. Among distinguished contributors it could boast Elizabeth Bowen (theatre), Evelyn Waugh (books), Malcolm Muggeridge, and as co-editor, Greene himself, a diversely energetic figure who had already completed nine novels, and in his 1980 autobiography *Ways of Escape* says, "the idea of reviewing films came to me at a cocktail party after the dangerous third martini."

Nor did my maturity seem to have suddenly overwhelmed Greene with *Wee Willie Winkie*. In an earlier May 1936 review of *The Littlest Rebel* in *The Spectator*, he had observed, "I had not expected the tremendous energy which her rivals certainly lack"; and with *Captain*

January had commented on "a coquetry quite as mature as Miss Colbert's" and "an oddly precocious body as voluptuous" as Miss Dietrich's. In such retrospect I find it odd my mother remained so unignited by earlier reviews as to give them no passing mention, yet permitted herself affront by Greene's *Wee Willie Winkie* piece.

Answering His Lordship's inquiry regarding Greene's whereabouts, Counsel Mr. Valentine Holmes said he did not know, but on behalf of magazine, publisher, printer, and author offered me deepest apologies for any pain the article would have caused me, had I read it.

Apparently Greene did not find the matter altogether hilarious, writing to his colleague Elizabeth Bowen: "I found a cable waiting for me in Mexico City asking me to apologize to that little bitch Shirley Temple." Had he done so, I would have wondered what for.

"This libel is simply a gross outrage," sputtered the notoriously severe Lord Chief Justice. "I will take care to see that suitable attention is directed to it." What could be found of the magazine issue was ordered destroyed, and $5,250 punitive damages were awarded to Fox and $7,000 to me, adequate wages for my alleged occupation. Twisting the knife, Fox insisted Greene contribute $1,500 himself.

"I kept on my bathroom wall, until a bomb removed the wall, the statement of Claim," Greene recalled in 1972, to which the editor of the 1985 *Night and Day* anthology adds, "The charges might have been even worse if he had not deleted from the typescript a comparison with Lady Macbeth."

In Greene's defense one colleague recently observed, "even at that distant period, the notion that children neither had nor could express sexual instincts was, to say the least, uninstructed." On at least one point, however, and fortunately for me, Greene's review seems to have erred. "The owners of a child star are like leaseholders," he wrote. "Their property diminishes in value every year. Time's chariot is at their back; before them acres of anonymity."

The whole event could be viewed as immensely fruitful. My punitive award was recycled immediately into 5 percent British War Loan Bonds to help arm sorely pressed England against a troubled Europe. Suddenly unemployed as a film critic, Greene was released permanently into the ranks of eminent novelists, and, finally, the saucy publicity tweaked British box-office interest, for *Wee Willie Winkie* prospered gloriously.

Important from my standpoint, the Royal Tribunal also confirmed me childless and nine years old.

☆

In my schoolwork Amelia Earhart's flight continued to be monitored daily, like a serial program on radio. With a sudden loop, the blue trackline on the map had reached Africa from Brazil and struck eastward across the sub-Sahara desert, straight as a string. On she had flown with navigator Fred Noonan past exotic place names such as Timbuktu and Fort Lamy. Leaping the Indian Ocean they reached Karachi on the Indian subcontinent. Along the plane's blue track were strewn subjects galore for my study. Getting me across India had taken me longer than it had Earhart, but finally we were both winging out over the Siamese temples of Southeast Asia, leaving land behind and skirting Indonesia's island empire en route to New Guinea.

Shortly before Independence Day on May 30, 1938, our blue line took off from Port Moresby, headed toward flyspeck Howland Island.

"Overcast . . . cannot see the island," read Earhart's early morning radio message intercepted by the U.S. Coast Guard cutter *Itasca*. "Gas running low . . . running north and south . . ."

Nothing more was heard of her plane, nor its occupants.

In a farewell letter to be made public in the event of her death, Earhart had written, "Hurray for the last great adventure! I wish I had won, but it was worthwhile anyway!"

For several days Klammy left our map thumbtacked to the wall, its blue line ended in mid-Pacific Ocean, a stark reminder of hope dwindling daily. As weeks passed the map became a static object of decoration. Then one day it, too, vanished.

16

The studio seemed to have been convinced it was far more perilous to return to the sentimental torpor of my thirteen previous scripts before *Wee Willie Winkie* than to follow the acting trail now being pioneered. My next film was announced as *Heidi*, a second dramatic role. Mother had mixed feelings, concerned that drama might confuse my personality growth. "We may take her out of movies when she begins 'acting' rather than just being herself," she observed.

Her reaction left me uncertain of her true wishes. To impose a constraint on professional growth was a puzzling phenomenon, so when asked, I hedged, saying that when I grew up, *then* I'd be an actress.

Heidi is an 1880 Johanna Spyri classic about an endearing and disarming child of the Swiss Alps. Although published in 30 million copies in thirty languages, including Siamese, Icelandic, and Afrikaans, to many Swiss nationals Heidi was someone to hate.

"She has become a symbol of everything about Switzerland that is no longer," said Dr. Franz Caspar, curator of the Heidi Museum in Zurich. "She enhances stereotypes that many urban Swiss would just as soon forget, a fiction that irritates them. Swiss no longer view themselves as rustics or mountain folk. Heidi is nothing more than a sentimental *kitsch*."

Despite Swiss opinion, the studio moved ahead, assigning Allan

Dwan as director. An ex-Notre Dame football hero, and since 1915 a prolific filmmaker, Dwan was the innovative engineer who conceived the "dolly" shot, a scheme for moving bulky cameras on floor rails.

"In a kind of left-handed way, Zanuck gave me *Heidi*," Dwan later related. " 'See what you can do with it,' he said. I liked to avoid children, especially those that were 'over.' She had hit her peak and was sliding fast when I started working with her. It was sad that the spark lasted only to a certain age. Zanuck would have liked to make a trade, but nobody was interested."

Perhaps Dwan did not know that at that moment Louis B. Mayer of MGM had begun dickering with Zanuck to get me for the lead role in MGM's *The Wizard of Oz*, but so far Zanuck was turning a deaf ear.

As had been the case with Wee *Willie Winkie*, during the making of *Heidi* I had a director who was skeptical if not annoyed at the prospect of working with me. As *Heidi* progressed, however, Dwan's initial attitude of resignation warmed perceptibly. In the end it was he who gave identity to my police force by replacing my "Junior G-man" badges with gilded ones engraved with the name of my force.

Dwan's initial skepticism, however, overlooked the facts. Screen rights to *The Wizard of Oz* had been acquired by MGM from heirs of author L. Frank Baum. Having just lost his key juvenile singer, Deanna Durbin, to Universal Studios, Mayer was without a star for the role of fourteen-year-old Dorothy and had asked Zanuck for me. Always a trader, Zanuck countered by offering to buy the story, intending to star me under his banner. Equally canny, Mayer declined, then dangled his own deal. If Zanuck would loan me, Mayer would loan Jean Harlow and Clark Gable to Zanuck. As a footnote to this exchange, I would then be loaned again to MGM to star with Gable in a subsequent film. Generally aware of the rumors rocketing around, Mother thought Mayer's idea a good one for me, particularly the last part.

Gable and I would have been a flashy twosome. *Fortune* magazine's first scientific opinion poll had just declared me the national favorite movie star of all American women. With male respondents, only Clark Gable was more popular.

Asked about the prospect, Gable had reservations. "Sure, we have dimples in common but she has three strikes on me from the start. I'm big and she's little. I'm dark and she's blond. And men still prefer little blondes. Then there's the great ear problem. Hers are hidden. Mine are naked, free to the wind. They should be hidden too!"

Death killed the possibility of a deal. When Harlow was struck down while filming *Saratoga* on June 7, 1937, her disappearance removed a key element of the proposed swap. Faced with Durbin's defection, my inaccessibility, and Harlow's demise, nothing was left for Mayer but to go with his already rejected option of Judy Garland. Sometimes the gods know best.

Dwan's comment that I was passé, however, neatly epitomized the ambivalence common behind studio closed doors. Enthusiasts and crepehangers could sit side by side. On one hand, I was ranked number one at the box office for a third successive year. On the other, some clairvoyants, even my director, believed I would soon disappear from the scene. I was central in an odd sort of split screen, dominant and moribund all at the same moment.

Unaware of either cheers from the box office or back-room lamentation, my only objective was to elevate my ability to the height of my energy. What really mattered was daily professionalism, sustained interaction among our total crew, the rhythm and celebration of work in everyday life.

For someone whose benchmark was excellence in her craft, *Heidi* had in store two jolts to my sense of achievement, both involving goats.

To approximate a Swiss alpine landscape, the film was made on location in a rustic mountain environment at Lake Arrowhead near Los Angeles. The Arrowhead Springs Resort Hotel, where we all stayed, was a fortuitous selection, owned largely by Schenck, Zanuck, and studio vice president William Goetz.

Time came when I was to be butted by a trained billy goat named Old Turk. Padding was stuffed into my pants and I was told to bend over. I shut my eyes for good measure. Old Turk needed no rehearsal. With a short quick rush, head lowered on target, he sent me up and forward, sprawling facedown in the dust. Wiping the dirt from my lips, I could see Mother had risen from her chair. Actually the butt was painless, and the sensation of flying pure fun. We had done it twice more when Old Turk's trainer stopped things by demanding his rental be increased from $1.50 per day to $5.00.

Several butts later Mother told Dwan a double must be found. Repetitive abuse like that could damage a girl. A boy my size was found, padded, dressed, and hatted in my clothes. Assuming my bent-over position with his face averted from the camera, he stole all my remaining fun. But the worst was, I could not do the job.

Forty years later the boy and I wound up sharing diplomatic duties in Africa.

"That goat was the worst thing that ever happened to me," he confided. "Dressed in your dress, blond-wigged and butted, was not fun. It was awful. My father was so scornful of my doubling for a girl, he eventually prohibited me from acting."

The idea of "doubles" was always repugnant to me too. No matter how minor, sharing a role diminishes the sense of achievement and, more significant to a child, dilutes the best excitement. When Heidi's horse carriage, for example, raced through a narrow stone archway, I was actually holding the reins myself, even though the horse knew the way. I was prepared to repeat that scene a hundred times.

The second goat to bedevil me was a patient female. Balanced on a three-legged milking stool, I was required to milk her. No matter how I squeezed or tugged, the bucket remained stone dry. Not one drop. The nanny just disdainfully turned her head and endured my efforts. I tried everything short of shuffling cards. Others had instructed me how to milk, but nobody told the goat what to do. I desperately wanted to get that goat to produce. It was my job.

A movie set has no such thing as a sacred goat. During my enforced absence at school, Dwan sent for milk, the old-fashioned kind with cream floating on top. Invisible to both the camera and me, a thin piece of flexible tubing was glued to the far side of the goat's udder. It snaked its way unobtrusively offstage and into the bucket of milk. With little to show for our rehearsal except tender teats, the goat was now automated.

Retrieving me from arithmetic lessons, Dwan said nothing about his scheme, dispensed with further rehearsal, and placed me on the familiar three-legged stool. The goat turned its head once to regard me with indifference as I approached that udder with renewed determination.

As cameras rolled I squeezed and tugged. Not a drop. I really had no idea why. In frustration I tipped up one teat to peer into its end. At that instant, back with the hidden milk bucket, a propman squeezed his rubber bulb, sending a stream of milk smack into my eye.

"Look!" I shouted, wiping my face with my sleeve. "I got some!"

Although the crew broke into shouts of approval, my exultation was brief. Inspecting the teat more carefully, I detected the tube and traced it from the far side of the udder, down the goat's hind leg, and away to the bucket. At first I told myself the joke was on the goat. We had tricked it by supplying the milk it wouldn't. Very quickly, however, I realized bottled milk had been required because I failed to get the real thing. Probably the goat went home to nurse its tender teats, but I went off to nurse an increasingly acute private regret. Put to another test with a goat, I had failed.

To compound my failure in both butting and milking, I was promptly entrapped in the necessity for dishonesty.

Unexpected events are always manna for studio publicists. Anecdotes of the milking incident released to the press omitted mention of a tube, extolling only the spontaneity of my comment upon achieving some milk. To reinforce the half-truth, Dwan gave orders that everyone stick with this sympathetic version in any casual conversation off the lot, and emphasized to me the importance of joining fully in the conspiracy.

I went along for two good reasons. First, silence helped obliterate my personal sense of inadequacy as a milkmaid. Second, since wavering uncertainly about untruth and teamwork when the *Captain January* crane had its feet nailed to the floor, I had come to believe that lots of institutional discipline was required to preserve our sense of internal integrity. Even dishonesty might be necessary to shield the art of make-believe from unkind exposure. The concept of teamwork demanded allegiance. In our common endeavor, protective falsehood could be seen as a virtue.

☆

Turning points in some movie careers occur to a blare of trumpets or the flutter of a pink slip bidding farewell. At other times it is a thin knife blade whose thrust fails to hurt until later. In *Heidi* one subtle script change tainted what otherwise would have been my second straight dramatic role.

Midway in shooting, a "dream" sequence was written in which I was miraculously transported from Switzerland to Holland. My standard fifty-six curls became two golden braids and a quarter-acre Zuider Zee appeared on the back lot, calm and coated with reflective oil. Along its banks I sang and clogged to a captivating number called "In My Little Wooden Shoes," a traditional Temple musical filler. Though a moment of charm, it marked the collapse of any studio resolve to build on the purely dramatic momentum first evident in *Wee Willie Winkie*.

The studio blamed Mother, saying the idea of returning to the tried-and-true past was hers. Quite the reverse. Several times recently and unsuccessfully she had petitioned Zanuck for roles which would require me to abandon my standard headful of curls. She knew that old credentials are a vanishing value. To have proposed elimination of the hair trademark only to urge revival of the dance trademark would have been wholly inconsistent. Her innate sense of timing told her it was time for broad change.

A little muddleheaded, director Dwan blamed me. "She helped invent that Holland dream sequence," he observed. "She thought that way. She knew it was a good spot for a musical number." Not exactly. *Any* spot is good for a musical number, but what really marshaled my enthusiasm for the idea was an aerial high wire that flew me, wooden shoes and all, across the Zuider Zee.

Dwan also missed the best reason for my enthusiasm for the scene. The dream called for braids and bangs.

It is improbable that such a mid-course change, whoever proposed it, did not carry the approval of Zanuck. Then at his pinnacle of power, he was a creative and officious man. It would not have been his only attempt to improve an an already time-proven classic, nor to manipulate his studio stars. To many studio heads, stars were an artistic commodity to be used, spent, or squandered as creative impulse might direct.

"In a very short time," Zanuck openly complained, "the business will be completely dominated by stars and agents. In today's market, it's only faces that count, not brains. We made the stars, but they've forgotten that ... faces, that's all they are, just faces!" He seemed to have forgotten that some stars were crowned not by him but by the audience.

For the sneak preview of *Heidi*, someone forgot to invite Mother, but Zanuck hastily wrote to assure her the oversight was unintentional, a song she had heard before. Beginning with the Long Beach sneak preview of *The Littlest Rebel* on November 11, 1935, my parents had been regularly excluded, always inadvertently, always with apologies.

When *Heidi* did premier officially I attested to its quality in my own way. On the screen, Heidi is being refused permission to return home to her grandfather. Although desperately anxious to go, the girl remains completely dry-eyed. Not so me, seated in the darkened audience. That girl on the screen was in a fix worthy of genuine sympathy. I cried copiously.

When the show ended Mother promptly started maneuvering me out of the still-darkened theatre. Pushing past knees and groping up the aisle, I glanced back at the title of the next feature, *Night Club Scandal*, starring John Barrymore. Now there was another film worth seeing.

In mid-July of 1937 came visitors worth seeing because they were so abhorred in advance. "More Commies," snorted Klammy. "They don't believe in God."

To arm me with useful Russian phrases, the studio had sent comedian Gregory Ratoff to tutor. Demonstrating "very good" in Russian, he sputtered the syllables, and like all short people, I caught his fine rain of spray, leaving me rehearsed and sticky all over.

Three of the visitors were short, two looming; all five were dressed alike, in drab suits with trousers flared at the bottom.

"I am Oumansky, chargé d'affaires from Washington," said one, his voice sonorous and thickly accented. "I translate."

"*Pashalsta!* Thank you," I replied, while everyone smiled politely.

"And I help," added Grigore Gokham, the USSR consul general in San Francisco, who took charge.

The other three men were aviators who had just flown in a single-engine plane 6,295 miles nonstop from Moscow across the North Pole, a world record for distance. The fliers had just landed in the early morning of July 12 in a pasture near San Jacinto, California, site of today's March Field Air Base.

"Know why they landed in a plowed field instead of the smooth nearby landing strip?" Gokham asked, then answered, "Because the air brakes were removed before takeoff to make room for a heavier fuel load. They had to use a rough field to help stop the plane." It all sounded exciting and logical.

"Yes, we pioneer commercial air route between our two countries," interrupted the pilot, Mikhail Gromov, a lean and attractive man wearing a small medal on a red ribbon. Noticing my interest, he stooped forward so I could see better. "Medal of a Hero of the Soviet Union, from the great world war," he told me. Although I hadn't studied the war yet with Klammy, I was mightily impressed.

"*Ochin Khorosho!* Very good!" I commented, tucking in my chin for the requisite guttural tone.

Actually the Gromov flight was the second Soviet transpolar flight. Severe head winds had forced the first plane to land at an army airfield near Vancouver, Washington. The U.S. commanding officer who took the three-man Soviet crew into his home was General George C. Marshall, later of international reknown. That initial long-distance record was short-lived, eclipsed by Gromov three weeks later.

"We flew three days," navigator Sergei Danilin began, reciting details, "precisely sixty-two hours and seventeen minutes. We have cyclones, ice, and fog over magnetic pole. Only one night dark enough for sleep."

"*Ochin Khorosho!*" I repeated enthusiastically although I was puzzled. We had not reached astronomy either. "Now I will lead you around the lot. First we'll see them making movies," I advised, and paraded the group onto the set of Eddie Cantor's *Ali Baba Goes to Town*.

Although polite to the cast, the visitors were obviously far more interested in technical equipment than chatting with strangers. Actors Tyrone Power, Alice Faye, Warner Baxter and Andy Devine stood in an attentive circle around the visitors, but one by one the fliers drifted aside to examine cameras, lights, and sound equipment.

The fliers were my excuse to attend my first baseball game. Along with 28,000 other spectators at Wrigley Field in Los Angeles, we watched a pickup Film Comedians team edge the Leading Men 7 runs to 6. Long forbidden to nibble between meals, I was not allowed to have hot dogs, and having only a meager understanding of baseball, I was reduced to watching others eat and play. It was one of the few moments I could remember when I could stare at other people without catching them staring back.

Sharing my disinterest in baseball, Gromov began to talk again. "Flying is like a game too," he said, while Oumansky translated. "We are a young country. We cannot remain behind." As he spoke he looked directly at me, his long fingers held just touching each other in a thoughtful pose. "World progress must be our progress. Maybe American aviators can better our record. So! We in turn once more may surpass *your* record."

Better than baseball, I thought. A simple contest, and perpetual. It intrigued and baffled me that so likable a person could bring horror into Klammy's voice. Despite obviously irreconcilable divisions of political philosophy, Gromov and I remained friends for years, and forty-five years later, in 1983, he wrote me of his hope that the "meteorological and political storms will soon subside, and we again will be able to share pleasant memories of meetings on your soil."

Inclined to take people on face value and unburdened by philosophical differences between capitalism and communism, I found the Soviet flyers far more exciting than I did the sudden reemergence of the indefatigable Jack Hays.

Grinding their way through the courts came his lawsuits seeking a slice of my earnings. District Judge Harry A. Hollzer had given both suits a double punch: first, ruling that the lower court that had first taken up Hays's charges was without jurisdiction and the suit was therefore stalled; second, that Hays's complaint had failed to establish a proper legal cause of action. Both rulings were promptly appealed and wound up before Superior Court Judge Robert W. Kenny, who fraternally upheld both decisions and added a touch of whimsy to the case. Observing that when the conflict had started I was only three years old and could hardly have been viewed a party in the suit, he ordered me released as a defendant.

Hays appealed all these adverse decisions to a panel including Justices P. J. Crail, J. Wood, and the same Marshall F. McComb who by chance had approved my original contract. Once again, Hays lost.

Still undiscouraged, however, for a fourth time he petitioned a different court, this time the California Supreme Court, a request finally denied on January 27, 1938. Six years of unsuccessful legal wrangling through five courtrooms might have vanquished someone who saw a less tempting target. This was far from his death rattle, however; Hays would shrug off the latest rejection and reload for yet another legal salvo.

My grasp of all this squabbling was limited to wonder at the flood of anger and hatred from my parents at any mention of Hays's name. To me he was only a memory, a hazy, faintly ominous silhouette who long before had demanded my obedience, gladly given. Old dust resettled had little interest and less appeal. Yesterday's events were as drained and lifeless as money once earned.

17

Had *The Wizard of Oz* trade matured, an incidental benefit to my studio would have been relief from the vexing responsibility of selecting my next screenplay. Again grappling with that chronic demon, Zanuck made a safe if uncourageous decision: recycle me through old hit movies of Mary Pickford's. My *Curly Top* had only been Pickford's *Daddy Long Legs* made during World War I, sterilized of swearing and stripped of its love scenes. Ahead would be *Fanchon the Cricket* and then *Pollyanna*, the tale of a perpetually happy girl, most recently a stage hit featuring Helen Hayes. But first would come *Rebecca of Sunnybrook Farm*, vintage 1917 and already repeated once by Fox Films in 1932 with Marion Nixon. Instead of dancing down a yellow-brick road to see a wonderful wizard, I would return to retrace the path I had already traveled. It was time to recall sacred cows and Zanuck threw wide the cow-shed door. Any promise of new directions drained away. I would be a rehash of somebody else.

Although never consulted on screenplay selection, Mother gamely climbed on the rolling bandwagon.

"Personally, I would like Shirley to do some of the things that made Mary Pickford's career so beautiful," she said. "Talk about Temple curls! Pickford's were very famous too!" But it was Pickford's style that she had in mind.

In fact, my standard curls became a casualty. "I'd like Shirley in a

198

film with long hair and a raggedy dress," Mother cautiously suggested. "But then, I'm only a mother. I don't shape her career. That's up to the studio."

As my contract gave her certain rights to devise my hairstyle, however, and following her opinion first expressed during *Heidi*, out the window went all fifty-six baby ringlets save one, the forehead spit curl devised to hide my bump fifteen films previously on *Stand Up and Cheer*. My new hairstyle was parted over the left eye and drawn back in long, loose waves over each ear. Mother kept likening it to Mary Pickford's dangling curls. I regarded it simply as progress.

Quite apart from discussing my hairstyle, direct contact between Zanuck and Mother had grown increasingly fleeting and superficial. A very few times we had visited him at his beach house so I could play with his three children. On such occasions he had always sat studiously apart, showing little interest in talking at length with Mother and none in speaking with me or getting to know me personally. My presence there was for his children, not him.

At other times, infrequent at best, I was summoned to accompany Mother to his office, and there Zanuck's demeanor had been similarly impersonal, with one exception. Perhaps experimenting with my spontaneous reactions, suddenly, he jumped up from behind his desk, uttered little animal gasps of terror, and ran to a corner. There he crouched, silently studying my reaction, with a stubby polo mallet held before him as if defending against a demon. It was all so odd, I just sat and watched. Humorous or testing, his behavior further reinforced a general impression that he disliked me. Whether he did or not concerned me because he was the boss, but not otherwise. My professional future had always seemed in my hands, not his. More realistically, Mother acknowledged our utter dependence on his whim, notably at option time each year, and always accorded him her most attentive demeanor.

First Lady of the American stage Helen Hayes came calling with a totally different idea for me than following in Pickford's footsteps, but a few weeks too late.

Any knock at our cottage door was, as always, a summons to duty. Hayes entered a step ahead of her daughter, Mary McArthur, a young girl my size, braids dangling from under a brown beanie. Both wore jodhpurs and ankle-high riding boots.

What did she want to see in Hollywood, Mother had asked Mary. "Well, first I wanted to meet her," she replied, pointing, "then I want to hear Lionel Barrymore belch!"

Brimming with vitality, Hayes explained that although she was out in Hollywood again, she really didn't like to make movies. Asked why, she answered because her face lacked character and range of expressions. Seated bolt upright on my undersized couch, she turned to me and asked if I ever dreamed of things I would like to do, but before I could answer she said, "When I was eight years old starting in theatre, I had a beautiful dream that I could someday be a queen on the stage." Her laugh rippled delightedly. "In fact, I just was!" referring to her play *Victoria Regina*. It was just as well she cut off my answer. Actually I never dreamed of things I would like to do, other than those I was already doing.

A standard stop on tours for children my age was a souvenir doll's house from *Curly Top*, now installed in our cottage bedroom. Piece by piece I demonstrated all its miniature equipment to Mary—the diminutive hooked rugs which lay on the parquet floors, the sheets covering each bed, and the bathroom commode with a lid that worked. Each door swung, every drawer slid open. Chintz curtains were tied back at each window, bric-a-brac cluttered the tiny tabletops, books lined the shelves, and fake food was in the refrigerator. We examined everything, preoccupied with the housekeeping details, as little girls would. Ghosts of vamp Lillian Harvey and sultry Gloria Swanson must have shuddered to witness what now transpired in their historic "Maison des Rêves" bedroom.

Hayes was still in animated conversation with Mother.

"Another of my pet dreams, despite my inexpressive face," she laughed, "is to start a brand-new career in films, like Marie Dressler." She fluffed her fingers through her hair. "What I would like best is to be a character actress playing the part of the nurse in *Romeo and Juliet*," her words came slowly, "starring Shirley Temple."

For a moment nobody spoke, everyone exchanging glances.

Mother broke the silence. "But that's a story about suicide, isn't it?" Whoever Juliet was, I knew I would not be playing her. "Besides, she's going to do *Rebecca of Sunnybrook Farm* next."

☆

My film must have had a special appeal for Mother beyond Pickford nostalgia and the reprise of my songs about animal crackers and the indestructible lollipop airplane, for she arranged that older brother Jack get a job as a third-assistant-director. Never having worked around movie sets before, he was supercargo and spent time thinking up things to take care of, one of which was me.

Among our dinner-table props on the film was a roasted turkey, sprayed with insecticide to keep flies away. With what I regarded as overkill, Jack loudly forbade me to sample the slices temptingly arrayed on the platter. Until that moment I had had no interest in eating something already announced as tainted, but Jack's assumption of authority scratched me the wrong way. Nobody in our family disciplined me except Mother and she didn't demand; she suggested. Jack had launched us both in new roles: his order was mine to thwart. Reaching for a piece of turkey, I popped it in my mouth and chewed. Despite a slightly bitter taste, it was good turkey and my disobedience was immensely satisfying. Jack seemed apoplectic, and shook me like a rag doll, as if to dislodge the mouthful. Director Allan Dwan interceded, saying rough action would get us nowhere. No elbows or sharp tongues on his set. Jack was dispatched on some errand.

On this point Dwan was not one to practice what he preached. Some directors need a private buffoon at hand, a sort of clown type to act as a lightning rod when tempers flare. Dwan had a script supervisor, a man who wore horn-rimmed glasses and a fixed grin regardless of what happened to him. If Dwan became exasperated over something, he would knock the script folder from his hand. Instead of flaring back, time and again he simply stooped to retrieve his scattered papers, staring up with the moist, mute apprehension of a whipped dog. Once or twice I saw Dwan punch him hard on the upper arm or grab a pinch of flesh and twist. Obviously physically pained, he kept grinning and accepted what Dwan dished out, as if humility were part of the job. The situation always struck me as odd. Why the man never fought back escaped me. Enduring physical mistreatment was not, so far as I knew, required by anybody.

☆

Rebecca of Sunnybrook Farm proved memorable for me less because of what happened on the set than away from it.

Uncle Billy sent a telegram saying he was en route by rail. Uncle Billy and Mother got on famously from the start when they discovered their mutual dislike of air travel. He always made the long trip to California by train, despite studio joshing that when his day came, he would go no matter where he was. According to *Mister Bojangles*, by J. Haskins and N. R. Mitgang, his reply was agreement, but "I don't plan to be up there on the pilot's day!"

"From the bottom of my heart to the *soul* of your feet," his message read, and when he arrived he had with him a special charm bracelet gift for me depicting himself with a cane and bowler hat and inscribed to his "best and smartest girlfriend."

Most relationships spawned on movie sets are thin as a slice of film, but Uncle Billy and his wife, Fannie, had been frequent guests at my parents' Sunday buffet dinners. Although I had never been invited to their home, it was a social curiosity not particularly strange as our guests seldom invited us back anywhere.

Photographically, however, I was all over Uncle Billy's home. Wrote one Harlem reporter:

The walls of his den are completely blanketed by autographed pictures... Katharine Hepburn, FDR, Marilyn Miller, Mae West, James Cagney, each inscribed to Bill. For each one of those others there are two of Shirley Temple. Shirley standing in one of Bill's shoes, presenting him a watch, another writing a letter together, and so on. In his living room there is a striking absence of photographs, except for one of Shirley and Bill in a silver frame, and looking down from the mantel one other, a dainty miniature of Shirley in a blue poke-bonnet.

In our current film the finale was a military crescendo performed to "The Toy Trumpet," the chorus costumed in striped pants, brass buttons, crossed brassards, and golden epaulets. To teach me the routines, Uncle Billy came down to the Desert Inn in Palm Springs, where we were nursing Mother's nagging bronchial cough.

Originally established as a recuperative sanitorium for tuberculosis patients in the warm dry desert air, by mid-1930 the Desert Inn was transformed into a playground for the healthy. A staff of two hundred attended the needs of two hundred guests. Comprised of a main building and detached cottages sprawled at the rocky toe of Mount San Jacinto, it slumbered in its own oasis under a kindly desert sun. It was here that Albert Einstein had tried unsuccessfully to explain to me why all energy in the universe is indestructible, an exercise which had left me skeptical but Einstein with a beatific smile of confidence.

That Uncle Billy was coming to the Desert Inn merited no second thought. Lots of Hollywood people did. Paulette Goddard was there wearing a racy black bathing suit and motherly attitude. In her charge were the two youthful sons of actor Charlie Chaplin, Sidney and young Charles. Although both boys had been to one of my birthday parties, I was wary of them because they had eaten the real flowers used to decorate my cake. Goddard wasn't their real mother, they whispered, only someone who used to live at their house. Their real mother still didn't live at home with their father either, but another woman was living there now. As a plot, I regarded it as confusing and dull.

Uncle Billy had arrived at midday at our bungalow. Our practice routine was long, incorporating jazz and blues with complicated nerve taps, all in an unbroken sequence. Even when we did the film I got a charley horse. Hobbling to the edge of the stage, I stood on one leg while Mother kneaded my thigh. In the resultant *Time* magazine cover photo, Mother's back blanked my face, leaving only my plumed hat and childish rump visible.

By early evening Uncle Billy and I were finished with practice. "What cottage are you staying in?" I asked him.

"Just staying . . . around," he replied casually.

After a moment I repeated my question. "Well," he said with a smile. "I'm staying alongside the entry road. You know, above the drugstore."

The annex quarters he described were reserved for hotel employees and personal servants of guests. "But that's where the chauffeurs sleep!" I protested.

"That's it," he exclaimed, as if making a sudden discovery. "The chauffeurs' quarters."

"But *you're* not a chauffeur." I was perplexed.

"Now, darlin'," he said reassuringly, "don't you fret. I've got a secret!"

"What?" I asked expectantly.

He leaned down, head cocked, and whispered, "I may be staying in the chauffeur quarters"—he paused—"but *my* chauffeur is staying there too!"

All secrets were good, but his message was unclear. Everyone was different, that I well knew, whether by sex, color, appearance, ability, or occupation. But I was unknowledgable of the reality that racial prejudice was part of a complicated and powerful social system that enshrined such inequity.

Also offstage *Rebecca of Sunnybrook Farm* gave me a short-lived career as a musician. Woven into our finale was a musical number played by the Raymond Scott Quintet. Following rehearsal, I had drifted up to drummer Johnny Williams, who showed me how to thump the bass drum, handle drumsticks, and clang cymbals. I loved those traps at first sight. Noticing my aptitude, Dwan decided to add a vignette to the film where I would play drums with Scott's musicians, and he ordered a set of traps delivered to the cottage for practice.

While waiting their arrival I had time to reflect. Playing musical instruments was not my strong point, starting with the diminutive three-octave pump organ in the cottage which had stood almost unused until Metropolitan Opera soprano Rosa Ponselle had visited.

"I'll sing and play," she had said in a voice like a controlled echo, "and you pump."

Spreading her hands, she had struck a heroic chord, then sung, *"Pace, pace, il mio dio..."* in powerful tones, her painted fingernails clicking across the keys, while I irreverently recalled Walt Disney's operatic hen who had trilled until she produced an egg.

"May I someday have the thrill of singing you to sleep," boomed Ponselle. I winced. "And next time may I bring my singing dog?"

The puppy proved small and friendly, formed his upturned lips into a tiny circle, and howled. It was a remarkable duet by a diva and her dog, but added nothing to my piano skills.

Later the studio had replaced the organ with an upright piano. Squeezed into my lunch hour, voice coaches came to the cottage for rehearsal instead of tying up a whole rehearsal hall. It was a deft studio move—cost reduction and some weight control, all at one blow.

Later a piano teacher appeared, Allene Chaudet, with her tweeds and her hair shingled up the back. Despite regularly getting my knuckles rapped, I never mastered reading music, simply memorizing her songs by laboriously picking out the notes by ear when she had left.

The end came during one lesson when she opened some untitled sheet music and bade me play. It looked familiar, so I began and continued almost flawlessly until the end. Unfortunately what I had played was Mendelssohn. The sheet music on the stand was Brahms.

Williams finally had set up my drums in our kitchenette and every noontime thereafter came over to demonstrate some new trick—how to crisscross my arms while drumming or some rapid-fire sequence on cymbals, bell, and wood block. Thumping and clanging was dessert to me, but Mother just got headaches. The more proficient I became, the more she despaired, finally complaining to Dwan that my posture was unladylike, sitting there with legs apart, bouncing around and banging at cymbals.

As usual, Dwan tried to persuade her otherwise. "Whenever I wanted anything from Shirley," he said, "I looked to the Mother. I'd seen it before with Mary Pickford and *her* domineering mother. Shirley was the product of her mother, the instrument on which she played."

Playing on me was of course not her problem, but *stopping* me was. An unexpected assist came from screenwriters trying to concentrate in neighboring bungalows who formally petitioned Zanuck to throttle my noise. The film sequence was scrubbed, and drumsticks and traps disappeared, a donation to the local boys' club.

☆

Shortly after this sad ending, nine men had appeared at our cottage gate, each wearing a snap-brim hat and with eyes slitted and stern. J. Edgar Hoover entered alone, a suddenly smiling man with dark wavy hair, while the others remained outside.

"I know about you," I said approvingly, "from *Gangbusters* on radio."

Hoover looked pleased. "And I've heard about your police department."

"Do you have a pistol?" I asked.

"No, but I brought you this." He opened a finger-sized leather bag. "A Minox camera, just like G-men use to take secret pictures."

"You should have brought me a tommy gun," I replied.

"Instead I've come to get your fingerprints," he said, laying out a card and ink pad on the tabletop. "Get up in my lap."

During the early 1930s big-time white-collar crime was minor, drug traffic tiny, and both blackmail and brothels regarded as local problems. Brutal kidnappings, however, had multiplied into an epidemic and bank robberies flourished like weeds. Into this freewheeling maze of crime and corruption had stepped Hoover, fresh from cleaning out the politicized and demoralized old Investigative Bureau of the U.S. Department of Justice. Now he had become the single-minded personification of the new Federal Bureau of Investigation, his job and his vanity.

Hoover understood how to manipulate the subtle levers of bureaucratic politics, having already bent publicity to his personal advantage with public enemies like Pretty Boy Floyd and Baby Face Nelson. His next target could have been "pretty baby" Temple.

From jawline to closely cropped dark hair, his whole impression was square. Long, level black eyebrows almost met over his nose, and his eyes showed white all around as they moved back and forth like a falcon's.

As he inked and rolled my thumb in its allotted square, I asked, "Are you married?"

"No, I live with my mother," he replied.

"Then I'll kiss you," which I did—the start of a long, close friendship.

Later we met at the Hotel Ahwahnee in legendary Yosemite Valley. There we watched the traditional evening firefall, caused by pushing a blazing signal fire off the crest of Half Dome mountaintop, sending a flickering cascade of sparks plunging earthward as embers ignited and died in their twisting descent toward the valley floor hundreds of feet below.

Hoover's lap was outstanding as laps go. Thighs just fleshy enough, knees held calmly together, and no bouncing or wiggling. One arm circled me protectively, and mine curled around his neck as I rested my cheek against his. For me the whole FBI was romantically encapsulated in his strong, quiet presence.

Following him around the golf course, I devised little disruptive actions, such as suddenly bolting across his line of sight as he lined up a putt. Along the fairways newly planted saplings were enclosed by narrow, tall tubes of wire fencing to discourage foraging animals. In retaliation for my bothersome conduct Hoover directed an accompanying agent to put me inside one of those wire jails.

"These are to keep deer out," I protested, wiggling my fingers at him through the mesh of my cage.

"Wrong!" he shouted. "It's to keep skunks like you in. The FBI always pens up skunks."

From that moment on Hoover sent me skunks. Skunks of cloth, skunks of glass, pictures of skunks. Big ones and tiny ones. The miniatures joined Mother's collection of animal figurines. The others piled up or were put away. Obviously once Hoover settled on a skunk, he never let the person forget it.

Shortly after Hoover's initial studio visit, Zanuck's secretary called to tell us that he was bringing over Vittorio Mussolini, son of the Italian dictator.

Mother was agitated on two counts. Much earlier my forthright solution to the Italian invasion of Ethiopia, simply to order Mussolini to stop, had been widely reported, and had resulted in her rejection while seeking Il Duce's autograph. Second, the unprecedented visit by Zanuck himself to our cottage filled her with anxiety. He was omnipotent but remote to our daily lives, and for him to visit was uncomfortably like an inspection for unknown purposes.

The epitome of casual California living, shirt open-necked, trousers double-pleated, and white kid shoes, Zanuck came striding in the lead, swinging his truncated polo mallet, trailed by Mussolini and a gaggle of studio staff. A blocky man, Mussolini scowled as he approached, walking with head thrust forward, looking down.

We met them at the gate.

". . . the son of Italy's ruler," announced Zanuck, with a backhanded sweep. As they walked up my path Mussolini's shoes made an unstealthy scritch, scritch sound.

Adulation or even curiosity was probably not the reason for Mussolini's visit, but pure politics. Hollywood producer Hal Roach had just negotiated a deal with Il Duce to film four operas in Italy, apparently undeterred by the 1936 Italian state banning of both Warner Bros.' *The Charge of the Light Brigade* and Twentieth Century-Fox's *Lloyds of London* on grounds that they were British propaganda. Reflecting a political tilt, Roach was reported combative toward Hollywood leftist intellectuals who were decrying Fascist Italy.

"Suave, gay dogs outwardly," he had complained, "but inside they are bitter and hate the film industry. They get a curious satisfaction by uttering Marxist phrases while drinking from long-stemmed champagne goblets."

Some speculated that the Mussolini visit, by displaying how reasonable Italians could be in the flesh, would blunt criticism and encourage
Hollywood cooperation in distributing Roach's four films. Naturally no
mention of this subject occurred, as Zanuck talked about moviemaking
and me and Mussolini sat almost silently, as if he either did not care
or could not understand English very well. As Zanuck referred patron-
izingly to the films I "had helped him make," Mussolini regarded me
impersonally, as if the visit was boring at best and irrelevant at worst.
Impatiently smoothing at his wavy black hair, he was the first to rise,
signifying an end to the visit. Nodding a single unsmiling good-bye, he
thrust out his chest and was gone, shoes still squeaking. Mussolini was
right. The visit was boring.

A curious aspect of *Rebecca of Sunnybrook Farm* was that it bore slight
resemblance to Kate Douglas Wiggins's original story, or even to Mary
Pickford's 1915 interpretation. All that was left were the title and the
names of the characters. This fact, together with its resounding box-
office success, must have convinced the studio that a program to repeat
me in Pickford classics was not requisite to my success, for that strategy
abruptly sank from sight. Screenwriters Harry Tugend, Rian James, and
Larry Rhine were assigned to prepare an original story in a modern
setting.

Despite the erratic switch in plans, Zanuck oozed compliments.
"Shirley Temple is endless. I'm knocked dead," he said. "It's beyond
the case of being a freak. I always thought when we dropped the curls,
this is the end, the gold mine has gone dry. Now, she's good for years."

Not everyone agreed. One national news critic observed, "She is
one of the most prodigious, unfailingly unbearable examples of infan-
tilism and bad taste in moviegoing masses."

Although my trail was meandering and public opinion divided, a
world of professional achievement still seemed ahead—certainly not
an ash heap.

18

S o this is where things stood four years after I crawled in under the Fox tent flap, a total stranger.

For a third consecutive year my name topped the 1937 Exhibitors' Box Office poll of popularity, trailed by Clark Gable, Robert Taylor, and Bing Crosby. None of us appeared on the U.S. Treasury Department list of top earners among actors and actresses. Although I was top box-office draw in the nation, my $112,500 salary was only one-third the $370,214 paid Gary Cooper, who rated only ninth. Popularity seemed unrelated to salary.

Japan had another notion of where the sacred cows were trudging. By the end of 1937 my name had dropped from first to seventh in Japanese box-office ratings, ". . . not so much from diminished popularity," explained the analysts. "It's the sameness of her vehicles. And the fact that events in Japan have turned our fans to sterner stuff."

In another sort of forecast the Bloomington, Illinois, Better Movies Committee, typical of local volunteer watchdogs, declared my pictures no longer fit for children because "there are too many adults in them."

Despite such straws in the wind, 240 million people, twice the population of the United States, had queued up for my films. An $11 million flood of products bearing my name and likeness were providing jobs and paychecks to manufacturers, tax revenues to the nation, royalties to me, and apparent satisfaction to consumers.

Numbers and magnitudes mean little to a child, particularly when they refer to the past. What was really important was a biblical downpour which struck California in March of 1938, producing widespread floods. Trapped in their ground-level hutch, six of my bunnies drowned. A studio gardener helped me scrape shallow graves in a patch of higher ground, and I solemnly arranged each tiny bedraggled carcass, head and paws arranged in an attitude of peaceful sleep. Leaving the gardener to cover the sad scene with soil, I slowly walked back to the porch, my shoes squishing in the mud.

By movie standards my next film, *Little Miss Broadway*, was unfailingly bland. Both the substance of the screenplay and its modest budget alarmed Mother, and one day her irritation overflowed. Dancer George Murphy, later a U.S. senator, had created the problem that so annoyed her. Detecting clumsy movement in the choreography of "We Should Be Together," he demonstrated his solution to dance directors Nick Castle and Geneva Sawyer with a short sequence of taps and turns.

Finally I piped up, "I think it should be changed, too. My *incense* tells me it's wrong!" Mother disagreed.

"Now she's got to learn a brand-new dance for the final scene. They just threw out the old one after everything was set. It's a good thing she loves this business. I'm the one it drives insane!"

Her annoyance was needless. As cameras rolled Murphy and I whirled around chairs and tables, and ended with a quick dancing run up and down a broad stairway. The watching crew burst into applause and called for an encore. The orchestra agreed, so everyone repeated the whole thing, this time purely for fun. Mother was right. I did love the business.

When director Irving Cummings called for a break Murphy stopped, but I kept on dancing by myself. Klammy called, "Come on now, Shirley," her clarion call for schoolwork, so I followed her off, continuing my solo and spinning through an archway with my skirt swirling about my hips.

Mother was watching. "She likes that skirt," she mused. "She can make it switch right up!" She had me right all the way.

The change from dancing to arithmetic was abrupt, but not difficult. To make my requisite staccato switches between stage and school, it helped to be able to keep separate activities within sharply defined mental compartments. After crying convincingly onstage, I could then quickly pull a prank, do a puzzle, or plunge directly into school lessons. Each activity dwelled comfortably in a cell of its own definition. Moving from one activity to the next was effortless. Picking up a new task simply meant leaving another sealed in its own vacuum. Freed from the mental and emotional impediment of overlapping concerns and divided attention, I simply clicked back and forth between activities.

One of these might have been eating. Several days before I had met socialite-entertainer Elsa Maxwell, a woman of mountainous spirit. "You and I have the most enviable positions in Hollywood," she had gushed. "We don't have to diet." Upon reflection I wasn't sure it was a compliment. My clothes were indeed tighter here and there, probably because I was outgrowing them. Mother speculated I might have a thyroid deficiency which could be cured by a pill. Tested, I turned out to be boringly normal. Perhaps it would help if I ate less of everything, she concluded, and nothing of some things, like candy.

Even Zanuck had begun to notice. Reviewing photos of me in proposed costumes, he observed, "You've got her looking like Mae West. Give her a streamline. Minimize her, back there. What do they feed her, Hershey bars?"

However therapeutic, the candy prohibition redounded. In the New York State Supreme Court the National Confectioners Association, an amalgam of 375 candy-makers and merchants, filed a half-million-dollar damage suit against the studio, claiming my dialogue in *Rebecca of Sunnybrook Farm* had implied I regarded candy bars as unfit food. Since others viewed me as a role model, it was claimed, the candy industry had been economically damaged.

"Say nothing to anybody," a studio lawyer admonished me.

"What if I told the truth, that I love candy?" I asked.

He stared, eyes like two dried prunes. "Not one word," he growled.

Murphy spoke so glowingly about our show to his actress-dancer friend Joan Crawford that she asked to come see for herself. A vagrant breeze outside had resettled her broad-brimmed picture hat, so as she entered she was still making minor adjustments to a black ribbon tied beneath her chin.

"Do you like candy?" she asked, presenting an elaborately decorated box of Austrian chocolates, "or do they make you fat?" I winced. At least Mother could eat them, I reasoned, and turned away to place the unopened gift on a chair.

"She takes my breath," Crawford was exclaiming. "What a shame for us to take the money." She was another of those adults who conversed while ignoring my presence. "Why, that child gives us cards in spades. I feel like a silly slug!"

No less apt self-description could be conceived for a woman so impeccably groomed and acutely self-conscious about every fold in her skirt. Her elbow-length black gloves were constantly being adjusted so as to be absolutely even, and her mannish suit of jet black elegantly framed the large golden cross suspended at her bosom. Altogether she was a beautiful and incandescent person, picture-postcard perfect.

Several weeks later Crawford visited me at home, herding two of her adopted children and trailed dutifully by current husband Philip Terry. Each child performed like a programmed wind-up toy. I had turned on my radio and was conducting a tour in my room. Christina cracked my closet door open and peered inside.

"Look at all those clothes!" she exclaimed.

"Those aren't clothes. They're costumes," I corrected, pushing the door closed.

Crawford was examining the shelves crammed with all Mother's fragile glass miniatures, but holding little Christopher by the hand. Without warning he drew back his fist and punched her hard on the thigh. Reaching down, she slapped him on the cheek, and of course he let out a wail which gained everyone's attention.

"He struck me," Crawford looked pleadingly toward her husband, "he struck me!"

On the radio Gene Autry had just begun twanging a nasal campfire song, not my favorite, so I raced across the room to turn him off. It was just as well the tour reached an abrupt end. Christopher was twisting on his mother's arm, and Christina had disappeared into my bathroom.

Crawford must have wanted to be neighborly. Late one evening her chauffeur delivered me a gift, a cocker spaniel puppy. It was lackluster and sleepy, so I cuddled it once, then put it in our laundry room with my own Pekinese, Ching-Ching II. By morning the puppy lay stiff and dead, gone with distemper. I had not even named it.

☆

In May 1938 the private world of Jackie Coogan split asunder, and in the process my parents were spurred to action. America gasped when Jackie, then twenty-three years old, broke and washed up, marched into court to sue his mother and stepfather, Arthur Bernstein, for $4 million, the total of his theatrical earnings, not one penny of which had he shared.

Coincidentally with Coogan's suit my parents and Twentieth Century-Fox amended the original provision of my contract relating to trusts. Future payments would now be made directly to my parents, not to the trustees. Father's partner, Ira Thomason, defended the change, saying, "In the future no one has any claim to the money, its investments, its proceeds, or disposition thereof . . . it eliminates any possibility of 'S' claiming any of [the money]."

Coogan's argument challenged California law derived from English common law written more than a century before. All income of minor children was given to parents to defray the expense of housing and clothing during minority. California failed to recognize any legal right of children to retain any portion of their childhood earnings.

That law was archaic, claimed Coogan, written when a child's earnings were a pittance, pennies for running errands or tending gardens. Movie industry earnings made the law a mockery. His earnings were what had kept his parents in a life-style their own skills could never have supported and enabled them to acquire capital estates in their own names. As for himself, he never had received anything beyond sheer necessities, and still had nothing.

Allegedly Jackie's movie contracts had never complied with the legal requirement for court approval. Although agreeing that Jackie's contracts were not binding without court approval, Coogan's mother claimed the approval process was less to establish a form of guardianship for the child than to protect the studio. Nothing in law, she claimed, was intended to safeguard a child's earnings for the child. That was left to parental discretion.

"Is it your position," queried Jackie's attorney, William Rains, "that all Jackie's earnings from any source during his minority belong to you?"

"That is the law, I believe," she had replied.

Ripples from the Coogan quarrel apparently splashed uncomfortably around my parents' ankles.

"That may be the law, but it is not our situation," Mother said. "Shirley's earnings are invested in three ways—paid-up annuities, government-guaranteed bonds, and bank-managed trust funds. The trusts will not all mature when she becomes twenty-one. Part will come then, another portion when she is thirty, and so forth every ten years thereafter. All are in Shirley's name," she said. "Under no circumstances can either I or Mr. Temple have access to her earnings. Besides," she added, "we already have more money than we need."

During the final stages of *Little Miss Broadway* wind machines set all the ceremonial flags and bunting gently swaying as our distinguished visitor Eleanor Roosevelt entered. Looking rather gray and bedraggled, she nodded and bobbed her way down our receiving line.

"I never realized before how the picture studios helped the employment problem," she exclaimed, regarding us with amazement. "What an army of workers!"

Following ritual handshakes and greetings, comedian Jimmy Durante asked her to dance. Neither looked very good, he shuffling back and forward while she attempted an impromptu hop-skip-and-glide maneuver. Despite low heels, she still loomed awkwardly above him, but she laughed and made refreshingly candid comments about her incompetence. That someone so eminent was prepared to meet our cast on gay, lighthearted terms came as a surprise.

"My first visit in Hollywood," she later wrote in her *My Day* newspaper column, "was with Shirley Temple, whom I had had the pleasure of meeting before. . . ."

Although gracious, the First Lady was in error. It was her first encounter with both Hollywood and me. Perhaps she had in mind a letter written by Mother after a Los Angeles celebration of FDR's fifty-sixth birthday and enclosing a slice of birthday cake. Politely acknowledging the note, FDR replied he had "eaten too much of it," but invited me to come see him if we ever visited Washington.

After her dancing demonstration Mrs. Roosevelt asked to see my schoolroom, so we climbed in my trailer and shut the door.

"Which do you like better, school or making pictures?" she asked brightly, seating herself on my little couch.

"I like them both," I answered. Her broad-brimmed hat looked smashed down on top. "But I guess I like geography best. Would you like to be a member of my police department? I'll give you a badge."

"I'd like two," she said, "for my grandchildren."

Never before having passed out badges as souvenirs, I hesitated. She was the First Lady, however, so I deputized her to faithfully inform her grandchildren of my rules, particularly the schedule of fines.

"Where does all the money go?" she asked.

"Into my milk fund," I answered. She looked puzzled.

"It's not really money for milk," I explained. "It's for teaching people to cook and make beds, like in the bungalow for Girl Scouts down in Santa Monica at Roosevelt School."

Brightening considerably, she glanced toward my bookshelves and asked which books I liked best.

"My autograph book," I replied, and immediately took it down and asked her to sign.

"I've left the top of the page for the President to sign someday," she said, returning my pen. "You do like dancing, don't you? I do too." She adjusted her fox-fur neckpiece. "I was so shy and awkward as a child, I thought dancing would increase my self-confidence. So I took ballet. I used to practice hard. That's why I appreciate the work that lies behind all your dances."

Continuing to speak of personal things, she recalled that when she was a child she dreamed impossible things, with a storybook quality.

"Is being married to a President like a storybook?" I asked.

She nodded, and then asked if I liked the President.

Not liking a President was something I had never even considered. "I like him because he starts all his radio talks with 'My friends,' " I replied.

A long black limousine was waiting for her departure. Bending down, she grasped both my hands. "Come to Washington and visit me," she said, and kissed me lightly on the forehead. Lots of visitors said goodbye like that.

With summertime fast approaching, Mother had announced plans for a motor trip to the East and Klammy quickly switched her curriculum to focus on the Boston Tea Party, Paul Revere, and George Washington.

"The wisest thing would be to stay home, but we like to travel like other people," Mother explained. "We will leave the same time Mr. Zanuck leaves on his vacation. Only we want to go up the Washington Monument and the Empire State Building, see Niagara Falls, and visit Montreal. Then maybe we'll find a hideaway in the Maine woods or return home by sea via Havana or Panama. A return motor trip will be rather strenuous and I'll need a rest."

"And I want to see Boston, where they poured the tea in," I added.

The studio dovetailed the Dionne Quints into this ambitious itinerary. Once before Zanuck had proposed a joint film with the Quints, an idea that foundered. When we would get to Callander, Ontario, he advised the proposal might be revived. By sheer good luck my director friend Allan Dwan would be there directing the Quints in their first film and singing debut, "All Mixed Up," a sadly apt title.

Since our vacation was being misread as a professional tour, financial offers for personal appearances quickly built to $350,000. As was their contractual prerogative, the studio methodically rejected each one. Mother had no difficulty supporting the decision.

"I have a horror of personal appearances and radio for Shirley," she said. "She is too young for such hard work."

Work really had nothing to do with it. She was fearful of anything "live." Weaned on moviemaking, where mistakes can be corrected by reshooting flubbed scenes and forgotten lines, Mother simply did not have confidence that I could escape some irretrievable mistake that would diminish my professional stature.

Among those with propositions, George Bernard Shaw cabled from London asking if I would assume the role of Cleopatra in his forthcoming London production of *Caesar and Cleopatra*. Suspecting some joke, a British theatre critic telephoned him for clarification.

"I have never seen Shirley Temple on screen," Shaw replied, "but I understand she is celebrated for playing juvenile parts."

"What about her American accent?"

"What about Cleopatra's accent?" retorted Shaw. "Nobody knows."

The critic would not be put off. "How old was Cleopatra when the action of your play takes place?" he asked.

"The Cleopatra I imagine was fourteen or fifteen years old."

"But Shirley Temple is only nine," observed the critic.

Shaw apparently was taken by surprise. "Even though I didn't know what an Egyptian girl was like at that age, I suggested Shirley Temple for the part." He paused. "Well, I *did* have an idea she was older."

Shaw's idea was stillborn anyway. British law prohibited children under sixteen from working onstage, one of the derivative principles which had come out during Jackie Coogan's lawsuit.

On the last afternoon on *Little Miss Broadway*, I was not surprised to be summoned back to the set. When a film budget was underspent, usually a cast party soaked up the remainder. Although it was only late springtime, we were decorated for Halloween, with corn husks, a crescent moon, and cutout owls. Everyone was there, cast and crew, wearing some scrap of goblin costume from the wardrobe department. Howls and caterwauling came from hidden speakers. Golden pumpkins and cardboard skeletons dangled. Owls hooted, wolves snarled, and false lightning flashed. Down from a catwalk crept a witch, outfitted with warts, pointy hat, brandishing a broomstick. From deep in the shadows came three other figures, masked and garbed in weird outfits, and trucking. Dance directors Castle and Sawyer were easy to identify, but only when they came within range and I fell in line did I recognize the third masked figure. The finger he held up in the trucking posture was black. My Uncle Billy was back, but, unknown to me, for a last time.

19

One of the triumvirate of screenwriters assigned to my next film, *Just Around the Corner*, came to the trailer to ask some questions and found me absorbed in painting a picture.

"Just a minute," I told him, "Mr. Farley is waiting for this airplane poster." The Postmaster General, whom I had met in Hawaii, had given me a job as a national sponsor of Airmail Week.

"Hurry up," he said.

"Don't rush me," I answered, continuing to paint. My progress in art had been marginal since *Mary Murphy and the Irish Potato*, a primer in which printed words were matched with tiny drawings. The prime virtue of my watercolor was originality, depicting me holding an envelope addressed to Farley and dragging a mail sack toward a waiting airplane with two protuberant engines. The wings drooped, causing *Time* magazine to later describe the plane as "a bug-eyed flying fish."

Printing my name carefully in a lower corner, I showed it to Mother. "There. *Now* do I get to fly in an airplane?"

"No," she said firmly. "You just be a sponsor on the ground."

"Well," I turned to the man in a spirit of resignation, "now I guess you can ask me your questions."

"What is the silliest question people ask you?"

"They all ask the same questions," I replied. "By this time they're all silly."

"Do they ever ask what you want to be when you grow up?"

"Always."

"What do you tell them?"

"I used to say a vegetable woman. Now I've got a much better idea. A G-woman!"

"You're not the type, Shirley," Mother interjected. "A G-woman would be tall and strong."

"That's why I'd make a good G-woman," I replied. "I'd fool the robbers. They wouldn't suspect me!"

Picking up a toy tommy gun someone had given me, I crouched and snarled, "This will teach you a lesson," then simulated a rat-ta-tat-tat as I sprayed the poor man with gunfire.

"That sure comes naturally," he said, hiding behind his raised arms.

☆

My pause between film assignments was usually brief, but being energetic as two squirrels, I found things to do. When I learned my next film would feature some dogs, leggy Afghans with soulful eyes, coiffed poodles, pinch-waisted greyhounds, and yappy terriers, I determined to get my own dog in the canine lineup. Ching-Ching I from *Stowaway* had expired under a careless heel at a veterinary hospital. Although Ching-Ching II was without film experience, director Irving Cummings agreed to include her as an extra at a beginner's salary of $5.00 per day. All she had to do was sit around with the other dogs.

Renting my property for props was nothing new, but as things turned out, assistant producer David Hempstead decided to expand Ching-Ching's part by having me bathe her. I balked.

"Five dollars is all right for an extra who does nothing," I told him, "but if she gets a bath, that means a bit part. She'll have to get more money." We settled on $2.50 additional. The haggling was enjoyable, but my request was a matter of principle. From observation I knew that any extra duty usually called for extra pay.

When the exact shape of *Just Around the Corner* appeared, what earlier had been only a gentle clang of alarm to Mother rose to a tumult. The plot was a political inanity in which I preserved capitalism with some timely song-and-dance. The hodgepodge cast included performers she characterized as "rubber-faced, rubber-bodied vaudevillians," plus a has-been or two, including Charles Farrell.

This was a switch. Ten years earlier Farrell had been one of her film idols. Since *Change of Heart*, four years earlier, he had been totally out of the limelight, his only notoriety, the origination of the "Folding Farrell" cocktail, now commonly known as a "bloody Mary." Located by director Cummings at the Racquet Club in Palm Springs, Farrell expressed surprise he was being sought.

"Why would Zanuck hire me?" he asked. "His studio *fired* me!"

Although Cummings prevailed with talk of a comeback, when Farrell accepted he was, ironically, cast as a failure.

Although Mother and I regularly shared such insights, I had little forewarning of how intensely she viewed the substance and casting of this film. One afternoon she returned to the cottage in an obviously agitated state and went directly to the medicine chest for her essence-of-peppermint bottle. She had just been to see Zanuck.

That she was even talking with Zanuck was big news. Years of intimate observation had made her familiar with tools and techniques of direction, recording, stage lighting, makeup, and costuming. Above all, she had a razor-sharp sense of what words and actions were appropriate to my age. However, much of this exquisitely honed judgment was destined by contract to exist in a vacuum, either unexpressed or ignored by uncommunicative directors and writers. Despite this fact, her leverage in the meeting just completed was impressive. Professionalism, a self-confidence born of financial security, and my top box-office standings were on her side. The studio still relied heavily on my success for its own. It was a combination of credentials warranting executive attention.

Apparently Zanuck had received her cordially and listened patiently. She had expressed the opinion that recent scripts were forcing me into rigid, stereotyped roles inappropriate to my growth. Typecasting in her view was one of the most persistent and destructive artistic traps. To seek Zanuck's agreement, she cited the early 1930s gangster phase, which he knew so well himself. For example she recalled how James Cagney's succession of brutal and vicious roles had so characterized him as a rough guy that when finally cast in a different role for *Mid-*

summer Night's Dream the public gave his new personality an indifferent reception.

Zanuck had cheerily admitted the sameness of my films. However, he noted the culprit was not typecasting but the star system. Studios were not organized by temperament or corporate interest to effectively nurture my growth, he declared, even if such was his personal desire. His studio was a production mechanism geared to produce a personality, or to capture one. His job was only to exploit that personality. When public tastes waned or changed, it was time to discard that personality and find a fresh one.

"Now she's lovable," he had said in a voice dead as dust. "The less she changes, the longer she lasts."

She felt as if struck by a rock, Mother recounted, dabbing some peppermint on her tongue. Zanuck had continued that audiences insist that their stars do not change. Public taste must be followed. He couldn't fashion it. His job was to make pictures that entertained. His only barometer was the number of people who bought tickets.

"You can't create a public fad," he had declared. "Once you have a fad, leave it alone."

To stress his point, Zanuck referred to his difficulty with Sonja Henie in *One in a Million*, when people were just getting the winter-sports craze. In cool northern countries it went okay, he said. In the south, it flopped. With her skates off she looked and acted like the "dame next door" so he'd told everyone to keep her on ice.

"Then we put her in *Thin Ice*; it caught the sports craze at its crest. Our longest run was in the Canal Zone! God, we had to sweat to make an actress out of her!"

Not sure she followed his logic, Mother asked, if he had been willing to change Henie from a skater into an actress, why resist moving me from baby girl to young womanhood?

Zanuck had ignored her question. Slanting off into the provisions of my contract, he said he could find nothing there to encourage Mother to concern herself with matters of artistic direction or control. It was a telling blow, and signified the end of their meeting.

An optimist at heart, Mother observed that by failing to indicate my subsequent film, he had left the door of hope ajar. Except for this glimmer, however, his volubility, obscure logic, and stinging contractual references had pushed Mother into a corner of exclusion and frustration.

What persuasive skill Mother may have lacked she made up for with a ladylike stubbornness. Deeply dissatisfied with the Zanuck visit, she decided to outflank him and take her observations directly to studio chairman Joseph M. Schenck, Zanuck's boss.

That meeting apparently went even more poorly than the first. Once removed from those production concerns which weighed so heavily on Mother's mind, Schenck greeted her entreaties with upturned palms of innocence and a grieved but helpless countenance. Schenck was sure Zanuck would do whatever he could. Pressed to intercede directly Schenck wound up expressing unequivocal support for his subordinate and refused to consider raising the matter with him. He was rock-hard and immovable.

Once again Mother returned to the cottage barely stifling tears. What she had devised as a clean surgical strike had obviously turned septic. With sharp tongues, icy eyes, and a double wave of executive wands, both Schenck and Zanuck had rendered her yearning for change irrelevant. Whatever the validity of her concerns, the twin assaults now made her part of the problem rather than its solution.

All I could do was share her obvious distress and hang on to her hand, while she uttered deep sighs and stared out the window.

Next morning outside the studio commissary we encountered Schenck walking the other way. A plain, oafish man, he nodded his head courteously and lowered his eyes, passing by in dignified, uncommunicative benevolence.

As a result of all this, Mother's attitude toward the studio suffered a noticeable change. Instead of bringing problems to heel, she now found herself being dragged along behind. So acute was her sense of failure that even disappointment drained away, leaving her in a thrall of acquiescence. Each of our minute decisions was soon being referred by her to studio staff for ultimate disposition.

An innocuous request from Mrs. Theodore Roosevelt, Jr., in New York, for example, asked if Mother would allow me to accept a doll's house from the Girl Scouts. It would be comparable to the world-famous Queen Mary's Doll House created in the 1920s by an army of English craftsmen, all its uncanny delicacy shrunk to the scale of one inch to a foot.

"The idea would be to make a really beautiful miniature home," Mrs. Roosevelt had written, "with design by a noted architect, and inside decoration by one of the best firms in New York... a work of art complete with electric lights that really worked. The house would be exhibited at the World's Fair in New York and afterwards presented to Shirley."

In her reply Mother hedged:

> The matter is up to the Fox legal department, which must give final approval. They advised that we couldn't work with all the requests and couldn't very well discriminate in favor of one without slighting others. As the decision of the studio is binding, I can therefore do nothing.

The studio said no. Undeterred, the World's Fair capitalized on my name in a contest involving 12,000 flowers from 150 growers. Top honors went to a spike of ruffled cream gladiolus crowned the Shirley Temple variety. The Owens-Illinois Glass Company was persuaded to erect an exact replica of the glass-block playhouse they had installed in our backyard. Outside stood an autograph "bar." For 50 cents a James A. Farley autograph could be purchased, or a J. Edgar Hoover or Eleanor Roosevelt. Clark Gable drew $1.00, Mahatma Gandhi $3.00, with all proceeds promised for his Indian Untouchables. Still uncooperative, the studio declined to release my autograph for sale.

In *Just Around the Corner* Uncle Billy and I did a closing number, rising and falling together on a hydraulically operated dance floor. Dressed in slickers and deluged under an artificial downpour we sang and danced to "I Love to Walk in the Rain." It was a literal watershed. We were performing in the movies for the last time, a moment which may have escaped us both. Leaving one final kiss on his shiny cheek, as I always did, I headed for my cottage and he toward the commissary. Later I was told that inside he paused to chat at the first circular table, where some other dancers urged him to sit. Declining with a customary chuckle, he had picked a single table against the back wall and eaten alone. There was one remarkable man, proud, self-contained and totally at ease with himself. Where he sat in life made no difference to him at all.

20

Early summer 1938 meant a studio shutdown for vacation. Embarking on a grand tour of Europe, Zanuck took along his wife and children, a maid, a governess, a press agent, and twenty-two polo ponies. We were off on a transcontinental motor trip, straight as an Indian arrow across America's midsection, with Father and Mother in the front seat and me alone in the back. A second car trailed us with the bodyguard Griff, Mabel, studio publicists, our baggage, a supply of Shirley Temple police badges, 2,000 still photographs, and 10,000 autographed cards.

Our trip had different objectives for those involved. For my parents it meant visits with my licensees in Chicago, Akron, and New York to help qualify the vacation as a tax-deductible business expense. For the studio my trip meant a carefully stitched network of newsworthy events, supported by advance men charged with arranging press contacts and local police protection. As a pot of gold at the end of our tour, I was scheduled to meet the Dionne Quintuplets.

"She is barely able to wait," read the studio release, "because playing with the Quints would be five times as much fun."

As what? I speculated, having little desire to play with five babies.

For me, the trip meant long hours in my solitary back seat wedged among games, books, and a special drop-leaf table. It meant doing the same sort of publicity I did all year at home. There was one new activity—steering things. I steered a donkey engine puffing up a narrow-gauge railroad to a Utah copper mine, and a steam engine on the cog railroad huffing our way up Pike's Peak as our whistle screeched out across the canyon.

In Chicago I steered a commuter train on the elevated railway. Visiting George Washington's home downriver at Mount Vernon, I steered a Potomac river launch. But when cruising around New York's inner harbor aboard Jock Whitney's motor cruiser, I had to fight to steer.

"A third of our immigrants entered through Ellis Island over there," Whitney had droned, steering away. "And there's the Statue of Liberty."

"Very nice," I said. "Doesn't her hand sticking way up there look like a man's?" Everyone looked so I squirmed between Whitney and his wheel. "May I steer?"

Swerving this way and that, all was fine until someone spotted a police boat nearby grappling for a corpse. When I went to the railing to get a better look, Whitney retrieved the wheel. Saying I was too young to see a dead man, he pushed up the throttle and sped away. I lost on two counts.

On the high seas traveling to Bermuda I steered an ocean liner, and while there a small launch, assisted by the owner's dachshund with his paws on the wheel. On a funicular leading from the dock 900 feet up a cliffside, I pulled the levers. I steered a horse hitched to a canopied surrey, a harnessed 600-year-old tortoise, and later in Boston a bona-fide police launch.

For someone with an instinct to steer, that summer was sheer heaven.

En route from California only three days, we came down out of the Rocky Mountains, traveling straight into the dust bowl of eastern Colorado and Kansas. The wind drove dense eddies of earth across the road while crowded jalopies with furniture and mattresses tied on top passed us headed westward. To protect Mother's hair from the hot, gritty air, we kept the car windows rolled up and put slabs of dry ice on the floor mats to cool us off as we drove.

At a filling station near Junction City, a reporter from the *Kansas City Star* caught up with us. "How do you like Kansas, anyway?" the reporter asked.

"Wonderful state," I replied, thinking how flat, dusty and empty it looked. "In *The Wizard of Oz* Kansas is the place where Dorothy was blown away from. By a cyclone."

Obviously disinterested in my comment, he asked for a topical picture. East of town on Highway 40, he stopped us beside the first photogenic wheatfield, and I was soon hip high in wheat kernels, straws, and beards. The photographer was shooting pictures rapid-fire.

"Just tell me 'when,' " I instructed. He was not playing fair.

"Go ahead and keep looking at the wheat," he replied, determined to get candid shots his own way. The shutter clicked again.

"Hey, you didn't say 'when'!" I protested.

"When!" he dutifully repeated, and took another picture.

"Do those wheat beards tickle your legs?" he asked.

"Not much," I answered, bending over. "The grass is sort of stickery, though."

He clicked without saying "when." That photo turned out to be my first cover on *Life* magazine, tantamount to publicity sainthood in those days.

Later an unhappy Kansas farmer complained the photo had been taken in his wheatfield.

"We love little Shirley," he wrote. "She would want us to have something. Give us a percent of what you got for the picture."

Free publicity is a commodity without cash value. What he sought was part of nothing.

Several days later, when approaching Washington, D.C., Father lost his way, providing me extra time to contemplate the press conference arranged at the Mayflower Hotel. Meeting reporters was nothing new, but I had been warned that the press corps in the nation's capital was somehow more aggressive than in Hollywood.

Press conferences are harder than one-on-one. Subjects shift instantly, rapport is difficult to sustain, and risks multiply as questions piggyback on one another. Weaned on a Hollywood press corps of over 450 accredited reporters, including sixty from foreign periodicals, grinding out 15,000 stories a year, I was no amateur. Early in the game Mother had stressed two inviolate rules of conduct with the media. One, I must be available, and two, I must respond. An evasive answer was acceptable, particularly in good humor, but unless leading the conversation afield, it would only buy time. Interjecting a "revelation" of some inanity was usually diverting, such scoops being like chopped liver for a kitty. But, above all, Mother urged, strive for control. Control of the situation, the pace.

I realized early in life that history in the raw is written by reporters, and, respecting such an objective, each encounter still served as a game no different from Chinese checkers or chess. Precisely the same as controlling the timing of an inoculation needle prick, my getting in charge with the press was critical. Of course within such rules lay room for both innovation and mistakes.

Once a reporter had asked my favorite comic strip. Actually it was a dead heat among *Skippy*, *Flash Gordon*, and *Tarzan*, but in a perverse mood I answered the *Katzenjammer Kids*.

He looked stunned. "Your *very* favorite?"

"Uh-huh," I answered. Actually it was Father who relished that strip, an unintelligible mix of puns and fractured German.

"But can you *understand* the *Katzenjammer Kids*?" the reporter bored in.

"I know Hans and Fritz."

"Why, it takes *experience* to know Hans and Fritz," he repeated incredulously. "All those outrageously clever plots to annoy their father the Captain. Always in trouble themselves or making trouble for others." Nodding agreement, I had stared back defensively.

"Can you understand all those words," he asked, "those queer ones, like 'dod-boggled'? Or mixed-up ones like 'Votder-dumgoozle'?"

Leaning against the arm of his couch, I was thinking hard. "I understand some of the words, sometimes all of them. Anyway my father explains them. Besides, I like jokes, even the ones I don't understand."

He was staring at me, dumbfounded.

"Can you play fish?" I asked. Manipulating interviews was easier to say than do.

On other occasions I had tried evasion, seasoned with a dollop of humor. Embarking on the SS *Malolo* for Honolulu the previous year, my brothers came aboard to say good-bye just as a reporter arrived.

"Try some new poses," he had urged, demonstrating.

"Some of them are goofy."

"Only this last day of work," he urged. "Then a whole month of vacation."

I beamed with anticipation. "I'm going to go native!"

"How will you like Hawaii after all the hard picture work you've done?" the reporter began. It seemed like a dumb start.

"Look, I lost a front tooth," I replied, smiling to display the gap.

Jack jumped in. "She doesn't talk much if she just meets you and you start asking questions," he explained. "Get her over a game of Chinese checkers. She'll talk your arm off."

The reporter had his own agenda. "Shirley, how do you like Hollywood?"

"I'm taking two trunks along, and I've got a book in one," I answered.

"Is that so?" he said with a grimace. "So, who's your favorite actor?"

"Black Beauty."

"Huh?" He looked gloomy.

"That's the book in the trunk. I've got a lot of clean hankies too."

He had started gnawing thoughtfully at his fingernail. Turning, he addressed George. "What do you want to be?"

"A veterinarian." The reporter had stopped writing. "Maybe it won't look so good in print," said George.

"What's that man doing up there with those birds?" I pointed toward the deck above.

"Carrier pigeons," the reporter replied. "See, he's fastening the other roll of pictures I just took onto the bird's leg. It'll fly them directly back to the *News*."

I grinned. "Maybe a newshawk will get the bird!"

Father was still lost trying to find his way to the Mayflower Hotel, and it was getting dark. Maybe the reporters in Washington would let me eat first. I was really hungry.

Two days earlier I had tried using my doll to divert the focus of another reporter's questions and thereby gain control. On this vacation I was traveling with two dolls, Susie Blockhead, a battered, scratched floppy favorite with loose elastics, and Jimmy, who enroute sun-blistered his face while sitting against a rock at the Grand Canyon. Now he was in Mother's suitcase, recuperating. At Marshall Field's department store in Chicago, Mother had purchased a girl replacement, beautifully coiffed and garbed and dubbed her Marsha after her origins. Pursued uncomfortably by one reporter, I had abruptly shifted the topic to my preference in dolls, and held up Susie Blockhead.

"Take her up on your shoulder," I said, a request with which he reluctantly complied after pocketing his pencil and notepad.

"There, see, her head falls on your shoulder, just like a real baby." He looked uncomfortable. "She may not be as pretty as Marsha, but she's very good to travel with. She has no hair to fix."

The press have not always found what they sought from me, nor have I been reported as I might wish. But over fifty-five years and several thousand interviews and news conferences, I am unaware of a single disastrous encounter with the media. Whether in parochial Hollywood, with more worldly press in Washington and the United Nations, or in Rome, Paris, London, or Beijing; whether in Moscow winter, steamy Africa, or remote Iran or Oman, or even while being interrogated by two Communist inquisitors posing as Czechoslovakian journalists, to this day each experience has always been exhilarating, often taxing, sometimes tiring, but never a drag.

By the time Father found the hotel, I was drowsy and bedraggled from our long day's drive. The reporters and photographers were there and insisted I be introduced even before going to our rooms. Sometimes life has no options. Carrying both my dolls I decided to do the best I could.

One reporter immediately suggested I pose in her lap "like Charlie McCarthy." Instinctively I knew it would be poor publicity to pose as a ventriloquist's dummy.

"I'm no blockhead," I cracked, "but here's one who is," and produced Susie, hoping to direct attention to a subject of my choice.

Another woman reporter then drew a silver cigarette case from her purse and casually held it open toward me. "Won't you have a cigarette?"

Obviously I sensed danger. "No, thank you," I replied; at least that was polite, adding "Marsha never smokes. In fact she has *no* bad vices." That got a laugh.

My wariness about smoking happened to be timely. Although health and tobacco had not yet been linked, the social acceptability of women smoking was a subject in fervent debate. Publication of my lighthearted response evoked a letter from a senior executive at the government National Research Council. "What a great example it would be for the world," he wrote, were I to "grow up to avoid the tobacco habit." The only women I had ever seen use tobacco were old colored women.

The first white woman I saw smoking was here in Washington. She was an actress. Now a lot of women smoke. Like sheep."

☆

J. Edgar Hoover's car picked us up, all seven and a half tons of it sheathed in armor and one-inch-thick bulletproof glass. His office was heaven. In a corner stood a tall American flag; plaques and garishly beribboned certificates plastered his walls, and an entrancing assortment of mysterious mementos was scattered on his desk and ranged along the bookcase. He pointed out two life-sized white plaster casts, identifying them as death masks of Pretty Boy Floyd and Baby Face Nelson. Never having seen a dead hoodlum, I examined each carefully, two pale old men, eyes closed and faces reposed in sleep.

Hoover was in command of the visit until I asked where his Shirley Temple Police badge was. Genuinely startled, he whispered something to an aide, then quickly redirected my attention to a giant billy club leaning nearby and asked me to heft it. I was about to return to my question when he proposed a tour of FBI headquarters, a public relations innovation commenced during the Boy Scout Jamboree the previous year. He personally escorted us up and down the file-case corridors where nine million fingerprints were on file, and through the identification laboratories, radio communication center, and physical fitness gymnasium, where at least I recognized familiar equipment, the barbells.

"About your badge . . . ," I began again. By this time his aide had retrieved it from Hoover's bedroom bureau and sneaked it into his hand. With a flip of his coat lapel, he demonstrated that everything was in order and turned us over to the director of the shooting range. This was even more to my liking than fingerprint file cases, microscopes, and radios. An instructor pointed toward one of the moving targets and handed me a gun. It was far too heavy for me to hold, so he propped the barrel on a chairback. Following instructions I pulled hard on the trigger. There was a shattering roar. I had missed the target completely, but the gun was still on automatic and as it recoiled, a trail of tracer bullets rose toward the ceiling.

The instructor had seized the gun. "Don't shoot up," he shouted above the dying echoes. "The Director's chair is just above us!"

While I was testing the FBI armory, President Roosevelt was also engaged in armaments, on a different scale. Plans had just been announced to construct four new battleships, four light cruisers, an aircraft carrier, and a fleet of destroyers and submarines. Complicating these warlike preparations, Ambassador Joseph P. Kennedy had just returned from London with a long, cheerless report about England's chance for survival if attacked by Hitler. Although keen to keep Kennedy's Irish-Catholic political prestige aligned with his views, FDR had just invited England's King and Queen to visit Washington, saying that America might soon be engaged in a life-and-death struggle and that Britain would be our first line of defense. Crammed among such concerns with military construction, threats of war, and Irish politics, somehow FDR found time to receive me.

At 9:30 a.m. on June 24 my parents and I passed through the White House guard post, and were greeted by presidential assistant Stephen T. Early, who asked us to wait until the President had finished his ceremonial signing of the Black-Connery Bill. The coincidence was startling. Elimination of American child labor was a linchpin in the President's legislative program. Borrowed from the English law, which had ruined George Bernard Shaw's offer to bring me to the London stage, FDR's law prohibited people my age from working at all. During congressional debate, however, an amendment had been attached which exempted all child performers in movies from the age limitation. Without inclusion of the so-called Shirley Temple amendment, a stroke from the President's pen would have put me out of work that morning.

Down the carpeted corridor we marched, past polished brass doorknobs, oil paintings of famous sea battles, and through a stream of people bustling around holding pieces of paper. Ushered past secretaries and into the Oval Office, we found FDR seated behind a big desk, so I came around and shook hands. A large man even in his chair, he was wearing a rumpled seersucker coat that didn't match his trousers, and he had jowls. A black Scottie was curled up nearby on the carpet, ignoring us all.

Whatever political ambivalence my parents may have felt about FDR, they were tongue-tied in his presence, standing stiffly until someone gestured for them to sit in the chairs pulled near his desk.

For a long moment he just held my hand and stared silently at me, waiting for me to say something. Looking sideways, I spotted a sailing-ship model. Noticing my glance, he asked if I liked boats.

"I like to fish from them more," I replied, and began to recount the salmon-fishing trip I had taken in Vancouver two years before.

"What kind of a hook did you use?" he inquired.

"I dunno. But I caught it."

Chuckling, he observed that sometimes ends were more important than means.

"Why aren't you smiling?" he suddenly inquired. "I thought you were famous for your smile."

"Smile for him," Mother urged, who up to then had said nothing.

"The reason is, I lost a tooth. See?" I pulled back the upper lip and went on to describe how the tooth had fallen out during a bite of sandwich. He threw his big head up and back and broke into loud laughter.

For me it was no laughing matter. The tooth had been left on my hotel bureau, later to go under my pillow for a "tooth fairy" reward. During my absence at the FBI maybe somebody had snitched it for a souvenir.

"It seems as if I have been losing teeth all my life," I said.

"That's the way with all of us," the President said, looking slightly uncomfortable.

Before I could ask about his dog, still asleep, it was time to go. Mother had brought along my autograph book, so locating the page where his wife had left room, he wrote, "For Shirley from her old friend."

"This is a very important book, now," I observed, shook hands, and left.

Outside in the hallway, we ran straight into Treasury Secretary Henry Morgenthau, who earlier had been among our visitors at the studio. As surprised as we, he invited us for lunch the following Tuesday, an invitation readily accepted.

"Did he like you?" Morgenthau asked, gesturing with his head toward the President's office through the open doorway.

"I don't know," I answered, "but I liked him."

He paused. "Do you still like yellow tomato juice?" he asked.

From deep inside the Oval Office we heard FDR's voice boom

impatiently. "Come on, Henry, there is always some woman holding you up. This is an important conference."

"Yes, Mr. President, but so is this one," Morgenthau called back. "I'm trying to find out what this lady wants for her lunch."

In the Secretary's private dining room, it was indeed butter-yellow tomato juice, and lamb chops. He ate with his fork in his left hand and used his knife to load it, upside down. Noting my stare he explained it was a European custom acquired when he lived in Turkey, where his father had served as U.S. ambassador.

"The President says you're a little diplomat too," he added. As if startled by his own remark, he turned to Mother. " 'Little Diplomat'! That's a good title for her next film."

On the road again and pointed northward toward New York City, I reviewed three things I wanted to do: first, visit Uncle Billy's home in Harlem; next, see the view from the top of the Empire State Building; and then a ride on a subway. I missed all three. Uncle Billy was in Hollywood opening a new dance studio and teaching tobacco heiress Doris Duke Cromwell to hula. The top of the Empire State Building proved to be closeted in fog. Subways were judged too dangerous. From my vantage point New York City had very little else to offer.

My bad luck almost changed one dinnertime when columnist Walter Winchell offered to take me on a night police patrol in his car, which was fitted with a red light and police radio crackling coded messages. A soft rain had just started, adding a spooky quality to what lay ahead.

Just as I was entering the car Mother pulled me back, saying it was past my bedtime. As consolation she offered to have Winchell's daughter, Walda, stay as my overnight guest in the hotel. Griff should take us back, she said, and with that she and Father joined Winchell in my place.

In the end it was Walda and I who had the fun. It was retribution that my parents spent three rainy nighttime hours cruising the streets, with nobody in New York misbehaving save one hapless drunk who was trying to force his way back into the Tombs jail to get shelter from the soaking rain.

At the hotel was where the action was. Walda was slightly larger than I and therefore contained more deviltry. After Griff closed us in the room, little time was lost. A heavy rain now slashed against the windowpanes and wind howled around corners. It was easy to convince ourselves the whole building was swaying in the storm. First came an exchange of the weirdest tales we could each recall. Then all available stock of hotel writing paper was consumed in inkblot contests, each interpretation more chilling than the last. The prize for the most horrendous tale was a forbidden Mrs. See's chocolate candy from Mother's secret supply.

Through the opened windows and past the ghostly dance of windblown draperies, we swirled paper airplanes made from pages torn from the telephone directory. Way down in the blustery darkness below secret accomplices awaited our messages. Room lights flashed on and off, hotel operators suffered anonymous screams and ghastly gargling noises over the phone, and in a crescendo we attacked each other in a water fight, creeping around the darkened room with full tumblers. In all this mayhem, Walda and I established a bond of friendship common to culprits the world over, while out in the hallway near our door Griff drowsed, his chair tipped comfortably to the wall.

Two days later, trailed by Fox Movietone News cameras, we visited Mrs. Eleanor Roosevelt at Val Kill, her 180-acre family estate at Hyde Park, eighty miles north from New York City. Calling on the First Lady required me to be in a starched frilly frock and white gloves. My lace purse was large enough for a customary hanky, my police chief's badge, and a favorite slingshot.

Val Kill actually is the name of a meandering brook bordered by water lilies which snakes past a small stone cottage containing a store selling pewter mugs and reproductions of Early American furniture. Mrs. Roosevelt's grandchildren, Sistie and Buzzie Dahl, were already splashing around in a swimming pond when we arrived.

She smilingly greeted us in a shapeless blue sundress cut loosely and low front and back, her hair concealed beneath a tied bandanna. Angular, thin, and informal, she looked at perfect ease in the woodland setting. She was not wearing either of the police badges I had given her during the studio visit, but I said nothing.

Well knowing that my curls and swimming did not mix, I chose to accompany Mrs. Roosevelt up a winding pebbly path on some errand to her house.

"You certainly have an unusual way of walking," she said after a moment, "swinging your arms in unison instead of in sequence."

I hadn't realized I was doing it. "My friends at home tell me it's a sign of being crazy." She looked at me, but said nothing, so I shifted to sequential swinging.

Her cottage fitted her appearance. A place of rustic simplicity, bare wood floors, and empty walls, it had no potted plants, knicknacks on tabletops, and not even a radio in sight. Upstairs, her bedroom was small, with only a narrow cot against one wall, a chair and bureau. Told she always got up early and made her own bed, I replied so did I. With a surprised look, she asked about our trip. Missing out to my parents on the police patrol through dangerous New York slums was still on my mind. Regarding me sympathetically, she agreed that whenever opportunity for broader experience arose, it should be grasped. Eternal contentment and stifled curiosity were, to her mind, fatal errors in living.

"But my father always said I had no right to visit slums for fear of bringing home diseases to my own children." Her voice was inflexibly gentle. "A wonderful man, so kind. He still seems alive, like someone in *The Blue Bird*'s Land of the Unborn Children." The reference was wholly unfamiliar, but the concept of such a land sounded spooky enough to remember a long while.

☆

Back near the pool the Fox cameramen were almost ready, engaged in their last-minute adjustments. As Mrs. Roosevelt and I waited at the lawn edge she seemed giggly and self-conscious, uncertain just what we should do, so I decided to help.

"We should start walking from way back here," I said, backing up a few steps, "then be waving at the camera when we come out." I demonstrated. "As we walk we can talk about flowers. When we pass them they'll still be following us, so then let's turn"—I showed her— "for a final wave together." She nodded agreement.

Next day in her syndicated newspaper column, she wrote her version of the moment: ". . . only Fox Films, with whom she is under contract, were allowed a few shots. I was amused when we walked out together for the first pictures to have her tell me just what to do."

With filming finished, I stayed with Mrs. Roosevelt as she was lighting charcoal in a portable brazier for our picnic.

"Where is your Shirley Temple badge?" I asked casually. Everyone had to keep their badge nearby, I said and reached in my purse to show her mine.

There were two badges, she reminded me, both already delivered to Sistie and Buzzie. Left them home in Seattle, the children answered when I asked. That means a fine, I said, so pay up. They both laughed, ran away, and jumped back into the pool.

Here was a serious problem. My force was no joke and the badges no everyday souvenir. It was a mistake to have deputized anybody else to explain obligations and penalties of membership. Confronted by hilarity while exercising proper authority of leadership left me privately annoyed and thwarted. Mrs. Roosevelt had gotten me in a fine pickle.

Everyone had by then congregated at the barbecue while the cooking meat sizzled and sputtered, sending up puffs of white smoke. "The children watched their chops broil," she later wrote, "and worried over the chance of their burning. I have never yet mastered the art of removing enough fat to prevent my charcoal fire from flaming up again as the fat burns."

Standing back from the fire, our hostess had to reach far forward with her fork to turn our chops, and when she did her sundress hiked up in the back. The target was irresistible, the range only a few paces, and the badge fiasco still rankled me. Edging backward a step, I slowly stooped and picked up a small rounded pebble. The slingshot was easy to slip out of my lace purse. Everyone was watching her, not me. Taking a quick sight along the fully extended elastic bands, I let fly. Bulls-eye!

Mrs. Roosevelt straightened with a jerk, holding her long-handled barbecue fork thrust upward like the Statue of Liberty. With the other hand she reached around in back and smoothed her dress over the target area. She never even glanced over her shoulder.

Nobody mentioned anything about the pebble during the rest of our visit, and even I had almost forgotten about it when the door of our New York hotel clicked behind us. But not Mother, who had seen it all. Brattish, she said. Quickly crossing the room, she spun me around and slapped me hard on the bottom, right where I had hit Mrs. Roosevelt.

"See how *you* like it," she scolded, and slammed the bathroom door behind her. My first physical punishment since babyhood spanking, it left me feeling younger, not older as I wished. Yet I had no regret. Mine was in defense of a worthwhile, moneymaking organization, in support of its rules, and to rebut a challenge to my authority. Nobody seemed to understand this, except me.

The whole incident was tactfully ignored by Mrs. Roosevelt, who summarized our visit saying, "All of us here are wishing for chances in the future to meet again. A well-brought-up, charming child is a joy to all who meet her. I have an idea whatever she does, she is always going to be a leader," she added with typical grace. "If I were asked to pick out the thing most characteristic of her, it would be her walk."

Within days my peculiar walking habits had a new twist—sea legs. Over a gentle ocean our two-day voyage to Bermuda was all bingo, shuffleboard, and mingling.

"Why does she hide all day under that bandanna?" asked fellow-passenger Vincent Astor, scion of the eminent New York family. A tall man with a large head and thick lips, he moved with a jerky motion, toes pointed outward like an awkward penguin.

"She feels the heat," Mother said. "It keeps her neck cool."

Actually it was because she insisted.

Astor's trousers had a tiny watch pocket at beltline with a hanging black-ribbon fob. Black connoted respect for the dead, he explained, pulling out a thick gold watch that had been found on the floating body of his father, drowned in 1912 when the SS *Titanic* sank after striking an iceberg. At his Bermuda estate Astor had a dachshund. Would I like to visit him?

Thinking about dogs made me lonely for Ching-Ching, boarding in a kennel. I told Astor the keeper had written that she rated "A" for politeness. "That's very important news," I said.

"Why?" he asked, cupping one ear with his palm.

"If she's polite, she'll be popular. If she's popular, she'll be happy. Nobody can be happy if people don't like you."

Wanting to be liked was one of my personal ingrained objectives. Not only was approval a step to happiness, but also a measure of professional success. Approbation served both, and had become a credo with implications beyond movie polls and fan mail.

It was not only people, I even wanted animals to like me. And other things, like that octopus in Hawaii. When I had rapped on his aquarium he sprang forward through the water, his domed head almost colliding with the glass. For a moment he stared at me, tentacles pulsing.

"He's watching your blond curls," said the attendant.

"He wants to kiss you," said Mother sweetly.

With one silky, slippery turn, he fled to the back corner of his tank, crouched to gather his tentacles then repeated his sudden rush toward my face.

His second charge made me step back quickly. "If he doesn't stop trying to kiss me, he'll get a sore nose!"

Rolling suddenly, he slipped sideways and expelled a dense cloud of black ink, which instantly obscured the tank.

"Well," said the attendant, "that proves he doesn't like you."

The attendant's conclusion was received as a harsh blow. To be liked was akin to respect. To be disliked, even by an octopus, was the same as an absence of respect.

As I was recounting the tale of the octopus to Astor, we kept eye contact. I thought he understood until he said he didn't care whether octopuses liked him or not.

Somewhere during my story he had fallen silent, staring down where the water slid by the ship's skin, his thoughts ambling away on their own. Looking at moving water is always a good place to think.

Winterhaven, the Bermuda home of Gertrude Lawrence, lay several miles distant from our hotel at Castle Harbor. By edict, no private automobiles were permitted on the island, so when we went to luncheon our taxi was horse-drawn, a vintage carriage with canvas parasol roof and yellow fringe. Sitting behind seemed too regal for my taste, so I got up on the postern beside the driver, a painfully courteous black man dressed in creased white clothing and a spotless panama. It turned out he knew all about my friendship with Uncle Billy and soon he gave me the reins.

Driving anything is more fun than being pulled along behind. As we clop-clopped along the twisty lanes toward Hamilton Town, nobody except me knew I was in charge, certainly not the horse.

Griff, the bodyguard, was pedaling his bicycle too far behind to intercept the barefooted boy who darted from a roadside hedge and began trotting alongside the carriage.

"I know the story of Wee Willie Winkie," he called up, and began reciting it from the start. A mile farther down the lane he was still jogging along at my elbow, and still loudly recounting details of the plot.

"I know the whole story," I finally called down, and flipped the reins to speed up our horse. If we went faster at all, the boy increased his pace to match, and kept up his soliloquy until we finally reached the gate of Winterhaven.

Restrained by Griff against following farther, he stood by the gatepost, calling after us. When his voice faded in the distance he had only gotten as far as the sword swallower at Koda Kahn's mountain palace.

Why Lawrence was curious about me may have stemmed from having made her own first stage appearance at age eight. Her *Tonight at 8:30*, with Noel Coward, performed two years earlier, had set the public tone for sophisticated love talk, as had her recent Broadway success, *Private Lives*. As things turned out, however, she was far more a playful kitten than big-city sophisticate. Kicking off her shoes, she chased me around the flower beds, ignored my parents, and wound up doing somersaults with me on the lawn. At her urging I got astride while she crawled around on all fours like a pony, uttering acceptable neighs until at last we collapsed in one mirthful heap, her shapely legs sticking out of her silk trousers, toes pointed toward the blue Bermuda sky.

Like most people, she seemed to have more than one personality. On the return New York sailing of the SS *Monarch of Bermuda* we were passengers together. Vanished was my informal and playful companion, the sloppy lounge clothes, and bare feet. Instead she appeared in a svelte leopardskin outfit carrying a see-through Lucite purse, and with tiny bells on her shoes jingling her presence.

At an evening showing of *Little Miss Broadway* in the ship's lounge, we sat beside each other. Even though she applauded politely, I felt as uneasy watching the film as I had in making it.

"I'm really sorry about this," I whispered. "There are some parts I'd like to do over again." Awe in the presence of one so exalted in the theatre had little to do with my expressed regret. I knew I should have done far better.

Once again landed in New York, Lawrence invited me to luncheon, and afterward I wrote down some comments about my regret that Lawrence's informality had vanished.

By nature Miss Lawrence is extemely nervous and has a habit of thinking that people are always staring at her. (This habit is acquired by most celebrities.) Miss Lawrence felt that people were staring at her during luncheon, and therefore she felt it necessary to put on a little show for them. She was wearing a dress of the very latest style, with loose drapes in the skirt, neck and sleeves. She was lavishly using her hands to push up her sleeves and readjust her respective drapes. Instead of sitting back and enjoying her little show, I had to interrupt her by saying, "My, you seem uncomfortable, Miss Lawrence, it must be because your dress doesn't fit too well."

Lawrence was simply another person, susceptible to the sardonic barbs of a ten-year-old. These, I confess, had too sharp an edge, as when I had once testily retorted to Grandmother Maude that I wanted her false teeth after she was dead.

Although *Little Miss Broadway* was courteously received at our shipboard viewing, except for me, from London came a negative reaction.

"Barbarism" wailed the London *Sunday Times*. "We resent cruelty in children and deplore its encouragement. Shirley pushing the manager of the flats into a swimming pool, and laughing her head off at his discomfiture. The same poor fellow shoved into the dirty linen closet . . . locked up . . . made a gull . . . the whole film cheapens Shirley by using a vulgar and cruel medium."

Also from England came a statement by Zanuck, then still vacationing in Britain. My next film would not be *Susannah of the Mounties*, as planned, but *Lady Jane*, a recent novel by C. V. Jamison set during Victorian times in New Orleans. Both titles came as total surprises to me. Following completion of *Lady Jane*, Zanuck announced that I would "tour the whole British Empire."

Reading in newspapers about my next film and associated promotional travel plans could only have emphasized the widening gulf between Zanuck and Mother. However, she said nothing, except to express the hope that neither film would continue the typecasting she so deplored, and that long trips were not as satisfying as they seemed.

Before departing New York for Boston we were breakfasting in the Waldorf-Astoria Hotel dining room.

"This applesauce tastes rotten!" I blurted.

Several nearby diners turned, regarding our table with annoyed breakfast expressions.

Mother grimaced and leaned over. "Eat it," she hissed, so I did.

We were driving along near Greenwich, Connecticut, under a lowering sky when from the back seat I yelled that I was sick. Father screeched to a stop, none too soon. Out the door I vomited. Propped ungracefully toward the roadside bushes with auto traffic whizzing by, I disposed of breakfast, the applesauce, and, for good measure, spit out another loose tooth.

"You have to stay well," Mother urged, as if I could control the situation. "Remember the press conference when we get to Boston."

Replying that I would try, I propped my head on a seat cushion, and eventually drifted off into a troubled sleep.

As he often did when approaching large cities, Father lost his way in the outskirts of Boston. Lying along the back seat, I listened while he and Mother quarreled about the easiest way to the Ritz Carlton Hotel. My view was restricted to upside-down visions of passing lampposts and buildings, including a fleeting glimpse of the gold-covered dome crowning the Massachusetts State House.

Long past dinnertime, we finally reached the hotel. Soiled and odorous, I was immediately sent off to bathe and don fresh clothes before appearing before the several dozen reporters and photographers patiently awaiting our delayed arrival.

"What do you think of Boston?" one began.

"How do I know? I just got here." My head throbbed and, despite a queasy stomach, I felt hungry.

The reporter persisted. "But you told them in New York what you thought of the city and the big buildings. Haven't you formed *any* impression of Boston?"

"Yes, I have." I put my clenched fist under my chin in a thoughtful pose for the photographers. "But I won't tell *you*."

Some of them smiled tolerantly, but wrote in their notebooks.

"Well, what do you want to see here?" another asked.

"Everything. But I don't know what you've got here. I'm thirsty." I genuinely wanted that conference to finish.

Someone then asked which of my films I liked best. "All of them," I answered.

"But didn't you say at some time you didn't like your last picture as well as the others you made?"

That question caught me by surprise. "No, not me." Could it have been my shipboard remark to Gertrude Lawrence? Luckily there was no follow-up. I had been nailed, flat-footed.

"What do you think of us reporters?"

"Swell," I replied, not entirely untruthfully, "but not when I'm tired and hungry!" Perfectly true.

The hotel manager, James Wyner, an impressionable type, recited the names of the dignitaries who had preceded us in our beds, including the Crown Prince and Princess of Sweden, King Zog of Albania and his accompanying Hungarian countess, whom Wyner characterized as "nothing."

Mother had thrust a thermometer into my mouth and recovered it for reading.

"One hundred three!" she wailed. "Oh, George!"

Relaxed and feverish, I let everything dangle. From the roof garden overhead came the rhythmic thump of dancers through our ceiling and the faint strains of orchestra music drifting down into our windows, thrown open to the humid night air.

Suddenly I sat bolt upright in bed and exclaimed, "I saw a golden dome!"

"Oh, George!" Mother cried again.

From overhearing her telephone call to Leo J. Madsen, our family physician in California, I learned that I was delirious and that he should catch the next airplane bound for Boston.

By dawn the hotel staff had summoned two other doctors from Massachusetts General Hospital. One wore a straw hat circled with a band of funereal black ribbon and carried a bulging medicine satchel. A step behind, perspiring and nervous, came his pediatric colleague. The doctor poked around my stomach with his fingers, peered down my throat, into nose and ears, and bent over to listen to my chest noises. Finally he removed his stethoscope.

"No pneumonia or appendicitis. Temperature elevated." He pursed his lips. "Perhaps it's grippe, or a change to our drinking water."

"I want to see what Bunker Hill looks like," I said. "Then Paul Revere's house. And where the men disguised as Indians dumped in the tea."

The doctor gestured for his assistant. "We'd better get a blood sample."

Approaching the bed slowly, as if I were contaminated, the other doctor took a cork fitted with a small scalpel blade and held my index finger. His hands were trembling. Misjudging the thickness of my skin, his first stab was too shallow. The second went too deep. Blood spurted rather than oozed. Quickly plastering an adhesive tape over the cut, he moved to another finger. Like a woodpecker, he tried several more times before getting a suitable sample. My fingers were sticky with spilled blood and several drops had fallen on the coverlet. It is not easy to take a blood sample from a movie star.

"Aren't you going to examine my dolls?" I asked him brightly. Marsha was pronounced in excellent shape, but Susie was obviously suffering from wear and tear. Like me, I thought.

Adopting a highly cautious view of my condition, Mother enforced a no-visitor status. The second morning Democratic governor of Massachusetts Charles F. Hurley was turned away at the hall door, and the same inhospitality greeted the neighboring governor from New Hampshire. Even Dr. Madsen found me asleep when he finally arrived, so he went off to bed himself.

Meanwhile, newspapers and radio had seized on my mysterious ailment with banner headlines and periodic bulletins, stirring up a daytime crowd which soon became so large that police erected barricades along Arlington Street. Everyone milled around quietly and peered upward toward our windows, as if undecided whether theirs was vigil or wake.

Little was left for me to do but lean indolently on the windowsill and wave occasionally at the upturned faces far below. Down through the treetops of the Boston Public Garden it looked like an oasis of cool green tranquility, and now and then I could make out a swan boat drifting around on the serpentine lake, like a colorful bug.

Several cloistered days would make any outing seem attractive, even a short walk from the hotel entrance over to the Commons and a floating swan boat cruise with Democratic Mayor Maurice J. Tobin. When I appeared at the top of the hotel steps, a rumbling roar rose from the packed crowd, which by then numbered over 10,000, everyone contained behind an array of ropes and barricades. Spaced all around the area were, I later learned, seventy-five uniformed patrolmen and eight police on horseback. With me mounted astride the formidable shoulders of Officer Stanley A. Slack, and escorted by a dozen policemen, we walked across the street toward the barricades, where the thick wall of bodies waited, children and shorter people placed forward to get a better view.

As we approached a sea of arms were upthrust, waving like tentacles, and from this packed humanity rose a pulsing cacophony of screams and reverberating growls. Inside the hotel's second-floor dining room, guests crowded against an open window to get a better look, dislodging a large screen, which plunged to the pavement with a clatter. A police horse nearby reared in terror, hooves flailing the air, his startled neighs adding to the general tumult.

Suddenly came the break. Down came the ropes, wooden barricades tipped and we were swallowed by the crowd's advance. Like scarecrows in the face of a gale the police in the cordon shouted and gestured. Unminding and relentless, the advancing crush of bodies squirmed sideways between the police ranks and swarmed against the officers in our flying wedge. Looking down I suddenly saw only a mosaic of arms and faces, mouths gaped open and shouting. Hands reached up to claw along my bare legs, tug at my shoes, and pull at my dress hem. It was a Boston version of Bedlam.

To steady myself, I clasped both hands across Officer Slack's forehead, knocking off his visored cap, which disappeared underfoot. The surging, incomprehensible roar made speech impossible, so I just locked my hands over Slack's forehead, unable to tell him Mother and Father had disappeared in the crowd somewhere behind. The muscled feel of his shoulders beneath my legs was reassuring, but for extra insurance I squeezed my knees tight against his neck as he plowed ahead. Roughly elbowing people aside, he finally reached the sanctuary of a narrow park entrance gate, leaving most of the mob bellowing and stalled, except for the more athletic, who scrambled over the fencing.

Not until we reached the jetty where Mayor Tobin awaited safely aboard an elegant old swan boat did the clamor begin to subside. By then Mother and Father had caught up, so we were quickly pedaled out into the sanctuary of the Frog Pond. The crowd re-formed along its sloping banks, like stadium fans into bleachers. Instead of their previous shouting behavior, they stood and sat unmoving and mute and watched as we slid across the water, the only sound a soft whirring of bicycle pedals where somebody in the stern was providing our motive power and steering.

Long after we returned to the hotel, aspects of the afternoon continued to nag at me. What happened to the kids and shorter people when the crowd broke in its hysterical rush? Handclapping was one thing, but why did they tug at my shoes, hold on to my legs, and shout so unintelligibly? The questions put to Mother, she stopped applying her lipstick and our eyes met briefly in the mirror.

"It's because you make them happy," she said, repeating a remark she made during my first experience with crowds at Iolani Palace in Hawaii.

This crowd didn't appear happy, I thought. Facing a theatre audience was not a new experience, but since Meglin Kiddie days the clapping in such circumstance had seldom been for me alone. Premiere crowds outside a theatre collected to see all the celebrities, not just one.

Crowd emotions had always puzzled me, but in Boston the experience was utterly new. First, I was not my usual self. Feverish and bedridden for several days, when I climbed on Officer Slack's broad shoulders I was a damp bundle, certainly too weak to repel Afghan bandits, as Wee Willie Winkie had done.

Second, and in particular contrast with the large Hawaiian crowd, the swan-boat ride was something I was obliged to do, not a vacation experience of my choice. Mayor Tobin had insisted he share in my first outing, and the swan boat seemed the quickest way to discharge that obligation.

Third, age provides one with greater sensitivity to the mix in most crowds between polite adulation and hysterical action. What we experienced in Boston was not exceptional; it was just that ten years old is a lot more sophisticated than seven.

Most importantly, after its long period of anxiety and curiosity, this crowd was understandably restless and its patience tinder-dry. The restraints of barricades and the presence of so many police may have ignited an attitude surely rowdy and bordering on the frenzied and irrational. Like a forest fire, that crowd generated its own momentum of flame and wind.

The best dancing partner: Buddy Ebsen, *Captain January*, 1936 *(Twentieth Century-Fox)*

Backstage training with Uncle Billy Robinson, 1935   *(Twentieth Century-Fox)*

Precision tap sequence with Jack Haley and Alice Faye, *Poor Little Rich Girl*, 1936   *(Twentieth Century-Fox)*

Construction laborer on
glass-brick demonstration
playhouse, 1936
(Twentieth Century-Fox)

John Griffiths ("Griff"),
bodyguard, 1935 *(Author's
private collection)*

Vittorio Mussolini and
Darryl Zanuck, outside
studio bungalow,
1937   *(Twentieth
Century-Fox)*

Baron Saburo Kurusu, later pre-Pearl Harbor Japanese emissary,
1936   *(Twentieth Century-Fox)*

Studio schoolteacher and dear companion Frances Klapt
("Klammy"), 1935 *(Twentieth Century-Fox)*

A treasured red and white racer from a treasured Uncle Billy Robinson,
1936 *(Twentieth Century-Fox)*

Frank Morgan stealing my line in *Dimples*, 1936 *(Twentieth Century-Fox)*

As a Bowery princess in
Dimples *(Twentieth Century-Fox)*

Playboy pal Robert Young in *Stowaway*, 1936 *(Twentieth Century-Fox)*

A fast hackney behind Little Carnation *(Twentieth Century-Fox)*

Afghan opponent Cesar Romero in *Wee Willie Winkie*, 1937
(Twentieth Century-Fox)

Evading the stampede, *Wee Willie Winkie*   *(Twentieth Century-Fox)*

Auld Lang Syne with Victor
McLaglen, *Wee Willie Winkie*
(Twentieth Century-Fox)

Transpolar Soviet flyers: Andrei Yumashev, Mikhail Gromov
(pilot) and Sergei Danilin, 1937 *(Twentieth Century-Fox)*

The original Ching-Ching in my bed, 1936 *(Twentieth Century-Fox)*

Bedroom scene featuring glass/china miniatures and Ching-Ching II, 1940 *(Acme News Pictures)*

Paulette Goddard, chaperon for Charlie Chaplin's sons, Palm Springs *(International News Service)*

G-Man J. Edgar Hoover, Fox studio, 1937 *(Fox Movietone News)*

Caged by J. Edgar Hoover like
a skunk, Yosemite Valley,
1938   *(Author's private
collection)*

Airmail poster requested by Postmaster General James A. Farley
(International News Service)

Brother George's welcome home from Hawaii, 1937 *(Author's private collection)*

Honorary colonel of the 27th "Wolfhound" Infantry Regiment, Hawaii, 1939 *(Author's private collection)*

Superdancer and later U.S. Senator George Murphy, *Little Miss Broadway*, 1938 *(Culver Pictures/Curtis Camera Press)*

Candy temptation from Joan Crawford during *Little Miss Broadway* *(Twentieth Century-Fox)*

My first visit with Eleanor Roosevelt during *Little Miss
Broadway*, 1938   *(Twentieth Century-Fox)*

With Helen Hayes,
First Lady of the
American theatre,
and her daughter
Mary, 1937
*(Author's private
collection)*

Indian signs with Martin Goodrider, *Susannah of the Mounties*, 1938 *(Twentieth Century-Fox)*

Chief Yellow Kidney instructing Bright Shining Star in *Susannah of the Mounties* *(Culver Pictures/Curtis Camera Press)*

Crowds and I had always seemed a harmonious twosome, each pleased with the encounter. But this crowd had one personality, I another. A fundamental fact of life was beginning to sink in. No matter its brilliance or how remote its location, any star can be devoured by human adoration, sparkle by sparkle.

☆

Understanding about his turndown at my room door, Governor Hurley had arranged a boat ride aboard a police launch down Boston Harbor to visit the restored USS *Constitution*. Once again true to form, I was behind the helm and operating the ship-to-shore radio in contact with reporters waiting for us at Charleston Navy Yard.

"Which boat do you like best," came crackling through the speaker, "police boat or swan boat?"

"I don't know, I hedged, "but I *am* steering this one."

The governor had been driven down to meet us in his sleek limousine. As we embarked for the ship tour, he immediately assumed charge. Back on the dock, a motley collection of local children had gathered to gawk, and as the governor ushered me into his limousine for our return, some of the kids crowded and leaned against his car, smudging moist handprints on its mirror finish. Visibly annoyed, Hurley shouted and roughly pushed them away. Back they came, pressing like waves against a rock.

"One more picture," called a photographer, so I pulled forward in the seat and smiled out the open door.

Just then the door slammed shut, catching the four fingers of my right hand. At my yowl of pain Griff leaped from the front seat, looking around for kidnappers. Once released, my fingers looked to be still attached, though dented and slightly crooked. Mother popped them into her mouth all at once, and began sucking on them.

"That door squashed my hand!" I cried. "Who did it?"

One of the children outside pointed at the governor, then turned and fled.

With my hand bandaged, I wound up our visit at a farewell lunch with six local girls, including daughters of both Mayor Tobin and the governor. Each got a memento bracelet from me, and I received a brass key to the State House, whose golden dome I had seen upon arriving.

"Are you a Democrat like my daddy?" asked twelve-year-old Betty Hurley.

"I don't know," I replied.

"You should be a Democrat," she insisted, "or at least a Republican. One or the other."

If I had to decide, I would. The logic of my selection was simple. The governor had slammed the door on my fingers, was a person who fretted about trivial matters like fingerprints on shiny cars, and manhandled anonymous little people as if they were unimportant. A natural antagonist, he was a Democrat. Therefore I would be the opposite, a Republican. It was as simple as that.

Hard on the heels of this private political decision, the U.S. Department of State proposed I become a goodwill ambassador, endorsing a request from the liberal bloc of the Argentine legislature for me to visit Buenos Aires. The Secretary of State urged I accept, implying to my parents that my insouciance might in a small way help sway Argentina away from fascism. Called on the phone, the studio declined on my behalf.

In a diametrically opposite development, a screaming newspaper headline on August 22, 1938, proclaimed that I had been assisting the Communists.

In testimony before the House Committee on Un-American Activities, headed by Representative Martin Dies of Texas, former Communist party worker James B. Matthews claimed that sixty senators and members of the House of Representatives and six motion picture stars had unwittingly served to spread Communist propaganda. As a former chairman of the League Against War and Fascism, an organization advocating closer friendship with the Soviet Union, and fresh from an internecine scrap within the American Communist Party, Matthews had turned government witness.

"Communists chuckle when a prominent person, in simplemindedness, lends his name to a 'front' organization," he testified. "Almost everyone in Hollywood except Mickey Mouse and Snow White has been signed up for some Communist front organization. They are the fathers of revolution, just as surely as Roosevelt's new drive to eliminate conservatives from the Democratic Party is playing into Communist hands."

Named with me were actresses Bette Davis and Miriam Hopkins and actors Robert Taylor, Clark Gable, and James Cagney. The charge against both Davis and Hopkins was membership in the League of Women Shoppers.

"Far from being a member of the league," Davis retorted, "I've never even heard of it!"

In fact, it had been formed the previous year as a protectionist organization to boycott Japanese silk stockings in favor of cotton lisle from America.

Matthews charged that I, too, had "lent my name to communism" by cabling anniversary greetings to the Paris daily newspaper *Ce Soir*, owned outright, so he claimed, by the French Communist Party.

My signature had indeed been included in a congratulatory cable sent by the studio publicity department the previous March, perhaps encouraged by Paula Walling, my previous tutor in French and now Hollywood correspondent for *Ce Soir*. Scoffing at the charge, Walling said the paper was far from being "Red" and was in fact owned by a group of French bankers supporting the French government.

Next to rise in my defense was the leader of the 75,000-strong American Communist Party. Arriving in San Francisco the day after the announcement about me, Earl Browder was indignant.

"Shirley Temple is not a Communist!" he declared. "The Dies committee is a great burlesque with sinister motives. It is a vicious attempt to destroy the unity of American progressive forces!"

Overseas, the Dies Committee charge was met with disdain. "Communism and fascism are both outlawed in Finland," said the speaker of Parliament. "We look to your country to lead the fight for democracy, but America's main cultural influence in Finland unfortunately still rests on the shoulders of that little girl, and your mouse."

It was a shabby moment for America. Thoughtful congressional testimony had been glossed over and subordinated to reeking, sensational claims.

After the committee concluded its Washington hearings, $25,000 of its budget remained unexpended. What remained of its appropriation would be spent on travel, announced the chairman. First stop, Hollywood. Before heading west the committee published its report in the *Congressional Record*.

"... Shirley Temple ... unwittingly served the purposes of the Communist Party. . . . The above testimony has never been denied by the screen star mentioned."

Years later the *Los Angeles Times* would observe, "Shirley Temple was ten years old at the time. Since then she has become quite respectable."

☆

Almost given a job to help fight Fascists and being charged with helping Communists were reasons enough to foreshorten my trip, but also out the window flew the planned publicity featuring me with the Quints. Someone belatedly felt I might be upstaged. I didn't care one way or the other, but missing Canada meant not seeing Canadian Mounties, and that was regrettable.

Leaving the hotel to catch our train, we drove up along the Common. As we turned past the Massachusetts State House, I remarked again about its soaring central dome, sheathed in gold. Mother cast me a sidelong glance, pursed her lips, and began to inspect her upturned fingernails.

Outside Old South Station a reporter asked what had impressed me most during our trip. "Boulder Dam," I answered, "especially down inside it. But I guess rather than live in a hotel, it's a lot more fun to have a nice yard, brothers, and dogs."

Away puffed the New England Express, westbound with our retinue of nine people, forty suitcases, and two sedans ignominiously strapped on a flatbed car coupled behind. The best thing about our trip was that it ended when it did; everyone was suffering from vacation fatigue. There was one bad aspect during our return. No opportunity presented itself for me to get up into the locomotive cab and steer that railroad train.

21

Delay and indecision are first weapons in the armory of movie-makers. As the summer vacation of 1938 ended, hope vaporized that Zanuck was prepared to select my next script promptly. Two competing titles flickered against the studio wall, the blood-and-leather frontier tale, *Susannah, a Little Girl with the Mounties*, and newcomer *Lady Jane*, a title which had struck Mother's fancy before she learned the story, simply because it combined nobility with my middle name.

Normal in-house discussion between writers and executives continued to swing to and fro. Just when they might have reached a decision, Mother set the dithering swinging again by introducing the *Little Diplomat* title suggested by Secretary Morgenthau. Within two days that idea was flip-flopping with the rest. Screenwriter Charles Beldon immediately submitted a story-line proposal. Intrigued, Zanuck instructed another of his writers, Eddie Moran, to write the screen version of Beldon's idea. The scattered clouds of studio indecision were gathering in one ominous, enormous thunderhead. Time was running out. Something had to be done. However, what could have been a deluge to alter the landscape turned out to be only a spatter of familiar raindrops. For the fourth time in eighteen months, the studio dramatically changed course. Blown back across its prairie went the foreshortened *Susannah of the Mounties*, into limbo faded *Lady Jane*, and off to the trash bin went *Little Diplomat*. For a second time I was to be reincarnated in Mary Pickford's image.

First stop on this flight backward into Pickfordiana was to be *The Little Princess*, Frances H. Burnett's Victorian saga of England and the Boer War in South Africa. Studio moguls had given up the prospect of making me fit the story and returned to making the story fit me.

In addition to Mother's revived admiration for Pickford, the size of the production budget was a cheering $1.3 million, six times the cost of my first film and enough for a blockbuster.

My role was a Cinderella in reverse. Initially a rich girl, I wind up a slavey lodged in a London attic and garbed in urchin clothes with torn stockings. To prepare this raggedy outfit, wardrobe conspired to destroy new shoes by sandblasting, and to artificially age a new dress, ripping out seams and scuffing the cloth with a wire brush.

"But that ruins it," I observed, watching my costume demolition. "Why not buy an old dress?"

The wardrobe lady shrugged and continued her aging process.

"How much does this dress cost new?" I asked. Told about $50, I muttered, "What a crazy business."

Props was also creating a Victorian doll, authentic to its waxen head, embedded with thousands of single human hairs in the old style. To save time and cost, I proposed to rent one of my own dolls.

The propman brushed my offer aside; authenticity was critical. If an 1850 antimacassar was used on a chairback instead of the appropriate 1899 version, some observant moviegoer was sure to spot the error and carp. Just any old doll wouldn't do.

Particularly with smaller props, the cult of authenticity was in full bloom. Zealots for the real thing, prop people collected stale bread crumbs, kippers from England, and for our mantelpiece a snowy white ptarmigan.

But that white is wrong, commented Klammy, and found a picture of a brown-feathered ptarmigan. Props was offended. It's a wonder of nature, he explained. To baffle its predators the bird feathers turn brown in summer and white when the snow flies. Ours was white because it was caught and stuffed in winter, precisely true to the season of our film.

His devotion to accuracy and truth struck me as right, and I began to measure things against the authenticity criterion. One day while inspecting exposed fasteners on one of my costumes, I asked director

Walter Lang if they had snaps like those when the Little Princess actually lived. A hurried consultation concluded that snap fasteners were invented in 1908, years after the period of our film. Showing his annoyance, Lang summoned a wardrobe lady with thread, needles, and supplies to replace all my snaps with period buttons. Everyone seemed upset. Lang glowered at the delay. Annoyed, the lady sewed with her head lowered in silence, once or twice furtively glancing toward me and scowling. In costumes, hewing the line of authenticity exacts a price.

Fidelity in costumes could also turn out to be plain bothersome. Each morning I became authentic from the skin out. When I was playing the rich girl, first came the cotton underpants, then an embroidered camisole buttoned up the front. Next, the garter belt with its array of dangling straps, then high stockings, ruffled pantalets, and high-buttoned shoes. Already encased and harnessed, I then donned a flouncy petticoat, often two. An inflexible hoopskirt followed, surmounted by the dress with its lace, ruffles, and bows. My authenticity was complete, all seven layers of me, but nature was not always to be denied. Sometimes I needed the bathroom.

Mine was hidden under the drop-leaf seat in my portable trailer, usually parked on the soundstage. Rudimentary, as well as ingenious, the facility consisted of a small, cold tin seat installed in a corner. Below the trailer hung a collector bucket, its telltale resonance always a clarion call of what was going on.

In addition to its built-in abuse of privacy, the contraption called for unusual agility in its use. Being a contortionist with one extra hand helped. First, the hoop and dress must be flipped up, and leaned against the wall. Petticoats need be pulled up and held, pantalets slipped down, attached garters moved sideways, and underpants eased free. Clearly a task for an octopus.

The most dangerous misstep, all you aspiring Scarlett O'Haras, is to inadvertently cover the toilet tissue when you are rotating the hoopskirt assembly out of the way. Awkward at best, laughable at worst. You'll never find it.

But by far the cruelest thing that can then occur in the process is for all desire to flee. For anyone really wedded to authenticity, wait until lunchtime when the set is empty. If absolutely necessary, pick a moment of maximum bustle and onstage noise, preferably with carpenters sawing. By all means, never attempt anything during the silence of someone else's scene. The wisest course: revere fidelity but cultivate thirst and avoid fluids. For those in period dresses, emulate a camel.

Everywhere I looked I started applying the measure of fidelity, even in the matter of the time clock, a new requirement of the Black-Connery wages-and-hours law. Installed just inside the set door, it included a battery of individual name cards. The first day, everyone found his name card and punched in. I looked but couldn't find mine, so I took my problem to Lang.

"Nope, you don't get one," he answered. "You're too little."

Exclusion from such routines eroded my sense of camaraderie and common purpose, an important bond linking me with the working crew.

Differentiation rankled. If we were doing mutually supportive things toward identical objectives, why should size exclude me from sharing in routines?

Lang well realized my chagrin, and the next day a card appeared printed with my name. Thereafter, morning and afternoon I lined up and religiously punched in and out with everyone else. Using it was a mark of maturity.

Getting wind of this innocuous exchange, New York headquarters of IBM capitalized on my enthusiasm, and constructed a special punch-card time recorder with my name embossed in silver and black and a supply of time cards bearing my photograph.

The gift was unwelcome on two counts. A personalized machine and special cards violated the fidelity of the process, made it a plaything rather than a businesslike, grown-up apparatus. Second, its existence again set me apart from the working crew.

After requisite publicity photos with the IBM machine, I refused to use it. Eventually someone took it away, and again I punched in and out on the regular machine. Unknown to me at the time, however, the studio payroll accountant had of course been ignoring my card all along. Like the IBM machine, my time card was part of a charade.

Insistence on an undifferentiated role with the working crew was an attitude which did not extend to performances onstage. There my normal competitive instincts galloped along, and on occasion, when I held the reins too slack, almost ran away.

Previously everyone had left me to compete any way I could within limits of energy and ingenuity. Losing, I had seldom brooded or resorted to spiteful tactics to win. In *The Little Princess* I did both.

Sybil Jason, a remarkably appealing child actress from South Africa, was cast as a feisty, humorous scullery maid with a heavy cockney accent. Although my role was longer and more varied she seemed to attract the best laugh lines.

"Down't you thynk its' toyme to cut the kike?" she said.

Her pronunciation caused a noticeable ripple of merriment among the stage crew. Director Lang called for a retake and quieted the laughter. Jason again recited her line, using the identical inflection. Lang called a halt.

"Flatten that out, that last word, for goodness sake! Say *cake*, not *kike*!"

Laughter again. Whatever she was up to was devilishly effective. I had been outmaneuvered for audience approval, and I had no idea why. Jealousy left me deadened.

Tolerated too long, envy onstage can reappear in dangerous costume. Still brooding, I moved to another scene. During my urchin period and in retaliation for a sneering remark from rich schoolgirl Marcia Mae Jones, I was to dump a scuttle of dusty coal ashes over her head and ruin her elegant dress. I relished the action almost as if I were getting even, although with the wrong girl.

Lang had ordered a single take. With true zest, I lifted the scuttle as high as I could and dumped its contents on top of her curls. She was taller, with long legs. Or perhaps it was the party dress. My envy was consuming, and her expression of distaste with all the mess was matched by my own enthusiasm. Sidling up to the director, I said I could do my part better if we tried it again.

It was already overkill. Scowling at me sideways, Marcia Mae was bent over, shaking the ashes out of her hair. Lang said no, and I recognized my spite had been misplaced and the mark overshot. Making amends, I asked her to share my ritual Coca-Cola from the props ice chest. Still dusty and perhaps justifiably peeved, she accepted, and our bottles were drained without much talk. As the next scene was due, Mother reached inside her oversized handbag.

"Here's a chocolate for extra energy," she whispered. I saw that

Marcia Mae had noticed but said nothing and kept squinting forlornly down the neck of her empty bottle. Something about her silence alerted Mother, for she extracted another candy. "And you, too, Marcia Mae," she said.

We chewed our candy in silence.

"I envy you a lot," Marcia Mae said.

The remark caught me off balance. It was *my* envy that had been the problem, and not even toward Marcia Mae.

"But you're a good actress too," I replied.

"Not that," she lowered her voice. "I envy you because you're always so happy."

To receive her *envy* when I deserved enmity was unsettling.

An assistant director had shouted, "First team in!"

"Well, watch me now," I replied. "I'm not happy at all. I have to cry."

"Sparkle!" Mother whispered.

"I can't. This is where I cry."

"You know what I mean, concentrate."

As I started off, building to my cry, I glanced back at Marcia Mae. She was smiling broadly.

The crying job actually began backstage while I waited to be signaled onstage by a flashing, low-wattage bulb. Mechanically simple, cue lights can be a powerful emotional mechanism for any actor. A silent summons, they are the trigger between illusion and reality. Out in front of the facade of scenery lies a true *Alice in Wonderland*, a land splashed in brilliant colors, with seductive music backed by intricately designed structures, while carefully costumed characters busily crisscross the stage speaking make-believe lines.

Behind that facade, however, lies the world of reality, a semidarkened shadowy place of temporary wooden supports for the false fronts. Empty soft-drink bottles stand around; in slouch hats and baggy pants, the grips and gaffers lean on things; microphones and other specialized sound equipment are strung up and hooked together in a spaghetti of electrical cables. The key link between all that onstage fantasy and the reality of backstage is that pale little cue light. Once that light flashes, Alice must come alive again, out of her rabbit hole into the stunning brilliance of make-believe.

My particular action required an entrance on cue and crying violently. Having been sobbing for years in all sorts of filmed circumstances, I was regarded as an accomplished crier, convincing and controlled. Theoretically the preceding action had built a firm basis for my grief, and so I was left alone in the shadows of backstage to embellish my sadness. However, as I recalled the script the reasons for my sorrow had been poorly drawn. Marcia Mae's stunning remark about how happy I always seemed was another reason my cry built far too slowly. Recalling someone's recent suggestion that a good way to attain grief was to get a cry started, and then switch to laughter, I decided to give it a try.

Using my usual system of an empty head, I managed to work up a modest cry. Still needing plenty more cry-power, I superimposed a laugh just as my cue light flashed. As I burst onstage, I was a spectacle of grief. Genuine tears poured down my cheeks and splashed off my chin, my whole body racked by sobs. The camera panned in for a close-up. My nostrils pulsed and flared, my face glistening with tears. It's a wonder I remembered my lines.

"Cut!" Lang finally exclaimed. "Great! Just great!"

The whole set broke out in applause. The scene was over for everyone but me. My combination of anguish and laughter kept going. I couldn't stop. Mother first looked at me puzzled, then alarmed. Quickly seizing my hand, she dragged me off to our portable dressing room and closed the door. I was totally out of control, classic hysteria. Holding my hands and speaking softly, she finally brought me back to normal.

Despite my overkill crying and laughing simultaneously was really a good system. In company with that cue light, I had stumbled onto a valuable new technique. What had happened was that I had outsmarted myself. Intensity of make-believe had simply overwhelmed me. Like many a kid, I learned the hard way by going too far. Stopping that crying was sad. When you get well started, it's really too bad to have to stop.

Refinement of my crying from childhood blubber to sophisticated hysteria was typical of progress for all actors. Continually probing for increased skill, from time to time I discovered challenges beyond my current ability. A dream sequence in *The Little Princess* required me to dance ballet. Possessed of neither adequate training nor swanlike neck, nor lithe, long legs, I was tutored by veteran ballet instructor Ernest Belcher. Unfolding a portable dance floor in our living room, he played

Nutcracker music and demonstrated, flexing up on tiptoe, leaping and twirling off the dance floor and among our chairs and tables. Several athletic weeks later I still was no ballerina, with little to show beyond tender arches and aching ankles.

Rather than scrub the whole number, however, studio dance directors Castle and Sawyer dressed me in tutu and ballet slippers, with thin pink ribbons laced around the ankles, and choreographed me in swoop, pivot, and twirl strongly backed up by a chorus of accomplished dancers. Everyone balanced on tiptoe except me. It was a one of those discouraging moments, posing beyond my real competence. To be found wanting after trying my hardest was even worse. To assuage my sense of failure, more than once I scrambled to find other ways to turn the situation to my advantage.

One action required that I ride a horse and jump seated sidesaddle. Before Horace, the stable hand, had disappeared over the horizon he had taught me how. Mounting the sidesaddle, one leg stretched down to the stirrup, I crooked the other around the pommel. Victorian women must have had longer legs than I did. My position was as uncomfortable for the horse as for me. Still I was surprised to be dismounted. Perhaps I looked insecure, for I was replaced before having had a real try, the job assigned to a double with a face round like mine and shiny riding pants. While waiting she told me her father was an MGM musical arranger working on *The Wizard of Oz*, and that she and the horse got $200 for each jump. I was shocked, not only because she was my double and by what her father did, but by her fee.

Remembering another scene which required a small horse lying in a stable, I offered to rent my pony Spunky. Lang said okay, so we settled on $10 for sleeping, which the pony did all day anyway. The straw bedding was dyed green, as technicolor turned natural yellow too stark. During his tryout Spunky's bilious-colored surroundings accentuated his own liverish approach to life. Lunging toward a propman, he refused to lie down, and even bared his teeth at me. It was doubly humiliating, first to be rejected as a rider, then to have my pony flunk his screen test and lose me a rental fee, but I knew that always trying to salvage failure was still the right thing.

On a soundstage disappointment comes in more cloaks than simply technical incompetence or a lost pony fee. Sometimes it arrives in the person of someone just passing by. Practicing the rollicking jig "Knock 'em in the Old Kent Road," Arthur Treacher, a reedy, hawk-faced butler type, was having trouble with one intricate movement.

"For anyone as austere and towering as I am," he complained, hiking up his pants, "well, it's too complicated."

The rehearsal was interrupted for us to be introduced to a man and woman, both thin and tall, with prominent noses and overbites. With his high forehead and lanky frame, the man reminded me vaguely of brother Jack. What set them apart was the name, James Roosevelt, eldest son of the President, and his wife, Betsy. Slightly inclined forward, he chatted quickly but about nothing. Overwhelmed with respect for his name, I tried to answer carefully. In poor taste, someone joked that one of my Tennessee fan letters had repeated a rumor that Mother had once been married to the same James Roosevelt. For proof one needed only to compare my brother Jack's strong resemblance to Roosevelt in build, facial structure, and high hairline. Roosevelt took the jest gracefully, but Betsy, judging by her face, found little humor in the comment. I was with her. Jokes were my stock-in-trade, but not where they deprecated the name of Roosevelt. To change the subject, I suppose, she turned to Treacher and bluntly asked what he thought of me.

Tugging at his nose and then pulling thoughtfully on his chin, Treacher replied, "You have no idea, if she were minded that way, she could be President of the United States."

Once again everyone tittered uneasily, except Treacher, who stood, shoulders thrown back, posing deadpan. Again I was annoyed. Flip remarks were more an insult to the President and his son than a compliment to me.

As the Roosevelts went around meeting the rest of the cast, I tagged along to eavesdrop.

"Did you get a police badge?" someone asked Betsy.

"No, does she give them away?"

"Well, your mother-in-law got some while she was here."

"That's different," Betsy replied. "We're the *un*important members of the family."

In my mind's eye the presidential family was a unity. Anyone who assaulted that unity insulted the whole. In my mind where the presidency was involved, nobody was unimportant. Tipping heroes from their pedestals offended me. When Betsy had jumped down from the pedestal, it left me disillusioned and resentful. I was less young than before.

At one point in the film I was an urchin relegated to dingy attic lodgings, and across the jumbled rooftops dwelled a magical swami, Cesar Romero, with his small monkey. The action required me to chase the little thing around and pick it up. Dodging artfully beyond my reach, it regarded me from deep-set black eyes, outthrust teeth frozen in a wary grimace. Relentless and coaxing, I had finally cornered it and lifted the muscular little body, which smelled of urine. Twisting, it grabbed my arm between its two leathery hands, ducked and dug its teeth into my forearm.

When I yelped the director shouted, "Cut!" Onto the stage leaped the animal trainer, cuffed the monkey hard alongside its ear, and spanked its bottom like a child. Squeaking and chattering, it fled on all fours under a chair, and stared out balefully, rubbing its bottom.

Kneeling, I tried to coax my tiny co-star to come out, but Mother wailed, "Now she'll have to have a tetanus shot!"

The director inspected my arm. "Not such a bad one, is it?" he said hopefully.

"It's not his fault," the trainer protested. "He bites when picked up that way."

"Why didn't you tell us!" snapped the director.

"Poor little thing," I cooed, keeping a safe distance.

And poor little me, I thought. It hates me.

The bite hurt and the prospect of an inoculation stung already, but the real problem was professional pride. My only achievements had been professional, and lacking respect derived from those efforts meant I had failed. The rationale may have appeared tenuous to others, but it was simple as only a child could make it. Unless I was liked, I had failed.

All during work on *The Little Princess* such unrelated events conspired to create a shadowy mood of personal uncertainty, like distant heat lightning without thunder. From a Civilian Conservation Corps mountain camp in southern Oregon, two enterprising young recruits wrote to the studio threatening me with bodily harm if $10,000 was not paid promptly. The money was to be used to learn to fly, they confessed to FBI agents. Remanded to a local grand jury, they were released on $50,000 bail, an amount which, incidentally, pegged their value to the state five times what my value was to them.

A different tack was taken by a fourteen-year-old girl who addressed a postcard to my mother from her little mining hometown in Pennsylvania saying, "Bring $320.00 to the below address if you ever want to see Shirley."

When the FBI knocked she too readily confessed, explaining she only wanted money to buy things. It was her second extortion try. The first was her note to her grandparents, residing in the same house, demanding 10 cents.

Yet another threat arrived, this time from Alabama, and again the FBI pounced, this time on a hardened criminal threatening me with dire consequences. Away he went for a ten-year sentence in federal prison.

Normally calm and composed, even Mother began to do little things out of character. Publicist Ray Dannenbaum arrived at my trailer step balancing a tall stack of beribboned and decorated gift boxes, all apparently empty.

"These are for Christmas photos," he puffed, leaning backwards under the light, ungainly load. Plump, balding, in tweedy clothes, he looked like a burgomaster.

"Christmas is months away," Mother needled him. "We don't have to do that yet, do we?"

Reaching out one long leg, she hooked the toe of her shoe under the edge of the topmost box and slowly tipped Dannenbaum's tower. As the pile tumbled helter-skelter, he grabbed, twisted, lost his balance, and collapsed among his jumbled boxes.

Popularity polls did little to reassure those uneasy with my growth. Although still at the top for a fourth consecutive year, I was closely trailed by Clark Gable and Sonja Henie. Mickey Rooney was fourth, catapulted from the deep hundred mark in 1937. The pack was closing fast on my heels.

On the lighted billboard atop Ideal Toy and Novelty Company's factory on Long Island, the lights had just flickered off my face. Soon the face itself disappeared. Since 1934, Ideal had delivered me doll royalties of $118,370. During 1938, however, royalties had plunged to only $4,017, off 80 percent from the prior year. The dolls knew a secret.

On the set, director Lang suddenly left our unfinished picture. Medical furlough, announced the studio, replacing him with veteran William Seiter. For several days cameraman Artie Miller complained in graphic detail about the pain he suffered from a cyst in his cheek.

"There must be a lot of trouble in the world," I remarked to Mother. "Everyone else has problems. When do I get to have some?"

22

Sometimes performers try too long. In my case it was no longer enough to be cute. What earlier was innovative and appealing now had begun to imprison me. Repetitive stories forged links to chain me in a former image.

Enthusing that *The Little Princess* was his finest film to date, Zanuck used past to justify present: "... twenty-one feature films, star in the last seventeen ... her films grossed $20 million ... the outstanding child star of all times ... by far the best picture she has ever made."

In contrast, Mother's eye was fixed ahead: "... no more backstairs waifs. It's time for Shirley to become a real child on the screen, with everyday problems of a child ... any in-between ratings are unacceptable. It will either be top of the heap or a graceful exit."

With Christmas and the day of peace came a toy machine gun that spit sparks from a flint wheel, four slingshots, a BB gun from the Daisy Rifle Company, and notification that *Susannah of the Mounties* would be next, a Canadian classic of wagon-train massacres and marauding Blackfoot Indians.

New Year's Eve 1938 coincided with my parents' midnight wedding anniversary, so as usual several dozen old friends gathered downstairs to eat and celebrate. To ensure a rested look for my job the next day as Grand Marshal of the Golden Jubilee Parade of the Tournament of Roses, I was sent off to bed early. As consolation my stand-in, Mary Lou Isleib, could stay overnight.

Most of my best girlfriends were daughters of Mother's closest friends, and Mary Lou was one of those. Well matched in appearance, we shared considerable empathy as well. Sometimes when I cried onstage, she would cry as she watched offstage. Stuck behind the photoelectric barrier at my bedroom door, we could hear the pulsing rumble of laughter and conversation downstairs.

"How do babies happen?" I asked across the dark separating our beds.

"They come from navels. They open up like a purse. The baby just pops out!"

"Then why do men have navels?"

"For something else, I guess," she answered, "but not babies. Only ladies' navels work for a baby."

That problem exhausted, I proposed we try to escape from the room. We both jumped out of bed. There must be some way to outwit that photoelectric beam. We pulled up a bathroom stool. Gathering my nightgown high, I leaped out into the hall, but only triggered the clanging alarm bell in Father's closet. It often malfunctioned, so we replaced the stool and dived back into bed, two angelic sleeping faces under chin-high blankets. Father came upstairs to disengage and reset the bell before the Brentwood police would automatically be enroute. Passing my door, he grumbled about the alarm and reminded us to go to sleep.

Our next attempt was to squirm beneath the beam. Halfway through, Mary Lou's rump tripped the bell again. Upstairs raced Father. Suspicious now, he scolded our two motionless bodies. Obliged to operate the projector for their ritual New Year movie downstairs, he said any further annoyance from us would result in punishment.

Despite his warning, faint sounds of film fanfare provided further incentive to escape. Perhaps very slowly obstructing the light beam would work better. I sneaked a finger over the recessed hole in the doorjamb where the electric-eye light was installed. Nothing happened, so I edged it across still farther. Still no bell. I covered it with my hand. Nothing. In his irritation Father must have forgotten to reset the alarm properly. We were free!

Creeping silently down the circular staircase, we could just see the movie screen mounted at the far end of our darkened living room. The film was a horror story called *Night Must Fall*, all about a human head hidden in a hat box and stored in the closet of Robert Montgomery, a cockney murderer. Crouched in the shadows, we peered transfixed through the stair rails like two caged animals. It was a long, grisly, spooky story, and at the end we scrambled back under our patchwork quilts.

Lying there captive to imagination I thought about a wide-eyed head being neatly sliced off. Suddenly I recalled a hitherto ignored Christmas present from France, a miniature toy guillotine mounted on a gallows with a sharp, weighted knife which could be wound up and released to plunge down onto a wooden chopping block. The trick was in a secret lever, activated to arrest the falling blade just before it severed whatever lay across the block. Mary Lou knew nothing of the toy, but agreed to play; however, we needed something to cut off.

Once again edging past the deactivated beam, we tiptoed down the back staircase to the kitchen, found a raw carrot, and crept back upstairs. In a shaft of light shining in from the hallway, we set up the guillotine.

"Make believe it's a neck with a head on it," I instructed, cackling softly in my best wicked-witch voice.

Winding up the guillotine blade, I secretly flicked the guard lever open and released the blade. Down it plunged, neatly slicing off the carrot end.

Mary Lou grimaced. "I don't like this game."

"Now put your finger on the block," I said. She hesitated. "Don't worry, I'll stop the blade by magic."

In slow motion she laid her finger on the chopping block and shut her eyes.

"No fair," I said. "If you don't open your eyes, it's no fun."

She was saved by Mother, whose approaching footfall sent the guillotine into hiding under the bed and both of us back under the blankets.

The guillotine and the movie did not leave me as unmoved as I made out. Although still stanchly regarding my body as a sum of parts, each expendable without damage to the important areas of human spirit, there was one exception. My own head. Mary Lou was not the only one repelled by the game. I had a morbid horror of decapitation, especially my own.

It was still dark when we were off to Pasadena for the Rose Bowl parade. President Lathrop Teischman of the Tournament of Roses Association had first pitched the deal by saying I could ride in a flower-bedecked coach, "like a modern Cinderella." He was wide of the mark until he mentioned I would also receive an ornate badge.

The float was a mountain of fresh rose blossoms with me perched on a chair at the peak. Just before I was to be hoisted up, a boy my age with upturned nose was pushed forward to me. His hair was trimmed high over the ears, and I vaguely remembered him as someone who had briefly visited the set of *Heidi*.

"My name is Billy Clark. My daddy's police chief in Oxnard. I get to pin on your official badge." He held out a giant rosette with golden printing and broad ribbons trailing to my waist.

"I now pronounce you Grand Marshal," he said, and the parade began.

Clipping along behind my float came Los Angeles Sheriff Eugene Biscaluiz and his mounted horse patrol. Mine was one of sixty floats sandwiched into a five-mile-long parade, each designed and decorated by volunteers and featuring tens of thousands of fresh, individual blooms. For three hours we inched along past deep crowds lining the entire route. My job was to keep waving right and left, but what I really enjoyed was ducking my chin to admire the badge and smell the flowers.

A snag in my happy New Year was Klammy's oversight in not having provided me a quick study on Indians. Twelve full-blooded Blackfoot chiefs showed up as bit players in *Susannah of the Mounties*. Decked out in beaded deerskins and plumed headdresses, they paraded onto the soundstage, suddenly hushed by their commanding presence. Chief Albert Mad Plume was the leader. Chief Many Guns was the youngest at forty-three, and the religious shaman was Chief Yellow Kidney. Five had never left their Montana reservation before, and only one spoke English—Chief Coward, the translator. Each was a picture-book Indian, leathery skinned, hawk-nosed, regal beyond expectation. During introductions they stood quietly looking ahead, arms folded, avoiding eye contact.

A Catholic priest in a shiny black suit appeared the next day, towing along a thirteen-year-old boy dressed in full tribal costume who said he was Martin Goodrider, another Blackfoot from the reservation.

"Hullo," I said.

"Hello," he replied. "I guess I'm going to play Little Chief." We traded stares.

"I just saw a movie," he said. *"Frankenstein.* There were a lot of murders."

"I have two machine guns," I replied.

He lowered his voice. "You know what's good for the nerves? Just have a fight." Suddenly he began waving his hand back and forth in front of my face.

"What are you doing?" I asked.

"I'm putting an Indian sign on you."

"Don't do that," I said. It sounded risky. "Take it off!"

"Don't you know it's just an ignorant superstition?" He radiated good humor. "You can have a lot of fun. Look, I'll show you how to do it."

Goodrider and I picked up companionship rapidly, but the chiefs remained uncommunicative and unsmiling. To help establish personal rapport, I proposed to enlist them in my police force. Scornful at first, they finally agreed, and gathered around me as if the swearing-in were just another in their daily chores. Holding up one badge, I delivered my usual admonitions on conduct, all duly translated by Chief Coward. Nobody smiled—a good sign. As tribal custom forbade wearing such a badge exposed, each man opened his deerskin tunic and I pinned it on the undershirt.

The yawning cultural chasm between the reservation and Hollywood was recognized by the U.S. Bureau of Indian Affairs, which threatened to impose a fine on the studio for any abuse to the Indian sense of pride. To protect themselves, the studio had purchased a $25,000 bond, assuring that each Indian would be presented to the movie public in a manner consistent with their traditional dignity, and meanwhile treated by the studio in the same fashion. This precept the Indians promptly tested on three levels: recreation, steak, and death.

Each Indian earned $55 a day, but payable only after his safe return to the Montana reservation. Lacking both money and knowledge of English, they remained bivouacked and cloistered on studio grounds, hardly a site for recreation. Periodic attempts to provide them movies, mainly inoffensive, short subjects, comedies, and cartoons, all met with a strong, prickly stream of contempt. Chief Coward relayed the complaints and specified the chiefs wanted to see *The Little Princess*. As with the general audience, it was a hit with the Indians and was requested on twelve separate occasions during their stay.

Food was the second challenge. On the reservation, cow meat was eaten thrice daily, and the studio fare of Hollywood sandwiches and potato salad was proving a cultural insult. Studio management balked, saying there was no budget for steak, so Chief Mad Plume, accompanied by Coward, took his indignation to the front office.

"When Blackfoot has visitor, visitor has all food he desires," translated Coward. "White man is bad-mannered." Mad Plume refused to leave the office until he got his pledge of steak every day.

More effective than movies and meat, death pointed up an even more profound problem instantly bringing our production to its knees. Routinely the chiefs had come to work garbed in traditional, fringed buckskin with eagle-feather headdresses. One morning they filed in wearing long, somber travel coats and broad-brimmed black hats. Coward explained that an important tribal official had just died back on the reservation. They all were honoring his death, Indian fashion, even if they were dressed in white man's clothes.

"Go get dressed in full regalia," ordered the director, "or be docked salary."

"We are in mourning," retorted Coward, staring back. "Pay has nothing to do with it."

With that all the Indians squatted down in a tight circle, where they remained, glum and uncommunicative. To utilize the fully mobilized set, our director tried to shoot around the Indians, but the rescheduling slowed us to a walk. For the next three mornings they appeared punctually but in their black garb, and sat around the set mourning away. Each day our shooting schedule underwent further erratic revisions. The unit manager charged with cost control mourned on his own account, because under terms of the fiduciary bond docking wages for mourning the dead was not permitted. Even Klammy was quick to complain that jiggling rehearsal schedules was seriously cutting into schoolwork continuity.

Without waiting a day, Father boiled over. Using attorney Loyd Wright as intermediary, he wrote Zanuck's boss, Joseph Schenck.

> ...The work of other players is usually done at night...leaving nothing but her work in the daytime...her schooling is rushed in between scenes.... Small periods of time such as four or five minutes are not counted by her teacher.... If we do not revise the shooting schedule, it will be necessary to report these things to Mr.

Thomas of the Board of Education. . . . Shirley's permit to work can
be revoked. . . . The studio may run into trouble.

Two other recent developments bothered Father more than my
schooling, which was merely a catalyst for his outburst. First, Zanuck
no longer spoke or wrote to my parents directly, but instead had started
to use vice president William Goetz as his surrogate. Son-in-law of MGM
movie mogul Louis B. Mayer, Goetz was apparently suffered reluctantly
by Zanuck, who reportedly once remarked that Goetz wouldn't know
a good script from a roll of toilet paper. "He's a born thumbtack; he
doesn't function when the thumb is missing," said Zanuck. Although
Father was already locked into a system of indirect communication with
Zanuck, he took it unkindly that Zanuck had designated Goetz as go-
between.

The second source of Father's irritation was that the studio had
transferred Griff, the bodyguard, from studio payroll to Father's direct
responsibility. The change was construed to mean that the studio no
longer felt it economically justified to provide me security, with all that
attitude implied for my future. It was also seen as a subtle move by
Zanuck to distance himself from direct contact with my parents.

Father was always quick to take offense or fling down a challenge,
and his thinly veiled threat to turn the studio in to public school authorities showed he was not adept at winning. Schenck ignored the
warning, in due course the Indians completed mourning, film scheduling returned to normal, and the basis for Father's concern vanished.

In step with the spirit of mourning, our next scene involved death
by immolation. Captured by Indians, Randolph Scott stood strapped to
a stake with tinder-dry brush piled high at his knees, ready to be ignited.
In full war regalia, our Indians shouted, leaped, and gesticulated, thumping away on tom-toms. Chief Yellow Kidney had strode forward waving
a firebrand and scattering sparks.

"Quick, somebody," I hissed, "get a *dis*tinguisher."

The remark was in deadly earnest, but everyone nearby laughed, so
director Seiter called a halt.

"Let's be serious about this thing," he said, staring pointedly at me.
Turning to the Indians, he instructed, "Pretend you hate him. You want
to kill him."

"Yes, *give*," I echoed.

Seiter called for a break.

"Come here, Shirley," he said. "Sit in my lap."

He had always been one of my favorites. Shiny-skinned, with eyes set so they could almost look backwards, everything on him tapered to the nose, as on a shark. I took his hand but remained standing.

"What's the matter? You used to sit up here." He slapped his lap. "Don't you like me anymore?" he taunted.

"Of course I do," I answered, "but you see, we're both much older now."

Reconciled to our passage of time, he got down to business. Did I have any other suggestions? I did.

"You know where Little Chief goes to sleep in the tepee?" He nodded. "Well, he takes off his clothes. Goodrider says Indians sleep right in their clothes."

"Then he sleeps with his clothes on," Seiter ordered.

Later, I asked Goodrider why he slept that way.

"It helps me smell like a man." He lowered his voice. "When I get back I may not bathe every day. Soap doesn't always work. Any man who depends on soap is at a disadvantage. On the reservation we acquire dignity other ways."

Goodrider fascinated me, someone who slept with his clothes on, fought to relax, liked *Frankenstein* movies, and regarded soap the wrong way to acquire personal dignity. Added to this, he smoked and rolled his own cigarettes from "twist," an aromatic, untreated tobacco. In one of our wigwam scenes he even puffed away at a peace pipe filled with real tobacco. Out of the blue, Seiter suggested that I, too, take a few puffs. Mother was appalled and refused, until he had an ingenious contraption rigged, a hidden tube taped to my off-side cheek but operated out of camera range. The proxy puffer was a set designer who, by chance, had staged the movie version of the great Chicago fire. It was *Heidi* fakery all over again, with smoke substituting for milk and my cheek for the goat's udder.

Synchronizing my exhales with his squeezes, however, proved impossible, so Seiter and Mother compromised. The real tobacco in the peace pipe was replaced by cubeb, a cousin to cornsilk, and the script now called for me to get queasy as a deterrent to any impressionable young audience.

Goodrider always carried a stubby, broad-bladed deer knife stuck in his belt and showed me how to use it in a thrust.

"I always believe in readiness," he told me. "I never walk from the reservation to town without my Saint Christopher medal in my pocket. But this knife is always in my hand too."

Sitting cross-legged in his tepee, he took the knife and gently faked pricking his own finger, then mine, and we commingled synthetic blood supplied by special effects.

"If this were all real," he told me afterwards, "you would be my blood-sister."

The following day I brought in a rubber knife from my home arsenal. A running gag in the film had actor J. Farrell MacDonald don a toupee as a decoy for his real scalp whenever Indians attack. He was seated alone, studying his lines. With a sudden whoop, I leaped on him, pretended to slice around his hairline and triumphantly held aloft the toupee while he yowled in fake pain.

The Blackfoot chiefs had eyed my joke in critical silence. Shortly after this Coward proclaimed that the chiefs in powwow approved of my scalping technique and wished to make me a tribal member. Squatting down between Chiefs Yellow Kidney and Iron Breast, I joined their tight circle, a motionless tableau of beaded, white buckskin, feathered headdresses, and squinty, weatherworn faces emblazoned with slashes of white war paint.

Chief Coward rose first and spoke in Indian language, a long, grave presentation, occasionally pointing at me. Yellow Kidney then took out a small penknife, poised it over his hand, and stabbed down into his gnarled, upturned finger. Blood oozed, forming a dark bead against darker skin. Before anyone on the sidelines could object, he turned, grasped my hand, and quickly nicked at my finger. A spot of blood appeared instantly, and he pressed his bloody finger against mine, his eyes closed. It was quick, if not totally painless. When it comes to taking blood samples, today's doctors can learn from Blackfoot chiefs.

With our fingers squeezed tightly together, Yellow Kidney then performed a long, singsong Indian benediction, half spoken, half sung, while the other chiefs grunted in cadence. When he had finished his chant we released our fingers; no trace of blood remained.

"Now, you blood-sister to Blackfoot nation," translated Coward. "Your name now Bright Shining Star." He unfolded a dress made of softened doeskin and held it up. "This your tribal dress."

"You could get an awful infection from that stab," lamented Mother. "Now you'll have to get a shot from Dr. Sands." Even that price was worth paying.

☆

Good things often end too soon. The film was winding up, and our Indian delegation was readying its return to Montana. Goodrider and I were saying good-bye when he offered to sing me a song.

"Like what?" I asked.

"Like 'Come Back Paddy Riley to Ballyjamesduff.' " He began in a clear, strong voice, his words laced with a brogue from the priest who had taught him. The lyrics were enchanting, the more so because he was singing.

"Will you ever get lonely out there on the reservation?" I asked.

"Oh, no," he replied quickly. "If I do, I just talk to myself." I confessed that sometimes I did the same thing.

"Would you like to keep on acting in movies?"

"I don't want to act at anything," he answered. Noting my scowl, he added, "You're sweet, and we ride and dance real good together. But you're civilized. I'm not, at all."

"Then what will you do?"

"Study until I'm thirty, and then be a Jesuit priest."

Much later, in the 1960s, I heard he had become an airplane pilot, then a religious mercenary in Africa helping Biafran rebels fight against the central Nigerian government. Flying in food supplies one day, he had crashed to his death.

Susannah of the Mounties received indifferent reviews: "Wee Willie Winkie among the Indians. . . A mediocre tale . . . Mass shots and spectacles . . . After the Technicolor success of *The Little Princess*, why revert to black and white? . . . The film's appeal abandons adults. . . . Addresses only the audience of Saturday-morning kiddie shows. . . . She is handicapped by having to repeat things done too many times in too many stories. . . . Shirley's growing up, but her stories aren't."

From the Blackfoot reservation in Montana came a distant cry of disappointment. Chief Coward had written the studio asking did I like the doeskin dress presented at the blood-sister ceremony? Nobody had bothered to answer. Finally another letter arrived, this one from the manager of the reservation trading post explaining that the chief expected a comparable gift in return. Recognizing its cultural error, the studio hurriedly dispatched a gift parcel. It must have stupefied the chiefs. Inside were fourteen samples from my dress licensee, all for girls and all for six-year-olds.

In Honolulu a young transit passenger went to see the film and missed his ship for the mainland.

"I really only stayed to play bingo," he explained at the juvenile detention home. "Sadly, they had already played it. Shirley Temple sure wasn't worth it!"

In a Chicago divorce court a woman charged that her husband had grossly mistreated her because she refused to accompany him to see my film.

"Shirley is *his* favorite," she protested. "I can't *stand* the rotten child."

Up the river at New York's state penitentiary at Sing Sing, I fared better. There, the inmates voted me their favorite long-term actress.

23

Upon completion of *Susannah of the Mounties* in late spring 1939, basic rhythms of my life altered.

Since age three only weeks had separated finish of one movie and anticipation of another. Now this principal rhythm of my existence ceased. Only background chords remained; daily studio tempos swirled by just out of my reach. Before this tantalizing backdrop of activity moved the principal actors in the drama of my young life.

Playing a lead was Zanuck. Flamboyant and seething, a man agog with ambition, he continued to be a distant and vague silhouette, someone far beyond my ken. His operating precepts were consistent. Retain my youth by keeping my skirts high. Pair me with the eternal moral verities of courage, love, and joy. Ignore my glands.

That course was perilous. No longer a cuddly child, I increasingly needed to establish my appeal to adult audiences. Yet the less I remained a child, the less my charm could be sustained for a new generation of children. Recent scripts flew in the face of both precepts. Although Zanuck crammed me backwards in time into childish molds, no practiced eye could fail to sense onrushing puberty. Story ideas bloomed and died, while he mustered a snake dance of screenwriters who advanced and receded with monotonous, incoherent regularity.

Once again *Little Diplomat* surfaced as a yarn of European troubles, co-starring Edward Arnold, fresh from portraying Diamond Jim Brady in *Man About Town*. Next whodunit writer Robertson White was hired to produce a mystery script. Jack Andrews was assigned to do a story with actor Al Jolson, fresh from his comeback try in *Rose of Washington Square*.

Zanuck then announced a public offer of $25,000 to anyone, anywhere for an acceptable story idea. Not to be ignored in this disjointed maze of activity, in floated Lady Jane, Zanuck's trophy from his London vacation, that wraithlike lady who already had swooped forward and faded. This time she had an original screenplay by Ethel Hill and Walter Bullock, and Zanuck assigned producer Ray Griffith and director Walter Lang for an April start in Technicolor.

Come April, for reasons undisclosed, Zanuck delayed his lady's entrance until June 26. Ten days before this debut she was stripped of her Technicolor. Two days before cameras were to roll, she was postponed for two weeks due to "script problems," blamed on Mother. It was a low blow. Mother had never even been introduced beyond the title.

"They don't consult me," she said. "I doubt if those who buy stories for her even look at her now. They just consult her old pictures."

Forty-eight hours later the lady was again jilted, this time for months, not weeks. A fourth consecutive period costume picture for me might be unwise, said the studio, leapfrogging Lady Jane forward to Thanksgiving. When her turkey did arrive, Zanuck's redoubtable peeress once again was pushed off, this time until Christmas week. The holidays brought her no cheer. Rebuffed for a fifth time, her start was indefinitely delayed.

In early fall studio indecision would still be dismissed by Zanuck in cavalier fashion. "It's a problem to find material for her. We have invested $150,000 to $200,000 in stories for her this year. She's a specialist limited to a few types of things," adding: "Specialists never last long."

Buried amid polemics and fitful studio behavior, back on April Fool's Day, Zanuck had purchased screen rights to Maurice Maeterlinck's *The Blue Bird*. First produced on the New York stage in 1912 and filmed in silents during 1918, the story was an undeniable classic. Columnist Louella Parsons had reported that the deal "lifted the deadly dullness of last week," a parochial comment, considering Mussolini had just leaped the Adriatic Sea to invade tiny Albania.

The clock ticked for us all, but Zanuck was boss.

Second player on that 1939 stage was Mother. Spreading softly with middle age, she still retained a remote beauty, her bosom heavy and shapely enough to attract admiring glances. Certainly no saint, she regarded the studio as both physical sanctuary and intellectual adversary. To ignore my plight today would have guaranteed it would be worse tomorrow. Whether wringing her hands in public or holding out those same hands in a plea for changed directions, she understood our limitations. When things went wrong she knew why. Beneath that gracious and groomed exterior were legs of steel. Poised at the center of emotional contagion, she cherished what she could, and never grew strident or self-righteous. Encircling me with affection, she looked to the future and never dropped her eyes.

My role in all this was less clear. For six months I had no lines to memorize at bedtime and rehearse in the morning, no call for costume fittings or even still photographs. In this professional vacuum, my academic grades showed sharp improvement, but existing so close to soundstage bustle with no call to work left me with an emptiness no rededication to school could totally fill.

Once in a while I had a duty. At the 1939 Academy Awards ceremony I presented to Walt Disney seven miniature Oscars for the dwarfs of his *Snow White and the Seven Dwarfs*, noting extemporaneously that Snow White had been overlooked in the award. The audience roared approval, not because of sexism, a concept not yet in vogue, but because I was right. Snow White had gotten a raw deal by being ignored.

A nice part of growing up is that you don't feel it until passing the big mileposts. Now I had observed that males had bumps in odd places, but so did women. Nothing unusual about that. While playing with boys, I had noticed little pointy things. Something to find out about, I thought, but it could wait. Hugs and kisses were only symbolic gestures. Other than my own, nakedness was a sight yet unseen. Nobody around home had yet explained babies to me. About sexual difference, I was completely blind, even in the case of birds.

My canaries, Ike and Mike, lived in an antique bird cage separated by a center grillwork. Twins even to their distinctive white tail feathers, they had a difference which escaped me. And the bars dividing them somehow were no obstruction to a conjugal visit. Soon Mike collected shredded newspaper from his cage bottom, made a nest, and laid some eggs. There was no good reason why Mike should not be a mother or conceive immaculately.

At my 1939 birthday party our parents were chatting away amiably in the downstairs library while upstairs we kids played murder and sardines. During one pileup in a closet I was pressed close to the Sir Galahad already favored by Mother. In the darkness his clumsy kiss missed my mouth. On general principles I wrestled free and landed a solid kick on his shin. With an angry snarl, he yanked me down again, threw me across his legs, and began spanking me, hard.

That something had gone wrong I knew, even before Mary Lou pointed and screamed for him to stop. Released, I fled to my nearby bathroom and slammed the door while she raced downstairs into the library.

"He spanked her too hard!" she wailed. "She's bleeding!"

Everyone came pounding upstairs. There Mother found me in the bathroom, standing there alone with my body and my newly discovered glands.

Nothing to worry about, she assured me, returning promptly with supplies and a printed pamphlet entitled "What You Should Know About Yourself."

"Now go on out and join your guests," she said.

"Whaaat!" I gasped, mortified at the thought.

"No cake for you if you don't."

Her rationale was compelling. Gooey chocolate cake is more important than the onset of puberty.

Father was the final important player in that 1939 hiatus, as he chuckled the days away. Neither spendthrift nor rascal, he seemed less spoiled by wealth than stunned. To his attorney were delegated most aspects of commercial business; to Thomason, all bookkeeping and tax matters. Cultivating his image as a canny businessman and set to the reassuring music of infectious laughter, he graced friends with loans, interest- and collateral-free, nibbled at real estate speculations, and savored penny mining stocks with the unshakable optimism of a sourdough.

One jarring note continued to intrude in his otherwise idyllic existence—relentless legal pursuit by producer Jack Hays. Playing croquet one day in Palm Springs, Mother and Father were accosted by a local constable bearing subpoenas for their depositions. Father scurried away around the corner of a cottage, leaving Mother trapped in the grass by her high heels. Three weeks later she appeared in court, refused to give testimony on advice of her counsel, and was assailed with a contempt-of-court threat by the plaintiff's lawyer, William C. Ring.

Meanwhile, Father had continued his flight to northern California. On a hastily arranged pretext, he appeared before the state Senate Judiciary Committee to offer testimony on a Child Actors Bill just introduced by Senator Robert W. Kenney. The intent of the legislation was to impound in trust all earnings of child entertainers until age twenty-one. Outraged by the miscarriage of justice in Jackie Coogan's tale of poverty, Judge Ben W. Lindsay, a renowned Los Angeles expert on juvenile court problems, had testified that "the committee should not see Shirley Temple and 250 other child motion picture actors have the same experience Coogan did."

In his March 29 statement, read at the final public hearing, Father agreed in principle that a child's earnings are the child's, but sharply criticized the bill as creating an unfair double-tax burden.

"Under California community property tax laws, the child's income can be split between both parents," his testimony read, "thereby reducing the total current tax bill. Under the proposed bill, higher taxes would be mandatory."

The committee disagreed. The problem to be cured was not taxes, but the risk in trusting parents to keep faith with their children. It recommended immediate passage by the legislature.

His duty done, if unsuccessfully, Father boarded a paddle steamer and floated overnight down the Sacramento River to San Francisco. He seemed impressed by the nude sideshow of fan dancer Sally Rand at the 1939 World's Fair but wrote Mother to "get the lowdown from Loyd when he thinks it safe for me to return."

Not yet, Attorney Wright advised. So under the public pretext of meeting brother Jack's college girlfriend, Mother and I went north by train, and our family was reunited on the top floor of the Benjamin Franklin Hotel in San Mateo, half the distance between Sally Rand and Stanford. Brother Jack asked to bring his sweetheart to meet us all.

A practice putting green had been set up on the sitting-room rug, the hole a tipped water glass. Father stroked a putt clunking heavily into the glass, just as a knock came at the door.

Miriam Ellsworth proved to be a pleasant-faced girl with the dark, bright eyes of a bird.

"What did you say your name was?" Father asked, not looking up.

"Miriam, but for short, everyone calls me Mims."

"Mims," he said. "How do you spell that?"

"M-I-M-S," she answered. "It doesn't mean anything."

He lined up another golf ball. "M-I-M-S," he spelled, then repeated phonetically, "Am-I-a-Mess." Stroking, he missed the glass entirely. "You sure are," he remarked.

Laughing unconvincingly, Mims glanced around at us while Father recovered his practice golf balls and, without another word, took his putter and went into the adjacent bedroom. Father's pick for Jack had already been made, the daughter of a theatrical agent, a person he described as "winsome, willowy, and wealthy."

Mims looked devastated. Father's tongue often stumbled with a pun. By the time she had married Jack, Father had grown to adore her, a gutsy woman of good nature, understanding, and charm. But for years afterward he slavishly resurrected this tarnished pun for his own merriment, never learning that humor can give off not only sparkle but searing heat.

Fleeing the process server turned out wise. Hays's suit was dismissed for lack of jurisdiction, leaving only one other legal action pending. It, too, was soon dismissed by federal Judge J. W. Vickers because Hays had failed to get his claim to trial within a two-year statutory limit.

Undiscouraged, Hays appealed the Vickers decision and filed a fresh suit, increasing his claim from $500,000 to $700,000 and again stressing that Father's repudiation of the original contract was "without justified cause, excuse, or consent."

Hays's latest hope flickered briefly when an appeals court met in mid-August and ordered Mother to answer under the prior subpoena. The case was returned to the lower court for further appropriate action. Hays's complaints seemed to have more lives than a cat, but after another year of legal maneuvering, Father's resolve to fight apparently drained away. Accepting precisely what he had resisted for seven years, he settled with Hays out of court, but for only $3,500. The wait was worth it.

Pocketing this thin slice of my earnings pie, Hays vanished from our concerns, reappearing briefly six years later when his wife, described in the press as a statuesque brunette, was being granted a default divorce.

"He choked me and slapped me," read her testimony. "I had bruise marks all over." For years Father had felt the same way.

Despite Father's contrary testimony, the California legislature enshrined into law a Child Actors Bill. Henceforth parents would be required to hold all their child's earnings in trust during minority. No retroactive provision was included, thus technically relieving my parents of compliance. However, on May 15, 1939, they executed a formal indenture between themselves expressly confirming that "certain monies" collected by them from my royalties and paychecks, together with accumulated interest, were really only being held in trust for me.

"Upon said minor, said Shirley Temple, reaching majority, said funds, in whatever form then invested, shall be delivered to said Shirley Temple," read the stilted text. That seemed to say it all. As joint, self-appointed trustees, however, my parents reserved all rights to use or dispose of such monies before my majority. Drawn as a declaration of good faith, the document actually surrendered nothing.

With little to absorb my energy except schoolwork, even visitors took on luster absent in busier times. Composer Irving Berlin came when Mother was busy. His interest in talking with me soon exhausted, he tarried outside, chatting amiably with Klammy, asking questions so personal she was mystified until his good-bye. "Well, it's been nice talking with you, Mrs. Temple."

On another occasion, responding to Klammy's call for school, I found a stranger waiting, his foot poised on the step of my trailer. He was introduced as Broadway playwright Noel Coward.

"Don't you ever get tired of people pushing, shoving, and loving you?" he asked. "And asking for your signature?" He held out his autograph book.

"No, I don't mind at all," I replied quite honestly. "It's all part of my job."

"Well, what are you studying in school now?"

"I was having Adolf Hitler. But today it's fractions, and they're hard. Why don't you come in and listen?"

Gingerly he stepped up into the trailer and looked about. "Where shall I sit?" he asked.

I pointed toward the narrow bench top divided into two cushioned lift lids. Hesitating an instant, he selected the left side, over the hidden commode.

Actually, both sides were important, and secret. Beneath the other cushioned lid lay my mother's box of Mrs. See's chocolates. With candy on my forbidden list, my fingers had become adept at cracking the lid upward, prying off the box top, making a tactile selection, and replacing things as they were found, all in one smooth, swift, operation. I learned both Chinese and French while seated above those chocolates. Something had to give way in later years. Luckily it was Chinese and French.

For several minutes Coward sat silently, listening while Klammy drilled me on arithmetic, his knees together, hands clasped in his lap like some English schoolboy waiting outside the headmaster's office.

"I never could do fractions either," he finally interjected. Obviously bored, he rose and said a polite farewell. As the trailer door closed behind him, I turned to Klammy.

"How do you expect me to learn about them in just a few weeks?" I tipped my thumb at our departed guest. "See, he must be over thirty and still doesn't know how!"

To further fill my time, Mother occasionally included me in her shopping excursions. A clerk at the pale gray elegance of Bullock's Wilshire department store called to advise the store had just received some things "which looked just like her." Almost every floor was polished hardwood or marble, except for red runners on the broad central staircase and luxurious carpeting in ladies' millinery. To relieve my tedium, I tap-danced around by myself, and eventually struck up a conversation with the floor manager. Mr. Goldie was a nice little man with red-gold hair, blue eyes, and blotchy complexion.

"Do you want to see a thief?" he said, and pointed, shielding his finger behind his palm.

Facing away from us stood a woman with blond, bushy hair peering into a showcase. Her pink suit was pinched at the waist and puffs decorated her high-heeled mules, but her purse was functional and bulky.

"Shoplifter," he whispered. "Just scoops things off the counter into that big bag. After she's gone, our salesladies make out charge slips and send them off to her husband. He never complains, just pays. A banker."

The woman was moving along the counter with a mincing gait.

Hurrying after her, I craned around for a secret look. The wrinkles were disguised under pale pancake makeup, and the eyelashes looked long and fake.

Returning to Mr. Goldie, I reported, "She's not very pretty. Why don't you catch her?"

His eyebrows arched. "Because she's happy. She thinks she gets away with something. Most of the time she's so busy shoplifting, she doesn't notice we're all watching her." He smiled. "She's like Santa Claus, except she's not seasonal."

"Her face looks more like Halloween," I commented.

Mother was delayed, so the rest of the morning I stalked that shoplifter but failed to see her steal anything. On subsequent visits whenever I spotted her, I always trailed her. We never made eye contact; not once did I catch her.

The end of the 1930s was fast approaching. Hitler's tanks had thundered into Prague, gobbling up Czechoslovakia. Roosevelt had pledged his support to Britain, ignoring congressional preference for American isolation. Like the 85 percent of Americans reported in Gallup polls, Klammy railed against armed involvement in "Europe's war" while in the same breath she urged more economic aid for England and France, the nations most threatened by Hitler. Besides, the studio makeup supervisor, Clay Campbell, complained, Balkan tensions had created a severe shortage of human hair for his wigs. Born to the crashing sounds of Depression and now racked by struggles for change, the decade now echoed warlike trumpets.

One day commotion arose at the main studio gate. Captain Fritz Weidemann, German consul general in San Francisco and key American confidant of Hitler, had arrived to meet with me, but studio officials were denying him entrance.

Remain in the cottage, we were instructed, and stay off the telephone. Drawing the curtains, we peeked out like pioneers surrounded by Indians. Only Mother expressed annoyance at what I took as an exhilarating chance to escape lessons. Why could Soviets and Mussolini get in, but not a German official? It was she who had approved the visit, following Weidemann's letter written on deeply embossed, crested stationery. German ethnic attitudes had nothing to do with an innocuous visit agreed to in advance. But Germany's exclusionary policy toward

American films was hurting us, reminded Klammy. They were commercial enemies. Outside in his diplomatic limousine, Weidemann fumed.

"What I wanted most down here," he bellowed, "was simply to be photographed with Shirley Temple! Any diplomat with a confirmed engagement would be outraged." That he was, and drove away in a state of high indignation.

Along with his annoyance, Mother's lived on, symptomatic of deterioration in her rapport with studio executives. On August 23, 1939, Zanuck was using his tongue on her like a woodsman his ax.

"Instead of bickering with us . . . the interest of Shirley Temple can best be served by closer harmony and cooperation. . . . Mrs. Temple has repeatedly taken the attitude that this studio, and myself particularly, are sitting up nights trying to find ways and means to ruin her daughter. . . . Mrs. Temple should direct all her energy toward 'playing ball' with this company, and recognize the fact that we have not stopped trying with Shirley."

Among other things to occupy my time were publicity layouts. Any *Life* magazine story was a public relations plum, even if paired with someone as currently controversial as Orson Welles. Author of a CBS-Mercury Theatre radio hoax based on H. G. Wells's *War of the Worlds*, he had seriously confused listeners with his narration of interplanetary invasion by Martians armed with death-ray guns who had landed in New Jersey and marched on New York City. Even his radio program colleague Joseph Cotten bade farewell to Welles, saying, "You are dead in the industry now."

Cast westward on this stage of notoriety, Welles arrived in Hollywood in a chauffeured touring car, exclaiming, "I'm rich! That's me! Just plain rich!"

A professional maxim in movies holds that a visitor, by the act of visiting, is thereby rendered inferior to the one visited. When the *Life* deal was struck, Welles demanded I come to his house for the job. Harry Brand, Fox chief of publicity, insisted I be host, however, leaking a rumor which reaffirmed my star status and branded Welles churlish and arrogant, an upstart with shaky credentials.

Outwaited, Welles finally caved in. Led to expect someone flamboyant, I found him the opposite. Formal in his double-breasted suit coat and pleated trousers, he looked faintly Chinese with his oval face, jowls, scraggly beard, and crescent of drooping mustache. Only his voice was distinguished, deep and reverberating, each tone treasured.

During my customary stable tour, the cameras clicked and Welles perspired, puffing heavily, with too much flesh sliding around beneath his bulky coat. The pose beside my diminutive merry-go-round bored him. A ride on the hundred-foot-long gravity roller coaster brought thick strands of black hair tumbling over his forehead and more gasping for breath. Sedentary photo opportunities might work out better, so I suggested croquet. Closer to the ball than taller opponents, I had regularly whipped most adults, even self-proclaimed expert J. Edgar Hoover. Alas, Welles was no beginner. With his pipe clenched firmly between his teeth, he stroked an excellent first shot. Photographers circled us and clicked away as we progressed around toward the final double wicket.

"What picture are you doing here?" I asked as he was bending over his ball. Distracting an opponent was fair game. He assumed a soldierlike stance, mallet at his side.

"A classic. Conrad's *Heart of Darkness*."

I shrugged. His shot was again good, and he waited until I was lining up mine.

"Did you hear my radio program about Martians?"

"Yes." I stroked my ball and scowled. It had stopped wide of the final wicket. "Nelson Eddy was why I listened."

Welles turned and leaned on his mallet, waiting. My evening routine included listening to Edgar Bergen and Charlie McCarthy, I explained, but when guest Eddy came on to sing, I switched stations and stumbled on his.

"Did you believe my program?" he asked, striking a pleasing pose for our photographers.

"No, I knew it wasn't true."

Taking careful aim, I knocked his ball slightly away from the mouth of the final wicket, leaving mine in good position.

His return shot caromed my ball away into a difficult lie.

"How did you know?" he asked.

Engrossed with my final chance, I said nothing and concentrated. I missed.

"Well," I replied resignedly, "if men from Mars had come here, why would just your program be broadcasting the news? That didn't make sense, so I didn't believe it."

In a patronizing gesture, he clumsily hit his ball wide of the final wicket, thereby assuring my win.

"From one champ to another," he wrote in my guest book, an accolade neither of us deserved. Magnanimous he may have been, but he won only my contempt. By throwing the game, he denied me the pleasure of an honest loss.

☆

Summertime and end of school left me with nothing to do and a future utterly blank, a situation never experienced since my start five and a half years earlier at Fox. Also never before had I had a real summer vacation. To my parents' surprise, I suggested that we go to Hawaii for a third trip, this time for change, not work.

Immediately after arrival we located a compact rental bungalow near Lanikai, a residential pocket on the windward side of the island, distant from the commercial bustle of Honolulu and Waikiki. Almost hidden behind a dense ti hedge at the end of a lane, it faced directly onto the ocean, and came equipped with a Chinese cook dressed in white and wearing a pillbox chef's hat, a smiling, enigmatic man who padded around silently on rope-soled sandals.

At first light in Hawaii it often rains, a sudden tropical downpour that thunders against the iron roof and overflows gutters in a crystal curtain of water, restorative to plants and human spirit alike. Passing as abruptly as it arrives, the rain leaves every petal glistening in the first cool shafts of morning sunlight.

Steps from our lanai stretched a lonely, sun-swept beach. There antic hermit crabs bearing borrowed shells scuttled about, diving down holes to evade my chase. Long-billed birds danced along the tide line, searching in the ebbing froth. Sand castles rose and were washed away, and a steady onshore breeze muted all sounds save the sea. What a joy to bounce waist deep in gentle surf or to mold myself a comfortable bed on warm sand at wave line, tasting sea salt on my lips, listening to the rhythmic thump and hiss of breaking waves, sensing the surge and retreat of water around my prone body.

All day through our permanently opened windows flowed a soft sea breeze until nightfall, when it reversed direction to steal down from the steep cliffs behind us, bearing a mysterious mix of scents from upland vegetation and flowers. Tropic dawn melted into tropic evening, day after day, until Hollywood seemed myth and Hawaii reality.

Next door to our hideaway cottage lay an empty lot used by local kids for softball games. Our regular umpire was a Hawaiian teenager, a trusty prisoner freed daily from nearby Wailua Jail for social work.

Everyone played barefooted, but Mother's rules called for me to wear shoes and a flared poke bonnet to keep my hair clean and the sun off my face. Despite such sartorial handicaps I soon figured out how to peer beyond the edge of my bonnet for an incoming pitch, swing the bat with authority, and run the bases almost as fast as my barefoot companions.

At first my new playmates treated me with a respect I resented, but gradually this formality eroded in our daily rough-and-tumble. A badge of acceptance came the day one ragamuffin kid on the opposite team teased me with "I see England, I see France, I see Shirley's underpants!" Swinging mightily, I drilled a two-base hit on the next pitch. My team cheered, and thereafter I was simply one of the gang.

Dawn to dusk, life flowed unstructured and sweet to the senses. The clock had stopped at a lovely hour. Then one afternoon a bicycle messenger pedaled up to our gate bearing a cryptic overseas cable. My next film would be *The Blue Bird*, and I should come home.

Before the bicycle had disappeared beyond our hedge, the old familiar sense of anticipation engulfed me. Hawaii once again was revealed as only a silky net suspending me temporarily above the real world of make-believe.

24

On the first day of September 1939 the final shooting script for *The Blue Bird* was delivered to my studio bungalow, almost at the instant of radio news that Nazi panzer divisions were slashing eastward into Poland, hapless victim for division between Stalin and Hitler under their nonaggression pact.

"So much for the bluebird of happiness," was Klammy's cryptic remark. "Let's hope Poland is no omen for us."

The rebirth of Maeterlinck's classic into an acceptable screenplay had already been arduous. Before arriving at Fox, the original had endured compression, expansion, and reshaping as ballet, pantomime, psychological drama, musical comedy, and monologue. The stage play consisted of 133 principal characters spread over six turgid acts, the longest stage show in American theatre history.

Chief screenwriter Ernest Pascal presided over the honing process for Fox, then added back in his own embroidery, a saucy sequence featuring Helen Ericson gowned in almost translucent chiffon as a new Spirit of Light. Despite the squeezing and massaging our tale clung to a predominant theme: happiness is found in the heart, not in external events.

True to character, Hollywood is not easily outspent or outmanned. Our $1.5 million budget accommodated spectacular sets and an army of three hundred children extras between the ages of four and fourteen.

Each morning a squad of thirty schoolteachers and chaperones appeared with their charges. Discipline was rigid, and misbehavior called for instant replacement. Dribbling noses or coughs meant suspension without pay. Keeping this tumultuous menagerie occupied when not working onstage presented a problem and a chance for me to earn some incidental income.

Normally playthings arriving in my fan mail were sent directly to a local charity. On *Blue Bird* I arranged for such gifts to be rented short-term for the children's play, at 10 cents per gift per day. The studio issued me a $200 payment in advance, the largest check made out in my name that I had ever seen. As always, Father took it for safekeeping.

As I was settling down to memorize the script, a Nazi juggernaut looped past the benighted Maginot line and stabbed deep into the French heartland. France and the United Kingdom had immediately declared war on Germany. In Hollywood we were also locked in a fight to the finish, fairy-tale style.

Some thought our film was conceived as a retaliation to MGM's *Wizard of Oz*. Zanuck stanchly resisted such innuendo.

"*Oz* is a musical comedy without any drama or sentiment," he declared. "*The Blue Bird* is strictly a dramatic fantasy. MGM made extravagant blunders and underwent financial tortures. We do not intend to copy *Oz* as to theme, or the mistakes that were made."

Although resolved to avoid errors, Zanuck was not immune to contention. For the forty-five days since our return from Hawaii, Mother had been nipping at his heels. For her, vacation had been therapeutic. Vanished was the acquiescent posture held almost uninterruptedly since her twin meetings with Zanuck and Schenck. Flooding back was her determination to achieve a change in my roles. By then no direct channel of conversation existed between my parents and Zanuck, so attorney Loyd Wright was enrolled to convey comments to Schenck, who then presumably relayed them to Zanuck. Rebuttals returned via the same circuitous route.

The first wrangle had been over just how repugnant I should be drawn in *The Blue Bird*. Mother urged that the writers make me impish, spoiled, and naughty. At first Zanuck had rejected the idea. Making me nasty was too risky. No audience would wish to see me obnoxious.

With every revised script draft Mother persisted. "If the crew hisses during rehearsal she will be in seventh heaven," she said.

Whether Zanuck grew indifferent or whether she wore the writers down or won them over, phrase by phrase my role became more shameful and despicable.

"They could have made her even meaner," Mother exulted to movie reporters. "She was tired of being good... getting bored. Her roles have been too monotonous... all sweetness and namby-pamby... difficult to believe... impossible to swallow." In some measure her views reflected mine. Just being hateful was not my objective, however; new characterizations were.

Another bone of contention between Mother and the studio concerned innuendos and symbolic touches occurring in the Land of Unborn Children sequence, well recalled from Mrs. Roosevelt's remark. Our scene was set in a heavenly forum of Art Deco benches and pillars, where boys and girls dressed in Roman togas and golden sashes milled about beneath a giant tent, each awaiting birth. It was a divine waiting room, where some children had tarried too long. The voice of "Studious Boy" Gene Reynolds, for example, was turning to baritone, and another child already sported a large vaccination scar.

The whole concept was elusive. Dead grandparents were comprehensible, but not unborn children. To complicate the situation, we all knew in advance that one six-year-old girl playing my sister was due to be born only so that she could quickly die. For someone so perfectly formed, a tiny soft-eyed clear-skinned little thing facing imminent death struck me as depressing.

Although Father was usually content for Mother to lead in squabbles with Zanuck, he, too, started to register opinions. Another in our unborn pack was young Abraham Lincoln, whose lines in our heavenly womb bore distinctive political undertones. Father complained to Zanuck via Wright. Why disinter the origins of the Civil War? FDR was waving the flag and talking about national honor as a reason to get in a fight alongside Britain, and were it not for our good isolationist Congress, we would already be at war. All this reference to war was inflammatory, he declared. Zanuck sent word back that he would "think it over."

Not only the shape of my role but others drew Mother's attention. In particular she was critical of Johnny Russell, a boy co-starring in some of my scenes. Although only six years old, he was an extroverted kid with a gift of mimicry. At my first encounter he sneaked up behind and cut loose a long, horrifying noise.

"Awrrrkk! The treasure is buried on the . . . awwkkkk!" he croaked, in a parody of Long John Silver's parrot. Like me, he had fat cheeks, sturdy legs, and a thick torso.

"Hi, shortie," I said.

He thrust out his chin. "I'm a man's man. I can do a man getting choked to death." Grabbing his throat he staggered backwards, gagging. "And a Chinese crook . . ." He switched to a singsong accent. "If you don't come out of that room, it'll be fatal," he shrieked once and rattled off gunfire noise.

The mimicry annoyed Mother, but I suspect she disliked his casting because Russell was younger and could potentially upstage me on that basis. What I needed was someone my own age she urged Zanuck, again through attorney Wright.

"Ridiculous," responded Zanuck. Two contemporary children meant I could not be the leader, as the story required. "If the boy were the same age, we would have to assume he was mentally incompetent or otherwise deformed if Shirley took the leadership away from him," Zanuck said in a burst of chauvinism. "A younger brother can cling to her for protection and guidance during the great adventure."

The "adventure" he cited was a combination gale and forest fire later described by a critic as "spectacular as the burning of Atlanta in *Gone With the Wind*." While lightning flashed and thunderclaps rolled, I led Russell by the hand as we fled along a forest trail past limbs hinged to sweep down to catch us. Whole tree trunks fell crashing and the wind howled. At last I detected a refuge in a hollowed tree trunk, dragged Russell inside, and there we huddled together, terror-stricken, until a lightning bolt ripped our shelter asunder, driving us once again into the spooky maelstrom of wind and rain. By that time the question of leadership had been well resolved.

"I was pretty scared," Russell later confessed, "with all that thunder and lightning and trees falling down. But she didn't say anything about it, so I didn't either." (Our issue of precedence was not in doubt then nor thirty-five years later in West Africa. By then I was a ranking U.S. ambassador, while Russell was a deputy chief of mission in a nearby nation, still my junior by one step.)

In 1939, however, who was being made the real star of the film continued to trouble both my parents. Once again a circuitous letter went off to Zanuck. "Shirley is the star of the picture," they wrote. "From reading the script at the end no one would guess such is the case," and went on to make invidious comparisons to MGM's *Oz*.

Zanuck exploded, again via Schenck and Wright.

"Beyond a shadow of a doubt, Shirley has 30 percent more to do and say than any other person in the picture, and for comparison, certainly more than Dorothy in the *Wizard of Oz*. We are at a loss to comprehend what you mean. The other characters are more or less puppets to illustrate her viewpoint. The real star of any story is the story itself. It cost us $100,000 to purchase it from Maeterlinck, and Paramount and the author have [has] been consulted. His first objection was that we had eliminated too many characters such as Bread, Water, Fire, and Cold in the Head. But we convinced him that the action of those characters was concentrated in scenes that did not include Shirley. She is the star. Her role demands she be the leader. I cannot accept your reasoning."

Obviously exasperated, he offered to "excuse me from appearing" in *The Blue Bird*, provided my compensation cease pending selection of another suitable story. It was a silken trap—straightforward suspension.

Offended that Zanuck had so personalized the matter, Father fired off his response via Wright.

"There is nothing the Temples want more than to cooperate with you. They have sought it for months. May I say frankly to you, if you were not so busy and you could take time to see Mrs. Temple, get her viewpoint, and go over the situation with her, many things could be ironed out and misunderstandings would not arise."

Privately, Wright advised my parents against accepting Zanuck's offer of suspension and recommended I proceed with the film.

"Then, I think we have a record," he wrote, "that will help us in the dog fight that will follow."

As these acerbic volleys went arching over my head unseen by me, down on the soundstage life seemed simple and our objectives clear-cut. With all the ingenuity, energy, and skill at our collective command, cast and crew were striving to produce a historic film, one to command widespread wonder and respect.

By the time we neared completion, however, a growing concern had arisen. The thematic complexities of our story line might be beyond the average moviegoer. Recognizing this potential weakness, marketing officials decided that favorable momentum was critical from the outset, and borrowed the "road show" merchandising concept used with *Gone With the Wind*. By concentrating heavy promotion and interpretative advertising in only a few markets, so went the theory, our film could be made more intelligible than if entrusted to scattered, variable promotional campaigns launched by theatrical chains. *The Blue Bird* must be merchandised like a jewel, not scattered like seed.

Accordingly, on November 8, 1939, *The Blue Bird* was withdrawn from its prior scheduled Christmas release and replaced by Sonja Henie's *Everything Happens at Night*. Held back for twice-daily performances in only three markets, San Francisco, Detroit, and New York, it was supported by a broadside of supporting advertisements and full-color spreads in magazines, billboards, and newspapers. Placards and displays were propped, pasted, and tacked up in storefronts and libraries. Book publishers Dodd, Mead, Grosset & Dunlap, and Whitman Publishing reprinted special editions of Maeterlinck's original story with our film photographs.

Faithful to her aversion, Mother removed me from duties on promotional tours. But to hype the film, a flock of studio personalities did wing off for personal appearances around the nation, among then Henry Fonda, Alice Faye, Linda Darnell, Don Ameche, and Brenda Joyce. Andre Kostelanetz was dragooned into an orchestral radio show featuring Tony Martin crooning that someday he, too, would find a bluebird.

Johnny Russell was among those sent out to hawk our wares, as usual interweaving his personal views with the standard pitch.

"I'll retire from pictures at twenty-nine and get married," he bubbled. "When I went to Hollywood I had thirty-seven girlfriends from ages five to twenty-nine. Now I only have one." Shirley? No. He could never marry me. Was it our age difference?

"I could outgrow that," he said. "It's just that people might think I was marrying her for her money."

Meanwhile the professional press had begun to draw uncomplimentary contrasts between *The Wizard of Oz* and *The Blue Bird*, suggesting our film was an attempt to ride piggyback on the earlier MGM success. Antipathy between Zanuck and Mayer over my aborted loanout for the *Oz* film seemed to be the taproot of the problem. Also, had not Zanuck lifted the idea for Eddie Collins's dog in *The Blue Bird* directly from Bert Lahr's lion in *Oz*?

A more considered view pointed up crucial differences. *Oz* appealed to both young and old, while *Blue Bird* was principally for children. *Oz* was a glorious, lighthearted musical based on reality, while *Blue Bird* drifted off into obscure fantasy. Dorothy of *Oz* was a naive Kansas farm girl knocked unconscious by a tornado, but her dream remained linked with the dust-bowl realities of home and a noble wish to help others.

Our bluebird went flapping off in a different direction. Like *Oz*, its takeoff point was reality, followed by a dream. However, there we got stuck, wallowing midway between vaudeville and a ponderous, barely intelligible spirituality.

Another major contrast was between selfless Dorothy and hateful me. My goody-goody image was in tatters, just as Mother had intended, with my full agreement. Gone was goodness; enter evil. The character appealed to me, a peevish, greedy, spiteful brat, the sort anyone would like to put over a knee and wallop. Arrogant with my parents, selfish about life, and covetous of the bluebird, I remained nasty until far too late into the film for successful redemption.

Just as Europe had hostilities, Hollywood had its own 1939 warfare, a highly personalized battle between MGM and Twentieth Century-Fox. Their wizard against our bluebird. In the end, it was more a battle between their cannon and our cap pistol.

Although shielded from extended tours sponsoring the film, I did what I could locally. In a rare exception to Mother's policy, I was permitted to appear on a Christmas Eve benefit radio broadcast of the Screen Guild Theatre, featuring me in a half-hour dramatic excerpt from the film and a "Silent Night" duet with Nelson Eddy. An untimely sore throat worried me a little, but I knew Eddy could carry me if my voice weakened.

My upstairs theatre dressing room faced directly onto a parking lot. Standing at the window I looked out while Mother fussed around with the back of my hair, and I saw a scruffily dressed woman carrying a large handbag come along below, peering up into each window as if searching. When she saw me, her face lit up with recognition. Scowling, she raised her fist and shouted something unintelligible.

"What is she doing?" I asked Mother, who simply dropped the venetian blind, and urged me to concentrate on my lines. As a general precaution, however, she reported the odd event to a theatre official. Jumpy about possible public disturbance, he in turn passed the word to local police, who upgraded the incident to a possible kidnap and involved the local FBI.

By the time the houselights had dimmed and the fanfare music swelled, both the woman and her vicious gestures were out of my mind. Standing behind the microphone, I swept the applauding audience with my warmest smile. Suddenly, there she was. The same frumpy, angry-eyed woman was seated in the front row directly beneath me, hardly an epitome of Yuletide spirit. At that moment the orchestra hit my cue, so I silently cleared my throat and launched into song.

Midway in the verse I detected two forms moving slowly down each aisle and glancing from side to side. Hardly ushers, I thought, not with those snap-brim felt hats.

"Oo-oo-oo!" I was warbling like a bluebird, then noticed the woman reaching into her handbag.

"Oo-oo-oo!" I echoed, this time with true urgency. She had extracted what appeared to be a small handgun.

A reed-thin microphone is a rotten place to hide, but the orchestra played on, so I kept singing, "someday you'll find your bluebird." My tones had gone slightly flat and timing way off, largely due to my out-stretched arms wagging like semaphores to direct the fedoras to the front row.

Slowly the woman rose, like one transfixed, raising her gun until it pointed directly at me. Now the two men had spotted the woman, and both came crowding and stumbling past the extended legs of seated patrons.

Moments like these would seem totally unreal were it not for a desire to vaporize into thin air. The stage wings were too far away. I might have elected to become a moving target, dancing quickly first right, then left. Or perhaps I could have flung myself into the orchestra pit, like some virginal sacrifice off a mountaintop, and sought shelter behind a tuba. Instead I just shrank down behind my microphone, my voice locked on another "oo-oo-oo."

Why the woman did not pull the trigger before being roughly seized by the two men is hers to answer and mine to bless. Disarmed and lifted bodily, she made no sound audible over the orchestra music, nor did the orchestra leader, his back to the disturbance, miss a beat.

It was a long evening. Apparently undismayed by the passing wrestle in the front row, the audience applauded appreciatively until Eddy began our "Silent Night" duet. Perhaps my chronic indifference to lyric voices had something to do with my performance, or placing us on opposite sides of the stage made harmony and matched phrasing difficult. A heavy cold is certainly no help, and perhaps the woman with the handgun was still in my thoughts. Whatever the reasons, my half of "Silent Night" would have been better left silent.

Next day an FBI agent called. The woman's gun had been loaded and she had indeed intended to kill me, for stealing her daughter's soul. Several hours before my birth, she had borne a girl, and at the very hour of my birth, her baby had died. My soul was in fact her daughter's, she claimed. To avenge the theft, she had set out to kill my body.

Although the tale seemed understandable to me, Mother would have known its crucial fallacy. My birthdate the woman was using was 1929, the one fabricated long before by Winfield Sheehan. In truth it was off by one year, so somebody else had stolen the soul.

Childbirth, death, and misplaced souls formed appropriate companions for *The Blue Bird*. Sophisticated enough for New York critics to tip a hat for our acting, the film was slammed hard for its screenplay.

"The acting is unanimously held to be big-league, but a case of movies slogging over Maeterlinck . . . a singularly maladroit transcription of a notable stage fantasy . . . an exquisite little fairy tale vulgarized by overemphasis on spectacle . . . as entertainment for adults, it's good fare for children."

On January 15, 1940, the bird that played the title role, at $50 per day, was reported missing from its cage at the Los Angeles bird farm of Coulson B. Glick. Lost, stolen, or flown, even the real bluebird fled for cover.

Summarized *Time* magazine, "*The Blue Bird* laid an egg."

Fate had one more twist in its blade. For Caryll Ann Ekelund, one of the children in our cast, life at home proved even more dangerous than on the set. A lighted birthday candle ignited her dress and burned her to death. With five older brothers acting as pallbearers, she was interred at Forest Lawn Cemetery. Her burial shroud was the unborn-child toga from her *Blue Bird* role, but ironically the theme sung by a graveside quartet was her favorite, "Over the Rainbow," from *The Wizard of Oz*.

Thirty years later our *Blue Bird* would receive critical acclaim as a film classic, but in the increasingly realistic time of 1940, it had to wait. Our film was conceived as a thing of the spirit, a beautiful kite sent aloft to inspire everyone with its mystic symbolism, a crosstown Hollywood spiritual response to the shallow optimism of *Oz*. We had all given a mighty tug to launch Zanuck's kite, only to see it fall back to earth.

25

When I get very, very old, I'll stay at home all day;
But I haven't quite made up my mind.
It's much too far away.
                                                        —From *Curly Top*, 1935

The New Year 1940 unfolded like a minefield across which only the most deft could clodhop.

The authoritative *Motion Picture Herald* ratings announced my plunge from first place to number five in popularity, trailing Mickey Rooney, Tyrone Power, Spencer Tracy, and Clark Gable. It was a masculine world now.

Undeterred by ratings, an eastern promoter offered me $10,000 per week for a personal appearance tour starting at the Hippodrome Theatre in Baltimore, then out on the Steel Pier in Atlantic City, and winding up the star in producer Mike Todd's *Hall of Music* revue at the New York World's Fair.

Still resolutely opposed in principle to such performances, Mother declared, "As long as I have anything to say about it, Shirley will never do a tour. She's too *shy!*"

Timidity would not have suited Todd's plan anyway, for he replaced me with a vaudeville act headlined by stripteaser Gypsy Rose Lee. Learning of this, Mother wrinkled her nose in distaste.

Like a jack-in-the-box, speculations kept popping up regarding what film the studio would select next. Mother joined the pack, by inference disclosing her assessment of films just completed.

"Her next should be modern, or a mystery, or something with a psychological slant. She's too old for cowboy-and-Indian stuff."

That attitude stifled a feeler for my loan-out to remake *The Virginian*, a western classic. Independently the studio squashed any further loan-outs with a flat statement that I was unavailable, and my next might possibly be *Rip Van Winkle*. Personal animosity between my parents and studio executives had choked off coherent communication, so Mother used the media to loft her javelins of indignation. In return the studio expressed its pique by doing nothing, but telling the world just that.

Continuing her refreshed assertive attitude, Mother publicly asked, "Why not co-star her with number two in the ratings, Tyrone Power? MGM casts Mickey Rooney with Spencer Tracy, and everybody makes a big hit. At Universal, Gloria Jean gets to appear with Bing Crosby. Why doesn't Fox pair its two biggest stars?"

Known for his skillful handling of women actresses, particularly in his recent hit movie *The Women*, and personally feuding with Zanuck anyway, director George Cukor threw a brickbat into the confusion.

"Cloud-cuckoo-land," he mourned. "Of all forms of cinema waste, the most extreme is tossing away talent. Even calloused souls with antipathy for child players let loose their complaints, not against Shirley, but those who choose and create her materials. The fate reserved for those with talent is vulnerability for the mistakes of the masterminds."

With the studio relationship sliding downhill rapidly, Mother publicly threw up her hands.

"I'm just waiting here for Shirley's contract to be over," she bitterly complained, "Whatever new contract she signs will stipulate only one picture a year."

"Will it permit you to sit in on choices of material?" she was asked.

"At present I certainly have no say at all," she answered. "If only they would realize it is time for realism. As long as the public will respond, the picture people seem willing to repeat that first Shirley."

"In other words, they are sticking to the personality which made her reputation?"

"Yes," Mother replied, "but it isn't her personality *now*. It may not be good to keep on acting a personality she is leaving behind."

Her statements lacked precision. My personality had not basically changed; my perceptions had. Klammy's system of parallelism in my studies, along with passing time, were sharpening my awareness of how closely distant events were coupled to life at hand. However, with this new perspective came restlessness, a vague dissatisfaction with the static character of my surroundings and tasks. Perhaps the familiar, slow pace of my surroundings was failing to match the physical changes occurring inside my body—and my head.

The sweep of my professional landscape may have looked bleak, but out of public sight and without my knowledge Mother had put into motion a plan to cope with my growth. On that very day *The Blue Bird* had commenced back in September 1939, she had applied for my entrance into the Westlake School for Girls.

Her timing was exquisite. Studio indecision, my declining popularity ratings, and her personal estrangement from Zanuck joined in funeral drumbeats for my Fox contract. Traces of my incipient boredom with movie work may have helped goad her to action. Drastic action was needed, something to shrug me free of the inertia gripping me. Girlhood stood a better chance of finding nourishment in natural surroundings than in the studio pasture of only adult companionship. Since gurgling infancy the institution of moviemaking had set my clock, served up my colleagues, summoned my services, and rewarded my efforts. Crumbling of this skeleton could well have been traumatic, but to ease my transition from young girl to adult, she had cleverly inserted Westlake, not to be a substitute but an overlapping institutional challenge to cushion the impact of rapid change.

On November 28, 1939, right after *The Blue Bird* finished, Mother disclosed her plan and took me to be interviewed by Westlake principal Miss Frederica de Laguna, someone who could have been a headmistress from any old movie. Stiff and regal behind her empty, polished desktop, dressed in shiny black taffeta, high-necked with a single brooch pinned above her ample bosom, she was a familiar, forbidding figure.

Why did I want to attend Westlake, she asked, resting both elbows on the desk, hands clasped together symmetrically like a belt buckle. To meet other girls, I guessed. Not to learn, she asked? That, too, I supposed. Headmistresses were nothing strange; I knew lots of them. Most had hair encased in a net and pulled back in a tight bun, and wore gold-rimmed spectacles balanced halfway down the nose. The trouble was, I hadn't memorized this principal's lines in advance, nor my own.

Inquiring from Mother details of Klammy's studio curricula, she listened with her mouth held in a thin line, impersonal yet not really threatening. Now and then she eyed me sideways, and each time I tried to round my eyes with intellectuality. Seated unmoving and erect, I felt like a piece of meat being weighed.

It was clear, was it not, that I would be entering school in midterm? Was I prepared to perform the requisite catch-up with my class? I bobbed my head enthusiastically, thinking less of homework than of the tantalizing glimpse of passing students as I had been ushered toward Miss de Laguna's office. All bore the three hallmarks of sophistication; height, good bodies, and lots of hair. I could hardly wait, catch-up homework notwithstanding.

When Griff let me out under the portico my first school day, curious faces were peering around window curtains, like stacks of billiard balls. Matching my step to Miss de Laguna's, I marched off to the routine daily morning convocation, a nondenominational potpourri of announcements, prayers, and group songs, concluding with the school processional. As the student body sang in a full-throated chorus extolling the joys of Westlake, my spine tingled. How I wished I had already learned the words, so that I could sing with the rest. Westlake was my spring latch to another world, and Miss de Laguna keeper of the keys.

Struggling under an armload of seventh-grade texts, I was assigned an unoccupied seat at a broad wooden desk in the rear row, one already shared by a plump girl with red hair. Smiling briefly, she slid sideways along our common bench to make room, then stared fixedly into her book.

From my vantage what I saw most were heads of hair, each styled differently from the other. As one whose whole life had been spent with two versions of ringlets, watching my classmates comb, preen, tease, twist, and fluff confirmed that I had been deprived. Within several days I had joined the group experimentation, using "rats" of crepe wool to create unusual contours and copying one schoolmate who swept her hair up in a looming pompadour pinned tight on the sides.

"That's not pretty," Mother commented sourly. "Your ears stick out. They're pointy." I took the hair down and tried to disguise my ears with the style called batwings.

Our class teacher was a spinster Miss Jessie L. Thornton, a woman with high forehead and clipped speech who moved quickly to establish her authority over me. My first day's recitation was an obstacle course, with odds heavily in her favor. Mathematics, in particular, was an initial humiliation. Although reasonably quick and accurate with arithmetic and fractions, I was slow with long division and tedious with equations, a disinterest always puzzling to Mother, who loved such things.

Clumsy and mortifying in my first oral answers, I was shown no mercy. Several days after I had joined her class she was reading aloud when she suddenly stopped and peered toward me.

"Why are you always smiling?" she asked. Some of the girls turned to look.

"Who, me?" I stammered. "It's natural, I guess. I always have this expression." The class tittered.

Her sweeping glance quieted the room. "Well, it's weird. You shouldn't smile all the time." Again titters. "Now, where were we?"

Unaware that my face looked happy in repose, yet anxious to please, I adopted a mildly troubled expression. After several days my deskmate asked why I no longer smiled, and one noontime Miss de Laguna stopped me in the hallway and inquired whether I was unhappy with Westlake.

Actually I felt the reverse. Luxuriating in the yet unrealized hope of companionship and unity with girls my age, I was the most delighted girl in the school. Book-laden students hustling crisscross in the corridors imparted a sense of purpose and obligation. Clanging school bells and regimented behavior fitted me like a comfortable shoe. Even the repetitious creamed eggs on toast greeted by student groans, seemed food fit for a princess. Yes, please, some seconds.

An entry in my personal diary tells the story.

"Perhaps it was because it was my first vespers, but tears came to my eyes. I looked at all those girls and knew I was one of them."

Within days, however, my sentimental generalization was bumping up against the phenomenon of homework. With Klammy the spoken word had always been dominant. Written texts, diagrams, and documents were used mainly as points of emphasis. Sudden dependence on reading homework was a marked departure, like eating my way through a pillow.

"What are you reading now?" Mother called one evening. Nibbling to finish my chocolate bar, I turned my radio down low.

"The *Junior Encyclopedia*," I answered, tones muffled by the candy. "I'm reading it through from the beginning."

"How far are you?"

"Well, I've hit a hard place, about 'acceleration.' It doesn't read fast."

"You're becoming quite a scholar already." She laughed.

"I'm supposed to read a little encyclopedia every day, but it's not what I'd like to spend most time on." We both knew the answer to that one, radio mysteries.

Reading itself was not a problem. For years I had read everything in sight, scripts, Bible stories, the *Oz* books, *Black Beauty*, and even sophisticated books like Arthur Koestler's contemplative story of a condemned Communist, *Darkness at Noon*, read with fascination if not total grasp.

A small antique cabinet near our dining room was a treasure chest of leather-bound volumes in gilded bindings. *The Complete Short Stories of Guy de Maupassant*, equipped with a crimson ribbon place mark, told tales which all seemed to start the same. Two men are seated comfortably before a roaring fireplace after dinner, before them a silver tray with half-drained brandy glasses. Perhaps someone's foot is propped on a gout stool.

"By the way," one would ask, "whatever happened to old Pierre. . . ?"

No, reading was definitely not the problem. Retention of homework reading was. Things read for pleasure were seldom forgotten, but those associated with work, such as a movie script, came effortlessly and disappeared the same way. Westlake homework was like a script, retained long enough to pass a test, then sent off into deep mental storage. My lessons could have been written with vanishing ink. With every sneeze I lost some statistic or a date in history, blew my mental cobwebs around, and resettled the dust. As with Koestler's principal character, Rubashov, years of solitary confinement in jail would have been necessary for me to reach into those subterranean mental levels and to restack and classify all those facts, studied and stored away.

My first week at school I was asked to play a role in a Christmas pageant. Instinct told me that playing show-off among amateurs would only earn enmity, so I declined. My refusal raced like wildfire through the school, feeding on itself, until it left me seeming not modest, but someone vain and uncooperative.

Scrambling to recover lost ground, I volunteered and was assigned as one of a pair of mantelpiece bookends in a skit titled "Minikin and Manikin." My companion was a classmate of American Indian descent, and rehearsing our shared activity promised genuine friendship. But once rid of our bookend costumes and acting obligations, she, like the others, withdrew from further cordiality.

Any alien celebrity suddenly plopped into a class of eleven ordinary girls could hardly expect effusive greetings. Long before my arrival everyone had sorted themselves into cliques, each coolly antagonistic toward the other. Brainy, mature girls stood aloof. They didn't need us. Sophisticated girls shared secret jokes and sneered a lot. Everyone else seemed to form up around shared past history together or special interests, which fenced them off from the others. Poorly groomed hair, pimples, or mismatched clothing were cause enough to realign friendship. It was difficult to see where I fitted, let alone worm my way in.

One lunchtime a classmate suddenly asked why I ate the way I did. "You shake your head from side to side to loosen the bite of sandwich," she said.

"What's wrong with that?" I asked.

"Most people bite and pull the mouthful away. They don't yank it free with that silly sideways head motion of yours. That's like a dog." Obviously, my battle was still uphill.

Sole exception in this isolation was my seatmate, Plump Girl. Enforced proximity probably evoked common ground, a jolly, extroverted view of things. From the outset her companionship saved me from being a complete loner. Having first stumbled into a bramble patch by being self-effacing, then confusing everyone and myself by trying to look sour when I felt happy, I realized the best course was to be myself—joyful, spunky, and competitive.

An opportunity to once again be myself presented itself in the recreation room of a Santa Monica church where our all-girl group was playing musical chairs. As the music stopped another Westlake girl and I raced neck and neck, and as she turned to drop onto the seat I applied a full hip, something I had plenty of. She landed flat-bottomed on the floor.

"I'm ashamed of you," Mother whispered afterward. "You were so anxious about winning."

That was the game, I protested. Somebody had to lose, and I was making sure it wasn't me. Mother remained critical, saying that sort of attitude was no way to make friends. Thinking about her view a long time, I agreed losing might be a way to make friends, but I would rather win.

Following this instinct during two successive holiday dancing parties attended by Westlake students did little to enhance my standing among schoolmates. Organized by the same Elisa Ryan of my childhood, our parties matched boys and girls under the watchful eyes of chaperones. Finding my partner shy and clumsy, I decided to lead, but standing on the outskirts of the crowd, Miss Ryan noticed, stopped the phonograph, and issued me a loud rebuke. Bored with an ensuing waltz record, I improvised again, adding a tap flourish. Again Miss Ryan leaped to stop the music, addressing me personally.

"Miss Temple, you will dance only what and when you are told."

If approval from schoolmates for being innovative was what I sought, I was disappointed. Most looked annoyed at delays in the dancing.

At Miss Ryan's next party everyone came disguised behind a black mask, and for the first time in my life I wore long silk stockings. After the mandatory waltz and box step, Miss Ryan called for a record with a faster tempo. Stepped on and stuck by pumping elbows, I escaped my partner's clutch and spun off alone, sending my long black pleated skirt flaring outward and up, confident that mask and swirling skirt made a synchronized, attractive picture. Told later why everyone stared so and laughed, I was appalled. It was the spectacle of elastic straps attached to my garter belt.

Eruption of my first facial pimple held renewed promise. The shared problem of acne might attract conviviality from those similarly afflicted. Pimples were a new experience. When mine first appeared Mother had treated it like a jungle chancre, packing me off to a dermatologist who solemnly picked off little flakes of skin with pointed tweezers and recommended I stop eating chocolate.

To my regret nobody at school wanted to talk about pimples—those with them from shame and those without them from aversion. Within days mine vanished, never to reappear, and I restarted chocolate with pent-up gusto. But my diminished status at Westlake still seemed secure. Most girls continued to look through me, leaving me standing in mid-greeting, superfluous and mortified.

One little girl was friendly, and I liked her very much, even after she got around to asking how to get into movies. Go to your father, I replied, knowing he was Robert Montgomery. Our cordiality eventually backfired on us both, she for cultivating an older girl and I for frater-nizing with a mere kid.

During one recess just before Christmas vacation I noticed a par-ticularly animated group, and came up from behind, hoping to join in. Suddenly the laughter stopped. One girl I knew was in the brainy crowd turned to face me.

"There's nothing we have to say to you," she sneered, "so we'd rather not talk to you at all."

From the first day that Smart Girl had proved one of my most inaccessible classmates. Particularly sophisticated, clever, and vivacious, she had scoffed that my slopey shoulders reminded her of a Coke bottle. That afternoon she was obviously organizing a party.

"You can come," she said, singling out classmates, "and you, and you."

I edged myself into her direct view. For one instant our eyes met. She raised her finger and pointed.

"But not her," she said impersonally, and turned away.

In all my life I had never felt so alone, and was seriously concerned that things might never change. At such fleeting instants my preference was to leave school and return to the relative warmth of Klammy and my friends around the studio lot. Continuous rejection for no apparent reason was a fresh and unsettling experience. My yardstick for achieve-ment had always been acceptance by others. Obviously I was flunking, and knew not why.

Smart Girl had resumed talking to her friends and was recounting what sounded like a riddle.

"You know how to break the ice with a boy?" she asked. "Well, just say in French, '*Voulez-vous coucher avec moi ce soir?*' "

She burst into laughter, but none of her listeners seemed to un-derstand the French. The joke was about to founder.

From Miss Walling's lessons I recognized the words, if not their implication. Pushing myself forward, I repeated her phrase, heavily laced with my own Parisian inflection, then burst into enthusiastic giggles. That made at least two of us who found the joke funny. Only Smart Girl really knew why, but she seemed relieved to have my support. After all, her riddle was falling flat.

Suddenly we had something to share. However, not one to give ground abruptly, she laboriously corrected my accent. Whether rightly or wrongly made little difference to me. Playing the willing student, I repeated the words until letter-perfect, her way.

"I guess you can come to my party," she finally said, a tiny wedge of light in the wall of indifference that imprisoned me.

26

Shirley's passing o'er the hill
To the setting sun
Ah! in time the passing years
Get most everyone . . .

Shirley's getting matronly
Shirley's getting fat;
At eleven all joints creak,
Life is just like that.

—H. I. Phillips
Washington Post, May 18, 1940

I f the Westlake School was the shaft of sunlight driving down from amid gray shapes overhead, Twentieth Century-Fox was a murky storm cloud. My contract was still running, but no future plans were announced.

On January 20, 1940, the chill factor dropped another degree when Miss de Laguna, acting as surrogate for Mother, refused to release me from classes to headline *The Blue Bird* film premiere in San Francisco, saying henceforth schoolwork would take precedence over publicity chores.

The plot of my professional life was starting to take more twists and turns than a Gothic novel. In mid-February the wind shifted slightly with my assignment to *Young People*, but the original screenplay by Edwin Blum and Don Ettlinger made cheerless reading. Again I would be an orphan, albeit older. Adopted informally by itinerant vaudeville veterans Charlotte Greenwood and Jack Oakie, I would dance and sing my way through the story, interrupted only by clips from my old films, culled to evoke past magic. The film's value amounted to less than the sum of its parts.

Our setting was Maine with a hurricane thrown in, and the director Sidney Lanfield, fresh from sick leave after guiding to completion the suspenseful *Hound of the Baskervilles*, launching pad for the "Sherlock Holmes" series. Our starting date March 1.

In late February, I was again onstage at Westlake in our *Valentine Vignettes* program for parents. My role was to pirouette as a nonspeaking Irish doll, and during intermission to hawk samples from our arts-and-crafts class to the captive audience.

At the studio, director-designate Lanfield lasted barely one week. He was replaced by veteran Allan Dwan and reassigned to *Public Deb #1*, a social spoof starring the real-life hostess Elsa Maxwell. Starting time was postponed two weeks to March 14.

During three months at Westlake things had taken a turn for the better, with stone walls to friendship fast crumbling. Acceptance by schoolmates subtly decreased the appeal of doing another movie. Hoping to have it both ways, I wrote Zanuck a letter, my first to him ever. Would it be possible, I asked, to reschedule the film start ninety days further until June? School would be out. He can be forgiven if he kicked at his wastebasket. His silence confirmed the starting date as inevitable.

My only recourse was to fall ill, which conveniently occurred the morning I was due at the studio. Checkmated by my fever, Zanuck pushed the starting date forward two weeks until April Fool's Day. Something must have triggered his second thoughts about the severity of my cold, for he immediately rescinded this extension and ordered me to appear for work two days hence.

Facing suspension without medical testimony of serious affliction, I reluctantly clicked off my radio and gathered up textbooks. Attended by well-calibrated coughs and sneezes, I reappeared at the studio cottage, where Klammy was prepared to tutor me in Westlake assignments during breaks in production.

Barely had I squeezed in behind my old drop-seat school desk than another spoonful of surprise medicine arrived. *Young People* was being scrapped. A massive search was under way for alternate material. With a grateful farewell cough, I repacked my books and returned to Westlake, my illness having improved dramatically.

One day later the renewed studio search ceased. My next vehicle would be *Schoolmates*, a tale based in a girls' school. Starting date, uncertain.

Less uncertainty was evident the next week. On March 26, 1940, the studio disclosed 1939 net profit after taxes had plunged to $4,146,000, off 44 percent from 1938. Hard on the heels of this ominous report,

Zanuck buoyantly proclaimed 1940–1941 plans. Fifty-six feature films were scheduled, the same number, Mother scathingly observed, as my old curls. More money would be spent on film production than ever before in company history, but not on me. In fact, forecasted budgets for films remaining under my contract would be drastically slashed.

While I stalled and Fox dithered, Mother was conjuring up an elegant building adjacent to our house. Dubbed the "dollhouse," but intended for my juvenile recreation, it was carved into the shoulder of a hillside, its appearance recalling an English stone farmhouse, with leaded glass windows, a steep roof sheathed in cedar shingles, and a turret with medieval window slits. The basement sheltered the valuable 1,000-item doll collection triggered years earlier by Winfield Sheehan, and a walk-in, steel-encased vault where Father secreted boxes of old documents, bottled water, and canned food against any apocalyptic emergency. Upstairs was a complete home theatre, in an ecclesiastical setting of vaulted ceilings criss-crossed by carved beams with scroll ends. Adjacent to the stage was an authentic soda fountain, with rickety wire stools, chrome levers, flip-lid counter storage for ice cream, and dozens of long-handled spoons and conical glasses. In cellar space not absorbed by dolls and Father's emergency rations was installed a foreshortened bowling alley with automatic ball return. Beyond lay a storage closet, designed as a mausoleum for movie costumes and memorabilia Mother had started collecting.

April Fool's Day brought bad weather, a roar of thunderstorms, pelting rain. Sheathed in rain gear and swaddled in scarf and galoshes, I sloshed off to cavernous Philharmonic Auditorium, which was clogged with an enraptured audience come to learn Mrs. Eleanor Roosevelt's vision of the world.

To honor her as national chairman of the Campfire Girls, our local Oki-Hi chapter had delegated three of us to greet her onstage. Donning Campfire beanies, we trooped up bearing broad smiles, long-stemmed roses, and a giant corsage. Shaking hands cordially, she said complimentary things about girl volunteers, and excused us back into our audience seats.

Centered mostly on social injustice, her remarks seemed so abstract and irrelevant to our own fortunate circumstances that they left little impression on me. Except for the Campfire Girls, she joked lamely, our nation faced uncertain times and needed experienced leadership. With her little pillbox hat, stiff posture behind the microphone, and padded shoulders emphasizing an already angular physique, she resembled some medieval figure from a playing card.

"Would FDR be a presidential candidate for a third term?" someone asked.

"Except in extraordinary circumstance, we should stick to our tradition."

"Would FDR drag us into the European war?"

Her chin seemed to recede in sadness. Again she answered equivocally, uncertain that democracy could be saved, yet confident it could not be destroyed. The audience whispered in dismay.

"What did you think of all that?" a reporter asked as we started out the door. Although her ideas had seemed terribly imprecise, and her view about democracy enigmatic, it was no moment for weighty discussion. I replied that I loved the United States and kept walking.

"Why?" he said, splashing along beside me.

"I love it because it's home." I ducked my head against the downpour.

"What else?" he persisted.

Perhaps frivolous answers would get rid of him. "Because I can get the best hamburgers and ice cream with chocolate sauce in the world in Santa Monica! I don't have to worry about having some bomb dropped on my house!"

My comment had ignored the studio. The following day word came of yet another breathtaking zigzag. *Schoolmates* was being abandoned, and *Young People* reinstated. Production would commence immediately. Recovering my well-traveled schoolbooks from Westlake, I transferred myself back to the studio.

When compared to my most recent films, things had shrunk noticeably, particularly budget and general cast quality. One thing had grown; me. Beyond the studio's averted eyes, either my costume hem was too short or my legs too long. With a little imagination, faint swellings could be detected in my breasts. Like a tadpole into a frog, I was changing shape.

"We're not little babies anymore..." our adolescent chorus sang. "We think children are an awful bore... we're young people." I really believed it.

Once again employing the circuitous link via Loyd Wright, Zanuck wrote Mother on April 2, 1940:

"We are planning to start *Lady Jane* a week after *Young People*. Please advise Mrs. Temple not to make any plans to take Shirley away because it will be necessary to start almost immediately with wardrobe fittings and rehearsals."

Father immediately sent back a quarrelsome reply. My December 1935 contract called for a full four weeks between films. Nobody replied to his challenge, perhaps because more important demands had landed on Zanuck's desk, including a bill from the Internal Revenue Service for $720,575 in delinquent 1935 taxes.

Confronted by Zanuck's silence and perhaps feeling protective, Father again started coming to the studio, but having nothing to do, he milled around with casual visitors, including a jewelry salesman. Jewelry peddlers frequently skulked along the wall inside soundstages. Gray, pallid-faced men with stooped figures, unobtrusive and uncommunicative, they shielded their open valises from casual view, like spiders. Attempts at secrecy are surefire to inspire a young girl's curiosity. Peering around their bodies I saw the man displaying a ring surmounted by a sparkling bluish stone.

"A small piece of the prestigious Cullinane diamond, progenitor of centerpiece gems in the English crown jewels," the peddler had enthused to Father. It was sale at first sight, but as a buyer of diamonds, Father was deceived. The ring he purchased was deep-sea blue; the Cullinane is clear white.

Asked later about the ring, Father's answer was muddy.

"Her mother paid for it," he replied, "but it's really Shirley's. We plan to give it to her on her eighteenth birthday. Meanwhile, it's just an investment." Neither Mother nor I overheard this curious explanation.

By now it was clear that differences between my family and the studio were irreconcilable. My professional emancipation had already begun with Westlake, and now Mother steadfastly pursued it. On April 10, 1940, she hired theatrical agent Frank Orsatti. His task: mend my 1935 contract with Fox or dismember it.

Why my parents ferreted out Orsatti when during the four years previous attorney Loyd Wright had represented them to the studio still is puzzling. When things do not go smoothly it is human nature to blame someone else. Perhaps the only place to shoulder off such blame was on Wright. Relishing his middleman role, friend to all and interpreting messages both ways, he was surely sensitive to the perishability of stardom and relative durability of corporations. A cagey lawyer does not bully potential corporate clients.

On the other hand, his role was that of a loser; neither side could wind up pleased. Even by the most bearish forecast, my broken contract meant surrender of assured studio net income. None of my films had lost money. For my family cancellation lay across a minefield of potentially explosive possibilities ranging from finance to professional future. One point was sure: from whatever vantage, Wright's status was seriously diminished by the Orsatti appointment.

A measure of my parents' desperation lay buried in fine print of the 1935 contract, which expressly prevented them from engaging the services of a theatrical agent in dealings with the studio. By hiring Orsatti they were automatically in technical breach of contract. As if blindfolded, they simply hurdled this legal prohibition without looking. The finish line lay ahead.

Orsatti had unusual qualifications. During Prohibition reportedly he brought a steady supply of liquor to MGM chief Louis B. Mayer. With repeal of the Volstead Act, he had left bootlegging and formed a theatrical talent business with brothers Vic, Al, and Ernie, representing among others Sonja Henie and Judy Garland. His most luminous distinction lay in broad and powerful personal connections within the industry, a preferential relationship with Mayer, undiluted since bootlegging days, and similar high-level access within the entwined community of movie moguls.

The simplicity of *Young People* allowed its prompt completion in early May. In the final scene I warmly thank my audience for past loyalty and announce my early retirement from entertainment. The pit orchestra strikes up "Auld Lang Syne," and we all sing and wallow in farewell sentiment until "The End" flashes on the screen. It was a shattering piece of symbolism.

At this moment Zanuck elected outright warfare. Locking away *Lady*

Jane forever in her dark closet, he leaked word to the press via his assistant, William Koenig, of a resolve to end my contract "by breaking the whole family." Simultaneously official studio leak holes dripped rumors that I "wanted to retire."

In her published response Mother denied the allegation and sketched out a solution to the impasse.

"We do not contemplate having Shirley retire. . . . She likes her work very much. . . . She would not think of giving it up. . . . We feel, however, that one picture a year, or possibly three every two years, would be the logical solution to the situation."

Events moved rapidly, leaving in their wake a lingering stench of catfight. On May 8 chairman Schenck was resting at his Arrowhead Springs Hotel, having just been charged by the U.S. Department of Justice with income tax fraud amounting to $283,083.

At the same time in New York City studio president Sidney Kent was huddled with Zanuck and vice president Goetz.

The next day Schenck flew east to join their discussions.

Two days later agent Orsatti flew to meet with them.

Three days later Hitler invaded the Lowlands.

On May 12 the wrangle spilled out of the shadows. Schenck announced I was being released from the remaining thirteen months of my contract.

"The Twentieth Century-Fox Studio will note the absence of Shirley Temple with regret," he said. "However, we are proud to have had the opportunity to present to the world the happiness and entertainment she provided."

That was a decent minimum, had he not appended a closing swipe. "I look forward to Shirley someday winning as great popularity as an actress as she has as a child star."

Ignoring his inference that children could not be actresses, Mother adopted a goat-footed policy to avert further acrimony.

"It's a matter of stories," she commented, "but there is another side to the whole issue. It supersedes any other. I do not think it wise for her to be deprived of normal, natural benefits from mingling and competing with other children. Shirley now takes part in life with other girls and boys her own age. She will not develop an isolated viewpoint, which often brings on an unhappy outlook on life. . . ."

As part of the contract settlement Schenck benignly reported he was presenting me with a $300,000 trust fund.

"It is the policy of the company," he announced unctuously, "to take care of our juvenile players by establishing these trusts."

Imprecise at the end, he got the numbers wrong. There were two trusts and together they contained only $125,000. The remaining $175,000 had flowed directly to Father, following their earlier May 5, 1938, contract modification.

The inaccuracy passed unremarked by Father, but what did arouse his ire was Schenck's implication of studio generosity in the settlement. A beneficent patron Schenck was not, Father declared; the funds were part of my regular past earnings. In any case, Schenck's presumption to the role of ethical fairy-godfather was short-lived. Found guilty of the tax-fraud case, he turned government witness against the Bioff-Browne gangsters, got his charge reduced to perjury, and would serve only four months and five days in federal prison.

The lump-sum release of trust monies had more searing implications than debate over parental responsibilities. No current income taxes had been paid on this income stream, and at current 1940 income tax rates the payment would largely devour itself. In 1935 my parents had rationalized the trusts as financial nest eggs out of sight of kidnappers. Now, five years later, they stood revealed as a savings account for Uncle Sam. Mine was the first case of "palimony." For seven years Fox and I had lived together, but it was the girl who paid dearly to get out.

Schenck's public proclamation of the payment contained two other inferences of importance to Father. Taxing authorities could quickly separate the funds paid into two streams, one comprising the $175,000 diverted directly to Father. Questions might arise. Why had this income not been declared in my prior income tax returns? On a purely practical basis, charging tax delinquency at lower rates might have turned out less productive for the government than taxing at new, higher ones, for in fact the government either didn't care or failed to notice.

The second implication was more subtle. What little remained of the payment after taxes helped disguise a disastrous family financial trend. Since 1934 my cumulative net after-tax income from all sources had totaled $1,395,978. Such a sum would normally suggest solvency, not a road to ruin. Yet in 1937 all my $351,000 current income was spent except $65,000. In 1939 all of the $335,000 income vanished in expenses except $32,423. In 1940 family expenses were *exceeding* my true income by $92,000.

Such trends were obviously all wrong. The settlement helped change our 1940 ink color from red to black, but thereby only deferred the need to change our habits.

As someone trained to believe it unladylike to ask or know too much about money, Mother claimed justified innocence.

"I haven't the slightest idea in the world how much we have, or what Shirley has. I know it's wisely invested. She will never come into it at one time. A protection against fortune hunters."

Her philosophy and mine ran in parallel. Freedom from serious want was satisfying, but not the main show. The chase and kill were more rewarding than the prize. What happened to earnings was of small interest to us. Managing money was a caretaker's job, one powered by statistics and paper forms, devoid of the human heartbeat so important to us both. Once earned, money turned stale as an old biscuit.

The last rankling fallout from contract termination was studio insistence that I had "retired."

Understandably, any movie company is loath to admit being baffled by a set of hormones. A more candid admission would have been that stars are a commodity. Once spent, forgotten. However, a less humiliating course was to contend I was quitting the profession entirely.

Studio news leaks also insinuated that large tax liabilities had inspired the desperate yearning for my release, artlessly inferring that the less I worked, the more money I would have.

Were it not for my eleven commercial licensees at the time, the debate about retirement would have been academic. Some companies were already resigned, having seen sales of products tied closely to my baby image fall dramatically with each inch I grew. In fact, between 1938 and 1939 my annual royalty receipts had slumped over 50 percent.

However, others were finding their markets still strong and several yowled in anguish over the rumor, tolling as it did a death knell for existing inventories and future sales. Nominally still handling licensee relationships, attorney Wright induced Rosenau Brothers, my licensee for dresses, to author a broadside letter to calm the commercial water.

"At announcement of retirement," wrote Sidney Rosenau, "I was deluged with queries from buyers as to the future of dresses bearing her name. As a retailer we do not want this profitable source suddenly cut off. Shirley is at an age where so much more can be done with the styling of her clothes that she is more valuable than ever before. Shirley intends to go on," his announcement declared. "I say this unqualifiedly. She will appear in pictures each year, and accept ones best liked by her parents."

At every chance Mother doused more cold water on the retirement rumor.

"We are constantly aware of Shirley's love for her work," she declared. "If an opportunity comes which spells advancement in a professional way, we will not ignore it."

So relentless became her public rebuttal that she stumbled sideways into an exposed position. Spotting this vulnerability and eager to protect its flanks, the studio then leaked news "angles" painting her as an archetypal moviemother, a voracious mercenary eager to harness her money machine back in traces.

Suddenly thrown on the defensive, Mother could only protest, "Work is not *my* theme song for her. Her song is, when do we go to the studio, Mom?"

One balmy late afternoon, May 27, 1940, Griff drove Mother by Westlake to collect me and to go empty personal items from the studio bungalow. It was his last chore. With no further need to protect an asset or maintain an intimate window on our home life, Zanuck had recalled his faithful friend from our employ.

The cottage door was ajar, and inside a woman was sweeping up and talking with Klammy.

"Take whatever souvenir you want," Mother told us. The old-fashioned, cast-iron school desk and a glass ashtray were all I wanted.

"What happens to the bungalow now?" asked Mother, pacing around and recording which items should be sent where.

"I hear no more stars will be assigned to the bungalows," Klammy replied.

"Will Rogers's is already an office for director Archie May. Musical director Alfred Newman is in Janet Gaynor's. Maybe they'll make this one another office."

Not quite. John Barrymore moved in, briefly. Wearing a broad-brimmed fedora cocked over one eye, he would pose in my backyard swing and quip that he could "just feel the dimples beginning to grow." Later the bungalow would become a dental office, and in 1955, a medical dispensary run by the physician brother of murdered mobster Bugsy Siegel.

"The studio has agreed to sell me all Shirley's old costumes," Mother told Klammy. "Dancing shoes, umbrellas, hair ribbons, the works. I'm going to add to our collection."

She turned again to the cleaning woman. "Please take whatever souvenir you want."

The woman glanced back with a wan smile. She was wearing canvas sneakers and a misshapen, faded green sweater. Shaking her head sadly, she lifted her broom and went outside.

Mother was saying, "Release! Here we are, *free*! And free we shall remain," adding carefully, "for a while."

All along I had felt free. "I hope I don't have to wait too long to make another picture," I added.

Klammy turned to Mother. "Did you speak with Mr. Zanuck?"

"Not for weeks," she replied. "No, months. I did get a short letter, posted on our unlucky May 13, or was it lucky? All he said was thanks and future best wishes. I wonder if he really feels much about all this, at all?"

For a moment Klammy said nothing. "It's your business, you know. I'd better not get involved."

"That's right," Mother agreed, lightly touching her shoulder. "Good friends don't grumble."

I went outside. The cleaning woman was seated on the front steps doing nothing, so I sat down beside her. She said she usually worked at night; that was why I had never seen her before.

"Don't they do something special for you, like a party?" she asked, pulling stray strands of hair away from her eyes and holding them pressed against her head.

"I guess not," I answered. "Besides, everyone around here works someplace different. It would be hard for all of them to get together."

"Don't the executives do anything, either?"

"I don't know. Besides, I don't know many."

"Is this the way they do with a star?" she said. Her eyes were shiny with emotion.

"Never mind." I tried to be comforting. "I've just outgrown it, that's all."

We drove Klammy as far as the studio school.

"Good-bye, Shirley," she said. "Don't forget me." Calm, dry-eyed, she wheeled around and trotted quickly up the steps.

We went as we had so often come, past the same main gate, blending into the stream of homebound auto traffic along Pico Boulevard. For several moments Griff drove us while we said nothing.

Finally I turned to Mother and said, "I wonder what *Lady Jane* would have been like?"

With one sidelong glance, she snapped open her purse. "Where's my essence of peppermint?"

"How did we ever get this far?" I mused.

She was looking down at the tips of her shoes. "Keeping you away from adults, I suppose." That answer surprised me. Adults had always been my principal companions.

"Mr. Sheehan had it right," she went on, "maturity shows in the eyes."

I stared off into the twilight. It was the end of the day, and the end of the line. I was unsure of just how everything had happened, but it really didn't matter. Nor who was to blame. I accepted it. Each day had been a glory. Each chore an exultation, doing what needed doing. There was nothing heroic in my attitude. Nor any slavish devotion to the concept of conqueror and vanquished. In this case, nobody lost.

I was eleven and unemployed. Ahead lay simple joys of maidenhood.

27

" First we get rid of the baby fat," said the little man seated behind the wide desk.

"Then new hair. Teach you to belt a song, and some decent dancing."

I sat woodenly and stared. Eight months had elapsed since leaving Fox in May 1940, and on this first executive visit under my new Metro-Goldwyn-Mayer contract, Mother and I were split up, she ushered away by general manager Louis B. Mayer and I left alone with producer Arthur Freed.

Best known as producer of the blockbusting *The Wizard of Oz*, Freed was rumored in some adult circles to have an adverturesome casting couch. At the time I knew none of this, nor would I have recognized such furniture even when sitting on one. To visit an executive of such stature was enough to send my spirits soaring.

"I have something made for just you," he continued, fumbling in his lap. "You'll be my new star!" That phrase had last been used when I was three years old in *Kid in Hollywood*.

Obviously, Freed did not believe in preliminaries. With his face gaped in a smile, he stood up abruptly and executed a bizarre flourish of clothing. Having thought of him as a producer rather than exhibitor, I sat bolt upright. Guarded personal exposure by both brothers and Father had maintained me in relatively pristine innocence. Not twelve years old, I still had little appreciation for masculine versatility and so

319

dramatic was the leap between schoolgirl speculation and Freed's be-
dazzling exposure that I reacted with nervous laughter.

Disdain or terror he might have expected, but not the insult of
humor.

"Get out!" he shouted, unmindful of his disarray, imperiously pointing to the closed door. "Go on, *get out!*"

Mother and I were en route home before I spilled my executive-
suite saga. Expecting her to be startled or angry on my behalf, I was
surprised when she had her own tale to tell. Not only had Freed cut a
figure, so had Mayer.

Ushering Mother to an overstuffed couch, Mayer returned behind
his desk and mounted a long-legged chair, a vanity which gave him
increased stature while seated. Wiping his eyeglasses on a silk handkerchief, he recounted how admiringly he regarded her. Every child
should be so lucky to have such a mother, he purred, a real mother,
yet someone sexy and refined. Usually solemn, his eyes glinted. Surely
she could recognize real sincerity when she saw it. Never forget, he
continued, at MGM we are a family. We take care of our own.

Slipping down off his chair, he approached the sofa and sank down
beside her, uttering a contented sigh.

Surely she was the most unique mother in the world, he said. Someone who should be a star in her own right. He grasped her hand,
pulling her toward him.

Mayer's opinion of his personal prowess was rumored to be over-
blown, but not the power of his office. Reluctant to test either, Mother
picked up her purse and retreated out the door, walking backwards.
Unlike my reaction of hilarity to Freed, hers was to be grievously af-
fronted. Not for nothing was the MGM lot known as the "factory," a
studio perfumed with sultry, busty creatures with long legs and tight
haunches, and more than its quota of lecherous older men.

Life at MGM would apparently move along at a brisk pace with some
signposts not to our liking, but for a while we drove along in silence,
thinking our own thoughts. Fortunately, flunking our initial trial runs
was irrelevant. My MGM contract had already been signed.

Straws in the wind tell little when the wind blows in circles. That
was how my professional activities had been swirling since departing
Twentieth Century-Fox. As I had passed through the gate, the same Lew

Brown involved in my initial audition seven years earlier had sought me for his new Broadway musical, *Swing Hansel, Swing Gretel*. Evoking her familiar litany of objections to live performance, Mother squashed the idea. The *Chicago Tribune* envisaged me singing "Finlandia" at Soldier Field Stadium, backed by a 150-piece marimba band, an international extravaganza enough to have merited more than Mother's prompt rejection. General Foods had dangled a six-year radio contract to push Cocomalt drink, but once again the offer foundered on the shoal of Mother's aversion to live radio.

Her concern for my competence before a live microphone still puzzled me. Reading a radio script is far less taxing than learning movie dialogue by heart. Rejecting radio offers had become so automatic that I was pleasantly startled when she had allowed me to appear on a *Lux Radio Theatre* program opposite distinguished actor Claude Rains. Later I learned why; she had finagled final script and cast approval, achieving a hitherto elusive goal.

No sooner had Westlake disbanded for summer vacation than author F. Scott Fitzgerald had arrived with a proposal to star me in a movie based on his highly acclaimed *Saturday Evening Post* novel *Babylon Revisited*, incorrectly judging Father the one to approach.

"Having just seen a girl-child through a difficult age up to a satisfactory fulfillment," he wrote, "I would like to give you the benefit of my experience, such as it is."

Possibly aware of the loggerhead relationship between Fitzgerald and his daughter, Scottie, Father had replied thanks, but no thanks.

On his second sally the author had skillfully approached Mother directly, and for several months thereafter they engaged in prolonged discussion.

I was very impressed with the kid—no trace of coyness or cuteness, yet a real dignity and gentleness ... if the personality that she has in private life could be carried *almost without heightening* over into the picture, I believe she would be perfect.... She has reached a point pictorially and by reason of natural charm where any attempt to strain and stress her reactions with clumsy "little mother" lines and unchildish prophetic conduct would seem a vulgarization.... Forget such old dodges as talking with tears in her voice, something

that a well-brought-up child wouldn't do twice in a given year and
then only under horrible stress—but that nine out of ten children
in Hollywood are taught as the proper, almost the only way of
conveying emotion . . . she is a perfect thing now in her own way,
and I would like to see that exquisite glow and tranquility carried
intact through a sustained dramatic action. . . .

Apparently dissatisfied with his own progress, Fitzgerald had fallen
into a strategic error, aligning himself with producer Lester Cowan to
help sell Mother on his idea. On July 29, 1940, he wrote about this to
his wife, as quoted in *Correspondence of F. Scott Fitzgerald*, by M. J.
Bruccoli and Margaret Duggan.

> The Temple thing is this. She's too old to have a child's appeal and
> though they've put everything in her last pictures—song, dance,
> sleight of hand, etc.—they fail to hold the crowd. In fact, the very
> last [*Young People*] is rather nauseous in its sentimentality.
>
> So this "independent" producer Cowan bought my "Babylon
> Revisited" for $900 . . . I should have held out for more but the story
> had been nearly ten years published without a nibble . . . in a beau-
> tifully avaricious way, knowing I'd been sick and was probably hard
> up, Cowan hired me to do the script on a percentage basis . . . *gave*
> me what worked out to be a few hundred a week to do a quick
> script. Which I did, and then took to bed to recuperate. . . .
>
> Anyhow I *think* it's been a good thing except for the health
> angle, and if and when he sells to Mrs. Temple and Paramount the
> script there'll be a little more money—if he doesn't think of a way
> to beat me out of it.

As quoted in the same publication, sixty days later Fitzgerald wrote
Cowan, indicating the deal was cooling on both sides.

> . . . This feeling was probably inspired by some interview I read with
> Mrs. Temple in which she said that she felt Shirley wouldn't do
> anything 'til after the first of the year—not realizing that she is
> growing right out of the part. . . .

Overlapping the Fitzgerald negotiation, Mary Pickford had proposed
she and I co-star in an epic based on her relationship with her mother,

a scenario hardly one to entice my own Mother's interest. Columbia Pictures had tossed out a barrage of propositions, casting me as a Barnum & Bailey circus clown in *Jo-Jo*, a bride in *June Moon*, and a melancholy maiden in *June Madness*.

Producer-director Buddy de Sylva then had proposed a Broadway play titled *Panama Hattie*. Created at blazing speed during fifteen days holed up in the elegant, isolated Samarkand Hotel in Santa Barbara, his show had been written expressly for me and stage star Ethel Merman, currently appearing in another of his hit Broadway plays, *DuBarry Was a Lady*. Having known Mother from five of my previous films, he had offered salary, percentage of earnings, and equity in the show. The script contained no double entendres, he assured her, and already-distinguished composer Cole Porter was writing the music.

"No other little girl would be able to play it," he had implored. "A sensational and distinctive part."

Although impressed by the story, Merman, and Porter, Mother told de Sylva she was still concerned that the hours would be awfully long for a child and that I might forget my lines. Me, Mother? Listening to her list reservations, I had been mildly offended.

"More and more she is becoming shy . . ." she had continued. By now I barely recognized myself, and de Sylva, who had known me since childhood, must have had similar trouble. Many long telephone calls later, however, he had given up.

While this variety of negotiations had gone zigzagging along without my participation, I had engaged in the work of all unemployed celebrities, helping bang begging bowls for United China War Relief and orphaned Greeks, and singing for the benefit of the local Children's Hospital as a member of the Nightingales, a group named not for voices but to honor Florence Nightingale, founder of battlefield nursing in the early nineteenth century.

Having returned to school in the fall, I realized my tonal quality was flattish, so Thanksgiving had been celebrated by losing both tonsils and adenoids at the Catholic St. Vincent's Hospital. General anesthesia was nothing new, but I had promised classmates to battle unconsciousness and report my sensations. Counting aloud to 99, and staring down a receding, narrow tunnel until blackness, I awoke looking down another tunnel, this one formed by the jutting, starched wings of a nurse's hat, at the bottom of which appeared a smiling little face.

The story was pretty dull, so to spice up my report I had opened wide to show off the bloody stumps where my tonsils had been. A senior girl had stopped to listen. Coltish, tall, and rawboned, she reached for both my hands in what I assumed was a gesture of sympathy, then suddenly spun me round and round in a circle, my shoes eventually clearing the floor. When she let go and sent me skidding off, I had started spitting up blood again, so back I had gone for more stitches with the realization that sympathy can be treacherous.

Schoolwork and personal things were what mattered as 1940 had drawn to a close. George had became engaged and enlisted in the Marines, claiming civilian life to be a bore. Jack became engaged to his college sweetheart and returned to Stanford. Sir Samuel of Speen lay down in his stall and died, and I took up chess. Meanwhile the buildup to war went on under our national noses, and in our cook's room. FBI Director J. Edgar Hoover had come to visit, and on this occasion noted how animosity was building toward Americans with names or accents obviously German. Not until many years later did I realize why Mother had averted her eyes and fallen suddenly silent. Her true maiden name was Krieger, vintage German. During World War I Grandmother Maude had altered it to a more Gallic-sounding Cregier to avoid the same guilt phenomenon.

Momentary embarrassment may have been Mother's but the joke was really on Hoover. While he had savored the coconut cake especially baked for him by our cook, out in her sleeping room that very night one of her relatives was holding a meeting of her cell in the German-American Bund, the ardently pro-German, anti-American society.

In the months since departing Fox, all sorts of experts had concluded that my public appeal was still vibrant and that I should be making another film. The only question, when. Driven by his embedded antipathy toward theatrical middlemen, Father had concocted a way to circumvent the loose arrangement instituted with Orsatti, who had negotiated the Fox contract cancellation. Father would become both my agent and producer.

As keystone in this scheme, he had formed a production company named Allied American Films, capitalized at $2.5 million. Of the authorized 750,000 shares, Father reserved 20 percent free to himself for promotional services. Electing himself chairman of the board at a $15,000 annual salary, he then hired as publicity representative Joe Reddy, a gregarious Irishman who had previously worked for screen comedian Harold Lloyd. As his initial film property, Father bought a $1,000 option on screen rights to *Lucky Sixpence*, a novel by Emilie and Alden Knipe. The company's articles of incorporation stipulated that "Mrs. Temple and I shall have sole right of selection and/or approval of story material, director, associate producer, and all supporting cast." Oddly enough, he forgot to reserve rights to select the star.

Confronted with Father's scheme to deal him out of the agent's commission, Orsatti, old hand from bootlegging wars, had retaliated with a trump card, the MGM contract. Two feature films starring me would be made within the next forty weeks. My salary would be $2,500 per week, with $1,000 for Mother. Finessed by such an attractive deal in hand, and with his company headed nowhere, Father dissolved Allied American Films as it had been formed, with a stroke from his pen.

However, when Mother had reintroduced her long-sought condition for script and cast approval, MGM had balked.

"If that is the deal," they told Orsatti, "forget it."

Before the contract had become final, Father pressed to eliminate the provision directing part of my earnings to a trust.

"We do not wish to be obliged to place a definite amount in trust for her," he observed. "Our income taxes are going to be a terrific burden." That may have been true, but again MGM resisted. Judge Emmet H. Wilson's eventual order approving the contract stipulated that 50 percent of my net earnings, after specified deductions, must be placed in trust for me.

In a last-ditch effort Father had proposed that my salary checks be issued in his name, a request rejected by MGM as contrary to the court order.

Hardly of concern to MGM, Father had a point in trying to generate immediate cash. Almost $300,000 would soon be due as taxes, only the tip of a chilling financial iceberg. In three years our family net worth had plunged 40 percent, from $1 million to $600,000. Every cent of what I would receive during 1940, except for the Twentieth Century-Fox lump-sum payoff, would be consumed by taxes. Viewed in a more dismal way, taxes due on what I earned were *twice* what I would be getting under the MGM contract.

Turning a totally blind eye to relentless erosion of our estate would have been inexcusable, and to his credit Father had made gestures to reduce family expenses. Usually this had taken the form of an afternoon meeting convened in the library by Father and his accountant partner, Thomason. Seating Mother and me on the couch like accused criminals in the dock, Thomason would obliquely berate our personal extravagance.

Over time we had grown calloused to his gloomy, moralistic negatives. Invariably at private showings of my latest film he would observe, worst one yet, never make a cent. As my $10 weekly allowance could hardly be analyzed for its extravagance, Mother and I both knew his scorching lecture was for her benefit. Pacing back and forth, he recited from department-store invoices, scattering bits of paper on the floor to dramatize the disarray of our finances—all to little effect. We accused bore his tirade with patience and carefully guarded humor. With all my earnings, Mother knew things simply could not be that bad.

After Father's carefully crafted program as independent producer had been shot to ribbons by the MGM proposal, and Mother's appeal for artistic control destroyed by the studio's obdurate resistance, in mid-December 1940 I had signed with MGM. But before reporting for work I had one prior obligation to discharge, on the Westlake stage.

Earlier I had realized I was only one of two actresses at school. The other was June Lockhart, a senior, daughter of veteran performers and someone whose stage debut had chanced to coincide in time with my first *Baby Burlesk*. Although not close friends, separated by the institutional chasm between older and younger girls, I looked up at her admiringly. Pert, fine-featured, with sparkling intelligent eyes, she always was ebullient and spoke with perfect diction, each word a crystalline gem of tone and inflection. In 1938 she had appeared in her first movie, titled *A Christmas Carol*. Not surprisingly in the world of coincidence, we were paired in a warm-up vignette for Westlake's Christmas vesper celebration.

Costumed as court jesters in tights, peaked caps, and long tunics with bells tinkling along our sleeves, we did a little dance down the staircase, waved jester sticks, and shook bells to make everyone laugh. True to Westlake philosophy which de-emphasized celebrities, the only two working actresses in school, one of whom had perfect diction, were the ones assigned to play their roles in total mime.

All these developments had provided a prelude for my first meeting with producer Freed in January 1941. Remake her in the Metro image, Freed decreed, so his backyard boys descended to transform my appearance, shape, voice, and skills.

That hairline gets raised, sighed stylist Sidney Guilaroff. Bobbing around my chair, he inspected me and scowled. That widow's peak goes, he announced. We need more forehead. No electrolysis needle for me, I warned. He grimaced. We have to straighten out the curls, he said. We lighten it, pull it all down to the side. He demonstrated. So it looks like Norma Shearer.

Across the aisle, perched in her own chair, was the startlingly beautiful actress Lana Turner, being fitted for a luxuriant "fall" of hair. Her own was cropped short, bleached, and looked broken off into crispy ends over the ears. They weren't going to hack me up like that, I resolved.

Guilaroff leaned back, inspected me unhappily, then finally muttered maybe we should try wigs. Thinking back particularly to the powdered wig from the minuet number of *Heidi*, I was delighted. Shortly I emerged as a Cleopatra, with straight black bangs and hair falling to my shoulders. While seated in my chair the mirror image looked exotic, but when I saw myself full-length it was appalling. Far too big a wig on far too short a girl.

Wigs later we finally settled on the original, my unflattering hairline, on my own rotten, brown natural hair, and my own obnoxious widow's peak. Hour by hour Guilaroff's smile had grown wan. At last he dismissed me from his chair, my hair and head intact, for better or worse.

MGM dressing rooms were little more than cells in a two-story wooden barracks, undifferentiated stalls strung down a long, narrow corridor. A locker-room odor clung everywhere, musty and damp, a pervasive concoction of pancake and well-exercised old clothing. Partial attribution of this aura came from an obligatory studio program of calisthenics and massage conducted by studio athletic director David

Loomis, a muscular man in a sleeveless shirt. Eventually I got my own gymnastics program moved home to my living room. There Mother included Plump Girl from school as a companion in my exercise regimen. If her presence was intended as incentive, the results were dispiriting. Plump Girl's flesh proved less tenacious than mine, and her excess fell away in miraculous fashion. Within months she developed so gorgeous a body, she was elected Westlake May Queen. My form just became more compact and muscular. The best I could do at Mayday ceremonies was to pull on my panty girdle once again and stand as an attendant to the Queen.

This MGM flurry of concern about my body was unnerving. Having always taken my appearance for granted, I felt suddenly misshapen. Even Mother, whose earlier comments had always been good-natured, joined the critical chorus. Lots of work was needed, she said, particularly below my waist. The MGM criterion was a beautiful body, and somehow mine was failing to measure up. Inspecting myself naked in the mirror, I didn't look so bad. Nice shoulders, oval thighs, decent breasts, a small, softly rounded stomach. To be taller and have longer legs would have been nice, but that was just an old speculation and fruitless. Stuck with myself, once again I resolved to stay friends with my body.

Next came the voice, beginning with instruction from one-eyed pianist Al Siegel, who had previously trained Sophie Tucker and Ethel Merman.

"I'll have you belting in no time," he said reassuringly, but before hearing me sing. After a few lessons he disappeared.

To keep me practicing, MGM provided a fold-out kit of songs for use during war-bond tours, which were de rigueur for us all. Noticing that people bought bonds willingly when I had barely said hello, I ignored the singing. No need to put at risk a sale already made.

Realizing I was still working the same bag of vocal tricks I had at age three, Mother was pushing for more intense vocal training. Unshakably devoted to the soprano antics of Lily Pons and Rosa Ponselle, she also envied the birdsong tones of actress-singer Gloria Jean. Several roles recently awarded her, Mother claimed, should have been mine. Clearly my voice was holding me back, and I would do better sounding like someone else.

Light opera is one way to train a voice, Mother speculated, and hired

Dr. Stetson Humphrey, a humorless metronomic man who played piano chords with one hand and waved a baton with the other.

"In one year I'll have you in the Hollywood Bowl," he said confidently. More likely a toilet bowl, I mused. When younger I used to warble pleasantly, but I was already old enough not to confuse baby noises with song.

The music doctor began to rehearse in the living room, with Ching-Ching II our lone audience.

"One love, one love, for you alone..." I began. "One magic night within his arms... Soon my knight will find me, softly steal behind me... With passion's flower unfurled..." It was difficult to control my laughter.

Ching-Ching II cringed and began a series of small yowls. Dr. Humphrey scowled and kept emphasizing the lyrics with vigorous strokes of his baton.

"Put me on his horse and carry me away..." I kept trying, but Walt Disney's operatic hen had nothing on me. The smartest thing for me to do was to lay my egg right there, before I laid one in public.

My first singing audition for MGM brass was almost the last. Huddled around a piano were stony-faced Mayer accompanied by a half dozen henchmen, plus two loyal patrons of Judy Garland, voice coach Roger Edens and Mayer's secretary, Ida Koverman. The character I was singing was from the proposed movie version of the stage success *Panama Hattie*, someone who required a big, strident voice.

I tried, but was not pleased. I was way off. To divine his reaction, the yes-men glanced sidelong at Mayer, who rose without changed expression or comment and departed, trailed single file by his entourage. Were I not already experienced in the business, the sepulchral quality of his silent exit would have been shattering. Koverman stared down at her nails, and I said nothing. Edens finally spoke.

"You have to learn to belt it. Like Judy." He was a tall, pleasant-faced man. "Judy's in a class by herself," he added.

"I'm not sure I can," I replied. "I've always been a lousy screamer. I'm a good crier, but I don't belt." It was not the audition either of us expected.

Hair, body, and voice having proved resistant to change, small wonder little progress was made with my feet. Choreographer Nick Castle had provided some fresh, saucy routines, and black speciality dancer Willie Covan was detailed to teach me. Unfolding his portable dance floor, he demonstrated a tap-rhumba. He was no Uncle Billy Robinson. Locking horns in some dumb argument, I balked. Petulantly, he folded up his floor and departed, leaving me to learn the rhumba by myself on the living-room carpet.

Midstream in MGM's unsuccessful transformation process came my twelfth birthday. Mother took me aside.

"You're not really twelve," she said, "you're thirteen."

"But yesterday I was eleven," I rejoined. "What happened to twelve?"

She recounted the early Fox scheme to make me younger than I was, and revealed that my birth certificate had been altered. "I don't want you entering your teens without even knowing it," she said.

"That proves the astrologist was wrong," I responded.

"What are you talking about?"

"That lady astrologist in Palm Springs, the one who gave us the book of forecasts." Mother nodded appreciatively.

"Well, she said I would lose both parents in an accident during my twelfth year. Now that can't come true, because there is no twelfth year." Mother shrugged.

"All that other stuff she told us," I went on, "about my having three children, and in middle life I would have a life-threatening disease. That's probably wrong too." As things turned out, of course, it wasn't.

To lose a year seemed less important to me than to gain one. "Now can I shave my legs and underarms?"

"Absolutely not!"

"Mary Lou does."

"Big deal. She's almost a year older," scoffed Mother. "The answer is no."

"How come? I'm menstruating, but can't shave."

"Once you start, you'll never be able to stop."

"That's okay on both counts." I pled, "Come on Mother."

Reluctantly, she agreed. "And please turn down that radio. It drives me crazy the way it goes morning, noon, and night when you're home. How can you study?"

"I do it better with shrieks and eeks in my ears."

"Bosh!" she replied in exasperation. She seemed to be taking my puberty harder than I was.

"There's only one time when she's still my baby," she wrote in her record book. "At night when she goes to bed. Her hair is pulled back, and she drops that little pose. She looks very sweet and small."

Wistful benevolence, however, she left at home. At MGM she caused the studio one giant headache. All her actions seemed viewed through the cracked prism of two desires: star roles rather than co-star, and some participation in story selection. The movie version of *Panama Hattie*, already partially cast with Ann Sothern, dancer Eleanor Powell, and comedian Red Skelton, was rejected as too ribald, carbon-copy to her reaction to the stage version. *Barnacle Bill*, with me cast as a motherless daughter adrift among seagoing scoundrels of the San Pedro fishing fleet, was "too coarse." Privately she told me that co-star Wallace Beery was a more dangerous and consummate scenestealer than Frank Morgan in *Dimples*.

How about *Topsy and Eva*, with Judy Garland in blackface, or *Babes on Broadway*, a musical with Garland, Mickey Rooney, and me? Mother again declined, explaining to me that bracketed between two talented hoofers and song belters was no place for my light to shine.

On my birthday in 1941, four months after first signing with MGM, my contract was revised. One film only, not two. The studio would select and cast the story; Mother would have to accept. MGM's patience was exhausted. They were washing their hands of me even before rolling a camera.

This was not exactly the way the official MGM explanation read. Three reasons were cited for the reduction in terms of my contract: my in-between age and appearance; the studio roster already had enough young talent, including Rooney, Garland, and fourteen-year-old Kathryn Grayson; and repeated script rejections by the family. From here on MGM would tell me what, when, and how. And for one film only.

In June 1941 I won the Westlake Posture Award by balancing a book on my head with the most dignity. Simultaneously I was summoned to start work at MGM on *Kathleen*. Grayson had already been announced as the lead, but was abruptly withdrawn in my favor. It would be a story about a motherless child's struggle to win the affection of her indifferent father, Herbert Marshall, thwart a gold-digging Gail Patrick, and play matchmaker for psychologist Laraine Day. Things were slowly changing. At last, I was only one-half an orphan.

Studying my script alone before dinner was a change from the way

Mother and I had always learned lines. Before bedtime we still did our customary duet, she taking all the other roles. Now, however, her part was largely mechanical, suggestions on my delivery few and far between, and interpretation of plot or meanings increasingly superfluous.

Her stance regarding the industry had also shifted. Recognizing that further top ratings were highly unlikely, she had reconciled herself that hereafter the measure of my performance must be solely against a personal scale of excellence. As this had been more or less my own yardstick since childhood, openly adopting this position seemed to relieve her. No longer did she see me locked in a nose-to-nose statistical game.

"I don't need to watch her anymore," Mother explained, "but I'm just interested. Whatever Metro does for her, I honestly hope she never again is number one. Too big a handicap."

On the first shooting day of *Kathleen*, as we approached the MGM main studio gate, our progress was blocked by pickets brandishing signs and waving placards. It was a warm morning, and several leaned in through our opened car windows snarling for us to turn back and shouting, "Don't be a scab! Stick with the workers!"

"Think of acid thrown in your face," hissed one man through uneven, stained teeth.

On the fringes of the crowd several uniformed studio gatemen regarded our encounter with clinical disinterest. Some of the pickets started lifting the fenders to rock the car, chanting for us to turn back. These men all looked like the same sort of crew I had always affectionately regarded as playmates and allies, certainly never antagonists. To my private relief and jubilant cheers from the pickets, Mother backed away, turned around, and drove us home.

Inquiring of the studio by telephone, she was advised the pickets were actually not crew members but from the Screen Actors Guild (SAG), then locking horns in a jurisdictional dispute with the union favored by MGM, the Motion Picture Alliance for the Preservation of American Ideals. They were all "Commies," she was told.

All very confusing, she replied. The SAG members she knew didn't seem like Commies. Anyway Communists were now our allies, having been savagely attacked by Hitler only days before. The studio spokesman was unmoved. Over there, they might be allies, he replied, but here, just troublemakers. It was a rocky start.

☆

Filming got under way following settlement of the labor dispute. Herbert Marshall, an English actor who had gallantly left one leg on a World War I battlefield, did marvelously well with his wooden replacement. An epitome of British courtesy, he interrupted our first scene together to ask why my brow was knitted when the script didn't require so troubled an expression.

"Because my foot aches," I replied, breaking into a grin. "You've been standing on it."

The next laugh was also on him. Psychologist Day and he were sharing an affectionate kiss across me, wedged between them in the front seat of his parked roadster. When the time came he was obliged to shift his wooden leg, roll up on his hip, and stretch to reach her proffered lips. Instead of the soft whisper of a decorous kiss came a muffled but unmistakably rattling noise. Glancing up, I saw the soundman monitoring the boom microphone remove and replace his earphones, as if to ventilate his head. Marshall remained seated, grasping the steering wheel, white-knuckled in embarrassment. Day kept her cool, eased herself out of the car, and stood smoothing her skirt. Everyone aware of the gaffe was gracious enough to ignore it except me. I took a long time to settle down and get back to work.

☆

During shooting on *Kathleen* it was clear that the traditional relationship between Mother and me while at the studio had altered in subtle ways. Instead of leading me by the hand, almost imperceptibly she had stepped back a pace. Even at home I had sensed her shoves becoming more gentle and her restraint less frequent. Welcome though such changes were, her physical presence at the studio was an invaluable passive psychological resource. Only once did she revert and become an aggressive defender.

During a dream sequence, I was a mulatto in a calypso straw hat, oatmeal pants cut short, and rigged with a bongo drum on each hip. A hydraulically operated dance floor rose and fell while the lavish dance-musical number pulsed and swirled in a mélange of tap-tango and tap-rhumba. For our large cast of actors and dancers the rehearsal was long, relentless, and sweaty. In a rare exception, I grew tired a few minutes before my statutory four hours of work had expired. Mother noticed. Approaching an assistant director, she suggested that as it was already evening, a break until morning would be good for everyone. The director construed her comment as related only to me and replied tersely that I should be ordered to work harder, not rest. Everyone was getting testy, including Mother. She refused to comply and told me to prepare to go home. Things came rapidly to a boil.

Voice coach Roger Edens was summoned, accompanied by a breathless, intense front-office type in coat and tie. Both urged Mother to order me to continue.

"Not when she won't do her best," she answered stiffly.

Nobody asked me if I wanted to continue, or anything at all.

Speaking in low, even tones but easily overheard, Edens said, "Look, this is Metro, Mrs. Temple. We work right through. Judy just had her eighteenth birthday and we worked her all night, until 4:00 a.m. She loved it! A mark of maturity."

"And wait until Shirley's eighteen," chimed in the other man. "We'll work *her* all night, just like Judy."

Mother turned, eyes glistening. "Well, she's not eighteen yet." She squared herself toward Edens. "I won't order her to do it. If *you* do, you'll get rotten results!"

That's just what they did, and that's just what they got.

Barring some miracle, I felt *Kathleen* was destined to bomb, and me with it. How wrong a guess. As reported by columnist Ed Sullivan, "Every New York critic, without exception, acclaimed her performance ... tremendous artistry ... bridged the hazard of being merely cute to genuinely artful ... she makes Hollywood glamour girls look like a bunch of Raggedy Anns."

The *San Francisco Chronicle* wrote, "A triumphant comeback ... baby Shirley doesn't live here anymore ..." and the *New York Times* added, "Please give her a machine gun for Christmas and a story with some bite to it."

In a subsequent survey of the leading 1941 films, the eight leading national trade magazines rated *Kathleen* second only to *How Green Was My Valley*, which had garnered five top Oscar awards.

Good and bad, film reviews and polls are part of the cut-and-thrust of Hollywood. Although Mother scrupulously continued to note current criticism, she never discussed my films with me in terms of either triumph or failure. Irrespective of the acclaim accorded *Kathleen*, my primary barometer of performance was how I felt about my performance. My opinion was that I had failed. In movies, however, failure is seldom final. The MGM experience was simply one in a long series. Taking one step backward when I must, a step forward when I could, I put the film on a shelf and redirected my energy to school.

In the fall I was formally elected class secretary, became president of the Campfire Girls chapter, served as a serious-minded reporter on the school paper, and authored long-winded poems about Hawaiian cliffs and flowers. While being initiated into the high school Freshman Club in the fall of 1941, I swallowed my aversion to the past and sang "The Good Ship Lollipop."

Equating maturity with personal dignity, I had begun signing fan photos "Your friend" instead of "With love" and conducting myself with the starchy mannerisms of a principle-ridden schoolgirl. Fairly quickly it became obvious that this veneer was less effective at catching boys' attention than my natural saucy, puckish self, so my studied maturity was short-lived.

At one of those punch-and-cookies school exchanges with Harvard Military Academy, a tall, uniformed senior with straw-blond hair and blue eyes cut in on the dance floor.

"I'm Hotch," he said, leading me in a series of swooping turns, which immediately gained covetous attention from my schoolmates. Not only a superb dancer, he was the most handsome boy I had encountered, someone whose conversation revealed a personality of high energy and bright humor. The austere veneer I had been cultivating was dropped flat and I invited him somewhere at the first opportunity, which happened to be Smart Girl's Thanksgiving barn dance, complete with blue jeans, checked shirts, and a punch bowl secretly laced with gin, rum, and whiskey.

Having no experience with alcohol, let alone such a weird concoction, I sipped away and flirted with Hotch. Suddenly I needed fresh air. Fleeing unsteadily outside into the night, I skidded on something mushy, lurched, and slid sideways into a shallow depression, landing on my hands and knees. Even in the darkness I recognized the odor of richly decomposed manure, a perfectly good place to vomit.

Having followed me in perhaps romantic anticipation, Hotch witnessed my performance from the bank above. When I had finished he reached down and hauled me up from the gluey clutch of the pit. Using a nearby hose, he washed me off, spread newspapers on his car seat, and drove me home. A charming date, for sure, and an unusual start to enduring love.

☆

A few days later Washington, D.C., newspapers announced the arrival of Saburo Kurusu, the newly appointed ambassador from Japan, the same genial diplomat who had visited at the Fox studio. Recalling to reporters previous American encounters, he listed me among them. His current job was to help defuse mounting international tensions in the Pacific. To anyone with an educated nose, things smelled ominously of gunpowder. My nose was not among them. Barely hours later, on December 7, 1941, the Japanese assault on Pearl Harbor descended with unanticipated suddenness.

Brother George was stationed with the Marines at Ewa Plantation, a target of Japanese air onslaught, and for days afterwards we heard nothing from or about him. In desperation, Father finally turned directly to FBI Director Hoover, who passed word to George to call home. We then learned his entire company had been invited to a Japanese wedding the evening before the surprise attack. Exuberant on sake and reeling homeward, George had finally fallen asleep on the grassy parade ground before his barracks and under a canopy of tropical stars. With dawn came Japanese dive bombers screaming down to strafe the buildings, and setting his mess hall afire. George had watched the horrifying spectacle from mid-field, propped up on his elbow.

At the tail end of a December 26, 1941, Elgin Watch radio show, I ad-libbed a whispered "Hello, George," the first of what became thousands of messages to servicemen overseas.

California had been seized with the imagined prospect of attack and invasion. Volunteering as a neighborhood block warden, Father began solitary nighttime patrols. Wearing a steel helmet painted yellow and firmly anchored by a black leather chin strap, he diligently searched for spies and infiltrators, flashing his light among the roadside bushes. California Attorney General Earl Warren issued a stunning edict to round up all ethnic Japanese in California for detention or resettlement elsewhere in the United States. My dollhouse was provisioned with extra bottled water and canned goods against probable enemy invasion. Each evening we assembled outside in the dark, heads craned back to search among the stars for Japanese bombers. I joined the Hollywood Victory Committee to help sell war bonds and stamps and went to local shipyards and airplane plants as a headliner during patriotic lunchtime rallies.

Overruling Mother's constitutional objections against live radio, I signed up for a long-term radio soap opera based on *The New Yorker* magazine series of "Junior Miss," later to become a highly popular Book-of-the-Month Club selection and Broadway production. For twenty-six successive weeks I carried on at the microphone, spoofing myself with such lines as "I can't stand that Shirley Temple. I think she's a drip!"

Sponsored by Ivory Snow and Dreft washing powder, "safe drying for wartime rayons, folks!" we finally washed ourselves away. Tallow used in the manufacture of soap was conscripted to produce nitroglycerine for bombs, so suddenly soap bars became a wartime shortage. There was no need to advertise for sale something in short supply.

"Hello, and good-bye," I quipped on our final broadcast. "Lard has gone to war."

28

Funerals are seldom hilarious occasions. That is, unless you are a fourteen-year-old high school freshman assembled with schoolmates at Forest Lawn Cemetery to bury headmistress Miss Frederica de Laguna. Respectful silence for the departed was shattered by the same minister who had presided several years earlier during last rites for the prior headmistress. In a cool, polished voice sent booming out among the headstones, he addressed the body before him by her predecessor's name.

Not much is required to start girls giggling. The prospect of the first headmistress getting buried twice, with Miss de Laguna left lying there waiting, was more than adequate excuse. However muffled our hilarity, it attracted the attention of senior class English teacher and vice principal Carol Mills. About to be promoted to succeed our departed principal, she correctly identified me as a ringleader and later summoned me to her office. Pale and thin-lipped, she resembled one of those medieval Flemish virgins found in books of art masterpieces. Every hair remained anchored in place no matter how quickly she swiveled her head to fix someone in her birdlike gaze. Standing or seated, her posture was unfailingly erect, when speaking, her syntax perfect.

First she lectured me on ladylike deportment. Days of giggling were over, she warned. If laugh I must, it should be gracious humor, carefully metered.

Much later I realized who was conspiring with Miss Mills. For someone so feminine to her fingertips as Mother, an adolescent hoyden forever climbing out on tree limbs must have seemed repugnant. Rough edges grated on her sensibilities, and my unbridled conduct screeched for some filing down. Time had come for me to acquire behavioral graces I appeared to lack, and Miss Mills impressed Mother as someone who could engineer the transformation.

A week after the funeral fiasco, Miss Mills caught me reading Kathleen Winsor's *Forever Amber*, a racy novel for its time, and poorly disguised within a school textbook wrapper. To punish me for my libertine taste in literature, she banned me from sports for two weeks, and confined me to study hall. Doubling as an English teacher, Miss Mills had devised a test on powers of observation and expression. Because several other sophomores were also being punished with study hall, she assigned us to make an unexpected disturbance. Her students present would be required to write their version of what happened.

Rather than punishment, her program had heaven-sent potential. One of my more hopeful techniques to create peer-group acceptance had been to play the clown. At the appointed moment I leaped up from my desk and raced around the room, tipping over empty chairs with a clatter, howling like a banshee and sweeping papers off desks. The English scholars sat rooted to their chairs, pencils poised in mid-thought, unaware that this peculiar behavior by me and my cohorts was in fact their test.

Noise and confusion were our only tools until someone more venturesome than most, perhaps I, set crumpled paper afire in a wastebasket. That did it. The first wisps of flame were a beacon to every student in the room. Swept up in genuine excitement, even the most scholarly joined our helter-skelter race, waving arms and shouting gibberish. Peeking through a cracked door, Miss Mills saw her test literally go up in smoke, and ran to trigger the fire alarm. With bells clanging, everyone poured onto the lawn to safety. Too bad no grades were awarded for our part in the test. Mine rated an "A."

Schoolwork had taken solid precedence over moviemaking since completion of *Kathleen* the previous summer of 1941. But by 1942, Father's antipathy toward agent Orsatti was propelling me into another film. Having stoutly refused to honor Orsatti's claim for $7,800 in commissions for previous radio work, and to extract himself contractually, Father had hired another agent. Frank W. Vincent was urbane, gray-haired, and silver tongued, charged with finding me a film job to finesse Orsatti's claim to exclusive representation. A convincing negotiator, Vincent had made a deal with independent producer Edward Small, collected his commissions in advance, and persuaded Father to settle with Orsatti on the basis claimed. Father had then tried to fob off on Small the *Lucky Sixpence* story, sole asset of the defunct production company. In so doing he collided head-on with Mary Pickford, still a principal owner of United Artists, the studio where Small had arranged to produce his film. Her choice was a remake of her last film, *Little Annie Rooney*, in which thirty-two-year-old Pickford had posed as a preadolescent with golden curls and glad-girl smile. During screenplay development, however, Pickford's interest flagged. The "little" of the title was dropped, and a successor story was written to replace the original. By whatever name, the *Miss Annie Rooney* which evolved would have been instantly forgettable had it not continued to glow like some nocturnal fungus.

"... between a paper doll and a sweater girl," later commented the *New York Times*. "Coy stances, self-conscious hip-swinging ... an adolescent phenom who talks like a dictionary of jive ... with quotes from Shakespeare and Shaw."

For some of us production had one saving grace, however: three glorious weeks of extended jitterbug rehearsal made necessary by dancing hang-ups of my appointed partner, Dickie Moore, sixteen-year-old acting veteran from *Our Gang* comedies. At one point, director Edwin Marin threatened to replace him with Dickie Jones, a rodeo stunt performer and off-screen voice of Walt Disney's *Pinocchio*, but eventually substituted Roland Dupree, another dancer, who did the scene disguised behind a molded-rubber facemask made in Moore's image.

Our use of the mask had an ironic twist. Due to wartime, a critical rubber shortage existed, and even our plot hinged on an invention to produce rubber from common milkweed. To cap things off, as we danced on June 19, 1942, President Roosevelt proclaimed "Victory Rubber Day," appealing for rubber of any kind to be turned in at depots located in auto service stations. If any of us around the studio had patriotic qualms about our use of rubber for entertainment, it failed to show.

Although he had been spared further embarrassment by his rubber-faced rival, Dickie Moore's misery persisted in the shape of a kiss, widely touted as my first.

As I fluttered my eyelids closed in anticipation, he strained across the car seat to land a peck on my cheek.

"I'd never even held a girl's hand before," he wrote in his 1984 memoirs *Twinkle Twinkle Little Star*. "Continence was in the air I breathed.... Shirley's breasts pressed hard against the party dress... legs firm and round, suggestively outlined beneath the skirt.... America's sweetheart was... sexy and seductive... I could not conceal the twitching of my facial muscles...."

"I sweated right through my suit," he recalled.

After Dickie made several floundering tries, Marin asked if he had inhibitions about kissing me.

"What are inhibitions?" Moore asked.

"If you knew what they were, you wouldn't have any," I interjected. Hardly a woman of the world, I was weary of his ineptness. After all, it was only on the cheek, and contrary to publicity hoopla indicating his as my initial kiss, months before someone had kissed me, and on the lips, in a horse corral.

Westlake freshmen had been matched in an exchange dance with boys from Thatcher School, an outdoorsy college preparatory school which required each boy to furnish and care for a horse. My blind date was Hugh Cover, a sturdy boy with blond hair. Best of all, his father was glamorous, a test pilot for Douglas Aircraft Company. Successfully eluding our eagle-eyed chaperones, we had sneaked out a side door of the gymnasium. Holding hands, we ran out to the moon-drenched dead center of the gymkhana field.

"Dear Diary," I wrote that night, "he kissed me."

After breakfast I had burst into Mother's room, where as usual she sat sorting and reading my fan mail. Kneeling by her chair, I whispered, "I'm in love!"

"With whom?" she said, never raising her eyes from the letter in her lap. I slunk away.

My date seemed equally unimpressed. The next day he had mounted his horse for a pack trip into the nearby Sespe Mountains and forgot about our romance in the old corral, forevermore.

Since that cataclysmic moment I had begun to paint my toenails red, experimented with eye shadow, and fancied charm bracelets and wedge heels. Boys were a pleasant contagion. Although Hotch remained my favorite boyfriend, a second lighthearted boy called Hunk, was running well in my disorganized field of flirtation. To maintain an equilibrium of envy between these two favorites, I encouraged each only when confident the other would find out. This tactic proved hazardous. Underestimating Hunk's possessive instinct while teasing him one evening about Hotch, I got slugged in the jaw. As blows go, it was more sobering than damaging, but it rearranged my cartilage so that to this day I still have an audible click. Rather than disqualifying Hunk for aggressive conduct, I was intrigued by the intensity of his affection, if leery about his temper.

Although Mother and I discussed everything else, sex never entered our conversations. Fortunately there was Smart Girl, whose worldly mother had already explained everything pertinent. Another schoolmate produced a contraceptive device, an item secretly inspected with profound interest at Westlake.

As my bust was fast developing, Mother said modesty demanded that I walk with my arms crossed or carry something in front, like schoolbooks. When I told Smart Girl that crossed arms were a symbol of chastity she answered that crossed legs would help more.

Anatomy class provided another forum for accumulating wisdom about such things. Teamed to reconstruct a jumble of bleached bones into a coherent skeleton we dubbed Miss Lilywhite, Smart Girl and I laboriously pieced her together on a table, but found one bone left over. Small, slightly curved and about an inch long, it obviously belonged somewhere in the middle plane. Exactly where eluded us, so, gleefully employing common sense, we decided it could only belong in the pelvic region. There it was placed, instantly converting Miss Lilywhite to a mister.

"Wrong," scolded Miss Ethel Jacoby, "The hyoid bone goes at the base of the *tongue*.

Gradually becoming attuned to all things sexual, at school we were fascinated by the public controversy stirred up when parents of an anonymous high-schoolgirl lodged a paternity suit against Errol Flynn. Admitting her earlier escapade aboard his yacht, she claimed to have enjoyed the moon through his porthole. Although valiantly trying to identify the girl as a Westlake schoolmate, the most productive we became was to compose a doggerel: "Twirl my nightie, tuck me in, here comes Mr. Errol Flynn."

Our wondrous process of self-education continued even in darkened movie theaters. After spending hours selecting what we should wear to a matinee at the Hollywood Egyptian Theatre, five of us were driven downtown, chaperoned by "Palmtree," my 225-pound bodyguard replacement for Griff. Actually he just sat in the rear row and drowsed. Well provisioned with bags of buttered popcorn and chocolate-coated peanuts, the rest of us settled into seats farther down front, eyes soon glued on the screen, where horrors of *I Walked With a Zombie* were unfolding.

Just when the man had pulled down the seat beside me I do not recall, although I was vaguely aware he wore a business suit and kept his hat on.

Converting someone into a zombie requires electrifying skills. Spell after spell need be cast on unsuspecting victims to reduce a normal person into a vacant-eyed automaton en route to commit some chilling act. A lady zombie was wandering among graveyard tombstones enlisting the dead, her diaphanous gown blowing gently in foggy night air. Suddenly the man seated beside me reached over, grabbed my wrist, and quickly pulled my hand into his lap. As I felt bare flesh I yanked my hand back. The man stared fixedly at the movie screen, as if nothing had happened.

Tugging at Smart Girl's sleeve, I whispered, "I'm sitting beside a pervert."

"What?" she replied, her attention riveted as a zombie was being raised from the dead.

"He pulled my hand into his lap! He's unbuttoned!" That got her attention.

Inclining forward, for a moment she peered past me in the half-darkness.

"With the hat? Doesn't look like a pervert." She wanted to return to the movie. "Look, if you don't like your seat, let's switch."

Settled in her seat, I, too, was soon mesmerized by the soft, eerie music and gruesome spectacles. Smart Girl gasped.

"See," I hissed, "I told you so!"

"Let's tell Palmtree!"

"No way," I answered. "He'll make us leave and we'll miss the movie. Let's move."

Already halfway up out of the seat, she whispered, "God, there are zombies all over this dump!"

By then graduated to a second-size brassiere, I was experimenting with Hotch. On a moon-drenched golf green at the Desert Inn in Palm Springs we got cooled off when the automatic nighttime water sprinklers erupted all around us. The next day we warmed up again while riding a tandem bicycle. Reaching from behind, he fumbled one-handed to undo my bra strap, taking far too long to allow me to show shock or even surprise.

Despite Smart Girl's tutelage and my own experimentation, I was still not exactly sure what precise degree of intimacy produced pregnancy. After the Desert Inn petting sessions, my menstrual period was late. Such things were seen as a calamitous harbinger. Immediate action was necessary, but hardly a subject for consultation. Scouting Mother's bathroom medicine chest, among her prescriptions for bladder infections and kidney stones I found one pill bottle labeled "Take as needed for delay."

Extracting one tablet, I swallowed it, retreated into Mother's room, and seated myself cross-legged before her full-length mirror like a monk about to perform a ritual. What would happen? Would I become a werewolf? Grow a beard? I stared, my heart beating faster. Would I die?

Nothing happened, of course. Nature soon verified that pregnancy was impossible in our cautious brand of necking, a discovery which encouraged us to take up where we had left off.

Naturally, Mother knew more of what was going on than we suspected. Accommodating the inevitably fickle will of her daughter, yet a stickler for propriety, she collaborated with Hotch to give me a finger-ring, a tiny amber-colored diamond surrounded by sapphire-blue petals with a tiny dangling tag reading "Forget-me-not." In retrospect, Hotch played his game with consummate restraint, leaving me chaste, if marginally wiser. He never was really imagined as a husband, any more than I as a wife. Our alliance was on the anvil, but never quite got forged.

Among her other attributes of maturity, Smart Girl smoked cigarettes on the sly, and introduced me to this habit of dubious merit. Whenever we could, we double-dated boys old enough to drive and smoke. Although honor bound to Mother for just the movie and a snack afterwards, even that tight rein had enough slack. At Simon's Drive-In people were often out of their cars wandering around. Once a drunken sailor came over and leaned through the rolled-down window, displaying a handful of what looked like cigarettes in brown wrappers.

"Wan' some marijuana?" he slurred.

Up to that point I knew only Lucky Strikes, Chesterfields, and Smart Girl's favorite Camels.

"Get lost, weirdo," our dates snarled in unison, so the sailor shrugged amiably, withdrew his hand, and went rocking away toward another car. Anybody who possessed marijuana, let alone used it, was really weird. Some people said drummers in bands, like Gene Krupa of the Casa Loma Orchestra, probably took it to make their drumsticks move faster, but that was just an occupational peculiarity, like doping horses at racetracks.

While I was gradually gaining confidence in sex and smoking, daily news reports of wartime horror and heroics kept churning up a general sense of uncertainty. Our Marines had just stormed ashore in a bloody Guadalcanal Island foothold, and Allied forces had invaded North Africa. Outside the gates of Moscow, German armor was poised, and southward the blitzkrieg had slashed into the French heartland. Hotch had become an Air Cadet in training. Both my brothers were enlisted sergeants, Jack in the Army Air Corps and George the Marines. Depression-era unemployment had vanished and few industries knew hard times anymore, including movie theatres, home to 90 million Americans driven there each week to escape bad news or to celebrate the good. The nation and Hollywood pulsed with activity and, on the sidelines, I was part of it.

My fan mail from servicemen overseas had swelled to a torrent.

Forty-year-olds treated me like a daughter. To those in their early thirties I was a sister. The younger ones wanted me for a girlfriend. On my behalf two full-time secretaries carried on hundreds of vicarious pen-pal romances, writing my thoughts, signing my name, and dispatching autographed photos by the thousands. My blown-up publicity photo was among those installed on the hangar deck of the aircraft carrier USS *Saratoga*, presumably to provide pilots a final reminder of home before flying off to battle. Like other celebrities, I regularly made cheer-up visits to military hospitals, gave peptalks in shipyards and defense manufacturing plants, and did regular duty at the Hollywood Canteen, mecca of memorable experiences for more than three million soldiers, sailors, and airmen from October 1942 until war's end. It was galling to be able to do so little for the war effort, but what also lay its heavy load on my stomach was realization that I was not even working.

To be sure, radio helped. By early 1943 I was well into a string of 66 radio programs to be completed during the 1940s, including dramatic programs sponsored to sell soap, cosmetics, toothpaste, and cigarettes, and guest-star appearances with comedians like George Burns and Gracie Allen, and Edgar Bergen with Charlie McCarthy and Mortimer Snerd.

To only Mother's surprise, I had been instantly at home in a "live" medium, jubilant under the tensions imposed by a large, theatrical audience replete with uniformed ushers and printed programs, and by the demand for split-second timing, and the unforgiving threat of a blown line. It was a new world. Gone were the grips, gaffers, and light men of prior years, replaced by technicians with earphones. Stripped of the customary weaponry of acting like eye-contact, facial expression, and bodily movement, I was left with only tongue and vocal tones. Timing was newly king; countdown came in seconds. Direction was new, a twirled hand signifying speed it up, a sliced-throat to end it all. Run too long, somebody else gets cut. Impromptu joking which uses up time does not necessarily make friends. Exchanging ad-libs with Bob Hope at March Field had our serviceman audience rolling in the aisles, but songbird Frances Langford's subsequent number had to be eliminated. Upstaging was done by the clock, not physical movement.

Rapidity exacts a toll. From first rehearsal to last line of a radio program was usually a day. Little time was available to me to detect the chink in Paul Muni's austere facade, or to understand the leaden truculence of comedian Jack Benny which switched to enduring humor when his mike became hot, or to share any unwritten conversation with widely revered Cecil B. DeMille.

Although strapped to the clock hand as never before, I luxuriated in these new tests of nerve and in the mystique of teamwork carried over intact from moviemaking. Radio experience piled on top of film work served me well, a launching pad for fifty television shows almost two decades later. And by exceeding Mother's expectations for me, I could give another soft tug at parental chains. Yet radio was intermittent and I remained restless.

In some lives the pleasures of retrospect and testimonial laurels hanging on the wall are comforting. For me past achievement is dry as dust, static memories best elevated to attic storage. Still yearning for gainful challenge, and fulfillment, I felt myself wallowing in the calm eye of a storm swirling all around me.

As always before, fate intervened. In May 1943 producer David O. Selznick called me asking that I visit him. Earlier that year, William Dozier, a story editor for Paramount, had referred to Selznick a series of letters written by Margaret Buell Wilder, a Dayton, Ohio, news-paperwoman, to her serviceman husband. In these she had talked about the problems of living on a military allotment, raising two teenaged girls, coping with loneliness, and her sense of personal uselessness. Selznick had been searching for just such a film vehicle to demonstrate both how much and how little the war had changed American life. In March he had purchased movie rights for $30,000 and brought the author and daughters Brig and Jane to Hollywood to assist in the screenplay he envisaged. By sheer coincidence both girls had been enrolled in my class at Westlake School. Still sensitive to the difficulties experienced by strangers in an established pack, I had gone out of my way to be friendly to both girls and we had become fast friends.

By late spring Selznick had taken Wilder's first-draft screenplay and begun to rewrite it, for sentimental reasons using the pseudonym Jeffrey Daniel, which combined the names of his two young sons. For expert assistance Selznick had then hired F. Hugh Herbert, author of the recent Broadway hit *Kiss and Tell*. A demonstrated expert on teenage culture, Herbert would prove invaluable in drawing an accurate character for

Brig, a shrewd tomboy lonely for her father and determined to help in the war effort.

Ringing Selznick's doorbell at his Santa Monica beachfront house, I was surprised when ten-year-old Jeffrey answered.

"I don't know you, but I like you," he said abruptly. "Father's in the den."

Selznick sat behind a desk, his form backlighted by a western sun low on the ocean horizon. Having dressed carefully in a white silk suit, tuxedo-cut with a low V neck, I had all the confidence clothing could impart.

"Please sit there, Shirley," he said, his mouth held in a wide smile, lips parted. Doing as instructed, I watched as his eyes moved over me slowly, from hair to feet and back again.

"Let me move to see you." He got up, and crouched down behind a potted palm. Adjusting his glasses, he peered out through the fronds. Moving slightly right, then left, for several minutes he continued this silent, furtive inspection.

Realizing he was engaged in some peculiar visual test, I remained motionless, letting him do the moving. After what seemed an eternity, he came around from behind the palm.

"You'll do. You're Brig." He laughed, a slightly liquid sound. "Jeff likes you, so I'm going to hire you."

Describing the role of Brig to me, he obviously was preoccupied with middle-class normality and the soda-fountain set. The screen dialogue would be peppered with accurate teenage slang and avoid any maudlin bursts, as he described them, of "dear Dad off to war." I liked what I heard.

Getting around to business, he offered to "test" me for one year at $2,200 per week. If all went well, it would be a seven-year contract at $5,000 per week. I had never heard of a test contract. Screen tests, yes, but one whole year of test? Despite my reservation, I accepted his terms, and as things turned out, I remained scared for a year.

Selznick had at least two other possible reasons to hire me, excluding Jeff's judgment: my youth and his general regard for women.

As quoted by Ronald Haver in *David O. Selznick's Hollywood*, five years earlier he had written, "The motion picture business belongs to youth. . . . We build our pictures on the emotions of the younger generation. . . . The great entertainment, propaganda, and social weapon of the motion picture is the weapon of youth, the weapon by which youth increasingly will bludgeon its elders into thinking its way."

As to his view of women, Selznick had consistently surrounded himself with articulate, sharp characters. Katharine Brown of his New York office was the one who had discovered the *Gone with the Wind* story, and Anita Colby, ex-New York model and top saleswoman for *Harper's Bazaar* magazine, had long helped polish the appearance and style of his future stars. Although his performing stable included several outstanding male regulars, it was with actresses such as Ingrid Bergman, Joan Fontaine, and, later, Jennifer Jones that he mined true gold. Knowing him by this reputation, to have been selected by him was profoundly satisfying.

My new contract brought cheering tidings to Father. Since my leaving Fox my fees from public appearances and radio had been our sole earned family income, although our standard of living had sailed along unchanged. Now this gritty fact was swept under the rug by the fresh stream of paychecks of my contract.

Mother was ecstatic for other reasons. Among all independent producers of the late 1930s, she really admired the work of only Samuel Goldwyn and Selznick. Part of that respect was entangled in a web of coincidence. Selznick had previously been involved with both our attorney friend Loyd Wright and with widely respected banker Dr. Attilio Giannini.

Prior to 1935 both Samuel Goldwyn and Selznick International Pictures had distributed films through United Artists, as did Twentieth Century Pictures. With the 1935 Twentieth Century-Fox merger, that supply of film dried up for United Artists. About the same time Goldwyn withdrew his productions in favor of RKO distribution, leaving United Artists hungry for productions. Mary Pickford and Charles Chaplin had offered Selznick one-third interest in their United Artists for $300,000 in return for Selznick's pledge to produce ten pictures for United Artists release during the next five years.

The deal also had a reverse spin valuable to Selznick. United Artists would loan the $300,000 right back to him for working capital, and accord any films in excess of the required ten the same preferential distribution terms given films produced by the original United Artists owners.

In the negotiation United Artists had been represented by Loyd

Wright. Though he was no longer our attorney, following an acrimonious farewell from Father in 1941 over the size of Wright's legal fees, his high personal standing with Mother had remained intact.

She also admired Giannini because of his relationship to the distinguished Bank of America family. A member of Selznick's board of directors at Vanguard Pictures, Giannini had assumed the presidency of United Artists. From Mother's standpoint the confluence of Wright and Giannini with David O. Selznick Productions, Inc., provided a luster of stability and business acumen in my newly established relationship.

An even more cogent reason for Mother's enthusiasm lay in Selznick's emphasis on quality, and on his widely expressed conviction that artistic pictures were also the best commercial successes. In 1935 discussions with reporters regarding his aspirations for newly formed Selznick International, he had observed, ". . . the day of mass production has ended . . . audiences are smarter than we give them credit for. . . . My object is to make the finer things, and leave the trash to others." He had succeeded in the judgment of his peers, and in 1939 the Academy of Motion Pictures Arts and Sciences had presented him its Irving Thalberg Award for the most consistent high quality of production. To be signed to work under such direction afforded me instant professional stature.

Perhaps the best measure of Mother's satisfaction was her abrupt abdication of her hitherto relentless demand for artistic control.

"We're leaving her career entirely up to Mr. Selznick," she flatly declared. "Whatever he says, goes."

29

Playing second fiddle in a good orchestra is sometimes better than doing a solo. That was my fortunate situation in June 1943 when Selznick completed casting for *Since You Went Away*. Top-star Claudette Colbert had been lured into becoming my mother, signed after a twinge of dismay at being found old enough for motherhood was softened by a $250,000 fee. Tall and ingratiating Joseph Cotten was also recruited, along with veterans Lionel Barrymore and Hattie McDaniel, companions from now ancient *The Little Colonel*. Breathless, blushing Selznick protégée Jennifer Jones was also selected, together with her husband, Robert Walker. Lined up for a principal-cast publicity photo, I was placed dead center, flanked by ten illustrious stars. My central position was not unnerving, although inconsistent with my actual subordinate position in official star billing. After all, I was still ahead of the other 5,035 supporting cast.

Embroidering on Mrs. Wilder's initial screenplay draft, Selznick was busy inventing characters and rewriting the 205 speaking roles, while from the soil of his back lot, under the gifted hand of architect William Pereira, rose a complete suburban house, its speckless beauty a far cry from Mrs. Wilder's original description of a place with dog hair on the furniture.

Long before shooting was to commence and seizing on her preferential position as co-owner of United Artists, Mary Pickford started angling with Selznick to produce my next film. Proposing *Junior Miss*, based on my recent radio series, she inspired little positive reaction. She then offered *Girls Town*, written by magazine writer Adela Rogers St. John, a tale of wartime dislocations and wayward girls. To lay a moral patina over this offbeat theme, she pledged all profits be sent to a charitable foundation for delinquents. Before either Mother or Selznick had time to even nibble her bait, the U.S. Office of War Information reputedly got into the act. Mute the delinquency angle, they urged; be patriotic. Pickford retitled the film *They're Only Young Once*.

Undismayed by the guarded reaction accorded her first two proposals, Pickford made one final thrust. At Selznick's social reception to introduce his new publicist, Mitchel Rawson, I met her for the first time. Before this moment the closest we had ever been was separated by several seats during a China War Relief extravaganza. Embracing me as an old friend, she adroitly steered us before the waiting lens of a *Life* magazine news team. What seemed just another innocent photo opportunity became an announcement. Confiding eloquently to the reporter, she revealed my next film as *Coquette*, a remake of her own 1929 starring role, with us appearing together. It was news to everyone but her.

However, if nothing came of her proposals, much came of our photo together. Combining nostalgia and future promise, our twosome received what was reported as the greatest single-day news photo coverage in movie history. Four and a half million copies of *Life* were sold, plus three million copies of photos in New York newspapers, and front-page news in 1,200 other papers served by Acme and Associated Press. Off all those pages we smiled over the caption "World's Two Greatest Has-Beens."

Connotations in both Pickford's proposal and the publicity caption evoked Mother's indignation. *Coquette* particularly winked a message of danger. At best it appeared a clumsy Pickford attempt at self-gratification, at worst her crude comeback attempt riding on my back. The *Coquette* idea disappeared into the same trash can as yesterday's newspaper.

Long before casting for *Since You Went Away* had been fully completed, Selznick had fastened his attention on my imperfections.

"Never mind studio drama school," he told me, lifting his upper lip to expose his front teeth, an expression intended to be friendly but instead appearing vaguely sinister. "I like you just the way you are. Except your hair. Thin it, drag it down with weights. It looks like an O-Cedar mop!"

To assist my transformation into someone more photogenic, he fobbed me off on his artistic director, Anita Colby, the supercharged, supermodel head of his one-woman charm school. Examining me slowly, skin, hair, and figure, she had concluded, ". . . stocky frame, close knit . . . thick muscles that can stand longer strain . . . less slumping and sag . . . a roomier torso to house a fuller intestinal tract . . ."

A more thorough analysis of screen potential is difficult to imagine, but she had continued, "More alimentary canal for food to store and linger in . . ."

For sure, I felt weird and unbeautiful, but she certainly had my attention.

Everyone at Vanguard Films, the unit Selznick had formed to discharge his United Artists obligations, had quirks demanding correction, Colby revealed. I should not be too sensitive. Electrolysis had been used to raise one ingenue's unsatisfactory hairline; thin wads of paraffin were inserted between the lower teeth and lip of another actress to fill out a jawline which caved in during photography.

"David wants you sweet sixteen, and in pinafores," she declared. "On such a short, thick body, never a long, gushy hairdo. Hair piled softly high is indicated." Her words came out a combination of Elizabeth Arden, Dale Carnegie, and a dean of Vassar College.

Sensing my immediate resistance to upswept hairstyles, she tried to enlist Mother's support for the change. Neither knew the true origin of my reluctance; Hotch liked long, loose hair.

As a fallback, Colby set out to minimize the mass of my hair by tucking my curls in at each side with a handsome pair of decorative combs festooned with roses in red and yellow gold. Visually that did help reduce the importance of my hair, dragging it down and in. The effect so caught Mother's fancy that she went off to the same jeweler and bought herself an identical set of combs.

Beyond her analytical skill, and tasteful ingenuity, Colby understood her employer when it came to feminine beauty. On the subject
of lingerie she had turned all flattery. "The most beautiful breasts," she
exclaimed, "better than Bergman, Fontaine, Jennifer, the lot."

Speaking of breasts, she offered some sisterly advice, a gong of
caution about Selznick. Be careful if I found him in stocking feet. I was
gathering the impression that casual sex could be a condition of employment, and resolved not to get myself in any difficult position, such
as prone.

Returning to breasts, Colby confided that a problem had arisen.
Selznick thought my figure too mature and curvaceous for the ingenue
he visualized. He had requested my bust be bound flat. Reluctant to
obscure two of my apparently scanty physical assets beneath muslin
bindings, again I rebelled. There was no good reason why I must be
flat-chested just because I lived in Peoria. For reasons I found uncon-
vincing, Selznick remained insistent and tried to draw Mother into
the debate. She sided solidly with me in a long meeting, at one point
of which her face suddenly became deeply flushed. Tugging at her
dress collar, she removed her necklace and complained of feeling ill.
Well briefed in Westlake hallways about such natural events, I was
astounded to find she had no idea what was happening. On our way
home I stopped by the San Vincente Drug Store for a copy of "All You
Need to Know About Menopause," a pamphlet I had already devoured.
The next day I went to Bullocks Wilshire Department Store for my third
upgraded brassiere, the pointiest one I could find. Selznick could just
be hanged.

While Colby and Selznick were concentrating on making me look
younger, Vanguard publicists were embarked on a patently uncoordi-
nated program to make me older and overtly sexy. Photographer Andre
de Dienes was assigned to pose me on a haystack at the nearby Arden
Dairy Farm, coincidentally the home of Tillie Temple from Tillamook,
my gift cow from a distant birthday. Dressed in cowboy boots, blue
jeans, blouse, and a bulky cable-knit sweater, I fluffed out my hair and
stretched out in what I assumed were seductive poses, most lying back
in the hay sucking on a piece of straw.

After a few rolls of film de Dienes complained that my outfit was
shapeless, and maybe too much. Rolling my jeans to the knee, I exposed
both calves.

Not just what he had in mind, he said. Let's take off the boots, for starters. Then, how about a little more off-the-shoulder with the blouse? For a third time, I rebelled. Pin-up photos were perfectly okay, particularly if the legs were like Betty Grable's. Contrived cheesecake was for starlets, and I wanted no part of it.

When shooting commenced in early September 1943 my transformation was still incomplete. That was the day the Japanese reported that I had been killed in a bombing raid on Los Angeles. On the verge of a riot, Tokyo had rejoiced. So far as I was concerned, I had joined my first labor union. At Vanguard complete unionization of production trades had been largely accomplished, and along with this, differentiation between management and labor thus intensified. I had always instinctively sided with the working crew, and as I was inclined to be suspicious of administrative types, my enthusiasm ran high with my official membership card in the Screen Actors Guild. My decade of apprenticeship had ended, ushering in over forty-five subsequent years of uninterrupted, faithful support.

Around home everyone was generally aware of studio efforts to rework my hair, reshape my body, and upgrade my sexuality, so brother Jack decided the pitch of my voice should be lowered in the interests of maturity. In league with Mother, he served up veteran drama coach Bob Paris to accelerate my aging. For my taste, Paris was a little too old to be teaching one so young. Consciously depress the voice, he instructed, banish the woo-woo habit, lose that pout. As requested, I rehearsed cute little love scenes with him, holding hands and sometimes hugging. After several days as a reluctant romantic and noticing his handy approach to my torso, I reminded him of my voice problem. Thereafter he coached from a distance, but his sessions left me with only an ill-deserved presumption of sophistication and a speaking voice one octave below normal.

Industrious as a fly, Selznick was there to watch our first filming, and heard me answer my initial cue with a newfound, serene, "How-now-brown-cow" technique.

He looked startled and inquired, "Someone teaching you voice?" When I replied yes, he blurted, "Stop it!"

"Go home," added John Cromwell, the taciturn British-born director, "and come back yourself."

That was the end of my other self, and I returned to the original, in more ways than one. Although aware of Claudette Colbert's standard prohibition against being photographed from her right side, I was reluctant to cooperate to my own disadvantage. One early occasion found each of us zigzagging backward toward a fireplace to avoid being upstaged by the other. Our respective movements resulted in the necessity for her right side to move into the camera. Suddenly she reached out and grabbed my chin. Firmly holding my head faced away from the camera, she rotated herself to a left exposure, a not-so-gentle hint from mother to daughter that she would not tolerate any tricks.

Just as forthright offstage, Colbert overheard me remark about a forthcoming date with Air Cadet Hotch and sweetly inquired wasn't he a little *old* for me. Starting out crosswise with another star would get us nowhere, so I ignored the edge to her remark.

"Maybe so," I replied, "but he *acts* young!"

If Colbert's temperament was potentially troublesome to some of us on the set, her private physical rhythms were a regular source of frustration for Selznick. More than once he laughingly announced that there was room for only one prima donna on the lot—him.

"Now she's demanding three days off," he lamented. "Miss Jones gets by on *none*. I would really appreciate it if Claudette would try to get by on *one*, for the duration. . . . Tell her there's a war on. . . . We all have to make sacrifices."

Not always the case with producers, Selznick constantly hovered around our set. Interjecting instructions, rewriting dialogue on the spot, or arguing with director Cromwell, he was a powerful presence. At one point he abruptly fired cameraman George Barnes for getting what he regarded unsatisfactory camera angles on Jennifer Jones. By then Selznick's personal preoccupation with her was common knowledge. Making no bones about where things stood, he had declared her career was his to build and protect. Although she was cast romantically opposite real-life husband Robert Walker, their marriage was fast falling out of its bed. Time and again during filming the undercurrent tensions in her personal life erupted in sudden, enigmatic behavior.

On one occasion we two sisters were being filmed in bed, carrying on a sentimental dialogue about Walker. Beyond expressing the required sentimentality of her lines, she wriggled under the sheets, a slight twisting and rolling of her hips. Suggestive movements really had no relationship to her specific lines, so at first I read this as simple scene stealing, ingenious at that. When the scene finished, however, she leaped from bed, burst into unrehearsed, copious sobbing, and fled to her dressing room. No road map was needed to show where events were leading, but she was having one hard time getting there.

The same reactions followed a subsequent love scene played between both Walkers in a haystack. Once again when the shooting finished she dissolved in tears, but this time Selznick was on the set and led her off alone to his office. Shooting stopped and everyone lounged around drinking coffee. Walker had disappeared, literally as well as figuratively.

Thereafter, Jones was regularly called to Selznick for long conferences, leaving the rest of us to hang around the set, waiting. To pass the time, I knitted one argyle sock.

As endorsement of his growing confidence Selznick usually emerged from these conferences to create new scenes around Jones, changes which caused consternation to those of us prepared for a now abandoned script and facing clumsy adjustments in filming schedules. Few of us could anticipate where the story was going; nobody could have guessed where it would end. Selznick continued to write, and each day the director was obliged to decide what we would do next. Selznick's way was a hard way. Every role except Jones's diminished. Personally, I detected little evidence that she was as exuberant as she deserved to be, with expanded opportunity raining down on her each new day. To the contrary, she always seemed to be suffering acutely, and her love scenes with Walker continued painful to witness, until Selznick mercifully rewrote him off to war and got him killed.

The inevitable rupture of the Walker marriage was certainly not unexpected. Perhaps I was mildly envious. Her absorption of Selznick's time and attention inevitably crimped my chance to gain equally intense professional supervision. Both Jones and I could have been seen as competitors for future ingenue roles with him. He obviously had chosen, and while I waited I got to knit the other sock.

Grumbling remained widespread on the set that his rewriting was diminishing the impact of the original tight script. At times what had started as a story of undaunted hope and bravery seemed in danger of dissolving into one large dose of choking sentiment. We were all wrong. Selznick's incentives may have been oblique and his behavior unnerving, but he was surefooted.

On February 9, 1944, 420 scenes later, after five long months and 127 days of shooting, *Since You Went Away* was completed. At the annual Oscar award ceremonies on March 2, Selznick was seated between Jones and me. As Mary Pickford presented the best actress award to Jones for *Song of Bernadette*, Selznick leaned my way and whispered he was picking up his option on my seven-year contract. Lost in a surge of happiness, I neglected to follow his gaze toward the podium until I heard him mutter that somebody had done a great embalming job on Pickford. She may have been approaching the end of her road, but as for me I felt reborn, just given a superb tonic. A nationwide poll of motion picture critics had voted mine the best juvenile performance of the year, and *Look* magazine had welcomed me to adulthood as the "most promising newcomer." But all such credentials paled beside the hard fact of continuity under Selznick's banner.

In early 1944, he proclaimed his next production, *Tales of Passion and Romance*, a three-hour epic to be co-directed by Alfred Hitchcock, Alexander Korda, and William Dieterle. The proposed cast glittered with well-known names—Ingrid Bergman, Jennifer Jones, Joan Fontaine, Vivien Leigh, and me to boot. Like many a good idea, this one foundered. Too bad; I would have been perfectly cast, in romance if not passion.

At the time my concept of female prowess was less physical than visual. My ideal woman would have been dressed in black taffeta, orchids in her hair, entering a room on the arm of some handsome uniformed soldier, preferably stolen from some other woman. Perhaps not qualified for the passion part, I certainly was for romance, with seven lively and well-rounded flirtations going on at the same time. Hotch was stationed in Wisconsin, a serious disadvantage. Locally my main pack of candidates included the belligerent but durable Hunk, a handsome bit actor I dubbed Beefcake because he couldn't

be called Brainy, and Smart Girl's brother. With each of these candidates I always agreed "to think about being engaged to be engaged,"
a thrice-removed semantic status which left me free to flirt to my heart's
content.

My letters were sealed with red lipstick prints and I did a lot of
scheming and dreaming. Along with my contemporaries, I had favorite
recording artists. Sinatra was nothing to collapse in my tracks about,
but give me that Dick Haymes or Johnny Johnston—there were a couple
of very "ritzy singers," I told my diary.

Occasionally even Mother conspired to help program my overlapping flirtations. If I was kissing someone good-bye at the back door,
she stalled the next visiting boyfriend with small talk in the living
room.

If my zest for flirtation became too consuming, Mother was sure to
intervene. Thirty-year-old James Melton, houseguest at ZaSu Pitts's next
door, occupied a room facing my bathroom window. My first clue to
his presence came one morning while brushing my teeth. Suddenly a
love song came belting across from his open window. Looking up from
my basin I saw both his arms extended in a romantic finale. In addition
to boasting a magnificent outdoor singing voice, he was an antique car
buff. Inviting me to accompany him on a ride in one of his heirlooms,
he managed, between gearshift, rubber squeeze horn, and ratchet brake,
to suggestively cling to my hand. Mother soon saw he was hanging
around too much for someone twice my age and sweetly suggested
that henceforth I would probably be too busy with rehearsals to see
him.

She was also keeping close track of Hotch, transferred to the Army
Air Corps training center in Wisconsin. Reduced to exchanging letters,
we had evolved a system of double-taping to thwart what we suspected
was Mother's audit. A vain hope. His love letters to me must have been
hidden haphazardly, for later specific queries indicated she had conducted private research in my sock drawer.

Another victim of Mother's protective attitude was a contemporary
in the Selznick stable, bit player Derek Harris, later to become John
Derek. A self-important young man, he had pleasing features, perhaps a little too sensitive for my taste. With a shock of dark hair
cascaded artfully over his forehead and his suit shoulders padded

out to disguise a rather delicate frame, he made a highly photogenic companion.

As an actor Selznick felt he had promise but so far little flair. Despite previous training, he still spoke downward and habitually missed his marks. Selznick had asked me to loosen him up. Not realizing the full extent of my task, I played the role of dramatic instructor. Relax, I urged. Ignore the audience. Never mind that twitch at your mouth or the one at the corner of the eye. Nobody can see it. Instruct and cajole him as I might, Harris would not, or could not, loosen up. On-camera he still came across wooden as a post.

Off-camera was another matter. The studio arranged for him to escort me around publicly, although one of us had our arrangement all wrong. On my fifteenth birthday he suggested lunch at fancy, expensive La Rue Restaurant. As the bill arrived he excused himself for the men's room.

Before long I detected he could be relaxed by necking. Neither of us was courageous about sex and we soon wearied of just kissing. As a replacement activity on the deserted moonlit playing field of nearby Riviera Polo Club, Harris taught me to drive stick shift in his jalopy and how exhilarating it was to floor an accelerator.

Realizing how susceptible I was to offbeat behavior, he produced a long knife, and stabbed around at invisible enemies. That surely beat necking. To embellish himself even further as an extraordinary fellow, one night he suddenly fell into an introspective mood and in rueful tones claimed to be the son of an undisclosed famous movie actress, but illegitimate. This pretext might have surprised his mother, had she overheard. As Delores Johnson, a hardworking actress, she was respectably married at the time to Lawson Harris, a songwriter. There in the moonlight, however, his unusual confession evoked awe and sympathy. Harris had set out to impress me, and he had. Not every girl gets to neck with a knife-wielding "bastard."

Apparently he put more lasting weight on our twosome than did I, for he pursued me relentlessly as I flirted my way elsewhere. On one Palm Springs family vacation he slept out on the desert sand in his sleeping bag and lurked around possessively to see whom else I dated. The knell to our relationship was sounded by a macabre gift, an original oil painting. Someone's bluish face was entwined in a surrealistic background of green seaweed. In his mystical, watery depiction Mother instantly saw a symbolic likeness between the disembodied face and mine. She forbade me to see him again, a tall order considering we were studio colleagues. But after thinking hard about her interpretation of his painting as a foretaste of undertow and death, I comfortably distanced myself, freeing Harris to skulk after more impressionable quarry.

While Mother thus tried to gently manipulate my romantic agenda, I kept winnowing my own romantic opportunities. To facilitate the process I collected photos of potential boyfriends in a three-ring loose-leaf binder, a handy way to quickly reorder their precedence. Not every kernel turned out golden. There was Tuscaloosa Tommy, for example, named after the place of his origin. An appealing, bubbling boy even without his incessant name-dropping, his personality was gradually outweighed by the inexorable forces of gravity. Everything about him hung. His hair was long and lank. His jowls were pendulous. He slumped, sitting or standing. The flesh even drooped at his armpits. When he wore swimming trunks private parts dangled visibly. It was as if some massive, geophysical tug were being exerted under Tusca-loosa Tommy's toes.

Newcomer Sergeant Jack, a gangling Air Corps recruit seven years my senior, was the brother of a Westlake classmate. His face contradicted itself, with glaringly blue eyes and a long, severe jawline suggesting strength, while at rest his mouth turned down at the corners in an oddly petulant scowl. Ann Gallery, my next-door neighbor and daughter of ZaSu Pitts, made the mistake of bringing him to one of my parties. Competitiveness was at the root of it all. From the outset nothing much more was in my head than stealing Sergeant Jack from Ann. The chase was the thing. Joyful describes the way I felt, and the contagion I helped spread.

Called by whatever name, I was one happy girl. Now securely one in a gang of a dozen Westlake girls, I was luxuriating in the same spirit of equality and conviviality that I had enjoyed with movie stage crews. We had not coalesced because of common social attitudes or intellect. Most of us were just weak B-average, playful girls who worked hard enough to sandwich ourselves securely between the brainy drones and the hopelessly inept.

In a Westlake assignment to discuss "my greatest asset," I wrote:

... to get fun out of everything I do. This may sound like a rather selfish asset, but by my having fun, other people see that I'm happy and will also have fun.

I can take a lot of sadness by feeling the way I do. You must have a lot of fun in you to be able to walk through hospital ward after hospital ward and see each uniform army cot containing its own personal problem and personality. I'm afraid a lot of my fun is turned on. When I first enter a ward, there's a deathly silence. I just have to start smiling and saying silly little things that will start them laughing and talking about their homes and ideas. Then I, too, begin to be happy. I no longer have to force the smile.

Perhaps my greatest asset is a rather common one, but it's important. Most people in the country are enjoying their troubles a little too much.

Indestructible schoolgirl cheer can come clattering apart, as mine did, upon learning of a classmate's death.

Although not a close friend, Maxine was rosy-cheeked, boisterous, and, like most of us, joyful. A few weeks before scheduled graduation she had simply disappeared from school, and in a matter of days we were told she had died, victim of a racing form of leukemia. The entire student body was conveyed to Forest Lawn Cemetery for her open-casket funeral. In contrast to Miss de Laguna's mirthful burial several years previous, this time I was profoundly affected.

Immaculate in her Westlake graduation dress, still apple-cheeked, every hair brushed into place, and both her hands gracefully holding a nosegay of spring blossoms, Maxine's lifeless body was in almost incomprehensible contrast to my memory of her. My light touch to the back of her icy hand produced a blinding realization of human mortality, life and death inseparably fused. Under her school yearbook photo the caption read, "She would give you the moon if she had it." I carefully inked in one word, "Dead." Genuine tears still watermark that page.

☆

By mid-1944, Selznick's time-consuming preoccupation with personal and business affairs made it vital that someone be added to oversee production of the twice-yearly Vanguard films required under his United Artists contract. Dore Schary, recently discharged from MGM, was hired to produce the wartime epic *I'll Be Seeing You*. In real life a strong-willed liberal intellectual with a penchant for injecting social criticism into his pictures, Schary soon collided with Selznick over the film's production. As quoted by Ronald Haver in *David O. Selznick's Holly-wood*, Selznick complained, "I deeply resent a man who is working for me, but not accepting my opinions, rejecting my criticisms. . . . For me to put up with this is not alone being tolerant and patient, it is being Christ-like, and I am *not* Christ-like!"

Selznick's run-ins did not affect us on the set, where Schary always seemed cheerful and competent, a nice enough man with a gap-toothed smile, like a Halloween pumpkin. A far more pressing problem was a puzzling antipathy toward me from Ginger Rogers. Someone whom I never recalled meeting before but whom I held in highest esteem as a luminous, accomplished pro, she seemed to have disliked me from a distance. Very early I gained an impression that she had wheedled some sort of cast-approval from Schary, for I was told she flatly demanded I be taken off the film. Apparently irritated by all this, Selznick sent me off to vacation at Palm Springs, presumably to resolve the impasse with me absent.

Hardly unpacked, I was summoned back the next workday, a Monday. Rogers was absent. Wearing ritual white gloves, director William Dieterle delayed our start from 8:30 a.m. to 9:00 a.m., until the moon conjoined with Jupiter in an auspicious planetary arrangement. Taking this to mean awaiting Rogers's late arrival, I brooded a bit, but the propitious moment came and went without her appearance. Down a long staircase I came dressed in a good-looking negligee and speaking dialogue that set the theme for the whole film story. Selznick had shrewdly resolved the controversy before it became a fight. Astrologically and practically, the film was locked in, and so was I.

It was Wednesday before Rogers returned to the set, noticed me with what I sensed as surprise, and left immediately in search of Selznick. Later I was told she had protested my presence. Too late. Our filming momentum was irreversible.

From that point Rogers and I regarded each other cautiously. Although several times I attempted to establish some offstage rapport, at

every point she seemed to resist intimacy. Usually she regarded me
silently, if at all, with her eyes narrowed, and occasionally she needled
me before others.

"Why, little Shirley," she scoffed one day, pointing at my bosom,
"you've grown up."

What could I say but, "Yep, couldn't stop myself."

"And those false eyelashes. They do *nothing* for you."

Over a ritual sixteenth birthday cake on the set, some cast members
gave me little remembrances of perfume or flowers. Rogers's gift was a
hat, elegantly boxed—a straw Chinese coolie affair surmounted by a
tepee of multicolored rooster tail feathers.

"There," she said, plopping it down on my head, "it does wonders!"
Unlikely, I thought, peering out from beneath the feathery brim like
some jungle animal.

Although Rogers and I later became friends, the reason for her
antipathy eluded me. I tried not to flare back. In fresh surroundings I
was desperately trying to do a good job to merit continuance with
Selznick. Competitive instinct was on short leash; what I sought was
approbation and companionship. It could have been only a pussycat
instinct of territorial sovereignty. Little could be done but disguise my
chagrin behind a mask of unruffled, good-natured bewilderment.

I'll Be Seeing You winds up with my emotional confession to Rogers
that I had tattled to her boyfriend that she was a convict. As rehearsal
progressed she prevailed on Dieterle to eliminate some of my dialogue
and to extend her final full-face close-up, which showed only the bushy
back of my head.

Reviewing final rough-cuts of the film after our company disbanded, Selznick expressed dissatisfaction with that last sobbing
scene and called in veteran George Cukor to direct a replacement
close-up, one which Selznick wrote featuring me full-face instead of
Rogers. Instead of recalling her, a blond-wigged extra was drafted to
stretch supine on the bed with her face averted. Kneeling at bedside,
full-face, I began to blurt out my sad admission. Suddenly Cukor shouted
to cut.

"Where did you ever learn this business!" he shouted, and without
waiting for an answer, added, "That's awful!" Removing his black, horn-
rimmed glasses, and letting both arms hang limp, he stared helplessly
at the floor.

For the first time, a director had openly declared me a dunce. That it came from someone long held in awe was both humiliating and alarming.

"Look," I replied, "all you want is a good cry. Give me five minutes and you'll get a good cry."

"Cry, nothing," he retorted. "I want emotion, not tears." There was neither other sound nor movement on the set, all eyes averted from mine.

The next try resulted in another Cukor explosion of disgust and dismay. Unnerved by his violent reaction, whatever capacity I had for emotional versatility simply vanished. Angered by his bullying direction and frustrated by my failure to please, my lines came out with increasingly hysterical inflection and, even by my thinking, less convincing impact.

By the twelfth take we both were on the far edge of exhaustion when, to my surprise, he put his arm around me affectionately. Finally he had exactly what he wanted. Never mind all those earlier harsh comments; that was only his style. Harangue and insult the woman, that was his way of getting results.

Neither technique nor rationale pleased me. Never before had I been bullied into an emotional reaction, let alone been able to deliver a better performance because of it. Theoretically any director who orders a dozen takes should be improving the product. After all, that's what directors are for. However, with each successive verbal buffeting I knew I produced a result less convincing. To this day I believe he picked the worst rendition of the lot.

Critics generally sided with Cukor, however. Applauding my final scene performance, Elsa Maxwell wrote, "A remarkable metamorphosis. Frankly, she used to bore me with her glibness."

Following *I'll Be Seeing You*, Schary left to become head of RKO. Simultaneously Selznick combined scripts, stock players, directors, and technical staff in a complete loan-out package to other studios on a 50 percent split of profits. Although my home base continued to be Vanguard and Selznick my mentor, for the remaining five years of my contract I became part of this loan-out concept.

On at least one subsequent occasion Selznick toyed with producing me in the lead for one of his personal blockbusters, *Portrait of Jennie*, based on the Robert Nathan novel. Having acquired screen rights in the fall of 1944 for $15,000, Selznick wanted me in a step-by-step transition from girlhood to adulthood. However, increasingly infatuated with Jennifer Jones after her success in *Duel in the Sun*, Selznick switched her into the role instead. As usual, his judgment was unerring. A more accomplished and beautiful actress than Jones in this role would have been difficult to imagine.

The collision of my growing yen for increasingly dramatic roles and an intuitive reluctance of producers to so cast me pointed up a fundamental problem, the difference between audience affection and admiration. My roles had traditionally been spunky, admirable heroines, a symbol of cheer and love for all ages. Yet with maturity had come interest in more complex and unsympathetic roles, maybe a harlot, profligate, or wicked bitch. After all, I was sixteen, an age when serpents are more challenging than angels. Besides, no actress worth her salt seeks audience love as her prime target instead of respect for mastery of her craft. Few in the Selznick organization seemed to share my ambition. One aide rebuked me by remarking that to cast me in a seedy role was akin to putting Mae West in a Salvation Army uniform behind the black pot. Once bestowed on a film star affection is not easily dislodged. Casting in a sharply different role can be construed as an insult to staunchly held conviction. In my case, audience adulation had become a straitjacket binding me to a treasured, unchanging film image.

My growing obsession with an offbeat opportunity so spilled over on Mother that we both lit up like beacons when Warner Bros. suggested Veda, a hateful and vicious juvenile in *Mildred Pierce*. Not only does this child seduce and kill her stepfather, she attempts to hang the murder around the neck of her self-made tycoon mother. As a role, Veda seemed concocted in heaven.

Although Warner Bros. easily lined me up for Veda, it ran into serious difficulty casting the mother. Bette Davis rejected it, then Barbara Stanwyck and Ann Sheridan among others.

As the idea languished, Mother genuinely shared my disappointment. As my inclination for independent behavior had increased, she had wisely drawn back, pace by pace, an accommodation which must have been difficult. My reaching toward new horizons could be without surrender of her companionship or the ready refuge it provided. On the other hand, her world was shrinking, influence over my professional decisions fast eroding, and customary small attentions from studio personnel all but disappeared. To cap things off, she was increasingly being edged away from my innermost thoughts. Emancipation of a child is usually greeted by a parent with relief and satisfaction. In Mother's case, however, I suspect it was not that painless. Her atypically intense absorption with details of my career and personal life over so many years must have made my liberation soul-wrenching for her.

Despite a relentless shift in the balance and character of our relationship, durable cords of affection and respect continued to bind me. Asked to compose a school composition in September 1944, for example, I instinctively cast myself as a mother contemplating a growing daughter.

I peeked into my daughter's bedroom and found her curled up on a small chair in front of her dressing table. She was earnestly studying herself in the mirror and talking in a very little voice. . . .

"You know, you're getting to be a very different girl . . . I've been noticing a big change in myself lately, and I'm not quite sure whether it's for the best or not. For instance, I've become very independent. When a girl is sixteen, she only seems to call for her mom when she is in some trouble. . . .

"Well, at fourteen I began to have a strong desire to leave her protecting wing and to test *my* wings. I'm a lucky girl because I can return to my nest. . . .

"Lots of girls my age are growing up too fast due to the war. They smoke and drink, and by the time they are twenty-one there is nothing new to them and they become bored and dull women. But I have nothing on my mind except schoolwork and high school dates. . . .

"I love to be alone . . . when one has lots of friends one wants to be lonely once in a while. You can afford to be lonely when you're happy, and the only type of loneliness that is unbearable is when you have no one to care for you or to love you. Is there anything more wonderful or relaxing than to curl up in your most comfortable chair and listen to a beautiful symphony, all by yourself!

"Goodness, I've been talking to my image in the mirror for

nearly a half hour. I guess that talking to one's self is due to old age. Well, sixteen, anyway."

Although apparently locked into a static movie image, by senior year my academic interests had dramatically shifted. Biology was an early favorite, particularly when dissecting laboratory rats and frogs, but the more intellectual the course became, the less its charm. Mathematics and its handmaidens of statistics, geometry and physics, were lost causes from the outset. Always a special attraction, literature continued as a favorite, but it was Hazel Hartley's history class that suddenly burst over me in a constellation of new discoveries. All at once there was a stunning reordering of my mental hodgepodge of civics, governmental mechanics, political process, and world affairs. Commencing with her focus on political democracy, we constructed a framework upon which to assemble my disparate recollections. The world carpet of history began to unroll in patterns of splendor, honor, and agony far more entrancing than any dozen radio thrillers. Without her, I might well have continued with surgery.

Like a fig leaf, her civics course at first pretended to cover more than it actually did. Then she introduced a *Time* magazine sales promotional program targeted at schools. Each Monday we were handed copies of the magazine to read cover to cover. Each Friday we were tested on what we remembered reading or seeing, including photos, names, places, and events, our answers entered in standard questionnaire folders provided by the publisher. Any weekly quiz stirred my competitive instinct, but this one had an impact more lasting than a good grade. The scheme helped gather all the straggling, unrelated recollections from six impressionable years of visits from all sorts of people from all over the world, and from skimming around on the surface of current events and historical subjects suggested by film screenplays. Everyone won with the *Time* program. Teachers were saved time and energy otherwise spent in composing a weekly syllabus. Many of us were subliminally hooked into becoming subscribers. For all the program glued together random information about what, who, where, when, and why, in some sort of coherent context. What I recalled from past exposure helped me immensely, and I forgot little of what was being learned. If one question was missed all year, I don't recall it.

On October 17, 1944, I had a chance to use my newly acquired understanding as an invited speaker for the annual *New York Herald Tribune* Forum in New York City. My theme was rebuilding the world on the wreckage of peace left behind by war, part of a series of appearances promoting the sale of war bonds. Also scheduled was a keystone appearance in Ottawa to kick off Canada's Seventh Victory Loan Drive.

While I was en route via Chicago, Hotch showed up at our hotel on a twenty-four-hour pass from his Madison, Wisconsin, air base. Either from pining away or eating serviceman's chow, he had grown lean and hollow-eyed. Although older on the calendar, he seemed younger in fact. From a playful, resourceful partner in puppy love, he now seemed to plead for repeated affirmation that he still rated number one. Perhaps what I saw was a junior airman trained to being bossed. However, the more subservient he seemed, the more I lost interest. The more obsequious, the less my affection. Obviously, we were two young people growing up in different directions at different rates. It was our first reunion, but I realized absence had helped snuff out the love light.

My prepared speech to the Forum proposed that movies be used as a tool in the postwar era. Reshape all those young minds overseas already warped into hating democracy, I urged. Planning ahead for propaganda, however, lacked the human touch which had so fired up my enthusiasm in other war-bond appearances. Absent was the clanging necessity felt while visiting a shipyard, or the cloying odors in a hospital ward, remindful of the horror of war. The only warm touch came from Smart Girl, recently transferred from Westlake to a New York finishing school and now seated in the front row. She ostentatiously sucked at a lemon, surefire to pucker up any speaker.

Things were less impersonal in the crowded Gracie Mansion office of Mayor Fiorello La Guardia. A voluble, perspiring little man, he demonstrated how to package home wastepaper for recycling for newsreel cameramen, Ethel Merman, and me. Hammering away on the need for constructive wartime conduct, he acted as if the hostilities would never end. No more ticker-tape parades, he said, pointing a finger at New York's dapper official greeter, Grover Whalen. Racing forms and obscene books collected by the police must be recycled for more patriotic purposes. His police commissioner smiled tolerantly. No shy rose her-

self, Merman extolled stamp collecting as a way to help our boys overseas. One 10-cent commemorative stamp bought a clip of .45-caliber
bullets, she boomed.

"You really should have taken *Panama Hattie*," she said, taking
me aside and mentioning that Buddy de Sylva had written his Broadway hit with me in mind. "And then came the MGM movie version,"
she said, with a sad, knowing glance to indicate I had really missed the
boat.

Even though war still continued to grind up humanity in Europe
and the Pacific, in a city of such size and diverse vitality as New
York everyone seemed eager to congregate for entertainment. Fifty
thousand people collected in the mall of Central Park to celebrate the
annual *New York Mirror* Sports Festival. Uncle Billy Robinson and I met
onstage, our first encounter since *Little Miss Broadway* five years earlier.
Appearing almost unchanged, he held my hands and suggested we
perform a dance for old times. His two-toned shoes flickered with the
same old magic I remembered so well, but I found myself laboring to
follow his lead. Dancing the shim-sham-shimmy in high heels is not
easy.

"Haven't done this since I was seven," I told him after we had
finished. "Excuse me if I wasn't so hot."

"Darlin'," he replied, with that familiar slanted smile, "you were *A*,
which means really sens*A*tional."

"Do I get a chance to visit you and Fannie?" I asked. A solemn little
cloud passed over his face. Removing his broad-brimmed white fedora,
he mopped at his brow, sighed, and waggled his head sideways.

It was an untimely moment to pursue the subject, but I wondered
why he was avoiding my visit. Many times he and Fannie had been
guests in our home, yet not once had I seen where they lived in Los
Angeles. Wiser by far about racism since my first awareness acquired
at the Desert Inn, I still believed that professional comradeship formed
an automatic bridge across a chasm dug between people in the name
of racial prejudice.

A second chance to get my answer occurred at the Harvest Moon
Ball in Madison Square Garden. In the audience he and I were seated
together, with Irving Berlin on my other side, a kindly, soft-spoken
man with ferret nose and twinkling eyes. Asking questions nonstop,

Berlin regarded any conversation with Uncle Billy as three-way. Although he was intriguing in his own right, Berlin's attention proved frustrating, as I sorely wanted to find out why Uncle Billy was avoiding a visit.

Toward the end of the show the audience began chanting Uncle Billy's name and mine. After Cab Calloway's orchestra struck up the lollipop song, we were really stuck. Performers generally do not like to "wing" routines without discussion with the orchestra, let alone between themselves. Just being onstage and smiling was obviously not going to satisfy the crowd, so lifting his hands for quiet, Uncle Billy announced we would perform a "paper and envelope" dance. For an instant I was startled. Then across a decade of time came zipping one of our old inside jokes. Standing immobile, we chimed together, "Stationery!"

Leaving the central platform, we held hands as we always had, and at the top of the aisle I again asked when I could visit. The last traces of applause were tapering off as he stopped and turned toward me, his face suddenly tinged with a calm, gentle expression.

"No way, darlin'." He gave my hand one reassuring squeeze. "Just no way."

☆

In Ottawa brisk, fall weather had arrived. To launch the Canadian fund drive, Prime Minister W. L. Mackenzie King had planned an outdoor ceremony on Parliament Hill. A bachelor, seventy years old and in his eighteenth year as Prime Minister, King had recently risen from a hospital sickbed and was bundled up in a well-worn overcoat and black bowler, like a man of modest means who had seen better times.

A carillon pealed, King produced his notes, reached inside his coat for a pince-nez, rubbed it on his sleeve, and read his speech. Pressing a doorbell button on the table before us, I symbolically launched nine ships somewhere in Canada.

Already informed that his life was as solitary as a lighthouse keeper's, I was surprised to be invited home for tea, and even more shocked by his inquiry, delivered without much small-talk as preamble: Did I believe women could exercise spiritual power on people

from beyond the grave? Although in fact mildly superstitious and inclined to believe in the existence of power beyond our normal
mentality, I took a cautious middle road in my response. We are re-
ceivers of facts and moods, I said, but from this point logic and common
sense usually take over. Shaking his head in disagreement, he pointed
to a nondescript wooden rocking chair and recounted a remarkable
tale.

Months earlier he had been strangely drawn to an unfamiliar
antique shop. Following this instinct, he had prowled aimlessly, and
in an attic salesroom had become aware of a powerful attraction
emanating from the very chair now before us. Returning home with his
purchase, he had inspected it carefully, and on the underside of the
seat had detected the identification of the original owner. Arising, he
upended the chair for my inspection. Burned into the wood and still
visible beneath layers of varnish and age appeared a woman's name
and a date.

"My grandmother," he said, replacing the chair upright. "It was she
who was telling me where her chair was, and urging me to buy it." His
sincerity was obvious.

"Let me show you something else," he said, putting his teacup aside.
Rummaging in his desk, he finally extracted a large, rolled document.
Spread on the table, it looked to be a hand-drawn chart of the French
Normandy coast, speckled with arrows and pencil notations.

"The Normandy invasion," he said, two fingers spread as if measuring something in midair. "The dates, the battles, the units employed,
points of resistance, even the eventual outcome. Everything is there,
just as it happened."

All those facts were well known, but I nodded thoughtfully.

"Do you know *when* this chart was drawn?," he asked. He pointed
his finger to a date written in the margin. "I annotated all this"—he
swept his hand across the map—"*months before* the actual invasion.
Entirely by precognition, psychic awareness of things to come. Someone
else had guided my hand." He eyed me carefully. "The spirit of my
dead mother."

Others have observed that King would rather have consulted his
mother than members of his cabinet. However cutting his critics, his
sincerity when we spoke together was obvious. What a refreshing per-

spective, a world leader unafraid to call up spiritual resources to predict events of international importance and unashamed to recount such events to a stranger!

Thoughts about King's psychic perceptions lingered fresh in my memory as our railroad train stopped at Niagara Falls en route home for a brief ceremony to celebrate resumption of nighttime illumination of the waterfall, darkened since the outbreak of war. The smoothly flowing sheet of water turning downward, the incessant roar as it pounded into the river below, and the dense cloud of spray that boiled and hung in the air before us exerted a powerful hypnosis of sound and sight. But my mind was drifting. I had noticed a solitary, thick jet of dirty brown water leaping from the rock directly beneath our viewing platform.

"Don't you think the falls are beautiful?" a reporter asked.

"Sure, but any newlywed can see a big waterfall. I really like that," I said, pointing down. "What is it?"

The reporter shot me a quizzical glance, as if I knew something he did not. "Sewer outfall," he replied.

Romantic detachment is usually short-lived in a sixteen-year-old. With Hotch unseated from his throne, the way was clear to elevate a successor. Two ranked even. Both boys had classic qualifications—tall, dark, good-looking, and attentive. That Hunk had hit me in a moment of jealousy was not in itself enough to disqualify so handsome a candidate. But Sergeant Jack was now a physical education instructor at nearby March Field Air Base and had a uniform with brass buttons. I worked to establish a dead heat. Allowing either to move ahead would have brought me perilously close to commitment, a state I wished to avoid. What I had not weighed sufficiently in the balance was Sergeant Jack's skill in endearing himself to Mother.

In her diary on November 15, 1944, she wrote that I was "quite excited" because Sergeant Jack was coming home, but it was Mother who was most impressed by his greeting.

"He took me in his arms and gave me a big hug," she wrote. "Then I stayed upstairs while he greeted her in the library. When I met him downstairs a little later, they both had tears in their eyes. He looks wonderful and was so excited about being home, he could hardly talk. I really don't know what she is going to do about all these boys. I think she likes them all pretty well, but is very much at-sea herself."

If I had them both fooled, maybe I could keep the rest of my candidates that same way.

The Little Princess première: My parents and I with Darryl Zanuck, 1938
(Author's private collection)

Oscar awards to Disney, seven dwarfs, but no Snow White, 1939
(Academy of Motion Picture Arts & Sciences)

Teaching Noel Coward fractions in soundstage trailer, 1938 *(Twentieth Century-Fox)*

Croquet challenge match with Orson Welles, 1939 *(Author's private collection)*

Departure for Honolulu: Jack, my parents, and George Jr., 1937   *(Twentieth Century-Fox)*

Clark Gable on MGM
lot during *Kathleen*,
1941   *(Metro Goldwyn
Mayer)*

Calypso routine from *Kathleen*   *(Metro Goldwyn Mayer)*

Signed with
David O. Selznick,
1943 *(Selznick
International Films)*

Wishful romance, with Lieutenant Joseph Cotten in *Since You Went
Away*, 1944 *(Selznick International Films)*

My sixteenth birthday on the set of *I'll Be Seeing You*: Joseph Cotten, Jennifer Jones, Spring Byington, Ginger Rogers, 1944 *(Selznick International Films)*

With Mother, 1944 *(Author's private collection)*

Old-time student,
Westlake School,
1944   *(John Engstead)*

Air Cadet Andrew D.
Hotchkiss Jr., my
first love, 1944
*(Author's private
collection)*

Wastepaper collection with Mayor Fiorello La Guardia *(left)* and Ethel
Merman *(right)*, 1944   *(The News*, New York City)

Clairvoyant Prime Minister
Mackenzie King of
Canada, Ottawa,
1944   *(Author's private
collection)*

MGM adolescents: Judy Garland and Mickey Rooney, with Louis B. Mayer, 1941 *(Metro Goldwyn Mayer)*

Serious talk with Ronald Reagan, father–lover figure in *That Hagen Girl*, 1948 *(Warner Bros. "Morgan")*

Martial arts with
Franchot Tone,
Honeymoon,
1946   *(RKO Radio
Studios)*

Cary Grant and Rudy Vallee during *The Bachelor and
The Bobbysoxer*, 1947   *(RKO Radio Studios)*

Newly engaged to be married, 1945 *(Press Association)*

Traditional wedding dress,
Los Angeles, 1945
(Edward S. Curtis Studios)

Sergeant Jack Agar at
the announcement of
our engagement,
1945 *(Author's
private collection)*

Firstborn Linda Susan,
Brentwood, Los
Angeles, 1948 *(John
Miehle)*

With Father at Brown Derby Restaurant, Hollywood, 1945 *(Robert Perkins,
Ettinger Co.)*

Marriage, 1950   *(San Francisco Examiner)*

My husband, as encountered in Honolulu, 1950 *(Hawaiian Pineapple Co.)*

Charlie Jr. (Barton Sunday), Bethesda, Maryland, 1952 *(Phil Raettinger)*

With my Lori Alden Black, Atherton, California, 1954 *(John Engstead)*

Family completed: Lori, Susan, and Charlie Jr., 1954 *(John Engstead)*

30

Four and a half years after my leaving Fox, my life was a clothesline strung with laundry for all to see. In one swipe away went comforts of studio life and with it the cohesion of job, working crew, and professional challenge. Suddenly I was immersed in peer-group problems as a schoolgirl, and in the enchantment of boys, all set to a staccato background of world war. Two feature films and intermittent radio dramas had provided only fleeting satisfaction. Then with Selznick, my course had at last wandered past choppy waters and into steadying seas and fair winds. My status had been summarized in a November 3, 1944, memo to his assistant, Reeves Espy:

> Shirley is exceedingly hot at the moment. We can't commence to fill demands for interviews and other press material on her from newspapers and magazines; and this is, of course, an indication of the interest of the public. At the preview of *I'll Be Seeing You*, co-starring Ginger Rogers, Joseph Cotten and Shirley, Shirley's name was received with the biggest applause of all three, despite the fact that the Gallup poll shows that Cotten is the great new romantic rage and that Ginger is one of the top stars of the business.
>
> Shirley's publicity in the New York press, both in connection with this appearance and in connection with her prior trip East to sell bonds, received more publicity—including, astonishingly, big

front-page breaks in the middle of a war—than I think has been accorded the visit of any motion picture star to New York in many, many years. Indeed, it is said (and I believe a check would confirm it) that her visit received more space than that of General de Gaulle!

She has made a great hit in *Since You Went Away*; and in her first grown-up part, that of *I'll Be Seeing You*, she is a sensational success. Her fan mail is greater than that of any other star on our list—actually exceeding by a wide margin that of Ingrid Bergman, Jennifer Jones and Joan Fontaine, who are the next three. . . .

Determined to protect my image of innocence Selznick almost aborted my next loan-out to Columbia for *Kiss and Tell* by demanding that he retain absolute script and scene approval, only giving in to producer Sol Siegel upon assurances that no suggestive dialogue would be included. Actually, F. Hugh Herbert's script was an uproarious comedy that would rack up a $4 million box office gross before 1949. Once again I was swept up in the daily delight of filmmaking. Walter Abel was much admired for his youthful good looks, and part of his charm was a head of dark, wavy hair. One day while idly twining some of those luxuriant locks through my fingers, up came a toupee. I yelped as if discovering a mouse. Unfortunately, the toupee was not from makeup, but from home. Nothing could be done about my gaffe but to help press it back in place, mumble an apology, and start talking about something else.

Despite Selznick's concern about premature sexiness, in the film I was required to kiss twenty-two servicemen sequentially, at a charity bazaar. The first boy in line was a returned veteran from Guadalcanal who confided that each of them was earning $25 for the job. However, to get the best photogenic angle, each kiss had to be rehearsed about four times. That put a $6.00 value on each of my kisses. Far too little, I computed, considering actual time and trouble of smudged lipstick, and I told him so. Startled, he replied it seemed a good bargain to him, a position instantly confirming for me it was a bad deal. However, I thought, to be judged competent by one's producer and appealing to two dozen virile military men is a stimulating combination, regardless of price.

Self-esteem and self-confidence had long since flooded back. Once again I was making business decisions, and just in time. Just completing some studio publicity decked out in a spectacular pastel dress with ruffles designed by already renowned Jean Louis, I was surprised when a messenger arrived to relay a request of studio chief Harry Cohn that I come to his office.

"I think he wants to formally give you that dress," the man observed.

Cohn's predatory instinct with women was legendary all over Hollywood. His quid pro quo for the dress might be something I was unwilling to pay, and I almost have it home already, I reasoned.

"Tell him many thanks, anyway," I said and kept on going all the way home, wearing the dress.

By early December 1944 freshets of new interest were combining in a powerful stream to bound me along at an ever-increasing pace. Foremost, I wanted to leave the parental nest, but eventually. Marriage did not yet enter my equation, but the concept of engagement connoted maturity, a leap toward further emotional independence from my parents. Hardly as a whim, I determined to be first in my school class to become engaged. Engagement ahead of my pack would be a symbol of competitive achievement, while still leaving me room to escape final commitment.

A major change was in my attitude toward war. Movie newsreels, media news, and dozens of sobering tours through military hospitals had done wonders to focus attention on fundamental moral and political questions involved, and equally complex questions relating to the peace now close at hand. Political origins of World War II had occupied much thought. In one hospital ward, plastered to the wall with surgical tape, I recall a doggerel dedicated to politicians everywhere.

> *Give'em all the same grub,*
> *And all the same pay,*
> *The war would be over and done*
> *In one day.*

To assert leaders were solely to blame for war was of course far too simplistic, but another troubling aspect shone clear: bugles, flags, and heroics always march lockstep with horror, prejudice, and suffering. The bent, maimed, and infected bodies I had encountered in hospitals were the counterside to exultant news of victory. Not only in European and Japanese cities and countrysides, but everywhere it touched war was leaving junkyards and physical rubble, plus a residue of prejudice, and vengeance. Despite my distaste for the cold character of my recent *Herald Tribune* Forum remarks, I had come to acknowledge that ahead lay a world political challenge of stupendous and complex importance. The defeated needed to be succored, what was destroyed needed to be rebuilt, and an equilibrium of understanding needed to be attained between victor and vanquished.

Reflecting on ponderous international problems did not take all my time. On the day the Germans launched the massive Battle of the Bulge counteroffensive with 600,000 men, the biggest single action of World War II, I was parked, necking with Hunk. Suddenly he produced a ring. By the dashboard light it glistened, two sapphires, one pale blue and one pink, cut in golden hearts and set side by side. It was too small for my engagement finger, so I shifted it to the little one just as he pronounced us engaged.

"No way," I replied, caught between cupidity and evasiveness. "Just a friendship ring."

Hunk was downcast. To cheer him up while ensuring possession of the ring, I struck a compromise.

"Okay, we can be engaged to be engaged," I said, thereby moving from my prior semantic hedge to protect me from doomsday, where I was only *thinking* about being engaged to be engaged.

Hunk's parents saw our deal in a different light. At a celebration family dinner even his father showed up, an indistinct personality and someone absent from home for long spells. Everyone purred contentedly, making oblique references to the handsome couple. Well aware I was skating around on thin ice, I thanked the good Lord: his ring fitted only my friendship finger.

On the day British forces stormed into the flaming city of Bremen, Sergeant Jack mounted his own offensive. We parked romantically among curbside shadows between a drugstore and the Eastern Star Old Ladies' Home; our car radio was softly playing the current pop favorite, "Won't You Tell Me When?"

"Marriage," he suddenly blurted. "Marry me before I go overseas and get killed!"

Both proposition and its reason were equally shocking. "But you're twenty-four," I protested. "I'm not even seventeen. And besides you won't get killed. And we haven't even been engaged. Mother would disapprove."

"Okay, let's wait to tie the knot," he agreed, skillfully finessing my objections. "Too young to wed is not too young to say yes."

That made sense. Carefully I reversed the Dutchman's ring so that the stones faced inward and stared thoughtfully out the darkened window.

"Here," he said, flipping the lid on a small box and extracting a solitaire diamond ring. "This will get us engaged."

That I could comfortably be in love with one or the other I well knew. But Sergeant Jack had the better cleft chin, and nobody else had ever given me a ring with a diamond. I agreed to be engaged to be married—sometime.

Disclosing our engagement on my birthday only eleven days hence would have been the best staging, but my secret lasted only one Westlake day. After all, I had better take no chances. I really wanted to be the first one in my class engaged.

"Give up movies because I'm engaged?" I answered reporters. "It depends on him. I've had all that long enough, anyway."

Holding my hand, Sergeant Jack beamed down. "No matter, either way. Certainly *I* have no idea of a screen career."

The maturity suggested when one announces betrothal might stimulate the more venturesome movie producer. Rising from behind his desk, Selznick had presented me with a huge box of congratulatory orchids and gladioli honoring my seventeenth birthday. It was chilly outside, but a cheery fire glowed on the grate. Pulling up a high-backed leather chair, he talked aimlessly about movies, and then marriage. Tipping back, he eased his shoes off and rested both feet on his desktop. In a flash I recalled Anita Colby's early warning: beware of stocking feet!

Her prophecy wasted little time coming true.

"I'm engaged." I laughed, circling first left, then right, around a chair.

"If you hold out," he threatened with breathless good cheer, "you could get loaned out!"

Keeping intact both virginity and contract is not always easily accomplished. Each of us, however, had too much riding on the outcome to allow pursuit and escape to devolve into a shouting match of accusation or recrimination. Within a few moments Selznick collapsed into his chair, kept his stocking-clad feet out of sight, and good-naturedly resumed his soliloquy about my movie career, sex mercifully left aside.

When Germany officially quit the war on May 7, 1945, we graduated at Westlake to a yearbook slogan "Wisdom is better than weapons of war." My sole honor was again the posture award. Holding myself straight and stretched was one of my few natural habits, intended to make me appear tall from the waist up. I intended to enter college, and my English entrance essay for UCLA described FDR as the most fascinating man I had ever met. Nobody tested my mathematics but surprises were in store. On an exploratory campus visit I was swamped by autograph hounds my own age, not exactly what I had in mind. Being "rushed" for sororities was equally grueling. Uncomfortable under personal inspection by sophisticated, potential sisters at sorority teas, I found only one group seemed my style, a houseful of ebullient girls, none too well informed but loaded with candidate material for homecoming queen. Sergeant Jack's sense of urgency also kept complicating my college plan.

"Why are we waiting?" he insisted. "Whoever heard of a married woman in a sorority house?"

All summer a vision of the eventual marriage ceremony kept flickering in my mind. A traditional evening wedding at the familiar ivy-festooned St. Alban's Church near home. The bevy of bridesmaids would be dressed in filmy gowns of blue exactly matching the color of the sanctuary wall, and be flanked by ushers, all photogenic. The bride would have downcast eyes behind a diaphanous veil, and would shed a sentimental tear as pledges were solemnly exchanged or perhaps during the triumphant wedding recessional from *Lohengrin*. My new sister-in-law, brother Jack's wife, would be matron of honor. I ticked off the bridesmaids, all Westlake classmates except dear friend and movie stand-in, Mary Lou. The casting was almost complete. Oh yes, the groom.

"It's silly to wait," Sergeant Jack insisted, leaving for duty at Geiger

Field in Washington State. "Those wolves will be out howling the instant I go overseas. It's pretty hard for a girl at home if she has no vow to keep her true."

Maybe he was right. One day I told Mother where things stood. Imposing the too-young argument, she was in quicksand when reminded that her own marriage certificate showed she was only seventeen. A fib, she admitted. Actually she was nineteen. The record was faked to win a competition among high school friends to see who got married the youngest. That crack in her armor was too tempting not to pry open. If she wanted to be the youngest, why shouldn't I aspire to be first in my class?

"I withdraw my objection," she sighed. "You'll be eighteen next birthday. I know you won't wait longer than that anyway."

On the day the Japanese surrendered unconditionally, President Truman's ninety-three-year-old mother said, "I'm glad Harry decided to end the war."

"Go ahead and get married," said mine. "You'll probably go broke paying off all those bets about waiting two years."

"Marriage comes first with me," I told the press, "but no longer need a girl vacate her career for the sake of the boy's. A boy should be proud if his wife can have one."

"From the bottom of my heart I believe in love," said Sergeant Jack. He spoke as if he believed in fairies.

"It's only because he's going overseas," I explained to another reporter. "I want to be his wife," adding prophetically, "even if it's only for a little while."

"We'll take over on details for the ceremony," Selznick announced. "A big one at Wilshire Methodist Church. Forget that tiny St. Alban's."

That I was old enough to marry stirred all sorts of public comment. A deluge of 36,900 letters swamped us during August, most sentimental and supportive, but others sharply critical of the precedent it set for other teenagers.

On my premarital visit to my personal physician for minor surgery and birth-control information, Dr. Lawrence Davidson had something else in mind. Gin rummy. His waiting room was full, but we kept playing. Finally he showed his real hand. I must stop smoking. There was a theory that it harmed unborn children. Convinced that smoking was equated with maturity, I was using a half pack of cigarettes each day. Try putting only five cigarettes in the case instead of the usual ten, was his suggestion. I departed physically prepared for marriage, a winner at cards, but unconvinced that smoking was dangerous or much different from any other pleasant habit, like laughter.

Meanwhile, Mother and her interior decorator were converting my "dollhouse" into a newlywed home, her idea not mine. One reason for my disinterest was discovery of another idyllic Hansel and Gretel honeymoon hideaway. Screened by shrubbery at the end of a private lane leading from busy San Vicente Boulevard, the tiny cottage was picture-book pretty, with geranium-filled window boxes and Dutch doors. I rented it immediately. Our sole visible neighbors were the landlords, a fastidious couple whose presence was sensed more than shared. She appeared only in glimpses, an egg-shaped woman wearing a smock, with permanently startled eyes peering from under a halo of spiky rag curlers. Her husband was the epitome of the small-time capitalist. Stolid and unimpressed by his tenants, he collected the monthly check without comment and walked off when we tried to make small talk.

The name was Wolf, and they kept four bull terriers. Our main relationship was with the dogs, a pathetic little troupe waddling around clothed in miniature rubber pants. To keep the house clean, was Mrs. Wolf's explanation. Around the yard they trooped, snuffling and wheezing, wiggling stumpy tails inside their diapers. Between the gregarious dogs and retiring Wolfs, the cottage promised to be an ideal balance of pleasure and privacy.

Sergeant Jack got a fifteen-day pass from Geiger Field to get married, despite a written protest to their commanding officer from other enlisted men, who complained they only got twelve days for the same thing.

On the evening before my wedding day I was alone while my betrothed was attending his final bachelor dinner. Answering a knock at the door, I found dancer Gower Champion standing in the splash of light. My unrequited crush on him had started when I was only six years old at Elisa Ryan's dancing school. Later, I had occasionally dated him, but Father disapproved twice over. First, because he was seven years my senior, and second, because on one occasion Champion had peeled flakes of sunburned skin off his arms and dropped them on the floor of

Father's latest Cadillac. For years thereafter Champion and I had carried on a low-tempo flirtation, intermittent and inconclusive.

At my suggestion we went next door to my dollhouse. Scrounging among the contractor's debris we lit some scraps of lumber in the fireplace to make things cheery and put on a phonograph record of "Dancing in the Dark." Already a spectacular choreographer and later to do the hit plays *Hello, Dolly!* and *42nd Street*, Champion was obviously a dream dancing partner. We were holding each other a bit too close when he suddenly asked me to dump Sergeant Jack. Before I could answer he kissed me—hard.

Like two alcoholics taking a last drink before abstinence, we confessed long-standing mutual affection, kissed again, and danced on. For true lovers it would have been a savored final moment of regret. In our case, it was more dumb than daring. Had I agreed to jilt Sergeant Jack, Champion would have been lost in the dust of his own departure. Our scene was loaded with drama, but ridiculous. Each comfortably immune, we swooped and swirled along the lip of the fiery volcano and peered over the edge with absolutely no danger of falling in.

Twenty-four hours later I was again kissing someone, this time Sergeant Jack. To the thundering crescendo of the wedding march, we paced back up the aisle, me skipping once to match my step with his and limping slightly from the misplaced lucky penny in my shoe. Benign expressions wreathed the faces of our 500 guests, some of whom I recognized. Even the church decorations of pink roses seemed to tremble with the pounding music and air of elation. Standing at the aisle in the last row was Selznick, beaming paternally. Habitually late, he had come puffing into the church after everyone else was seated and slipped into a pew beside California Governor and Mrs. Earl Warren. The church organist had been vamping, awaiting his arrival, a stall evident to us all. Smart organist. Selznick was paying.

No care or expense had been spared to create a memorable wedding celebration and photogenic cast. Drafted as best man, brother Jack's initial appearance was found wanting, a government-issue sergeant's uniform with the pants too high and buttons off-line. Tall, lanky, and slightly stooped, he was no supply sergeant's dream. Mother had him measured up by a commercial tailor who used genuine drab and standard-issue buttons to make him the best-dressed sergeant in his unit.

My bridesmaids were dressed in glorious concoctions of soft blue silk organza and satin, hems trailing to the floor and necklines deeply cut. For the large and unruly outside crowd spilling onto Wilshire Boulevard and delaying traffic, the dresses proved tantalizing souvenirs, in whole or part. Smart Girl lost a sleeve, partially exposing one bosom. My sister-in-law was likewise scavenged, losing ribbons and ruffles, and fled to her car defensively clutching her brassiere. Both found enough needle and thread at our home to repair themselves sufficiently to join the receiving line set up on our outside patio. Under a clear, starry sky, florists had tediously wired 780 hothouse blooms on our empty rose-bushes, setting a scene of excitement and celebration with only one regret. Missing from our wedding guests was Uncle Billy Robinson, in the middle of a New York engagement and unable to attend, he wrote Jack. "You ever hurt this girl, I'll come and cut you!"

Look magazine chose that moment to present me the first copy of their book, *My Young Life*. A rehash of morgue clippings, publicity releases, studio photos, and third-person interviews, it reads like fiction, a mélange teetering somewhere between banality and idiocy. At least it came well published on good paper.

In a traditional hail of rice and popping champagne corks, the bride and groom at last escaped to the Town House Hotel in downtown Los Angeles. To everyone's surprise and our chagrin, we had no room reservation and the hotel was supposedly full. The studio, it turned out, had indeed booked the bridal suite, but under a nondescript alias. Nobody told the drowsy night clerk, who gave it away to the first honeymoon couple in the door that evening. After waiting in the lobby for half an hour, we were finally ushered to a double-bedded room. For the next hour our doorbell jangled as a procession of bellhops arrived with fruit baskets, champagne, flower arrangements, and chocolate candies, atonements for having so massacred the arrangements. To stanch this procession of nocturnal courtesies, we finally refused to answer the door knock and instructed the telephone operator to cut off all calls. After all, we were newlyweds and it was almost dawn. We both fell on the bed fully dressed, exhausted from felicitous wedding guests and bountiful room service.

At that hour the phone was jangling in Mother's bedroom. Apologizing, the AP wire service regretfully informed her I had been killed in a grisly auto accident, a plunge off a hilly Westwood road into a deep rocky canyon. Unable to penetrate the blackout on our room telephone, or even to gain confirmation that we had checked in, Mother roused the local police. Treating her as a distraught crackpot who imagined herself my mother, they promised to look into the matter and hung up. Far too late to compensate for her anxious hours, the AP day shift apologized for its mistaken identity of the accident corpse.

In our room, Jack and I engaged in our first quarrel.

"You said you were a virgin," he accused.

"I was, until three days ago," I snapped. "Don't yell at me. Discuss it with Dr. Davidson."

Two days later we had sorted ourselves out, for I wrote Mother from the Samarkand Persian Gardens in Santa Barbara, assuring her that married life was "terrific." I peppered my letter with unkind references to the diet kitchen and the plethora of graying shuffleboarders, women in broad-brimmed gardening hats decorated with roses, and men with thick eyeglasses, Hawaiian sport shirts, and a tendency to wheeze.

"There are about a hundred people here, but ninety-six of them are dead..." I wrote. "Yesterday morning I took too hot a douche and darned near killed myself! I've finally learned how to use those 'tampons' too. When we left the Town House to come to Santa Barbara, I had the cotton tampon *plus* the cardboard container up inside... *most* uncomfortable during the long drive...."

"I'm sorry to say I haven't missed any of you.... Jack is the most wonderful husband in the world...." Signed, Shirley Agar, Jr.

Ten days later my romantic world caved in. Humorist Robert Benchley, author-cohort from *Kiss and Tell*, honored us at a candlelit dinner party at his San Fernando Valley home. Jack was dancing with a starlet type, a bit player from a recent low-budget movie. Lithe and rangy with cascades of blond hair and widely flared, sensuous nostrils, she had already made biting remarks about my compact stature. Unflattering comments could be handled in good grace, but not the spectacle of my husband at center dance floor embracing her in a long, passionate clutch, lips locked.

Seated alone at our table, I was the target of all eyes, searching for reaction. All I could do was stare meditatively off into space, draw measured pulls on my cigarette, and release the smoke in slow, ladylike exhales. Inside I was shattered.

Driving home to our honeymoon cottage, Jack was merciless.

"Always wanted to marry a long-legged model," he said. "Not someone like you."

Already stunned, I could hardly believe my ears. But playing second fiddle was against my nature. "Trouble with people who have those nineteen-inch waists," I replied, "their other measurements are small too. Including the head."

Our verbal exchange was as dismal as it was fruitless. Nothing could purge the memory of my public humiliation, nor the damage punched home by his private jibe. Reluctant to consider his conduct and commentary symptomatic of our future, I blamed both on inadvertence from liquor and on the perpetually dangerous social environment of Hollywood.

Viewed in the context of Los Angeles during the middle 1940s, local social groupings fell into three imprecisely defined parts. The dominant stratum was peopled by a highly productive, but sometimes self-centered commercial and financial elite. Swarming almost everywhere else was a vast, inchoate population of ordinary working people, many with simple expectations, most of modest behavior and guided by homespun virtues. This was the group in which my family had their origins. Even after film success had introduced us to Hollywood our linkage had remained strong with old friends, traditional attitudes, and simple pleasures.

The third grouping, called "Hollywood," was wedged in between the elite and the pedestrian. An aberrant subculture led by movie businessmen and artists originally emigrated from the East Coast to utilize California's year-round brilliant outdoor sunshine, it was a pulsing, blood-red creative chunk of humanity that kept largely to itself. Enormously productive at what it did, the movie industry spun off its share of profligacy, self-aggrandizement, and human abuse. It was into this treacherous aspect of Hollywood life that Jack had dipped a toe, my convenient rationalization for his exceptional conduct. Besides, I ruminated privately, had I not romantically kissed another man on my marriage eve? However innocent my intentions, was not that incident good reason to overlook Jack in one frivolous encounter?

Before Jack's military leave expired, Selznick honored us with a farewell party at his home. Toasting our future, he raised his glass to me. "Never would have cast you as a bride," he chortled. "Too young for the role."

Meant as a compliment, I suppose, the comment was personally diminishing. He failed to notice and turned to my husband.

"Jack is ready for movies," he said.

"You did look awfully well in your first movie," I whispered, having just seen films of our wedding at a local newsreel theatre.

"I hope I don't have to do it again," he replied, "at least until our golden anniversary."

Not everyone named Jack was reticent about working in movies. Mustered out of the army, my brother Jack showed up at Columbia Studios as an assistant director assigned to a film ironically titled *Framed*.

As always, brother George had struck off in his own direction. Still content with his muscles, motorcycles, and carhops, he resigned from the Marine Corps to become daytime wrestling coach at Santa Monica High School, his alma mater. By night he wrestled professionally, usually billed as the "good guy" in tag-team matches with new colleagues like Nebraska Wildcat and Swedish Angel. One errant weekend he slipped across the Mexican border to Tijuana and married an ecdysiast dancer from Detroit who had become a groupie trailing him from arena to arena.

Confronted with radical change in the lives of her sons, Mother said, "Young George seems to like his life. Jack won't need any help. But Shirley probably will. With her career, that is."

Capitalizing on my married status, Vanguard created and published my "Ten Commandments for Teenage Marriage," an optimistic list whose full compliance would have rendered most marriages utter failures.

Asked which rule was most important, I observed the most valuable one was not even on the published list: a good sense of humor.

My remark was not flip. I still regarded as my first duty to others to create happiness. By that I did not imply the sort of high spirits associated with self-indulgence. Nor did I relate happiness to any crystalline state of moral rectitude. In fact, it was already my opinion that too often moralists poisoned life with their fear. Morals that left one dreary must be wrong. My conviction was that in joy is goodness. Whether the senseless mirth of children or the good humor required of newlyweds, happiness rouses in everyone a purity of thought and strength of heart without which any existence turns sour. My own sense of humor would be sorely tested during the next four years, almost to a day.

During January 1946, Jack was shuttling between army camps in Washington, Utah, and California, imminently to embark for the Pacific. Knowing that the latest replacements overseas would be the last to finally return home, Father invoked every powerful acquaintance he knew, not excluding J. Edgar Hoover, to get Jack's orders rescinded, all to no avail. Bureaucracy finally resolved the matter by altering the point-system for discharge. Due to his prior service, Jack became automatically immune from an overseas billet.

During this military yoyo game I had visited Washington, D.C., to address the national convention of the General Federation of Women's Clubs. Child delinquency was the subject of their meeting, and they presented me prepared remarks that movies led children astray and producers were bogeymen. Feeling quite differently about the matter, I abandoned their text and spoke extemporaneously. No Hollywood clique can elevate the quality of movies unless the general public demands it, I said. Kids are not delinquent by nature, nor are producers. Movies mirror the times, they do not create them. For movies which found strong disfavor, it was the public that was delinquent, not producers. My remarks received such scant applause I concluded by saying, gee, I hope it snows outside. It was certainly cold inside.

Apparently the negative reaction to my theme was short-lived, for in company of a gaggle of busty clubwomen wearing flamboyant hats, I got inside the White House for a second time. "Come in and take off your shoes," Mrs. Truman greeted us. "Make yourselves at home."

Over teacups and dainty cookies, the clubwomen repeated their local good deeds for the sick and needy while Mrs. Truman nodded and smiled approval. Nothing was said about child delinquency, or for that matter the atom, or the United Nations. Obviously America was fast forgetting about the war and looking inward toward local concerns. This retreating tide left me stranded. If our action in joining the war taught anything, it was about shared problems beyond national boundaries. Zigzagging back home through war-bond rallies in Denver and Salt Lake City, I pumped the slogan "Finish the Job of Victory," somehow feeling vestigial, a relic calling for sacrifice while the rest of the public raced ahead to new parochial challenges.

In early February, Jack threw away his khakis and donned sports jacket and slacks, and together we began life as a civilian couple. Realizing I was no good in the kitchen, I enrolled in a quickie cooking school and soon was producing fried meat patties, baked potatoes, and chocolate roll with whipped cream almost every night. The monotony of my menus arose not from dislike of cooking but boredom arising from Jack's reaction to the process and its results. As a cook my pleasure came not only from preparing tasty food, but from companionship in the kitchen and appreciation at the table. Unfortunately, my husband always seemed to be away during the drudgery of chopping, mixing, and stirring. Whenever he returned, there I was in a spotless kitchen in an attractive, organdy apron. The laundry was done, house cleaned, and every hair in place. A picture-perfect wife, just as in the movie magazines. Idyllic. If only he had kept me company in the kitchen, or said how good everything tasted, even if it didn't.

"What will you do for a living?" he was often being asked. "How about a screen test?"

"No, thank you," he always replied. "One star in the family is enough."

☆

Like all my springs, that of 1946 meant another upsurge of appeals for items suitable for celebrity auctions. "Any personal wearing item," the letters pleaded, a euphemism for something of real value. Certainly nobody wanted cast-off underclothes or stockings with runs. With metronomic predictability the appeals piled in, and with equal regularity my two fan-mail secretaries dispatched photos instead of mementos. Even a partial response would have left my bureau and closet bare.

Several times I caught Jack shaking his head with wonderment. Public life was obviously new to him, still.

Predictably, *Honeymoon* was selected as the title of my film commencing production in March. In an event I hoped was not symbolic, I nearly blinded myself getting ready. Seated before an ultraviolet sunlamp while putting up my hair, I neglected to don smoked eyeglasses. At midnight I awakened in agony, my face misshapen and eyes almost swollen closed.

"You may never see again," intoned the cheerful emergency-room physician at Santa Monica Hospital. He should have been more optimistic, for after three days of severe apprehension I did reappear on the studio lot, worse for wear. One quick look at my puffed face and squinty eyes forced director William Keighley to order night lenses on all cameras, blurring the image of my swollen features. Close-ups were postponed, long shots in. Among those was a sizzling samba performed with dance director Charlie O'Curran. Perhaps Keighley hoped all the wiggling, stamping, and twirling would divert attention from my face.

Mother came on the set infrequently now, in deference to my marital status if not my seventeen years, and offered few comments about my performance, unless pressed. While there, however, she found other things to do, such as playing the horses. As a banker Father was repelled by gambling, except his own golfing wagers, and probably assumed the family followed his lead. However, bookies covered soundstages like horse blankets, skulking around. One could walk up to a bulging corner curtain or call out to an electrical distribution box and somehow the bet got placed. If there were winnings, money materialized without comment from some stranger's hand. Mother's current favorite was named Stagehand, nosed out in the classic encounter with Seabiscuit. Never having bet money on anything before, I followed her lead, picking a long-shot horse named Honeymoon, of course. When it came in first I took the win as an omen of luck that would spill over onto my real marriage.

To my disappointment, actor Joseph Cotten had gone on suspension rather than get paired with me in *Honeymoon*. Far too young, he had complained. Maybe he had underestimated youth or just hadn't read the whole story. At one point the script called for me to apply jujitsu, fling him to the floor, and pounce on him for a kiss. The role went to

Franchot Tone, who suffered from no such misapprehension. As an American vice-consul in Mexico trying to assist me, he got wrestled around instead.

In perfect synchrony with my film antics, brother George chose this moment to resign his job as a high school wrestling coach and enter professional wrestling full-time. At his debut Father sneaked into the last row at Ocean Park Arena to watch him eventually pin someone called Iron Duke Works. Instead of congratulating his son at ringside, Father stamped home in a huff, apparently more repelled by the whole environment than pleased with his son's win.

Mother picked up his sense of chagrin, so I tried to intercede. "Look, Mom, getting flung around is just the entertainment game. There's more action in the ring than in some four-star movies. I'm in the business, why not him?"

Eventually Father begrudgingly accepted the inevitable, but Mother stood irrevocably against the whole idea, the profession, the people, and the places he wrestled. When George filed for divorce from his wife, citing "extreme cruelty" for having produced an eight-pound baby boy only six months after their wedding, Mother was quick to point out how right she had been all along.

To no one's surprise and with monthly regularity, the press asked me about a baby. No scrap of information was too small to stir up a rumor. During the latter days of *Honeymoon* it had become necessary to remove two of my lower wisdom teeth, both impacted. One socket healed poorly and became infected. A puffed cheek is unacceptable for camera work, so we called in a dentist, a rotund, shiny-cheeked little man, high in fee and low on charm. Hustling in with his black bag, he took one look in my opened mouth, recoiled slightly, and shook his head.

"Pronounced swelling," he muttered the obvious, and ordered me off to my dressing room, where he lanced the infected area. My stand-in, Mary Lou, had missed the dentist's arrival, and when she asked what was wrong I replied that my jaw was pregnant.

Some half-eared interloper heard the magic word. The next day gossip columnists announced I was expecting a baby. Months of diligent denial failed to squash the rumor, only put to rest when my waistline remained slim and unchanged.

Press interest also intensified on details of our private life, many questions centering on Jack's as-yet-undetermined occupation and his contribution to family finances.

"Budget?" I replied to repeated probings from columnist Hedda Hopper. "Certainly. When Jack married me he stipulated all household expenses would be his. We live on his resources, not mine."

Fate had removed him momentarily from the invidious posture of an indigent husband living on his wife's earnings. His deceased father's will provided for a bequest of $10,000 upon marriage, a windfall sufficient to obscure the real facts.

Once again custodian of increased cash flow from my paychecks, Father was ebullient. Honoring my role as homemaker, he raised my allowance to $75 a week. However, the assumption by others that with marriage had come discretionary control over a substantial estate began causing me new problems. Like any urban center, Hollywood had no shortage of pious souls tirelessly filtering through the community seeking donations for one charity or another. Chief among these chiefs was Ida, tenacious friend of the local Jewish Home for the Aged. A formidable woman with jutting chin and intimidating bosom, she bore extra clout as a sister of MGM boss Louis B. Mayer. One day she cornered me for some serious talk.

"Dearie," she cooed, eyes narrowed and expectant, "Mother was always so good to us. So good. We need you for a personal appearance. Down she sends you. She should get a mezuzah award. How the dear old people loved it."

How well I recalled. Those unfortunate residents, used up by life and now propped in chairs and beds, pathetically wide-eyed and slack-jawed as I paraded by. I would swirl to move the curls and dimple my best.

"What a cute bottom!" someone invariably said. "See her bottom." I would have preferred their attention on the front, but whatever made them happy was acceptable to me.

"Now you are a grown girl, dearie," Ida continued. "Now you control your own money. What you give from the heart comes back a thousandfold blessed." Her eyes glinted. Before I could observe she was wrong about my financial discretion, she said, "When are you coming through?"

When I reminded her that, as a minor, my finances were still being controlled by Father, she threw her head back and clucked in disdain.

"Oh, come on, dearie. You're married now. You're emancipated by law." She held up a single warning finger. "Come across, or you're dead in the industry."

31

I'm Nobody!
Who are you?
How dreary to be Somebody!
How public, like a frog,
To tell one's name, the livelong June
To an admiring bog!

—Emily Dickinson

Conventional wisdom says the first year of marriage is a joy, give or take a few compromises. In our case this wisdom got knocked on the head. In a nutshell, I was somebody and Jack, nobody. There was the rub. Part of his compensation may have been reassurance in drinking and public flirtation, both conducted in excess of what I would have wished, yet neither tendency a death knell to our union. We had adequate incentives to sort ourselves out and little cause to prematurely shovel earth on the coffin of our marriage. In my heart no doubt existed that, given a spell in the intensive care unit, our patient would soon revive. Instead of mourning, my 1946 New Year's resolution was to scramble and salvage. I would compromise where I must, fight where needed.

Of course his position was trying. Being joshed as Mr. Shirley Temple touched a tender nerve, and being ordered off the set of *Honeymoon* by the director as a distraction assailed both his masculinity and pride. Although one columnist cheerily wrote we were a cinch to make a go of it, "Look at Dale Evans and Roy Rogers," Jack responded by idly threatening to hire his own press agent. More than I he seemed to be struggling under the long shadow of little Shirley Temple. From my standpoint she had passed away about 1941, and a new person had appeared—me. Psychiatrists, please stop squirming. She and I have always existed in harmony and understanding. We both know who we are. But in many respects her image seemed constantly stepping on Jack's toes.

Doubtless the first five months following our wedding were difficult times for him, with neither job nor disclosed occupational interest. Rummaging around for clues and tidbits, the trade-paper press even began to drop unflattering inferences about his true intentions, putting us both on the defensive. Columnist Sheilah Graham uncharitably referred to his job as "golfing," a characterization drawing my strongest objection.

"How about acting, then?" she asked, to which I replied confidently that not once in serious conversation, not a whisper during pillow talk, at no time had Jack and I ever discussed the possibility he would enjoy acting, or even want to try.

"One thing we are sure of," Graham then wrote, "it won't be in the movies."

Twelve days later, on April 14, I swallowed hard. Out of the blue came a press release from Selznick, my own mentor. Jack was being placed under his contract at $150 per week and assigned to acting school to learn the profession.

My disappointment was severe, but not over the substance of the release. Employment of any sort was as welcome to me as to him. With his fine features, if he could learn acting, perhaps a satisfying future lay ahead. Nor could Selznick be faulted for going about things behind my back. Personal loyalty and professional courtesy are often submerged by commercial considerations. What bedeviled me was betrayal of trust between man and wife. Annoyed by my initial reaction, Jack stormed out of our honeymoon cottage. At an early morning hour he returned, red-eyed, and aggressively clicked on the bedroom lights. Again he railed about my attitude. The subject of unshared confidences never arose again. Perhaps it should have.

Publicly, I tried to dust the whole matter aside.

"He's a natural. That's why I married him. That, and a couple of other reasons," I added cheerfully.

Privately, however, I speculated on what had prompted this sudden veer toward acting. Because he was asked, he retorted, handsome jaw outthrust. And anyway long ago he had decided on an entertainment career, and years earlier had made a brief appearance as a nightclub singer at a small Chicago nightclub. All fresh news to me, I brooded, not so much criticizing his decision as his stunning lack of candor.

A few days later, on my eighteenth birthday, I tried to put a good face on things by propping up Jack's self-esteem. In a public declaration I called our union a patriarchy. "The studio can make me work after 5:00 p.m. now. I'm not sure I'll like that. I am my own boss now," I declared, but nodded toward Jack, "except for him."

My eighteenth birthday was no time to let down the bars, was the simultaneous comment of Women's Christian Temperance Union President Mrs. Leigh Colvin, a proclamation delivered without the chuckle it deserved. Ever since its setback in sales stemming from the movie *The Lost Weekend*, the liquor business had been redoubling its efforts to glamorize drinking in movies. Noting that the script of my forthcoming *The Bachelor and the Bobby Soxer* required me to take a cocktail, Mrs. Colvin branded the scene a disservice to American youth. If I could drink, why not everyone? RKO studio officials protested it would really be only iced coffee, and that I would spurn the drink after one taste. Mrs. Colvin was scornful. That was just her point. It showed me *trying*. Trying was what the WCTU was against, not whether I liked it or not.

Although I was not yet old enough to drink in public legally, the WCTU ruckus convinced Mother it was time for Father to mix me a real manhattan cocktail. Seated comfortably in a library armchair, I swirled my glass in the light, inspecting the decorative cherry like a connoisseur admiring vintage wine. Slowly I took a large gulp. Reacting as I did in the eventual movie, I raced to the bathroom and spit it out.

Settled into acting school at the studio, and social routines at the golf club, Jack had developed a "nineteenth hole" camaraderie with Ben Gage, a tall, wisecracking TV variety-show host and his statuesque wife, Esther Williams, ex-Olympic swimmer and actress. Bursting suddenly upon me for a home-cooked dinner, this jolly trio would clog the doorway jamb to jamb while I just smoothed my apron and expanded the place settings already laid out for two.

"Little Miss Marker, my child," Gage would guffaw with emphasis on the diminutive.

"Don't keep calling her that just because she's younger," cooed Williams, giving me a reassuring pat on my cheek while both men would hoot approval.

Being too young to drink legally was not in itself bothersome. What offended me was the derision it inspired; what hurt was being regarded an alien in the group. Driven by the professional necessity to be regularly seen in public, Jack and I willingly patronized Hollywood nightclubs. For me it was a disquieting mismatch. In such a sequined, sleek environment of self-indulgence, frenetic table-hopping, and bar flirtation, women tend to become more feline and men more macho. Once while I was seated in solitary splendor at our nightclub table, Jack having wandered elsewhere, I suddenly found standing by my side a stranger, who introduced himself as Kirk Douglas. Bowing in courtly fashion, he asked me to dance. Recognizing him by reputation as a recently arrived Broadway actor and egocentric man's man, I accepted. At first we circled decorously along the edge of the dance floor, saying nothing. But when the music stopped, Douglas stepped back and clearly stated what he wanted to do to me. The only time I had heard such graphic language was in the Westlake bathroom.

"What?" I blurted.

Tipping his handsome head back, the better to display his cleft chin and toothy, confident smile, he repeated.

"Wow!" was all I could answer. "All I want to do is return to my table."

Such bracing encounters were, however, exceptional. Instead I usually wound up ignored and feeling out of place. Night after night spent in glittering nightclubs is fused in my memory in a tableau of liquor, lust, and paper-thin gaiety.

Tending this nightly trapline of nightclubs was frittering away our personal capital in public, so I determined that more congenial home surroundings might compensate for instabilities imposed by our requisite evening duty. As part of this program we relocated from our rented-cottage household into the dollhouse, now elegantly converted to a residence.

Counting on beautiful surroundings proved a false hope. Jack chafed under the fenceless proximity of my parents. In a move that had not helped, the previous December Father had insisted that Jack execute a formal quit-claim deed confirming all my premarriage assets as my separate property.

Then, there was Mother. Although still carried on my payroll as a

$7,000-per-year teacher, she obviously seldom appeared, but despite her effort to remain unobtrusive, the specter of her personality hovered just beyond the property line.

After less than a half year of marriage, Jack and I were still drifting rather than making progress, beset on both sides by irregular work schedules which helped rupture chances for regular routines together. As far as I knew, he was attending acting school at Vanguard, but I was at RKO, assigned to make *The Bachelor and the Bobby Soxer*. As I was often held at the studio until late in the evening, producing a workday well into darkness, scant time remained on our mutual clock to exchange private concerns. Differing work demands also deflected energy and concentration from the personal problems clamoring for attention. Ours was a highly charged backdrop for intimacy. Too often, I wound up digging my toes into shifting sands. I sincerely loved him and wanted to understand and ease his problems. Yet, not infrequently, I wanted to wring his neck.

Unrelieved irritability in a household can be contagious, and has a way of spilling over at work. I was not immune. A unit manager at the studio reminded us, ad nauseam, that we should minimize walk-through rehearsal, speed up scene changes, and make our number-one priority bringing the film in on budget. I was already burdened with private emotional baggage, and now, harried to place primary attention on money rather than performance, I found my onstage tension amplified.

Veteran actor Ray Collins and I were doing a belligerent scene, he square-jawed and threatening to take me over his knee for a spanking; me combative and angry-eyed. We were mired in miscues and false starts. First he blew his lines. Then I bobbled. When he flubbed again the director exploded. Collins had been a successful character actor with forty years experience on stage, radio, and movies. There was no reason except the pressure, and I was little help.

"You're too old to be working," I muttered.

"Bitch," he retorted, "dirty little bitch," and turned on his heel.

My ears regarded my tongue with amazement. In all my movie years, I had never had an onstage blow-up. Something was markedly wrong, I knew perfectly well, and in my home.

A decade earlier my parents had been inundated with financial and commercial problems resulting from my success. Then they had sought refuge with a family physician. My own doctor was skilled with coughs and muscle strains; perhaps he could also dispense wisdom with his pills.

One glance at my sorrowful face, and Dr. Davidson locked his office door and pulled out the gin-rummy pack.

"You have everything," he counseled me after a few hands. "Health, good looks, a job, splendid home, and an attractive husband."

It was all true.

"Sometimes I feel like a dumb cook," I replied. "Plenty of ingredients to work with, but I don't know how to bake the cake."

"That's negative. Think of the blessings," he said, clicking his tongue against his teeth.

"A very good life," I agreed. "I just can't stand it."

"Nonsense," he replied. "Some failure is part of anyone's lot." He put his cards down, covered them with both hands, and regarded me with a steady gaze. "Any well-lived life attains balance and direction. What we must watch out for is becoming self-centered, particularly when beset with uncertainties." Fleetingly I wondered if he meant me, Jack, or both of us.

"Your problems are not so tough." He pushed back his chair. "First we address his liquor."

Crossing the room to a wall cupboard, he returned with a tiny, unlabeled vial containing a small amount of brownish liquid.

"Slip all this into his next drink," he instructed.

The next Saturday afternoon I poured Jack a whiskey in the kitchen, and we sat together in the living room watching television. His glass was half empty when he remarked that he felt awful and left, one hand held to his stomach. I heard the outside door slam. Following, I saw him on his hands and knees among our rose bushes, vomiting violently. Shaken and pale, he finally reentered the house, declined dinner, and collapsed forlornly on the couch.

"You know, you really have a drinking problem," I observed, but he only groaned and waved me away as one would a bothersome child.

Net result: he drank more often away from home, claiming the liquor was better. Once poisoned, twice wise was my sad conclusion.

☆

During our infrequent personal discussions my relative youth kept bobbing up in conversation. Even when Collins had called me a bitch, he had emphasized the word "little." Immaturity is not easy to overcome, but I speculated that change might create the same impression, starting with my appearance. Since early films my ears had been buried under curls, and later by bouffant hairstyles. It didn't bother me if mine stuck out like a baby fox's. Compared to other movie ears, like Gable's batwings, mine were not so bad. Exposing them might startle everyone into thinking I had grown more mature, and so I adopted a stark, upswept coiffure.

"Unacceptable," clucked the studio makeup expert, appraising my exposed ears. "If they stay exposed, they must be stuck back." Applying mucilage, he held my ears pressed to my head for several minutes. Odd-looking, I thought, but maybe better on-camera.

"The glue is good for several hours, more than enough to get you through the sexy scene with Cary Grant," he assured me.

Our scene was a close-up, with lights shining comfortably warm on my skin. We were slow getting started while director Irving Reis and Grant bickered about details of delivery and stage position. Their wrangles about words or stage direction were getting commonplace. Much of what Grant proposed was meritorious, mostly ad libs and little routines. However, for every added embellishment, Myrna Loy would excuse herself to the portable dressing room and bring back suggestions to enhance her own role. Grant was known as someone obsessively concerned with nuance and detail, and Loy as someone not easily finessed. In the middle was Reis, unwilling to be superseded by either of the two warring contestants.

Waiting for Grant and Reis to sort themselves out, I sensed my ear glue might be weakening, but before assistance could be sought, Reis impatiently instructed the cameras to roll. Midway in shooting came an audible sucking sound as the glue gave way. Out popped one ear, trailing looping, goopy strands. The soundman on the boom heard before the camera saw, and filming stopped.

Back came the makeup man with his glue pot. Throughout, Grant watched the repair with bemused gallantry, but Reis paced back and forth, obviously distressed by another delay.

Once we had gotten by the scene, I pried both ears out where they belonged. Not so bad, I thought. Why all the fuss? They're built right for listening.

☆

In June 1946 at Bikini Atoll in mid-Pacific the venerable World War II aircraft carrier USS *Saratoga* was sacrificed in the world's first underwater nuclear detonation. The photo blowup of me laminated to the wardroom bulkhead was incinerated and drowned in a ten-million-ton atomic water column. That cataclysm was symbolic, if reduced to the tiny dimension of our soundstage on that date.

Grant and Reis had bubbled over. In a huff Grant had disappeared into his portable dressing room. Little could be done about the personal animosity, so Reis again shut the set down. For a few minutes we all milled around aimlessly, chatting and drinking coffee, then Reis carefully rolled both his white shirt sleeves to the elbow and rapped sharply on Grant's dressing-room door, ordering him to return. Grant did pop out at once, but not to work. Off he stormed without a backward glance. Going directly to producer Dore Schary, he threatened to quit unless Reis was fired. Buckling to the pressure, Schary replaced Reis with himself, releasing publicity that Reis had collapsed from physical exhaustion. Several days later Reis seemed to have recovered dramatically, for he hosted a reception for cast and crew members, Grant notably absent. The party was held at his home, one of those aeries clinging to the steep side of a Beverly Hills canyon, and the candlelight disclosed our host quite healthy and philosophical about his replacement.

Although some residual disharmony continued to plague the set, Schary coped with Grant's perfectionist tendencies and tolerated his abrupt absences to count or rewrite lines. As was my custom during such intermissions, I hung around joshing with the crew, far preferring some activity to nothing. That's how the trouble started. I started to mimic Grant. Egged on by the crew's applause, I soon was doing an impromptu show. Taking center stage where the lights were ready for our next close-up, I tipped my head, put on a quizzical smile, and started a soliloquy in a deep-throated, cockney accent. Swaggering across the set, I executed a typical Grant double-take, careful to point out that I was showing only my right profile, a well-known minor vanity. The crew had been laughing and cheering, but suddenly turned silent as tombstones. Beyond the edge of the light's glare, I detected Grant's face. I was caught red-handed.

Again he stalked away, this time directly to Selznick, who sent word for me to come at once. Grant was quitting the film unless I went, and Selznick was fuming at yet another personality clash on an already troubled set. Mimicry is immature, I was lectured, leaving a clear impression that if anyone left the film, it would be me. Never having been fired, to say I felt chastised would be a yawning understatement. Trembling with apprehension, I made my way back to the set. As had been the case with Lionel Barrymore in *The Little Colonel*, my only salvation lay in a personal apology, one fortunately accepted by Grant. By then his annoyance level had subsided, and with a grave nod of his head he accepted my remorse, turned, started off, then stopped.

"By the way," he said, cocking his head in an exaggerated version of my mimicry, "it was a pretty good imitation."

Still devising structures to shore up our home life on our first anniversary, Jack and I joined in a pact to avoid alcohol altogether, for him a sacrifice, for me a gesture. We also resolved to refuse further publicity or stories bearing on our personal homelife or to permit photos to be shot inside our house. To honor his primacy, I officially switched my professional billing to include my married surname. Still convinced a more mature appearance would enhance my acceptability as his companion, I styled my hair in an even more adult manner than my recent exposed-ear version. Although his reaction was generally approving, he discouraged me from further experimentation, saying, "Never mind trying. You'll be a bobby soxer until age eighty."

To accompany his backhanded compliment, he surprised me with two ruby circlets to guard my wedding ring. My RKO studio hairdresser was a practical woman. Inspecting the rings I proudly displayed, she laughed.

"Garnets, dear, not rubies," she said. "I know. I'm married to a jeweler."

To reinforce the amount of time Jack and I spent together, I decided to become his companion on the golf course as well as off. In the end, however, he proved too strong a player to tolerate twosomes with a duffer. Before long we were back where we started, except I had a bag of golf clubs and spiked shoes.

Throughout the fall of 1946 the rhythm of our home life swung erratically between idyllic moments, bitter exchanges and reassuring gin-rummy sessions with Dr. Davidson. Even when striking an equilibrium between the good and the annoying in our married relationship I shot off on furious bursts of silver polishing or housecleaning, as if energy and activity could somehow demolish my tenacious sense of foreboding.

Soon after our arrival at a 1946 Christmas party given by producer S. P. Eagle, Jack had drifted off with some other woman on his arm, leaving me seated alone in the library with only a cigarette, a soft drink, and a magazine. Constant attentiveness was not expected of my husband, but neither was casual rejection. For a while Robert Montgomery sat and talked with me, and as he rose to leave he said, "Well, nothing changes much in this town."

Nothing much had, except my figure, which was becoming fabulous. All that crying at dinner and pushing away half-eaten meals was doing wonders for my weight. So there was something good about a tumultuous home life.

"Maybe a baby would help too," suggested Dr. Davidson. To my surprise, Jack was enthusiastic and announced it should be a family of two boys and a girl. Hopefully not at the same time, I laughed. The prospect of a child exerted a powerful and quieting influence on us both. For his part, independent social behavior diminished and self-discipline increased. On mine, prospective motherhood endowed me with a renewed sense of responsibility and determination to make things work. Calm and tender moments between us became more frequent. As a by-product, my sense of humor, not well exercised for months, returned. Likewise a sense of professional compassion flourished in place of the testiness demonstrated with Ray Collins. Peter Lawford needed both that humor and compassion during a national live radio drama sponsored by Lady Esther Cosmetics.

We were reading from "sides," single script pages mounted on stiff cardboard to avoid rustling noises over the microphone. Midway in Act II he somehow skipped sides, leaping the action from Scene 2 to Scene 4. The moment was a horror of horrors for performers on a live mike, but his expression suggested everything was still in logical order. Absolute concentration is a must for actors. Diluted concentration telegraphs instantly to an audience. Lawford's concentration had vanished. He could not have been listening to his own words, let alone my responses. Disaster was imminent.

Putting my stack of sides on the floor, I snatched his away and tried to figure out where he had scrambled things so badly, ad-libbing into the mike all the while. It is not easy to make up lines while trying to rearrange another story coherently, and Lawford was zero help. To that moment, I really believe he had no idea of the problem. It required perhaps a minute to correctly reshuffle his scrambled sides and to point out with my fingernail where we should be. Somehow by racing through the remainder of the script, we finished before being cut off for a commercial.

Under normal circumstances, I would have been furious. Any decent actor deserves to expect professionalism from colleagues. The new calm between Jack and me in contemplation of a baby, however, placed a soft edge to my tongue, and Lawford escaped with a kindly "forget it."

Spring of 1947 arrived in a crescendo of compatibility at home. On April Fool's Day, I acquired a male lovebird with a mirror to keep it company, and dubbed it April. Later I added a mate called Angel. They fought from the outset. Small wonder, as both turned out to be males.

Unlike April and Angel, their patrons prospered, thriving on fresh routines and reestablished mutual affection. When Selznick placed Jack in his first role as an actor, a small part in a coast-to-coast radio show, it was a tonic to his self-esteem. His good-natured understanding and affectionate behavior made my heart sing for our future. God could not have contemplated a happier home to bless with a baby, but somehow nobody told the rabbits at the medical laboratory.

Every few weeks I underwent their examination for pregnancy, and every time they turned ears-down.

Just prior to my nineteenth birthday, on April 23, a long shadow of our past reappeared. There had been dinner out, some sharp words, and I returned home alone. Just before dawn he appeared, tieless, and his collar smeared with lipstick. Throwing his clothes on the floor, he came into our bed and immediately fell into a snoring sleep.

Lying awake, I felt a searing stab of pain in my left chest and suddenly had to fight for every breath. Pain, palpitations, the works. Heart attack. Reaching for the phone, I wakened Dr. Davidson and recited my symptoms.

"Well it's 5:30 now," he advised. "Come in at 8:00 for a cardiograph." He sounded sleepy. "You are a strong young woman, and I know you will be fine."

When I arrived, apprehensively clutching my hand to my heart, his nurse was red-eyed and sobbing.

"Never mind," I said. "I feel a little better."

"Not you," she cried. "The doctor. They found him in the bathroom this morning, stone dead. Heart attack. Come back tomorrow, dear. We couldn't get a decent reading on you today anyway."

I remained standing before her desk, eyes brimming. She blew into her handkerchief and looked up.

"Well, maybe Dr. Bradbury down the hall will do you. The rabbit tests too. I'm sorry, dear." Holding the handkerchief to her nose, she went back into the doctor's private office, hunched over and weeping.

By noontime my own crying had eased, the pain had disappeared. Once again I realized I must face up to life alone, almost.

For some time I had sneaked off to St. Alban's Church and sat alone thinking. Attending group church services had always been a trying experience. Avidity from gawkers and fans inevitably tainted the mystique of religion for me, and perhaps others as well. Consequently I had become a loner, sometimes spending several hours just staring at the sky-blue wall of the sanctuary and the two tall windows flanking the altar. Far too much a determinist, I sought neither religious favor nor spiritual solution. My problems were never parked at the church chancel railing. Each visit was not so much escape or search for salvation as simply spiritual relief, a period of concentrated calm. Problems were still visible, but held suspended to one side, freeing my mind and spirit to contemplate life unencumbered by niggling concerns.

Perhaps my concept of marriage was idealized, forged in a copy of my own parents', or perhaps romanticized by the stilted soap-opera influence of movies and radio. Plots that had begun in tumult but received generous applications of good cheer and ingenuity always reached a happy conclusion.

The mutual immaturity characterizing our married relationship was not in itself disabling. Collisions of will were inevitable, Jack from insecurity and me from a lifetime of self-motivation. Despite the tawdry implications of that recent night, I quietly left St. Alban's refreshed, at peace with Jack and myself and again determined to make a go of things.

Selznick's business organization was in a mess, further confusing our respective futures. On May 1, 1947, he had written his top executives, as quoted in Rudy Behlmer's *Memo from David O. Selznick*:

"Beyond *Portrait of Jennie* I will not go," he wrote to an associate. "Whether we liquidate or not . . . assume we must lend out each and every one of our people until and unless we get a top general manager. Trying to function without one is too idiotic, and is a strain upon me which I no longer will endure. . . ."

Reflecting this palliative for his troubles, I was among those to be loaned out, this time to Warner Bros. Steadily and subtly, administrative distractions had begun to distance me from his golden touch.

Lying on top of my bed reading each page of the screenplay of Charles Hoffman's adaptation of Edith K. Roberts's soap-opera novel, *That Hagen Girl*, provided a welcome refuge from hard realities. I savored every word, and my position. Stretched out was where I always had my most creative thoughts. Standing up was where I was most productive. Lots could be done with the role, a lip-smacking case history of an adopted, illegitimate girl in a small town. Gossip and taunts bloom into total social ostracism and culminate in her attempted suicide. Then there is a gallant rescue and eventual happy marriage to a man long suspected of being her father. For convoluted plots, this one bulged and groaned. But therein lay opportunity.

Speculating how to play my suicide attempt in the local river, I had few clues. Short of the plunge, it was a totally alien concept. Perhaps the zombie syndrome would be useful, vacant-eyed and slightly sad. But after my hero had bravely pulled me to shore and wrapped me in his bathrobe and pajamas, I would have to brighten quickly, especially when he revealed he loved me and proposed marriage. From suicide to exaltation in the time it takes to dry off would be tricky. Played right, it had high dramatic potential.

The opposite lead was to be Ronald Reagan, who looked to be about twice my age. If only he looked younger, or I older. But then he had to be convincing as my father as well as my lover. Well, I had better look my best. Putting the script aside, I ruefully admitted so far I was definitely not looking my best.

Despite discouragingly negative rabbit tests for pregnancy, I had been putting on weight in the wrong places. If the rabbits had said yes, it would have explained my increase, but apparently it was just too much food. Enrolling at a local Terry Hunt's fitness gym for three weeks, I had lifted weights, taken steam baths and heavy massage, and performed endless pushups and squats. My exercise companion, actress Jeanne Crain, always departed scrubbed, sylph-like, and radiant, while I shuffled out feeling awful, my body aching and my waistline unchanged. The only way I could have lost weight was to let one of those exercise machines tear a leg off. To my dismay, at the end of the three weeks new sets of hooks were required on my skirts.

The only one who appreciated my medieval proportions was studio boss Harry Warner, who enthused I was getting a wonderful, mature figure, ideal for his blockbuster idea about Marilyn Miller, the celebrated Broadway star, now dead a decade. Finish this picture, he said, and we start the new one pronto.

Reagan and I had met only once before, during dedication of the Motion Picture Relief Association Hospital. Newly elected as president of the Screen Actors Guild (SAG), he had immediately recalled the accusation of the 1937 House Select Committee on Un-American Activities (HUAC) that I was a Communist "dupe." I burst out laughing at his recollection, a jovial view in which he seemed not to share. As we were speaking together the 1946–47 successor committee, under the chairmanship of Congressman J. Parnell Thomas, was scheduled to recommence loyalty hearings that fall, sure to be of intense interest to the movie industry. Reagan, as head of SAG, had keyed his remarks to the seriousness of the Communist infiltration, making repeated references to "dupes" and "pinkos" as no laughing matter, leaving me mildly uncomfortable about my earlier jocularity.

Reagan is reported to have detested the *That Hagen Girl* script, which cast him in the ridiculous position of first being rumored my father, then my lover. Jack Warner apparently brushed his objections aside, advising Reagan that as a contract player, he do it or face suspension.

His casting found almost as little enthusiasm from Mother. She still read the trade papers religiously, and her general impression of Reagan was someone long on quips, short on talent, and mired permanently in the never-never land between anonymity and success. I didn't care one way or the other. Warner Bros. held the whip hand, and if they said it must be Reagan, that was that.

Shooting commenced in early June, and within two weeks we were into the scene depicting my despair and attempted drowning. It was soppy, set in a pelting rainstorm. Like a lifeguard Reagan plunged into the river to rescue me. Dissatisfied with the staging, director Peter Godfrey kept us going in and out of the water for several hours. Drenched, bedraggled, but happy to be busy at work again, I enjoyed the splashing and flailing around. However, Reagan fared less well on our diet of rain, rescue, and romance. The next morning, June 19, he called in sick and disappeared for several weeks. Godfrey groused each morning and rescheduled shooting in a potpourri of unrelated scenes.

Perhaps as emotional compensation for my embedded uneasiness about things at home, I missed no chance to put a comic spin on everything. In a turgid high school Shakespearean adaptation of a playlet within our story, I was a virginal Juliet capped and gowned in pearl-studded white chiffon, required to sentimentally regard the splay-legged, prone corpse of Romeo. Each manly curve of his body was visible beneath clinging tights.

"Oh, happy dagger!" was my line, impossible to deliver with a sorrowful expression. Repeated unsuccessful efforts compounded my difficulty, and soon Romeo and the crew exploded in laughter each time I tried. For the moment our scene was a lost cause, drowned in humor, as if the drab outlook at home simply did not exist.

On July 12 I had an important visitor, Dr. William C. Bradbury, successor obstetrician from down Dr. Davidson's hallway. A square-jawed man with soulful eyes and shaggy hair, he apologetically extended farmer-sized palms and explained that lab technicians had been botching laboratory tests, including mine. A laboratory full of rabbits had died, not, he added with a smile, because of the quality of the submissions. The tests must be rerun, and he had come for yet another urine sample. To atone, however, he offered to telephone results directly to the set. Unwilling to share such a message over the usual loudspeaker, I arranged a verbal code: red roses, either to be delivered or announced as not yet available.

Two days later, on July 14, Reagan reappeared, amiable but sunken-cheeked. His past four weeks had been traumatic. Following our suicide scene, he had collapsed and entered Cedars of Lebanon Hospital with viral pneumonia. Eight days later his wife, actress Jane Wyman, had delivered a baby girl three months prematurely. Within twenty-four hours the infant was dead. Bedridden himself, Reagan could lend no direct support to his wife during her ordeal, a bleak footnote to his tragedy.

Our first rehearsal the morning of his return did not involve him, but had me up on a stool and leaping off like any schoolgirl answering a telephone ring. During a break the real telephone rang. It was for me, with Dr. Bradbury's message: roses arriving next January. My heart soared!

There was no time to share my news before shooting recommenced. On the next run-through, instead of jumping off the stool, I gathered my skirt and dismounted as carefully as an old lady. No miscarriages for me, thank you.

Godfrey was disgusted. "Act like a teenager, for Pete's sake! You got a crush on the guy. You're ecstatic! Leap off the damn stool!"

No secret is more poorly kept than a happy one. All rehearsals stopped in their tracks. Joining fully in my celebration, Reagan left the impression he had no private sorrow. In all truth his own recent bereavement sailed high overhead and unnoticed by me.

Along with long-stemmed roses of congratulation, Selznick enclosed a contract offer for my signature which would have placed my unborn "he, she, or them . . ." under his exclusive artistic control. I took it as a lighthearted joke, even when I later learned that he did not.

Roused from its nine-year silence, my old licensee, Ideal Toy Company, proposed manufacturing a doll in my baby's assumed image. Using a doll to make money was a concept with which I found no quarrel. In fact, Mother had always happily referred to our Brentwood home as the "house a doll built." But Ideal's current objective was not mine. I had always believed, dating from childhood, that I worked to create pleasure and happiness. My motivation was abstract—to please. Material results, however useful as yardsticks to measure success and failure, were never the reason for my effort.

Ideal's proposition, to reduce my pregnancy to a money-spawning venture, struck me as obscene. It was one thing for a child to elect, either by demonstrated interest or volition, to commercialize itself, but meanwhile I would protect the prerogative of free choice for my unborn baby.

"We'll name him after me," Jack enthused, prematurely. Once again our relationship was steadied and healed, with expectation of diapers, weaning, whooping cough, and eventual grandparenthood.

As expected, the media swooped down in a feeding frenzy, focused on the possibility that motherhood might interfere with my career. Never having even considered the possibility, I used a standard response: answer but direct the next question to a new topic:

"Baby notwithstanding, why should I quit? Motherhood might impose radical new responsibilities, but not to the total exclusion of work. What *would* make me stop would be the necessity of accepting unimportant roles for the sake of working. There would be no kick in that. Would I like to direct? Sure, someday. Why not? Women have more imagination than men, and sometimes they are more convincing liars."

Pregnancy imposed a subtle problem on my acting beyond physical restrictions. As a profession acting often allows people to be what they are not. Libertine ladies in fact can learn gestures of sainthood. Wimps transform themselves into swashbucklers. Empty heads spout profundities. *That Hagen Girl* drove the point home. The difference between expectant mother and schoolgirl ingenue was so extreme that I really had to stretch to perform as someone I really was not. In the process lines became as digestible as raw octopus, my acting turned stilted, and the director evidenced concern. Whenever time permitted he sent me off for sessions with a dramatic coach.

"Take off your shoes and walk around barefoot," the man instructed. "Make love to the carpet. Sexy footprints mean sexy feet, mean sexy knees."

Inspecting my bare feet with newfound respect, I paraded around on the carpet, searching for sexuality in the woof and warp and wondering if the director wanted his ingenue to become a vixen.

As several times before, my voice was also judged too youthful. Grinding eggshells with a mortar and pestle into a sandy consistency, the coach instructed me to swallow several spoonsful. "Your voice will be fuller and deeper, lush!" he said.

Gagging, I did as I was told. Bits of shell stuck in my teeth. "Doesn't a canary do this with cuttlefish bone?" I cheeped. "Maybe it will help me lay an egg in the film."

Grimacing, he struggled on. "It's only to help you reach down in your throat to draw on experience." A numbing analogy, considering my bouts of morning sickness.

Mercifully shifting his attention from my feet and larynx, he pressed his fingers into my midriff.

"Use the gut when you speak," he ordered.

"I already have," I laughed. "Got a baby in there."

He ignored me. "Find the character. Find it in your diaphragm of souls." That instruction I'll never forget.

Who my tutor was, how he got there, where he went, or what bare feet, eggshells, and soulful diaphragms did for my acting, I know not. What I thought I had been doing since age three now appeared to be terribly complicated. Years ago someone should have told me that I wasn't qualified.

If onstage my pregnancy stirred up problems, offstage it seemed to make me more desirable, at least to my makeup man. Armed with sponges, paint pots, and a fistful of brushes, as usual he stood ready to attack my shiny skin, and misapplied cosmetics. Fresh from a retching bout of morning sickness but greeting him in my new eggshell contralto, I mounted his chair and let him adjust my bib.

Youthful, fuzzy-haired, and cow-eyed, given to loose-fitting clothes and moving in an aura of chic, soap, and cologne, he had tried on prior occasions to recount unhappy aspects of his recent marriage. Before he could get into details I had blunted his soliloquy, lest I become his mother confessor.

That morning he ostentatiously broke the seal on some expensive imported lipstick and slowly began painting from the corners toward my cupid's bow.

"Two minutes on set," shouted an assistant director, rapping on the closed door.

"She'll be there when I'm through!" retorted Makeup, bending over closer, until I had a strange inkling he wanted to put his lips on mine, instead of using the lipstick.

"You're taking too long with the mouth," I said.

Cracking open a box of fresh pancake, he extracted a new sponge from its crinkly, plastic wrapping, both highly complimentary gestures in the world of makeup. Freshly opened packages and new sponges theoretically reduce the chance of cross-contamination from someone else's skin.

He began to apply the pancake. Suddenly he grasped my hand. "I love you," he blurted.

"Waiting on set!" yelled the assistant director, rattling the doorknob.

"Give me the sponge," I said.

"Come on, Shirley," persisted the assistant director, pounding the door.

"I love you," whispered Makeup.

"Coming," I yelled, smearing the remaining pancake around, and pulled off my bib.

"I love you," he whined, standing dejectedly by his empty chair with nothing in hand save lipstick and brush.

Godfrey wanted to retake the suicide scene. As I edged down a slippery path with wind-driven rain pelting my face, all trace of makeup vanished. The water was murky, but at body temperature and chlorinated, prophylactic measures for both Reagan's recent infection and my current condition. Gingerly wading out into the river, I stopped, took a deep breath, and ducked under as my hero came flailing through the shallows like a bull elephant. Lifting my sodden, bedraggled form, he removed it to his place rather than mine. In the miracle of movies, I became dried off, clothed in his oversized pajamas, and wrapped in a predictable on-camera clinch. As movie kissers go, Reagan was good.

"I love you," he said, holding me close, eyebrows arched either in mock sincerity or utter disbelief in the lines he spoke.

"Just think," I whispered into his off-camera ear, "you've just saved *two* people."

Not all movies are winners—a distinction shared by *That Hagen Girl*. In his closing lines on-camera, Reagan levels a final blistering retort to the local gossipmongers, who have confused him as my father rather than my lover.

"You want me to speak at the school graduation exercise, after all you've said about me and Mary Hagen! You have a very convenient kind of justice. When you go, open the windows. I want this place to air out!"

The cameras had stopped, but Reagan kept rolling.

"And on the opening night of this picture," his voice rose exultantly, "I'm going to have my two kids in the balcony whistle when I say *that*! It's their daddy's big moment!"

Time magazine of November 10, 1947, joined the accolade.

When the Hagen girl jumps in the river,... the plot hauls her out, but sends the picture to the bottom, like a stone. After reels of behaving like Shirley's father, Reagan suddenly exhibits unpaternal passion and breathlessly marries her. Moviegoers with very strong stomachs may be able to view an appearance of rebated incest as a romantic situation.

Even the Communist *New York Daily Worker* paid tribute. "Shirley is just Shirley," it observed helplessly, "but that Reagan! A philosophic father and sweetheart to the same girl? Odd."

Seldom one to bumble his timing, Selznick moved to capitalize on the happy-couple public image. Jack would play his first movie role opposite his real-life wife. The film was an 1866 military horse opera called *Massacre*, after the novel by James Warner Bellah and featuring a he-man lineup including John Wayne, Ward Bond, Henry Fonda, Jack Pennick, and Victor McLaglen. John Ford would direct and the screenplay was by Ford's son-in-law, Frank Nugent, erstwhile gadfly of Zanuck.

As filming progressed *Massacre* became *War Party* and finally *Fort Apache*. Although the title changed, Jack and I remained as we started, an uncomfortable duet. Despite his crash course in acting, there was still lots to learn. My acting edge was also dulled, fearful that one extra cinch on the corset or inadvertent thump on horseback would induce miscarriage. Both of us seemed to enjoy saying clever, sweet things to each other, some with a quiet bite. Commenting about kissing me, he said he would "not feel at ease making love to another girl, before the cameras, that is."

Displaying the soft, shrewd side to his otherwise gruff character, director Ford called for more love scenes between us than the script actually contained. "Not that I intended to keep all this nonsense in the final print," he later admitted. "Just wanted to keep up the morale of the youngsters."

A Western potboiler from start to end, *Fort Apache* turned into blue-ribbon box office. Jack's performance was treated kindly by the critics, if not with enthusiasm. While elevating me to no new heights, the film did little damage. In a Motion Picture Research Bureau national opinion poll, June Allyson and I ran in a dead heat for the title of "America's Girl Friend," with Elizabeth Taylor trailing third.

With the film behind us, Jack and I drifted away on our relatively rosy cloud of expectation. Nary a ripple disturbed our family tranquility during fall of 1947, if one omits the grace note of excitement provided when brother George momentarily married his second wife, only to promptly abandon the union when she admitted she was already married to someone else.

Shortly before Christmas in the final stages of pregnancy and pleasurably uncomfortable, I had retired soon after dinner and Jack had gone off to play a few hands of poker with friends at nearby Riviera Country Club. Shortly after midnight I awakened to the sound of loud, jolly voices audible through the wall separating our bedroom from the living area. Moments later the door was flung open and lights suddenly bathed the room. Jack swooped unsteadily to my bedside and tugged at the blanket.

"Get up!" he said. "Let's have a party."

Framed in the doorway behind him stood a strange woman with long, tousled red hair. Lounging one voluptuous hip against the doorjamb, she grinned uncertainly and hoisted a drinking glass in my direction. "C'mon," she urged, "les' go party!"

My first instinct was to leap from bed and yank her red hair by the roots. On second thought about my almost born baby and my bowling-ball shape, I decided to roll over rather than fight. Shielding my eyes, stupefied by this sudden assault on my privacy, I averted my face and hitched the bedclothes higher. The light switched off and the door slammed. Her shrill laughter grew faint as they left by the front door and a car drove away.

Lying there alone in the dark, I rolled back and stared at the ceiling, in a vortex of fury. As if annoyed by the interruption, the baby shifted heavily. Even measured against the most bizarre standards of conduct, my husband's actions were proving him uncommonly complicated. Instead of salvaging his ego by acting opposite him in *Fort Apache*, had I simply underscored his relative incompetence? Compulsively gregarious, lacking in self-esteem, zigzagging between loving husband and insensitive wastrel—his case would be meat and potatoes for a psychologist. But despite everything, I loved him, and desperately wanted him to love me.

While recycling such vexations, I could not spare myself. Perhaps my expectation of faithful love was unrealistic. Should all the structural niceties of marriage I offered, the clean, chintz curtains, varied menus, even myself, should all these be served up without condition, without expectation of acknowledgment? Could it be that my continual patience with his foibles was actually counterproductive? When I forgave and forgot his betrayals, was I guaranteeing their repetition?

Addressing the ceiling that night, I asked whether continued struggle in such unrewarding conditions was worth it. But even before the answer came back, my dander rose anew. No, I was not some tremble-lipped sentimentalist, content to slosh about in tears of self-pity. No, I would not be beaten down. I come from solid peasant stock. I am a fighter.

Ah, yes, but what to do?

Whatever was going on now, it was wrong. Once again, the idea of a doctor flashed to mind. This time it would be Bradbury, the obstetrician and bearer of good news. Unemotional and practical, when he spoke the words rang crystal clear and to the point. Might not Jack be persuaded to sit down and listen to such a counselor, someone graying at the temples and with medical diplomas on the wall?

The baby shifted and kicked. Just possibly Bradbury was the one to counsel us with our mutual problems. Help might be at hand, courtesy of our yet-unborn child.

32

"Be good and you'll be lonesome."

—Mark Twain

At four in the winter morning of January 30, 1948, Jack and I switched customary roles, he fast asleep in our bed and I cautiously nosing my auto through darkened Santa Monica streets.

Earlier that evening Dr. Bradbury had hurried over to assess my report of labor pains, which inconveniently ceased upon his arrival. Seated quietly, he read a book while Jack alternately slumped before television or paced aimlessly around the room. Staring moodily into the fireplace embers, I waited for another pain, and thought. Involving Bradbury in our problems had really solved nothing. Although I still hoped for some miracle of understanding, Jack had stoutly denied he was culpable on any score, and Bradbury had only observed what we already knew, that there was trouble ahead. His most pointed suggestion was to get rid of all my caged birds.

Some women, when unhappy or pregnant, buy hats or eat pickles with ice cream. With me, it was buy another bird. To our chattering lovebirds, April and Angel, I had added a blue mountain lorikeet, which trilled and ate mashed bananas. Then came a raucous Mexican cardinal with a piercing whistle. When Bradbury had mentioned the health hazard posed by parrot fever, I returned all my caged companions to the pet store, which promptly resold them at twice my original price because they had once been mine.

Shortly after 10:00 p.m., Bradbury yawned. "Well, maybe it was in-

416

digestion. You're not going to deliver tonight. Here are a couple of sleeping pills. Take one if you get antsy. Good night."

Reluctant to miss anything, I set the two pills aside.

"I'll take them," Jack said, reached for his highball glass, and popped both pills down.

At 3:30 in the morning my contractions began in a rush. No fooling this time.

"Wake up." I nudged him. "We're going to the hospital."

Stirring, he mumbled incoherently, rolled over, and returned to sleep. Rising alone, I donned my maternity dress for the final time, collected a bag of necessaries, and slipped into high-heeled shoes. Big as a watermelon in front, tottering uncertainly on spiked heels and jackknifing forward with each labor pain, I mounted the hospital front steps carrying my own bag. A sleepy desk attendant pointed me toward the elevator. Inside, a janitor was up on a short stepladder changing ceiling light bulbs.

"Good morning," I said, and leaned against the wall.

"Morning, ma'am," he responded, glancing down. "Say, aren't you Shirley Temple?"

"Yes," I said. "Does this elevator work?"

"Sure. Just changing bulbs. Push the floor button and ignore me up here. Come to think of it, can I get your autograph?"

"Okay," I said, just as a contraction hit. Dropping my purse, I clutched at the stepladder for support.

"Never mind the autograph," he said nervously. "Say, shall I come down and push that button?"

"Nope." I reached sideways like a crab. "Thanks, anyway."

With a jerk, the elevator started up while I hunched over embracing the stepladder legs. Above me the man continued to screw in fresh bulbs. Both of us could hardly wait for the elevator to arrive.

With dawn, Linda Susan appeared.

Because the hospital nursery was being painted, the baby's bassinet was installed at my bedside. Her hair was wispy and reddish, and when she opened her almond-shaped eyes they were brown and calm. Instead of a cry, she produced a series of soft, resonant "Oooh-la's." Thirty-three years later, her own baby girl would make exactly the same unusual sounds. During feeding and cuddling time we studied each other carefully, she with a slightly troubled uncertain stare. That we would always share a special firstborn bond there was no doubt. Drifting on a sea of contentment, I realized children were what life was all about.

When Jack arrived, his face still creased from sleep, and inspected her, he found four dimples, one on each cheek. Uncle Billy Robinson telephoned, asking if he could be godfather, a role already given away to John Ford, so we settled on adopted godfather. Within days a present arrived from him, a tiny ermine coat and matching bonnet with a note saying he just wanted to live long enough so he could make Susan dance like I had. Brother George celebrated by falling off his motorcycle at high speed, skidding across the Mojave Desert on his head, and winding up in his own hospital bed.

On February 8, 1948, Louella Parsons gushed, "Tonight, I salute Shirley Temple, the finest little ambassador Hollywood has ever had. Shirley is the perfect answer to those forever denouncing loose morals, loose thinking, and loose living. What a lesson she offers for those girls constantly hitting headlines with many marriages, divorces, and so-called 'romances.' " Reading this, I felt a twinge of regret, a bittersweet recognition of chronic problems still surging beneath our surface happiness.

Time for a second honeymoon, Bradbury counseled. Leave the baby with its nursemaid; go away and speak frankly. Rekindle the original flame.

Dutifully, we motored northward to the Del Monte Lodge at Pebble Beach, an idyllic resort nestled amid towering pines at the edge of rocky Carmel Bay. My golf shots were still erratic and fell short, while down the fairway Jack leaned impatiently on his club and a following foursome yelled to play through.

Horseback riding proved equally unsatisfying. My first time on the trail, my docile horse, Old Spook, suddenly veered off and plunged straight down the face of a wind-slicked sand dune while I arched back toward his rump and sawed futilely at the reins. Soon we were clopping along alone through a strange, quiet pine forest. Having given up trying to steer him, I crooned, "Home on the Range." Looking back, Spook flattened his ears and bit at my foot. Arriving at the Del Monte Stable next morning to give riding another try, we found Spook quietly lying down under a moldy gray tarpaulin.

The stable groom shook his head sadly. "Started to saddle him. He just laid down, wheezed once and died."

"How old?"

"About nineteen."

So was I, I thought. Neither one of us is doing very well. Being married to Jack was neither good nor bad, like bathing in a tub with its porcelain chipped. It did the job, but there was no joy.

Following our return, it became clear that no shared child, however lovable, could by her presence soothe Jack's sensitivities or reinforce my patience. Even things done in innocence evoked reactions from him far more intense than justified. When I was asked to present an Academy Award Oscar for a "Merrie Melody" comedy entitled *Tweetie Pie*, he was given a seat in the rear row, refused to stand beside me during the reception afterwards, and went home alone.

When a national news service asked my pick for U.S. President in the forthcoming fall election, I selected General Douglas MacArthur, believing he would best uphold our interests abroad. A humanitarian and soldier seemed a good combination. Jack seemed shaken because the reporter never sought his opinion about anything. Later, when MacArthur lost the nomination to Thomas E. Dewey, he took unnecessarily smug notice.

Our caldron of petty irritation finally bubbled over, at the hand of our cook. Squat and rotund, with thick arms, a bull neck, and lumpy jowls, she proclaimed herself both Christian and teetotaler, pursing her mouth and clouding her eyes at every appearance of whiskey. Frequently during her soup course I would dissolve into tears at some remark from Jack, throw down my napkin, and flee behind the locked bedroom door. In retaliation he would stomp into the kitchen, castigate me to the cook and the walls, and wind up in a sullen stupor, slumped before television.

One morning after one such an episode he rose first and went into our main room for breakfast. Baby Susan was in her crib waiting for her bottle. Still pouting a bit, I had just stepped into my slip when loud shouts from the living room brought me scurrying to the connecting door.

The scene was eye-popping. Stumbling backwards in clumsy retreat around chairs and tables scrambled my husband, pursued doggedly by the cook brandishing a thick butcher knife over her head.

"You dog," she hissed, chopping menacingly at the air, and lunged forward.

"Oh, God!" Jack cried, eluded her rush, and bolted up and over the couch back.

Opening the door a crack, I wondered what to do. Supposing she outmaneuvered him and whacked off a slice of flesh? What then? Blood all over the freshly laid, deep-pile Chinese carpet. A mess. She was an excellent cook, but Jack was my husband.

Wading out into the fray I came, barefooted and bare-handed. Crouching at a respectful distance, I tried to cajole the woman into stopping, but she ignored me. She seemed to have him momentarily cornered between our tropical fish aquarium and the baby grand piano. Now was the moment for my move.

"Now, there," I crooned, "dear friend. Let me have the knife." Reaching out slowly with both hands, I kept talking, then grabbed. Her wrist was trembling.

For a teetotaler, she reeked of whiskey. Between sobs and mutterings her story finally became clear. Distraught by the inhumanity of our dinner-table bickering, she had retired with Jack's bottle. After brooding and nipping away the night, she had greeted first light with blood in her eye.

Dismissal was inevitable, but she got a good letter of recommendation: an excellent cook; fine housekeeper; please, no phone inquiries. In retrospect, I might better have fired him and kept her. Good cooks were hard to find.

The glinting knife blade introduced a chilling urgency for corrections to home life, and a possible threat to baby Susan. Slicing through my relatively complacent, stupefying confidence in happy endings, the incident shouted for more drastic action than hope alone.

The more I weighed options, the more I detected hidden minefields. Analyzing my side of the problem, I might be suffering from an insidious form of jealousy, fear that I was unloved by the one I loved. This speculation was troublesome because it lacked a principal target for my jealousy. The women with Jack were only figures that briefly appeared and then faded from sight, like ducks in a shooting gallery.

Jealousy, however, cuts both ways. If it goaded me to compete more effectively for his affection, why could not the field be reversed? Could I not inspire *him* to be jealous of *me*? And to sidestep the practical peril of getting involved with a real suitor, why not keep the whole thing on a fictitious plane?

Perhaps greater caution should have attended my reflections. Blurring off into the distance went the truism that jealousy seldom induces true love. Optimism and hope overwhelmed uncertainty. Self-confidence, I told myself, could control any dangerous moments ahead. Thus fortified by my own rationalization, I embarked on a perilous journey at whose conclusion I would nearly sup with the devil.

First would be the suggestion that a secret suitor existed. Mr. Ruser ran an elegant Beverly Hills jewelry shop which catered to a clientele with lofty taste and bulging purse. Selecting a $350 gold-banded wrist-watch, I inscribed a card to myself from "an admirer" and directed that the expensively wrapped package be chauffeur-delivered at our din-nertime.

When it arrived Jack admired the watch, ignored the card, and re-turned immediately to complain about my lack of proficiency in golf. For days I wore the watch ostentatiously, but my mysterious suitor proved to have no clout.

Next, I tried an unexplained overnight absence, in my view some-thing inevitably provocative. Smart Girl from Westlake had moved into a rustic cottage on her mother's heavily wooded property. Without saying good-bye to Jack, I drove off after dinner. Smart Girl's bird dog came romping up in the blustery darkness, took my outstretched hand softly in his jaws, and led me down a pathway and across a narrow wooden footbridge to her cottage. Always ready to help a friend, Smart Girl let me spend the night, with County snoring and snuffling at the foot of my bed.

Returning home next morning, I found nobody there save the baby and her nurse. Jack had missed me, however. Telephoning my parents at midnight, he had easily roused them to a frenzy barely short of an all-points police bulletin for a kidnap. Going off elsewhere to share his concern with acquaintances, he, too, failed to return home. As usual, things were at a standoff. My plow had twice bitten soil, but so far nothing productive had been planted.

Although I still spent time in contemplative communion at St. Alban's Church, my friend the May Queen from Westlake had long been en-couraging me to join the Christian Science church. What intrigued me most in reading *Science and Health With Key to the Scriptures* was its transcendental approach to human problems, of which I had my share. In the end, however, religious belief and resolution of secular problems continued as separate entities. The May Queen's proposition languished.

Parallel to my other efforts, the hours we felt obliged to spend at nightclubs gradually decreased in favor of entertainment at home, my hope being to eliminate my husband's casual flirtations, which I had found so irritating. At first most of our guests turned out to be refugees from the golf club, ornate, leggy blondes with saucer eyes and feather heads clinging to the arms of tanned, golfing lotharios wearing gleaming smiles.

Reflecting on this period, I always view it as life in an aviary. There was Egret, tall, plumed, stepping carefully as if already posing on the stage to which she obviously aspired. Round-eyed Flamingo, with her neck arched like Cleopatra and feathers the color of the sunset, could be counted on to swoop from group to group. Starlings flitted around, noisy and black-sheened. Mademoiselle L'Oiseau pouted, hunched her shoulders to better dramatize her plunging neckline, and trilled in a French accent. Magpie, straw-blond and muscular, mimicked whatever he heard to whoever would listen. Informing everyone about everything was his concept of universal popularity. Occasionally, the Screech Owl came, a watchful sort who regarded everyone with fatigued benevolence. The most innocuous glance or casual comment would cause him to cock his head sideways and blink thoughtfully.

Our aviary roof shielded them from the newshawks always circling and watching for takeoffs, changed formations, or landings. With all inhibitions released, this exotic crowd regularly drank, tittered, and posed, ignoring the Little Red Hen, who was me. Younger by apparent light-years than my guests, I clucked and scratched around, refilling the ice bucket, providing buffet food, and emptying ashtrays.

Occasionally, as a parlor activity this gaudy, demonstrative flock would settle down together for dramatic readings among themselves, trading unabashed embraces around my breakfast table and excusing excesses in the name of professional practice. Not one bird ever turned to the Little Red Hen to ask for a critique, and not once was she offered a part, an exclusion she found extraordinary. So far as she knew, of all the aspiring actors and actresses in the aviary, she was the only one working regularly.

A henhouse with the door ajar is bound to attract visitors. Strutting like a cockerel, one of those salvaged by Jack from the country-club flotsam was an unhappy husband. Chattering incessantly about his woeful homelife, he was invited by Jack to stay overnight in the cook's unoccupied room. Our hospitality, food, and lodging found such favor that Cockerel lingered several days, pecking away at his life from every angle. Hearing in exquisite detail how other hens had so abused him provided me a perverse sense of satisfaction, and I gave his repetitive chattering my sympathetic attention. Having all but abandoned attempts to elicit Jack's jealousy, I overlooked Cockerel as another appropriate vehicle, according him only commiseration. Cockerel viewed my interest differently, as I would later learn.

Against this frenetic backdrop, my twentieth birthday rang a knell on my teens, and once again a new film helped deflect my eye from personal concerns. Selznick had cast me as a suffragette in *Baltimore Escapade*, later named *Adventure in Baltimore*. The role fitted my mood like an elbow-length glove. Based on Christopher Isherwood's 1900s tale, the rise of a cleric, played by Robert Young, to the bishopric is sorely hampered by the political activities of his daughter. Inserting Jack into a third-billing position and in conformity with his new practice of packaging, Selznick dispatched us all to RKO Radio Studios for production.

Selznick was still suffering. Shifting public tastes, resulting from the vigor of infant television and an uncertain churning within traditional motion picture circles, was exacting its toll. Chafing also over his inability to eliminate wastefulness at Vanguard, Selznick finally had opted against any further personal productions, grieving that he didn't want to make any more films personally unless and until he became properly organized.

One crisp day Cockerel, the confident one from our aviary days, strutted boldly and alone through my henhouse door. Standing in the foyer and without preliminaries, he blurted out a hitherto hidden tale of affection for me. His sudden romantic outpouring was interrupted by a jangling telephone bell.

It was Mother, next door, sounding an almost hysterical alarm. Seizing a loaded gun from his bedroom arms cache, Father had just bolted downstairs and was hurrying toward my house. For some time I had been generally aware that Father loathed Cockerel as a person of base intentions. Addicted to peeking from windows, he had surely witnessed Cockerel occasionally come and go in our flock of visitors. What ignited him on this occasion was someone so despised approaching my doorway alone.

No sooner was the receiver replaced than an urgent, heavy pounding sounded at the door. "Open up or I'll kill him!" came Father's shout.

Cockerel stood rooted, terror-stricken. It was a stupid predicament for everyone. Darting to the door, I threw the bolt, then tugged the almost immobilized Cockerel into the living room. A furtive glance out a side window confirmed the situation as desperate. Father had just retreated to the low, stone wall bordering our driveway, where he now sat, glancing malevolently between my front and kitchen entrances. In his hand, its long barrel pointed menacingly at the sky, was a Wild-West .45-caliber pistol.

"This way," I hissed, gesturing toward the tall French doors that opened on a back verandah.

Cockerel needed no urging. Bolting outside, he leaped down the long stone stairway, and went plunging and crashing through the underbrush like an animal, only fleetingly reappearing as he raced across my dusty riding ring and scaled the far rail fence in one headlong plunge, never to be seen again.

In explanation of Father's impetuous action, I later learned he was already exasperated before Cockerel's sally, having just been served a subpoena as co-defendant in a legal suit in which an elephant was the other named defendant.

"A what?" I had asked, after we had cleared the air over the gun episode.

It seems a traveling circus had strung its banners across a midwestern main street, proclaiming "Shirley Temple Is Coming." People had flocked to the tent to glimpse me, and when told Shirley Temple was only an elephant, had threatened to run the circus out of town for misleading advertising. Before this could occur a little child, obviously thinking Shirley Temple should be sweet, offered her peanuts, crowded too close, and the elephant had stomped on him.

"Now the child's parents have sued us for not preventing the use of your name." Father heaved a sigh of genuine disgust. "It's all in Grant Cooper's hands now—a good lawyer in nasty situations."

They say an elephant never forgets. Nor would the Little Red Hen when it came to remembering Cooper's name in time of need.

Emphasis on social activity at home rather than in public had demonstrated serious drawbacks, so once again we drifted back into the nightclub habit, arriving stylishly late after dinner, and lingering until closing hours. For those preferring to stay out rather than go home, after-hours joints were available. Low-ceilinged and cluttered, they were usually without music or entertainment and with lighting so low it left everything in half-shadow. All were indistinct, smoky places with stale air where tongues loosened easily and sudden cordiality reigned.

At Dave's Blue Room one night we met retired New York City detective Barney Ruditsky. A nonstop talker, he had worked police crowd-control during my 1938 visit ten years earlier and produced a blue-and-gold official detective badge as evidence. Without it he could have passed for any refrigerator salesman.

Across the dimly lit room Ruditsky pointed out mobster Mickey Cohen, a pale lugubrious man surrounded by beefy henchmen in a sideshow of conspiratorial behavior, heads inclined together or raised to sweep the room with unmistakably hostile glances.

The staircase to the upstairs bathroom was narrow and steep. I had started back when Cohen came pounding up, head down and alone. We met at mid-stairway, his chunky body pressed sideways facing me. As we stood fitted together like sardines, he said he had noticed me with his friend Ruditsky and how much he liked my films. In such close proximity to a genuine underworld insider, my imagination raced ahead, but then he was gone. His elevated heels clomping on the bare wooden treads, he was off on a mission more pressing than chitchat.

When Ruditsky recognized how impressed I felt near seedy characters like Cohen, he whispered that he had a treat in store. A combined posse of Los Angeles police and county sheriffs was planning a marijuana bust at a Mandeville Canyon hideaway of actor Robert Mitchum and actress Lila Leeds. Would I like to come along in his unmarked car?

It was a tough decision. What was Ruditsky's role? Why was a retired New York cop involved at all? Were Cohen and he really friends? Why hadn't Jack been included in the invitation? How would it read in the papers if I were spotted riding "back seat" during a drug-bust? All the answers remained as murky as the air in Dave's Blue Room, so I said no.

The decision was right. Couched in lurid prose and embarrassing photos, the raid was splashed across the next day's front pages. My presence, innocence counterpoised to the sordid event, might have increased news coverage but befouled my public image.

On another late night at Dave's Blue Room Jack had returned from the bar with someone he requisitioned to accompany me home. Offended by the arrangement, I left them both and collected my wrap. When the doorman brought my car, a blue Cadillac with raised tail fins, I roared away in an evil mood.

Halfway home I noticed the light gray fedora on the seat beside me. Pulling to the curb, I inspected the hat carefully, found no identification, then noticed the car upholstery was not mine. On the floor in back lay a long, locked, black leather case, soft to the touch but with something hard inside. It was a very wrong car.

When I returned to the nightclub the valet tumbled over himself with gratitude. What he had delivered was Mickey Cohen's look-alike Cadillac. Still annoyed, I switched cars and went home, thereby missing the action. Cohen and his phalanx of bodyguards had appeared at the doorway requesting his car. As the doorman stood aside the whole group was suddenly sprayed with automatic gunfire from the opened window of another car speeding past.

In mid-fall, Jack was preparing to leave for location for *She Wore a Yellow Ribbon*, his third film and first without me. He told a news reporter he was deadly sick of still being "Mr. Shirley Temple," only a tail on the kite of his famous wife. Starting with this current film, he declared, he would do no more double-bills with me, nor would he give further press interviews about his married life. Behind these declarations lay a confrontation of cataclysmic importance for us both.

On our third wedding anniversary, it had been another evening of brittle, impersonal gaiety at the Mocambo nightclub, followed by a high-tempo argument over something trivial with neither of us willing to let go, even after we returned to our bedroom. I saw the blow coming as he lunged. Twisting half around, I fell to the floor. Which of us was more surprised I cannot say, but without a word he left the house, slamming doors behind. For a long time I sat where I had fallen, a disheveled woman with an aching heart and crumpled spirit. It was growing ever harder to keep the lamp of love lit.

A crucial factor in the relentless process of making a movie is that it leaves little time left over to contemplate personal miseries or cope with them. Hard on the heels of *Adventure in Baltimore* and after an eight-year absence, in early November 1948, I returned alone to the Twentieth Century-Fox studio lot to begin *Mr. Belvedere Goes to College*, cast as a widowed young journalism student in hot pursuit of a publicity-shy professor. A "Welcome Home Shirley" reception was hosted by Darryl Zanuck in the Cafe de Paris commissary, always off-limits to me in earlier years. In a peculiar coincidence, and although invited to attend, Mother chose that day for elective surgery to correct a minor female problem she said had resulted from her nine-hour labor at my birth. The revelation made me feel guilty until reassured by her doctor that the situation was related to age, not childbirth. Her timing had an obvious measure of convenience. Rattling old skeletons with Zanuck would certainly offer little appeal.

Visiting old haunts is hard on memory. Things shrink, change, and disappear. My cottage had become a dental clinic. All sorts of stage crew hurried past, but all strangers. Only grizzled gate guard Al Turney recalled the days eight years earlier. Flashing a slightly tarnished badge from the old Shirley Temple Police, he recalled with a note of pride that he had once pinched me for speeding in Uncle Billy's racing car. Zanuck's official welcome was impersonal, and his remarks perfunctory, as if we shared no common past at all. Somewhat more wistful, C. Aubrey Smith, my gruff military commander and grandfather from *Wee Willie Winkie*, observed that time was racing by for us all. Sixty days later he was dead.

On November 5, 1948, our cast and crew were bundled on an overnight train to Reno, Nevada, for location work. As Jack had already gone to his own shooting location in Monument Valley, I quipped, perhaps unwisely, that our simultaneous departures in opposite directions was just the sort of thing to start a divorce rumor. I should have thought again about feeding rumors myself.

As our train went clickety-clack through the desert night, several of our film company, including the Wizard, gathered for a club-car nightcap. Hardly the mogul he aspired to be or sometimes chose to pose,

Wizard shoveled compliments in my direction, covering everything from appealing looks to yet-unrealized dramatic potential. Toward midnight the group thinned out and he offered to walk me to my compartment. Only two ways to go on this train, he laughed, and I'm going yours.

As I turned in my opened doorway to say good night, he roughly shoved me back inside and slammed the door shut. In one hulking maneuver he toppled me onto the bunk previously made up by the car porter. The swiftness of his attack shocked me from my head to my high-heeled pumps, one of which fell off. His breath was heavy with a sickly aroma of whiskey, and with his free hand he was fumbling at his clothing.

Good God! I thought. I'm going to be raped!

33

Shirley: What's a lawyer?
John Boles: Well, a lawyer is a person who gets
              you out of trouble.
Shirley: Oh, my! I could use one almost every
              day!

              —From *Curly Top*, 1935

Immediately following my arrival at the Mapes Hotel in Reno, I telephoned my Los Angeles agent at MCA.

"Trouble," I recounted. "Call him off or I quit the picture."

Within the hour Wizard knocked, bearing a bouquet of long-stemmed roses and shouldering in without being asked. I wanted to be done with the encounter before it started, but he quickly seated himself and observed how tense I looked, probably true under the circumstances.

"Look, I'm going to be a big executive," he said. "We're going to have to get along." He held up both palms in a gesture of inevitability. "What I had in mind was just a workplace informality."

"It may be in your contract, but not mine."

"Sex is like a glass of water," he went on, using the clinical tones of a doctor diagnosing an affliction. "You get thirsty, you drink. You want sex, you have it."

Trying to lighten the conversation, I observed that eight glasses of water a day were healthy, but that his concept sounded excessive.

"Sex before a close-up makes the eyes ... luminous," he continued, the first and last words rolling over his tongue.

Sure that under such circumstances my eyes would be heavy-lidded and lackluster, I told him so. "Look, for seventeen years in movies, I've never needed that formula," I said firmly. "I'm not starting now."

The Wizard only smiled benignly. In a final remark thrown over his shoulder he said to think it over carefully, after we all returned to Los Angeles.

☆

By Thanksgiving our film company had been reestablished on the home lot. A star's dressing room had been prepared for me, complete with nook refrigerator, fresh flowers, a newly installed bathtub, and a long, comfortable couch. Wizard's other shoe was not long in dropping.

My old friend the hairdresser was repairing me at the end of a long day when he entered, unannounced. Accompanying him came a uniformed waiter bearing a tray of champagne and two glasses. The waiter was an old man I vaguely remembered as bringing food trays to the cottage years before. As he placed my glass on the dressing table, our eyes met, reflected in the mirror. A surge of shame crept over me that his image of me must be shattered by the compromising scene around us.

"I'm going to be someone very big at this studio," the Wizard repeated, raising his glass. "I'll make you a big star!"

Choking softly on the first sip, I whispered to my friend, "Don't leave." Savvy and loyal, she kept snipping, combing, and rebrushing my hair.

Pouring himself another glass, the Wizard paced and ostentatiously glanced at his wristwatch.

"A little more bleach there, maybe?" I suggested. Bit by bit my hair was growing lighter and lighter. "Right here too. Just a little."

The Wizard had begun to chronicle the kind of roles which would guarantee my star-sparkling future.

"I've got to go home and cook my husband's dinner," my friend whispered.

"Not on your life," I hissed. She knew I meant it.

Film and Wizard wound up together. On our final shooting day Jack had returned from location and together we went to dinner at Wizard's home. Ostensibly the purpose was to meet his wife, who turned out to be a lovely lady, cultured and intelligent. After dinner, as we prepared to depart, I went upstairs alone to retrieve my coat from his wife's bedroom. The Wizard followed, stepping softly. Just as I was lifting my wrap from her bed, he suddenly seized me from behind. With a quick twist, he spun me around and backwards on top of the piled fur coats.

For a second time I found myself an unwilling entry in a wrestling match. Exasperating and abusive though it was to me, his actions disgraced his charming wife, only steps away with her guests, and was a gross effrontery to my husband. Yelling "Murder!" would have only further inflamed a dangerous situation. Pushing up on his chin with both hands, I flexed a knee and struck with all my might, a blow which proved that microsecond lust can be switched off as quickly as on. Smilingly shaking hands good-bye at the front door, the Wizard might just as well have drunk one of his metaphoric glasses of water.

Despite its brutish character, and perhaps because Jack and I were growing increasingly less candid with each other, I kept what had happened to myself. The film was finished and it was Christmastime. So far as I was concerned, the Wizard had simply melted away in the heat of his own ardor.

However, for me the Hollywood chase scene had not ended. As I was gathering up my things to leave Fox, George Jessel came hustling into my dressing room. Riding high from his mammoth musical success, *Bandwagon*, he was casting his next film, *Dolly Sisters*. He asked that I come to his office to discuss a key role in his film. It was early evening and the second floor of the administration building was deserted. Jessel answered my knock and escorted me into an inner office, rattling on with nonstop innocuous chitchat.

"I've been looking at the *Mr. Belvedere* rushes," he said tonelessly. "You're very good. What I want to talk about is starring you in my next film."

We were standing a pace apart, eyeball to eyeball. In one swift movement he opened his trousers and, with a sudden reach, encircled me with one arm, his face, droopy and baggy-eyed, looming directly into mine. I could feel his other hand groping to lift my skirt. Hard on the heels of the Wizard, this new assault seemed unreal, but little could I do but thrust my right knee upward into his groin. A blow enthusiastically pointed for his chin, it effectively knocked us apart. Pain, disgust, and hate flickered across his face, but I felt no mercy. More and more the adult movie business seemed populated with a bunch of copulating tomcats.

A few days prior to Christmas, Selznick requested I come to his office at ten o'clock the next Sunday morning.

"I'm thinking of making *Little Women*," he said, a comment delivered without humor.

I thought he referred to the Louisa May Alcott book, and indeed he did have a very rough script. Midway in my reading, however, he raised his hand to stop me and abruptly veered off into another subject.

"Rumors," he said, sighing. "Public love can turn to public hate overnight. Just spatter on your image, you'll see. A terrible backlash." He crumpled a scrap of paper and dropped it to the floor. "It would be curtains," he said, flicking the corners of his mouth dry with both fingertips.

Coming around to my side of the desk, he continued in a less accusatory tone. "Of course you have to be smart about it." He reached and took my hand in his. Glancing down, I saw the telltale stocking feet.

Pulling free, I turned for the door, but even more quickly he reached back over the edge of his desk and flicked a switch I had learned from Colby was a remote door-locking device. I was trapped.

Like the cartoon of wolf and piglet, once again we circled and reversed directions around his furniture. Blessed with the agility of a young dancer and confronted by an amorous but overweight producer, I had little difficulty avoiding his passionate clumsiness.

"It's just the grease that oils Hollywood's wheels," he laughed, feinting ineffectively. "Makes them run smoothly."

"Not grease," I answered, grasping for a metaphor. "Acid."

In contrast to my encounters with the Wizard and Jessel, banter was more effective with Selznick than a knee. In this case humor eventually cooled his hot pursuit.

Raising both hands in mock surrender, he told me to take the script home, return the next day and let him know what I thought of it.

Determined to avoid a more resolute confrontation with my boss, I arrived tugged by my three leashed dogs: Duke, a fawn-colored Great Dane; Chris, the barrel-chested boxer; and Lanny, a shifty-eyed collie. All muscle and eagerness, they plunged up toward Selznick's desk, gagging and snorting.

Knowing him to be partial only to toy poodles, I was not surprised to see him bug-eyed with dismay. "Okay," he laughed, moving behind his chair out of range, "I'm not going to bother you."

That trip was the first useful duty any of my dogs had performed. For all the food I had shoved down them, they preferred to nuzzle rather than bite. One night a tramp had sought temporary shelter in our garage, but rather than alert the household, vicious Chris had curled up beside the trespasser, just to keep him warm.

Realizing the dogs were a genuine concern to Selznick, however, I commanded, "Down, down!" Chris sank to his haunches stiff-legged, but continued to stare belligerently at Selznick.

"Sit, sit," I repeated, until the collie obediently curled up at my feet and tucked his pointed nose under his furry rear haunches. Duke remained standing, his long, hairless tail pounding a friendly tattoo on a nearby chair arm.

Overnight I had read the entire *Little Women* script and was enthusiastic about the part of Jo. Selznick said he intended to go ahead, and we agreed the role was mine. The conference concluded. I started to rise, but he patted the air, indicating I should remain seated.

As we had spoken the only other sound was from Duke, his lustrous, long form unmoving by my chair, pinkish tongue lolling out the side of his gaped jaws, whimpering in excitement.

Selznick had switched subjects. After this film, he said, forget America. What my career needed was Italy. "They are on a naturalistic kick, the Anna Magnani thing. Be a femme fatale." He shot me a sidelong glance. "Some people think you are anyway."

I was beginning to feel like travel-stained luggage that had never actually gone anywhere.

From a moviemaking perspective he may have had a point. Playing a film vamp, a sex symbol in an Italian vineyard, just might have commercial possibilities. What his suggestion really tested was the strength of my desire to, first, change my image, and, second, to commit to an endless career making movies. I remembered the Italian option for months, my artistic heart hankering after something my head knew could not be. In the end Selznick was the one who took his own advice.

☆

Next door, Mother had hardly remained unaware that tugs in different professional directions now placed new and threatening strains on my marriage. Helpless to influence the tide of events, but stubbornly the optimist, she registered her thoughts in her diary on Christmas Day 1948.

Tomorrow will be better. When you think you are at the end of your rope, tie a knot and hang on. Tomorrow will be better.

Both of us knew full well that the past year had been one of sharp change and severe stress. Perhaps as a self-cleansing mechanism, I wrote her a letter, coincidentally dated the same as her diary note.

Dearest Mom, I know I haven't been too great a daughter this year, but I've tried my best. I've made many mistakes, and your advice to me has always been right, but I just have to learn the hard way. I do feel that I've advanced myself in certain lines, and, as you know, I'm completely wrapped up in my work. . . .

If I've hurt you, I'm truly sorry, for no girl has ever had a more wonderful, understanding mom. But please remember that the things that you've taught me have stuck, and I'm not going to do anything foolish. I love you and Susan more than anyone else in the world, so, Merry Christmas from your daughter, who is just beginning to realize how perfect you've always been, and are, and will be, in my life.

All my memories of 1948 were not rollicking. Misjudgments had been racked up, and several times I had been seared. However, if the sky was not crystal clear overhead, passing clouds seemed no more dense than before. I failed to see that the heavens were actually black with chickens coming home to roost.

☆

As the New Year rang in the Hollywood Women's Press Club nominated me, after Rita Hayworth, the second least cooperative star in the industry. The vote came to me as a thunderbolt. My lifelong conviction held that a critical aspect of professionalism was popularity, including popularity with the working press, upon whose opinion the public relied. Mother recommended I apologize. Father said I was in enough hot water with gossip already; leave it alone. Their friendly publicist, Joe Reddy, also urged I do nothing. How one can waste big gobs of time asking everyone for opinions on what to do! Someone shouts from the sidelines, you turn to listen, and the whole game gets away from you. Ignore it, laugh and look the other way was certainly one option. But bearding the press in its own lair was more straightforward to my way of thinking. The nomination stuck in my throat like a bone.

At my request, on January 5, 1949, I met with the entire club. The reception was sincerely unfriendly. Epithets like "stinker" and "always totally unavailable" were delivered, albeit with a smile. One writer claimed to have tried unsuccessfully for an interview for three years. Only columnist Hedda Hopper rose to shift the blame, saying officious underlings of the Selznick studio had rejected press inquiries without consulting me. In rebuttal another woman snarled things would never change; I was simply terrified to speak candidly with the press.

"How about now, this afternoon?" I called back from the podium.

Far too late to rescind my award, the group apologized as individuals, and lined up to schedule exclusives. Far from an egotistic exercise, my appearance recognized the pervasive power that the Women's Press Club exercises, its opinion echoing in unexpected Hollywood crannies, as I soon found.

Several weeks later Jack and I had attended an evening party at Errol Flynn's secluded estate, two in an uncongenial but glittering guest list. Diversions included a racecourse for white mice, complete with croupiers and pari-mutuel betting, and in midevening a tiny crisis when a *Look* magazine reporter covering the party allegedly stole a loaded pistol from Flynn's desk. Apprehended by other guests in mid-theft, he denied guilt by producing his own gun and asking rhetorically why would he want another.

Spurred by diffidence, boredom, or perhaps a desire to be clean, at midnight Flynn had retreated to his walk-in steam bath. There, clad loosely in a towel, he held court, waving a hazy welcome or adieu to those seeking their host. As Jack and I were departing, I opened the door a crack to say good-bye.

"Come on in, Shirley." He gestured to the plank bench at his side, "Just you."

Although Flynn's reputation was of never having spoken to a woman he didn't wish to seduce, I declined for even more practical reasons. "Steam gets my hair frizzy. Just wanted to say good night."

Through the haze I could see his inviting expression turn scornful.

"So that's why the press voted you most uncooperative, eh? Good-bye, kid!" he said, and waved me away with a sweeping gesture.

Hard on the heels of my misunderstanding with the local women's press, the Harvard University *Lampoon* listed *Adventure in Baltimore* among the ten worst movies of 1948, singling me out as the "worst all-time hoyden, with the most nauseating screen voice." Apparently the eggshells had not worked wonders at Harvard. Critics are different from the reporting press. If you believe critics when they call you tops, then they must be believed when they call you rotten. Over many years I had found it more satisfying to ignore movie reviews, so the *Lampoon* left me unmoved.

Not so gossip columnists, who deal on a far more dangerous level than either reporters or critics.

Their realm was rumor and inference. It was wise to pay attention. Helen Gould suggested it was "time Shirley took a close look at the tragic case of Judy Garland," implying booze, pills, and nervous break-downs. Regarding it a cruel cut, Joe Reddy concocted a press release to emphasize my moral rectitude by criticizing two currently well-established sex symbols, Yvonne de Carlo and Peggy Castle. Both were vociferous proponents of cheesecake photos.

"Between leg art and acting," Reddy quoted me, without asking, "I take acting."

Both women promptly blasted me as a prissy nincompoop. "Girls who won't pose for cheesecake won't be eating it, either," Castle quipped.

By the start of 1948 a snowfall of breakup speculations had started appearing in the press, interleaved with photos taken in better times but now bearing wild-whisper captions. Columnists probed and peered, searching for significance in each eyelash flicker. Jimmy Fidler cited an unnamed "swelling list of details." Edith Gwynne lyrically referred to "sounds of distress . . . their marriage bark is foundering." More straight-forward than most, Sheilah Graham dryly observed, "After three years, it's time for divorce." Reading this sort of gossip, each time I used to die a little.

Politics and acting were a poisonous combination, so went current Hollywood dogma. Support of humanitarian struggle against some disease was safer. A March of Dimes national fund-raiser for the National Foundation for Infantile Paralysis was scheduled to coincide with the inauguration of President-elect Harry S. Truman on January 20, 1949. As centerpiece in a national radio hookup from the White House his daughter, Margaret, was urging support, flanked by North Carolina democrat Betty Smith, author of *A Tree Grows in Brooklyn*, Republican Senator Margaret Chase Smith from Maine, and Jack and me as the only apolitical luminaries. Assembled in a small east-wing conference room with Missouri relatives descended in a flock from Blair House across the street, we were greeted by Bess Truman. Explaining she was saving herself for more important receiving lines yet ahead, she shook hands with her left one. The radio announcer identified us all as Truman's family and closest supporters, to which we all responded with an obligatory cheer.

Now established as family guests of the incoming President, we applauded warmly each time he lashed out at Communists during his inaugural address and yelled approval at each scornful, bellicose phrase. All the face cards of Washington politics seemed to be present. In corners and strung along the Capitol corridors after the ceremony, little clots of distinguished-looking people spoke animatedly among themselves. Their eyes wandered through the passing crowd like wolves inspecting a flock of sheep. All those fixed flashing smiles, darting glances, and hands extended in predatory greeting formed a lasting remembrance of power and ambition in action.

FBI Director Hoover had invited us to view the parade down Pennsylvania Avenue from the vantage of his office window. Well appreciating my delight with police paraphernalia, and adopting his best Santa Claus smile, he opened my purse and dropped in a tear-gas gun disguised as a black fountain pen. Not a toy and not available to the general public, he warned, and cautioned me on its use, his face stern and iron-jawed. Under no circumstances reveal where I had obtained it, and never point it unless ready to fire. It was the first time I had walked around with a loaded gun of any sort, and I relished the feeling.

The official Inaugural Ball was held in the cavernous National Guard Armory. Drafted by the Democratic Host Committee to be an usherette passing out programs, I had a steady exposure to all those self-possessed guests ebbing and flowing in their competition for recognition and access.

No egos were checked at the door, including mine. Along with every other recognizable face, I was trapped into autographing programs. Caught up in the spirit, I decided to get the President's signature. Any autograph hound knows he must provide the pen. Yet the only one I carried in my beaded evening bag was Hoover's disguised weapon. Inevitably, the next fan seeking my autograph lost his pen in exchange. Thus equipped, I approached the presidential box. Several yards short of it, a Secret Service agent stopped me. Taking the real pen from my hand, he tediously disassembled it and peered down the barrel. The more lethal pen remained hidden in the folds of my hankie.

Despite passing the security cordon, I was still unable to directly approach Truman, whose presidential box was slightly elevated above the dance floor. Standing directly below his line of sight, however, I waved my program. Noticing my wigwag, he leaned forward over the railing and cupped his ear to hear me above the din. Learning what I wanted, his face froze.

"You ought to know better than that, Shirley," he called down. With a sour grin, he waved me away and settled back in his chair to speak with someone else. Well, obviously I didn't know any better.

During the March of Dimes program, the Capitol swearing-in, visiting the FBI, and at the Armory, Jack was present. I think. By some trick of imagination he seemed a paper-thin presence. I knew he was there, yet when he spoke it was soundlessly. Although visible to me as he stood smiling and shaking hands with strangers, when I had turned my head he vanished as a presence.

En route home from Washington, the private railcar of Illinois Governor Adlai E. Stevenson was hitched onto our regular train. Learning I was aboard, he dispatched Richard Coleman, an accompanying railroad official, to summon me for a private visit. Greeting me warmly although we had never met, he showed me to a chair. His wife was courteous but cool, watching both of us unsmilingly as the train jounced along. After several moments of inconsequential talk about the Washington ceremonies, he suddenly narrowed his eyes.

"Tell me everything you know about the movie industry, in one minute," he said like a prosecuting attorney.

I sat stupefied, grateful that the porter chose that instant to lean down and softly inquire if I would like something to drink. A Coca-Cola, with bourbon, please. That took ten seconds of my allotted minute; for the rest of my time I repeated what I knew about the dislocations being caused by television. Stevenson didn't want to let his subject go, so for several minutes we carried on. At length his wife interrupted and changed the subject. Stevenson was openly irritated.

"Dear," he said, drawing out the word in a fatigued, patronizing tone, "this is the first time I have met Shirley. I can look at you anytime."

Cruel words, spoken without a smile. Words which made me feel suddenly thrust between warring parties. Words which, by substance and tone, told a tale of a relationship in collapse.

That moment was catalyst to my own midnight thoughts as the train went ticking through its darkness. Beyond doubt, my hope to induce Jack's jealousy and recapture his primary affection had foundered. Rather than savior, perhaps I had been executioner, helping crush our love under the vain pretext of nourishing it.

Our pattern of life had been shattered. My vision of love, home, and hearthstone was unattainable. Lasting personal bonding between us had turned out a remote, romantic fiction. Our baby girl was the sole beautiful legacy from a world changed largely for the worse.

Losing is painful. If at a young age one is really good at something and knows what it is to win, that pride carries over to adulthood. Failure, any failure, becomes a highly unpalatable pill, and harder still to shoulder off on someone else. What had overtaken us was not solely his fault. I shared responsibility, and had contributed to the problems. The damage we had done to ourselves was irreparable. The only common ground remaining between us was square one. Staring upward in the darkness, I could see the faint outline of the streamliner berth where my husband lay softly snoring. It was the end.

Although my decision helped unclench my fists, dissolving marriage would not be quick or easy. Obviously, Jack might object. From a professional view the separation must also be staged so as to preserve what was possible of the public image which had been my livelihood since age three. Far more fragile than mine, his image must also be protected. Seizing and holding the initiative would be the keystone if I were to succeed on both counts. The man in the bunk above must learn of my decision only at a moment of my choosing. The situation screamed for expert help.

Within hours of arrival home I contacted the lawyer who had defended Father and the rogue elephant. Without preliminaries, I confided my plans to Mother and arranged that Father pay a $10,000 advance retainer to Grant Cooper's firm: his task, terminate a marriage that had already ended.

Both parents were stunned by my decision, and horrified by its professional implications, long doggedly clinging to a blind hope that somehow we could salvage ourselves before catastrophe. Cutting them both out of this fraying loop of my life had not been simple. However, I was resolved to wrestle this demon with my own hands. This was a time of final emancipation. Total severance of the umbilicus which had linked my life with theirs, it was to be hoped, would free each of us to move to deeper bases of mutual regard.

Marriage was not my only era of importance drawing to its rocky close. On April 7, 1949, Selznick put his whole movie operation on the block. Two weeks earlier he had consummated a final million-dollar loan-out deal with Warner Bros. that bundled off Gregory Peck, Jennifer Jones, Joseph Cotten, and me for a film called *Pretty Baby*. His Vanguard facilities were to be abandoned, all equipment auctioned, and the flag hauled down from the flagpole.

Selznick's problem was industry-wide. The boom years of traditional Hollywood production were ending. Television was forcing a revolution in entertainment habits. There were now fifty television broadcast stations nationwide, and before year's end 35,000 TV sets were expected in Los Angeles alone. The number of movie theatres had dropped 17 percent since 1941 and attendance was falling dramatically.

Warner Bros. announced in late April that instead of *Pretty Baby* my next film would be *Always Sweethearts*. I winced. Neither title was apt, but either called for an inescapable delay in proceeding directly to divorce. Should Jack elect to contest, trial proceedings would collide with movie work, and my contract brooked no delay, no matter the reason. In order of precedence, filing for divorce must wait.

Always Sweethearts turned out to be a multiple romance involving a horse with its authentic Irish trainer, Barry Fitzgerald, me, speaking in a brogue, and Lon McAllister, current craze of all bobby-soxers. As an ingenue, I was not at my best, again sounding like a Westlake schoolgirl trying to be ladylike. The role was preposterous for someone long married, a mother, and secretly traveling the road to divorce.

Belatedly recognizing the risk in using "sweetheart" as a true-life title, Warner's switched the title to *The Story of Seabiscuit*. Anyone wanting to know all about Seabiscuit the horse could learn a lot. Otherwise, the film was best for a matinee.

Like a mad dog chasing its own tail, I was immediately assigned to do *Kiss for Corliss*, for the second time stalling my still confidential plans. That film was star-crossed from the outset. Independently produced by relative newcomer Colin Miller, it was a wobbly sequel to *Kiss and Tell* but lacked the gifted pen of F. Hugh Herbert, author of the original. Rewritten and repaired, the script turned muddy with shaky witticisms and strained dialogue. Before shooting started a major financial backer reportedly withdrew, carrying the film-company checkbook. Holding the bag was the other major creditor, faithful Dr. Attilio Giannini of the Bank of America, forced to protect his original investment by financing the film to conclusion.

Another ponderous albatross hung draped from Miller's neck was the state of mind of his two principal stars. For different reasons both David Niven and I were impaired. Again miscast as a bobby-soxer bubbling brightly whatever the script inanity, I was required to execute a heroic switch of personality each morning. Responding empathetically, my body held up production three times, once to cope with infected wisdom teeth and twice with suspected attacks of appendicitis, which proved to be only stomachaches.

Niven struggled under a separate burden. Because he had joined the company late and desired to finish early, his scenes were compressed into a rushed, lumpy mass, without continuity. A gray, tense mood settled over the whole production.

"Today we do scene 425," director Richard Wallace would announce.

"Oh, God!" Niven would reply. "I didn't prepare *that* one!"

Everything would grind to a halt except the coffee machine. Niven would retreat somewhere to learn the appropriate lines, invariably reappearing with the triumphant clarion call, "I've got it!" Usually he hadn't. The more he fluffed, the more impatient I became. Working over his shoulder and off-camera, I took to smiling superciliously at the crew as he blew over and again. As he was an experienced actor with brains and wit, Niven's problem was not incompetence. What I neglected to acknowledge with my snide glances was that he detested this job. At MGM his last two films had been catastrophes. Blaming the studio, Niven had sought early release from his contract. Rebuffed, he now may have seen this loan-out as MGM punishment.

My comeuppance came. Lulled into expectancy of yet another Niven failure, I was not alert when he finally *did* get it. The surprise was so complete, it was I who then blew the scene by flubbing *my* lines. Each for our own reason, neither of us could do the film justice. London *Observer* columnist C. A. LeJeune wrapped up things aptly:

> *Sometimes I think David Niven,*
> *Should not take all the parts he's*
> *given.*
> *While of the art of Shirley Temple,*
> *I, for the moment, have had ample.*

Beset by his string of misfortune, Miller simply could not reverse his luck. Later he elected to release *Kiss for Corliss* coincident with my announcement of divorce. Tickets to see a teenager cartwheel happily across the silver screen are not easily sold when in real life daily newspapers trumpet the explosion of her private life.

For these among other reasons producer Miller fled Hollywood for the life of academe, winding up a scholar in Slavic and East European studies at the University of California. Had his intellectual interests extended to superstition, he would have known *Kiss for Corliss* was my thirteenth film since leaving Fox. It was his first movie production. For each of us, it was the last.

On the morning after my September 19 fourth wedding anniversary, at long last I instructed my attorneys to get me out from under a blanket of silence.

The Soviet Union had just exploded their first atomic bomb when I detonated the fuse of my own firecracker. In late afternoon of October 12, 1949, Jack entered the house. A tall, unsmiling stranger was waiting, attorney Cooper's partner, George Stahlman.

"Shirley wants a divorce," he said calmly. "No, she does not wish to discuss it with you."

Like human gestation, that moment had been nine months from conception to fruition. Years later in 1982 Jack commented on his reaction, as quoted by Lester and Irene David in their *The Shirley Temple Story*:

"It hit me right between the eyes. I felt that while there had been problems . . . there weren't any that couldn't be resolved . . . left without seeing Shirley and drove to my mother's house. I told her what was going to happen, and I remember she cried . . . then the roof caved in . . . the newspapers never stopped calling . . . reporters did everything to get me to talk even offering me large sums of money. . . . I was raised to be a gentleman . . . what everybody was demanding of me was certainly not gentlemanly. . . ."

My action stirred consternation in the skeletal remains of the Selznick organization, to which I was nominally still under contract.

"You can't," pled publicist Charlie Pomerantz. "You just got an award as Mother of the Year!"

"It says 'Mother,'" I pointed out, "not 'wife.'"

Both *Story of Seabiscuit* and *Kiss for Corliss* suffered momentary box-office shock, as if I had misled an audience who loved me and I should be punished. Although *Kiss for Corliss* continued to drift sideways, a potboiler to the end, *Seabiscuit* rebounded quickly. Within thirty days it was pulling in the top movie receipts in the entire nation.

After the flurry of publicity began to subside, my cherished dance partner Bill "Bojangles" Robinson came to Los Angeles for a one-night charity performance. Dismissing the significance of my impending decree, he disclosed that he and Fannie had separated some time before, and that he was now happily remarried and had a ten-year-old adopted daughter.

"But she can't dance," he said, cocking his head sideways and flashing that same wide-eyed, toothy smile so indelibly imprinted in childhood memory.

"I'm in hard times now, and gray too." He ruffled one hand over his hair. "But after all, I'm seventy-one."

For a while we sat together, contentedly recalling the happy past we had shared.

"Both of us come a long way since that first staircase dance way back in 1934." He gave a delighted, rolling chuckle. "Still plenty to laugh about."

Within several days, on Thanksgiving, Uncle Billy lay dead. Penniless, the newspapers reported. In an outpouring of affection 30,000 people lined New York City streets as his funeral cortege wound through Harlem, led by a brass band of trumpets, tubas, and trombones, stepping slowly in lockstep. What they played was not a dirge, however, but music Uncle Billy would have wanted, dance music in slow motion. Our entertainment careers were ending just as our duets always had, in good time and in step.

Two weeks later, on December 5, 1949, I climbed the Los Angeles County Courthouse steps, flanked by attorneys Stahlman and Cooper and my friend and witness, Mary Alice Franklin. The divorce action would be uncontested, and in fact everything had been carefully worked out in advance. Sole custody of Susan was mine, along with my restored maiden name. Under California's community property law Jack shared half of my 1945–49 net earnings. Part of this amount he agreed to use to establish a fiduciary trust with Susan as sole beneficiary. Everyone's legal fees and court costs would be paid by Father, who assured me my $75 per week household allowance would continue, no matter if there was one less mouth to feed.

In granting the interlocutory decree, the judge intoned that, "The integrity of the family lies at the very foundation of the welfare, tranquility and good order of our society.... The evidence offered here, the plaintiff's demeanor, and the very evident sincerity with which she testified have convinced the Court that the grounds are serious ... and that the plaintiff has made a very reasonable effort to save her marriage. . . . It is therefore the judgment of this court that an interlocutory decree of divorce be granted. . . ."

"If the Court please," responded Jack's attorney, Clore Warne, "when differences arose, Mr. Agar acted at all times as a gentleman . . . it is in order for me to say on behalf of Mr. Agar that he was, and is, concerned for the welfare of his child, and from here on out, with the welfare of both parties in whatever area their respective lives shall take them."

Speaking in *The Shirley Temple Story*, Jack reflected that he looked back on those years as though it all happened to a stranger, "a kid from Chicago . . . tossed into a lifestyle unlike any I had ever known . . . Shirley was even more than a movie star, she was a national institution . . . I was beyond my depth . . . we had it all, Shirley and I, for a while, the beautiful home, complete with tropical fish, dogs, parakeets, a swimming pool, even an outdoor refrigerator . . . everything except what was needed to make it all work. . . . I didn't have the background, nor the experience, nor the maturity to handle my marriage to her. . . . I was made the heavy in the case. The press, as well as the motion picture industry, aimed a lot of potshots at me. I took the strongest barrage they had and survived. I am at peace with myself. I wish her nothing but the best. The past is past. I do not look over my shoulder often, if at all."

Following my court appearance I revisited the solitude of St. Alban's Church for prayer and contemplation. Seated alone in my customary pew, I stared at the Romanesque blue wall of the sanctuary, letting my eye trail up, where it joined the curve of the roof, then across above the tall narrow side window, then down again toward the altar. Nothing had changed since prior visits, yet everything else about me was new. Far from being an invention of the devil, divorce was rebirth for us both. Four years of uncertainty, turmoil, and vexation had left me emotionally drained, yet somehow strengthened. A dreadful mistake had been expunged, spattering both Jack's and my public image with some churned-up mud. But in the erosion and eventual destruction of our mutual love I knew my character had grown, and I prayed his had as well.

A door opened and closed somewhere, then the uncanny silence descended again. I closed my eyes to give thanks for my baby girl,

Susan, a blessing worth any thousand agonies. How long I prayed I do not recall, but when I raised my head a man dressed in white vestments had entered the church in silence and now stood in the side aisle not far from where I sat.

Catching my eye, he spoke softly across the empty pews between us. "May I help you?"

My heart was still tingling with spiritual gratitude. "Thank you," I replied. "I've already been helped."

34

Dwell in the past, you lose one eye;
Ignore the past, you lose both.
—Russian Proverb

My New Year's resolution in 1950 gave thanks for having had modest good luck juggling motherhood, marital crisis, and movie work. But critical professional decisions still loomed. Warners had announced my next film as *Career Girl*—wishful thinking, I thought. Everything about my career was in flux. My last film had been prickly fare and my performance bland. Selznick had dangled the Italian option. Renewal of his contract in midyear seemed implausible. His Hollywood operation was almost totally collapased, and he himself had departed for Italy. With such eggs still to unscramble, where a more salutary environment than Hawaii, that magical, fragrant refuge from battle, a place to pause and drift while deciding?

At dinner with my parents I announced we would all be celebrating Susan's second birthday on January 30 in Honolulu, and go by air.

Spoons clattered to plates. Mother gasped, "Fly?"

"Why not?" I said. "You get seasick on ships."

Recording her emotions, she later wrote:

". . . I felt as if I were walking to a death cell as I approached that big monster. . . . After we took off . . . interest and pleasure . . . the entire trip . . . not the least bit nervous about landing . . . I couldn't understand myself!"

Mynahs still chattered high in the ancient banyan tree at the Royal Hawaiian Hotel portico. The same gentle air so well remembered from

447

my three prior trips drifted along hotel corridors, open to the sea. Only the people were new, polite but under my circumstances, cloying.

On February 7, 1950, Mother wrote, "... really hectic for us, especially Shirley and the baby.... They couldn't go out of the room without people rushing for their cameras and taking pictures from every angle ... very annoying when you are trying to eat ... everything modern and lavish ... neon lights.... Time marches on."

Within days we had found a two-bedroom rental house. The dormant volcano of Diamond Head separates glitzy Waikiki from quiet residential Kahala, a foreshore reaching eastward several miles between mountains and sea. Its far outer tongue is called Niu, a narrowing strip dense with coconut palms and facing on a shallow bay.

"One room for you and Susan," said our friend Henry Ah Chan, "and one for your parents. Off the kitchen in the back, a maid's room for the baby's nurse."

Great, I thought. But the beds got reshuffled. Mine would be the maid's room, by any other name a reconstructed broom closet. Airless, furnished only with narrow, rump-sprung cot and rickety, wooden lamp table, the room at least boasted a stall shower and wall-hung utility sink. All mine. Except for unsociable cockroaches that scuttled around in the dark and one tropical spider, long-legged and black, which lived behind the cold-water faucet. When the bedside lamp was on Spider emerged. Tiptoeing across the ceiling he came down the wall behind my bedstead to read over my shoulder. Sharing quarters with Spider was a price willingly paid for privacy. After all he lived there all the time. Hard decisions regarding my career were momentarily deferred. There in my broom closet, I was surely the most contented maid in Hawaii.

Island communities can have a pleasantly incestuous flavor. As friends and business associates gravitate to one another at work and play, their inventory of conversational subjects turns stale. Personal opinions become predictable, and life becomes as comforting as an old shoe. Sea, sky, and cloud-topped mountains blur with familiar faces and tongues in one contagious, lulling monotony. Interruptions to this silky, repetitious rhythm arrive conveniently with each plane- or shipload of visitors. I was one. By the afternoon of Bam Rastatter's reception on February

7, I was concluding eight daytimes of constructive indolence with my baby girl and early evenings with Spider.

Among Bam's arriving guests, I noted one man in particular. Tall, deeply tanned, with a brilliant smile and thick black hair, he introduced himself as Charlie Black. His handshake was firm, and cool.

"You're new here, aren't you?" he asked brightly. His eyes were blue-green, like the sea beyond him. "Somebody's secretary?"

At first I thought he was putting me on, but then I realized this athletic-looking stranger with the clear gaze was sincere. I told him my name, adding my occupation as actress.

"Wouldn't look so stupid if I'd gone to that cocktail party somebody gave in your honor last week," he said, appropriately chagrined, "but the waves were up."

"Up?" I asked.

"The surf," he replied. "The waves were good for surfing."

"Hope it was worth it," I replied. He nodded enthusiastically and we both laughed.

Overhearing us, others began to rib him for not recognizing me on sight. In his defense he said he had never even seen any of my films. That was why I was a stranger.

"Then I don't owe you any money back!" I rejoined. "You probably go for Charlie Chan."

"Nope." He looked thoughtful for a moment. "But when I was twelve, I did fall in love with Lupe Velez, in *Cuban Love Song*."

"One of her many suitors," I replied, a little bitingly. "Didn't you see *any* of my movies? I made them all through the thirties and forties."

Again he shook his head, saying he had been locked up in an eastern boarding school—"You know, the strict kind where professors smack you on the head if you miss a Greek conjugation. Even listening to a radio was grounds to get kicked out of Hotchkiss." That name, of course, rang a bell.

"My first boyfriend's great aunt founded that school," I said, raising a subject he clearly was disinclined to pursue.

"Anyway, that's how I missed you when you were a starlet," he said.

"A *what!*" My eyebrows arched in genuine indignation.

"Well, weren't you a little kid in the thirties?" He looked defensive. "Isn't the diminutive of star 'starlet'?"

A thimble could hold what this man knew of my business. In Hollywood's professional pecking order for actresses, stars reign majestically on top of the heap. Way down there at the bottom scuttle legions of luscious starlets, all hopeful, some with round heels or empty heads. To call a star a starlet is demeaning. Perhaps he could be excused. His ignorance was certainly sincere.

Actually it was a novelty to encounter someone with no preconception of what I looked like. More often I met the fawning type, those who recite plots or drool over my performance. In contrast, here stood an undeniably intelligent man unable to recognize my face and totally ignorant of films produced over two decades of stardom. To cap things off, he offered no apology, as if he valued little of what he had missed.

Turning the tables, I learned he was staff assistant to the president of Hawaiian Pineapple Company and originally from San Francisco, where his parents still lived, and had attended Stanford and Harvard. His older brother, married with a family, also worked in Honolulu. A younger sister, widowed when her submarine husband had been lost in the Pacific, was now remarried to Charlie's first commanding officer in motor torpedo boats during the war.

Before conclusion of the reception he proposed a trip "around the island" the following Saturday. It sounded impersonal, a tour guide offering interesting sights, but gossipy local girls quickly sneered at the idea.

"Whatever you do, don't go around the island with him," one advised. "That's synonymous with having a pass made at you. With him, it's a real waste of time. He already has some hot thing back on Telegraph Hill in San Francisco. Out here, he's never serious. Just surfs."

Neither his sublimations nor surfing were important to me, and certainly romance was not on my mind. It was vacationtime and he seemed lively and interesting. No more, nor less.

Early Saturday morning he appeared at our Niu cottage driving a battered old maroon Dodge with its canvas top folded down. His appearance was no more prepossessing than his car. Barefooted, wearing khaki shorts and a faded green T-shirt letting go at the side seams, he failed to favorably impress my parents. Father employed his thin smile, and Mother a sweet, genuinely apprehensive expression.

Bathed in sunshine, we drove slowly along the cliffs beyond Koko

Head and along a ribbon of lonely road between steep hillsides covered with ochre scrub grass and seaward the surf pounding and creaming against black boulders. Skipping over his failure to see my films during sequestration at boarding school, I inquired why this grievous deprivation had continued *after* graduation.

"By 1937 I was off to China as a merchant seaman," he replied. I had to admit this guy had a knack for getting my attention. How come the wild jump from schoolboy to sailor, I asked?

"I thought I was headed for Stanford, but apparently my educated pretentions didn't sit well with Dad. Now he's a bigshot businessman and a community leader, but before college he was a mule skinner in the high Sierras, six-shooter on his hip to fend off marauding bears and rogue mountaineers. Probably he engineered it, but instead of college I wound up shipped out on a steamer bound for the Orient. By the way, I remember we were tied up across the Aloha pier when you arrived from the Coast in 1937, with all that hoopla."

"My films were very big in China. How come you missed them there too?"

"Sailors ashore don't head for movie houses," he chuckled. "Besides, our ship was bombed when the Japanese invaded Shanghai, so eventually I came home. Already behind my regular college class, I scrambled through four years of Stanford in three, then crammed in a year of graduate work at Harvard before the military draft caught up with me in 1941. All that hurry left no room for movies. Sorry."

Academic credentials and war stories impressed me less than his flashing white teeth and smoothly muscled arms and shoulders. I wasn't going to let him get off so easy.

"So much for my films before Pearl Harbor. Did you know I made thirteen major films *after* 1941?" I asked.

He glanced sideways, uncomprehendingly. "No, I didn't. Running PT boats in wartime in the southwest Pacific and crawling around in the jungles—well, no movies there, that's for sure." He pointed. "There's Makapuu Point up ahead."

A steep arrowhead of land came into view, tipped with a light beacon. As we cut through a shoulder in the headland, a large cove opened up, streaked with ranks of waves racing shoreward and smashing onto the sandy beach in a churning boil.

"Do you bodysurf?" he asked.

I shrugged noncommittally.

At Lanikai we peeked through the ti hedge of our rental cottage occupied ten years earlier. Later we visited with his good friend James Norman Hall, co-author of *Mutiny on the Bounty*, browsed through a vacant ancestral home of the prestigious Cooke family, and foraged in a roadside sugarcane field for a sweet chewy stalk. At a small, lonely beach I splashed hip deep while he porpoised about me in circles. Mostly we talked, about everything.

His hang-ups were easy to spot, chief among which was his job, where he felt underutilized and insufficiently challenged.

"Not fair," I chided. "All you seem to do is work, surf, and seek independence by sidestepping everyone you have most in common with." The day was too lovely to exchange troubles. "Do you like to dance?"

"Sure, but I'm not keen about dancing in a hotel ballroom," he answered.

I thought that one over. Since childhood my dream prince had always been blessed with blue eyes and blond hair, a non-taxing intellect, and was a superb dancer. Except for the eye color, Charlie was far from my ideal. Yet, there were compensations. All his outgoing self-confidence and ebullience did not seem put on. Obviously he was just an independent type, broadly opinionated, stubborn as a boulder, needing little from others to be happy and productive. One refreshing clue to his personality was the absence of name-dropping. Either he knew no one of importance or had no desire to impress me. Not once did his conversation take a ride on anyone's coattails.

Dinner was consistent with the simplicity of the whole day: hamburgers and milk shakes at the local Kau Kau Korner Drive-In. Fourteen hours from our start, he brought me to my darkened kitchen door, brushed my cheek with one darting kiss, and was gone before I could return the gesture. Reviewing things with Spider, we agreed Charlie seemed interesting, perhaps even a scalp worth going after.

☆

The swimming idea was all his. Like a turtle under his shell, he arrived carrying a skiff on his shoulders, and we were off to explore the fringing reef which lies in a shallow pancake a half mile offshore from Kahala

Beach. The swimsuit I donned was an old but seldom-used article of clothing. After he had rowed us out among the coral heads he detected a cavernous hole in the reef which seemed worthy of exploration. Gesturing me to follow, he slipped overboard like an eel, leaving me alone in the gently rocking rowboat. Holding white-knuckled to the gunwale, I peered down into the vague shapes and shadows below. This was the realm of razor-edged coral, things hiding in rocky crevices with long feelers and eyes like marbles. Eels would be panting open-mouthed for a white foot to arc past their hiding holes. Down there existed a slow-motion world of slippery, squishy things with claws, sharp spines, and poisonous tentacles. Swimming on top, let alone undersea, was just not my stuff. The motions were familiar, and I could swim as long as I could hold my breath. The system worked fine, up to a point; then a handhold on something solid was useful while I got my next breath.

Charlie may have misread as flirtation my iron-willed decision to slide over the rail and follow his watery lead. To clutch repeatedly at him while I switched breaths might have added to his confusion. Romance was really not my purpose in swimming. Flailing around in that hole in the reef was just another challenge to respond to. Far better to take my chances and sink than shrink for lack of courage.

Unseen back on the beach, Father had stealthily trailed in our sandy footprints. Disguised under the heavy noonday shadow of a coco palm, he now secretly watched our every move through eight-power binoculars. Seeing me slither out of the rowboat, only he could have been more surprised than was I.

Mutual inspection takes time but Charlie and I lost little. Each workday at sunset the venerable, prewar roadster turned into our driveway. Following routine pleasantries and an inconclusive bounce on his knee for Susan, who regarded him warily and without affection, we would drive off into the gathering evening. Our second weekend began earlier, and ended later.

How my parents assessed this sudden preoccupation gave me little concern. Although Mother kept up gentle conversational probing and I assumed Father still prowled out of sight, listening around corners and peering into lighted windows, each of us knew that romantic decisions, fair or foul, were mine alone.

Providing an assessment, Mother wrote brother Jack, "Shirley is trying to persuade Dad to stay another week. Three guesses who will win. . . . You see, she has met a very handsome young man. . . . It seemed to be love at first sight. . . . He has never married . . . according to his story, he has been in love only once before. . . . Don't say anything about this to anyone yet. Of course, when she returns home, this romance may wane. . . ."

What our relationship lacked in duration was being made up in intensity, but to be reported in love less than sixty days after receiving my decree of interlocutory divorce presented a double threat: the unpredictable public-audience attitude toward such precipitous behavior, and the risk of somehow being judged an unfit mother and thereby losing sole custody of Linda Susan.

Buck Buchwach, an industrious *Honolulu Advertiser* reporter, was a constant reminder of the first risk, pursuing us goodnaturedly, tailing our car and eavesdropping behind potted palms in search of his scoop. Leaving few trails and casting a pall of secrecy over our activities dovetailed with Charlie's instincts and suited my purposes. Best of all, by concentrating on privacy we lost little time learning about each other.

One evening he asked if I would like to *read* instead of talk. From a battered steamer trunk he exhumed a half dozen misshapen pocket-sized notebooks with faded and worn canvas covers. "Here's what happened, things I've thought, sort of journals," he said. He handed me the stack and gave a little chuckle. "Skip the parts about women." Fat chance.

That night in my broom-closet bedroom Spider and I began to read. The pages were thumb-stained, soiled with coffee-cup stencils, and when turned gave off a musty aroma of age and the tropics. In contrast to their graveyard appearance, the books contained vividly written observations, anecdotes, and squibs of purely decorative description. Nothing was chronological except the numbered pages. Little was tactful or discreet, as if never intended to be read. Starting with Ensign Black, naval intelligence officer at the time of Pearl Harbor, the notebooks carried on through four years of combat experience in the motor torpedo boats and as a scout in coastal jungles, winding up with five years as a beginning businessman in California and Hawaii. What emerged was Robin Hood, egalitarian and jolly, along with Huckleberry Finn, insouciant, daring, and self-propelled. It was a nine-year-old personal window on someone growing critically important to me.

"You skip over the military decorations," I asked, returning the books. "You don't say what for."

Shrugging, he went back into the trunk, where almost everything of personal value seemed stored. Rummaging around for a moment, he extracted a squashed leather box, pried open the lid, and held up a medal in the shape of a silver star with a clasp of red-white-and-blue ribbon.

I inspected it carefully. "Gallantry in action, it says. What for?"

"For not getting killed." He laughed. "You want it?"

Dropping it in my handbag, I remarked about my habit of collecting military insignia as trophies. Pocketing his silver star, however, I had an eerie feeling. It was not only me doing the collecting.

The marine aquarium at Waikiki is a small, rectangular citadel crouched alone in a grove of palms separating the roadway from the sea. With darkness it becomes a sanctuary for parked lovers, each auto discreetly spaced beneath a canopy of palm fronds languidly rustling in the breeze creeping down from the mountains. Thirteen years earlier, at the same spot, I had imagined an octopus wanted to kiss me. This time everything was different. Ours was a rushed romance, only twelve days from introduction to betrothal. Alone, we seemed to be going nowhere; so we kissed and agreed to go there together.

To seal the deal we switched rings, his gold signet ring for mine from Westlake. His fitted me like a collar and mine was too tiny for him. It would be our only mismatch in the next thirty-eight years, so far.

Despite the quickening current, recent scars still told me a tale of submerged rocks along any course laid out solely by a heart without a head. This time, I knew, reason and romance must dance hand in hand. There was one last out, something to be done after my return to California. Depending on the outcome, I could either proceed confidently or disentangle myself, however ungracefully. My allies were geography and time.

The day before departure Laurence M. Judd, ex-territorial governor, well informed that I had been witness to several local surgical procedures, invited me to visit the leper colony of Kalaupapa, assuring me unequivocally that the disease had recently been proven noncommunicable. My interest in hospitals was genuine and well known. Touring orthopedic wards as a child of five, I had recognized that my job was to spread good cheer in any circumstance, just as I had on film. Surrounded by crutches, leather harnesses, and steel braces, I would chat in reflective mirrors with children who could only look upward, feed those with paralyzed arms, and perform tap dances, always acutely self-conscious of my comparative mobility.

During wartime my motivations had shifted. By walking military wards I enlisted in the battle, the only way available to me. Following Hawaii in 1950, I would volunteer at Children's Hospital in Los Angeles. Armed with an *American Pocket Medical Dictionary* and utilizing my only therapeutic skill, a knowledge of phonetics, I would help in speech rehabilitation for young patients with cerebral palsy.

Small wonder I accepted Judd's invitation. Except for me, it was also no surprise that my visit plunged me headlong into a local political controversy hinging on whether or not leprosy was really communicable. Judd and others wished to move the colony from its uneconomic location to lower-cost facilities in Honolulu and were attempting to quiet public apprehension by asserting the disease could not be transmitted. Many experts fervently disagreed. Congress had dispatched a delegation to resolve the matter, which apparently had resolved nothing. Press coverage of my daring presence at Kalaupapa was greeted by cheers from one side and sneers from the other, with the ravaged patients I visited somehow ignored in the middle.

Kalaupapa merits more than a solemn memory. Seesawed between religious fervor, medical mystery, and public contention, Hawaii's lepers were a heartrending symbol of the mystique and frustration surrounding a plague whose cause was poorly understood and cure unknown. From tramping hospital wards, I well understood wartime combat injury and peacetime trauma from fistfights and falling off ladders. Leprosy was something else entirely, and Kalaupapa helped drive into my subconscious the specter of international suffering without hope. There it would lie dormant under layers of more immediate concerns, only to erupt three years later in a highly personal context.

Put mildly, six Hawaiian weeks had upended my personal life. Sporting a broad-brimmed coco-frond hat at the airport, I waved farewell to 1,000 autograph seekers, turned a demure cheek for Charlie's kiss, and slumped into my plane seat, crying. A man seated ahead turned, stared, and commented, "My God. I've never seen anyone so sad about a vacation!"

Lined up at the chain-link fence beside the runway Charlie stood with Buck, the peripatetic newspaper reporter, and surfing pal Al Long.

"What did you do this morning, Charlie?" Buck asked casually as they watched the plane roar down the runway.

"Got up."

"That was some polite peck you gave Shirley," Buck said.

"She's up over Diamond Head already," reported Al.

"More significant," said Buck, "you kissed her mother." If only he had known, Charlie had presented Susan a tiny finger ring.

"There she goes," said Al. Our plane turned eastward. "Now she's gone. Well, looks like you're going to be a lonely kid, pal." He slapped Charlie on the shoulder. "At least, we get you back up on the surfboard!"

35

What now needed doing was obvious as daylight. After unpacking from the tumultuous 1950 vacation, I penned a breezy letter to Charlie Black in Hawaii.

... a real-life drama. Does love live in a pineapple? Tune in next week, find out. Did Mr. Black escape from his sinister company superior? Will she write? (Who cares!) Will she find a heart under her pillow? How will she smuggle him away from the L.A. Airport when he arrives? Will they marry? This drama is being brought to you by the Ace Detective Agency, who always get their man. Will she? ... I can't remember ever having been so in love. ...

Buried under all those jaunty words, my mind was marching in lockstep with my heart. Two thousand ocean miles separating us was a geographic moat, with time on my side. My second action was to place a call to the FBI.

Fifteen years earlier J. Edgar Hoover had winked to begin a long sub-rosa bureaucratic policy of kindness to my family. To vet a prospective husband for a longtime friend was hardly in the FBI charter, but I felt no impropriety to ask, nor did they to listen.

Leaving my heart in Honolulu did not yet keep my feet anchored at hearthside in Los Angeles nor eliminate my teasing, as I shared in a letter to Charlie:

... Friends took me to dine at a place called Tahiti. One of the native musicians there said he knew of some band of Tahitian musicians in Hawaii ... Charlie Black? Sure, he recalled, but not in the islands, in San Francisco. What does he do for a living, I asked? A guitar player by profession, he replied. And sings, too. But he just goes from one bar to another. Never amount to anything.

Charlie's letter had crossed mine in mid-ocean.

... Rusty nails reach out to snag me. Is her heart on the rebound? Am I a symbol of her desire, not the essence? Should I sit on the fence and yell my pleasure at my nosy Japanese neighbors, or just keep moaning at the empty mailbox? Unanswered questions flip over and over like flapjacks. Last night I stalked my room, read half a page, played half a record, drowsed for half a minute ... suddenly remembered the sleeping pill you left me. ...

Brought up within sight of Mother's stunning lineup of prescription drugs, I had no aversion to taking medicine when needed. At an opposite pole, Charlie pushed self-reliance to what seemed to me illogical extremes. If he needed anything beyond half an aspirin tablet, it was a humiliation to the self-healing properties of his body. Apparently he felt in dire straits.

I popped the pill and stretched out expectantly. ... Meanwhile a gusty wind arose, sucking and slamming at my shower door ... I staggered up in the darkness and crashed headlong into the wall ... veered right, groped for the familiar kitchen ledge, and fell sideways into the iron stove. On all fours by now ... blood running down my forehead ... struggling erect again, I careened past the bathroom and plunged headlong through the opened shower door. Bleeding and bruised, half-witted in the grip of your pill, I finally staggered back toward the bed. ... Someone lay there. It was *you*, your skin filmy-white where the suntan stops, arms outflung, your face like an indistinct Valentine on my pillow. I expected to smell perfume, but could only taste blood. ...

While the FBI snooped around Telegraph Hill in San Francisco, a neighbor and former Westlake schoolmate had returned from Honolulu with disquieting news. Grown into a gangly but sensuous woman, she reported a bathing-suited encounter with Charlie on Waikiki Beach. Employing suggestive behavior and her considerable good looks, she had frankly tried to involve him in an indiscretion which she could then report as disloyal to me.

"What happened?" she asked rhetorically. "Nothing!" Before I could express relief, she added with a smile, "You know why? Because he doesn't like girls!"

Several days later a local FBI agent telephoned and asked to see me. Chewing on my lip and waiting, I silently cursed my old schoolmate's evil tidings. All needlessly. Smart, clean as a hound's tooth, patriotic, reported the FBI agent. From a fine family, highly regarded by everyone around. Regular American applesauce, joked the agent, reviewing his written notes. Maybe a little spicy but applesauce still. Leaping to my feet, I kissed his cheek. He looked pleased but perplexed. Maybe FBI agents don't often get kissed for helping a friend.

Were anyone more deadly cautious about Charlie than I, it would have been Mother. In early April 1950 she wrote me another of her notes posted from next door:

Shirley, Darling,

I am writing this because I know you are sick and tired of hearing me lecture, and believe me, this is the last word from me on the subject.

Shirley, you have been the most wonderful daughter anyone in the world could ever hope to have. You have carried me to the greatest heights of happiness, to the very bursting point. I have been so proud and have loved you so, it has hurt. All in all for the past twenty-one years you have been my very life.

Since your marriage, I have tried to be understanding, to just help you if I were needed. I think you will agree with me on this.

Through happenings during this unfortunate marriage, you have sent me down into the deepest depths of despair. You have been in those depths yourself. We have all been crucified.

Now everything looks much brighter. Great happiness is in store for you, and I hope for your father and I, too. I have just one plea to make. For God's sake, make no more mistakes or indiscretions or all will be lost. You have really been very lucky, but don't push this luck too far. Time will seem to drag, but it will actually be moving very fast.

That is all I have to say, Shirley. I hope you will understand my reason for writing. Maybe in some little way you can reassure me.

Lovingly,
Mother

Going next door, I gave her a hug. Trust me, I urged. She burst into tears, not exactly an expression of confidence, so I hugged her again and we both cried. Nobody seemed sure how this romance would work out—except me.

Although my heart was firmly on course, my mind was far from settled when it finally returned to wrestle the basic question of whether I would continue in films. Staying with movie work was given a sparkling lift by longtime friend Taft Schreiber, then a senior MCA executive. On March 23, 1950, I recounted the luncheon conversation in a letter to Charlie:

Warner Brothers wants me to sign a seven-year contract at $3,000 per week with no options, to make two pictures a year. Whew! . . . Another offer from Paramount, now just listen to this! A ten-year contract at $3,000 per week and only one picture yearly. . . . I choked on my coffee, affecting a bored look, and said, "But I'm planning to retire the end of this year." He returned my glassy-eyed stare, then choked on *his* coffee!

From seven years ago when he was acting as my agent, he treated me like a little sister . . . long talks when I decided to sign with Selznick . . . warned me about him, not as a producer but as a man. Also warned me about Agar, begged me to go to college instead. After I married, he tried unsuccessfully to dissuade Agar from going into acting. Deaf ears all around.

After my divorce filing, he urged me never to marry an actor again, nor *anyone* connected with the business (my sentiments since age six). . . .

While Schreiber dangled his bait, down the corporate MCA ladder my personal agent, George Chasen, was anything but sanguine. Nothing of current interest, he said, adding quickly that of course MCA wished to renew my exclusive representation with them for another three years. It would have been tactless to mention the earlier proposals from his boss, Schreiber. Everyone was playing games, and so could I. When I again dropped the word "retire," it was as if I had suddenly laid a dead rat on the table.

"You can't do that," Chasen spluttered. "You owe your life to Hollywood and the public. You're an institution!"

"How I detest that concept," I wrote Charlie. "Makes me feel like an insane asylum or a marble building."

As we had planned, in early summer Charlie resigned his job and left for California. Before meeting his plane, I had one commitment to fulfill, scattering some burial ashes. My courtroom character witness, Missy Franklin, and her husband were under a friend's deathbed instruction to cast his cremated remains into the ocean from a promontory near Point Dume, near Malibu. Drafted to hold the box of ashes during last rites, I stood solemnly at the cliff edge. A fresh onshore sea breeze went streaming upward past our ears and far below the surf came boiling in among the rocks. As the eulogy ended I loosened the box lid and flung the whole thing seaward. For an instant it seemed to tumble slowly downward in midair, disgorging its contents in a smoky cloud of sandy particles, instantly blown back up the cliff face, stinging my cheeks, mixing in my wind-tossed hair, and sifting down my V-necked blouse. Poor fellow. He deserved better.

Fluffing him out of my hair and wriggling him free of my underclothes, I went off to collect my live man. Perhaps I still visualized the partially empty cremation box wedged in a rocky crease halfway to the sea, or perhaps I was in love. In any event, upon leaving the airport with Charlie, my sense of direction vanished. I turned south toward Mexico instead of north toward home. Twenty miles later I executed an abrupt U-turn. Never mind, I assured him, just wanted to lose anyone tailing us. The excuse was lame, but fitted in neatly with the program of secrecy commenced in Honolulu. It also presaged eight months of furtiveness in a game where the only ones fooled were ourselves.

Mutual yen for privacy had a practical edge. Under California law governing interlocutory divorce, the custody of a minor child can be upset during the year-long waiting period before final decree if the custodian is seen as an "unfit mother." Plunging into fresh romance as the ink was drying on my temporary decree did not necessarily render me "unfit," but the whole question was a legal pitfall better skirted. Keeping our romance out of sight minimized the chance that my multicolored balloon of happiness might pop.

For this good reason I insisted that Mother invite Charlie to be her long-term houseguest. My brothers' room was unoccupied, except for some abandoned clothing, a pair of barbells, and one warped tennis racket. Having quit his job for love, and faced with an eight-month wait to marry a woman who had not finally made up her mind about her career, Charlie found a temporary job as a sales executive with a television station. Thus, cloistered during off-hours behind high stone walls and wrought-iron gates, our extended family settled back into pedestrian routines, sober, quiet, and uneventful.

Bachelors, even those who skulk around, can underestimate how watchful a household can be. Hungry for a snack one night and naked as a jaybird, Charlie went sneaking down the darkened back staircase to raid the family refrigerator. Mother's housekeeper was curious as a cat and an insomniac. Detecting a creaking footfall on the stair, she rose, slipped into a wrapper, and tiptoed silently across the kitchen to the bottom of the stairs. Suddenly she flicked on the light switch. Her horrified scream was a sentinel cry that tumbled Mother and Father from bed and sent them racing headlong to the top of the stairwell, he with revolver in hand. Like a rat trapped among three cats, Charlie calmly pressed himself face-first against the wall, mumbling all he wanted was a glass of milk.

For someone accustomed to anonymity, Charlie was beset from all sides. Very little escaped the peripatetic housekeeper, my watchful mother, or my relentless Peeping Tom of a father. Also, for nocturnal protection from thieves who never came, we had employed a prowling, ham-fisted outdoor watchman. An ex-cowboy, replete with bandy legs, Buffalo Bill handlebar mustache, Colt six-shooter, and towering ten-gallon black hat, he was also armed with a spool of black thread. Like a weaving spider, he rigged his web in gaps between shrubbery, across pathways, and at building corners. Each night our entire property was encased in an unseen cocoon of traps to detect movement.

Charlie's worst problem, however, was my boxer dog, Chris. Like his mistress, the dog immediately adored him. Trotting everywhere at his heel, sprawled at his feet, or patiently drowsing outside the last door he had entered, Chris was an infallible telltale. To locate Charlie, find Chris.

Our total isolation from public view was of course a delusion. To meet Charlie's family in San Francisco, we timed the visit to coincide with what was predestined to be his final Bachelor's Ball. In the gilded elegance of the Palace Hotel we swooped around to a Viennese waltz, he stepped on my toes and ended his front-stage ordeal as soon as he could. Already encountered in Charlie's journals, both his parents seemed old friends at first handshake. Chairman of the board of the giant Pacific Gas and Electric Company, his father looked the role. A square-jawed, friendly man in a conservative, double-breasted dark suit, his every word conveyed the simple wisdom characteristic of self-made men whose original personality survives enormous success.

Although leaving a perfumed note of welcome pinned to my pillow, his mother proved to be the penultimate frontier woman, gracious and jolly, but practical and iron-willed. To media inquiries she was cordial but elusive, saying, "I've met Miss Temple. A nice little girl. No, nothing to it at all!" Writing her daughter, however, the song was different. "Keep these news clippings, Sis. My baby boy still isn't old enough to fool me."

Consistent with her line I, too, joined in the improbable denials. "I like Mr. Black very much. What? It's impossible to be engaged. I'm not yet divorced!"

At home Jack's court-authorized visitations with two-year-old Susan continued to leave me dispirited, and probably him as well. Scowling and undemonstrative, Susan's practice with strangers, she ignored the toys he brought as if booby-trapped, and responded to kindly overtures by burying her head in the folds of my skirt. Buoyed by self-confidence in newfound romance, I was no less forgiving. An indirect birthday remembrance from him, sent perhaps in a spirit of contrition if not reconciliation, was a pair of pearl earrings.

"To Mommie," read the accompanying card. "All my love, Susan."

The time for sentiment between us had long passed. Several times he probed about Hawaii rumors, but graciously accepted my silence. We both knew our life together had ended.

To allay general curiosity about Charlie among my family's oldest friends, we produced him for inspection during our 1950 traditional July the Fourth barbecue around our pool. Ira Thomason, still Father's business partner, was the last to arrive. Descending the serpentine flagstone steps from our main house with that rolling gait common to the overweight, he steered his wife, Ora, with one hand, the other held high in a generalized greeting. Picking her way toward the nearest couch, Ora sank among the cushions and sighed. She always settled quickly and seldom moved more than necessary. With her mouth pursed in a kindly turtle grin, she fluffed and spread her skirt until her shoes disappeared, the picture of a Russian tea cozy.

In contrast, Ira went nodding and bobbing his way among the guests, finally drawing Charlie aside and engaging him in conversation.

"What was that all about?" I later asked.

"Nothing important," Charlie replied. "What went wrong with Stanford football last year. A few jabs about supercilious Harvard graduates. Nothing about Korea." We both found this surprising, as only four days earlier President Truman had sanctioned full use of American military forces to stem the North Korean invasion. Ira was making some sort of assessment, his own way. As our traditional prophet of darkness, he had always viewed things in painful detail, eyes shaded. During those periodic lectures to stem Mother's and my "frivolous" expenditures, I would inspect those grizzled features through his pall of cigarette smoke, watching his lips flick open and closed like a trapdoor, never certain if he was profound or simply sly.

Toward the end of our swimming party, Ira took Father aside and delivered his private verdict. Staring at his two-toned shoes in mock embarrassment, he declared Charlie to be a talentless bum. He gave our romance six months.

Skewering Charlie to my parents seemed a lunacy to me, but I knew it was potentially infectious. Both of them still lingered in Ira's thrall, which made the situation tricky for all. To that instant ours had been a dating game, a couple outwardly in love, but with formal commitment withheld. Only we regarded our marriage a foregone conclusion. So far as my parents could observe, we each were reserving our options. The best antidote to Ira's brand of poison was to formalize our intention before my family.

Once again patronizing my Beverly Hills jeweler friend, Mr. Ruser, I arranged a $3,000 limit to match what I knew to be Charlie's budget for an engagement ring and invited him to come calling with diamonds for Charlie's selection. The process had my ghostly guidance, for a marquise-cut diamond was positioned dead center in the sparkling array laid out on the black velvet.

"Here goes my wartime savings," said Charlie, putting his fingertip over the diamond I already wished.

"For you the setting will be free," Ruser added.

On July 14, 1789, the royal Bastille prison in Paris had fallen to victorious democratic revolutionaries, ushering in irrevocable change. Now, 161 years later, my bastion of final retreat likewise collapsed. In the presence of my parents and whimsically hidden in a cranberry-red water tumbler, his ring symbolized both an end and a beginning.

Where to live and work was already central in our discussion of the future. By 1950 business had become enormously unsettled for the movie industry. Live broadcast television was continuing to siphon off major audiences and entertainment dollars, and between January and June, 600 movie theatres shut their doors. The typically good spring season had turned unusually bad for film production. Performers and producers churned around among themselves trying to adjust to the long shadow of television and changed public habits. Despite this bearish environment, brightly bound movie-script proposals continued arriving at my door. Almost without exception my role was murderess, madwoman, or fallen angel of various hue. Being a youthful divorcée from a mildly messy marriage seemed to have suggested a new image. In years past when undeniably pristine, I had regarded any evil role as a feast. Now, blemished a bit by life, I could hardly pitch those weird scripts aside fast enough.

A more intriguing proposition arrived from Peter Lawrence, Broadway producer of *Peter Pan*. Flying in from New York, he proposed that I replace Jean Arthur in the lead role. She was a brilliant actress, but her emotional seesaws were causing him fits. Noting that the role called for skin-tights and flying around the stage on wires, Mother again revived her haunting refrain of disapproval, emphasizing fatigue in a daily grind, the no-mercy quality of live performance, and, of course, my unsuitable shape. "Peter's supposed to be a kid with skinny legs," she said, unlimbering her traditional big gun.

Long ago having made peace with my body, and sharing neither her fear of performing live nor horror of getting tired, I reread J. M. Barrie's original story. Peter Pan had opted out of the cycle of growing up in favor of perpetual childhood. Fox had concocted just that program for little Shirley. It didn't work then, but this Peter had stopped the clock. I liked the story and the prospect of soaring around on high wires. The big uncertainty was how a Broadway career would mix with what Charlie elected to do, and where.

Neither yes nor no, I told Lawrence; I'll let you know.

My repeated disinterest in proposed film scripts was exhausting my agent's patience. In late summer MCA summoned me and announced they were not renewing the contract appointing them my exclusive theatrical agents. Although having toyed with the idea of my dropping them, just because they had stolen the initiative, I dug in my heels.

"Wait a minute," I objected to the man across the desk, a relative stranger. "Stars drop agents, not vice versa."

"Maybe so," came his icy response. "But this time, we fire you."

"Why?" I yelped.

"Because you're through." His eyes were unwavering, inky black. "Washed up."

I started to cry.

"Here," he said, pushing a Kleenex box across the desktop. "Have one on me."

What rankled me most about that encounter was not being told good-bye or even the fact that I had lost the initiative of decision. It was my emotional weakness in brimming over. Their business position was understandable. For six months I had rejected every suggestion they had made. I would miss the ritual Christmas fruitcakes, nothing more. The opinion that I was finished as a performer and the crude quality of its delivery had cut deeply. Not that I believed it. That anyone could say it, let alone believe it, was what really twisted the knife.

Within hours I was on the phone to producer Lawrence of *Peter Pan*.

"Wonderful," he enthused. "Jean is ill again. We prefer you to her understudy, Betty Fields. When can you fly back?"

Apparently Arthur was aware what Lawrence had in mind regarding a replacement and that I was in her New York audience that night. Her eyes kept sweeping the audience from the stage in a purposeful manner. Midway through the performance she suffered another of her debilitating attacks, was removed by ambulance, and Fields came on to finish.

My phone was jangling as I reentered the hotel room.

"Don't take *Peter Pan* away from me, please!" cried the voice, without introduction.

"Stop. Who is this?" I interjected, guessing full well the identity.

"You know who I am," the voice cried. "I'm Jean. I'm Peter Pan." Then she hung up.

Her dismay saddened me, but did nothing to dampen my interest. But the idea continued to wind up in a tumbled heap when I tried to visualize how to integrate the logistic and romantic implications of Broadway for Susan, Charlie, and me. In the washup, I declined.

☆

By October 1950, Korean War casualties were streaming back to base hospitals just as in World War II. At Travis Air Force Base in the Sacramento River delta the wards so recently vacant were suddenly repopulated. As if in sorrow, unseasonal torrents of rain drenched northern California, drowning farmlands and rural communities in major floods. War wounded and natural disaster were more than adequate reason to revive programs for Hollywood personalities to visit hospitals and stricken areas. I, along with others, volunteered.

The stretch limousine picked up Hearst gossip columnist Louella Parsons last. Preceded by two suitcases and a hatbox for our overnight trip, she entered the car clutching a rosary, Saint Christopher medal, and a full-length black mink coat.

"Do I look all right in my new Don Loper dress?" she asked, twisting heavily in her seat for our inspection. "The news today is that Bette Davis is so happy with Gary Merrill. I know he's eleven years younger and it probably won't last, but who cares? I'm glad Bette is happy now! Are you all ready for Travis Air Base?"

A two-engined C-47 from World War II awaited us, but the scheduled 9:00 a.m. departure was apparently too early for Margaret Whiting and her current consort, Buddy Pepper. The crew captain went off with our two dollars to buy a canasta deck and we all waited and played cards in the ready room.

At last, as we roared off the runway, Louella clasped her religious medals with one hand and her safety belt with the other. "What a headline it would be," she shouted above the takeoff din, "Hearst motion picture editor and former child star die in each other's arms."

It was a macabre speculation.

Approaching Travis, beneath us spread a surrealistic platter of flood waters, unbroken to the horizon except for an occasional lonely barn roof, treetops, or hillock of land poking up from the flat, gray expanse. I pointed out the window and Parsons looked, apparently unimpressed.

"Are you going to marry Black before Christmas?" she asked, leaning close to my ear.

Sensing another "Heavens, no!" coming on, I resisted. "We have no plans," I shouted back. "Look at all that devastation."

"Does Agar visit Susan?"

"Not for the past four months," I replied. "Where are all the people and animals?"

Clearing her throat, she leaned closer. "Then you must be letting Susan call Charles 'Daddy'?"

"Impossible." I shook my head.

Conversation in the uninsulated cabin was difficult, so we continued to exchange sweet glances, eyeball-to-eyeball. She would write whatever her imagination dictated. She knew it, and so did I.

Had not my professional window been creaking closed of its own accord, the U.S. Navy would have smashed it shut. The war in Korea was not going well. Still a lieutenant commander in the U.S. Naval Reserve, Charlie received notice one fall day that he would soon be recalled to active duty. An unwelcome meteorite in the middle of our constellation of unanswered questions, his formal orders were received soon afterward, directing him to report to Washington, D.C. Charlie promptly appealed, citing his four years of prior duty under arduous circumstances. Precisely, came the answer. Your experience, plus your single marital status mean the appeal is denied. Show up within ninety days.

The probability of hostilities winding up soon, with consequent demobilization, kept us from undue concern. General Douglas Mac-Arthur had been rolling the North Korean invaders back, saying "the war is very definitely coming to an end shortly." Confident he would escape call-up, Charlie initiated another ping-pong round of pleas and refusals with the Pentagon. However, on November 24, 1950, the Chinese entered the war, swarming across the Yalu River border and sending our U.S. First Marine Division reeling forty miles backwards. Shortly thereafter the South Korean capital of Seoul fell to the Communists for the second time. On Thanksgiving, Charlie received a registered letter unequivocally ordering him to report for active duty within thirty days. The calendar showed twenty-one days until my final divorce decree was to be granted. Suddenly all else in our lives together was subordinated to twin deadlines—one military and one romantic.

36

St. John's Chapel at Del Monte could have been at home in the pages of *Grimm's Fairy Tales*. Couched in a protective grove of oak and pines a stone's throw from passing highway traffic, it was a diminutive building of granite and redwood shingles laid in flowing patterns remindful of a medieval woodcutter's cottage. Not far from the adobe ranch house Charlie's parents used as a weekend retreat, the chapel would be an exquisite setting for our wedding, an event of monumental importance for us.

The church was approached through a covered gate of ornately carved granite bearing filigreed iron lampstands and surmounted by a crucifix, then a sinuous pathway of stepping-stones worn uneven with age. The structure itself looked more the handiwork of woodland deities than an Episcopal architect. Long pine branches swept down, almost brushing the gabled roof and arched stone entry. The twin doors, ajar as if in exclamatory welcome, were surmounted by a single, large rose window depicting St. John the Eagle. Viewed from the churchyard, the entry gave the impression of a startled Cyclopean deity.

Our irreverent contemplation ended with the appearance of Chaplain Reverend Theodore Bell. A gnomelike, jolly Englishman, craggy-cheeked, with a domed forehead and lightly tousled gray hair, he extended both arms in greeting. Once the purpose of our inquiry was made known, he escorted me from the top of the aisle toward the polished wood altar, pacing slowly in hesitation step, like a father with a bride on his arm. He explained that the chapel dated from 1891, built as an adjunct to the then new Del Monte Hotel.

"Every redwood plank was milled from some tree felled on the spot," he recounted. "A Mr. C. A. Black donated our organ." Eyeing Charlie sideways, he pointed toward the transept. "Your father, perhaps?" Charlie winced, but managed to shake his head.

Paused at the iron chancel railing, we peered respectfully upward where a stained-glass window depicting the Good Samaritan arched behind the altar.

"Spiritual symbol of our little chapel-of-ease," murmured Bell, "a patron to help travelers in need."

"That's us." I laughed.

"My pleasure, indeed," he rejoined. In a courtly mix of business and spirituality, he gestured us both into the sacristy.

The room was tiny, doubling as an office despite its stored chalices, the tall processional cross, eucharistic candlesticks, and chancel lamps.

"Let me fix us some tea." He rummaged around and plugged in a teapot. "Tell me about yourselves. I already sense yours will be a marriage made in heaven." He gave an elfin chuckle.

"Well, it probably makes no difference," I began, "but I've been married once before."

He turned slowly, exposing his lower teeth in a grimace, and audibly sucked in a long breath. "Oh, but that does make a difference, don't you know." He looked truly crestfallen. "I can't perform the ceremony, then."

Charlie and I exchanged morose stares. The sacristy was silent except for the soft gurgling of tea water. Through the small-paned window a lacework of tree branches made inky silhouettes against the late afternoon sky. Clicking on his desk lamp, Bell seated himself facing us, shook his head slowly, and sighed.

"I am truly sorry." He poured the tea. "Do you take sugar? It's obvious you are very much in love." His smile was a benefaction, the kind older men reserve for a mother holding her baby.

"At least I can give you some counsel." Reaching back, he selected a small book which he laid open on the desk before him.

"This is what it would be like if I could," he said, adjusting a pair of rimless spectacles on his nose, "which of course I can't."

Clearing his throat, he began to read aloud, "Dearly beloved, we are gathered here together..." Someone out of sight rang a Sanctus bell, testing.

"...do you, Shirley, take Charles..." He paused and looked at me, eyebrows arched inquiringly.

"I do," I replied.

"...do you, Charles..." He peered over his eyeglasses and paused.

"...I now pronounce you man and wife." Charlie and I kissed. He gently closed the book before him.

"That's the way it would be," he said. "I wish I could have." The Reverend Bell retired the next month, his life's work done.

The second time we married was in surroundings equally sylvan. The Black family cottage "Mesita" was a whitewashed hideaway which hugged its solitude at one edge of an open mesa falling steeply on three sides in thickly wooded slopes. Its architecture reflected the historical heritage of Monterey, a blend of Spanish mission fathers' adobe brick and curved red roof tiles with the wooden slat shutters and mullioned windowpanes from New England.

Indoors one found the same happy inheritance. Its single main room was heated by a wood-burning fireplace at one end, and at the other squatted an antique, cast-iron coal-burning stove. Timbered ceilings, polished wooden furniture, and Indian throw rugs on plank flooring pockmarked by boot heels suggested a frontier ranch house of old California.

By day two horses pastured on the mesa under live oaks festooned with Spanish moss. Columns of quail scuttled between thicket and brush pile, and sunshine drenched the brick patio, with its purposefully low-maintenance rows of potted daisies and cactus. A distant cry of a hawk overhead, bubbling coos from doves hidden nearby, or a silky breeze sliding through the pine tops, all were grace notes.

By night wood smoke from Mesita's chimney slowly drifted and disappeared among the trees while the mesa was silently recaptured by brown-tailed deer, raccoon, and opossum. When tide, wind, and surf matched just right, one could hear the rhythmic pulse and thump of waves on distant Monterey beach. Once in a while, feral cats shredded the nighttime peace with snarls and screeching over some territorial sovereignty, or a wood rat creeping under the roof tiles thumped a staccato warning with its tail. Mesita's strength was in its simplicity and its concealment, a harmonious place of restoration for the soul amid diurnal songs of nature, beast, and man.

My last night unmarried was spent in a lower bunk bed in a tiny, spartan room painted turkey-red. A romantic ladder of moonlight came through the tipped wooden blinds beside my headboard. Flickering distant memories of another marriage passed behind my closed eyes, the looming stone church on Wilshire Boulevard in Los Angeles, pounding organ chords reverberating into the trusses high overhead, ranks of benign, smiling faces as the bride and groom walked up the aisle. Crowds outside, seething, shouting, and gesticulating behind the restraining yellow police ropes, a glittering, staged spectacle.

Just when I became aware of a noise outside, I was unsure. It might have been only a breeze drifting dry leaves, I thought, but unlikely on so calm a night. There it was again, a gently placed footfall, a slow scuffling and crackling in the bushes beyond my open window, followed by measured, heavy breathing. My Romeo was not beyond such a romantic gesture.

"It's bad luck to see the bride before the ceremony," I whispered, drawing the blanket up under my chin. There was no answer.

"Lo," I intoned softly, lest Juliet arouse the senior Blacks sleeping beyond the wall, "What manner of man tarries beyond yon window sash?"

A long sigh answered, terminating in a soft snort.

"Blow your nose, Charlie," I cautioned.

A horse's head came thrusting through my window, its nose pushing the slatted shutters aside.

"Criminy," I gasped, wiggling quickly away toward the wall, "and you need a shave too!"

The head swiveled toward me, batting Disneyesque eyelashes, and gave another quiet snort through its rubbery nostrils.

"Out," I hissed, waving both hands in the darkness.

With a last, long look and indifferent sigh, it obliged, and slowly withdrew its head. I could hear it stepping carefully off through the dried oak leaves. It's nice to be loved by a horse, but my next dance was taken.

☆

And so, on the cool gray afternoon of December 16, 1950, Charlie and I were married by a local justice, standing before a fireplace bedecked with pine boughs. No public notices, no church, no organ music, no crowd, no police, and no press. Only a dozen family members and friends.

The single, sentinel light on the verandah of the compact little Cypress Point Club beckoned like a lighthouse. Happy honeymoon castaways, we curved off the lovely 17-Mile Drive, our car's headlights slowly sweeping past rows of densely ranked pine trees, tires crunching over carefully raked gravel into the forecourt.

Before we had stopped a spidery man in a shiny black coat emerged from the shadows, addressing us by a prearranged alias.

"Welcome, Mr. and Mrs. James Fogarty from New York," he recited. "I am Lawrence. We are all alone tonight. Just we three." His mouth was held fixed in a crooked half-smile, shrewd and discreet.

Escorting us up a broad, plank stairway, he recounted how some newsman had telephoned earlier, inquiring if we were expected. "Which you are not," he added, flashing another engaging grin. "Ah! Here's your room."

The twin beds were separated unromantically by a stubby bureau, but a log fire snapped and crackled, a small dinner table was set for two with lacy white linens, wineglasses, and a single candlestick.

Striding across the room, Lawrence unlatched the doors and swung them wide. "Nobody will bother you tonight, except them." He gestured off into the darkness. From a distance we could hear deep-mouthed barking of seals, plainly audible above the nearby sound of waves that broke, slid, and hissed among the boulders in a darkened cove directly beyond our room.

At exactly half-past eight, I proposed a toast. We had been married four hours.

"Most exciting thing that's happened since PT boats," Charlie rejoined.

What a long meal. Bolting the door, we snuffed the candle, banked the fireplace logs, and pushed the two beds together.

Came a loud knocking at the door. "Your night water," called Lawrence.

We listened as his footsteps retreated along the verandah and went ticking down the steps. Through the darkness beyond our balcony came the rhythmic thump and swish of waves in the cove, an occasional distant bellow from a seal readjusting his bed, and hanging over us like a constellation the distant, thrilling roar of the ocean. A moist night wind had risen, whistling softly across the sand dunes, and two owls called back and forth in nearby cypress trees. I heard part of their secret.

Beneath our window the next morning, a dove had wandered erratically across the close-cropped golf green, leaving footprints in dew not yet cleansed by the sun's first low rays. Like an elf, Lawrence magically appeared with newspapers and breakfast trays, which we took to our porch beyond the French doors.

Ironically, the morning *San Francisco Chronicle* front page was dominated by two items: a four-column notice of our marriage and a three-column proclamation by President Truman of a national emergency, citing threatened world conquest by Communist imperialists. One hundred thousand Chinese had again smashed U.S. forces, snatching back our bloody Hungnam beachhead in northeast Korea. Charlie began to deplore what was happening in the world.

"The happys have it," I said, trying to refocus the first early sunray off my diamond ring directly into his eye. We were waifs, temporarily marooned in a pleasant oasis, laving ourselves in the treasure of at last becoming man and wife.

It took an auto accident to bring us to ground. Two days later, at the residential San Francisco street corner of Buchanan Street and Pacific Avenue, we tangled fenders with another car. No matter that the other driver was underage with his braking leg encased in a plaster hip cast, we all wound up on the city police blotter. By dawn we were trapped, hostage to several dozen newsmen and photographers in the 945 Green Street family apartment where we had sought overnight refuge.

"I'm Shirley Temple Black now," I said with the appropriate emphasis, "and I'm officially retiring from the screen."

Flashguns popped and everyone crowded close, as if our announcement were as important to them as to us. "Nineteen years is enough," I amplified. "No, nothing wrong if others choose to combine marriage and acting. I don't intend to."

The press conference was a grueling experience for my husband.

Assiduous pursuit of privacy was important to him. This was in direct contrast to the uncomplaining availability to public curiosity I had always accepted as normal. To be hoisted on laps, pinched by incredulous strangers, to occasionally get my curls tugged, to be cooed at, photographed, and quoted—all this was part of the job. Even in my more mature years, to be assessed, discussed, and rumored rarely bothered me. Hem length, nail color, and physical measurements were served up willingly.

In fact, privacy had seldom been my lot, even at home. My bedroom was never more than a few yards from my parents' room. After my marriage to Jack a glance from their neighboring window told when my house light clicked on or off and who came and went. Stolen moments of solitude were frequent and had always meant a great deal to me, but fading away into anonymity was simply not in the cards. Our balancing act might be a superstunt, conducting public and private lives simultaneously with minimum abrasion between, but talking it over, Charlie and I saw no reason why we could not have it both ways.

Southward from San Francisco toward distant Palm Springs, the highway slides along the margin of the bay, then twists gently upward over Pacheco Pass past meadows reborn by winter rains into an emerald carpet of meadows studded with picture-book cows. Beyond lies the massive agricultural bowl of the San Joaquin Valley, verdant and populated to the eastward, but along the western side we traveled, lonely and dry. For one hundred miles our road undulated over shallow foothills, cleaving through rock and hardscrabble on both sides, a sweeping watercolor wash of a landscape, dun-colored and empty. Only overhead was there color, where piles of platinum clouds steeplechased across a stridently blue sky.

At the bottom corner of the valley sits the tiny town of Taft, in 1950 barely a huddle of somnolent frame cottages dominated by a dozen sentinel oil derricks clothed in sun-parched, wooden latticework. As we passed down the main street it looked deserted. Over any long highway stretch at constant speed, the harmonic drone of car noises can become narcotic. In its unearthly tranquility, Taft appeared an apparition, false-fronted and fragile, awaiting only fresh winds to uproot its frame houses from the sandy soil and topple the delicate towers. Like tumbleweed, it could all go gracefully bouncing and rolling away into the distance, an antique movie set scheduled for demolition.

The comparison was apt. When we returned to Brentwood there would be much to do, and quickly. Like mystic Taft, my surroundings would be collapsed. All five servants would be dismissed, memorabilia packed for long-term storage, copies of all my films sent to film vaults, film costumes and 1,000-item collection of dolls loaned indefinitely for public display at Exposition Park in Los Angeles, a car and a house to be sold. From all this I would reappear, phoenix-like, as a navy wife in some second-story walk-up apartment on a side street in wartime Washington.

Unraveling almost twenty years of accumulation need not be disheartening, nor would it be for me. Change of drastic proportion can be therapeutic. The past, with all its paraphernalia, had no bonds too troublesome to sever. As always the future, whatever its form, was the essence of what appealed to me most.

We flicked on the car radio, by chance tuned to the booming voice of J. Edgar Hoover speaking from Washington. "The United Nations are defeated in Korea. . . . No U.N. member responded to the call, except America. We stand alone against communism. We are the Gibraltar of Western civilization. We must arm ourselves to the teeth!"

I looked at Charlie. "Praise the Lord and pass the ammunition," I said. "He means us."

37

Not the quarry, but the chase,
Not the laurel, but the race,
Not the hazard, but the play.
Make me Lord, happy alway.
　　　　　　　　—Author unknown

Charlie's tiptoe into details of Temple family finances was inevitable. Current tax returns needed to be filed as a married couple, and basic information was required. My voluntary ignorance concerning personal income, assets, or net worth was almost total. Legal emancipation had produced only two relevant changes: one, a minor addition to my $75 weekly allowance from Father for household expenses; and the other, legal title to the renovated dollhouse.

Between Father and me it was a dead heat who was least interested in seeing me financially independent. I had never inquired about money, and certainly nobody offered information. Income was solely a benchmark of productivity and success. Investment, expenses, costs, and fiscal conservation were of scant interest, happily and wholly left to the province of Father and his partner, Thomason.

Although Charlie's questions required answers, I knew getting the necessary data was a process speckled with hazard. Father's stunted education and resultant insecurity in the hurly-burly of business were factors in the risk. Confronted with probing questions about anything, business or current events, Father's style had been to skirt substance and disguise himself behind the mask of exuberance common in winners. Faced with this peculiarity, we concluded Charlie's meeting should be held in the businesslike quiet of the Temple-Thomason office.

Talking finances might well pry open the lid of a Pandora's box, but for the first time I was becoming curious to see what was inside. After all, presumably it contained presents and Christmas was two days away.

Continuing our drive south at the tail end of our honeymoon to the planned rendezvous with my parents and Susan in Palm Springs, we sped across sagebrush country near Lancaster as dusk fell, twisted through the mountains above San Bernardino, and dropped down toward the desert. There a friend had offered us his family's unoccupied cottage. Perched on a spine of bare scrabble reaching from the foot of Mount San Jacinto out toward the valley floor, it was a secluded Spanish stucco with weathered tile roof, one end of the building obscured under a luxuriant mantle of purple bougainvillea. An ideal hideaway, if one were to discount a vagrant rattlesnake slithering across the hillside scree and up and over the low wall to share our sun-drenched patio.

My parents had already arrived with Susan, Christmas-tree ornaments, brightly wrapped packages, and recent news clippings, one of which primly announced Charlie's expulsion from listing in the *Social Register*. Anonymously printed in New York, the thin, black book listed people nationwide judged the upper crust of what is called "society." One cardinal rule seems to have been that no actress could get in the book, or stay in. Meaning nothing to Charlie, and less to me, his was an exclusion we both could bear.

On Christmas Eve we announced to my parents our comprehensive plan. We must respond to Charlie's navy orders immediately, sell our home, and effectively cut some ties with California.

"But after the war is over, you'll return home?" Mother asked, visibly depressed by the ring of finality in the word "sale." Extracting her hankie, she dabbed her eyes. "I don't like all this, at all."

When Charlie asked if he might come by the office for some information needed for our tax return, Father stared fixedly at the carpet, making little sucking noises through his teeth. From our decorated tree lights winked a multicolored message of titanic change.

Depending on whose characterization is accepted, Charlie's early January 1951 visit to the Temple-Thomason office was either a raid or a revelation. Both Ira and Father declined to answer his questions or offer assistance beyond suggesting that Ira do our married tax work the way he had always done mine. Sensing failure, Charlie suggested a family conclave in my parents' library, where my presence would confirm his right to probe into my finances, a proposal Ira and Father reluctantly accepted.

Accordingly, the next day we all met, attended by ponderous ledgers and bulged file folders. Seizing the initiative, Ira started off with a torrent of generalized statements regarding the complexity of accounting and tax law, until at last I decided to see what my Pandora's box held.

"Where is my money?" I interrupted. Ira looked as if thunderstruck. "And how much do I have?"

To answer those questions, I was told, we must start at the beginning. I lit a cigarette and relaxed.

The first revelation I already knew. Ira preferred to look at my child-star period first. I had no ownership of any kind in any of my films. The producers had hired me, paid a wage, and bade me farewell. My gross earnings from wages and royalties between 1931 and 1941 had been $3,118,000. Three-quarters of that was eaten up paying bills, leaving $930,000 as net savings. Viewed another way, out of every dollar earned I had 25 cents left over.

"Fine, where is it?" I repeated.

Ira seemed not to hear, instead raising his voice to recall the unexpected $239,000 federal tax burden in 1941 imposed by the Fox lump-sum payoff, the time when Father got his first stomach ulcer.

"Okay." I wanted to skip along. "From 1941 to now, how much did I earn?"

Father fanned through some accounting sheets, sucked the end of his pencil, and started adding columns. "From everything? Check me on this, Ira. $1,000,000. Saved? Well, $27,823."

Three cents were saved on each dollar earned; it was easy to compute. How uncanny it was that each year for the nine years of my adult work our family expenses almost exactly matched my net income.

Ira interjected the obvious. "That's because ninety-seven percent was spent," his voice rising in a note of patronizing triumph.

"Worse," he clicked along. "Take 1950. Salary, $93,487. Expenditures, $121,613." He stared malevolently at first Mother, then me. "Instead of earning, you lost. Thirty cents lost on every dollar earned!" Again that exultant, accusatory stare, as if it were all Mother's and my fault.

Wallowing in this sea of accounting irrelevancies threatened to leave my central question stranded. Seated beside me, Mother shifted position and entwined her fingers. Starting again at the beginning seemed the wisest approach, so I asked:

"Ulcers and deficit years aside, how much have I earned since *Baby Burlesk* days?"

Father calculated while Ira looked over his shoulder. "The answer is $3,207,666."

"And after all bills were paid, what's left?" Again silence, save for little mumbles as they consulted and subtracted aloud.

"$811,000."

At last we were making progress. "Fine," I said. "Where is it?"

Ira seemed to have anticipated this moment, for he started reading from a piece of paper. "I have attempted to explain to Charlie the historical and tax considerations involved in and behind that question." His tones were kindly, as if speaking to fools.

"Only one thought guided Mr. and Mrs. Temple, as well as myself, and as long as he was employed, the attorney, Mr. Loyd Wright. How, under the existing high rate of taxation, could the maximum amount of savings be accumulated lawfully." He paused. "And morally, for the ultimate benefit of the minor child earning the money."

The rhetoric was flawless, if unresponsive to the question asked. Silent until this moment, Mother turned toward me, repeating that tax savings were the reason behind everything that had been done. Pointing toward Father, she asked was this not true?

Bobbing his head once, he quickly muttered something about California community property law and how splitting my income between Mother and himself ended up saving me money.

Things were becoming too technical. "Well, where is the $811,000 now?" I asked, returning to my original line of inquiry.

"Invested," answered Father sourly. "Stocks and bonds, mostly."

"Where are they?"

"Safe in a vault, underneath New York," added Mother uncertainly. "Isn't that right, George?"

Father nodded silently. The location seemed imprecise, but I was determined not to digress further about vaults.

"Who *owns* them?" I asked.

That question evoked chaos. Dialogue rocketed crisscross among them, their voices tumbling over one another in explanation. The outburst finally subsided, with Ira looking belligerent and Father pacing and agitated. Mother had sunk back against the cushions, her face shrouded in bewilderment.

"Well," I repeated, "do I own them?"

Ira answered. "No, you do not, because as I tried to explain to you before—"

Mother cut him off. "But I thought they were *all* Shirley's," she said, looking toward Father, who was staring at Ira, who began again.

"As I said earlier—"

Again Mother interjected and turned to Father. "But George, how about her trust?"

Judged by his reaction, a noise midway between a mumble and a burp, the subject of a trust was not on Father's agenda. To me it was a completely unexpected subject, so I asked for details. Bit by bit the blurred background came into focus.

In approving my 1940 MGM contract in February 1941, the State Superior Court had ordered a specific portion of my salary be given to a corporate trustee for preservation in trust for my eventual benefit. Procedurally, MGM was directed to pay all my salary directly to my parents. They, in turn, were ordered by the court to deposit to the trust one-half of my net earnings. That term being defined as salary, less taxes, and less 5 percent for schooling, 10 percent for an agent, and 7.5 percent for management. In approving my Selznick contract on April Fool's Day 1943, the Superior Court bound Vanguard to the same formula as MGM, and renewed my parents' obligation. The trust, said Father, was number 2433 at the California Bank and had a current balance of $44,000. All agreed this was my property.

That balance seemed a pretty small residue from all those lush, active years with Selznick, but before another diversion, I wanted my prior question answered.

"Back to the $811,000," I reminded. "The stocks and bonds. If they are not mine, whose are they?"

I had struck the Achilles' heel. The securities were theirs. All my earnings since Day One had been appropriated by my parents. The only amount restored to me was upon my 1945 marriage, when they transfered title to the dollhouse, representing a $45,000 gift.

Where I stood now was becoming easy to calculate. Of my $3,207,666 gross earnings, I retained $89,000, half in cash and half in a house. My rate of salvage was less than 3 percent over nineteen years effort. Not included, of course, were far more important assets: a treasured daughter, three dogs, a canary, and a husband who claimed to adore me. Many women have less.

Ira had returned to gnaw on his favorite bone. "Bear in mind those taxes," he said, index finger raised. "These, and all your expenses we can tabulate, so you can see exactly where the money went."

I shrugged. Dusty records were not on my mind. Current worth was. And at last I had an answer.

Ira and Father departed together, ledgers and file folders underarm, leaving Mother and me seated together on the couch. She placed her hand gently over mine. "I'm truly sorry, Presh. I'm just dumbfounded."

No more so than I. But for reasons some may find inexplicable, I felt neither disappointment nor anger. Perhaps years spent ignoring such matters had insulated me from disillusion. The spilt-milk parable surely played a role in my equanimity, as did the power of bloodline and family ties.

Father had wrestled with his demon far longer than I knew at the time. Thirty years later I came upon his testamentary codicil executed in 1940 when I was leaving Fox.

Article Sixth:

> Having a daughter of such success and fame as Shirley has been both gratifying and difficult, difficult because her tremendous popularity has made it necessary for all our family to live on a different plane than we otherwise would have preferred.
>
> There will be those, upon my death, who will without knowledge of sacrifices my family and I have willingly made, accuse me of the wrong course as the parent of Shirley to take her earnings. . . .
>
> Notwithstanding this, we endeavored to so handle Shirley's earnings to enhance her ultimate estate. For this reason we have exercised rights given us by law to take the earnings of our daughter. For this reason we have elected not to be appointed guardians, for restrictions on investments under guardianship laws made it impossible to enjoy safety or advantages of enhancement to the extent we enjoy it by investing as individuals, free of court mandate.

This course has been necessary too, because law necessitates all documents filed in such matters being open to the public. Periodic reports of Shirley's earnings would result not only in tremendous annoyance and demands upon us, but in something much more serious.

On that enigmatic note, the article ends, leaving forever unanswered whether he feared kidnap or perhaps something even more damaging. Perhaps it referred to my understanding of what was going on.

Answers require prompt action. There was no question now. My dollhouse home was promptly listed for sale, its windows sparkling, all shrubbery pruned and preened, cushions fluffed, shoes lined up in the closet. Maybe the real estate market was truly soft, or perhaps the sales agent was shaking our resolve to hold firm to our price, but nobody came. Nobody even looked, not one offer. I was almost reduced to standing in the street and waving cars into our driveway.

At last one potential buyer appeared and caught me in the kitchen, simmering stew beef and diced vegetables. The air was filled with a homey fragrance, only fleetingly marred by an aroma of gin as the buyer and agent trailed past me into the main room.

In our family, stew is popular. Several days later, when the two women returned for a second look, another batch was cooking on the stovetop.

"Still cooking the same stuff?" the customer gibed.

"Nope," I muttered, "just stewing in my own juice." But they had already passed by.

On her way out the woman again paused. "Actually, I like stew," she said. "Certainly more than the house."

I should have invited that one to dinner. By the front gate our "For Sale" sign kept swinging and creaking forlornly.

☆

Ira's promised tabulation arrived in a bound volume. For some, poring over statistics and tables is akin to plunging into an intellectual black hole. Most of the time I knew where *I* was, but not what else was there. Temple-Thomason's thick book analyzing my historic receipts and disbursements was no exception. The shadows of its authors fell heavily across each page as its numbers meandered through an anthill of financial tunnels and switchbacks. Bank and brokerage accounts opened, multiplied, then vanished, while Little Shirley earned, paid, and supported. Baby bountiful from childhood, she purchased clothing, a parade of automobiles, every dog bone, golf ball, and diamond for seventeen years. This had been my domain: parents, brothers, twelve household staff, until death a demanding grandmother, and two paternal uncles, whom I vaguely remembered collecting handouts at our gate. Implacably generous, I loaned cash, interest-free, to penitent friends of my parents and faceless names like Hap Nutts and Fanny Sniff. Few repaid. Summing up, I did.

Picking over such corpses of the past is like the task of a carrion crow, disheartening and fruitless. Whether siphoned off as expense or investment, my salary checks had ended up in other purses. Through all those hoary records one human theme pulsed loud and clear: keep dancing, kid, or the rickety cardhouse collapses.

However, among pinpoints of concern lingering from our earlier confrontation, one continued to flicker. Was the $44,000 balance in Trust 2433 *all* that remained from nine years of working for MGM and Vanguard? It seemed so little for so much work. Flipping around in the Temple-Thomason statistics, I added up $891,067 of gross salary. As stipulated by the court, one-half went to my parents, outright. From the remaining half, I deducted taxes and the stipulated percentages for agent, school expenses, and business management. That left $356,000, the amount which my parents were ordered to have deposited in the trust. Yet it now contained only $44,000. Somewhere, obviously, $312,000 had vanished.

The more I checked my figures, the more inescapable became confirmation of my gnawing fear. For years Father had flagrantly disobeyed the Superior Court order. Commencing in 1942 he simply ceased depositing anything to my trust, a delinquency continued for eight years.

Once the implications of this fact had sunk in, I found myself stretched out on a spiky bed, with critical questions humming and clanking through my brain. Why had he done it? Did he gamble that avoidance of the court order had slim chance of discovery? Did escape from detection over many years somehow condone the illegality, as a bad dream fades away after daylight? Was he unable to forget lessons of the Depression years, when nest eggs were vital? Like Mr. Micawber, the Dickens character, had he religiously counted on something to turn up to redress the problem?

Perhaps his malfeasance had something to do with the way our family operated, always in a tight circle of mutual need and support. As a child I needed Mother's crucially important maternal and professional influence. She needed Father for business administration. He, in turn, relied on me to produce the income stream. Brothers and relatives needed the family merry-go-round for their own sorts of rides. By some psychological twist, had Father seen only sharp outlines of a single-family process, with all separate interests fuzzed?

However complex his motivations, my options were clear. I could privately go to him and request restitution, probably a Pyrrhic victory no matter what its tactical success. Being brought to task would constitute a dangerous humiliation for a proud man. Already showing signs of consternation and disappointment, Mother would receive this latest damaging revelation as a whiplash. Vindictiveness tears at family seams. That option was poor.

Hardly worth considering either was the legal ax approach, involving charges of contempt of court or breach of fiduciary trust at a minimum, imprisonment for fraud at the worst. Unworthy visions, all were discarded at once. Blood revenge is deadly dangerous, as unforgiving to accuser as to victim. Far better to just store the matter away, along with any other family skeleton.

From all these revelations some may conclude I had too little too late, or too much too soon, and that's why I am the way I am. Whatever I am, that's not the reason. My attitude has always been, get it over with, and get on with life.

The best and only solution was obvious. Do nothing. Avoid piggish action contrasting now and what might have been. Until death removes any chance of embarrassment to the living, neither word nor gesture. Charlie and I did not hesitate. Born of a sense of compassion, honoring family unity over material cupidity, ours was a pact to be faithfully kept. This ugly genie would stay securely stoppered in its bottle.

38

"You did fine, honey."
The bedside voice was familiar, but not the surroundings, a room sterile and fuzzy in the gray dawn light slanting through the blinds. Then, like a turned page, things slipped into focus.

Susan, Charlie, and I, a world of paraphernalia crammed jigsawlike into our venerable Dodge roadster, with only our dogs missing; the long drive eastward across desert stretched like a saucer between bare upthrust mountains, skirting gorges and canyons of the Colorado River, then pushing out onto rolling midwest plains, following Route 66 straight as a string under a lowering sky. The steady west wind ruffled tail feathers on magpies balanced on roadside fence posts, mile after mile whizzing by. In the dying sun at our back lay the world that had both christened and chastened me, while bequeathing a treasure trove of recollection and professional satisfaction. Off in the darkening horizon ahead lay a true-life role of navy wife during Korean wartime, and a family seedbed awaiting cultivation, hopefully with a future harvest of mutual love and interdependence.

At noontime, near the tiny farming town of Prague, Oklahoma, we stopped at a roadside store for a ham sandwich. A bitter, fleeting aftertaste was soon forgotten. Charlie was driving and suddenly he laughed.

"To think I thought you were rich! Like all movie stars! I could see the swimming pool, and maybe a cattle ranch in Nevada."

"Don't blame me," I rejoined. "*You* were billed as heir to a pineapple fortune, just because you worked for the company. But I found out. You were really a shy, San Francisco socialite, but still wealthy. And then I got a firsthand look at your total savings from World War II. Poof!"

Ribbing each other was enjoyable ever since reciprocal financial realities had revealed our pauperdom.

Above and behind our heads, Susan clung like a monkey to the supporting crossbar of the canvas roof, listening uncomprehendingly. Reaching backward, I touched her face, and she turned to kiss my fingertips. My other hand I rested on Charlie's thigh. Wealth wears many disguises.

The western sky was blood-red as we slowed in the outskirts of Tulsa and pulled into the Will Rogers Motel, selected for its name. At check-in the first pain struck, a rolling, twisting knob low in my right abdomen. Acute appendicitis, ruled the physician at Lawrence Hospital emergency; take her straight to surgery. It was my decision too. Losing an appendix was like having a tooth pulled. Save it as a souvenir, I had instructed.

Now the jumbled pieces were all back in place. Turning toward Charlie, I asked about Susan.

"Stashed away happily with old Boge's family," he replied. A wartime friend in Tulsa had responded with instant hospitality upon learning of our emergency. "Understand it was milk and cookies at midnight."

"Bless him. Where's my appendix?"

Reaching for a stoppered glass flask, he held it up to the light. Inside was a scrawny, shriveled thing, more a dry pea pod than something ready to explode. "Doc says it's the most perfect one he's ever seen," said Charlie.

That remark took a moment to sink in. "But he told us it was about to burst, a life-threatening situation."

"Yeah," came the quiet answer. "The tune changed after the operation. He took it out to be on the safe side. Said you being a celebrity, he couldn't risk missing the diagnosis."

"That's sure what he did," I observed dryly. "What was wrong then?"

"Something you ate, he thinks. Just a stomachache."

"Stomachache," I blurted, raising my head off the pillow. "Ouch!

Where does he get off! Carves up *my* belly to protect *his* reputation!" Casting a baleful glance at the specimen jar, I said, "Send it back. He needs a souvenir more than I do."

The bill was twice what we expected, hardly a consolation. Acceptance as just another navy wife wholly dependent on my husband's salary was gong to be no easy hat trick.

The point was underscored two weeks later by a child autograph-seeker. The day was a typical Washington spring afternoon, steamy and overcast. We were curbside before our slightly shabby, second-story walk-up rental apartment at 2009 Wisconsin Avenue when she came running up holding out a fan-mail portrait for my signature. Resting the photo on a car fender, I carefully scribbled Shirley Temple Black. The child's face fell. "But this isn't worth *anything*!" she exclaimed, fixing me with a disgusted stare. It was an inauspicious start in the new neighborhood.

Our apartment building was blocky and functional, its only pretension the mock-Georgian portico at the top of the steps, an adornment too shallow to shield anyone except from the gentlest rainfall. To one side crouched a shingled cottage behind a single maple tree. On the other rose a stolid, red-brick house, once stylish but it, too, now losing white paint around the windows. One rain gutter had detached itself from the eaves and drooped forlornly.

Inside, our apartment was a far cry from my Brentwood dollhouse. Gone the cathedral-timbered ceilings, the deep pile carpeting, the elegant, expensive overstuffed furniture. Absent the gleaming sterling ashtrays scattered casually on polished end tables. Vanished the lush vistas of flower blooms, the shielding green hedges, towering pines, and eucalyptus, the swooping California pepper trees. By contrast, our new home was a cubbyhole, three rooms, a cramped bathroom and a slender Pullman kitchen too narrow to permit bodies to pass without squeezing against each other, an acceptable penalty actually. The front room boasted one circular throw rug, its nap flattened by former feet, and several unmatched wooden chairs peeling varnish. The previous tenants' thumbprints were engraved on the doorjambs. All was Spartan, secondhand, and slightly soiled. It was also heaven.

In the rear room we installed Susan, her bed almost engulfed by unopened shipping boxes, stacked there to avoid storage expense. Our single large mattress, an inviolate selection as years would prove, filled the front bedroom wall-to-wall, making even a change of sheets an acrobatic feat, like making one's bed while lying in it. Eventually we moved ourselves to a sheet spread on top of the parlor rug. This was long before the popularity of home air-conditioning, so we opened the front sash wide to the hot and humid night and let a purring electric fan drive the damp air across our bodies where we slept splay-legged on the floor.

Once I hired a woman to come in to clean up the dinner dishes. She was superfluous in such compact quarters. Her fate was sealed when I caught her profile in the kitchen, head tipped back, draining the last of Charlie's beer. Neighbors studiously ignored us except for civil encounters on the staircase. Next door in the cottage, however, dwelled Patinka Foscott, a sprightly, graying woman from Tennessee with an encyclopedic knowledge of the neighborhood. From her I learned that the two-story red-brick house across the street, the one with two dormer windows and its shades always pulled down, was in fact an annex of the embassy of the U.S.S.R. Now, there was a neighbor to watch.

In Washington, as elsewhere, apprehension regarding Soviet institutions was at the boil. Our wartime alliance with Russia had unraveled and everywhere communism seemed relentlessly on the march. English scientist Klaus Fuchs, a member of joint Anglo-American nuclear projects and confessed spy, had passed critically important secrets to Moscow. The Soviets had detonated their first atom bomb. Chinese Communists had already kicked the demoralized remnants of Chiang Kai-shek's army off the Asiatic mainland. In the United States diplomat Alger Hiss had been judged guilty of perjury by denying he had passed the infamous "pumpkin papers" to Whitaker Chambers, alleged to be a former Communist spy.

Responding to wrathful partisan insinuations that his administration was "soft on communism," President Truman had several years earlier signed an executive order creating "loyalty boards" to screen charges brought against employees of executive departments. Treason and sabotage were obviously grounds for dismissal, but the order also emphasized another type of important evidence: "Membership in, affiliation with, or sympathetic association with, any foreign or domestic organization . . . or combination of persons designated by the Attorney General as totalitarian, fascist, communist, or subversive . . ."

The implications of that order were sweeping. Epithets like "pinko" and "fellow traveler" could shatter careers, rolling up the blameless with the bad. Guilt by association was legitimized, setting loose a hound-dog chorus in which Senator Joseph P. McCarthy's now-discredited list of "known Communists" working in the Department of State was only one yowl. Respected columnist William F. Buckley, Jr. may have depicted McCarthyism as a movement behind which men of "goodwill and stern morality can close ranks," but to me McCarthy remains a dismal footnote to history, not as to intent, but as to method.

As cries of sedition, spying, and treachery rose as one widespread tumult, and everywhere the poison of communism was portrayed as seeping into America's bloodstream, I was in the front rank of those concerned. On at least one prior occasion I had even offered my services to the FBI as an infiltrator and informer.

Two years earlier, Sig Arno, comedian, light-opera star, and an accomplished portraitist, had been painting a series of Hollywood stars under commission from a Paris gallery. Asked to pose, I was flattered. The deal was upscale, and the portrait would be mine, a no-fee deal.

The first day I had driven alone up a steep curvy driveway in the bohemian section of Benedict Canyon. Arno met me with his wife, an alert little person with home-cut bangs and no makeup. Telling me that today we would do the body, he said he envisaged me as a woman of another century. Someone in a purple bonnet, crocheting.

Way wide of the mark, I thought, compared to my actual personality; anyway, I went into the bedroom to change into his required costume. Opening the closet door to hang up my clothes, I almost tumbled backwards. Leaned against the back wall was a life-sized portrait. Dressed in military tunic, staring at me full-face, was the chief communist of them all, Joseph Stalin.

Before returning on the second day I called the FBI: Guess what? "Well, thank you, Shirley," the agent replied, "very useful. Keep track of things."

That day Arno painted my face, but neither in his conversation nor actions was there anything to report to the FBI. Tomorrow we do the eyes, he said.

By the third and final day I had myself convinced I was a central player in an international dragnet to catch an elusive foreign espionage agent. It was my last chance to entrap him in some incriminating deed or comment. All that happened was that I ruined his portrait. Instead of the contemplative gaze of a crocheting gentlewoman from another era, what came glinting through were the eyes of a female Sam Spade, everyman's detective, eyes slitted, eager to unfrock yet another pinko masquerading in the heart of patriotic Hollywood.

It was just as well the FBI never called back. I had nothing to say. Arno continued to act and paint, Stalin may still be in the same closet for all I know, and the portrait of me rests permanently in my attic, eyes still narrowed, still searching for something in the dusty darkness.

Notwithstanding my failure with Arno, what a happy hunting ground Washington seemed for someone like me, concerned about Communists and nurtured by almost two decades of enjoying plot and counterplot on radio and in the movies. Although the importance of United States broadcast radio still eclipsed the ten million TV sets in use, of which we had one, television had added to my inventory of plot and drama with spy programs like *Foreign Intrigue*. Trench coats buttoned high, Copenhagen streetlights fuzzy in a cold, blowing fog, cobblestones shiny wet, guttural accents, I can still hear it all, and see it all. That program was my weekly visit to the subculture of prowling and pursuit. Now, courtesy of Patinka, we had a real-life spy operation across the street. Like any Minuteman, I volunteered in my nation's defense.

Sleeping on the floor as we did, there could be no "Reds under our bed," but creeping in the late hours to our darkened windowsill, I could peer long and hard across the street where real live Reds lived. Frustrated by shades drawn against the light, I listened to typewriters softly clicking through the steamy night air, and silently deplored the languid behavior of the FBI. Through brother Jack at the FBI, I had offered our parlor as a convenient stakeout to keeps tabs on the ominous embassy annex across the street, but nobody had called. Impatient with bureaucratic lethargy, I had then called FBI Director Hoover himself. Within hours two snap-brimmed, stern-faced agents had appeared, spending the better part of a week furtively peeking from my window and noting coming and goings. Now they, too, had gone.

Within weeks we were melting into the unexceptional ebb and flow of Washington life. Daily, Charlie went to work on a bus. I hauled groceries home in a paper bag. Too young for school, Susan was my constant companion, a delightful grasp loosened only when we hired a sitter for a night out with navy friends. I cooked, cleaned, and got a $5.00 ticket for crowding a fireplug in front of the apartment. "Little Miss Marker is no great shakes as a parker," quipped the *Washington Post*.

In a letter to Mother, I wrote, "The days fly. I feel like I've been a resident of Washington since Abe Lincoln." We were a small knot embedded in the fabric of a large middle class. Occupationally, financially, by heredity and taste, that's where we belonged. Our California house still drifted on the market without a bite. In fairness, we did keenly miss the Collie, sold to a happy home, and our remaining two big dogs, boarding still with my parents. Susan did too. As usual we had spread out the morning newspaper to practice her reading. Laboriously reciting, she read, "Shirley Temple getting a beautiful new house." She looked up inquiringly.

"Here. This little apartment," I explained.

Characteristically calm and trusting, her eyes went round, eyebrows arched. "Is *this* a beautiful new house?"

Gossip about our moving somewhere else continued to fly, rooted in the erroneous public assumption of my wealth and in disbelief that anyone who could would not flee such modest surroundings. One local columnist took off on a particularly fanciful flight, writing that we were about to purchase a sprawling country estate from a breakfast-food heiress, a monumental spread with rambling mansion, paddocks, gardens, stables, and guest cottages. Uniforms for my staff were already being designed by a famous Paris couturier, the report read. Ignoring drivel was easy, particularly as I had just gotten off my knees from swabbing down our bathroom.

With the advent of Lewis and Marion Parsons, however, everything changed. New rooms opened, filled with new people. Perhaps it was an elegantly appointed corporate suite in the posh Carleton Hotel downtown, or a drawing room in some baronial residence where old masters on the wall gauged new masters and mistresses arranged on brocaded parlor chairs before them. Occasionally the room was a chandeliered dining room with serving waiters in livery and carefully matched couples of sleek, scintillating women and men with resonant, authoritative voices.

Lew was the courtly vice president and Washington representative for U.S. Steel Corporation, then among the largest and most prestigious American corporations. Curiosity may well have motivated Lew and Marion to seek us out, along with courtesy to a director of the corporation, who chanced to be my new father-in-law. Despite its generational gap, our relationship over time bloomed into a deep-seated companionship ended only by their deaths.

Despite Marion's constant scolding, Lew puffed too many cigarettes for his own good and drank scotch hard, fending her off with deep rolling chuckles of good cheer. Quick to scoff at pretense, and with boyish enthusiam for derring-do, he had the idea for me to invade the sacrosanct premises of stanchly antifeminist Burning Tree Golf Club. This we did on the day it was usually closed, including a sweep through the slightly malodorous locker room. Rules may prevent female entry, but even so masculine a bastion has no defense against the unseen intrusions of old golfing shirts and socks.

The F-Street Club was another sort of redoubt, and again Lew provided a passkey. Domiciled in an erstwhile corner residence, little distinguished the building from its neighbors. Approached by a flight of wide, brownstone steps flanked with carefully painted iron railings, it squatted on a slight hillock and stared through its drawn muslin curtains at pedestrians hurrying by.

The ambassador from Cuba had described the membership. "They are four hundred power-elite, all industrialists, diplomats, politicians, and public figures. No place for the usual five percent commission man. You have to be at least a *fifty* percenter and connected with something big, like steel or oil."

That profile seemed apt the first time Lew shoehorned us onto the guest list for a dinner jointly honoring Perle Mesta, ex-U.S. ambassador to Luxembourg and prototype for Ethel Merman's smash Broadway hit *Call Me Madam*, and Joseph Pew, powerful patriarch of Sun Oil Corporation. For anyone reading the local newspapers regularly, each introductory handshake clicked with recognition. Just being present left us with the feeling of being surrounded by a powerful and brilliant coterie, the sort of people one would intentionally select if chance permitted.

Charlie was quick to lump them all together as "bigwigs," a reflection of academic training and business exposure which automatically classified people on the basis of corporate or government office held. I saw things differently, a blessing from years of chance encounter with preeminent persons, where name or title was dwarfed by personality traits. To me Washington political and business celebrities seemed no different from celebrities anywhere. Products and ideas need to be peddled, things need doing, politics need to be pursued, and sometimes self-delusion and pretension need be served. What interested people like me was the people themselves. Origins, office, and posturing be hanged. The elastic response of individuals to ideas and events is what provides the bottomless well of discovery from which people like me can drink.

However, like most quasi-social gatherings, this one proved a mixed bag. Some guests were men with minds shown by conversation to be precise, clean, and dry. Some were obviously achievers and gentlemen, and others desirous of being so regarded. A few had gone to seed with visions of self-importance, some with an edge of malice in the voice. Like earthworms in a box, they entwined among themselves, chatting as if each derived sustenance and wisdom only from contact with the others.

On that evening to my left was seated a senior political official. "When I was a punk Cadillac salesman in 1936, we drove out from Oregon," he related, "and camped on your doorstep. Nobody was home. My wife insisted we wait. My daughters both worshiped you, and the Quints."

A diversionary comment about the jellied salad failed to derail what promised to be a boring anecdote.

"You and your mother finally drove up, in a Cadillac. She's much better-looking than you are." He smiled. "You said, 'Mom, I'm tired,' but she said, 'These nice people are all the way from Oregon. Give them your autograph.' "

"Where did you get that nick in your ear?" I asked, pointing to an obvious scar.

"That's only one of my five wounds from World War I," he enthused, mercifully embarking on a narrative of the battle of Belleau Wood.

To my other side sat Philippine Ambassador Joaquin Elizalde, conducting in a running soliloquy about sugar quotas and international conflict. Between breaths he apologetically observed that I probably knew or cared little about international politics.

"Not so," I replied. "It was I who mediated the key cease-fire between Afghan leader Khoda Khan and the British at the Khyber Pass."

His Excellency shot me a speculative, sidelong glance and forked in another mouthful of salad.

"I know more," I continued. "During the Boer War in South Africa, I had occasion to meet on a personal matter with Queen Victoria." He had ceased eating. "And I sat on Abraham Lincoln's lap." Earning conversational credentials is not easily achieved in Washington.

Sometimes we fared poorly. By reputation my luncheon hostess was one of the best-financed, most compulsive local party-givers. Energetic and youthful for a middle-aged woman, her shiny black hair pulled tight, she listened well, head swiveling from speaker to speaker, eyes fixed on the speaker's lips.

"You would know her, dear. Now, let me think. Her name—oh, you know. Acapulco. Let's see—Rosita—lovely mother and father. You would remember. Marti, maybe. Marti?"

"Marti, Marti?" she interjected. "Well, one of the Martis I know . . ."

Perhaps misreading my interests, shortly thereafter she telephoned to invite us to a formal dinner. "And I look forward to seeing your handsome husband," she added.

While in general agreement with her assessment, I casually mentioned Charlie was sporting a large fever blister on his upper lip. There was a sudden silence on the line.

"Well, dear," she resumed, "perhaps you'd better not come this time. This party is only for the *beautiful* people."

Apartment life seemed to be grinding hardest on Susan. At home, doors had opened outside, not on stair landings. Little friends were hard to come by in our new neighborhood. No school, no pets, no dirt, no mud, no butterflies, no bugs.

I wrote Mother:

> The poor babe, with flu for five days, has had nothing but ginger ale, Coca-Cola, skim milk, dry toast and crackers . . . Charlie and I were totally unprepared on Saturday afternoon when he walked into Susan's room. She was out of bed reaching for "Fido" who had

fallen on the floor, and as she got up, she rocked back and forth . . . fainted, giving her head a resounding bang on the back. Charlie quickly put her on the bed and raised her legs, and she came out of it in a few seconds. Naturally, I was upset, but it couldn't compare with the grief Charlie went through. . . . I've never seen any two people more crazy about each other than he and Susan are. . . .

Suspended in temporary lodgings, we faced an equation familiar to all young couples on the move: a house there that wouldn't sell, and no extra money here to buy another.

Back in California, my parents were confronting the reality that no longer would I be providing an income stream. Far too fair to continue to erode what remained of my accumulated earnings on their unaltered life-style, they were shortening their own sail. The family Brentwood property was subdivided down the middle, separating the more luxurious home from the dollhouse. By good luck, the big house sold instantly, and so they bought ours at the asking price.

At last unleashed to house hunt locally, we settled on a whitewashed brick cottage, slate-roofed and snug, with blood-red shutters and a wishing well complete with bucket. Situated near Potomac, Maryland, a rural crossroads of wooded hills and fenced pastureland, the location promised privacy and unlatched doors. Our two dogs arrived, followed by a new canary and an aquarium. A waterfall of wild honeysuckle vines all but buried one stretch of the board fence that otherwise encircled us, built low enough to be sportingly leaped by panting hounds and galloping horsemen who, by custom, would come baying and thundering across property lines in pursuit of some hapless fox.

The house had been designed and built by a handyman hardware-store employee, a man strongly given to afterthought and quick to utilize building materials left over from customers' orders. How else to explain our exotic bathroom, tiled in an eye-jarring rainbow of colors and haphazard dimension, or its commode, installed directly beneath the shower head.

Living for the first time in a climate where winter came early, and remained long and cold, I found some things innovative. The parquet oak flooring had been laid over a cement pad radiantly heated by circulating hot water. When winter did arrive little could beat leaving the dinner dishes in the sink and stretching out on that hard, warm surface with my loved one while *Foreign Intrigue* hummed softly on television and outside the wind howled under the eaves and drifted snow up against the door.

Heaven may also have been the assessment of Duke, the Great Dane. As reported in my roundup letter to Mother shortly after moving in, however, he was still a dog.

> As for the rest of the household, it has gone to pot! I've just brought the fish through a siege of "ich," after losing seven during the process. Bing III the "boid" has diarrhea and mites, but I'll spray him tonight. As for Duke, we've practically disowned him. It seems the females are in an early heat, and our son, Duke, for the past week has made a disgusting spectacle of himself with two bitches. He and his eight male dog friends have put on a day and night display in our front and back fields. They don't eat or sleep, and of course, Duke is the worst, because he's the biggest of all the other mutts. The poor little bitches can't get home because every time they get up to walk, well, you know what happens. Mean old Duke won't even let the poor little female rest, and pulls her up by the neck when she falls exhausted to the ground. He's thin and awful looking, and if you want the dull-eyed thing back, I'll be glad to pay his plane fare!

Our summertime situation was in fact idyllic, except for a luxuriant crop of ragweed pollen which drifted and dusted the neighborhood. Initially I had thought the pretty yellow blooms ideal as a centerpiece for our table and arranged a pretty bouquet for my husband. Between sneezes he instructed "get rid of it."

Obediently I borrowed a tractor fitted with sickle mowing bar, donned work clothes, and bound my hair tightly under a red bandanna. Clattering off in a cloud of diesel fumes, I began to chop our front pasture to the earth. Back and forth, swath by overlapping swath, my bar sliced under the dense mantle of bunchgrass and foxtails and laid them down in a tidy green coverlet.

I failed to notice the family who had parked their car at roadside and were now all arraigned by size along our board fence. The man had begun to wave his arm in quick, sweeping gestures and shouted something unintelligible to me above the roar of my tractor engine. Turning, I drove down and stopped in front of the group. The man's camera was unsheathed, lens cap off.

"Not there," he shouted in disgust. "Get out of the way."

All of them were staring fixedly past me and across the field up toward the house. Following their gaze, I could see nothing unusual.

"Move away, you're lousing up my picture."

"What picture?" I called.

Lowering his camera slightly, he tossed me an irritated glance. "A picture of her house. That's where Shirley Temple lives."

"Oh, her," I replied, and ground backward in reverse and out of range.

Anonymity can be regarded as a bane for movie performers. Conversely, recognition from strangers is an anointment. Prompt visual identification had usually been my lot, but when I did go unnoticed it was of no concern. Acknowledgment and privacy each had value in my life, and I never much worried about their relative proportion. Not so with Charlie, of course, with his deep-seated penchant for privacy. Several times when approached by strangers in department stores inquiring if the woman with him was me, he had replied no. I really didn't care. Better than anyone anywhere, I knew who I was. Who else knew was of little importance.

The presence of knowledgeable strangers perched on my fence, however, added a fresh dimension to my notion of privacy. An isolated location such as ours was vulnerable to unwanted visitors. The nearest police and rescue squad were a half-hour distant, at full siren. Anyone possessed of sufficient gall or evil intent could simply trudge or creep across our open pasture and instantly fall upon our innermost citadel.

Responding twenty years earlier to the twin bugaboos of kidnap and extortion, my parents and the studio had devised a system of stone walls, locked iron gates, electric eyes, and armed bodyguards. Now the risk equation was slightly altered. On one side we had two dogs of doubtful wariness. I had an alert and aggressive husband, unfortunately away weekdays on navy duty. On the other side existed the old incentive of my presumed personal wealth. Now the pot of gold was augmented by a little girl to kidnap. Interwoven in such grisly speculations, of course, was the irony of it all. Ransom money simply didn't exist. But nobody knew this but us.

An easy way to have reduced the risk level would have been to publicly set the record straight regarding my true estate, a disclosure sure to shatter Father's image as conscientious father and canny banker. As this option was already well considered and solidly rejected, the next obvious way was to get a gun.

Mine was a small, snub-nosed Smith & Wesson .38-caliber pistol, duly registered. Under regular weekend tutelage by a U.S. Marine friend, I practiced squeezing off rounds at isolated stumps and river rocks. Under recoil the serrated wooden grip tore up my tender palm, a situation cured with sandpaper for the gun and a glove for me. If never threatening the mark of Annie Oakley, my accuracy did increase, along with my general comfort level.

Personal reinforcements might logically add another line of defense, but these had drawbacks. Our home was too tiny to justify a household helper, our budget too tight to easily accommodate one, and I was frankly possessive about the kitchen. Despite an initial reluctance, I culled employment agencies for a woman to work, someone not too proud to share my drudgery, somone young enough to play with Susan and be ever mindful of strangers.

Rosa seemed to fit the order. Short of stature, broad-hipped, square-faced, with a wide, toothy smile, from any angle she seemed anchored to the earth, a convivial woman of simple needs and animal watchfulness. Never mind the luxuriant, silky black hair worn in a stylishly primitive pigtail, the too-tight satiny blouse, the exotic fragrance eddying in her wake, or those almond eyes, half enticement and half warning, like a lynx. I understood. All women are closely related to cats. Her presence was reassurance, until a gossipy neighbor toppled everything.

When blustery weather had coincided with Rosa's day off from work, she often elected to remain, a gesture I had construed as loyalty. When the weather turned fair, however, she again outfitted herself in vivid colors, dangling earrings, and a looped necklace of polished silver links. I would watch admiringly as she strode down our long drive, a sultry, burnished creature with an impudent hip-swinging gait.

There's where the problem starts, the neighbor whispered, down at the gate. She thumbs rides, not in itself remarkable, but she accepts lifts only from men driving alone. Instead of offering to share the gas, she propositions the driver.

Confronted with the accustation, Rosa's eyes flashed. I was intruding into her private business, she shouted, actually the case.

"You're fired," I said evenly.

"I quit," she snarled, raising one clenched fist before my face. "You bitch!"

The only other time in my life I had been called that in person was during *The Bachelor and the Bobby Soxer*. Her aggressive posture and sharp tongue confirmed that she would have made a fine watchdog, had not her entrepreneurial spirit intervened.

Dispensing with Rosa again increased our physical risk and in early November 1951 I probably compounded the problem.

Bess Truman, folksy wife of the President, had requested I come to the vaults of the American Security & Trust Company to model for a publicity photo plugging a forthcoming "Court of Jewels" fashion show to benefit the Washington Home for Incurables. The job sounded routine, the cause worthwhile, and the auspices superb. Dramatically positioned front-page in the three leading Washington daily newspapers, our ensuing photo portrayed Mrs. Truman admiring a necklace, eloquently described as "a pear-shaped, double diamond and valued at three-quarters of a million dollars."

On my way home I realized that publicly parading in such opulent jewelry could well reinforce the public vision of my personal wealth. Conceivably the photo could provoke someone to strong-arm robbery in our relatively exposed circumstances. Not only did publicity draw attention to the erroneous probability that I had something worth stealing, I had in fact just acquired a ring of exotic character, valuable if not priceless.

Still altering her life-style and to help generate the cash which I no longer earned, Mother had decided to sell her blue diamond ring. Long admired by me for its beauty, and worn regularly by her since first purchased by Father in waning days at Fox, it was now on consignment in the shop window of Ruser, our friendly Beverly Hills jeweler. Either she had forgotten or had never heard Father's public declaration that the ring was actually mine, given Mother only for safekeeping. Equally unaware, I found the proposed sale outside our family repugnant on other grounds. Short of most dire cash necessity, it should not, for sentimental reasons alone, be sold.

I'll buy it myself, I offered, an extravagance we could ill-afford but could not avoid. A deal was struck at the original price, my pleasure undimmed by the knowledge that I was buying it for a second time.

Several weeks had passed since the "Court of Jewels" publicity and my companion acquisition of the blue-diamond ring. A cool gusty wind was stripping trees of their last dried leaves and sending rumpled woolly clouds scudding across a sunless sky. While teaching Susan how to delicately clean bottom debris from her tropical fish aquarium, I was jolted to hear the front doorbell chime. Nobody was expected.

Standing back from the stoop appeared a man about my age, casually dressed, with his jacket collar upturned against the breeze.

"Hi, Mrs. Black," he said in a tone of familiarity. "Is your husband home?"

The question was civil enough, although most husbands are at work in midafternoon on a weekday. Something else about him made me hesitate, his headlong cordiality contrasted with the opaque, hooded quality of his gaze.

"Yes, my husband's home," I lied, "may I help you?"

From the adjacent room Susan's voice called, "Mummy, the fish."

"In a minute . . ." I answered, but the man overrode my reply.

"Is that the little girl?" he asked brightly.

Obviously he had foreknowledge of Susan's presence in the house. Flicking through my head went the vision of my handgun, locked inaccessibly in a bureau drawer. In a pinch I would be down to teeth, nails, and knees.

Closing the door slightly, I asked what he wanted.

"I've come to tune your piano." He stepped forward but paused when I said we had no piano, also a lie.

"That's funny." He started to search his pockets. "I have an order somewhere." I noted he carried no tool kit as had other piano tuners I'd known.

"Sorry, wrong house," I said, firmly closing the door just as he advanced one foot as if to block my movement.

Strangers, even a zany fan, appearing in a workplace context had seldom rated my second thought. An unrecognized visitor at our home doorway, however, stirred the instinct of a lioness at the mouth of her den.

As the man drove away in his dark blue van, I memorized the license plate and placed a telephone call to the police in Rockville. Normally I was not one of those edgy housewives quick to cry wolf, but my action had been stimulated by an earlier call from my friend Drucie, daughter of Secretary of the Treasury John W. Snyder.

A stranger had telephoned, and coincidentally another friend, with the same inquiry, asking details of my financial worth. Identifying himself as an insurance salesman, the caller had on both occasions probed about annuities or coverage on Susan. His interest seemed so peculiarly centered that Drucie thought I should know.

Several days after my encounter with the strange visitor, two plain-clothes detectives with proper identification visited me. Aided by the license number, they had quickly located the young man, whose answers to general interrogation cracked the lid on an unexpected situation. The man's purpose in visiting was to spot the telephone line point of entry, our interior room layout, and where Susan slept. The accomplice and brains of the scheme was a middle-aged insurance salesman, also now in custody. Appropriate federal authorities had taken over, as the case was a planned kidnap.

From that moment my front-door habits changed. Unexpected or unrecognized callers were greeted through a locked door and redirected around the corner to a kitchen window, where at least a screen separated us while I made up my mind.

A snowfall blanketed everything on our first anniversary. Trudging happily off into a nearby woods, we chopped down our Christmas tree and dragged it homeward with Susan cheerily riding astride and both dogs leaping through the drifted snow like porpoises at sea. While I cooked, Susan sat cross-legged before the TV watching *Rebecca of Sunnybrook Farm*, the first of her mother's films she had ever seen. During dinner she criticized my singing voice. In explanation, I related that in the movie I was supposed to have lost my voice.

She remained unconvinced. "Well, anyway, Mummy, you sure didn't sing very well."

Later, as she was curled comfortably in her daddy's lap in a rocking chair before a crackling fire, they were fashioning imaginary pictures in the flames. The chair was new, upholstered in tufted blue leather. In late summer Lew and Marion had invited us to spend a weekend as their guests at the Rolling Rock Country Club in the green hills of Ligonier, Pennsylvania. There, in room Double-D, we had admired the chair. Learning its design was proprietary to the Duquesne Club of Pittsburgh, we had forgotten about it, until it appeared as a gift at our door.

"Sit ye, rock, and think," read the message enclosed, "something for all ages and all moods."

In its monotonous squish-squish and squeak-squeak, bogeymen did indeed vanish. Lulled by the slow, salubrious rocking, body and soul became enveloped in the quietude so essential to natural health and peace of mind.

Staring dreamily into the fire, Charlie asked Susan what a new baby should be named, if one appeared. Without hesitation she replied, Barton Sunday. Why did you say that? Because it's a good name for a boy. Where did that name come from? From something recently read? No. Television? No. How do you spell it? She couldn't. What's it mean? She did not hesitate. Because it will be a boy and he'll be "born on Sunday." Give or take a phonetic sound, she was on target. Our visit to Ligonier had bequeathed us more than the rocking chair. Again I was pregnant.

☆

In any presidential election year, Washington vibrates early. Truman was beset with problems. For almost two years the Korean bloodletting had dragged on, producing 100,000 casualties and a seemingly endless drain on the American economy. The military draft was exacting a high price in voter goodwill, and sour notes of political corruption clanged frequently, to the apparent delight of the reporting press and sorrow from almost everyone else. The principal theme resonating in Washington was the forthcoming 1952 presidential primary election.

It was intellectually exhilarating, if not spiritually uplifting, to be repeatedly included by Lew in his gatherings of the power-elite, usually small enough to induce a degree of candor otherwise imprudent. How else could I have heard directly from Admiral Louis Denfeld, an old salt with blood in his eye, when, how, and why Truman had just sacked him as

Chief of Naval Operations? Or when could I have presented my views directly to balding Senator Robert Taft, who had extolled isolation, deplored the United Nations, and spoken scornfully of Eleanor Roosevelt's preoccupation with civil rights, all positions to which I was ardently opposed?

Where else could I have stood between veteran Democratic Secretary of the Senate Stephen Early and Vice President Alben W. Barkley, the latter widely acknowledged as Truman's favorite candidate for the Democratic presidential nomination, while they assessed Republican chances in the fall elections? A good shot at it, with Korea still around our neck, Early said. Barkley shook his big head sideways, craggy features clouded over. Spies and wars aren't what's important in this election. It's the stomach, and he patted his. And the pocketbook, he added, reaching around under his coattail for another pat. Let them nominate any leader, he declared, then they have a good chance.

Those guest lists were always a name-dropper's delight, a sprinkling of jurists, cabinet officials, legislators, warriors. Men of title and clout, their heads inclined together in animated confidentiality, with much jowl-shaking for emphasis and fingers raised in admonition. With few exceptions, it was a galvanizing concentration of authority and prestige, a rare opportunity for any local sparrow like me to consort with eagles. Occasionally their conversation seemed almost alien, flashing with references to people and events, details skipped as if all within earshot knew the background anyway. I often didn't, and would find myself flitting owl-like between groups, listening but rarely uttering a word.

Once I said yes, and it spelled eventual deep trouble. Dan Kimball was a gregarious southern California aircraft manufacturing executive, recently confirmed as Secretary of the Navy. He cornered me one evening and proposed I have my baby in Bethesda Naval Hospital, citing the morale-boosting potential of such an event for all navy families. And besides, he said, it's free. His reasons seemed sound, so I agreed and wrote Mother the news.

The Navy is going to turn itself inside out to make my "confinement" in their hospital a pleasant one. They are very, very publicity-minded and ever since the unfortunate Forrestal suicide in their hospital have done everything possible to treat their V.I.P.'s with the greatest care and kindness. I will have the top Navy O.B. man in the country (who happens to be a captain stationed here). He will see me for the remaining months and be on 24-hour call when delivery time rolls around. I will have a private room and can stay for seven to ten days if necessary with my own nurses around the clock. All in all, it will be a much better deal than I could get or afford in a local hospital. And I'd like to see a reporter or photographer get into the flagship Navy hospital of the United States. Ha! They would probably be shot on sight . . . from a public relations standpoint, we couldn't be in better hands.

All that was correct, but neither Kimball nor I could have imagined into what a glue pot both we and the medical Navy were about to plunge.

By my twenty-fourth birthday I was round as a butterball, attending a National Day reception at the Dominican Embassy and scattering rum-cake crumbs over my yet unborn child. Later, at the Norwegian Embassy, Ambassador Munthe de Morganstierne piloted me to his honored guest, Sonja Henie, under the mistaken belief we were dear friends instead of old acquaintances. More bosomy than I remembered, she was wearing a feathered hat that radiated out like a halo of icicles. Although we were co-workers at Twentieth Century-Fox at the same time, our brief Washington conversation was more extensive and cordial by far than any encounter while working within hailing distance.

Traveling our route on the social side of diplomacy and domestic politics, I was taken by surprise to be visited in springtime of 1952 by gossip columnist Hedda Hopper, arrived to generate a movie-magazine story. During the past year I had become a little weary of newspaper reporters asking mundane questions about pressure cookers and posing me with Sunday comics before the fireplace. Inevitably the question had come, what did I think of when I saw little Shirley Temple on television? Equally inevitable was my answer. There is nothing schizo about our relationship. She is a relative and nobody knows her better than I. But what she does is her business, and what I do is mine. We are mutually supportive. She helps me and I help her, as any good mother should.

Seeing Hopper again brought into focus how far afield from parochial Hollywood my interests had shifted. Nobody believes it when a Hollywood star declares retirement, she said. Did I miss acting?

"No. That fire bell doesn't ring anymore. I acted to learn, and did my best along the way. But acting was only part of my life. For twenty years it was good for me. But now it's behind."

Noting that her expression hung midway between skepticism and sympathy, I went on. "So much else exciting is going on, Hedda, the international problems, the politics. From my spot in the last row of the third balcony, down on the stage it looks great."

Did that mean I would never return to pictures?

"Never is such a final word," I replied. "But I don't think so."

The interview completed, she adjusted her trademark hat, a floppy-brimmed number crested with a spray of silk spring flowers, and we walked outside where her long limousine waited. With one smiling wave she was gone, down the long gravel drive toward River Road, and out through the stubby fieldstone gateposts crowned by masthead lanterns salvaged from a navy surplus store. Her car turned right toward Washington and disappeared from my sight.

Hopper had wanted to learn specifically what lay ahead for me, but I really could not help her. I was no creature of unfulfilled yearning, someone driven to claw my way up some new ladder. Under professional contract for nineteen years, I was trained to wait. In the beginning Mother had hustled my movie roles, but I never did. Things just happened. Passive I may have been, but not fatalistic. My habit was to resist stagnation by preparing myself temperamentally and professionally for whatever opportunity might knock at my door. If others viewed me as capable, I'd be asked.

So far I hadn't missed much, except mumps and chicken pox. Contented in the regularity of my life and the reliability of Charlie's affection, I was already blessed with one treasured daughter and soon a Barton Sunday. Enormously stimulated by my Washington environment and supremely healthy in body and spirit, I had no idea what the future held.

Nor that within two weeks I would stand at death's door.

39

March 15, 1955
Auditorium of the Burlingame High School

More than five years had flown since I'd left the set of my last movie. Meanwhile two new children had been added to our family, Charlie's tour of navy duty had ended, and we had resettled in a small town in northern California where he was employed by Stanford Research Institute.

For the first time since leaving Hollywood I was involved with the performing arts. Armed with a flashlight, symbol of authority, I was an usherette, taking tickets and seating several hundred children for a performance of *The Wonderful Wizard of Oz* staged by a volunteer women's organization of which I was a provisional member.

The auditorium lights dimmed, and the last babble of childish anticipation died. Swinging the double doors shut, I briefly tested my flashlight and seated myself to watch, again an onlooker, not a player.

First appeared Dorothy and her dog, Toto, in a Kansas farmyard setting. Then, with footlights blinking and to the roar of recorded wind noises, a cyclone whisked them off to the Land of Oz. Snatched away from comforting surroundings to an alien land, beset by harrowing obstacles as she sought a way home again, Dorothy would be sustained by unquenchable optimism. Good entertainment so far, judged by the squeals of delight from the audience. How true to life was our little allegory.

A couple of years before, in 1952, I reflected, a figurative cyclone of events had swirled me away in Bethesda. Blame for what happened along my yellow-brick road might better be assigned to refried beans and spicy tortilla than to a cyclone.

Yearnings of pregnancy had led me to a dingy and ill-lighted road-house, which served dinner sauces like molten fire. At midnight I awakened Charlie with news of birth pangs. As planned, we put Susan, half asleep, in the rear seat and drove off to the U.S. Naval Hospital at Bethesda. There waited the captain, whom I call Queeg. After X rays he stretched me out on an examining table just as my pangs ceased altogether. A fatherly man with sufficient rank to suggest skill and inspire confidence, he listened with his stethoscope, occasionally offering some sardonic remark about "noises in there." My medical care would rest solely in his hands; no other doctor would be involved, certainly none more junior or less experienced.

Placing his ear directly against the drum-taut mound of my stomach, he remained motionless in this restful position for so long, I suspected he had dozed off. A few quick breaths jiggled him alert, whereupon he announced my fetus was full-term, weighed eight and a half pounds, but that its umbilical cord was unfortunately looped around the neck, evidenced by a faint, distressed heartbeat. We received his analysis with disbelief. Although sleeping quietly at the moment, my unborn child had always kicked and shifted normally, just as Susan had before.

You can go home, Queeg said, but the fetus may die. He recommended an immediate Caesarean section.

To delay for a corroborative diagnosis would obviously be offensive to Queeg, and would also place our unborn baby at mortal risk. So, at 2:16 a.m. on April 28 I was delivered of a baby boy. His dimensions and condition must have surprised Queeg. The birth weight was of six pounds, eleven ounces, not eight and a half pounds as predicted. The umbilical cord lay in a normal position, and healthy yowls proclaimed a healthy newborn child. Queeg had made a mistake. The X rays had been incorrectly interpreted, and a heartbeat had been misread against the background tumult of refried beans and tortilla. No matter the unwarranted surgery, Barton Sunday was our enormous blessing, and we gladly overlooked the knife and stitches.

Almost as it occurred, Mother sensed trouble from afar.

"Feel something going wrong ..." she had written in her diary, commencing on May 1, "... although a nurse informed me it was only usual 'third-day' troubles ... doctor going to remove stitches and clamps .... For some reason or other, I feel very uneasy about her ... how I wish I were with her.... She is not feeling very well. Incision opened slight bit ... a little inflammation in wound. What is that doctor doing to my precious? ... Expects to be in hospital two weeks longer.... Has pain in her back.... I am sure she is not letting us know how sick she is...."

As usual, Mother was prescient. Five days earlier Queeg's basket-weave of sutures and old-fashioned clamps had given way, and I had partially eviscerated. To disguise his error, and despite my painful and surgically dangerous condition, he had insisted I walk to his private examination room, where he administered a whiff of ether and sewed me up again. Within hours peritonitis had taken hold, followed by an embolus which lodged in my right lung, introducing pneumonia and pleurisy. Architect of this surgical disaster, Queeg kept mixing a mortar of incompetence with my blood, administering massive injections of Aureomycin and installing plastic tubes both in and out of me, stubbornly maintaining my care in his hands rather than disclose his problems to others more competent in postsurgical complications.

At times I sensed I might die, seeing myself from a detached perspective, as if part of a drama being played out. Alternating between leadenly painful sleep and glassy-eyed wakefulness, I became aware of Uncle Billy Robinson, dead three years, whose round, shiny face materialized in the center of my lazily revolving wall fan. His eyes were filled with the clear and childlike friendliness I recalled so well, and I heard his voice calling, as if carried on the wind from a distance:

"Come on up, darlin', it's fine up here."

Shivering, I turned my head, blinking the vision away. At least he had said "up."

Exhausted by pain and spiritually drained, I was still determined to cope alone, and purposely had misled Mother. Lew Parsons was the one who spilled the beans, and both parents had flown East.

On May 11, Mother wrote, "Mothers' Day today. Saw Shirley ... so *very, very* ill ... dear little precious ... baby boy is adorable.... What has that terrible butcher of a doctor done to her?"

Blanching at her first sight of the plastic tubes trailing from my nostrils and taped to my forehead, Mother failed to spark to my view that this was a novel way to lose weight. Nor was her first encounter with Queeg reassuring. He had entered holding a spray can of air deodorant, which he squirted around in graceless fashion to demonstrate how easy it was to freshen the room atmosphere. After his three fruitless tries to find my veins for a blood sample, Charlie bluntly asked him to send someone else, risky talk from a junior officer to his senior. Staring back belligerently, Queeg said if he got sick, probably nobody would send him flowers like my friends had; they'd send stinkweed. Picking up his deodorant can and syringe, he stalked out.

"Dear God," wrote Mother, "save Shirley for her wonderful husband, her precious babies, and us."

Prayer, and belated recognition of my dilemma by navy brass, arrested the downward slide. My care was shifted to surgery, beyond Queeg's fumbling clutch. Like a black cat, one day he crossed Charlie's path in the hallway and urged him to tell Secretary Kimball it was all a misunderstanding. As Lieutenant Commander Black, Charlie luckily thought twice before smashing his fist into Captain Queeg's senior face. As for Queeg, his problems were more serious than we knew. Within a short while an undiagnosed, racing brain tumor would kill him.

Surgeon General Admiral Pugh, glistening with gold braid, was obviously determined to make amends the navy way. First he felt my pulse, then stood me at bedside attention and ordered removed from the wall where I had pasted it up a horrifying medical commentary on side effects from Queeg's antibiotic panacea, Aureomycin.

By then news reporters were hot on the scent, with late reports spread by workmen on scaffolding rigged to inspect the suicide-proof window screens installed following Defense Secretary James Forrestal's suicide plunge years earlier.

"Guess who's on the tenth floor," one was quoted. "Esther Williams! And guess who's visiting her. Shirley Temple!"

Although I steadily improved, family tragedy continued to stalk Mother. On the very day she had entreated God to intercede for me, bad news had arrived from California:

"... emergency call from home ... George, Jr., critically ill with blood clot in the brain ... paralyzed on right side ... lost power of speech. ..."

Subsequently and to everyone's apparent surprise, George regained enough mobility to move home, but within weeks returned to Sawtelle Veterans Hospital with an embolus lodged in his lung, just like mine. Recovering slowly again he went home, but when the paralysis worsened he returned to the hospital, a seriously ill man with complex symptoms not well understood. As a footnote to her season of sorrow, Mother's own mother slipped into a coma and died just before Thanksgiving.

Later I would meet Dr. Augustus Rose, an eminent neurologist at the UCLA school of medicine, who diagnosed George as having multiple sclerosis, a disease poorly understood, cause and cure both unknown. Slashing indiscriminately at men and women in the prime of young life, MS condemned its victims to a fitful, relentless course of physical debility.

According to Dr. Rose, systematic analysis of worldwide incidence and correlation of the snippets of medical research now barricaded inside national boundaries were fundamental steps to understanding MS better. Spurred by the predicament of my brother and buoyed by Dr. Rose's vision, in 1953 I became involved in a local MS chapter, and then the national board of the Multiple Sclerosis Society. Now, as National Chairman of Volunteers, I was spearheading a fund-raising campaign.

Forty-nine days after my 1952 Mexican dinner, scarred but lacking a purple heart for wounds in the line of duty, I had collected Barton Sunday from the nursery where he had been parked and pampered. My favorite nurse wheeled us out to go home.

"Until you got well," she confessed, "I didn't know how sick you had been."

Well, all that was two years ago, I reflected, my attention suddenly diverted by a commotion several rows ahead in the auditorium. Kids were standing up, a few crying out in dismay, while onstage the Witch of the North was offering Dorothy magic silver shoes for her trip down the yellow-brick road to Emerald City. Forced to choose between watching the show or obeying a summons from nature, one child had opted for both at the same time. Somewhere I found a carton and paper towels and was on my hands and knees as our stage play rolled on. Cleaning up after children in dramatic settings was once again where

I now stood, or more aptly put, kneeled. Seated once again in the last row, I pressed the flashlight under my chin and daydreamed in the darkness.

Onstage Dorothy, the Scarecrow, and Tin Woodsman had been joined by a Cowardly Lion, and arm-in-arm they were dancing along the yellow-brick road, a bewildering, pot-holed, ditched route. Everyone traveled that sort of road, I reflected, obstacles overcome, rivers forded, old friends and places left behind and new ones encountered along the way.

Before departing Washington in 1953, the President had graciously invited us to say farewell in the Oval Office. Five-year-old Susan spoke first, piping an utterly unrehearsed "Good morning, President Eisenhower, Man-of-the-Hour," which set a jolly mood for the visit, with the President still basking in his recent landslide victory over Adlai Stevenson. Before saying goodbye he signed my baby's memory album, "To Barton, good luck and a long life."

Our long drive west was a cocoon of contentment, anticipating we knew not what, and already bathed in a sense of bittersweet nostalgia. But then a stale melancholia came when our road had finally looped back to Los Angeles. Repeatedly, I was challenged regarding my zest for being a mother and wife, as if anyone so inclined were either stupid or devious. That someone bathed in stardom for nineteen years would voluntarily turn a shoulder on filmmaking was judged incomprehensible.

"Yes, I do my own housework," I had protested. "There is nothing else I would rather be doing."

Not even movies?

"I won't say I'll never act again," I had replied, "but right now the only thing I'm interested in is running my own home and leading a normal life."

From all sides incredulity reigned. Seen one day in swimming trunks, his torso a crisscross of jagged scars from earlier gorings, the famous bullfighter Dominguín told me that he would never enter the ring again.

Bending forward, he had regarded me mockingly, and spoke slowly.

"And you? You will never act again? In all life, ¿quién sabe? No?"

Although I had surely left the movie business, in some respects it had not left me. Were it not for my ulterior motive to persuade Twentieth Century-Fox to convert my 35-mm film library to more manageable 16-

mm format, I would probably have declined the headline spot at a November 1953 Screen Producers Guild testimonial banquet honoring Darryl Zanuck. Seven hundred guests had crowded into the Statler Hotel ballroom, tanned, full-bellied men with darting eyes and sleek women with swirling skirts and heads tossed back in explosive laughter.

My personally prepared comments were rather lyrical, likening Zanuck to king of an enchanted fairyland in which every little girl could imagine herself a princess. The connotation seemed to please him. On a more lighthearted note I joked that his married daughter Darrilyn Jacks and I were forming a production company to be called Black-Jacks whose product was baby stars. The jest was not farfetched; I was five months pregnant.

Rounding out our children at three was an idealized concept. It was as if I lived under a compulsion, unaffected by recollection of the near calamity in my second childbirth. Looking back to Captain Queeg, I could easily recall his head resting against my protuberant stomach, and how at the time I suffered from some unexplained tension, as a rheumatic joint can anticipate an approaching storm. This time, however, there existed no reason to chew such a melancholic cud. Calm and wry, my old colleague Dr. Bradbury was an elixir of confidence. Neither apprehensive nor queasy, I agreed to another Caesarean incision, this one the modern horizontal Pfanensteil. Joined to my existing old-fashioned vertical scar, the final pattern would form an anchor, to memorialize the naval hospital, not the departed Queeg.

Even Santa Monica Hospital had a favorable mystique. My room would be where I had been born, and Susan after me. The floor supervising nurse, a rangy, motherly woman with a soft sentimental gaze, had attended Mother at my birth and me at Susan's. In my mind's eye the people were all beneficent, the walls protective, and the outlook joyously upbeat.

The clock hands stood at 6:30 p.m. on April 9, 1954. With the punctuality of a Swiss railroad train, I was rolled through the swinging green doors leading to surgery. Thirteen minutes later, to my tingling delight, was born our second daughter, Lori Alden Black. Her sex was no surprise to Mother, who had redecorated a wicker bassinet with pink ribbons, nor to me. All the infant clothing already had pink trim.

"Welcome to your world," wrote her father. "We live on a pinnacle of happiness ... cloud seven. ... Never mind that a third hydrogen bomb has just been exploded at Bikini atoll ... or that the Soviets are reported building a *nitrogen* bomb ... or that Cubans are protesting British use of the Bahama Islands to test germ warfare ... for sure, the next few years will open your eyes wider than they are today, and maybe ours as well."

Within a week, and hardly the worse for wear save my anchor scar, I was marching home with Lori in my arms.

But Dorothy was still having her troubles getting home. The Wizard turned out to be a humbug from Omaha, Nebraska, the winged monkeys were too parochial to fly her away, and the hammerhead people were obstructing her from reaching the land of the Good Witch of the South, for one last chance. Our volunteer chorus struck up the finale:

> *Could Glinda the Good be good enough,*
> *Would you think that she understood enough*
> *To get a girl back to Kansas ...*

She could. Following instructions, Dorothy clicked the heels of her silver slippers together three times and repeated the words that there was no place like home. The backdrop of Oz was pulled offstage, revealing a barnyard with a painted milk cow. Dorothy was barefoot, her silver slippers lost en route to Kansas. Everything back to normal.

Within the limitations of a high school auditorium, our finale was smoothly staged and seemed well appreciated by the children, who shouted and clapped approval. Putting my flashlight aside, I joined the applause. The story, in all its mutation, rang as true to me as when Father had first read it aloud while Mother gave my curls their Sunday evening shampoo. The message was clean and unchanged. Bizarre things can happen to anyone. Sudden cyclones can whisk a person away, forcing a journey along a meandering yellow-brick road with new companions. In fact each brick, each person, and each encounter are only extensions of the realities of life, momentarily left behind.

Now the houselights were bright and the audience seething in a tumult of childish chatter as a tide of small bodies clogged the aisles, surged up toward the doors opening out the rotunda, and streamed past with barely a glance in my direction.

My role as an unnoticed usherette was no surprise to me. Professional bonds loosened by passing time had been replaced by others, including a stable home life, a felicitous, loyal husband, and three children radiating health, happiness, and mischief. Opportunities abounded to work as a political activist, to volunteer in traditional community services, and to help in a small way to solve the riddles of international health.

With liberation from the past had also come a profound and sustained peace of mind and spirit, my days spent in sweet contentment and nights in careless slumber. Dreams of yesterday, the undimmed good and bad, inspired neither longing nor regret. Visions of an indistinct future evoked no apprehension.

What was happening was the rational consequence of a natural, pendulum-like phenomenon. I was moving in a period of relative calm between crests of activity. Cradled in a comforting hollow, I remained content to wait until lifted by the next wave.

Being a wife and mother I loved.

Me in charge, but not alone.

Thanks, Mom.

Filmography

The Runt Page (Educational Films Corp., 1931). *Producer:* Jack Hays. *Director:* Roy La Verne.

From the same film studio, and producer; variously written, and directed by Charles Lamont:

> ***War Babies [What Price Gloria]*** (1932)
> ***The Pie Covered Wagon*** (1932)
> ***Glad Rags to Riches*** (1932)
> ***The Kid's Last Fight*** (1932)
> ***Kid in Hollywood*** (1932)
> ***Pollytix in Washington*** (1932)
> ***Kid in Africa*** (1932)

Merrily Yours (Educational Films Corp., 1933). *Producer:* Jack Hays. *Director/ Writer:* Charles Lamont. *Principal Cast:* Shirley Temple, Junior Coughlin, Helene Chadwick, Mary Blackford, Harry Myers, Sidney Miller, Kenneth Howell.

Dora's Dunking Doughnuts (Educational Films Corp., 1933). *Producer:* Jack Hays. *Director:* Harry J. Edwards. *Screenplay:* Ernest Pagano and Ewart Adamson. *Principal Cast:* Shirley Temple, Andy Clyde, Blanche Payson, Florence Gill, Fern Emmett, Georgia O'Dell.

Pardon My Pups (Educational Films Corp., 1933). *Producer:* Jack Hays. *Director:* Charles Lamont. *Screenplay:* Ewart Adamson, based on a story by Florence Ryerson and Colin Clements. *Principal Cast:* Shirley Temple, Junior Coughlin, Kenneth Howell.

Managed Money (Educational Films Corp., 1933). *Producer:* Jack Hays. *Director:* Charles Lamont. *Principal Cast:* Shirley Temple, Huntley Gordon, Junior Coughlin.

What to Do? (Educational Films Corp., 1933). *Producer:* Jack Hays. *Director:* Harry J. Edwards.

The Red-Haired Alibi (Tower Productions [Columbia], 1933). *Director:* Christy Cabanne. *Screenplay:* Edward T. Lowe, from a story by Wilson Collison. *Principal Cast:* Grant Withers, Merna Kennedy, Theodore Von Eltz, Purnell Pratt, Fred Kelsey, Shirley Temple.

Out All Night (Universal Studios, 1933). *Director:* Sam Taylor. *Screenplay:* William A. McGuire, from a story by Tim Whelan. *Principal Cast:* ZaSu Pitts, Slim Summerville, Shirley Temple, Laura Hope Crews, Shirley Grey, Billy Barty, Gene Lewis.

To the Last Man (Paramount Studios, 1933). *Director:* Henry Hathaway. *Screenplay:* Jack Cunningham. *Principal Cast:* Randolph Scott, Esther Ralston, Shirley Temple, Buster Crabbe, Noah Beery, Jack LaRue, Barton MacLane, Gail Patrick.

Carolina (Fox Film Corp., 1933). *Director:* Henry King. *Screenplay:* Reginald Berkeley, from *The House of Connelly*, by Paula Green. *Principal Cast:* Janet Gaynor, Lionel Barrymore, Robert Young, Henrietta Crosman, Shirley Temple.

Mandalay (First National [Warner Brothers], 1933). *Director:* Michael Curtiz. *Screenplay:* Austin Parker and Charles Kenyon, based on a story by Paul H. Fox. *Principal Cast:* Kay Francis, Ricardo Cortez, Warner Oland, Lyle Talbot, Ruth Donnelly, Reginald Owen, Shirley Temple.

As the Earth Turns (Warner Brothers, 1933). *Producer:* Robert Lord. *Director:* Alfred E. Green. *Screenplay:* Ernest Pascal, adapted from a novel by Gladys Hasty Carroll. *Principal Cast:* Donald Woods, Jean Muir, Russell Hardy, Emily Lowry, Dorothy Appleby, Shirley Temple.

New Deal Rhythm (Paramount Pictures, 1933). *Principal Cast:* Charles "Buddy" Rogers, Marjorie Main.

Stand Up and Cheer (Fox Film Corp., 1934). *Producer:* Winfield Sheehan. *Director:* Hamilton McFadden. *Screenplay:* Lew Brown and Ralph Spence, based on story idea by Will Rogers and Philip Klein. *Principal Cast:* Warner Baxter, Madge Evans, Shirley Temple, James Dunn, John Boles, Ralph Morgan, Tess Gardell.

Now I'll Tell (Fox Film Corp., 1934). *Producer:* Winfield Sheehan. *Director:* Edwin Burke. *Screenplay:* based on life story of Arnold Rothstein, as told by his wife. *Principal Cast:* Spencer Tracy, Helen Twelvetrees, Alice Faye, Shirley Temple.

Change of Heart (Fox Film Corp., 1934). *Producer:* Winfield Sheehan. *Director:* John G. Blystone. *Screenplay:* Sonja Levine and James Gleason, after a story by Kathleen Norris, *Manhattan Love Song. Principal Cast:* Janet Gaynor, Charles Farrell, James Dunn, Ginger Rogers, Shirley Temple, Jane Darwell.

Little Miss Marker (Paramount Pictures, Inc., 1934). *Producer:* B. P. Schulberg. *Director:* Alexander Hall. *Screenplay:* William R. Lipman, Sam Hellman, Gladys Lehman, based on a Damon Runyon story published in *Collier's* magazine, 1932. *Principal Cast:* Adolphe Menjou, Dorothy Dell, Charles Bickford, Shirley Temple.

Baby Take a Bow (Fox, 1934). *Director:* Harry Lachman. *Screenplay:* Philip Klein and E. E. Paramore, Jr., adapted from the James P. Judge play *Square Crooks. Principal Cast:* Shirley Temple, James Dunn, Claire Trevor, Alan Dinehart.

Now and Forever (Paramount, 1934). *Director:* Henry Hathaway. *Screenplay:* Vincent Lawrence and Sylvia Thalberg, from a story by Jack Kirkland and Melville Baker. *Principal Cast:* Shirley Temple, Carole Lombard, Gary Cooper, Charlotte Granville, Sir Guy Standing.

Bright Eyes (Fox, 1934). *Producer:* Sol M. Wurtzel. *Director:* David Butler. *Screenplay:* William Conselman, from a story by David Butler and Edwin Burke. *Principal Cast:* Shirley Temple, James Dunn, Jane Darwell, Jane Withers, Judith Allen, Lois Wilson.

The Little Colonel (Fox, 1934). *Producer:* B. G. DeSylva. *Director:* David Butler. *Screenplay:* William Conselman. *Principal Cast:* Shirley Temple, Lionel Barrymore, Sidney Blackmer, Hattie McDaniel, Evelyn Venable, John Lodge, Bill Robinson, Alden Chase.

Our Little Girl [Heaven's Gate] (Twentieth Century-Fox, 1935). *Producer:* Edward Butcher. *Director:* John Robertson. *Screenplay:* adapted by Stephen Avery from "Heaven's Gate," a story by Florence Leighton Pfalzgraf. *Principal Cast:* Shirley Temple, Joel McCrea, Rosemary Ames, Lyle Talbot, Erin O'Brien Moore, Margaret Armstrong.

Curly Top (Fox, 1935). *Producer:* Winfield Sheehan. *Director:* Irving Cummings. *Screenplay:* Patterson McNutt and Arthur Beckhard. *Principal Cast:* Shirley Temple, Rochelle Hudson, John Boles, Arthur Treacher, Jane Darwell, Etienne Girardot, Esther Dale.

The Littlest Rebel (Twentieth Century-Fox, 1935). *Producer:* Darryl F. Zanuck. *Director:* David Butler. *Screenplay:* Edwin Burke from the play by Edward Peple. *Principal Cast:* Shirley Temple, John Boles, Karen Morley, Bill Robinson, Jack Holt, Guinn Williams, Bessie Lyle, Hannah Washington.

Captain January (Twentieth Century-Fox, 1936). *Producer:* Darryl F. Zanuck. *Director:* David Butler. *Screenplay:* Sam Hellman, Gladys Lehman and Harry Tugend, based on a novel by Laura E. Richards. *Principal Cast:* Shirley Temple, Slim Summerville, Guy Kibbee, Buddy Ebsen, June Lang, Sara Haden, Jane Darwell.

Poor Little Rich Girl (Twentieth Century-Fox, 1936). *Producer:* Darryl F. Zanuck. *Director:* Irving Cummings. *Screenplay:* Sam Hellman, Gladys Lehman and Harry Tugend, based on the stories of Eleanor Gates and Ralph Spence. *Principal Cast:* Shirley Temple, Alice Faye, Gloria Stuart, Jack Haley, Michael Whalen, Sara Haden, Jane Darwell, Claude Gillingwater.

Dimples [The Bowery Princess] (Twentieth Century-Fox, 1936). *Producer:* Nunnally Johnson. *Director:* William A. Seiter. *Screenplay:* Arthur Sheekman and Nat Parrin. *Principal Cast:* Shirley Temple, Frank Morgan, Robert Kent, Delma Byron, Astrid Allwyn, Stepin Fetchit, John Carradine, Herman Bing.

Stowaway (Twentieth Century-Fox, 1936). *Producer:* Darryl F. Zanuck. *Director:* William A. Seiter. *Screenplay:* William Conselman, Arthur Sheekman and Nat Perrin, from a story by Sam Engle. *Principal Cast:* Shirley Temple, Alice Faye, Robert Young, Eugene Pallette, Helen Westley, Arthur Treacher, J. Edward Bromberg.

Wee Willie Winkie (Twentieth Century-Fox, 1937). *Producer:* Gene Markey. *Director:* John Ford. *Screenplay:* Ernest Pascal and Julian Josephson from the story by Rudyard Kipling. *Principal Cast:* Shirley Temple, Victor McLaglen, C. Aubrey Smith, June Lang, Cesar Romero, Michael Whalen, Constance Collier.

Heidi (Twentieth Century-Fox, 1937). *Producer:* Raymond Griffith. *Director:* Allan Dwan. *Screenplay:* Walter Ferris and Julian Josephson, based on the book by Johanna Spyri. *Principal Cast:* Shirley Temple, Jean Hersholt, Sidney Blackmer, Arthur Treacher, Helen Westley, Mady Christians, Pauline Moore, Delmar Watson, Marcia Mae Jones.

Rebecca of Sunnybrook Farm (Twentieth Century-Fox, 1938). *Producer:* Raymond Griffith. *Director:* Allan Dwan. *Screenplay:* Karl Tunberg and Don Ettinger, based on a story by Kate Douglas Wiggin. *Principal Cast:* Shirley Temple, Randolph Scott, Jack Haley, Gloria Stuart, Phyllis Brooks, Helen Westley, Slim Summerville, Bill Robinson, Alan Dinehart, J. Edward Bromberg, William Demarest, Franklin Pangborn.

Little Miss Broadway (Twentieth Century-Fox, 1938). *Producer:* Darryl F. Zanuck. *Director:* Irving Cummings. *Screenplay:* Harry Tugend and Jack Yellen. *Principal Cast:* Shirley Temple, George Murphy, Phyllis Brooks, Jimmy Durante, Edna Mae Oliver, George Barbier, Jane Darwell, El Brendel, Donald Meek, Edward Ellis.

Just Around the Corner (Twentieth Century-Fox, 1939). *Producer:* Darryl F. Zanuck. *Director:* Irving Cummings. *Screenplay:* Ethel Hill, J. P. McEvoy and Darrell Ware, based on a story by Paul Gerard Smith. *Principal Cast:* Shirley Temple, Joan Davis, Charles Farrell, Bert Lahr, Bill Robinson, Franklin Pangborn, Cora Witherspoon.

The Little Princess (Twentieth Century-Fox, 1939). *Producer:* Darryl F. Zanuck. *Director:* Walter Lang. *Screenplay:* adapted by Ethel Hill and Walter Ferris from the novel *Sara Crewe*, by Frances Hodgson Burnett. *Principal Cast:* Shirley Temple, Anita Louise, Richard Greene, Cesar Romero, Ian Hunter, Arthur Treacher, Marcia Mae Jones.

Susannah of the Mounties (Twentieth Century-Fox, 1939). *Producer:* Darryl F. Zanuck. *Director:* William A. Seiter. *Screenplay:* Robert Ellis and Helen Logan, from a story by Fidel La Barba and Walter Ferris, based on a book by Muriel Denison. *Principal Cast:* Shirley Temple, Randolph Scott, Margaret Lockwood, J. Farrell MacDonald, Martin Good Rider, Victor Jory, Maurice Moscovitch, Moroni Olsen.

The Blue Bird (Twentieth Century-Fox, 1939). *Producer:* Darryl F. Zanuck. *Director:* Walter Lang. *Screenplay:* adapted by Ernest Pascal from the play by Maurice Maeterlinck. *Principal Cast:* Shirley Temple, Spring Byington, Gale Sondergaard, Nigel Bruce, Eddie Collins, Johnny Russell, Russell Hicks, Sybil Jason, Gene Reynolds, Sterling Holloway.

Young People (Twentieth Century-Fox, 1940). *Producer:* Harry Joe Brown. *Director:* Allan Dwan. *Screenplay:* Edwin Blum and Don Ettinger. *Principal Cast:* Shirley Temple, Charlotte Greenwood, Jack Oakie, Arleen Whelan, George Montgomery, Kathleen Howard, Darryl Hickman, Mae Marsh.

Kathleen (Metro-Goldwyn-Mayer, 1941). *Producer:* George Haight. *Director:* Harold S. Bucquet. *Screenplay:* Mary C. McCall, Jr., based on a story by Kay Van Riper. *Principal Cast:* Shirley Temple, Herbert Marshall, Laraine Day, Gail Patrick, Felix Bressart, Nella Walker, Lloyd Corrigan, Guy Bellis.

Miss Annie Rooney (United Artists, 1942). *Producer:* Edward Small. *Director:* Edward L. Marin. *Screenplay:* George Bruce. *Principal Cast:* Shirley Temple, William Gargan, Dickie Moore, June Lockhart, Guy Kibbee, Peggy Ryan, Roland Du Pree.

Since You Went Away (United Artists, 1943). *Producer:* David O. Selznick. *Director:* John Cromwell. *Screenplay:* David O. Selznick, based on a novel by Margaret Buell Wilder. *Principal Cast:* Shirley Temple, Claudette Colbert, Jennifer Jones, Joseph Cotten, Monty Woolley, Robert Walker, Lionel Barrymore, Agnes Moorehead, Keenan Wynn, Nazimova, Craig Stevens, Guy Madison.

I'll Be Seeing You (United Artists, 1944). *Producer:* Dore Schary for Selznick-International. *Director:* William Dieterle. *Screenplay:* Marion Parsonnet, based on a radio play, *Furlough*, by Charles Martin. *Principal Cast:* Shirley Temple, Joseph Cotten, Ginger Rogers, Spring Byington, Tom Tully, Chill Wills, Derek Harris [John Derek].

Kiss and Tell (Columbia, 1945). *Producer:* Sol C. Siegel. *Director:* Richard Wallace. *Screenplay:* F. Hugh Herbert, based on his play of the same name. *Principal Cast:* Shirley Temple, Walter Abel, Katherine Alexander, Jerome Courtland, Robert Benchley, Porter Hall, Tom Tully, Virginia Welles, Darryl Hickman.

Honeymoon (RKO-Radio, 1946). *Producer:* Warren Duff. *Director:* William Keighley. *Screenplay:* Michael Kanin, based on a story by Vicki Baum. *Principal Cast:* Shirley Temple, Franchot Tone, Guy Madison, Lina Romay, Grant Mitchell, Gene Lockhart.

The Bachelor and the Bobby Soxer (RKO-Radio, 1947). *Producer:* Dore Schary. *Director:* Irving Reis. *Screenplay:* Sidney Sheldon. *Principal Cast:* Shirley Temple, Cary Grant, Myrna Loy, Ray Collins, Rudy Vallee, Harry Davenport, Johnny Sands.

That Hagen Girl (Warner Brothers, 1947). *Producer:* Alex Gottleib. *Director:* Peter Godfrey. *Screenplay:* Charles Hoffman, based on Edith Roberts' novel *Mary Hagen*. *Principal Cast:* Shirley Temple, Ronald Reagan, Rory Calhoun, Lois Maxwell, Dorothy Peterson, Charles Kemper, Conrad Janis.

Fort Apache (RKO-Radio, 1947). *Producer:* John Ford and Merian C. Cooper. *Director:* John Ford. *Screenplay:* Frank Nugent, suggested by the James Warner Bellah story "Massacre." *Principal Cast:* Shirley Temple, John Wayne, Henry Fonda, John Agar, Irene Rich, George O'Brien, Victor McLaglen, Dick Foran, Guy Kibbee, Grant Withers.

Adventure in Baltimore (RKO-Radio, 1948). *Producer:* Richard H. Berger for Dore Schary. *Director:* Richard Wallace. *Screenplay:* Lionel Houser, from a story by Lesser Samuels and Christopher Isherwood. *Principal Cast:* Shirley Temple, John Agar, Robert Young, Josephine Hutchinson, Charles Kemper, Johnny Sands.

Mr. Belvedere Goes to College (Twentieth Century-Fox, 1948). *Producer:* Samuel G. Engel. *Director:* Elliott Nugent. *Screenplay:* Richard Sale, Mary Loos and Mary McCall, Jr. *Principal Cast:* Shirley Temple, Clifton Webb, Tom Drake, Alan Young, Jessie Royce Landis, Kathleen Hughes.

The Story of Seabiscuit (Warner Brothers-First National, 1949). *Producer:* William Jacobs. *Director:* David Butler. *Screenplay:* John Taintor Foote based on his story "Always Sweethearts." *Principal Cast:* Shirley Temple, Barry Fitzgerald, Lon McAllister, Rosemary De Camp, Pierre Watkin, William Forest.

A Kiss for Corliss (United Artists, 1949). *Producer:* Marcus Low, Richard Wallace and Colin Miller. *Director:* Richard Wallace. *Screenplay:* Howard Dimsdale, based on the Corliss Archer character of Hugh Herbert. *Principal Cast:* Shirley Temple, David Niven, Darryl Hickman, Tom Tully, Virginia Welles, Gloria Holden, Robert Ellis.

Index

About the Author

September 19, 1988

Shirley Temple Black is currently writing the second volume of her autobiography. Aside from her literary efforts, she seldom looks back or narrows her vision of the future.

She has been married to Charles Black for thirty-eight years, and is the mother of Lori, Charlie Jr. and Susan and grandmother of Teresa Falaschi. Her longtime family residence is a small rural community south of San Francisco. Active in local civic and cultural affairs, she has also served on the boards of directors of six major U.S. industrial and financial corporations, and during 1959–61 she performed in fifty one-hour television programs.

In the mid–1960s, Shirley Temple Black rededicated herself to work in an international context, a natural extension of her childhood exposure. This year marks a point of equilibrium: she is completing her nineteenth year of government service, equal to her nineteen years as a movie actress.

Following Shirley Temple Black's 1969 appointment by President Richard M. Nixon as a U.S. Representative to the 24th General Assembly of the United Nations (New York), she became successively Deputy Chairman, Preparatory Committee, and member of the U.S. Delegation to the U.N. Conference on the Human Environment (Stockholm); member of the delegation negotiating the U.S.-U.S.S.R. Treaty on the Environment (Moscow); and Special Assistant to the Chairman of the Council on Environmental Quality (The White House). In 1974, President Gerald R. Ford appointed her U.S. Ambassador to the Republic of Ghana, and later Ambassador and U.S. Chief of Protocol, the first woman in U.S. history to hold this position. Recipient of honorary academic degrees from Santa Clara University, Lehigh University and College of Notre Dame, and an official of numerous international organizations, she is also an officer and founding member of the Board of Directors of the American Academy of Diplomacy (Washington, D.C.).

For the past seven and a half years, the author has served as a Foreign Affairs Officer/Expert for the Foreign Affairs Institute, U.S. Department of State (Washington, D.C.).

On November 23, 1987, U.S. Secretary of State George P. Shultz recognized the abilities of Shirley Temple Black by appointing her the first Honorary Foreign Service Officer in the nation's history. The citation reads:

THE SECRETARY OF STATE
OF
THE UNITED STATES OF AMERICA
TO
SHIRLEY TEMPLE BLACK

In recognition of your distinguished contributions to the diplomacy of the country you have so ably represented at home and abroad, and with grateful appreciation for your willingness to share your experience, insights and wisdom in the training of virtually every first-time ambassador appointed since January 20, 1981. Truly, it can be said that you have had an excellent effect on your country's interests abroad.

I do hereby appoint you an Honorary Foreign Service Officer of the United States of America.

(Signed)
George P. Shultz